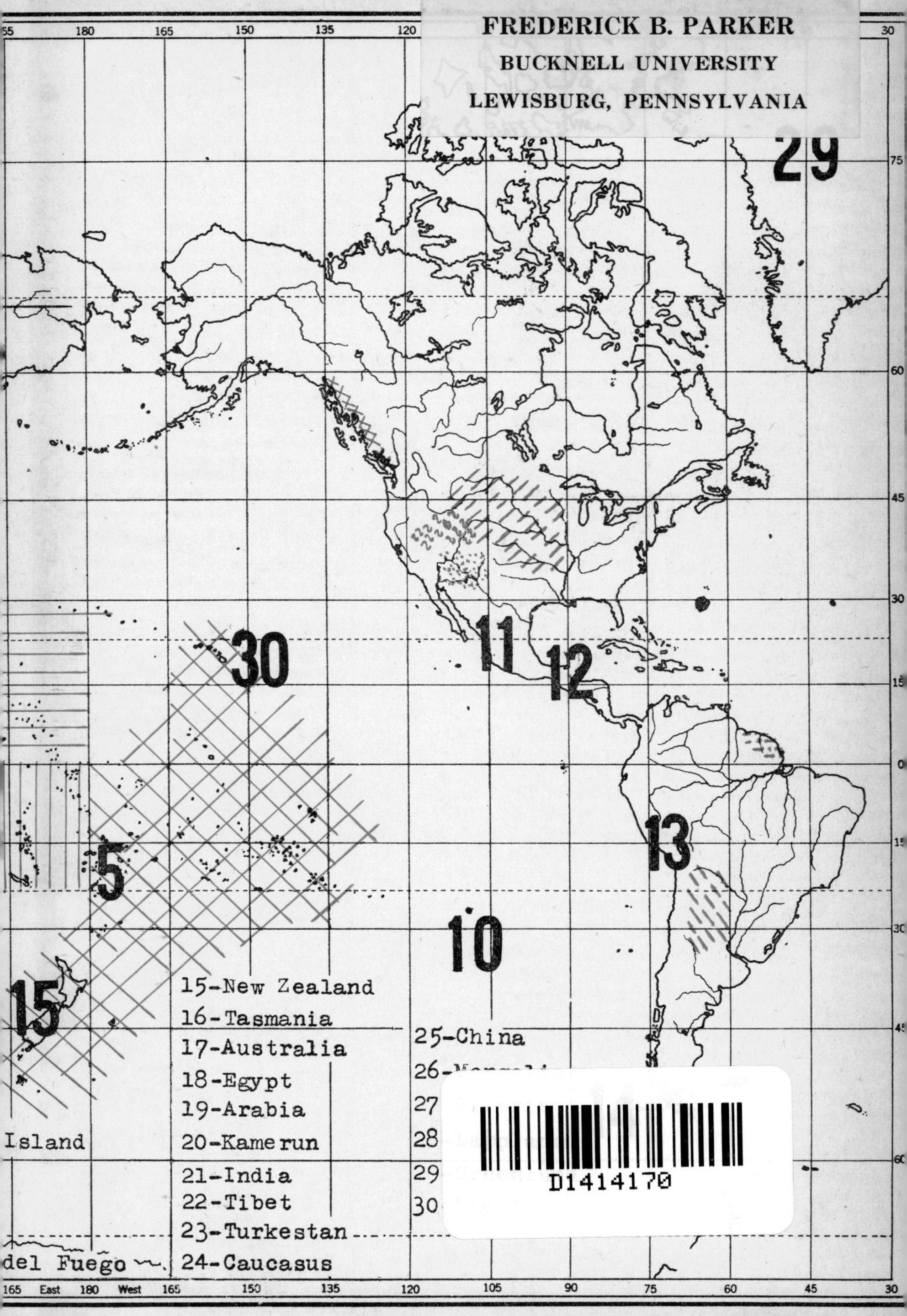

Map I: Important Areas and Countries

AN INTRODUCTION TO CULTURAL ANTHROPOLOGY

AN INTRODUCTION TO CULTURAL ANTHROPOLOGY

A NEW AND ENLARGED EDITION

BY ROBERT H. LOWIE, PH.D.
PROFESSOR OF ANTHROPOLOGY
UNIVERSITY OF CALIFORNIA

FARRAR & RINEHART, INC.
PUBLISHERS NEW YORK

PRINTED IN THE UNITED STATES OF AMERICA
BY J. J. LITTLE AND IVES COMPANY, NEW YORK

TO MY WIFE

PREFACE TO THE SECOND EDITION

The original purpose of this book was to provide a topical survey of culture, with the emphasis on elementary facts. For lack of such preparatory orientation, I believed and I continue to believe, advanced students of the social sciences, including anthropology, and even young scholars launched on a professional career, remain pitiably at sea. They are sometimes found working with the subtlest problems when they have not the faintest idea how these fit into the general framework of civilization. Apparently the book has fulfilled its humble mission in the English-speaking world; and the French translation, *Manuel d'anthropologie culturelle* (Paris: Payot, 1936), is said to have proved useful in France and in South America.

However, teachers of anthropology in this country have urged amplification, requesting chapters on Language and Theory, as well as descriptions of typical cultures in their totality. The present edition is meant to satisfy these demands without undue enlargement.

The tribal sketches, which occupy a large portion of the supplementary space, have received special care. First, I have tried to demonstrate the range of cultural possibilities by bringing out qualitative differences as well as varying degrees of complexity. Hence, chapters on Albania and Western civilization no less than on Fuegia and Australia; on incipient and on intensive farmers; on cultivators of rice and of maize; on hunters and on herders. But pedagogically little is gained by a multiplicity of names; for that reason the number of these sketches is limited and, so far as possible, tribes already rather fully considered in the topical survey are reintroduced in Part II so that cross-referencing may economize space.

Second, even at best descriptive completeness is not possible and should not be aimed at even in outline. Indeed, the effort to treat all peoples according to one scheme distorts the pictures. The proper procedure is to view any one group according to its distinctive emphases: government cannot be ignored in the merest sketch of the Shilluk, but requires no explicit discussion in a chapter on Fuegians. On the other hand, cultural individuality is best depicted by contrast, and accordingly comparisons have been freely used.

Finally, the peoples dealt with are not merely so many specimens of social patterns, but also exemplify broad principles of cultural process. Accordingly, these have been stressed at the close of the several chapters.

Careful perusal of what is now Part I did not suggest the need for radical revision, but some supplementary information is offered under the head of Addenda. In compliance with special requests I have also added an Annotated Reading List over and above the Bibliographical Notes.

To the several firms and institutions that authorized reproduction of copyrighted illustrations I once more express my obligation—above all to The American Museum of Natural History, which provided the half-tones for the chapter on Art; to Field Museum (Chicago); the Baessler-Archiv (Berlin); Anthropos (formerly St. Gabriel-Mödling bei Wien, now in Fribourg, Switzerland); Institut d'Ethnologie (Paris); F. A. Brockhaus (Leipzig); Albert Bonnier (Stockholm); and the University of Minnesota (Minneapolis).

ROBERT H. LOWIE

Berkeley, California
April, 1940

PREFACE TO THE FIRST EDITION

Considerable teaching experience indicates that most students of cultural anthropology and other social sciences are very slow in acquiring an elementary knowledge of culture history, and that many fail to acquire the relevant facts and concepts even years after they have launched on a professional career as anthropologists. The result is prolonged and needless floundering. This book is an attempt to forestall such wasteful confusion. Deliberately avoiding theoretical discussion, it endeavors to present the essential facts topically. Naturally there can be differences of opinion as to what is essential for an introductory treatment. According to my own feeling in the matter, it is indispensable to stress the simplest tribes, such as the Fuegians and Australians, and, on the other hand, to link the culture of illiterate peoples with the higher civilizations, past and present. Both these objectives have been rather consistently kept in view.

This definition of aim throws open a great mass of good descriptive material for possible use, and selection has to be made. Tribes have been chosen mainly for two reasons: because they illustrate significant points and because they have been thoroughly described. For example, the Shilluk illustrate contiguity to a higher civilization and selective borrowing, as well as a sharply definable conception of royalty. Further, they have been described by a veteran British anthropologist, a German ethnographer-linguist, and a German missionary who resided in the country for years.

I have further attempted to feature groups that have not been made to do constant work by general writers in the past. The stressing of the Murngin, Ona, Maricopa, and Shilluk and the virtual exclusion of the Arunta will possibly be appreciated as a relief.

In a work of this sort footnotes and an excessive bibliography would be pedantry. Citation of literature has accordingly been relegated to an Appendix, works constantly utilized preceding more specific references for each chapter.

To my wife I am indebted for keen criticism of the manuscript and for invaluable help in the selection, arrangement, and execution of the illustrations.

To the several firms and institutions that have authorized reproduction of copyrighted illustrations I desire to express my profound sense of obligation. I am specially indebted to Field Museum (Chicago), the Baessler-Archiv (Berlin), "Anthropos" (St. Gabriel-Mödling bei Wien), Institut d'Ethnologie (Paris), F. A. Brockhaus (Leipzig), Albert Bonnier (Stockholm), and the University of Minnesota (Minneapolis).

ROBERT H. LOWIE

Berkeley, California
August, 1934

TABLE OF CONTENTS

PART II: ILLUSTRATIVE CULTURES

APPENDIX

LIST OF PLATES

PART I

CULTURE: ITS NATURE AND ITS PHASES

I

INTRODUCTION: CULTURE, RACE, AND PROGRESS

Culture Defined. In the scientific sense "culture" does not mean unusual refinement or education, but the whole of social tradition. It includes, as the great anthropologist Tylor put it, "capabilities and habits acquired by man as a member of society." Culture includes *all* these capabilities and habits in contrast to those numerous traits acquired otherwise, namely by biological heredity.

Differences of Culture. Passing from one social group to another, we at once discover differences that can not be due to anything but social convention. An American who travels in England finds that afternoon tea is a fixed institution and that cars drive on the left side of the road; in Denmark every one is riding a bicycle; in Madrid, café patrons sit outdoors to sip their coffee and are pestered by itinerant bootblacks and peddlers of lottery-tickets. These are not American phenomena, but represent minor cultural differences. If we travel to the Orient or put ourselves in imagination into ancient Greece, the disparity becomes much greater. All the influences of a machine age and of Christianity drop out, and strange ideals are thrust upon us. Nevertheless, even the Chinese seem relatively close as compared with the illiterate hunters of Australia or the North American Indians as found by Hudson and De Soto. Yet every one of these lived in a social group which passed on information to its young about tool-making, woodcraft, moral conduct, and belief in supernatural beings. All, therefore, technically are "cultured" and the proper subject for study by culture history; and the business of such a study is to define what sort of culture belongs to all human groups past and present and, so far as possible, why their social traditions vary.

Racial Differences. Every human being, however, has traits which he does not get from his society. Australian elders can teach a boy to throw a boomerang, but they can not permanently alter his chocolate skin by smearing paint on it. Skin color and other physical traits are inherited, not socially but by biological heredity. An Australian child brought up by a white rancher tends sheep instead of throwing boomerangs at kangaroos; he may learn to write, as do white children, and to drive an automobile. But no matter how much he associates with whites the color of his skin, the shape of his skull, and the width of his nose remain unaffected because they can come to him only from his parents. Thus, every human being has a social and a racial (biological) inheritance. The two may be in some measure related, but they are different.

Races. Modern man belongs to a single species, *homo sapiens,* subdivided into races, which correspond to a zoölogist's varieties. From very early times human groups have freely intermarried, and all intermarriages have proved capable of producing fertile offspring. As a result, absolutely pure races no longer exist; and this by itself makes it extremely hard to distinguish existing groups on a racial basis. No one criterion can be safely used. The skin color of "Caucasians" is not the same in Sicily and Sweden, and that of woolly-haired Pygmies is much lighter than would be expected in Negroids. In stature North Europeans, Zulu Negroes, Hawaiians, and Plains Indians differ very little. The character of Australian hair resembles that of Europeans rather than that of the Negro. For our purposes a very rough orientation will be sufficient. We may distinguish four major divisions, the Australoid, Negroid, Mongoloid, and Caucasian races.

The Australoid has a very wide nose, with a marked

depression of the root, chocolate skin color, dark hair that may be curly but never woolly, a long skull, and heavy bony ridges above the eyebrows. This race is generally taken to include not only the Australian himself, but certain groups in and near India, such as the Vedda of Ceylon (*Pl. 2, fig. 4*).

The Negroid differs from the Australoid by his woolly or frizzy hair and lack of heavy brow-ridges. He generally resembles him in his dark skin color and long skull, also in being wide-nosed. His protruding, thick lips are characteristic. But there is great variability. Around Lake Chad the natives are round-skulled, and in South Africa the Hottentot and Bushmen have yellow skins. As for stature, the shortest and the tallest peoples of the world are Negroid. The Negroid race includes, roughly, the natives of the southern two-thirds of Africa (*Pl. 1, fig. 2; Pl. 2, fig. 1*); the dark and frizzy-haired Oceanians—the Melanesians and Tasmanians; various Pygmy groups, such as the Negrito of the Philippines; the Andaman Islanders southeast of India; and the Bambuti of the Congo.

The Mongoloids are distinguished by their straight and coarse hair of the head, sparse facial and body hair, and oblique eyes. The yellow skin, wide faces, and round skulls credited to them are frequent but not universal, though this probably holds for all racial criteria whatsoever. Mongoloids are made to include the Chinese, Tibetans (*Pl. 1, fig. 1*) and many other Asiatics, the Malays (Indonesians), the Lapps, the Eskimo (*Pl. 1, fig. 3*), and the American Indians (*Pl. 2, fig. 2*). But even the American natives alone are extraordinarily variable. Eskimo heads are very long, those of the Colorado River Indians excessively broad. Some California Indians average only a trifle over 5 feet in height, while Northern Plains and Patagonian tribes are about 8 inches taller.

"Caucasians", or "whites", likewise vary a great deal; so much so that many scientists split them into several supposedly distinct groups. Their skin color is on the whole lighter than that of other races, though the pigmentation of a Sicilian differs much from even a North Italian's, let alone a Swede's. On the whole, they present facial and other features that depart most widely from the apes'. The Caucasian race would include various Western Asiatics, such as the people of Northern India (*Pl. 1, fig. 4*), the Arabs and Persians; North Africans, as for instance the Egyptians; and the various European populations.

According to taste one can either divide the latter into Caucasian subraces or treat them as separate races: viz., the Nordic, Alpine, and Mediterranean, to which some add a Dinaric. The Nordics (or North Europeans) and Mediterraneans are both relatively long-headed—though not so decidedly as, say, Australians—but the Nordics are much taller and fairer. The Alpines, who are typically represented in central France, Switzerland and southwestern Germany, sharply contrast with the foregoing by their broad skulls. In stature and complexion they are intermediate. The Dinarics, typically represented by the Yugoslavs, are swarthy, very broad-skulled, and quite as tall as the Nordics.

Polynesians (*Pl. 2, fig. 3*) can not be fitted into any of the four major divisions of mankind. They never have the Negroid woolly hair, but flat wide noses are common among them. Actually, scientists report a mingling of Caucasian, Negroid and Mongoloid strains in Polynesia.

Classification is obviously an appalling task. No race has remained pure, though some are less mixed than others. Also, assuming a time when races *were* pure, we do not know how variable they may have been. For instance, the Shilluk of the upper Nile (*Pl. 2, fig. 1*) have intensely dark skins, almost attaining true black in the physicist's sense. On the other hand, the Bushmen are yellow-skinned Negroids. Does this mean that the Negroids are capable of varying in skin color to that extent? Or are the Bushmen a mixture of Negroids with some lighter race?

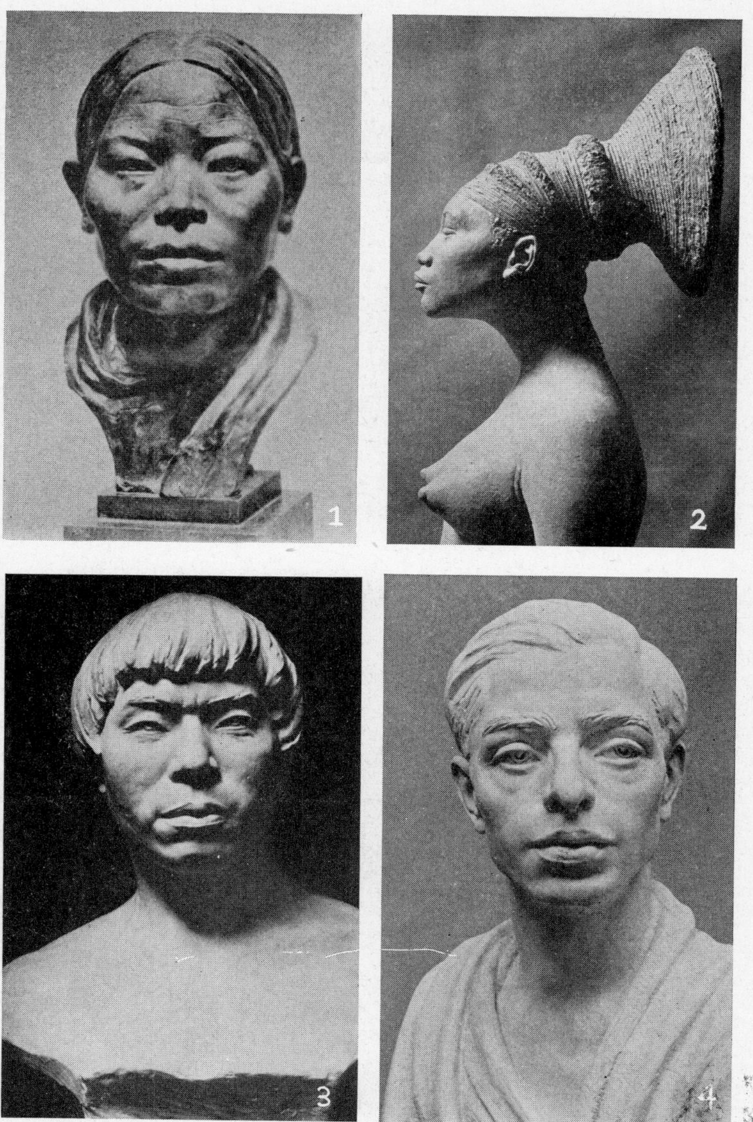

Plate 1: Racial Types.

1. Tibetan Woman 2. Mangbettu Woman 3. Eskimo Man 4. Man from Bengal. (The photographs on this page are reproduced with the permission of the sculptress, Miss Malvina Hoffman, and Field Museum of Natural History, Chicago. Copyrighted by Field Museum.)

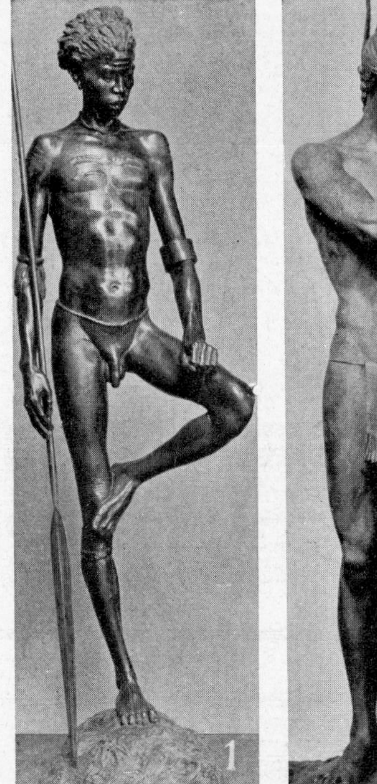

Plate 2: Racial Types.

1. Shilluk Warrior 2. Blackfoot Indian 3. Polynesian Surf-Rider 4. Vedda from Ceylon. (The photographs on this page are reproduced with the permission of the sculptress, Miss Malvina Hoffman, and Field Museum of Natural History, Chicago. Copyrighted by Field Museum.)

The outstanding fact is that no human division falls completely outside the range of other divisions. The Pygmies are not Lilliputians; they are conventionally defined as groups with an average male stature of 4 ft. 11 in., or below. In other words, the average Pygmy has the height of an extremely short American white, but nevertheless such as we occasionally see. On the other hand, the tallest Negroids are not giants, but average somewhere between 5 ft. 11 in. and 6 ft. 1 in. This overlapping holds for other traits as well.

Grading of Races. If races are to be ranked as higher and lower, it must be for their mental traits. Fair hair and long heads have no intrinsic value, though conceivably they may be *signs* of superiority. The only physical feature that directly suggests mental worth is the brain because in the animal kingdom a better brain does go with a higher status.

Here, however, there is again overlapping. Mongoloids are not inferior to Caucasians at all; Negroes somewhat; Australians more so, yet without falling below the more poorly equipped whites. There are really groups with larger and smaller brains, just as there are taller and shorter groups. While some Negro brains equal French or British brains, the average is lower; the largest Negro brains do not equal the largest Caucasian brains, the smallest in the Negro series fall below the smallest in the white series.

Nevertheless, this result can not be interpreted directly in terms of psychology. While very great differences in the brain are significant, lesser ones are not. In civilized countries autopsies sometimes prove criminals to have large brains while some great men were found to fall below the normal. A difference of merely a few hundred units is thus not decisive, and the smaller brains of Australians or other races are no positive proof of inferior faculties.

Races and Mental Traits. The only way to get positive results as to the inborn endowment of races is to test a sufficient sample of each race under similar conditions. Two difficulties meet us here. In the first place, the behavior of a tested individual is partly due to his training. No European visitor can equal a Samoan in his native waters because the Polynesian has been taught from infancy how to behave there. The European would get dangerous cuts from live corals and be dashed against rocks by a wave, where a Samoan falls forward over it or submerges under it according to circumstances. By his inability to respond properly to cues any Polynesian considers obvious, the white man would be rated an imbecile. The tests hitherto applied to aborigines have been almost always tests first devised for whites and without any insight into the preparation of the aborigines. Consequently they are no fairer than would be a Samoan test of European intelligence on the basis of swimming about for sea food in the South Seas. So far, then, this difficulty has not been overcome. Perhaps future psychologists can cope with it.

Secondly, in order to mean anything the tests must be applied to at least fairly pure groups. We may regard Andaman Islanders and Swedes as sufficiently pure when put beside each other to warrant comparison provided the first difficulty is solved. But we can not compare any European group with any other at the present time because if Nordic, Alpine, and Mediterranean once were pure they have long ago become mongrelized. Sweden is the purest Nordic country, but not twelve per cent. of its people simultaneously present fair hair, blue eyes, long heads and tall stature. What is more, we could not segregate those Swedes who shared these traits and hope to determine the mental traits of the original Nordics from them. According to biological theory, the several traits that may be inherited are inherited *independently of one another,* hence a person who looks Nordic may have a racial psychology that is largely Alpine or Mediterranean.

To sum up, at the present moment we know nothing

helpful about the inborn racial differences of man. Our only hope is that psychologists may discover tests to eliminate the factor of training when comparing exotic races with Caucasians. As for scientific proof of any differences among Caucasian subraces, only a miracle unscrambling the present mixtures could help.

In short, whether racial differences *exist* or not, at present cultures can in no way be safely *explained* in terms of racial psychology.

Culture and Race. This negative result can be directly supplemented by another: innumerable cultural facts could not be explained by race even if racial differences were enormous, because culture changes far more rapidly than race. It is not an inborn urge that makes civilized Europeans eat with forks, because a paltry few hundred years ago every one ate with his fingers. It is not an inborn trait of Nordics to be Protestants because when they were purer racially than now they were Catholics, and when still purer, pagans. The relatively pure Nordics of Caesar's time were barbarians to the Romans, and they stood far lower than the Arabs in 1,000 A.D. The Arabs, on the other hand, who are more or less racially what they were then, have fallen from their high estate.

Since biological change occurs slowly and cultural changes occur in every generation, it is futile to try to explain the fleeting phenomena of culture by a racial constant. We can often explain them—in terms of contact with other peoples, of individual genius, of geography—but not by *racial* differences.

Perspective of Culture History. All races possess some sort of culture, and that alone suggests its great age. As early as 3,000 B.C. the Egyptians were a civilized people, with writing, domestic beasts, cultivated cereals, ploughs, metal tools, and towns. These did not spring out of nothing. Some two thousand years earlier the natives of Badari in the Nile valley already tilled the soil with hoes, raised barley and emmer wheat, made pottery, and ground ax blades. Their culture was lower than its successor because it lacked a script, metallurgy, and ploughs, since these later inventions supplied the same human needs as their earlier equivalents and did so more effectively. For writing fixes information more permanently than oral tradition; metal tools cut or chop better than stone knives or hatchets; and a plough drawn by an ox saves human energy.

However, even the Badarian level was infinitely beyond that of recent Australian and Fuegian hunters, who knew nothing of pottery and farming, being thus more than seven thousand years behind the ancient Nile dwellers. In this they were like forerunners of the Badarians whose remains in the form of rough stone tools are sprinkled over North Africa. Wherever man lived over ten or twenty thousand years ago his condition was that of a modern "savage". If an archaeologist digs below the surface in sites long ago occupied, the landmarks of higher development drop out as he goes deeper. The uppermost layer may harbor bones of cattle or sheep, as well as remnants of cultivated grain; farther down there are traces of nothing but wild game and roots. Near the surface pottery sherds turn up, below them only fragments of basketry. Metal implements overlie stone tools, and these generally grow cruder near the bottom.

Taking all humanity as a single unit, we can mark off certain rough eras in culture history. Though we are not sure when culture began, it certainly dates back to an age of animals that have long been extinct and that required a very different kind of climate, for tools of a definite shape are found together with the remains of this ancient fauna. If the beginning of tool-making is set at about a hundred thousand years ago, savagery was the universal condition of man for by far the greatest part of his existence; for there is no evidence that he farmed anywhere or raised live-stock much over ten or fifteen thousand years ago. Throughout this extensive period man roved about hunting, fishing and gathering wild vegetables. His implements were of wood, bone, shell and stone. Because the last of these materials is most durable, scientists have found a great many of the stone tools, so that the era is often called the Old Stone (Paleolithic) Age.

In the second main period the most progressive peoples raised crops and made pottery, a craft adapted to the settled life of farmers. Later they also bred live-stock and developed a new tool by grinding the edge of ax blades. This last comparatively unimportant invention came rather late, but because of it the entire era is commonly called the New Stone (Neolithic) Age. About 4,000 B.C. the advanced residents of Egypt and Babylonia spurted ahead, beginning to smelt copper and thus ushering in the Metal Ages. Possibly a thousand years later they discovered that their tools were greatly improved by mixing tin with the copper—whence the Bronze Age. With it also came the earliest writing, the plough, the cart and the potter's wheel. At last, probably after the lapse of another millennium some people, perhaps south of the Black Sea where nature offered great supplies of iron, found that this metal was superior even to bronze. We of today are still profiting from this discovery, for our saws, knives, axes and chisels all go back to it.

Accordingly, we may roughly summarize as follows:

Period	Duration
Savagery (Old Stone or Paleolithic Age)	100,000–10,000 B.C.
Dibble and Hoe Farming (New Stone or Neolithic Age)	10,000– 4,000 B.C.
Copper Age	4,000– 3,000 B.C.
Bronze Age	3,000– 2,000 B.C.
Iron Age	2,000 B.C.– present

In this table all dates are mere approximations. Still more important, they deal with mankind as one whole. Only the most favored groups emerged from savagery somewhere about 10,000 B.C.; the Tasmanians were still savages in 1850. In other words, when a step forward was taken in some area the invention may have traveled and gone far, but it did not necessarily reach the remote parts of the world. Thus, iron smelting got to most of the African Negroes and the Scandinavians, but never as far as the Western Hemisphere or Australia. Only during the last century white traders, missionaries and governments systematically spread European civilization to the four quarters of the globe. Thus, for the first time, a certain drab sameness has come to most human groups. Tahitians, African Negroes and Crow Indians have learned not only to cipher and read but to drive automobiles; they have learned to strike matches, thus making fire in a way much superior to anything known to our own great-grandfathers. This recent diffusion, then, shows in the most glaring manner how rapidly culture may change under proper conditions and without the slightest change in the biological make-up of races.

Another point must be stressed. Progress has been achieved, but not at a uniform rate. For by far the greatest part of his existence man was unable to rise above savagery, while the last century witnessed one striking invention jostling another. If we look at particular peoples, we see still more clearly that man has no inborn urge to forge ahead. Roman civilization crumbled into the condition of the early Middle Ages; the Arabs, once the most cultivated people in the world, are now loitering far behind; the Mongols, whose empire was admired by Europeans in the Thirteenth Century, have long since become has-beens. Thus, peoples have their ups and downs. Progress is therefore nothing inevitable and can be maintained only at the cost of labor.

II

HUNTING, FISHING, GATHERING

Economic Life and Population. For us hunting and fishing are sports; but during most of human history they were man's sole means of support, eked out only by the picking of berries and digging of wild roots. Moreover, this "savage" condition lasted until recent times. A little over a century ago vast parts of the earth were inhabited wholly by people on this level—all of Australia and Canada, for example, and all our Pacific and Basin states.

Savage hunters need larger territories than skilled farmers or herders. African Negroes commonly raise crops and breed cattle, hence they have been able to found kingdoms with vast populations. Along a narrow strip on the upper Nile there are concentrated at least 60,000 Shilluk, which means possibly 600 souls to a square mile. If they were deprived of their herds and seeds, they would have to spread over a very much larger area. California ranks as a hunters' paradise, but its aboriginal residents are set at less than 150,000—about one person to a square mile. In less favorable conditions savage population was far scantier: 2,500 Tasmanians roved over 26,000 square miles, while a bare quarter of a million blackfellows spread over the whole of Australia, an area not much below 3,000,000 square miles, the density of some sections falling to 38 square miles for every person.

Hunters, then, must work much harder to live than tillers and breeders, but their backwardness does not prove them dunces. Often conditions prevent any other mode of life. In Tierra del Fuego, Antarctic currents and snowfall bar agriculture; on the alkali-stained shores of western Mexico the Indians can not raise corn because no one could. In such cases the natives do not deserve censure for failing to farm but earn our admiration for the way they turn to account such resources as nature allows them.

Hunting and Nomadism. Savages are not all alike. For one thing, they are not all nomads. Everything depends on how they have adjusted themselves to circumstances. If they depend on wandering game, of course they, too, must roam. There are the Ona of Tierra del Fuego, who live on the flesh of the guanaco. This wild, deer-sized camel forever shifts its quarters, so the Indian must follow in its wake, crossing large tracts to bring down his quarry. The men chase a herd, their families live on the kill, then every one moves to new hunting grounds. Large settlements are not possible here, for great bodies of food-seekers would very soon destroy all the game in a district and then die of want.

Even such simple groups, however, do not wander aimlessly. Each Ona is born into one of thirty-nine bands. He has the right to exploit the district claimed by his own band, but not to trespass on the land of its neighbors, who would treat him as a poacher if he overstepped the well-defined boundaries. So in Australia a blackfellow stuck to his hereditary soil. There he knew the habits of plant and animal species, the position of the water holes; outside he felt lost. Such attachment to a particular region was not merely due to fear of enemies and a sense of one's ignorance in a strange environment; there were also sentimental reasons. Ona and Australian based their ownership on descent from certain ancestors and keenly resented separation from the spots hallowed by their presence. That is why Australians, who made capital sheep herders within their old home territory, lost heart as soon as they had to tend flocks elsewhere. That is why neither they nor the Ona ever conceived war as an attempt to gain new land. Their old land belonged to them and they belonged to the land, and no good could come of taking over what had not been passed on to a group through the ages.

Even nomadic hunters, then, roamed only a definite region. But many "savages" made a quite different adaptation. If they fed mainly on fish, they might easily lead a settled life. Thus, salmon-catching Indians of British Columbia put up solid plank houses in permanent villages; and their whole social structure is far more complex than anything to be found in Australia or Tierra del Fuego. Handicrafts are perfected, wealth is created; and instead of being communities of equals, tribes are split up into nobles, commoners and slaves.

Resourcefulness. A great diversity is thus possible among "savage" communities. In other words, man did not stagnate during those tens of thousands of years simply because he lacked plant and animal husbandry. These particular inventions he did not happen to make until fairly late, but he achieved progress in other ways and solved any number of practical problems. If he was pushed out into a desert region, he had to make the most of his new setting or go to the wall. He could not hunt rabbits by the technique that served for buffalo. In South America he doubtless lost arrow after arrow by shooting at birds in the trees where the arrows got stuck; but at last he made the point blunt and could then recover his dart. When primitive man had discovered a good method he tested it in an experimental fashion. Many South American Indians shoot fish with bow and arrow, and so do the Andaman Islanders. The Samoans use this weapon mainly against pigeons, but they will also let fly their arrows at a fish near the surface. On the other hand, nets seem made for fish; but the Samoans sometimes catch pigeons with the hand nets used to intercept leaping mullets, and the Pygmies of the Congo drive antelope into nets, whereas natives of California enmesh rabbits.

Primitive people also turned to account features of

culture that seem to bear no direct relation to the chase. The dog was man's earliest domestic animal and often developed into a great aid in hunting. In the woods and mountains of Tierra del Fuego dogs are indispensable; they scent the guanaco, track it and bring it to bay so their master can hit it within a comfortable range of 40 to 60 feet. If a wounded beast flees, the barking dogs follow, attack it and prevent its escape. Yet the Ona himself deserves much credit. He knows by what paths guanacos travel to their watering-places, lets his dogs drive them down the mountains and lies in ambush ready to shoot them from cover. When several men join a hunt, the dogs scour a wide tract to bring a herd closer, the sportsmen taking allotted places. Thus, the Ona combine observation of the guanaco's habits, marksmanship, intelligent use of the dog, and a coöperative spirit.

Planned Hunting. Elsewhere organization was on a grander scale. Plains Indians killed whole herds of game by chasing them down steep banks. Another way was to drive them into corrals, where they could be shot at will. Such a hunt netted hundreds of buffalo, but it required much forethought. Before the whites brought in horses, it was not so easy to get the beasts started for the place they were supposed to go. Some beaters had to be sent behind the herd in order to get them moving, perhaps by firing the grass. To keep the victims from escaping, two long lines of rocks or posts were made to converge toward the pound (*Pl. 3*). In the intermediate spaces old men and women did sentry duty, waving robes so as to frighten the game back into the "chute" whenever they tried to break out of line. Thus, almost every one in the community had an allotted task, and the corral for so many buffalo also required joint effort. What is more, it was important that no one should do anything to startle the herd before everything was ready, or the buffalo would make their getaway and the Indians might starve. Accordingly, during the hunt a police force issued orders to the entire tribe and had the right to punish severely

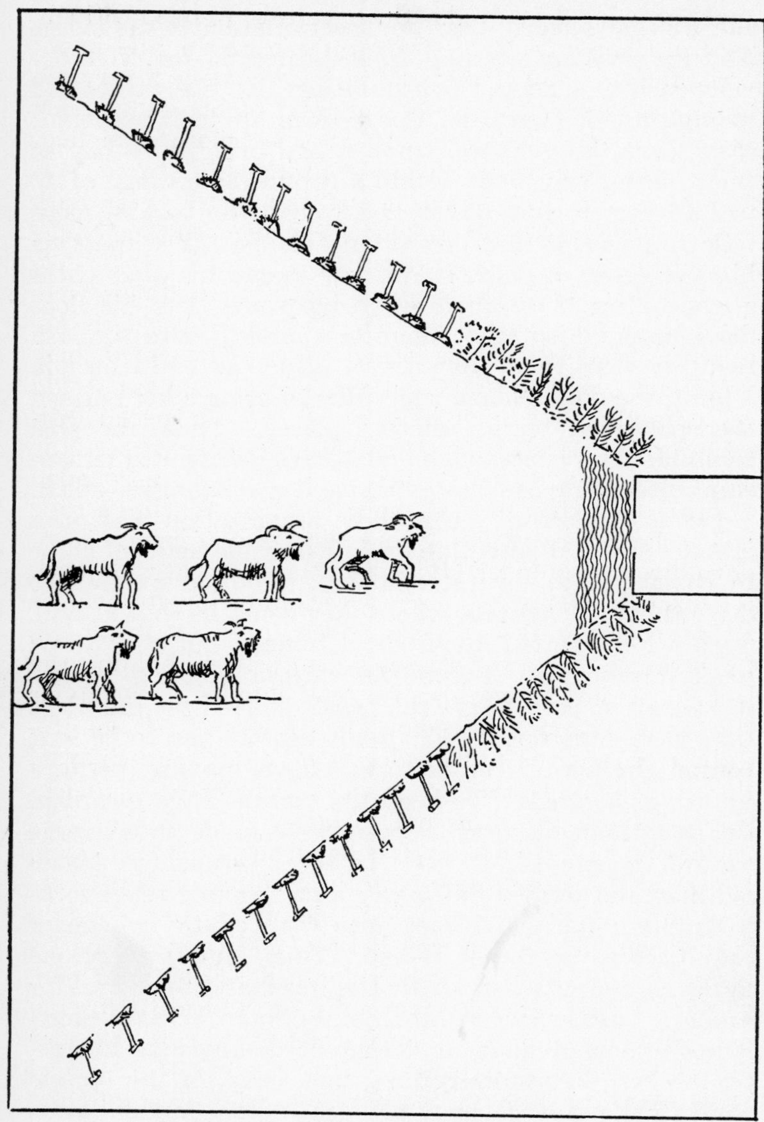

Plate 3: Early Woodcut Showing a Buffalo Drive.
[Umfreville (43)] *

* *In legends the figures in parentheses refer to titles of references for illustrations at the end of the book.*

any one who disobeyed. Such corrals were effectively used in Canada, east of the California Sierra, and in Siberia and Lapland. Impounding may thus be a very old human device for wholesale catching of big game, such as antelope and reindeer. An actual enclosure, in fact, was not indispensable. The Californians of Owens Valley scoured a large tract, firing the brush with bark torches and closing in to drive the deer into a circle, where they could be shot down.

For killing large game many ingenious methods were devised by hunting tribes. The Bushmen of South Africa with crude sticks dug large pitfalls and covered them with light twigs, so that an unsuspecting elephant would come toppling down. African natives have a special aptitude for snares, traps, and deadfalls. On the upper Nile a log is spiked with a heavy spearhead and suspended over an elephant run. As the pachyderm touches a rope below, he releases the log and the weapon comes down deep into his shoulder (*Pl. 4, fig. 2*). A world-wide trick is to sneak near the quarry while imitating its own or some other harmless beast's appearance. A Bushman, for instance, disguises himself as an ostrich, holding the head of a bird above his own, and mimics its behavior till he is within arrow-shot of a herd (*Pl. 4, fig. 1*). California Indians put on deerskins and antlers, pawed the ground, pretended to graze, always keeping to leeward of the game so as not to be scented.

Chasing big water animals calls for methods of its own. In the coves of the upper Nile the Shilluk kill hippopotami with a harpoon. This is simply a spear with a barbed and detachable iron head (*Pl. 34, fig. 2*) that is fastened to a strong rope carrying a float at its far end. The hunter is paddled by an assistant and waits for the first hippopotamus to show its head, when he at once hurls his weapon into its neck (*Pl. 5, fig. 2*). The enraged beast makes a dash for its enemies, who dive into the water and swim for the bank. There they watch the float, which shows the movements of the hippo. After a while

Plate 4: HUNTING DEVICES.

1. An Ostrich Hunt as Shown in a Bushman Rock Painting, South Africa [Stow (41) p. 82] 2. An Elephant Trap, Nyassa District, East Africa [Lindblom (23) p. 96]

a second rope fastened to the bank is tied at the end to the float, and the hunters pull at both ropes till the beast is landed and can be speared. Though the Shilluk no longer live by the chase alone, they are here using an old invention, for bone harpoons were favorite weapons toward the end of the Old Stone Age, possibly twenty thousand years ago.

Fishing. Some savages disdain fish, but the majority are only too glad to vary their diet by this means. In several regions, in fact, hunting is of less importance than fishing: the peoples of the lower Amur River are, above all, fishermen; and from Alaska to Puget Sound the Indians of the coast feed largely on salmon, cod and halibut. As a consequence, primitive folk know in principle most of the tricks familiar to civilized fishermen. The Australians, for instance, spear or harpoon sharks and dugongs; they net, hook, or cage smaller fry, and sometimes drug fish by dropping narcotic plants into the water. The last is a common primitive device for painlessly obtaining food; South Americans systematically tried out the species in their flora to test their stupefying powers. Some forms of fishing required as much coöperation as a game drive. Thus, several Australian beaters will go upstream and frighten fish into nets stretched out by their companions. Still more remarkable are the dams of these blackfellows, with narrow stone passages, the current sweeping the fish where they can be caught easily. At one site there is a vast stone maze, able to withstand heavy floods, in which thousands of cod have been trapped. The natives spent enormous labor to construct this dam, and regularly repaired it, proving that they are neither so dull nor so improvident as their reputation makes them.

Survival of Hunting and Fishing. Because men crave variation in their food, peoples who have long since taken up farming or stock-breeding continue to hunt and fish. For example, the Shilluk hunt the hippopotamus although they grow millet and maintain cattle. As a mat-

Plate 5: MISSILES.

1. Man Throwing a Spear by Means of a Spear-thrower, Queensland [Thomas (42) p. 82] 2. Shilluk Throwing a Harpoon [Hofmayr (13) Fig. 24c]

ter of fact, they go to great trouble about it, risking their lives and exposing themselves for months to the most mosquito-ridden districts of their country. However, there are reasons. They love meat, but the African custom is not to slaughter domestic beasts except for offerings to the gods. Accordingly, the Shilluk must go hunting, and the flesh of the hippo happens to appeal to their taste. For corresponding reasons the peoples of Oceania turned to fishing. True enough, most of them breed pigs. But they can not afford to grow enough vegetable food for very large droves, hence pork is a luxury which as a rule is served on a large scale merely at great feasts and ceremonies. Very few wild animals exist in the South Seas; but the waters teem with fish and the natives proved equal to their opportunities. A Maori net actually measured by a European proved to be over two thousand yards in length; and Captain Cook's sailors had less success at angling than the natives.

It is a very fortunate thing that as a rule farmers and herders did not forget the old hunting and fishing methods. Crops fail when there is a drought, and plagues destroy even large herds. In such emergencies the only way to survive is to turn to the humbler food-getting methods of the savage.

Gathering. As agriculturists like a relish of game or fish, so the savage wants some kind of plant food to vary the monotony of his fare. Even the Ona with their guanaco diet and the Eskimo, who live largely on seal and caribou, are eager to get berries. In other areas wild vegetable food becomes a very important item. Australians dug roots with a pointed stick and collected nuts and bulbs, while similar eatables were gathered in abundance by Bushmen and by many of our Indians west of the Rockies. Indeed, in central California the acorn was the staple, with the pine nut taking its place east of the Sierras. Each group of the Owens Valley people claimed a tract of pines, and trespassing formerly meant war. Large parties would winter in the mountains to lay in a supply. They pulled down the cones with hooked poles, individuals carrying off as much as forty bushels apiece. Apart from pine nuts, bevies of women would collect quantities of seeds, knocking them into large conical baskets with plaited beaters. In addition, there were dozens of species of roots, bulbs and berries.

This same method of gathering could procure some forms of animal diet, such as shellfish. It was also sufficient for capturing beetles, grubs, caterpillars, grasshoppers, snakes and lizards, which were quite acceptable contributions to the menu of Australians and Bushmen. We must not be over-squeamish in judging them. Tastes in cookery differ. The Ona were horrified at the thought of eating pork; and some East Africans despise any man who will touch a chicken or an egg.

Gathering wild vegetables and the lowlier animals is almost everywhere a feminine task. In Australia the women dig up wild roots; among the Ona they pick berries and mushrooms, and so forth. Men, on the other hand, are generally responsible for the supply of flesh. This represents possibly the earliest division of labor.

As farmers keep on hunting and fishing, so they do not by any means drop all interest in wild plant products. The Maricopa of southern Arizona grew a little maize, but during the proper season women picked the wild mesquite beans until the bushes were stripped, for mesquite remained the staff of life. However, uncultivated vegetable food is still eaten in civilized countries, even apart from berries. In times of dearth European peasants use the meal of acorns as did the California Indians, while in Corsica and other Mediterranean areas chestnuts are still a mainstay of the poorer classes.

III

FARMING

Women and Farming. Because women foraged for wild roots and seeds they observed the vegetable kingdom more closely than did their mates and thus doubtless became the earliest gardeners and farmers. Hence the foregone conclusion of many recent tribes that women must provide the vegetable fare and men flesh food: as Australian wives bring in wild bulbs, so East African women are responsible for the banana crop and squaws in the eastern United States were the corn-growers. By common-sense arrangement the heavy work of felling trees for a clearing was the men's share, but planting, weeding and harvesting were feminine tasks. There was, of course, no natural law about this division of labor, so in the course of centuries a good many shifts took place. In West Africa and Polynesia men often shared in farming or even took over the bulk of the work. However, the major change generally occurred when agriculture became a people's principal support so that hunting dropped out as an important occupation. Then the men turned farmers, as among all the higher American cultures from Arizona to Peru; similarly in the ancient civilizations of the Near Orient and the modern ones derived from them, such as our own. The plough, the symbol of advanced tillage, is pretty uniformly guided by men. Yet here, too, special conditions have sometimes modified custom. Traveling in France in 1787, Arthur Young was shocked at the condition of peasant women "ploughing with a pair of horses to sow barley. The difference of the customs of the two nations is in nothing more striking than in the labors of the sex; in England, it is very little that they do in the fields except to glean and make hay; the first is a party of pilfering and the second of pleasure: in France they plough and fill the dung-cart."

Effects of Farming. We must not exaggerate the *immediate* effects of farming either on population or on the general mode of life. Our Eastern Indians raised crops, but only incidentally, remaining hunters at heart. Instead of exploiting their land as white farmers would, they planted only the tiniest fraction of it. Hence the density of population was much less among these tillers than in such favorable non-agricultural regions as California. Only the Pueblos of New Mexico and Arizona and the Indians of southern Mexico and Peru made the most of the cultivable land. Nor can we draw a sharp line between settled farmers and roving hunters. As shown, hunter-fishermen often live in permanent villages, which means that they are as likely as agricultural folk to work at crafts dependent on fixed dwellings. On the other hand, primitive farmers are not nearly so stable as European peasants. Knowing even less about treatment of the soil, they exhaust it more readily and must then make a new clearing, often after only a few years.

The tremendous importance of farming, then, lies not in what it did for mankind when first introduced but what it was capable of achieving after being itself greatly improved. The expert farmers of Peru could maintain a population of possibly three million. This meant a chance for more geniuses to be born, and for part of the people to enjoy leisure during which able craftsmen might perfect their art. But to raise agriculture to such efficiency took thousands of years. The earliest farmers were much more like the Maricopa Indians, for whom corn meant simply a little extra food while they still relied in the main on game, fish, and wild mesquite.

Origins. Indeed, the earliest farmers are best pictured as merely people led by steady observation of the vegetable kingdom to do a little more than merely gather.

Even West Australian natives not only collect a kind of flag but burn over the ground and thereby improve the next crop. In Owens Valley the Californians knew nothing of cultivation, but they did increase the natural yield of wild seed plots by irrigation. We do not know where the crucial step was taken of deliberately planting seeds or cuttings. At Badari (p. 9) barley and emmer were grown at least seven thousand years ago, but it may be mere chance that we have such ancient evidence for this area and not for others. Possibly the beginnings of agriculture have to do with entirely different regions and plants. For all we know, cereals came later than tropical plants, which often yield fruits without much labor.

Implements. Of one thing we are certain: the first cultivator did not use a plough, which appears only about the Bronze Age plane of civilization. The earliest farming implement was doubtless a dibble (*Pl. 6, fig. 1*)—a pointed stick for making holes in the ground; in other words an adaptation of the savage's root-digger. Modern Samoans jab one stick into the ground and loosen the soil by levering up the butt. A thicker stick enlarges the hole, where grow the tubers of the taro, their chief plant. Their fellow-Polynesians, the Maori, had a similar tool ending in a three-inch wide, spade-like blade, the main improvement being a footrest (*Pl. 6, fig. 6*) lashed on to the shaft. When breaking new ground, a row of men would drive these dibbles into the ground and turn over the earth with them. After that the clods were broken up, pulverized with clubs, and cleared of roots. Then natives formed little mounds and planted their sweet potatoes. Our Pueblo Indians also used a dibble with a footrest, but the Maricopa merely had a cottonwood stick flattened chisel-wise at the lower end.

In addition to a dibble the Tanala of Madagascar have an iron spade (*Pl. 6, fig. 5*), to be swung with both hands and driven into the ground to lever out a piece of earth. Hoes being unknown in Madagascar, they use this to construct terraces and to prepare the earth be-

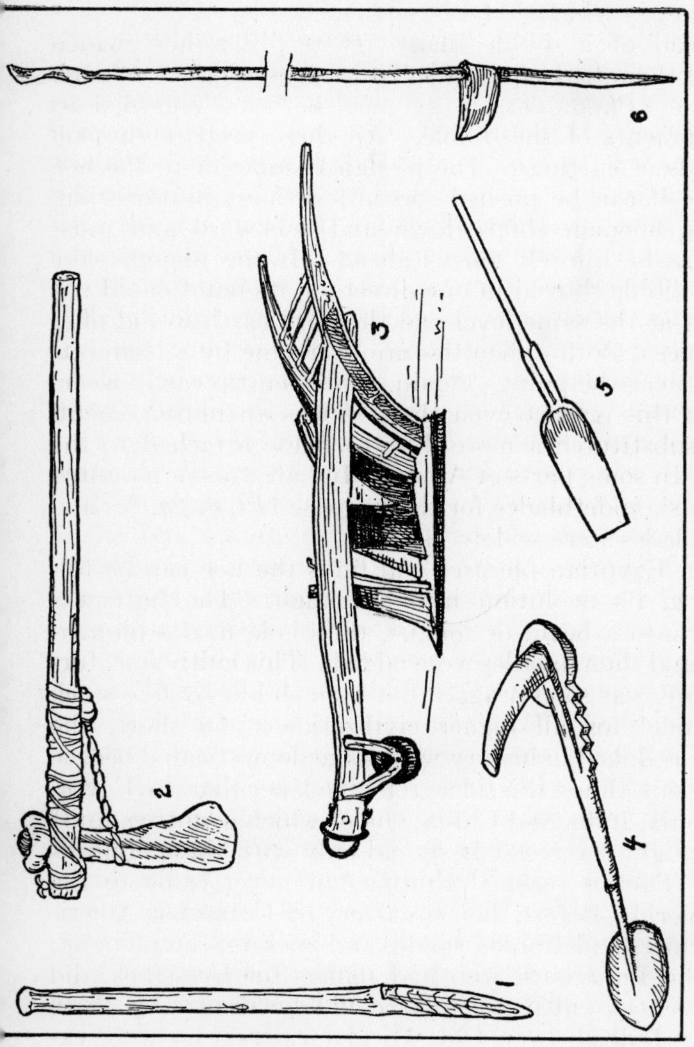

Plate 6: Agricultural Implements.

1. Digging Stick of the Hidatsa [Wilson (46) p. 12] 2. Primitive Hoe, Hidatsa [Wilson (46) p. 12] 3. Daniel Webster's Plow [Rogin (31) p. 15] 4. Spade from the Jur, Upper Nile [Schweinfurth (37) *Plate II, No. 20*] 5. Spade from the Tanala, Madagascar [Linton (24) p. 41] 6. Dibble with a Foot-rest, Maori [Best (2), p. 160]; this dibble is about 5 feet long.

fore planting wet rice. On the upper Nile spades are used not only as agricultural implements but also as a medium of exchange (*Pl. 6, fig. 4*).

Instead of a dibble many tribes ply a hoe, which enables them to scrape the soil after loosening it. Plough and hoe (*Pl. 6, figs. 3, 2*) may both be regarded as developments of the dibble. All three prepare the soil for seeds or cuttings. The plough is superior to the hoe because it can be pushed forward without intermission, while a hoeman chops down and backward and must pause as he himself moves ahead. If the plough were only a dibble shoved in one direction, its point could not be kept at the same level and the hard earth would offer resistance. Both difficulties are overcome by a beam attached near the point. Again, a wooden tip easily wears out; in this respect even the hoe was an improvement, for it substituted a more durable blade attached to the shaft. In some parts of America Indian women mounted buffalo shoulderblades for the purpose (*Pl. 6, fig. 2*), and stone blades were widely used.

From Egyptian pictures and finds the hoe can be followed in its evolution into a plough. The haft was turned into a beam or tongue, the blade into a ploughshare, and then handles were added. This cultivator, furthermore, was soon dragged not by men but by live-stock —a model for all higher civilizations. In short, the plough is linked in history with large domesticated beasts. In ancient times this idea remained peculiar to Egypt, Babylonia, India and China, one of which countries must have taught the rest. It spread only with these civilizations. Thus it reached Europe but never came to the New World. Before their discovery by Columbus American farmers had dibbles, spades and hoes, but no ploughs; even the Peruvians, who had llamas for live-stock, did not invent a cultivator that could be drawn by these beasts. Indeed, even Old World farmers who were exposed to the invention failed to profit by it. The Shilluk of the upper Nile were favorably situated for borrowing an idea developed farther down the river much more than four thousand years ago; but their farming and their live-stock remained two separate departments for them. Indeed, even by primitive standards, this tribe is strangely backward in farming. Weeding is for them proverbially the hardest labor known. Their difficulty, however, is quite unnecessary; it comes from the short handles of their tools, which force a worker to kneel painfully on the ground. Other Negroes in the vicinity do the same work in convenient standing position by simply lengthening the handles of their weeders. But the Shilluk cling to their own style of tool. As champion harpooners (p. 18) they are certainly not lacking in deftness. Their case merely shows that men have their blind spots; not only do they fail to create fruitful ideas themselves, they often balk at taking them over ready-made.

The same tribe astonishes us by its ingenuity in one respect and its lack of intelligence in others. Civilized people show the same blend of insight and dullness—hence are often advanced in one respect and backward in others. In the Eighteenth Century France was intellectually the most brilliant country in the world, but in many ways it fell far below the British level. Immense tracts of arable land remained waste, whole streets of provincial towns were without a glass window, and Paris itself lacked paved streets.

Farming and Stock-breeding. American Indians and Oceanians prove an important fact. Thousands of them had been farmers for centuries before their discovery, yet most of them had no live-stock whatsoever. The Peruvians, to be sure, raised llamas, but agriculture is certainly older with them. On the other hand, though swine are common in Polynesia and Melanesia we know that hogs are everywhere bred only by farmers. Thus, there is positive proof that man did not have to be a stock-breeder first in order to develop into a farmer. He developed from a gatherer of wild roots into a dibbler and hoer; and in some other regions he developed from hunting to stock-breeding. Finally, in Egypt or Babylonia he combined the ideas of plant and animal husbandry. Of course, oxen or horses had to be domesticated before they could be harnessed to a plough; but ploughing, we have seen, is only a special and comparatively late form of tillage.

Food Plants. The foremost aim of planting is a more reliable food supply, and the number of species raised is legion. The main crops of Western civilization have been wheat, barley and millet, with millet dropping behind as human food in Europe and America though it still holds its own in Africa. In southern Asia and Indonesia rice is the great staple for hundreds of millions. Aboriginal America depended largely on maize (for which manioc was substituted in the tropical forests) while the potato loomed large in Peru. In various parts of southern Asia, Indonesia, Oceania and West Africa we find as staples yams, taro, bananas, coconuts and breadfruit.

Vegetables and fruits may be briefly mentioned. Some of our favorite vegetables are of American Indian origin (p. 31). Apples were raised about 2,900 B.C. in Babylonia, where dates, figs, grapes and pomegranates were also very old, while pears and almonds were at least known if not grown. Egypt had dates, melons and gourds, also cabbages, cress and artichokes. The olive-tree flourished in early Syria and Palestine, while apricots and peaches come from China.

Nature of Primitive Farming. Primitive farming is not scientific agriculture. The Lango, neighbors of the Shilluk, know little of rotating crops and waste much timber by clearing new patches when the old plots are exhausted, as they inevitably soon are. But there is a brighter side to their efforts. They know that weeds are harmful and that their millet would rot if exposed to rain. Accordingly, women and children are recruited to clear the plots and help with the harvest, while the younger generation also play the part of scarecrows. Since large beasts are likely to do considerable damage, the Lango set up stout palisades to keep out hippopotami and elephants. In New Zealand the swamp-hen was kept out by much lighter barriers. But the Maori deserve credit as keen observers of the soil; they sometimes even carried quantities of gravel from distant spots to improve their sweet potato plots. Other Oceanians terrace their hillsides for gardens and artificially water them by dams and channels. In New Guinea one 60-foot long flume of hollowed logs serves as an aqueduct over a gorge 30 feet deep. So the rice terraces of the Ifugao in the Philippines constantly amaze white travelers. Even if they should have been modeled on those of higher Asiatic civilizations, the natives manage them with admirable skill. For one remarkable achievement primitive farmers deserve the sole credit. The bitter manioc is a plant peculiar to South America, and in its natural state contains prussic acid. Yet the tropical forest dwellers ingeniously grate the pulpy parts, squeeze them in a basketry press to get rid of the deadly poison, and drive out its residue by heating. Thus a positively harmful species is transformed into a staple crop.

The outstanding thing about primitive agriculture, however, is not this or that clever device. What counts is that every single cultivated species of any importance goes back to illiterate peoples. With all our knowledge of botany and soil chemistry we have done nothing but improve varieties of plants, while the simpler folk turned the trick of bringing them from the wild into the cultivated state. Potatoes, the best kinds of beans, squashes, maize, tomatoes and pineapples were wholly unknown to Europeans until they borrowed them from the American Indians. Millet, barley and wheat go with the ancient civilizations of Egypt, Babylonia, India and northern China, but they were first raised when these countries, too, had a primitive population. Thus, we owe an immense debt to the forerunners of the old Oriental cultures, and even to members of other races. Without the

American Indian, Ireland and eastern Europe would lack their mainstays, the potato and maize, respectively.

Planting for Non-dietary Uses. Although agriculture serves above all for getting food, it does more than that, for many plants are grown for other purposes as well or even exclusively. The banana, for instance, has supported millions of African Negroes and Oceanians; but in the Philippines an inedible species, popularly called "Manila hemp", furnishes fiber for cordage and weaving. In Polynesia the paper-mulberry was grown for its bark, which could be made into cloth; and East African trees were used in the same way. In the Near Orient and the countries influenced from that source linen was the great textile, and it was derived from flax. The Chinese equivalent was hemp, while cotton spread from India, even reaching some of the African Negroes. Independently, the Peruvians grew cotton, which was carried as far north as the Pueblo Indians.

Nor must we forget stimulants. Early Egyptian kings already kept vineyards, and both on the Nile and in western Asia the vine was grown well before 3,000 B.C. Barley yielded a beverage as well as bread in the Near Orient, the earliest known recipe for brewing beer going back to Babylonia of 2,800 B.C. In Uganda, millet—elsewhere the staff of life—is only grown for brewing, and while the banana is the staple food there, some of its varieties are raised for beer. Most Polynesians cultivated the pepper plant known as "kava" in order to prepare a beverage from its roots. From India eastward through Melanesia the chewing of a palm nut, the "betel", with lime and a pepper plant, took the place of kava. American Indians had many varieties of tobacco; even some hunters learned enough gardening to raise this weed. The Chinese have grown tea from time immemorial; the coffee tree is a native of Abyssinia; and the Spaniards first learned to drink cocoa from the Mexican Indians.

These milder stimulants suggest the sugar-cane, which came to be cultivated on a larger scale because of them.

It was first discovered by Europeans on Alexander the Great's excursion into India in 327 B.C., but was only introduced a thousand years later by the Arabs, remaining a luxury until the Eighteenth Century. Many Oceanian tribes raise the plant, chewing the stalk without being able to manufacture sugar, while the Samoans grow it mainly for house thatch.

The coconut, too, has varying uses. In the low coral atolls it is the South Sea Islanders' staff of life, but in better favored parts of the area its dietary value is completely overshadowed by other uses. The natives plait its leaves into baskets or mats; carve weapons from its wood; use the shells for cups and bowls; smear their bodies with the oil till they fairly glisten; and make from the fibers of the husk a superior cordage known as sennit. To take another case, the Maori cultivated the gourd (*Lagenaria vulgaris*) for a marrow-like dish that could be prepared from the fruit in its early stages; but water and food containers made of the ripened fruit were of more account.

Diffusion of Plants. After men had come to depend on planted vegetables they did not readily drop the achievement. When they had to migrate they took with them the parts necessary for cultivation. Thus, the Maori carried various species from central Polynesia into New Zealand. They had no success with the tropical coconut and breadfruit, while the paper-mulberry ceased to be significant, being unable to thrive in a temperate climate. The yam, important in Samoa and Tonga, proved too delicate except in the northernmost sections; but taro, though no longer a staple as in Samoa, could still be grown widely in the North Island. Most instructive is the history of the banana family. All its cultivated members are grown from side-shoots, never from seed; hence if bananas are raised anywhere in the world where no wild form exists men must have brought the shoots there and planted them. Now wild bananas extend only as far east as Tahiti, yet bananas are cultivated thousands of miles farther, in Easter Island, so the Polynesians must have imported them to this last outpost of their race. Also, botanists tell us that the wild bananas of Africa, with their inedible fruits, large seeds and lack of side-shoots, could never be made into the African *cultivated* bananas that support millions of Negroes. Accordingly, the side-shoots must have been brought there from southern Asia, where cultivated bananas and their possible wild ancestors flourish side by side.

But cultivated species did not spread only by migration. Often contacts with a foreign culture are sufficient. In 128 B.C. a Chinese general traveled to parts west and brought home the seeds of the grapevine and alfalfa. In recent times the Lango became acquainted with the banana through raids into neighboring regions and introduced it on a small scale into their own country. About prehistoric borrowing we can have no direct record, but we can prove it by botany. Thus, maize has no wild relative in North Dakota or New England, hence the cultivated plant must have spread from the one region where a possible ancestor exists, namely, southern Mexico. But for this no wholesale migration was essential; within the last 200 years Indians from Montana visited corn-growers of North Dakota, exchanging skins for the ripe cobs. Such visits could easily lead to deliberate planting of borrowed kernels, and so the species might be spread widely even without major movements of tribes.

In modern times whites have systematically spread cultivated plants very far from their original home. Though coffee is a native of Abyssinia, the Arabs took over its cultivation; later the Dutch introduced it into Java, and finally the major center came to be in Brazil. Soon after Columbus's voyages European seafarers began to introduce what had been exclusively American plants wherever they could be profitably grown. Thus, African Negroes who have never seen an Indian nowadays are growing manioc, maize and tobacco; Ireland is as unthinkable without the potato as the Balkans without Indian corn; and the pineapple is associated in our minds with Hawaii instead of tropical America. On the other hand, Old World species such as bananas are now grown in tropical South America, and wheat has ousted even Indian corn among the Maricopa.

Multiple Source of Farming. Clearly, there has been a great deal of both spontaneous and organized diffusion of cultivated plants and many peoples have been nothing but borrowers. One naturally asks whether all of them have got the idea from a single source, such as Egypt. This would imply that American Indians remained hunters until some mysterious Old World travelers arrived to give them a course in agriculture. In fact, on this theory every attempt in the world to grow any species would be an imitation of the first cultivation, possibly ten thousand years ago.

Now our hundreds of species of food plants, fruit trees, and textile species are certainly not the result of so many independent ideas. We *know,* for example, that rye was not. At first, it was rated merely a disagreeable weed that insisted on attaching itself to desirable cereals. But in the loftier parts of western Asia it was found to yield fruit where wheat crops failed or were uncertain. Hence rye was deliberately planted, and the discoverers of its utility added an important food plant to humanity's stock. This was undoubtedly not the only case in kind. When early farmers had successfully planted one species they tried the same processes on others. Accordingly, we do find that, whatever the staple, other plants are grown alongside it. Thus we have the trio of wheat, millet and barley in the Near Orient and northern China, and the comparable "three sisters" of North American Indians—maize, beans and squashes. However, it is a far cry from this to saying that *all* cultivation the world over has a single origin.

For "cultivation" is really not at all the same thing in every case; it is only a blanket term to suggest that fruits are produced by intelligent planning. But how are they produced? Sometimes by sowing, sometimes from tubers, sometimes from shoots. Egyptian and Babylonian farmers sowed wheat, barley and millet broadcast. The people of northern India, we now know, were in touch with the Babylonians and grew wheat in about 3,000 B.C. Quite possibly they applied the idea to a wild plant within their range and so came to grow rice, with the adjustments proved desirable by the peculiarities of the species. But causing seeds to sprout is something utterly different from lopping off the side-shoots of a banana to set them in the ground; and growing sweet potato or manioc tubers is again another matter. Sowing wheat might suggest rice, but never planting a banana shoot; and vice versa.

The history of farming is therefore a complex matter. It goes back about ten thousand years and developed independently in several centers. In the Old World, barley, wheat and millet are very ancient, but tropical species such as the banana or the breadfruit may, for all we know, be still older than any of them as cultivated species. In any event, the farmers of the New Stone Age were not ploughmen but dibblers and hoe-gardeners. However, with their simple tools and in their illiterate condition they laid the basis of our own economic life by achieving agriculture.

IV

DOMESTIC ANIMALS

Domestic animals differ from their wild ancestors in no longer being shy or hostile toward man. However, that is only a minor distinction. Australians catch frogs or rats and tie them up for playthings, and Brazilian Indians hang up lizards in their huts, but these are mere pets. Nor does the difference between "wild" and "domestic" hinge on the usefulness of the beast. In India and Indochina elephants do a great deal of heavy work, yet they are only "tame" not "domestic", because they do not reproduce in captivity as do cattle, horses, or sheep. There lies the rub: the majority of species will not breed freely except in freedom, and in scientific language only those which can are "domestic". In contrast to the hundreds of cultivated plants, their number is very small. Disregarding forms such as the cat and the bee, which do not affect human life very deeply, the important domestic species can be counted on our fingers. Dogs, cattle, sheep, goats, pigs, horses, donkeys, camels and reindeer very nearly exhaust the list.

Domestication of the Dog. The dog stands in a class by itself as the earliest species permanently linked with man. Actual remains of the animal are not known from sites earlier than the transitional period between the Old and the New Stone Age, but that is because so far only western Europe has been thoroughly explored. Neither Denmark nor England nor Portugal, where the finds occur, is likely to be the original home of domesticated dogs. Far more probably that lies in Asia; and since it must have taken savages some time to wander from there to the shores of the Atlantic, we may set the beginnings of domestication a little further back, in the latter part of the Old Stone Age. This does not make it one of the most ancient traits of culture, yet it places dogs several thousand years before any other domestic beast. The dog's comparative age is strongly indicated by its distribution, which none of its competitors even approaches. Cattle, sheep, goats and swine were bred in the Near Orient 6,000 years ago, but none of them had spread to America by 1492, while the dog existed there in three main and sixteen lesser varieties, being found as far as the extreme tip of South America. From comparative anatomy we learn that all these breeds go back to a single ancestor in Asia. Indeed, all dogs in the world are probably descended from an Asiatic wolf, except that the greyhounds of early Egyptian dynasties may have the jackal for their ancestor. The Indians therefore must have brought dogs with them from the other side of Bering Strait, and this must have happened thousands of years ago to explain the numerous varieties that sprang up in the New World. To turn to other regions, even the Australians kept dogs, though of peculiar type, the "dingo"; and this they, too, must have brought from the mainland of Asia. Comparatively few primitive tribes lack the animal, and in most such cases clearly because they *lost* it. The Polynesians, for example, failed to transport dogs over the thousands of miles to Easter Island; but they got them safely to New Zealand and everywhere else. Only of such extremely rude people as the Tasmanians can we believe that they never owned dogs. They doubtless wandered off to their remote island before any men had achieved domestication at all; and later they were so far away and so poorly equipped for travel that they no longer shared in the advances made by other human groups.

What difference did the dog make in the savage's life? As already shown, it was of the greatest utility to the Ona; at a pinch even a woman could get game by setting her pack to track, chase and kill a guanaco. The Vedda of Ceylon hunted deer with dogs; the Shoshoni of Idaho, mountain-sheep; the Hottentot of southwestern Africa, antelope.

The Polynesians, hard put to it by the dearth of mammals, ate dogs. So did Peruvians, Aztecs and Iroquois, who had no such excuse, hence evidently relished the flesh for its flavor. But many tribes recoil from such practices. The Maricopa, who dream of dogs, regard them as persons, give them names, and will not beat even annoying curs. Indeed, primitives carry such sentimental attachment to great lengths, as when a Vedda once killed a fellow-tribesman for bewitching dogs. By way of contrast, the "pariah" dog of Palestine and Anatolia is left roaming about half-wild to devour carrion as the public scavenger.

Barking turns into an asset for the savage master, for it announces the coming of a stranger, a possible enemy. At a higher level watch-dogs aid in tending live-stock, as when a Lapp uses them to guard his herd against wolves. But such service depends on the breed. In east Siberia dogs are still so wolf-like that they would tear up any reindeer entrusted to them. On the other hand, animals may well be useful even if ferocious by nature so long as they are docile with their owner. Early travelers complain of the fierce Plains Indian curs, yet the natives broke them to carrying burdens. Crow warriors packed their moccasins on dogs' backs, and before white men brought horses a dray of two converging poles was tied to the beast's back, the butts dragging along the ground (*Pl. 25, fig. 4*). There was a netted frame between the two sides, and to this could be fastened a load of firewood, or even a little child.

In some areas dog traction grew into a more important feature. Men can not ride dogs, but they can make teams draw vehicles with or without passengers. An Arctic dog enables his master to travel over the ice in loaded sledges at the rate of four or five miles an hour for ten or twelve hours. On trade journeys in search of raw materials not obtainable in his own district an Eskimo finds his "huskies" an invaluable possession; and they also put the Arctic hunter in a position to scour a much larger area for game. But dog traction has lingered on in civilization. French Canadians still journey in dog carts, and in Hamburg as late as 1924 vendor after vendor could be seen pulling his vegetable cart to a city market with the aid of his dog.

Shaggy breeds have sometimes furnished a decorative material. In New Zealand the long hair of such dogs was sometimes sewn on cloaks.

In short, dogs enriched savage life, actually and potentially, in a number of ways: they made hunting easier and could themselves be eaten; they protected their master and his possessions; they could be used as pack animals or to haul a sledge; and their hair and hide sometimes ornamented clothing. Indeed, for such people as the Eskimo and the Ona, to possess them might become a matter of life or death.

Pigs and the Cattle Family. No one knows when and where the next wild animal came to be domesticated. Honors were long divided, or rather disputed, between Egypt and Babylonia. But the pig may well have been first brought under control in China or India. Recent discoveries in northwestern India prove the inhabitants to have kept cattle, sheep, buffalo and pigs about 3,000 B.C., while in New Stone Age sites in China vast numbers of the bones of domestic pigs have been found. It is not even clear whether the earliest live-stock breeders were already farmers or still in the hunting stage. At one time hunters were considered too nomadic to keep animals, but that argument implied too low an estimate of the savage. Since many hunters lived in fixed villages, just as primitive dibblers did, and constructed pounds for catching herds of buffalo, they were also able to build corrals for a few wild cattle. However, it is an error to speak of domestication in general as if conditions had been and were alike for all species. The pig, for instance, can not be driven over large distances in droves; hence pastoral nomads never raise the pig along with their flocks and herds of sheep, horses, cattle and camels. It is uniformly associated with agriculturists. Transporting swine in boats was simple enough, so we usually find Melanesian and Polynesian dibblers with a trio of domestic animals—dogs, pigs and poultry. Quite conceivably, then, the earliest hog-raisers were primitive farmers. But this does not prove that the first reindeer- or cattle-breeders also had to be agriculturists.

The history of pigs suggests various interesting points. Though kept at a very early date in the Near Orient, they were apparently put to no use whatsoever. Among recent Melanesians they were indeed eaten, but as a rule only at feasts and ceremonies. On the other hand, Jews and Mohammedans taboo their flesh completely, while with the Chinese pork is the outstanding flesh diet. This, however, is coupled with another fact: though the Chinese have kept cattle for several thousand years their aim was not to get beef, which seems a specialized development of modern civilization. The ancient Babylonians rarely ate beef, which was far too precious for common fare; and the Kirghiz of Turkestan deliberately disdain such meat in favor of mutton and horse flesh. The latter, by the way, was still generally sold at European markets in recent times. The eating or not eating of pigs seems to have been tied up with religious and social attitudes rather than with the availability of the animal.

Whatever may have been the earliest use of cattle it was not that of feeding the population with their flesh, since that was not customary either in China or the Near Orient. These two centers differed in one essential feature. The Egyptians and the Babylonians milked their cows as early as 3,000 B.C., as may be gathered from ancient Egyptian pictures. The practice is also characteristic of India. On the other hand, the Chinese never have milked any female animal, nor have the Japanese,

Koreans and Indochinese. Now domesticating wild cattle must have been a very difficult thing to do and probably was achieved only once. The early Chinese, living farther west than today, doubtless came in contact with the outposts of Babylonian civilization and learned about cattle from them. Why, then, did they not take over dairying as well? For the simple reason that this always comes relatively late in domestication. Milking is a quite artificial practice since a cow's udders are designed only for the calf's use. That is why most cattle-breeders can get the cow to yield milk only in her offspring's presence. In East Africa, if the calf has died its stuffed skin is brought before the mother beast to trick her into supplying milk. In other words, when the Chinese had a chance to get cattle from the Babylonians, *no* nation in the world had yet mastered the secret of milking. Thus, the Chinese presumably acquired the one idea they and the other ancient civilizations share, that of harnessing an ox to a plough. And since ploughing is itself an advanced trait, we may guess that the very first domesticators of cattle neither used them in tilling nor for their milk, nor for their flesh; that they probably kept them for sacrificial use.

Some illiterate peoples have come to exploit their cattle more or less. On the one hand, there are the Negro and Negroid cattle-breeders of East Africa, either themselves farmers or living among farmers; on the other, the pastoral nomads of Asia. The Africans keep either a variety that originally came to them from ancient Egypt or a humped breed, the "zebu", which must have been derived from its old home in India. In either case, they never use cattle for ploughing, and eat their meat only at feasts; cows are an economic asset because of their milk, an important feature of the native bill of fare. Yet Negro dairying is backward; cheese remains unknown, and even butter often serves only as a cosmetic smeared over the body. Although the natives have not progressed to regular stall-feeding, they take good care of their animals, washing the udders after milking, burning fires to keep off insect pests, and tending sick beasts. Some tribes have regular veterinaries. Throughout this area there is a love for cattle that surpasses belief. Natives are known to have committed suicide because of the loss of a favorite cow. The Shilluk pay cattle for a wife, sing poems in praise of a cow, and honor a friend by addressing him as "my ox". Yet they are far from getting the greatest possible profit from their stock. Their small cows yield little milk; cattle being slaughtered only in religious sacrifice, beef is eaten only when an animal happens to die; and oxen normally are used for nothing whatsoever. The natives lavish enormous labor on massaging the humps and twisting the horns into fanciful shapes, thus proving that men work hard from other than practical motives.

The Kirghiz also rarely kill their cattle, mutton being considered superior to beef. But otherwise they have gone much further than the Shilluk. They not only milk their cows, but prepare a set of dairy products—soured milk, curd and cheese. Oxen are pack-animals, sometimes carrying loads of 400 pounds when the camp moves. They are also ridden by children and shepherds, who guide their mount by a halter tied to a nose plug.

When the zebu and our common cattle were once under control, men living in particular regions tried to apply the same idea to other members of the same zoölogical family. Thus, in the arid highlands of Tibet the natives managed to domesticate the yak from a considerably larger wild form. They have made it into a beast of burden and a mount. But they also depend on it for food, eat its flesh, milk the females, churn, and make cheese. Its hair is used for ropes, tents, and blankets; from the hide they make bags and trunks, even boots; above the timber line the dung serves for fuel. To the nomadic Tibetan, then, the yak is an animal of outstanding value; and where the native has turned farmer, he again patterns its use on that of the ox by harnessing it to a plough.

Another cousin of our cattle is the true buffalo—not our American bison, which has never been domesticated, but the water-buffalo of India or carabao of the Philippines. It is better suited to swampy regions than common cattle and has accordingly been transported rather widely from its home in India, where it seems to have been bred as early as 3,000 B.C. Its exploitation differs characteristically in different regions. Since the people of India already milked zebus, they naturally did not scruple to do the same to the buffalo, transferring their dairying technique to its yield. Not so in Indochina and Indonesia. Here the East Asiatic prejudice was too deeply rooted for any such development. In the Philippines, for example, carabaos are essentially beasts for sacrifice; elsewhere they were sometimes harnessed to a plough. It is worth noting that the true buffalo was introduced into Europe about 1,200 A.D. It is still an animal of some importance in the Balkans and Italy.

Pigs and cattle, then, can be useful to man as food (provided he wants to use them in this manner), as religious offerings, as a source of pride and social prestige. In addition, cattle may be milked, although milking is comparatively late, or harnessed to a plough. They may also be used for packing loads too heavy for a dog. Finally, hides are of value for clothing, tent covers, and other articles. In the course of time mankind extended domestication to related forms, namely, the zebu, the yak and the buffalo.

Goats and Sheep. For all we know, goats and sheep may be older than domesticated cattle. In any case, they appear in equally early Egyptian representations and remain extremely important in southern Europe. The two species are generally linked, actually and in thought. The Kirghiz go so far as to pasture them together and to mix their milk indiscriminately. Sheep yield less milk than goats, hence in European sites of the New Stone Age there are more evidences of goats than of sheep. By the

Bronze Age, however, the development of wool (see p. 52) and of weaving had led breeders to prefer sheep.

Sheep-breeding is the principal form of animal husbandry in Turkestan, where the Kirghiz breed a variety with a fat tail weighing up to forty pounds and painfully dragged along the ground. In a wild state no such sheep could survive. The natives, acknowledged masters as mutton cooks, slice and boil the tail, prizing it as a delicacy. They make various dairy products, including cheeses, and beat the wool into felt (see p. 119) used for rugs, mats, tent covers and clothing. In Africa sheep and goats are not so important. Some African tribes do not eat the meat at all, using only the skins.

Transport Animals: The Camel, the Horse, and the Donkey. Babylonia registers domesticated two-humped camels at about 1,000 B.C., the one-humped dromedary being mentioned in 854 B.C. as a native of Arabia. Horses appear in Babylonian records about 2,300 B.C., some 500 years earlier than in Egypt. The oldest of the three animals is undoubtedly the donkey, which was used extensively in Egypt by 3,000 B.C. and must have been domesticated somewhat earlier. The domestication of the horse probably resulted from the earlier success with its more docile cousin, the ass. But even so, breaking in the first horse must have been no mean task.

In certain areas the same ideas were applied to camels. In the dry steppes of Turkestan the camel provides an enormously convenient transport, the more sensitive one-humped variety being used in the South. Where the nomads turn tillers they plough with the camel, imitating their neighbors' use of the ox. While the flesh is not highly esteemed, camels' hair ranks above sheep wool. The milk of the camel is rich in fats and, when fermented, yields an extremely nourishing drink.

For the Central Asiatic nomads, with their sheep, goats, cattle and horses, the camel is only one beast among others. Not so for the Arab, in either his homeland or North Africa. To him the dromedary is absolutely indispensable. True, he piques himself on his steeds, but they are mainly for mere show. For unlike the Kirghiz, the Arab neither milks mares nor eats their flesh; and as for travel, after two days in the desert no horse can keep up with a camel, which for several weeks doggedly makes its three or four miles an hour for eight or ten hours a day. Without the camel Arabia would be largely uninhabitable. The endurance of this animal passes belief. When fresh pastures are available, it can forego water for a month. In fact, in Kordofan the herds are driven into waterless wastes for two or three months and return in fine condition. The herders in the meantime live almost entirely on camels' milk. In Arabia itself many a desert dweller has saved his life by killing his beast and squeezing out the water from its paunch to quench his own thirst. In short, the camel serves the Arab for food and drink, as pack and mount, provides hair and hide for rugs or clothing, and dung for fuel. But with all its virtues it was not an easy beast to bring under control, and even today handling it requires expert skill. The camel is difficult to mount, and the saddler must be very cautious since any injury to its hump might prove fatal to the creature. Danger also looms in traveling up and, still more, down hill, for the camel's fleshy toes give no hold and it may easily break a leg. Further, it is disconcerting to a rider when his mount suddenly flings itself a-wallowing in the soft, loamy soil.

The Arab sets his non-utilitarian horses on a pedestal high above the indispensable camel. At times his own flesh and blood must thirst in order that a favorite mare shall not suffer. He thus illustrates the common human trait of exalting mere luxuries.

But, as proved by the Kirghiz case, that is not the rôle of the horse in other cultures. During a four months' season the Mongols and Kirghiz milk their mares six or seven times a day—a dangerous task performed only by men. The milk is fermented into "kumyss", on which the people virtually live all summer. consuming enormous amounts of this slightly intoxicating beverage, which satisfies hunger as well as thirst. These nomads not only live on kumyss for months, but prefer the flesh of young mares to any other meat. They also cut the skins into cords for bridles, whips, and belly-bands. Rich Kirghiz, owning up to a thousand head of horses, ride only geldings, while the poorer classes mount stallions or mares. With their vast herds the Mongol, Turkish, and Tungus nomads became superb horsemen and developed cavalry tactics, by which they often threatened and sometimes overthrew the superior civilization of China. Cavalry, however, can not be proved to have existed anywhere in the world before 860 B.C., when it appears in the Assyrian army; and horses as mounts are first mentioned in Babylonia in 1,130 B.C. In earlier times the Babylonians merely used their horses for drawing war-chariots, and about 1,700 B.C. this use was introduced with the animal itself into Egypt, where horses were neither ridden nor harnessed to a plough or common cart. The Babylonians knew of horses as early as 2,300 B.C., but linked them with the wild mountaineers to the north and east; even some 300 years later they escape mention in Hammurabi's code. In other words, the positive proofs for domestication of horses do not go back as far as for cattle, sheep and goats; the oldest references indicate some Central Asiatic group of nomads as the first domesticators.

American Indians in the plains of North America became expert horsemen after the Spaniards brought horses to the New World. They hunted buffalo more effectively on their mounts, but never took to eating horse flesh or to milking their mares.

Donkeys are still the favorite pack animals throughout the Mediterranean world. Even in the center of Madrid the braying of donkeys still blends with the tooting of automobile horns. They appear single, in pairs, or four in Indian file, sometimes drawing a two-wheeled covered cart, sometimes straddled by their master or mistress, with a big hamper dangling on either side. The donkey has been used for threshing grain ever since ancient Egyptian days, and is occasionally harnessed to the plough in Palestine and Syria. However, its function is, above all, that of a beast of burden. In that capacity it occurs even among the primitive Masai of East Africa, who pack donkeys rather than oxen. But elsewhere the increasing use of horses and camels, which latter probably did not exist in North Africa long before the birth of Christ, made the donkey somewhat less important.

The Reindeer. The history of the reindeer is hotly disputed. Some scholars hold it to be the first of all livestock species; others insist that it was the very last, not much antedating our era. The earliest literary reference to its domestication is indeed very recent—in a Chinese source of 499 A.D. Irrespective of controversy, the positive facts are highly suggestive. Here is an animal abundant in northern America and widely hunted there as the "caribou", but never domesticated by Eskimo or Indian; the Alaskan reindeer were all imported by the United States Government to aid the aborigines. But from Lapland in northernmost Scandinavia to the Chukchi and Koryak on the west side of Bering Strait we find one tribe after another of reindeer-breeders. Some features of their animal husbandry are uniform; in other respects there are wide differences. Thus, most of the groups use the lasso with the herd, all of them know that human urine lures the reindeer and binds it to its master, most of them geld the males.

The part played in native life by the reindeer varies enormously. For some Tungus groups in eastern Siberia it is only indirectly of economic value. They can not afford to slaughter their beasts, which are few in number, but they *ride* them and thus cover a larger territory than would otherwise be possible. In other words, their livestock assumes the rôle of the horse for the American Plains Indians or the dog for the Eskimo: it enables them to scour wider territory for game. They thus remain essentially hunters though they keep stock.

Not so the Chukchi of northeasternmost Siberia. They breed reindeer not yet thoroughly tamed, hence difficult to corral and harness, but they own large herds and accordingly can slaughter and subsist on the flesh. Though they do not follow the Tungus riders' example, they harness reindeer to sledges. Since the reindeer is both larger than the dog and does its own foraging, the Chukchi thus enjoy a superiority over the Eskimo, who has to carry provisions for his huskies. The Lapps have gone a step further. Probably taught by Scandinavian neighbors, they milk their stock, churn butter, and make cheese from it. Their reindeer thus yield both dairy products and meat, and largely serve the same purposes as our cattle.

Independent Invention versus Borrowing. In many ways reindeer domestication seems to follow older models: the Siberian sledge to which it is harnessed is derived from the dog-sledge, reindeer-riding is an imitation of horseback riding, and milking was suggested by the milking of cows. This is characteristic of the story of domestication as a whole and exactly parallels the case of cultivated plants. Not every single animal presents a wholly novel invention; often there is simply extension of an old idea. As wheat, barley and millet are all sown broadcast in the Near Orient, so people who had once learned to milk cows would try the trick on sheep, goats, camels, reindeer, or even mares; if they succeeded in ploughing with oxen, they might experiment with horses and camels; if asses could be mounted, a daredevil would straddle a horse, and so forth. Yet here, too, some discrimination is in place. The donkey might suggest packing a horse but hardly a chicken; and neither would be likely to lead to cricket-breeding, in which the Chinese have for centuries indulged on a large scale. In other words, telescoping as we will the diverse ideas of animal husbandry, a number of irreducible inventions remain. The dog did not lead to an abstract idea of "domestication" as a pattern to be applied equally to horses, cats, and silk-worms.

Here again the American data are significant. In contrast to Old World peoples our Indians had very few domestic animals. They never attempted to do more than hunt the buffalo (bison) or reindeer (caribou), and though it is interesting that the Mexicans kept bees and turkeys their lives could have continued quite as well without these luxuries. Apart from the dog anciently brought from Asia, the Indians had only two beasts of any importance, the llama and the alpaca, both derived from such dwarf camels as the wild guanaco. Moreover, these were limited to the area of the Peruvian empire and even there never played the basic part of the camel in Arab life or of horses and cattle among the Kirghiz. Had the notion of domesticating these beasts come from Asia, the Peruvians would have borrowed the ideas that accompanied domestication there. But the Peruvians neither produced ploughs to which to harness llamas nor did they milk or develop into pastoral nomads. They remained farmers, who packed their beasts with small loads, ate the flesh but not as a staple food, made the dung into fuel where wood was scarce, and sheared the wool for textile work but without ever beating it into felt. Peruvian stock-breeding thus never blossomed forth into a definite type of economic life as did its Arab, Mongol, or Turkish equivalents. Nevertheless, it was an *original* development. The impulse could not have come from the higher Asiatic peoples, who would hardly have failed to transfer their concrete ideas about the use of domestic beasts. It could not have come from the South Sea Islanders, who had only the dog, the chicken and the pig, none of which would serve as a model for a domesticated dwarf camel!

To put it briefly, there has been a great deal of borrowing in the history of domestic animals. Man traveled with his beasts as he traveled with his tubers or side-shoots, and in strange lands they were transmitted to new neighbors or looted by them. Ingenious spirits would try out some of the old ideas on new species, harnessing reindeer instead of dogs to sledges, riding reindeer instead of horses, or horses instead of asses. But such originality was not all lavished on adaptation. Peculiar circumstances would lead a people to observe a special group of animals and achieve their independent domestication. The Chinese, for example, who have always shown an extraordinary interest in insects, have from time immemorial raised silk-worms, a very different activity from breeding camels or cattle. The Egyptians kept cats before 2,000 B.C., viewing them with such religious awe that they were buried in mummified form in cemeteries. One feature, their use as retrievers, was doubtless modeled on dog training, but the origin of cat domestication was distinct. Not only are the habits of the two species very different; but while the dog has been diffused all over the world the cat until quite recently had a very small distribution. Even in Europe it was not known until the beginning of our era.

Motives for Domestication. The story of the common fowl also offers much food for thought. In Oceania, where flesh is scarce, chicken is prized, sometimes as an economical substitute for pork. But tribe after tribe in Africa makes no *practical* use of it whatsoever. In Urundi, for instance, all castes despise its flesh, and all except the lowest have a horror of the eggs. Here, the sole reason for keeping poultry is a religious one; they are dissected because the people believe that the color of the entrails reveals the future. Here we have a clue to the ultimate origin of other species, too.

In Burma, the very area where according to zoölogists chickens were probably first domesticated, their most prominent use is in divination and cock-fighting. *The motives for breeding them, then, are ceremonial and sportive.* This recalls some facts about other species. Milking, we noted, is never an early development and may even, as with mares, remain a dangerous enterprise. Beef does not figure much in the household economy of the Chinese and only rarely among the ancients of the

Near Orient and modern Africans. The plough was invented later than the domestication of large stock. Wild sheep have no wool. Horses were not ridden until fairly late times. What, then, could have been the motives for the earliest domestications?

Evidently, the original reasons for keeping animals were not practical ones. No primitive intellect could foresee that some time sheep would evolve wool or that cows would come to yield abundant milk even after giving suck to their calves. These practical considerations could not, then, have acted as motives. Practical uses are the result of domestication, not the cause. But, as shown (p. 37) even lowly tribes keep pets; some South Americans maintain veritable menageries from which they derive no benefits except in the way of amusement or sentimental satisfaction. In the Orinoco area parrots, mice, turtles and small deer are caught when young and raised with the utmost care; elsewhere ostriches are the children's playmates. Biologically, we may assume, only relatively few of the many species thus kept by primitive folk proved capable of permanently associating with man and breeding in human society. These, and only these, became domesticated. In domestication they assumed new traits, such as wool, which *at a later stage* made them of practical value.

Historical Effects of Domestication. But this value varied widely in different areas and attains its maximum among the pastoral nomads of Central Asia. The Kirghiz have all their economic wants supplied by their flocks and herds of sheep, goats, camels, asses, cattle and horses. Vegetable food, traded in or raised by sedentary branches of the people, is a desirable addition but not a necessity where the larder teems with kumyss, cheeses and mutton. Like all good things in this world, this, too, has its negative side. The pastoral nomad is dependent on his herds and their comfort. He is obliged to wander with them in search of fodder and shelter; a reindeer-herder must follow his stock to the coast when they try to escape insect pests, and back to the interior in the winter. Again, a plague may suddenly bereave him of all his wealth. Thus, reindeer Lapps have been forced to turn to fishing by the sudden loss of their stock. Where pasturage is limited, one group of herders comes into conflict with another, and there may be actual war of nomad against nomad tribe.

More significant, however, have been the inroads of pastoral people on peasant populations. Mobility gives the nomad an advantage, which is increased when he rides horses and commands cavalry. Thus, the comparatively simple Mongols and Tungus harassed and conquered China, and the former overran half of Europe. They, like the Arabs after Mohammed, proved able to absorb the higher culture of agricultural and urban civilizations and themselves formed centers of culture. In the Thirteenth Century Marco Polo found nothing in Europe equal to the institutions of the Mongol empire; and in 950 A.D. Arab culture in Cordova was incomparably superior to anything in Christendom. The historic rôle of the herder, ultimately based on his use of domestic beasts, can thus hardly be overestimated.

V

FIRE, COOKING, AND MEALS

Fire

Uses of Fire. Probably no single feature of material life so definitely lifted man above the animal plane as the use of fire. By burning grass savages were able to drive herds of big game toward cliffs or pounds; food often became edible only by cooking; and without means of warming himself man could never have settled in the colder zones of the globe. The hardy Ona makes shift with scant clothing and a mere wind-screen for dwelling, where a flurry may leave him covered with an inch or two of snow by dawn. When tired from a day's march he does not even bother to put up his shelter. But a fire he must have, not only for comfort but for survival.

Apart from these basic uses, fire alone enabled man to develop his crafts. The carvers of British Columbia made huge dugout canoes from hollowed cedar trees; but in order to get the desired width they had to force the sides of the log apart, and that could be done only by filling it with water and dropping heated rocks into it. There could have been no true pottery without fire; and no metallurgy at all, for smelting, casting and alloying require directed heat. No wonder that humanity treasured such a valuable possession and almost everywhere built elaborate myths and rituals around it. From Peru to New York State there were Indians who periodically made new fire in a ceremonial way. The ancient Greeks had their story of Prometheus; and even the Australians and Basin tribes of North America explain how fire was once hoarded by a selfish being, from whom it was at last snatched by trickery.

Early Methods of Fire-making. Fire was evidently discovered tens of thousands of years ago, for in some very old sites occupied by the long extinct Neanderthal type of man archaeologists have found charcoal and charred bones. What lucky chance taught humanity to make the discovery we can only guess; but all recent tribes when first met by whites utilized it. The Andaman Island Pygmies did, though they were unable to make fire at will, and hence had to watch their fires to keep them going. The Bakango, Pygmies in the northeastern Congo, were recently found in the same situation. But their next-door neighbors, also Pygmies, have got further. In sitting posture they hold down the ends of a pitted piece of dry wood with their feet and rapidly twirl a stick twelve inches long in one of the pits. The constant rubbing removes wood meal and heats it till a spark, dropped on the dry bark spread for tinder, can be blown into a blaze. This *fire-drill* (*Pl. 7, figs. 3, 5*) is the commonest implement for the purpose in human history. The Egyptians used it in dim antiquity, and so did the ancient Greeks and Romans. Widely known in Asia and Australia, it is almost universal in Africa and America. Under perfect conditions it yields a spark in ten seconds; Ishi, a California Indian, turned the trick in twenty-two. But there is a knack to twirling the shaft without making it come out of the pit, which gives the dust a chance to cool off. For this reason a beginner will feel his palms smarting before he sees as much as smoke. Nor are all primitive folk equally expert. Often two men take turns at the job, or one man holds the lower piece while the other revolves the drill. Also, circumstances are rarely ideal. Humid weather and damp sticks interfere, and unless there is good tinder to catch the spark all the labor will go for naught, a condition that holds for all the aboriginal methods. Some primitives, notably North Siberians and Eskimo, devised an improvement that saved blisters. Instead of twirling the shaft directly with their hands they twist the string of a bow around the stick and then rotate it merely by moving the bow (*Pl. 7, fig. 1*). This invention was also known to ancient Egyptians. With a sharp tip this instrument can be used to drill holes, which also applies to one type of drill found in Madagascar (*Pl. 7, fig. 2*), the pump-drill (see p. 117).

Some Australian tribes drill, but others saw, fire, which is also the favorite way of Indonesians (*Pl. 7, fig. 4*), with a bamboo bed and saw. Australians substitute a shield on the ground held with the feet and a wooden spear-thrower (p. 214) vigorously drawn back and forth over it. The wood dust is separated, the tinder prepared, and the spark tended much as in drilling. South Sea Islanders typically "plough" fire, i.e., they push a pointed stick back and forth on another so as to rub a groove and thus continue till the friction generates heat, smoke, and at last a spark (*Pl. 7, fig. 6*).

Some Asiatics learned to strike fire, obviously a more effective method than either drilling, sawing, or ploughing it; though ceremonially the Hindus retained the drill until fairly late times. The strike-a-light was the method of our great-grandfathers. To quote Henry Adams, the grandson of one of our presidents: "The flint and steel with which my grandfather Adams used to light his own fires in the early morning was still on the mantelpiece of his study." Strangely enough, the Tierra del Fuegians, among the simplest of American aborigines, used the same principle. Of course they had no steel, but pyrites took its place in every adult Ona's bag along with the equally indispensable lump of flint and dry fungus for tinder. This method was fairly ancient in Europe. In the New Stone Age and even in the immediately preceding period archaeologists have found pyrites and flint in the same sites, a discovery which strongly suggests how fire was produced.

Notwithstanding the skill primitive men often attained, they never enjoyed having to produce fire at a pinch. Accordingly, they took pains to keep one going when it was once kindled and carried slow-matches on

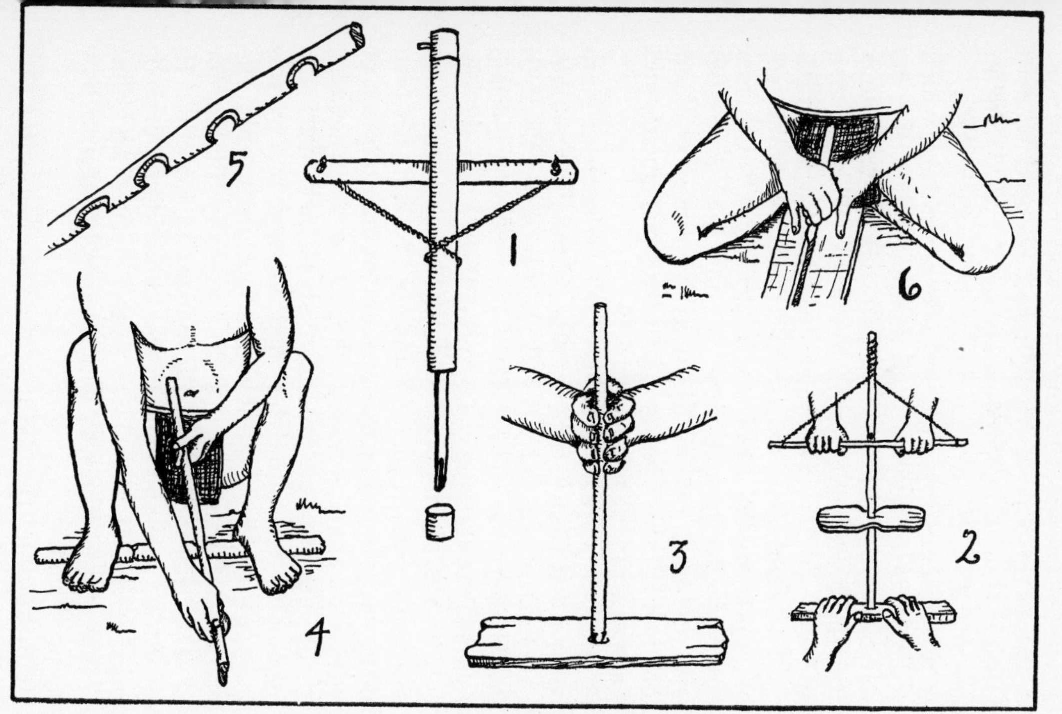

Plate 7: Fire-Making Techniques.

1. Yukaghir Bow-drill [Jochelson (17) p. 429] 2. Madagascan Pump-drill [Linton (24) p. 65] 3. Madagascan Palm-drill [Linton (24) p. 61] 4. Madagascan Fire-saw [Linton (24) p. 61] 5. Hearth, Queensland [Roth (33) Fig. 14] 6. Melanesian Plough-drill [Lewis (22) *Plate XX, No. 2*]

the march. The Havasupai of northern Arizona took with them six-foot coils of cedarbark rope tied together at intervals and from time to time blew on the smoldering end to keep it alive. This dislike for unnecessary work survived into the flint and steel period of modern Europeans. Sixteenth Century Scandinavians kept fire burning overnight at the cost of much timber, or borrowed fire from a neighbor at the grave risk of starting a conflagration in the thatched roofs of their houses.

Modern Matches. Only the early years of the Nineteenth Century saw a real advance over the primitive fire-drill, fire-saw, fire-plough, and strike-a-light. It was discovered that splints of wood coated with sulphur and potassium chlorate ignited when dipped into sulphuric acid. For some time such matches remained impractical because they were unsafe. But at last phosphorus was combined into a harmless mixture, which was applied to the surface on which a match was to be struck. And finally in 1844 John Edward Lundström built the first Swedish match factory. Until then the most progressive nations of the world were very little ahead of the Tierra del Fuegian in the matter of fire-making.

Cooking

Primitive cookery is underrated by the ignorant. It has its oddities, but also its peaks of achievement. A Russian governor kept a Kirghiz to prepare mutton for him; Baron Nordenskiöld found the roast fish of the Chaco Indians equal to any he knew; and according to Dr. A. B. Lewis a yam as cooked in Melanesia excels our baked potato while the roast pork from a Melanesian oven "has a flavor that more civilized methods of cooking can not produce."

Cooking without Vessels. Certain tribes are hampered by lack of vessels. The Ona have none, hence are unable to boil food. They hang slices of guanaco from a stick bent toward the fire and turn the meat this way and that until it is evenly broiled. Fish and rodents are gutted and then baked in the hot ashes; so are birds, after having larger feathers plucked and smaller ones singed off. Australians used similar devices. They threw gutted fish and plucked birds on the fire and roasted kangaroos by cooking one portion after another. But locally they displayed greater ingenuity. In the west a native would wrap the fish in bark and slowly bake it in heated sand covered with hot ashes. Among some of the blackfellows a regular oven was in vogue: they strewed wet grass on hot stones, put their birds on top and covered them with the grass, then added more hot rocks and covered everything with earth. Kangaroos were also steamed or baked after this fashion.

The earth oven, however, is distinctive of Oceania. In some islands it was the only means of cooking, and it has survived even the introduction of metal vessels. The New Zealanders—ignorant of pottery as were all the Polynesians—dug a shallow pit and lined it with stones to keep the wood together. A fire was kindled and fuel heaped on, with stones on top. When the fire had burned down, green leaves were put on the hot rocks as a resting-place for the food, another cover of foliage followed, and water was sprinkled over all. Then came a covering of mats and finally of earth to confine the steam; and after two hours the dish was cooked. The Samoans as a rule did not cover the oven with earth, preferring to let some of the heat escape through interstices between leaves. Also they cook entirely by dry heat, never sprinkling the food or stones. The hot stones are conveniently handled by tongs made of a doubled piece of coconut leaf midrib.

The Oceanian oven had great advantages over parching or broiling. It was more economical of firewood and prevented direct contact with charcoal, ashes, and smoke. Even pottery-making Melanesians generally cooked only small quantities of food in their earthenware and fell back on the oven when preparing a feast. Dr. Lewis witnessed the opening of a Fijian oven containing half a ton of taro and yams as well as two large eviscerated pigs, baked whole; and this was considered very meager compared with the capacity of ovens in earlier times.

Stone-boiling and True Boiling. But people without pottery need not forego boiling altogether. One can not wrap up liquid food, hence the Polynesians put it into wooden bowls and drop heated stones into them. Stone-boiling, however, was far more important in Kamchatka and North America. In British Columbia hot rocks were put into wooden boxes; the Californians cooked in water-tight baskets; the Plains Indians in pits lined with hides, and the Canadian tribes in birchbark vessels. As might be expected, people did not at once wholly give up an old practice for an innovation. Thus, fairly recent potters, such as the Havasupai of Arizona, to some extent kept on cooking in baskets even after clay vessels had become popular for kitchen use. But strangely enough the ancient method survives in Europe, too, where earthenware has been made for thousands of years. Modern Basques of Guipuzcoa, Spain, occasionally stone-boil milk in wooden pails, whereas Yugoslavian herdsmen use bark containers.

Native ingenuity is illustrated by Havasupai travelers, who improvised a vessel from the barrel cactus by burning off the spines, cutting away one end and removing the pulp, so that hot stones could be put in.

Cooking in pots is less laborious and cleanlier than the use of stones. But the same result is achieved without earthenware throughout Indonesia, where a bamboo tube takes the place of earthenware, a custom extending to New Guinea. When primitive man had attained true boiling, he had virtually a complete set of cooking techniques. As a rule, he applied them all, as we do, not indifferently but according to the dish required. The Havasupai boil corn meal, squashes, beans and squirrels; they roast rabbits in ashes; and they toss wild seeds about in a basketry tray with live coals, thus winnowing the food from the lighter charcoal, which is tossed up and blown away.

Preliminaries and Relishes. Food often requires more than heat before becoming fit to eat. Even ignoring such special cases as manioc (p. 31) and acorns, vegetable fare must generally be treated by some preliminary process. The Maricopa pounded their staple, the mesquite bean, in a mortar and then ground it on a quern (hand-mill). Mortar and pestle (*Pl. 15, fig. 7*), quern and muller, are widespread means for making flour. Some people use both, others specialize in only one of them; and gatherers of wild seeds employ them no less than farmers. The Euahlayi of Australia, for instance, grind seeds on flat stones and make them into cakes, the querns being treasured as family heirlooms. Often the same process is repeated over and over again. The Shilluk pound their grain four or five times, then grind it on a hand-mill and mix it with milk.

From barley and wheat flour the Egyptians and Babylonians baked bread in very early times and all manner of cakes as well, though Syria seems to have excelled as a land of pastrycooks. The Egyptians were the first to leaven their dough, passing the art on to Greeks and Romans; the Chinese, as in regard to milking, developed along distinct lines and have never taken to a ferment for bread-making. The Pueblo Indians make "wafer bread" out of a batter of corn meal. A Hopi woman spreads some of this with her bare hand on a stone slab propped up over a fire and a minute later removes a thin sheet, which she rolls up into parchment shape or folds into a "loaf". It tastes not unlike corn flakes; the natives prefer it to our bread and a huge pile of "loaves" is set for ready use at any family meal.

Pounding and grinding are only two of the most outstanding processes. The Samoans have many others. They cut up raw fish or pork with bamboo knives; strip green bananas and grilled breadfruit with wooden or bamboo peelers; scrape taro, yams and breadfruit with half coconut shells cut to an edge; grate coconuts on a piece of sharpened coconut shell mounted on a tripod the cook can straddle; and strain liquids free of chewed or scraped solids. They even use a primitive mincing machine—a number of strips of the skin of a coconut leaf midrib—for cutting up the soft flesh of the immature coconut. One of their favorite vegetable dishes well illustrates how processes are combined. They cook breadfruit on the open heated stones of an earth oven, removing the charred rind with peelers and putting the cooked fruit into a bowl. There it is mashed with a pounder, and the immature seeds are flicked out with a strip of coconut leaf midrib. Coconut cream is added as a relish, with or without sea water, and finally the hot mass is deftly divided by pinching off smaller pieces and rolling them into balls ready to be served.

Condiments and relishes have varying importance according to the nature of the diet. The Ona meat-eaters require not even salt, and after weeks of straight guanaco fare Father Gusinde, too, found himself no longer needing it. Many primitives, on the other hand, covet salt and get it at great inconvenience to themselves. Thus, some of our Southwestern Indians made special expeditions for salt-gathering, while in Africa it is a standard article of trade. Natives of New Guinea make a several days' journey to the coast, bringing back salt in the form of sea water, which they sometimes drink to gratify their craving. Some collect the ashes from burned driftwood, mix a portion with water and after settling pour off the salt solution for use in cookery. Certain plants are burned in order to extract salt. The Shilluk, for example, leach the ashes of durrah stalks, place them in a perforated gourd and pour in water, which drips through, charged with salt.

For the epicures of Polynesia coconut cream and its many derivatives are indispensable for meat, vegetables and puddings. Mixed with sea water and cooked in a wrapper of banana leaf, the cream thickens like curds and thus turns into sauce used with all of 17 distinct dishes, while the oil separated by further heating is essential for a taro dainty.

In the cookery of Spain and other Mediterranean countries olive oil largely replaces our butter. Tibetans, on the other hand, drop butter into their tea as an essential part of their diet. African Negroes as a rule only smear butter on their bodies for a cosmetic, but the Shilluk prize it as a first-rate relish with a vegetable course.

Storage. Reports of primitive improvidence are grossly exaggerated. Even the Australians put nuts and seed-cakes aside for future use. Since fresh meat was not always available, Plains Indian hunters knew enough to dry buffalo flesh after a drive, pound it up, mix it with smashed chokecherries, and pack it away in rawhide bags. To seal this "pemmican" against insects and moisture they poured melted buffalo tallow over it. By itself the dried pulp of berries smashed with stones was similarly stored. The Hidatsa of North Dakota, who farmed part of the year, kept corn, beans, and squashes in sizable jug-shaped pits—the larger ones deep enough to require a ladder. A single household might have four of these cellars, using the same ones year after year except when mice spoiled them. The observant women of this tribe also discovered that it paid to gather from a good crop enough seed for two years. If the following year's yield was of poorer quality or suffered from frost, they would still be able to plant good seed the third season. The Klamath of southern Oregon sun-dried their fish, strung them on poles and put them on high stages, where they were covered with boards and bark. Seeds were stored wholesale in communal pits three feet deep and fifteen in diameter; and an ill-smelling plant known to deter even grizzlies was buried with the food. The Maori raised storage huts on piles about four feet high, but put their staple, the sweet potato, into pits. Great care was needed, since decay set in with the slightest bruise and soon spoiled the whole mass. In the Marquesas, too, the

Polynesians took elaborate precautions against a famine. Into leaf-lined storage pits averaging four feet across and three feet in depth they lowered enough fermented breadfruit paste to support a family for a year; while the great tribal pits were thirty feet deep and half as wide. There in theory food kept almost indefinitely; the natives, at least, considered it edible after fifty years.

Meals

Timing of Meals. The time and nature of meals differ greatly even in civilized countries. An American in Madrid enters his hotel restaurant at nine in the evening only to find himself the first dinner guest. But he need not hurry, for his motion picture show will not begin before ten-thirty or eleven. In Vienna dinner is in the middle of the day and supper at eight-thirty; and since the curtain of a play is likely to go up an hour or two earlier, the theater-goer avails himself of the first intermission to take a meal in the café conveniently located in the theater itself. Primitive peoples differ still more in their customs. The Ona have no fixed meals; the fire is kept going all day and any one so minded roasts himself a snack, usually at short intervals. Tribes of the Rio Pilcomayo district farther north also eat when the fancy seizes them, by day or by night. Queenslanders take their main meal about sundown, but otherwise eat whenever they choose. However, two fixed meals a day are common. The Shilluk breakfast at about nine and dine at seven. They are content with a single course provided it be an ample one. Meat is never served by itself, but cut up and mixed with some flour preparation. Maori and Samoan likewise found two meals adequate. Normally the latter left for their gardens at dawn and returned about eleven for a hearty breakfast-lunch; dinner followed sunset, when men had come back from their fishing and the flies had retired. But Samoans were not hide-bound in this respect and were quite ready for an extra repast whenever food was abundant.

Utensils. Table manners also vary enormously in space and time. Forks were probably quite unknown among all primitives except that in Fiji they were used with human flesh. But we must remember that they were very recent in Europe. In 1423 a Spanish nobleman pointed out that the two-pronged and three-pronged implements in vogue for carving would help convey meat to the mouth without having one's fingers greased. Italians are credited with forks a century or more earlier, but in both countries they were extremely rare and precious objects confined to the highest circles. In 1295 Pope Boniface VIII had four large and three small golden forks; and sixteen years later Pope Clement V owned two large and three small ones. In more northerly countries this refinement appeared much later. A motion picture quite correctly shows Henry the Eighth of England tearing a chicken apart with his bare hands. Until 1600 polite French society knew nothing of forks, in fact, the middle class did not take to them until the Eighteenth Century. Thus, the Ona who seizes a lump of guanaco meat with his hands and tears off morsels with his teeth is only two hundred years behind the most advanced Caucasian nations. And these were millennia behind the Chinese, who used ivory chopsticks in the Chou dynasty (1,122-247 B.C.), and wooden or bamboo ones before that.

On the other hand, knives, spoons and ladles are widespread on all levels of culture. For milk and flour dishes the Shilluk carves and bends horns into spoons, other food being eaten with simpler shell implements. While four hundred years ago a party of civilized Western Europeans thought nothing of drinking from a single glass, every Shilluk in a household has his own individual gourd, while a large calabash bowl takes the place of a plate. Before and after each meal one of the women brings a pitcher with water, so every one can rinse his mouth and wash his hands. The Chané Indians of the northern Argentine are also reasonably cleanly, each eating from a separate bowl, washing his mouth after a repast, and then squirting the water over his fingers. Other Chaco tribes are less meticulous: the Ashluslay mix their mashed fruit in a large calabash, each grasps as much as he can with his fingers, sucks at it, and then expectorates it back into the common container. If these Indians depart widely from our standards, genteel Samoans largely conform to them and greatly outdo us in formality. They serve food on flat oblong trays of coconut leaflet; but if a distinguished chief is to be honored he alone receives such a platter, others being served on mere leaves. One or two taros and a breadfruit go to each platter, then follow the fowl, pork, and other viands; each guest gets a drinking nut. While both hands are used for other dishes, the favorite taro leaf preparation must be eaten with a piece of coconut leaflet midrib. Attendants anticipate the guests' wishes, fan them, and keep off the flies. When the visitor is done, he pushes his tray away; it is quickly removed, and he receives a bowl of water for washing his hands. At a banquet the portions far exceed what one person can consume, so behind each guest sits a member of his family, who stows away the remains and takes them home in a basket.

Etiquette. Here and in Polynesia generally, the etiquette of eating merges into something like a religious ritual. The Maori had a strong prejudice against eating inside a dwelling. Also their women always ate apart. This latter custom has also been noted among Greenland Eskimo, Melanesians, Chaco Indians, Shilluk, and many other peoples. The Samoans, ever intent on class distinctions (see p. 91), prescribe precisely how each recognized section of a pig is to be distributed according to the rank of the guest. For this reason they often hand out raw pork, not because they prefer it that way but because too much cooking blurs the exact boundaries of the ceremonial divisions—a grave error on the part of the superintending chief and his chefs. "A failure in ceremony can not be remedied, but underdone pork can be recooked." Accordingly, the visitor need not eat his half-raw portion but may take it home to have it heated up. By an equally odd rule Samoans never serve to a high chief any part of poultry but the legs. Again, it is a terrible insult to be offered an uncropped chicken; only a few years ago a cook's negligence in this respect all but precipitated a strike of the builders' guild.

Comparing the ceremoniousness of the Samoan with the informality of the Chaco Indians, we note once more how widely primitives differ in custom. Comparing Samoan usage with our own, primitives often are discovered to be not less particular, but particular about different things.

VI

DRESS AND ORNAMENT

Three main motives exist for dress—modesty, protection, and improving one's appearance. In addition, it marks status in the community: one's sex, tribe, married or single condition, and rank.

Modesty. As for modesty, probably all peoples have strong feelings on the subject, but this sense of shame expresses itself about other things than nakedness. Thus, in Brazil the Swedish scientist Nordenskiöld met an Indian woman who was perfectly at ease without a stitch of clothing, but completely put out when she found herself without her usual nose ornament. California Indian males, and especially old men, constantly went naked in the old days except when it suited their convenience to do otherwise. On the upper Nile, Shilluk women wear a leather apron, but men walk about wholly nude. Adult Melanesians rarely go that far, but their young commonly remain unclad until puberty. In other words, there is no instinct that makes human beings everywhere ashamed to expose themselves. In some regions and periods it is highly improper, in others perfectly correct.

Protection. Protection against the weather is a real motive for the use of clothing, but human groups have sometimes shifted along with the scantiest dress in a severe climate. Thus, much of Australia, as well as all of Tasmania, lies so far south of the equator as to be subject to cold winters. Yet many of the natives wore nothing but a large shell or a tassel of fur string. Most remarkable of all is the case of the Tierra del Fuegians. The Ona chases his guanacos through the snow without

Plate 8: PRIMITIVE FULL-DRESS COSTUMES.

1. Boy from the Chaco [Nordenskiöld (29) p. 120] 2. A Shilluk Man [Hofmayr (13) Fig. 29]

any garment, and at his great initiation ceremony he will stand outdoors nude for hours. At best he wears a stiff cloak of guanaco-skin, and that he fails to wear with the warm woolly part inside. He has hardened himself enough to survive the climate, but no human beings could be comfortable in the circumstances. Accordingly, the Ona shivers in the Antarctic blasts even if he manages to live on. He certainly can not depend on his dress to keep him warm. When drenched by rain he folds up his cloak and squats naked by the fire; and if a long spell of cold plagues him, he gets relief by smearing his body with a thick layer of guanaco fat and red paint. In other words, even bleak latitudes do not *mechanically* produce ample clothing. There are two alternatives: weaklings perish; and physically fit groups live on, but in discomfort. The same holds for all geographical influences. Man must adjust himself somehow in order to survive, but he may solve his problems as a master or as a bungler, or with any intermediate grade of skill.

While the Fuegians merely muddle along, peoples in corresponding parts of the northern hemisphere coped with the same problem in truly elegant fashion. The Kirghiz of Turkestan have a winter costume of sheepskin robes, fur caps with ear protectors, leather breeches, felt stockings, and high heeled top-boots. The Aleut wear rainproof clothes made from the guts of sea and land mammals. Siberians and Eskimo (*Pl. 11, fig. 5*) have a complete outfit of leather clothing in the summer and furs in the winter—aprons, trousers, boots, coats, scarfs, caps, chin protectors, even goggles against snow-blindness (*Pl. 11, fig. 2*). Tropical regions also may suggest suitable protection. On the upper Nile helmets plaited of human hair and topped with ostrich feathers (*Pl. 12, fig. 7*) are edged with feathers and worked into a sun-protector.

It is not always against the weather that man must guard himself. In the tropics he often wears sheaths to keep insects from entering the openings of his body.

Combs (*Pl. 12, fig. 4*) are decorations but also welcome weapons against vermin. Californian women carried burdens by a pack-strap over the head and wore a cap to prevent chafing their foreheads. A Samoan gets his soles toughened from infancy, but if he has to wade inside a reef with extra sharp coral he dons bark sandals. Similarly, Bolivian natives find sandals convenient in regions with plenty of prickly plants; and on the Pilcomayo River, which is infested by fish with razor-like teeth, they put on thick stockings. Footgear in general serves as a protection in traveling. Californians usually went barefoot except when on a trip outside the village; and the same holds for the Maricopa of southern Arizona. Indeed, the same is true of people on a much higher plane: the ancient Syrians and their neighbors put on sandals or slippers only before a long journey. Here is also the reason why the Indians of the British Columbia coast rarely used moccasins—they traveled mainly by boat. For walking over snow and soft ground the natives of eastern Siberia, northern Japan, and North America as far south as the Sierras of California put on snowshoes. On the other hand, skis—now a favorite sport of ours and of our Canadian neighbors—were unknown to American aborigines. They were invented in northern Eurasia and are used from Lapland to the Amur River and eastern Siberia, where a native straps on his long thin boards and can then keep up with a reindeer. As skis and snowshoes are special devices for traveling afoot, so the boots of Asiatic nomads were developed with horseback-riding, illustrating how closely footgear goes with travel.

Materials and Style. The materials for protective covering vary greatly, often depending on other features of culture. Hunters of large game, as for instance the Ona and our Plains Indians, largely use the hides of animals more or less carefully prepared for the purpose. For obvious reasons the material could also be employed by stock-breeders such as the South and East African Negroes. On the other hand, only stock-breeders could

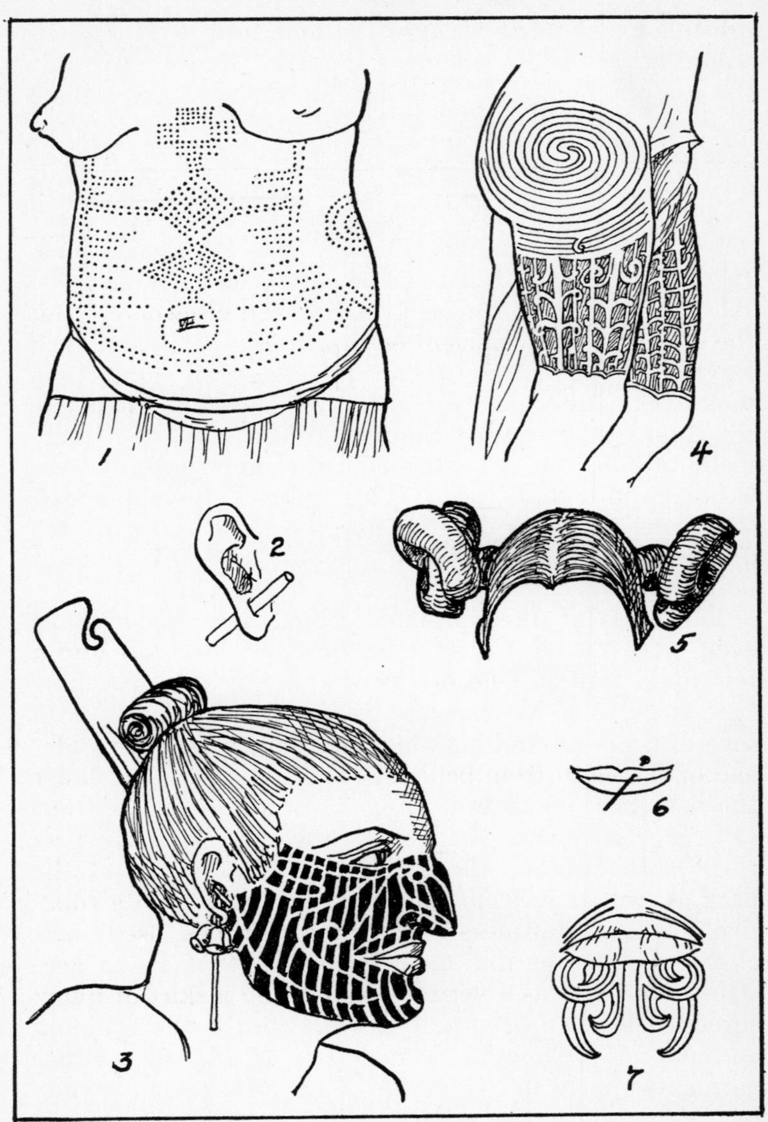

Plate 9: Body Decoration.

1. Abdominal Scarification, Congo Pygmies [Schebesta * (36) p. 96] 2. Ear Plug Worn by Congo Pygmy [Schebesta * (36) p. 201] 3. Maori Man with Tattooed Face, Headdress, and Ear Ornaments [Best (2) p. 210] 4. Maori Tattooing on the Hip and Upper Leg [Best (2) p. 220] 5. Hair Dress Worn by Unmarried Hopi Girls (From a Photograph by Lowie) 6. Lip Pin Worn by Congo Pygmy [Schebesta * (36) p. 200] 7. Maori Tattooing on the Lips [Best (2) p. 220]

** The writer is indebted to F. A. Brockhaus, Leipzig, for permission to reproduce these items.*

use felt for clothing because the hair from wild animals would never yield a sufficient supply. Accordingly, only the pastoral nomads of Asia developed such dress, though in lesser degree it spread to China and southern Europe (see p. 119). Again, cotton and linen garments depend on two features of higher level, farming and the art of weaving. Accordingly, in America cotton fabrics occur only in the more complex cultures, from Peru to Arizona. In the Old World, India raised cotton as early as 2,700 B.C., and thence it spread to Africa and elsewhere. But the at least equally ancient civilizations of Babylonia and Egypt had flax instead, whence linen costume; and China took over neither flax nor cotton but developed hemp as the chief textile species, though clothing was also largely made of silk. On a lower plane the inner bark of trees is beaten into cloth (see p. 120). The Polynesians used the paper-mulberry for the purpose, East Africans the fig-tree, and various tribes in Celebes and South America indigenous species.

The style of the garments from these materials is even more varied, nevertheless most of them fall into a few main types. One of the simplest is the masculine "gee-string": a Melanesian man wraps his bark cloth several times around his waist as a belt, passes the wider end of the cloth from behind between his legs and under the belt part, and lets it hang down apron-like in front (*Pl. 12, figs. 1, 2*). In Guiana the men similarly pass their cloth between the legs, bring up the ends at the back as well as in front, and suspend them from a rope-like girdle. Marquesan women sometimes used bark cloth precisely as did their husbands, that is, as gee-strings, but also as a veritable skirt; and a skirt of finely shredded leaves fastened to a waist cord is the common garment of Melanesian women (*Pl. 12, fig. 3*). Other garments appear in Polynesia. Thus, Marquesan women passed two corners of a bark cloth sheet round the neck, tying them over either shoulder; and the men fastened their sheets as a cape over both shoulders. Shirts occurred for gala dress among Plains Indians, and woven shirts were widely used in South America with Peru as a center.

In principle the simpler peoples jointly got as far as the higher civilizations of ancient times, which contented themselves with simple raiment. The Mesopotamian men of 3,000 B.C. wore only a loincloth, though later they adopted the women's practice of covering the left shoulder with a piece of cloth, leaving the right side uncovered. Ancient Egyptian men are pictured with linen loincloths, the women with a skirt reaching from the hips to the ankles. Sleeved shirts appear in Mesopotamia about 1,500 B.C. and proved a practical innovation since they left both arms free for work. Classical Rome and Greece were content with draping the body.

In contrast to these the Eskimo, the simpler Siberian primitives and their neighbors, achieved true tailored clothing, that is dress fitted to the body. The ancient Scythians, whose culture was that of the Asiatic pastoral nomads, had tight-fitting and tight-sleeved sewed coats, plaited trousers, leather boots, and peaked caps covering the ears. They were thus closer to our costume of today than were Greeks and Romans.

Decoration. Decoration is extremely old, for sites estimated to date back more than 15,000 years contain necklaces of teeth and perforated shells. Among modern tribes it is important, whether they are scantily clad or wholly nude. Siberians and Eskimo take great trouble to trim, fringe and embroider their fur costume (*Pl. 11, fig. 5*), which is also provided with tassels and bone or metal pendants. Plains Indian women made geometrical designs in quill embroidery on leggings, moccasins (*Pl. 30, fig. 4*), and dresses, while robes were painted. In the Philippines, Mandaya craftsmanship attains its peak in the silver breast ornaments of both sexes (*Pl. 11, fig. 3*); and Bagobo women load their arms with brass bracelets (*Pl. 11, fig. 4; Pl. 12, fig. 6*). Melanesians favor mother-of-pearl ornaments for the forehead (*Pl. 12, fig. 5*) and

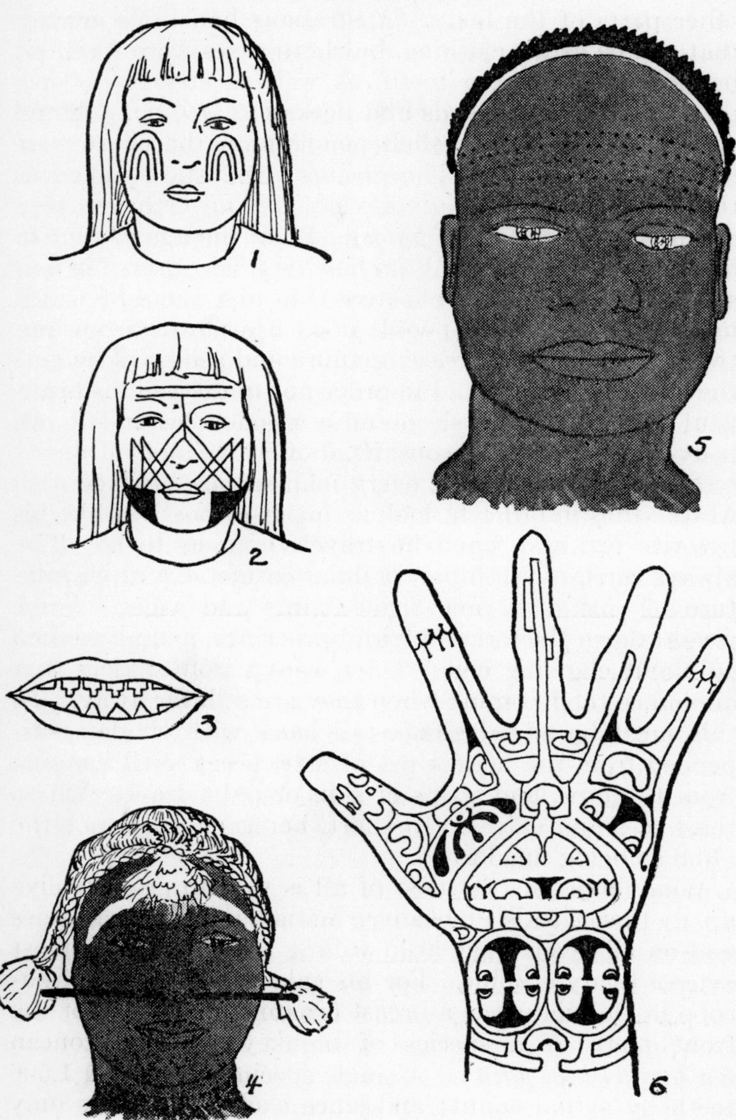

Plate 10: Body Decoration.

1 and 2. Painting of the Face by Colorado River Indians [Kroeber (19) p. 732] 3. Filed Teeth from the Philippines [Cole (5) *Plate XIIb*] 4. Nose Plug and Hair Ornaments of an Australian [Thomas (42) p. 68] 5. Scarification Marks on Forehead of a Shilluk [Hofmayr (13) *Plate 27b*] 6. Tattooed Hand from the Marquesas, Polynesia [Handy (11) *Plate III*]

other parts of the body. Australians had little enough that can be called clothing, but both sexes wore forehead bands with kangaroo teeth, as well as strings of such teeth around their heads and necks (*Pl. 10, fig. 4*); and cord necklaces with a shell pendant on the chest were especially esteemed. The Shilluk men, stark naked as they are from our point of view, are nevertheless fops of the first order (*Pl. 8, fig. 2*). From the age of four or five a boy begins to think up how he might dress his hair and ever after devises effective coiffures, some of which make him look like a poodle dog. He powders, kneads, twists his hair with grease, manure and ashes till he gets the effect he wants; and in order not to disturb his beautiful work of art he sleeps on a wooden headrest. All body hair, however, is considered offensive and ruthlessly scraped away. Further, every man smears his face with white ashes in order to look as much as possible like his favorite ox; and when he travels or goes to court he always carries with him a popular cosmetic, a dried mixture of cow dung and urine burned to ashes. Some weight down the forearm with brass rings, and all women go about clanking eight or ten heavy iron anklets that announce their coming when they are still far away. To this must be added giraffe-tail hairs with ringlets suspended from the neck, rings of ostrich egg shell hanging from the hips, and strips of skin or palm leaves tied to the knees and calves. In short, being naked is not the same as being unadorned.

What impresses us most of all is that in order to live up to their ideals of beauty, human beings in all ages and on all levels have been willing to undergo the most extraordinary trouble. For his gala dress a young Chacobo in Bolivia needs a breast ornament made up of the front teeth of a species of monkey and red toucan feathers (*Pl. 8, fig. 1*). A single specimen required 1,506 teeth by actual count; and since each animal has only eight front teeth, this means shooting 189 monkeys. What a waste of animal life and of energy, to boot! For

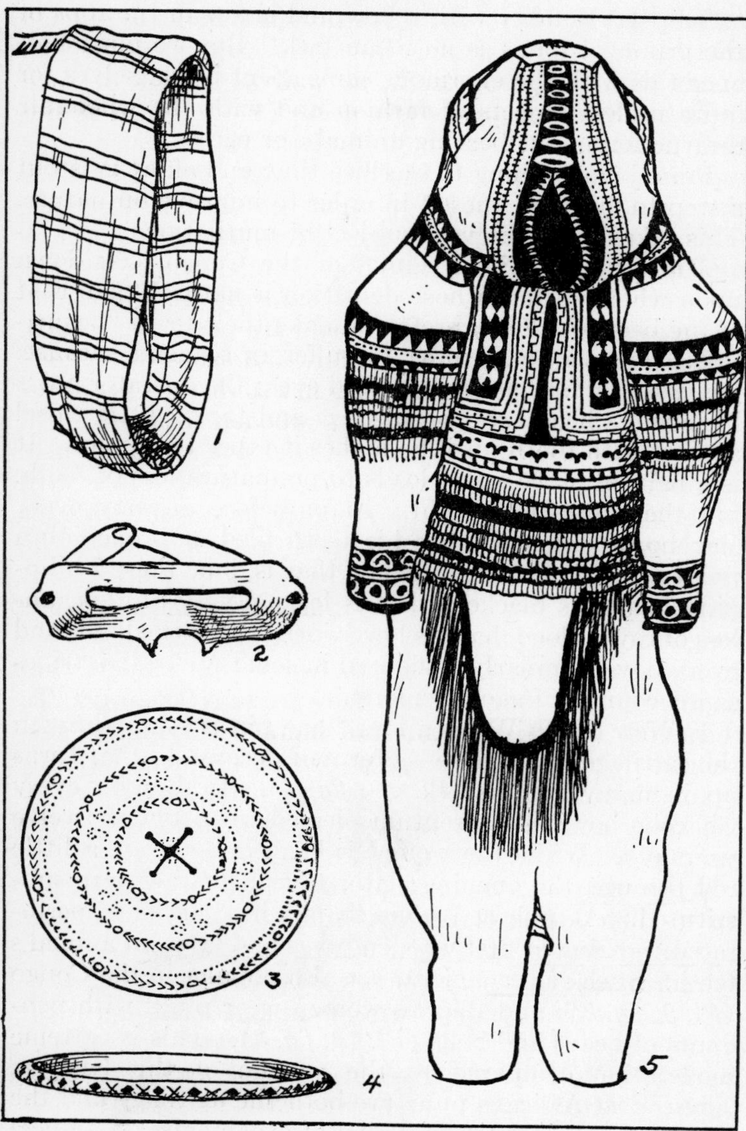

Plate 11: DRESS AND ORNAMENTS.

1. Baby Sling, Chaco [Nordenskiöld (29) p. 160] 2. Eskimo Snow Goggles [Mathiassen (28) p. 195] 3. Silver Breast Ornament from the Mandaya, Philippines [Cole (5) p. 191] 4. Brass Bracelet from the Bagobo, Philippines [Cole (5) p. 58] 5. Eskimo Dress [Mathiassen (28) p. 175]

to kill that number with a bow and arrow in the tops of the primeval forest is no mean task. But we must balance this with the enormous sums spent by ourselves for quite useless objects of fashion and with the wholesale destruction of fur-bearing animals, or egrets.

From being willing to sacrifice time and effort it is but a step to disfigure oneself in order to improve on nature. This takes us to the vast subject of mutilations.

Mutilations. The Pygmies of the Congo look down upon white visitors whose dentition is natural "like that of the beasts". *They* prefer to make their teeth "beautiful". The victim, willing to suffer in so good a cause, lies down on his back with closed eyes; the operator holds his client's head between his legs and taps a little chisel against each tooth until he makes it taper to a point. It is a painful process and leads to premature loss of teeth, but that bears no weight. At or before puberty every Bagobo of either sex has his teeth filed or broken to a point (*Pl. 10, fig. 3*), and when that is done these Philippine Islanders blacken what is left. Every Shilluk, unless of royal blood, has his lower incisors knocked out, and every boy is similarly disfigured in some Australian tribes at his coming of age ceremony.

In New South Wales a long bone pin is stuck through the cartilage of the nose—a form of decoration that turns up in many regions (*Pl. 10, fig. 4*). In Bolivia every Chacobo boy has his septum pierced when ten or twelve years old. While the wound is healing he wears a little rod through the opening; later toucan feathers are substituted. At puberty a youth has his ear lobes perforated, wearing at first wooden plugs and later an animal's teeth. Such ear ornaments are also popular in the Congo (*Pl. 9, fig. 2*); and Bagobo women wear plugs with pendants of beads and bells (*Pl. 12, fig. 8*). This is extreme moderation compared to the custom of the Kikuyu. These East Africans puncture both the cartilage and the lobe of the ear for the insertion of ornaments. A typical man's decoration would include various earrings fastened to the edge of the cartilage, while a spiral of iron wire in cylinder form with pendent chains is put into the lobe, which might accommodate a large orange and has been dragged down to the level of the chin.

Similarly in the Congo area Negro and Pygmy women wear large ivory disks, rods (*Pl. 9, fig. 6*) or rings, in the upper lip, thus at times acquiring a strange duck-bill. Father Schebesta witnessed the perforation performed on a ten-year-old girl. Several women held her so she could not stir while one of them pierced her lip with a porcupine quill, the victim screaming with pain. As soon as there was a hole, increasingly larger objects were put in until it was large enough for an arrow-shaft.

Not only facial features but the whole shape of the head is sometimes artificially altered. This may happen unintentionally, as among the Hopi of Arizona, who lash their infants to the cradle in such a way as to flatten the back of the head. Elsewhere, however, it is a matter of deliberate choice. In the Columbia River area only a slave would fail to have his skull artificially deformed.

Status Marks. Some of the mutilations are meant to improve looks, but often another purpose is added or substituted; and this holds for all artificial changes of appearance. Over and above any ornaments he may choose according to his taste, every Shilluk bears on his person the badge of his tribe. Sets of little gashes are kept from healing by rubbing soot and fat into the wounds; thus they come to swell up and form lines of scars (*Pl. 10, fig. 5*)—three being usual for boys, four for girls. Other Africans scarify to a much greater degree, forming numerous and elaborate patterns on the chest and abdomen (*Pl. 9, fig. 1*). The method can, of course, also be used for purely dandyish reasons. Thus, Ona adolescents of either sex cauterize little circles into the left forearm without any thought of proclaiming their tribe. Here, however, at least adult males are marked, for at puberty every youth receives a head-ornament of guanaco skin, which he must ever after wear on the march or hunt.

Decoration or mutilation may thus indicate not merely the people to whom a person belongs, but his sex and station as well.

A great many facts come under this head, including many that belong to our own and other high civilizations. Caps and gowns mark academic degrees and the universities that confer them; judges wear robes or gowns, and in England wigs also; swallow-tail coats mark gentlemen or waiters; silk hats, gentlemen and coachmen. Primitive tribes generally stress status more than we do, hence naturally have more and more rigidly enforced outward symbols of such social differences. A Hopi girl wears her hair in large whorls over her ears as a sign of her maidenhood (*Pl. 9, fig. 5*). Her Kikuyu sister in East Africa gets a browband of beads and shell disks at initiation, a necklace as a token of betrothal, an iron collar as a wedding gift, and spiral copper ear-rings when she herself is old enough to have an initiated child. Marriage is shown by shaving the head except for a small tuft of hair in the back, and even that must go in old age; a white woman is stared at as a curiosity because of her full head of hair. As the foregoing are symbols of life's stages, so other signs are used elsewhere to betoken prestige. A Sioux scalp shirt originally belonged only to recognized leaders in the military societies, while feathers at the back of one's head showed one's deeds against the enemy, which demonstrated one's social position.

Tattooing, like scarification, may indicate sex, tribe, and social position. Throughout Polynesia tattooing was practiced by highly esteemed and well-paid experts. Maori women generally had tattoo only on the lips and chin, while a fully decorated man's face, thighs, and buttocks were covered with designs often of the same spiral pattern that prevailed in native painting and carving (*Pl. 9, figs. 3, 4, 7*). The artist traced his figures. then

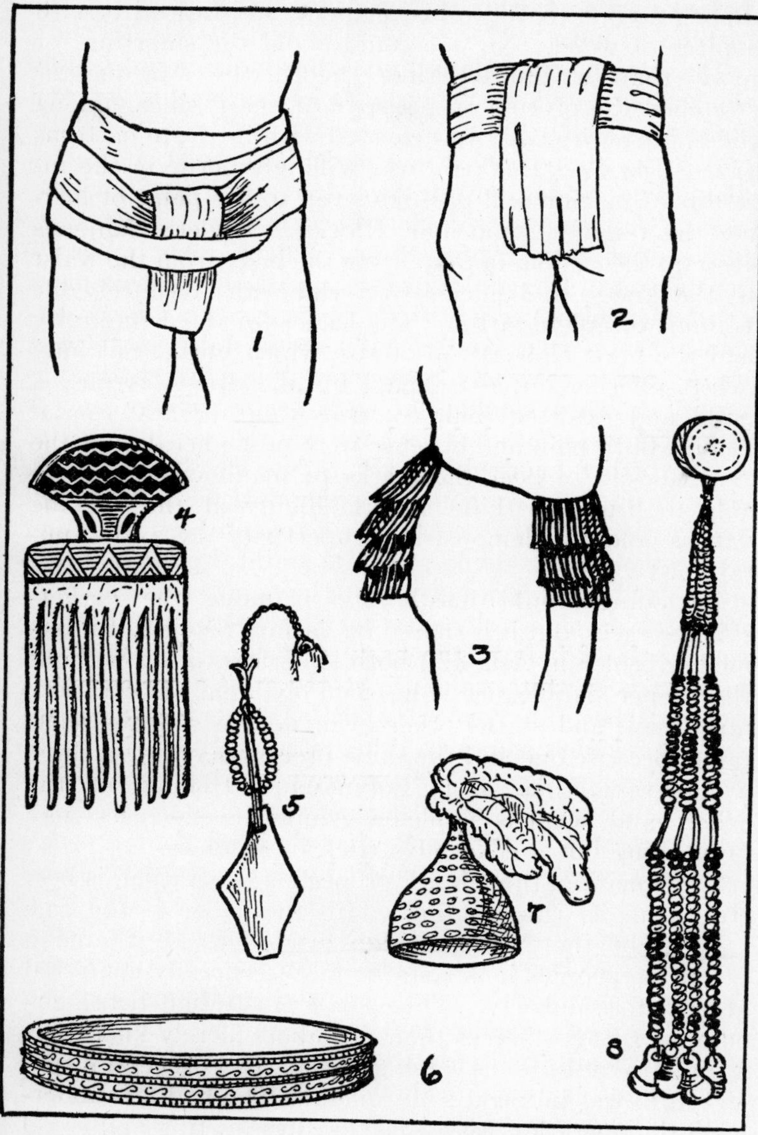

Plate 12: Dress and Ornaments.

1 and 2. Gee-string, New Guinea, front and rear views [Finsch (7) *Plate XVI, Nos. 1 and 2*] 3. Grass Skirt from New Guinea [Finsch (7) *Plate XVI, No. 9*] 4. Wooden Comb from Kamerun [Von Luschan (44) *Plate XXIV, No. 19*] 5. Forehead Decoration of Mother-of-Pearl, Bismarck Archipelago, Melanesia [Von Luschan (44) *Plate XXXV, No. 9*] 6. Brass Bracelet from the Bagobo, Philippines [Cole (5) p. 58] 7. Feather Hat from the Dinka, Upper Nile [Schweinfurth (37) *Plate 1, No. 2*] 8. Ear Plug with Bell Pendents, Mandaya, Philippines [Cole (5) p. 169]

dipped a bone tool into his pigment, and tapped it with a piece of wood. No one could stand the smarting for more than a limited time, hence the Marquesans stretched the process over a span of years, since, among them, the entire body was covered with intricate patterns (*Pl. 10, fig. 6*). But pain was willingly borne in the interests of fashion and prestige, even to the point of having the tongue tattooed in Hawaii. Modern Samoans keep up the custom of decorating the body from the waist to the knees, and anciently a chief was inconceivable without complete tattoo. The leaders of the community had the most elaborate patterns, which meant not only extra suffering but extra pay, for the artists formed a guild and extorted high compensation for any special labor. Both pain and expense were borne because of the "keen desire to bear the marks of manhood and to be able to hitch the kilts a little higher at the evening dances and so demonstrate superiority over the untattooed".

Tattooing would hardly show among the darker-skinned races, but it is shared by various peoples of intermediate color in Asia and both Americas, often without the deeper significance it has in Polynesia. Decoration, mutilation and status tokens can not be sharply separated, because one and the same process may be all three at the same time, as in Polynesian tattooing; on the other hand, what is a solemn symbol in one place may be nothing but a coxcomb's trick in another.

Circumcision, though not properly a decoration, is best treated under this heading. It is the badge of the true religion of the Mohammedans and Jews, but among primitive peoples it is a status mark generally conferred at or before puberty. Thus, some Australian tribes circumcise a boy, whereas their neighbors merely knock out a tooth to indicate his coming of age. In Polynesia a special form was in vogue; Marquesans who had not undergone the operation were considered disgusting and could not get married. Many African tribes, too, make circumcision the essential part of initiation prior to which marriage would be out of the question. Here, as in the matter of food preferences, a difference in custom becomes the object of scorn. The Arabs despise the uncircumcised heathen, while the Shilluk mock the Mohammedans and any renegades of their own tribe in pungent satirical songs.

Temporary Decoration. While tattooing, scars and circumcision are permanent tokens, many changes of appearance are made only for special circumstances. Thus, white men and women wear crêpe for mourning, dinner jackets for semi-formal evening meals, high-heeled shoes for dances and low ones for tennis. Primitive men are often organized into clubs and fraternities each with its special regalia, to be worn at meetings or public performances; ceremonies require special costume; so very often do widowhood, war expeditions, secular dances. To give a few typical examples, the members of a California cult put on a hair net, Crow Indians who had killed an enemy blackened their faces, a Boulia Australian warrior covered his face with gypsum and drew boomerang figures from the shoulder to the waist. The Ghost societies of Melanesia and West Africa have disguises and sometimes elaborate masks, which is also true of the Pueblo mummers who impersonate the ancestors of the tribe. In the Plains the Indians rarely masked themselves, but each military club carried or wore such badges as hoof-rattles, sashes, owl-feather headgear, headbands with kit-fox jaws; and during their processions any tribesman saw at once whether the paraders were of the Dog, Kit-fox, or Lumpwood organization.

Painting is a popular form of temporary adornment. Often it becomes an art comparable to tattooing; the natives not only smear themselves with pigment but work out decorative patterns. Thus, on the Colorado River young women rarely appear in public without striking red or yellow designs on their cheeks (*Pl. 10, figs. 1, 2*). This was merely for decoration; but in Plains

Indian organizations, painting becomes a marker of status. For instance, members of the Dog club of the Arapaho tribe (Wyoming) had red face paint and over it long black lines crossed by shorter ones, along with black stripes on the forehead. Finally, among the Ona art activity is largely centered on the painting of the body, which attains its climax in one act of the great initiation festival (*Pl. 37*). One typical design used on that occasion is named after a diving bird; it consists in vertical rows of white dots from shoulder to knee, the points being framed by white lines. According to the Ona all patterns painted come down to them from the mythical period. Such religious sanction for decoration is common among American Indians; on the Plains simple ceremonial designs for face paint are said to have been revealed in dreams or visions. Because of this very special origin the patterns are regarded as patents; an Ona chooses only from among the samples his home district obtained in the ancient period, and for ceremonial appearance a Plains Indian would shrink from painting a simple cross on his cheek unless he had seen the design in a dream or bought the right from some one who had (see p. 281).

General Remarks. Certain interesting general points stand out from the mass of facts considered. Of the motives for covering parts of the body modesty is comparatively weak if we consider the whole of mankind, past and present; the need for protection seems stronger, yet often strikingly fails to assert itself; while artificial changes of appearance, for their own sake or to mark status, have been tremendously important. Men and women willingly undergo expense and even torture in order to embellish themselves according to their lights, to indicate their social status, or to show how superior they are to others. Fashion and social standards have their victims on all levels of culture. Individual savages sometimes die from the effects of the operations performed at initiations or otherwise with crude surgical tools, but civilized whites have crippled their feet by unhygienic shoes and injured their health by tight lacing. The follies of costume show all humanity to be kindred spirits.

VII

HOUSES AND SETTLEMENTS

In the earliest parts of the Old Stone Age that we know anything about the climate of western Europe was warm so that man could live in the open. Somewhat later it grew colder and he sought refuge in caves, as demonstrated by the remains of fireplaces, stone tools and cracked bones of game animals. Since such shelters are readymade, they rank as the lowest type of residence. Nevertheless, they are still used by the Vedda of Ceylon, a simple hunting tribe; and temporarily even people able to construct good dwellings occupy caves. Indeed, Indian rock shelters existed in and near the present boundaries of New York City.

True structures may be considered under several heads, such as economic and geographic influences, functions of buildings, forms and materials, evolution of higher from simpler types, and arrangement of single buildings in settlements. These topics are not entirely distinct, however, but merge into one another.

Economic Influences. A hunter can not have a fixed abode because he must follow his game, and a herder is bound to wander with his stock. Hence buffalo-hunting Indians and South Siberian nomads lived in tents. On the other hand, people who are above all fishermen may well occupy definite villages, at least for a large part of the year. Thus the Salish of interior British Columbia made a large excavation, built a conical roof over it, and covered it with the earth dug up. This semi-subterranean house was entered by a notched-tree ladder and was warm even in the coldest weather. Only in the summer when the natives did not fish but went deer-hunting and root-gathering was there any need for tents. Similarly the Klamath of southern Oregon had permanent winter settlements of earth houses in spots where fish could be taken all the year, but when scattering for the summer they took to small dome-shaped lodges covered with mats.

People who combine farming with hunting may lead a similar double life. When the Omaha of Nebraska hunted buffalo they had to travel in tents like their neighbors; when they looked after their maize they had fixed earth houses. Seasonal arrangements are even common in Europe, where agriculture goes with special forms of stock-breeding. Norwegian peasants live in the valleys; but in the summer their cattle are driven to higher levels, where the women in charge occupy temporary quarters.

Geographic Influences. Geography affects first of all the materials for building. It favors some regions, so that mere superiority in this regard does not test efficiency. The southern Ona build huts while the northern branch of the tribe has only windbreaks; but the reason is simply that in the north there are no beech forests. So in northeastern Bolivia the Indians can make huts waterproof with a minimum of effort by shingling them with the leaves of a certain palm; a little farther south this species no longer occurs, and we can not blame the natives for their poorer dwellings. The point holds for higher cultures. The Egyptians are not superior to the Babylonians because of their ampler use of stone architecture: they had plenty of the material at hand, while in Babylonia it was extremely rare, so that brick largely took its place. Even trade relations could not change matters on a large scale; it was easy enough for Egypt to import quantities of cedar wood from Western Asia, but transporting masses of stone was a different thing altogether. In modern times Italian peasants, having plenty of stone and little wood, naturally build in stone; northern Europeans just as naturally exploited their timber to an extent varying regionally according to the supply. In Denmark it began to run low in the Sixteenth Century, so government ordinances tried to prohibit new log cabins, though with tardy success. However, the very structure of a Danish house depended on the available wood: where it was plentiful heavy ridge poles supported the roof; otherwise it rested on pairs of rafters meeting at the top and spread like compasses below. Norway was amply stocked, and towns like Trondhjem are still largely made up of timber houses, with even the royal palace wholly of wood. Other details grow out of natural conditions. Danes were able to thatch their homes; but in Norway, where only five per cent. of the total area is arable, straw was far too valuable. The typical Norwegian roofing was accordingly of turf, where the local flora freely grew and sheep were allowed to pasture.

Besides dictating what materials shall be used, the environment may suggest reasonable adaptations, but men vary greatly in using such hints. One adjustment is against overflowing streams or swampy ground. From the New Stone Age until today men have raised their houses on piles, some of the prehistoric Swiss lake-dwellings and modern Venice being famous examples. As late as 1868 the Russian city of Kasan had whole streets of pile dwellings to protect residents against annual inundations; and on the Portuguese coast fishermen occupy whole villages of this type, much like those of primitives in New Guinea. In the Malay Peninsula a pile hut is raised high enough to allow an elephant to pass below without bumping against the floor. Should he attack the posts, the residents flee to a platform prepared on a neighboring tree (*Pl. 14, fig. 4*).

The Eskimo snow-house well illustrates human resourcefulness at its best. The snow must be neither too hard nor too soft nor in layers causing blocks to break, so the builder first tests his material with a wooden probe. Then he cuts his blocks with a special knife where the floor of the dwelling is to be. The cutting automatically forms the foundation of the wall; then the first row of blocks, possibly 30 inches long, 20 in height, and 8 inches thick, is laid in a circle and shaped with the knife so as to lean slightly inward and to fit one another. After the first course the upper surface is cut away at a slope so as to form the beginning of a spiral with props for the next layer. Standing inside, the worker goes on building up his spiral, fitting each block to its neighbors on the side and below. The blocks are inclined more and more inward, and the windings are shortened to produce a dome, the last block being at the top. When finished the builder is entirely shut in and cuts his way out, the opening being afterward widened into the doorway. This hut differs from our domes in that one can stop at any stage without having the walls tumble down. Such structures melt in the spring and must be abandoned for tents, but with the coming of autumn they are the only comfortable residence for the Eskimo. A single man can build one within an hour and a half, and an expert has been known to do it in 26 minutes. More commonly two men coöperate and finish the job in 40 to 60 minutes. The hut lasts a month or longer during the cold season and if lined with skins may survive a winter. Inside it, one is comfortable when the thermometer stands at 50 degrees below zero outdoors. Without this shelter winter travel would be impossible: a hunter caught in a snowstorm would perish unless able to put up this type of shelter in a hurry. Early explorers were mainly handicapped in winter travel because they had not learned from the Eskimo how to build a snow-house.

However, as in the case of dress (p. 70), geography by itself does not create adaptations. The Mackenzie River Indians lived in crude tents or windbreaks that gave meager protection; and the shelters of the Ona, even where they use beech wood, fail to keep out the snow. In the Chaco the rain comes pouring through the Indian hovels, drenching the inmates, who fail to provide a covering of earth to make their grass roof waterproof. Thus here, too, some primitives show marvelous skill, while others are bunglers.

Conservatism. Often maladjustment results when people cling to what was once a good arrangement but has ceased to be such from change of circumstances. So long as the Chukchi of northeastern Siberia hunted sea mammals they could live in fixed houses. When they took to breeding reindeer they had to follow their stock in movable dwellings. But they tried to pattern a tent on their old style of home, producing a clumsy result. Again, pile dwellings are found among South Americans who live on perfectly dry ground. The best explanation is that their ancestors came from a region where piles were necessary.

However, some survivals are not unreasonable, an old method being put to new uses quite as practical as the original ones. In Oceania the space between piles is used as a pig sty; and structures on posts make excellent storage huts. The people of Kamchatka and the lower Amur made theirs do double service, for storage and for summer homes. So European peasants in Switzerland and Spain, in Scandinavia and Russia, raise granaries above the ground, and here and there use them also as bachelors' dormitories. In the Solomon Islands, Melanesia, huts were elevated for protection: the humidity safeguarded against firing, and stone axes made little headway in chopping down a house defended by its inmates.

In general, builders must be admitted to proceed in the old way from sheer inertia. This holds for higher civilizations also. Modern court-houses, banks, and parliaments still largely ape Greek temples or other historic forms. Only rarely have modern architects evolved new patterns, like the skyscraper, as a response to modern needs and technical equipment.

Conservatism in matters of housing sometimes resulted in disaster. When people began moving from the country into towns they preserved many customs appropriate enough in their old setting but fatal in crowded centers. Thus Danes thatched their roofs, with the result that their towns were constantly being wiped out by fires. Notwithstanding these sad experiences, the practice was kept up in defiance of royal decrees until well into the Nineteenth Century. Stockholm developed more sanely, not because Swedes are more progressive than their fellow-Scandinavians but because of an unusually energetic monarch. King John III not only issued orders but saw that they were carried out. As a consequence Stockholm in 1582 had 429 stone houses out of 658—a ratio that put the Swedish capital even ahead of London. This example well illustrates the effect of a single powerful personality.

Functions. The building technique may be applied to various ends. Even simple cultures have distinct kitchen and canoe sheds, places of worship, assembly houses and dance halls. The Maori, for instance, who strongly object to eating in their homes, put up special cooking-sheds. The Samoans also prop up a separate roof to shelter the earth oven; and, in addition to their everyday dwelling, men of quality need council chambers for the entertainment of guests. Chiefs vied with each other in the splendor of such houses, which fostered the rise of expert architects, who organized into powerful guilds similar to our trade unions (see p. 107). Here we see one phase of culture influencing another. Because prominent men crave to outdo others, they require the services of trained artisans, creating a new social class.

Ceremonials also give a new direction to building. The dance snow-house of the Eskimo is either a particularly large structure or a combination of such huts; and the Crow of Montana perform their Sun Dance in a gigantic lodge shaped like their conical tents. The chapels of the Hopi are of the same oblong plan as their homes, but underground. Elsewhere houses of worship are more definitely marked off. Here again architecture may be linked with social institutions though in a manner very different from the Samoan. Hawaiian temples, like those of the ancient civilizations of the Near Orient, could be finished only by the joint labor of many subjects recruited for the purpose. One Hawaiian example was surrounded by stone walls 224 feet long by 100 feet wide. On three sides the enclosure towered up to twenty feet, narrowing from a base 12 feet thick to a stone walk of half that width at the top. On the seaward side the height was only 7 or 8 feet. Inside the walls were several terraces and an interior court with the image of the war god and a high wickerwork tower, which the king's prophet entered to get an inspiration.

In short, as culture grows complex, buildings of special functions arise while the simpler forms linger on. Egyptian plebeians were still living in mud huts when princes dwelt in palaces and had put up pyramids. The Aztec similarly continued living in plain mud and wattle houses when their public buildings were of stone.

Progress is not equally shared by all classes of the population but often only by a favored few. Peasants even in western Europe have frequently continued living in the most primitive manner in modern times. In the winter Scandinavian dwellings of the Sixteenth Century were shared with the live-stock. Stray travelers whose beds were spread on the floor had pigs grunting at them and licking their faces, and infants were suspended high enough to elude prying goats. At that time glass window panes were a novelty even for the upper class; as a matter of fact at a much later time they were not yet universal in the most progressive countries. In 1787 a British traveler through France and Italy again and again noted the complete absence of glass windows in otherwise good houses of stone and slate; a town important enough to be the seat of a bishop had a long street without a single pane. Rational housing for the masses is an extremely late ideal of Western civilization and has not even yet been completely carried out. Thus, families

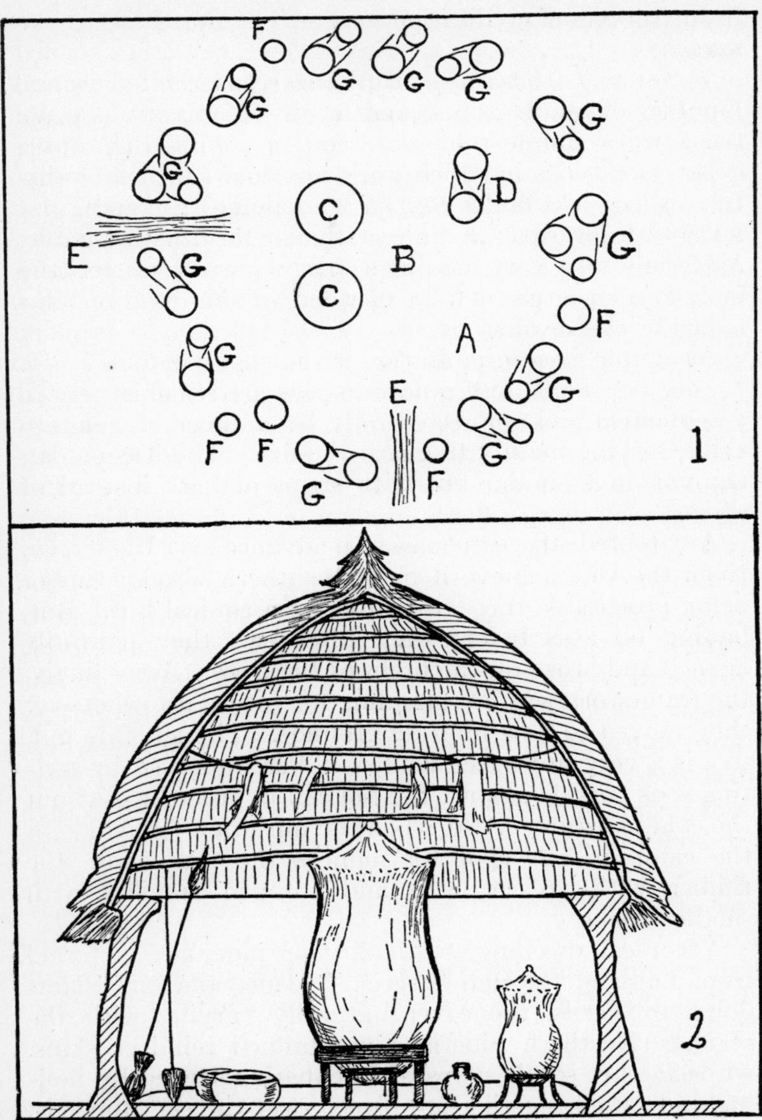

Plate 13: VILLAGE AND HOUSE PLANS.

1. Plan of Shilluk Village [Hofmayr (13) Fig. 15a] A—Village tree; B—Free place for dances or cattle; C—Stables; D—Temple; E—Paths to villages; F—Single dwellings for old people; G—Family dwellings.
2. Cross-section of a Shilluk Thatched Hut [Hofmayr (13) Fig. 16b]

in the centers of civilization may still be found living like savages.

Types and Materials. Buildings conform to a small number of main types and their combinations. We recognize a simple roofless screen; a conical hut and a dome, two types in which walls and roof can not be distinguished; a cylinder topped by a dome; a rectangular form with flat roof; and a rectangular form with a gable. Materials also vary within a fairly narrow range: the body of a structure may be of wood, of sun-dried or kiln-baked bricks, or of stone.

As simple as any habitation is the Ona windbreak (*Pl. 14, fig. 1*). Some half a dozen sticks are set obliquely in a semicircle and connected only by a cover of guanaco skins, serving mainly to guard the fire. The Tasmanian equivalent is similar but with strips of bark instead of skins.

Any roofed structure marks an advance over the screen. Even the Ona achieve it in the southern woods; timber being procurable there, they put up a conical hut. But, having no axes before their discovery, they painfully lassoed and broke off the limbs of the trees. Accordingly, the framework was left standing for future use whenever they moved to new hunting grounds. Though this hut, too, is a very imperfect shelter, it was improved by putting sods outside against the bottom in order to shut out the cold moisture. Also, when the initiation festival kept the camp in one spot for months the Ona chose the timber with greater care and stopped crevices with smaller sticks.

A conical dwelling, stationary or movable, is found from Lapland through Siberia, Canada, and our Plains down to Texas, the cover naturally varying with the region. Northern Siberians use tanned reindeer skins, while farther south strips of birchbark softened by boiling and sewed together are placed over the skeleton. In the forests of the Altai region the bark of pines and larches appears, but peoples in open country substitute felt. This characteristic cloth of Asiatic nomads also forms the Mongol tent cover. The northern Canadian dwelling often strikingly resembles Siberian patterns. More elegant is the "tipi" of the Plains, with its taller poles and the neat regulation of the smoke-hole by two flaps held in place each by an outside post. The vent could be opened or closed at will by moving these exterior poles.

A beehive type of hut also can not be divided into a roof and walls because the two merge. Such was the wigwam of the Atlantic Coast Indians. They stuck poles into the ground, bent them over, intersected them with similar poles, thatched this dome with grass or covered it with reed mats or bark. A hole in the center allowed the smoke to escape. This type occurs in circular or oval form in the Gran Chaco, likewise among the Pygmies of the Congo and other Africans, for instance the Hottentot and Zulu. The Eskimo snow-house, though of quite different construction, falls geometrically under this head.

If a cylindrical frame is topped by a cone, the result is the Mongol tent. Its cylinder is a lattice frame about 3 feet high, pairs of crossed sticks being set in a circle and connected with cross-bars (*Pl. 14, fig. 3*). To these are tied the butts of poles converging upward with their tops held together by thongs. A tripod of heavier poles dug into the ground around the fireplace supports this roof. The Mongols cover the structure with felt, but other Siberians substitute reindeer skins. Turkish tribes, such as the Kirghiz, top the cylinder with a dome, a variation of the Mongol form.

Cylindrical walls may, of course, be joined to a conical roof for a fixed house, a frequent African development. Likewise the construction, the materials and the proportions can be varied. For the cylinder some Nile dwellers plant posts at short intervals and fill the interstices with clay. Only inferior Shilluk huts follow this model; a good house has a solid clay wall rising over five feet and a half from a foundation of earth and sand. The roof is made separately of eight or more bent rafters, converging at the top and fastened to hoops placed inside and out, the interior ones numbering up to thirty-five; the skeleton is then thatched with steppe grass (*Pl. 13, fig. 2*). A dome-shaped roof, with a mushroom-like total effect, results. The Shilluk and the Mongol-Turkic dwellings thus show similar shapes coupled with entirely different modes of construction.

Some of the simplest structures known are oblong. Chaco Indians, who normally sleep in the round huts already mentioned, have four-cornered unwalled sheds with flat thatched roofs for kitchens and for sleeping-quarters. The elaborate Samoan houses do not exclude crude rectangular sheds with a sloping roof for a carpenter's workshop. In Guiana the Galibi build reception halls with three forked posts supporting the ridge pole (*Pl. 14, fig. 2*), the rafters resting on smaller forked posts. But this geometrical form allows of infinite variety. The tribes of the British Columbia coast build walls of split cedar planks, the gable roof resting on heavy posts and beams. An old-fashioned house may be forty by thirty feet, with the roof ten feet high at the ridge. An excavation several feet deep forms the floor and daytime sitting-room, while sleeping platforms run along the walls. The fireplace is in the center, with the smoke-hole above it. From the center of the front gable end there rises a lofty pole with heraldic carvings, a hole in it forming the door.

In Indonesia and Oceania oblong gabled houses were common. The ordinary Maori hut of light poles and thatched roof was of this type; while the more pretentious houses and public buildings resembled the house of British Columbia in having plank walls, though the roof was always of reeds.

The Hopi build flat-topped oblong rooms, the walls being made of irregularly laid courses of sandstone plastered with mud, which also supplies the flooring. Anciently the house was entered by climbing an outside ladder and then descending by another through a hatch-

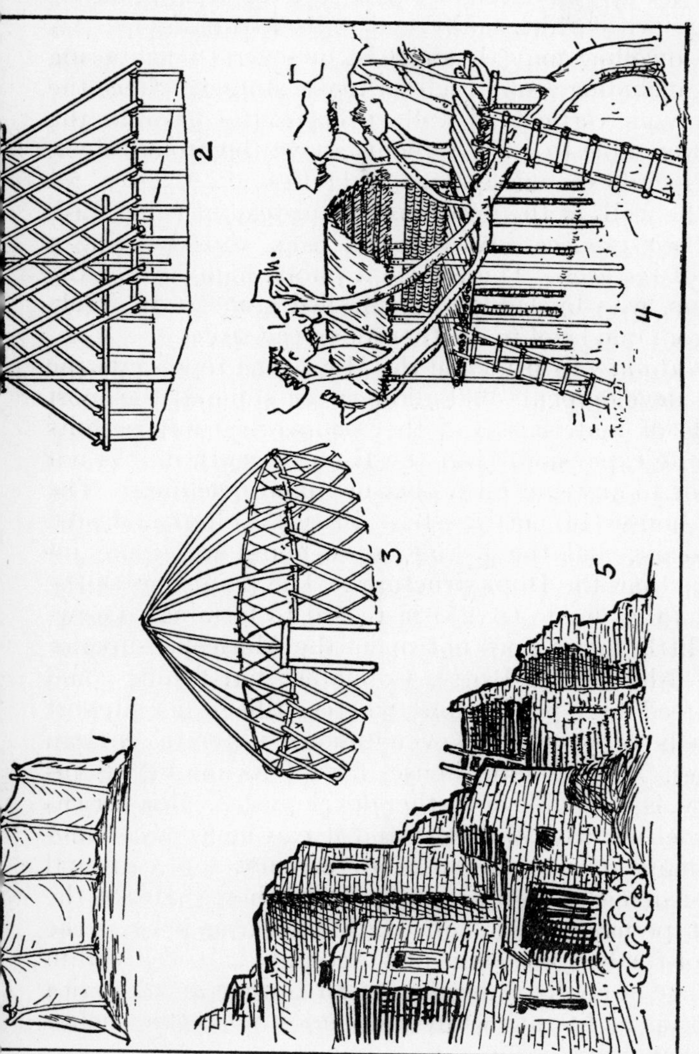

Plate 14: TYPES OF HOUSES.

1. Ona Wind Screen [Gusinde (9) p. 198] 2. Framework for Guiana Oblong House [Roth (33) p. 262] 3. Framework for Mongol Round Felt Tent [Jochelson (16) p. 197] 4. Pile Dwelling, Malay Peninsula [Schebesta* (35) p. 55] 5. Stone Dwellings, Hopi (From a photograph by Lowie)

* ***The writer is indebted to F. A. Brockhaus, Leipzig, for permission to reproduce these items.***

way in the roof. Within are doors to connect adjoining rooms, for one advantage of this style of architecture is the ease with which additional units can be added. A family dwelling may thus consist of several neighboring rooms, including a small cell for maize storage. Since the type favors vertical as well as horizontal growth, the Hopi were able to achieve rooms above the ground floor, the principle of our apartment houses (*Pl. 14, fig. 5*). Only the walls of the upper stories, instead of being flush with their predecessors, were set back, thus creating a series of terraces. These form a public highway for the villagers, who by ladders or unrailed stone steps freely pass from one level to another along the street.

Evolution. In principle the Hopi type represents the higher developments of building; for stone is the most durable of materials, and the rectangular unit permits indefinite expansion. But the Hopi masonry unit is not superior to any and all timber or round dwellings. The plank houses of northwestern British Columbia lasted fifty years; and the Eskimo snow-house was more ingenious than the Hopi structures. The point here is the same as that made (p. 25) in regard to farming. Growing a little maize does not make the Maricopa superior to the fishermen of British Columbia; but fishing could never feed large populations, whereas tillage can support hundreds of thousands even among illiterate African Negroes. So the snow-house, for all its marvelous ingenuity, is incapable of further development. It is perishable, melting with the sun; and it can never accommodate many inmates because one can not top a ground floor of domes with a second story of them. Hence the Hopi type makes an advance only insofar as it bears the germ of further development. Actually, it is well within the range of civilized dwellings. In Europe and America thousands of literate white men enjoy no better shelter than that provided by Pueblo homes.

In fairness, we can compare and judge builders only if they meet the *same* conditions. The Eskimo had no giant cedars, hence could not invent plank houses; the Norwegians and Babylonians lacked stone, hence built wooden and brick houses, respectively; while the Egyptians had little timber but abundance of stone. In studying the development of architecture, the proper way is therefore to take countries with a long history and to trace the steps by which in each one the simpler dwellings assumed more and more complex forms. Thus, in ancient Egypt the earliest type is a simple structure of mud or wattle and daub with a wood-framed doorway. Later sun-dried and kiln-baked bricks formed the material for private buildings. In subterranean tombs the brickwork lining yielded to stone, the structure was translated above ground, and putting one unit on top of another resulted in the stepped pyramid. Correspondingly, Greek temple porches first had wooden posts, which were later transformed into stone columns, while the main structure was first of sun-dried brick, later of limestone or marble.

Again, in ancient Mesopotamia a very early method of spanning the space between walls is by "corbelling": courses of bricks are made to overlap, each projecting a little farther inward than the one below until the two sides join. Such a false arch was as far as the Indians of Yucatan got, but the Mesopotamians progressed to the true arch before 3000 B.C., roofing tombs with wedge-shaped bricks, the last of which, or "keystone", held the whole arch in place. Much larger spaces could thus be more safely spanned than by corbelling.

The great achievements in building are not inventions of single minds. They result from the combined experience of centuries and of different peoples. Most of our architectural principles come down from a hoary past. We did not invent columns, but got the idea from the Romans and Greeks, and the Greeks borrowed it from Egypt. The vault, too, is not a recent creation of ours, but goes back to Rome and even to ancient Babylonia.

Furniture. Roving hunters such as the Ona have no real furniture. Their bed consists of brush or grass, with their cloaks as blankets. The fire, though indispensable, is bound to be temporary. Congo Pygmies are similarly unequipped: they lie down on two or three slabs of wood with a log to prop up the head. Mats or blankets are unnecessary; of a cool night they, like the Fuegians, put their trust in the fireplace. The Eskimo require more: platforms of snow take the place of our beds, chairs, tables, and shelves; and on them a sleeper rolls himself up in a skin rug. For heat and light there is a soapstone lamp of crescent shape with a moss wick for burning seal blubber (*Pl. 15, fig. 3*); over it the natives hang a soapstone kettle for cooking, or dry their clothes on a frame. In northern South America a set of three clay cylinders sometimes supports the cooking utensils (*Pl. 15, fig. 6*).

The Banyangi Negroes of the Kamerun keep many gourds, pots, and wooden containers (*Pl. 15, fig. 5*) in their houses, but little true furniture. Three or five stones set in the floor form a hearth, above which are several shelves for storage. Opposite the door and on either side rise clay benches, which mats and log-pillows convert into beds (*Pl. 15, fig. 1*). A true couch of unusual construction (see p. 136) appears in the Nile-Uelle watershed among the Mangbettu (*Pl. 15, fig. 8*), who also use the less pretentious backrests of their neighbors (*Pl. 15, fig. 4*). Platforms are common among Indians (see p. 96), but beds were not wholly lacking. Early French travelers to what is now Mississippi found the Choctaw sleeping on cane settees raised three to four feet above the ground and used also as tables and seats; a deer- or bear-skin took the place of a mattress, a buffalo-skin that of a blanket.

Natives of tropical South America invented the hammock. In the Chaco it is not a practical substitute for a bed because of the cold nights; also the tribes there could not sling it in their cramped huts, though some make a daytime lounge of it. Headrests of bamboo or

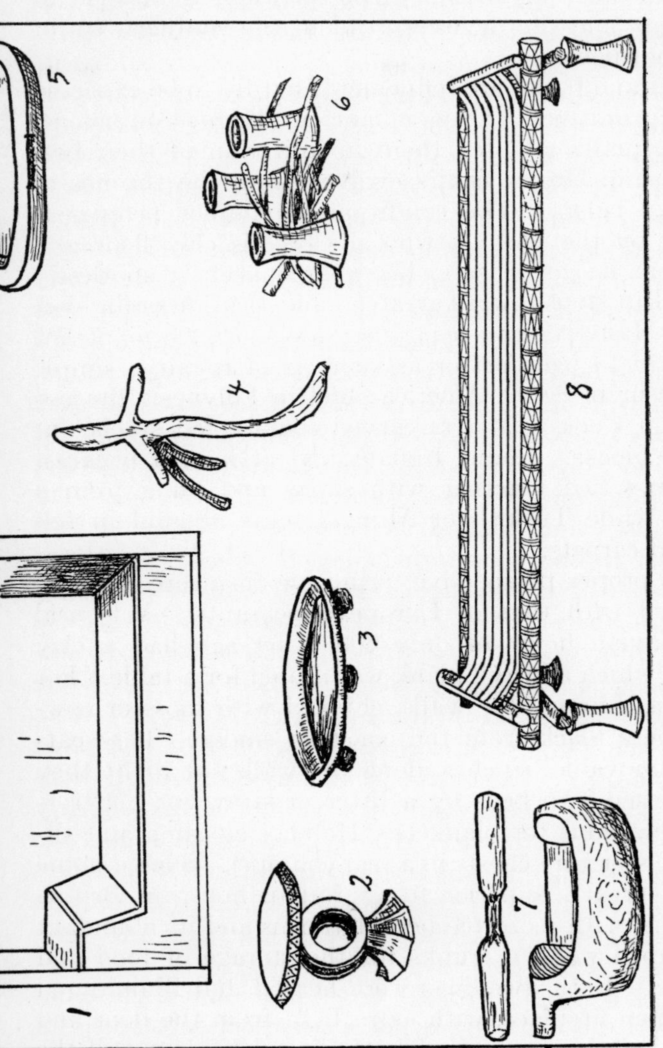

Plate 15: Household Furniture.

1. Clay Bed from Kamerun [Staschewski (40) Fig. 68] 2. Carved Wooden Stool from the Mangbetu [Schweinfurth (37) *Plate XVII, No. 9*] 3. Eskimo Blubber Lamp [Birket-Smith (3) p. 91] 4. Back Rest from the Azande, Northeast Congo [Baumann (1) p. 78] 5. Wooden Dish from Kamerun [Staschewski (40) Fig. 75] 6. Hearth with Clay Supports for Cooking Pots, Guiana [Roth (33) *Plate 75c*] 7. Mortar and Pestle from the Azande, Northeast Congo [Schweinfurth (37) *Plate XIII, No. 23*] 8. Bed from the Mangbetu [Schweinfurth (37) *Plate XVII, No. 18*]

wood are in vogue among Melanesians (*Pl. 22, fig. 6*) and Samoans. Egyptians slept on them thousands of years ago, and the device spread to the southern tip of their continent.

Chairs and tables are refinements hardly to be expected among primitives. Even in ancient Egypt commoners only gradually adopted them in imitation of their betters; and in Greece chairs evolved from the thrones of gods and rulers. The condition of simpler peoples is typified by the Shilluk, who sits on his clay floor and eats from it; to be sure, his women keep it spotlessly clean. But steps toward greater sophistication occur elsewhere. Many African tribes use stools (*Pl. 15, fig. 2; Pl. 22, fig. 3*) for comfort or as symbols of royalty; simple seats occur in South America; and in Polynesia the Society and Cook Islanders carved four-legged stools out of solid blocks. Plains Indians had at least a backrest of willows tied together with sinew and hung from a tripod; while Turkish or Mongol tents abound in felt rugs and carpets.

For a proper perspective, primitive furniture must be compared with that of European peasants. A typical Scandinavian home of only 300 years ago had a clay floor, in which a heavy plank was rooted for a table. For lack of a chimney the walls, chinked with moss or cow-dung, were black from the constant smoke. The seats were immovable benches along the walls; at night they were turned into beds by a litter of straw for mattress and a few skins for blankets. Holiday clothing and silver were stored in chests in a rear chamber. Such a home was not greatly superior to an Indian house in British Columbia, with its settee-bed platforms and its abundant well-shaped wooden trunks for the storage of food and treasures. Both dwellings were heated and illuminated by an open fireplace, with extra light from the door and a small hole in the roof. The Indian fishermen and the Nordic farmer were not far apart in their accommodations.

Settlement. Residence involves more than a building technique. First of all, there are the basic requirements of all camping: water, food, fuel. When not one small family but a whole community must be provided for, the matter is naturally complicated. For a big initiation with possibly several hundred participants, the Ona carefully determine the site. There must be plenty of drinking water and game; failure of guanaco at once causes a shift of quarters. The indispensable necessaries of residence, however, play a different part according to geographical conditions. In arid countries water is *the* factor. The Hottentot in South Africa scorns good grasslands for his herds because he dare not move too far away from the Orange River. So in Turkestan habitation is linked with the supply of water: where it is abundant, population clusters; and if cities are destroyed they are rebuilt on the same sites. The Caribou Eskimo, on the other hand, find fresh water almost everywhere so that suitable snow for huts in the winter and the movements of their game determine the distribution of their settlements.

Modes of settlement are variously influenced by environment. Chaco Indians live in villages, but among the Yuracáre of Bolivia single families form a settlement, separated by miles from their nearest neighbors. Living in the tropical forest without clearings, they found it hard to create large plots for cultivation without the white man's axes.

But man has to contend with enemies as well as with nature, and this may make him forego comfort in favor of safety. The Hopi, harassed by marauding nomads, built their homes on steep ridges overlooking the desert plain. Their women had to carry every drop of water up the heights, and the men traveled several miles to their cornfields; yet from conservatism most of them continue this inconvenient arrangement even today when hostilities are no longer to be feared. For protective purposes our Eastern Indians often surrounded their villages with palisades, as did the Maori. These latter, however, often combined the advantages of a lofty site with a stockade. Many of their settlements were very effectively fortified, considering the weapons available for an attack. There were scarps, ramparts and trenches. In a sample village sketched by Captain Cook the besiegers, after battering down an outer palisade, would have to face a deep trench; above it rose a rampart with another stockade and a lofty fighting-stage, from which the defenders could hurl rocks and spears.

The Yuracáre case shows single families constituting a settlement. More frequently there are several families in a single large house. In British New Guinea Dr. A. B. Lewis found a communal structure 490 feet by 117 feet, and 70 feet high. Such coöperative tenements for a whole village occur in the northwest Amazon region, where 200 or more persons reside in a common dwelling. Naturally, special subdivisions are allotted to individual families.

Often, however, the family unit is set aside for residential purposes, cleavage following other lines. Melanesians often have a dormitory-club for all the adult men, while women with their daughters and as yet uninitiated sons occupy their several homes. So in Bolivia the Chacobo men sleep, work, lounge and dance in a big hall flanked by two long structures for the women of the settlement. Still another plan is followed by Australians, who often have a separate encampment for the bachelors, while the Andaman Islanders segregate not only bachelors from married couples but both from the adult single women.

Where a settlement comprises more than one structure, many tribes require no definite arrangement. But the Plains Indians usually pitched their tents in a regular circle, the Omaha even allotting special segments to particular clans. A Shilluk village was similarly laid out, with family dwellings in a ring enclosing the dance ground with the sacred tree, the temples, and stables (*Pl. 13, fig. 1*). On the other hand, the coastal peoples of British Columbia had their residences in a single row facing the beach some distance above high water; and West African Negroes sometimes build fairly regular streets of strung-out oblong houses.

In Europe the need for walled protection deeply affected the growth of towns. Inevitably houses and streets were cramped within the fortified area. Occupants of upper stories in British towns could shake hands across the street. Given a cramped space, Scandinavian builders naturally made their gables front a main thoroughfare so as to have a maximum number of houses in contact with it. The famous boulevards of Paris date back only to Louis XIV, who tore down the ancient bastions; and the complete break with medieval narrowness was only inaugurated by Napoleon III in 1853. In Vienna progress lagged, though the old restrictions of space caused terrible congestion: in the first fifty years of the Nineteenth Century, the population rose from 220,000 to 431,000, but the number of houses in 1850 was only 8,898 as against the earlier figure of 6,739. Not until 1858 were the fortifications razed and the way paved for the magnificent "Ring" avenue now girdling the "Inner City".

The change from rural to urban life created other problems that were only slowly solved. As already indicated, old-fashioned buildings were often firetraps, so that whole towns were again and again destroyed. In Norway it was not feasible to replace timber with stone, so another solution was hit upon. Towns, as Bergen and Trondhjem, were laid out in wide intersecting thoroughfares so that conflagrations might be more easily prevented from spreading to new quarters. Yet there were other perils. Until the last hundred years sanitation remained everywhere on a very low plane. In the Sixteenth Century pigs roamed freely over such cities as Copenhagen and Berlin. As late as 1860 Viennese citizens drank water that had sometimes come trickling through cemeteries; and guide books still warn travelers against the polluted water of French cities. In 1787 Paris lacked foot-pavements, so that a shower made walking horribly inconvenient for men and impossible for a well-dressed woman. Even without rain pedestrians would inevitably be splashed with mud by the passing coaches. With such constant accumulation of dirt and with hygiene and medicine lingering far behind progress in other respects, one plague naturally followed another in the history of Europe. Between 1550 and 1554, for example, the schools of Copenhagen had to be closed and the court fled from the capital, which seemed about to be depopulated. Yet ten years later an epidemic reappeared in the North on a still larger scale, corpses were buried day and night and, if interred at all, were thrown helter-skelter into large pits. Altogether, thirteen major plagues devastated Scandinavia within half a century. In the light of such occurrences, conflagrations almost loom as benefactors since for the time being they destroyed the germs of disease.

In short, when men began to live in large communities they had to meet the same old problems of camping but under far more difficult conditions. A camper escapes danger if he takes elementary precautions about water and fireplaces; and primitive rovers such as the Ona changed their quarters so often that disease could not be fostered as it needs an inadequately cleaned town. It has required all the resources of modern science to make urban centers safe and comfortable places to live in; and even today city planning still admits of much improvement.

VIII

HANDICRAFTS

Conditions of Craftsmanship

Skilled Labor. Even in the rudest societies some individuals greatly excel the rest in manual skill, so that difficult tasks are entrusted to them. All Ona men must spend most of their time hunting, hence no one can set up as a professional artisan; and at a pinch every one must know how to make all the implements considered indispensable. Nevertheless, even these Fuegians recognize superior talent and honor it by a special term. Such "masters" have no regular customers, but they are paid for delicate work—for putting the finishing touch on an arrowhead or making the bridal bow that takes the place of an engagement ring. Even the germ of trademarks appears, for each arrowpoint chipper has some technique of his own and can be at once identified by his product.

More complex societies carry specialization much further. The Shilluk have blacksmiths, boatwrights who are also tomtom-carvers, and roof-thatchers; and in Polynesia the tattooers, architects and canoe-builders were true professionals. Samoan chiefs had to coddle their builders lest they leave in a huff; for they were organized in trade unions and no strike-breakers could be found to finish the job. These artisans thus formed a favored class. Elsewhere certain occupations are treated as contemptible. Notwithstanding their value to the community, blacksmiths are the outcasts of the Masai of East Africa; they must camp apart, may be abused at will, and are never allowed to marry a Masai proper. In other parts of East Africa, as well as in India, tanners are similarly treated. Crafts are thus sometimes linked with differences in social rank.

Sexual Division of Labor. As hunters' wives supply vegetable fare, so there is among nearly all peoples an industrial division of labor between the sexes. This frequently has nothing to do with the inborn aptitudes of men and women, but is a matter of convention. To us tanning does not seem a feminine kind of work, but in most of North America it is woman's distinctive occupation. In the Southwest, on the other hand, men do whatever is connected with hides. North American baskets are mostly made by women, but among many South Americans the craft is masculine, though at the tip of the continent the Ona women are again responsible for basketwork. In Arizona the Hopi men spin and weave, jobs which their next-door neighbors, the Navaho, allot to women. Indeed, extremely few generalizations hold for the whole world. However, men usually carve, work metals, plough, and turn pottery on wheels, while women are by far the most common makers of hand-made earthenware.

Tribal Specialization. Less common, yet far from negligible, is local specialization. In New Guinea many tribes own pottery, but it is manufactured in relatively few villages, which act as distributing centers. Some depend for food wholly on their neighbors, whom they supply in return with their earthenware or shell trade specialty. Another region of intense specialization is Guiana. There all the tribes use hammocks, canoes, curare poison, and manioc graters, but each concentrates on producing a particular article. Curare was especially produced by one group, which was handsomely paid for it with finished blow-guns. Sometimes several distinct groups inhabit the same country, each plying its own trade, so to speak. This happens in various parts of East Africa, where a race of herders have subjected the native peasants, who perform all the useful work except stock-breeding. In Ruanda, Congo, a third class is added

—the Pygmy hunters, many of whom have settled down and apply themselves to such industries as pottery.

The natural effect of localized concentration is intensive trading. This in turn brings together diverse populations and spreads other features than those primarily sought by the traders.

Geographic Influences. Some crafts are limited or excluded by natural conditions. Although stone was generally worked by primitive man, its importance has been overrated, for considerable stretches of territory are and were without this material. A few miles from the Andes the Chaco is wholly lacking in stone; the natives simply substituted bone, shell, teeth, and hard wood, for rocks can not be conveniently imported. For like reasons, natives of Oceanian coral atolls had to make their adzes of shell. By no means all stone is equally suitable for implements, hence again the need for travel and trade. In Central Australia axes were ground only if the natives were near diorite or could get it in exchange. Ona arrow-makers preferred a slaty rock for their points and would go great distances to secure it from favored spots. In other cases a craft can exist only by continued intercourse with the outside world. Since Sweden has no tin, for instance, only foreign trade lifted the prehistoric Scandinavians to the bronze-using level.

Tools and Devices. Every craftsman requires tools, and every trade has its tricks. Primitive workmen lacked many aids that are obvious to us. Nails, for example, were largely unknown; Polynesian architects lashed rafters and beams together with cordage, and so did South American builders. Even the Peruvians, who had small copper nails, used them very little. Again, needles are limited to a few areas; bone ones existed in western Europe toward the end of the Old Stone Age and are used by modern Eskimo. And the Peruvians made copper needles before their discovery. But when an Australian woman did any sewing she punched a hole with an eyeless pointed bone and pulled through it a thread of opossum or kangaroo sinew. Similarly, an Ona seamstress pierces two strips of skin with her bone awl, then moistens a sinew fiber and pushes it through the hole. Only a few years ago one could watch Plains Indian women doing the very same thing. Scissors are peculiar to higher civilizations; Europe was without them until after the beginning of our era. As for the simple idea of patching a hole, even the Peruvians mended only by darning.

The most common and typical primitive tools are: knives; axes, often used as adzes, i.e. with the edge running transversely to the long axis of the handle; scrapers; and drills.

A Queenslander's tool-kit includes natural pebbles. Fixed into a handle (*Pl. 17, fig. 8*) one of these will crack hard nuts and loosen sheets of bark from trees; unmounted, it strikes flakes from a core of rock (*Pl. 17, fig. 9*), which thereby assumes a characteristic appearance (*Pl. 17, fig. 10*). The same piece of stone may yield short stumpy and long thin slivers, suitable for scrapers and knives, respectively. Sometimes several hundred blows are struck before a single good knife flake is obtained. Still another type of tool in this area, blocked out first and then ground to an edge, is an ax or adze according to the method of fixing it to a handle (*Pl. 17, fig. 6*), being used, respectively, for felling a tree or hollowing a canoe.

A stone knife might be awkward to hold; Queenslanders and other Australians embed the head in a lump of cement (*Pl. 17, fig. 7*) for a grip, sometimes eking this out by a flat piece of wood. Such knives make no headway with hard materials but do cut flesh and skins. Thicker and longer flakes of the same type were mounted as pick- or spear-heads (*Pl. 17, fig. 3*).

The Australian at times produces something vastly superior. By pressure with a bone tool he can make a flake into a spearhead the whole surface of which is nicely chipped. Such "pressure-flaking" appeared much later in the Old Stone Age than the striking off of flakes

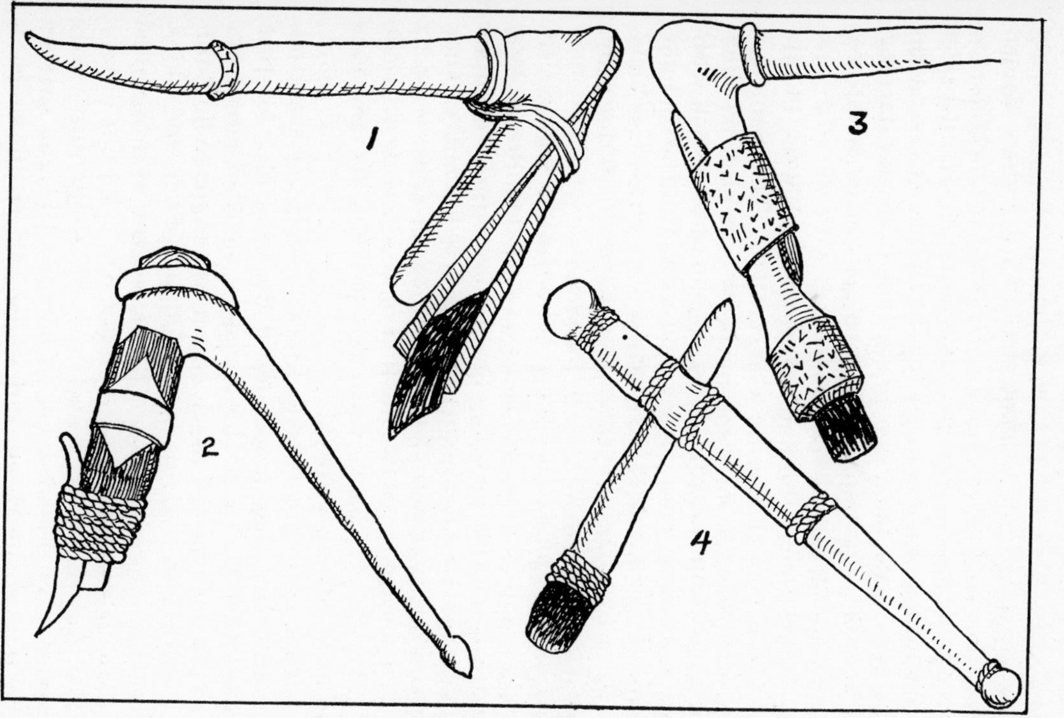

Plate 16: Methods of Hafting a Stone Ax.

1-4. New Guinea [Finsch (7) *Plate I, Nos. 3-6*]

from a core, and obviously it demands far greater skill. But we can not grade people by their knowledge or ignorance of this art. The Polynesians, in many ways supreme among illiterate peoples, knew nothing of it, while the simple Fuegians were adepts, first blocking out their arrowpoints by blows on a lump of slate with a stone hammer, then delicately pressing off slivers with pieces of guanaco bone (*Pl. 17, fig. 2*). By such pressure-flaking California hunters made superb obsidian blades sometimes well over a foot long.

As stated above, the importance of stone work in human history must not be exaggerated. The Samoans shaped stone tools for some purposes, but grooved shell with *natural* slivers of basalt and cut up flesh or fish with a strip of bamboo. In the stoneless Chaco the Indians simply used hard wood for scaling or gutting fish, and on the coral atolls of Micronesia the shell of the giant clam made a good substitute for stone.

Stone axes or adzes with ground edges are widespread but were unknown to the savages of the Old Stone Age, and a fair number of living peoples do without even an equivalent. In procuring the timber for his hut an Ona had to lasso branches and break them off at the crotch, hence he kept the framework standing mainly to save himself this troublesome exertion. Californians split logs with an antler wedge driven by an unworked stone maul. In the southern part of the state even this device was absent so that trees were never felled; the Mohave tied stones to handles and hacked away smaller limbs from willows, burning the brush about the butt to kill the tree and leaving the stump standing.

The earliest ax, dating back in western Europe perhaps 100,000 years and more, was not ground but merely worked from a mass of rock by striking off chips from it; the remaining core was then wielded as a hatchet without handle. Crude and heavy at first, these cleavers became more shapely and lighter in subsequent periods. But it was not until well into the New Stone

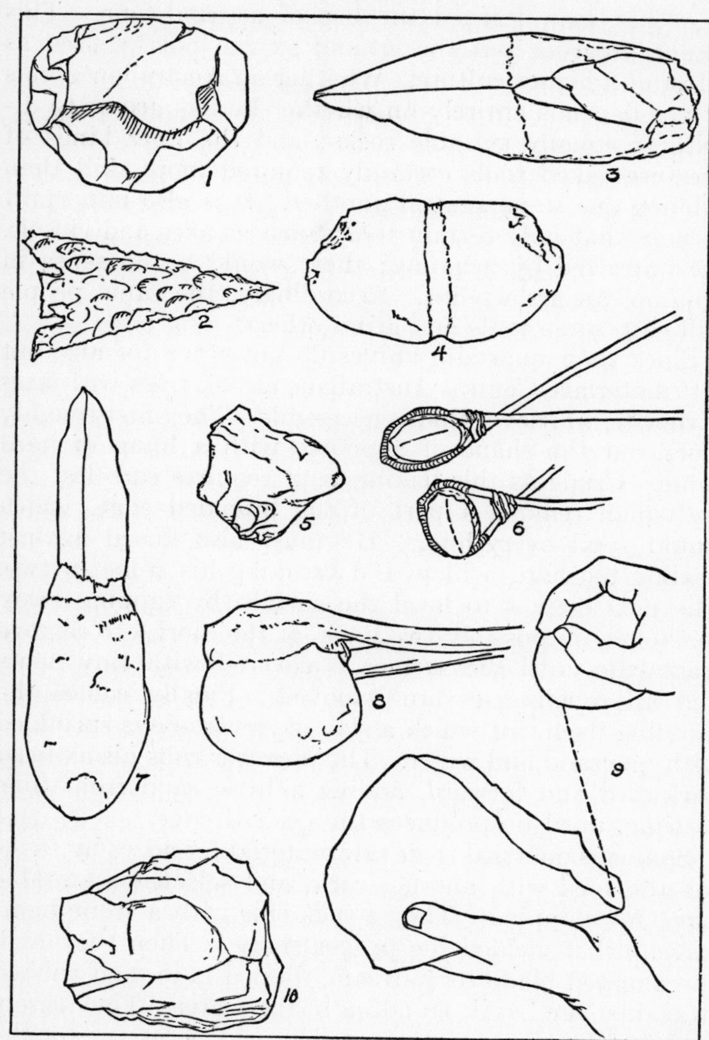

Plate 17: STONE TOOLS.

1. Fuegian Scraper [Lothrop (25) *Plate 8a*] 2. Fuegian Arrow Point [Lothrop (25) p. 113] 3. Flaked Spearhead, Queensland [Roth (32) Fig. 41] 4. Celt, Queensland [Roth (32) Fig. 62] 5. Scraper, Queensland [Roth (32) Fig. 96] 6. Hafting of the same celt in two ways, as an ax and as an adze, Queensland [Roth (32) Figs. 56, 57] 7. Knife, Queensland [Roth (32) Fig. 132] 8. Hammer, Queensland [Roth (32) Fig. 154] 9. Hammer stone in the act of striking a core with a view to removing a flake, Queensland [Roth (32) Fig. 23] 10. Core, after removing a flake, Queensland [Roth (32) Fig. 35]

Age that man learned the use of a grindstone. This meant progress, but the ground ax can not be used as a test of a higher culture. Whether an Australian grinds or not depends entirely on whether he has access to diorite or equally suitable rocks; and the finer kinds of pressure-flaked tools certainly required more skill than rubbing one stone against another. It is also important to note that only certain tools, such as axes and chisels, are improved by grinding; there would be no sense in grinding an arrowpoint. Accordingly, the same people will chip some tools and grind others.

Since their quartzite knives do not serve for any but soft materials, Central Australians attack trees with axes of diorite, whenever that is accessible. They first roughly block out the shape of a pebble with a lump of hard stone. Crude as this flaking is, it requires care lest the craftsman remove a part of the intended edge, which would spoil everything. He must also guard against dealing too hard a blow and breaking his stone in two. The next step is to level the surface by tapping away for hours, on possibly two days, at the diorite to remove fragments until the surface is covered with tiny dents and all roughnesses are removed. Finally comes the grinding itself, for which a slab of sandstone is sprinkled with fine sand and water. The operator rubs his ax head backward and forward, adding a little sand from time to time, until he produces the desired edge.

Samoans quarried their raw material for adzes by striking the rock with another rock, and selected a suitable piece for chipping. They struck this with a stone hammer until it yielded the proper shape. Then they took the chipped blade to a stream, dipped it in, and rubbed it against the basalt standing in the water. They rarely bothered to grind much more than was necessary for the cutting edge, but many other Oceanians nicely polish the entire surface. Since this in no wise added to efficiency, the extra labor must have been put in on behalf of aesthetic effect. Clearly, then, ground tools are produced by first using the Old Stone Age process of striking off slivers of stone and then adding a sharp edge by the lengthy and arduous process of grinding.

In contrast to the fist-hatchet of the Old Stone Age, the axes, adzes, and chisels of later and recent periods were hafted (*Pl. 16; Pl. 17, figs. 6, 8*). This added power and relieved the tiring rebound of the hand in wielding the tool. The blade can either be stuck into the handle, or tied to it, or pierced for a handle to be put through the hole. Some Swiss blades of the New Stone Age were set in a slit of the handle, a method also used at times in Australian picks. But Central Australians usually heat the middle of a stem to make it pliable, then bend it double around the blunt butt of the stone and tie the two halves together, fixing the blade with resin, which covers the bent part of the withy. This is a crude method, for a hard blow cracks the resin and loosens the ax head. Far superior is the Polynesian way of lashing on the handle with cordage, the elbow of a tree limb being fitted to the blade. Melanesians vary this (*Pl. 16, fig. 2*) with more complex devices by which the blade is directly attached to a separate holder that is tied to the shaft (*Pl. 16, figs. 1, 3*) or stuck into a perforated shaft (*Pl. 16, fig. 4*). Some of these specimens enable the worker to turn his cutting edge. A special subtype, found occasionally in Australia (*Pl. 17, fig. 4*), very common in North America but rare in prehistoric Europe, had the stone grooved so the cord could be firmly attached. Drilling a hole through a stone ax was difficult for Stone Age technicians, hence relatively rare and applied to igneous rocks rather than to flint.

In the Bronze Age of Europe the bronze blade developed wings which ultimately united to form a socket. This implied, of course, that the blade was no longer stuck into the handle but vice versa. The form continued into the Iron Age. In America socketed copper axes are known from the Argentine, Peru, and Ecuador, and a sample in gold has been found in the last-mentioned country.

Scrapers are common wherever skins are worked; they go back to the middle portions of the Old Stone Age of Europe, occur abundantly in archaeological Fuegian sites (*Pl. 17, fig. 1*), and are highly characteristic of North American and Siberian life. The Caribou Eskimo alone have several types, each for a special purpose, but all held in one hand and moved away from the worker. One kind serves to free the skin of the tissue below the outer layer and to remove remains of flesh and fat. The material is of the shoulderblade or some similar bone of a caribou or musk-ox. For crushing the fibers of the skin there is a beak-shaped stone tool made from sandstone hewn with another rock and then ground. For thinning a skin the natives anciently had very sharp scrapers of hard bone; and sometimes they soften stiffened skins with an antler tool sharpened and cut with parallel sides except for a short curved branch left at the top for a grip. Plains Indians likewise have several implements for dressing hides, notably a chisel-shaped flesher for cleaning the inner surface and a stone blade set in a handle of elk antler for removing the hair. A common "beaming" tool consists of the sharpened long bone of a deer or similar species broken lengthwise; in typical fashion the Havasupai worker grasps it with both hands and draws it down the hide hung over a smooth pole. Australians made the short slivers knocked off from stone cores into scrapers, some of them worked into a concave edge for sharpening the tips of wooden spears (*Pl. 17, fig. 5*).

Drills are easily made of sharp bits of hard stone, shell or teeth, suitably mounted. The Havasupai and some Melanesians twirl the wooden shaft exactly as they would in fire-drilling (p. 55). Other Melanesians and also Polynesians improved on this by setting a perforated wooden flywheel on the lower part of the shaft, and above the disk a crossbar tied by each end to the top of the upright. The operator begins by twirling the shaft so as to wind up the cords from which the bar hangs, thus raising the bar. Pressing down on the handle, he unwinds the cords and makes the upright revolve so that the cords are wound up in the opposite direction. Thus the shaft goes on revolving back and forth. This is the pump-drill elsewhere used with a blunter tip (p. 56) for making fire (*Pl. 7, fig. 2*). The Eskimo and Yukaghir, who revolve their fire-drill with a bow, use the same appliance for boring holes (*Pl. 7, fig. 1*). The Eskimo even substitute this process for sawing bone, making one hole beside another and then wedging the bone apart. But rude cultures had still another method at their disposal—that of boring with a hollow reed; this naturally caused a hole by the dropping out of a cylindrical core. Primitive drilling was generally aided by the use of sand and water.

Processes

Certain crafts figure so prominently in history as to require separate treatment. These are: the preparation of skins, felting, bark cloth manufacture, basketry, weaving, pottery, carving, and metallurgy. They are not uniformly distributed over space and time. Some exclude others: skin clothing militates against woven fabrics, and bark cloth tends to limit both skin and loom work. Basketry appears on most levels, but pottery and loom-weaving rest on a technical basis that makes them improbable on a hunting plane.

Some craft developments can be plausibly accounted for. Peru had both excellent textile material in the form of wool and also specialization, some young girls virtually devoting their lives to weaving. Other cases are not so clear. While the people of western British Columbia had splendid timber, their carpentry was disproportionately superb as compared with that of otherwise comparable tribes. North American skin dressing is greatly superior to that of African Negroes even where the latter are otherwise technically more advanced and live in similar geographical conditions.

The several crafts considered below, some of which affected the evolution of art itself (p. 182), instructively illustrate man's inventiveness in various environments.

Preparation of Skins. People who use hides generally try to increase their resistance to weathering and rotting, either by mechanical, or by mechanical *and* chemical, means. The combination of the two is called tanning and results in leather. Pelt is converted into leather by vegetable or by mineral materials, by both jointly, or by oily substances. In tanning the mechanical preliminaries uncover that portion of the skin, the "corium", which is chemically altered.

When an Ona has flayed a guanaco hide, his wife stretches it for drying and after several days lays it on the ground, wool side down. She kneels on the stiff rawhide and laboriously scrapes off the fatty tissue and the transparent layer below it with her quartz blade. After a while she kneads the skin piecemeal with her fists, going over the whole surface repeatedly and even bringing her teeth into play until it is softened. If the hair is to be taken off, that is done with the same scraper. In order to improve the appearance, the woman smears a mixture of red earth and fat over the hide. The Shilluk likewise mainly knead and rub after fleshing the stretched hide with stones; dung, ashes, and fat render it flexible and there are frequent applications of fat. While many Eskimo groups steep skins in a vessel with urine, the Caribou Eskimo use only mechanical means, though very fatty hides may undergo some unintended chemical change. Though not treated chemically, the fresh skins of these people are said to be quite on a par with the tanned skins of Canadian Indians.

Typically, however, North American natives tanned with some special preparation of brains. After beaming (p. 116), the Havasupai soak, rub, wring out and pull the skin, whereupon it is ready for tanning. Two balls have

Plate 17A.
Dakota Man's Skin Robe with Black War Bonnet Design. (Courtesy of American Museum of Natural History.)

Plate 17B.
Decorated Skin Bags for Pipes and Tobacco, Dakota Indians. (Courtesy of American Museum of Natural History.)

been prepared, the first to be used being from roasted deer brains, the other from the marrow of a deer's spinal canal. The ball is worked up in water into a soapy liquor, which is sprayed in mouthfuls over the hairy side and the ends of the fleshy side. The skin is rolled up and set aside long enough to be soaked with the tan, then it is spread, dried, and vigorously rubbed and pulled until soft. Similarly the Plains Indian leather-maker rubbed oily brains of game animals into the scraped and fleshed hide and allowed this material to soak in with exposure to the sun. Many tribes give a final touch to the manufacture by smoking the leather over a smoldering fire.

Instead of using brains the Kirghiz steep pelts for days in a mush of flour and sour milk or in a pap of the ashes from burned steppe grass. In classical antiquity tanning was due to the tannin of oak and other barks. Similarly, in India the mechanically prepared skin is formed into a sack and filled with bruised bark; the tanner pours in water, and this gradually saturates the skin.

Hides, raw or tanned, play a large part in the manufactures of some peoples. Leather bottles are typical of Asiatic nomads; South and East African Negro tribes use skin clothing and shields. The Plains Indians dressed in skin robes, shirts, dresses, leggings and moccasins; they covered their tents, cradles and shields with skin, stored smoking outfits and sundries in soft buckskin pouches, and preserved meat in rawhide cases.

Felting. Felting is the typical industry of Turks, Tibetans, and other nomads, whose herds provide them with ample wool and hair. The essential process is rolling, beating, and pressing the material into a compact and even mass. This technique spread to ancient India, China, Greece and Rome. The ancient Greeks wore rain cloaks and tight-fitting conical caps of felt, and the Romans borrowed the practice. The Chinese adopted the industry from the Turkish and Mongol nomads to the north, though the wilder peoples of the south, such as the

Lolo, still wear a felt blanket or sleeveless coat throughout the year. However, with the true Chinese, as with Greeks and Romans, felt was a minor trait that could have been eliminated without deeply affecting their lives. In contrast to them the Tibetans dressed in felt before the Chinese fashion of silk garments found favor, and still wear felt boots, rain ponchos, and hats. Felt rugs, tent covers, mittens and mattresses are common among the Turks, and the medieval Mongols even worshiped felt images. The following account gives the details of manufacture in a typical case. The Kirghiz spread the wool over a mat, sprinkle it with water, then beat it with rods, roll up the mat as tightly as possible, and tie it with cords. This package is rolled back and forth, pulled along the ground with a rope by experts, and pushed with the feet. When unpacked, the wool is rolled up and rerolled for hours while water is continuously sprinkled on it. There are usually two layers, a lower of cheaper brown wool and an upper of white wool. These are finally spread out and dried in the sun, making a smooth felt cloth.

Bark Cloth. Felting was never practiced outside of Asia and Europe. Neither the Egyptians with their sheep dating back thousands of years nor the Peruvians with their llamas ever invented the process. But the comparable technique of beating bast, i.e. the inner bark of trees, into cloth is found in Africa, Central and South America, Indonesia and Oceania. The universal tool is a wooden mallet, usually grooved. The Bakuba of the southern Congo wear bark garments only for festivals, the men's costume being made of a single piece while the women's is a mosaic of small bark patches sewed together with palm fiber. In Uganda, on the other hand, everyday dress was of bark cloth, and it was a man's duty to clothe the household just as it was the wife's to feed them bananas. The worker first made incisions around his tree and lengthwise, put a knife blade under the bark, and peeled it off. Then he scraped the outer side, left it overnight, scraped it again inside and out, and then took it to a special shed. There he spread the bark on the smooth surface of a 6-foot log sunk in the floor and began beating it with mallets grooved with different grades of fineness. He continued until he had a sheet as thick as paper and measuring seven or eight feet wide by twelve feet long. Pieces with flaws were cut out, other pieces being fitted in and neatly stitched.

Northeastern Bolivia is one of the outstanding centers for this industry, both sexes manufacturing cloth from the bast of certain trees. Shirts for men and women, carrying-straps and bags are all made of this material. However, not all species provide suitable bark, hence the art is geographically limited. On the other hand, its great development naturally eliminates the need for woven fabrics, so loomwork is meager in this area.

Though in Uganda only men make bark cloth, its preparation is a feminine industry in Polynesia. The plant generally exploited is the paper-mulberry. After the bast has been peeled off, a Samoan scrapes it with various tools made of a special shell. Then she smooths, dries and folds her strips, each separately, pressing out as much moisture as possible. Now comes the actual beating on a wooden anvil, which is followed by stretching the sheets while damp and drying them. Patches are pasted over any holes, and the separate sheets are similarly stuck together into desired sizes and thicknesses. In eastern Polynesia the bast is soaked in water for a considerable time, allowed to drain, and then beaten out in one continuous sheet to the required thickness. In other words, the strips are joined by the felting together of the fibers. But in Samoa the bast is soaked only for a brief time and is soon scraped with shell tools. Hence it is so dry that when several strips are beaten together, the material from each comes out separately; in other words, it is not felted to that of other strips. The mallet also differs in the two regions, the Samoan form being either plain or only coarsely grooved. In the east, plain beaters are used only in the preliminary pounding, the worker always finishing her cloth with closely grooved mallets. Beaters of the latter type have been dredged up in a New Zealand harbor. The Maori, therefore, brought the eastern Polynesian art of bark-cloth making to their new home but abandoned it because the paper-mulberry would not thrive in that climate.

Basketry. Basketry differs from felt in consisting of two regularly connected sets of elements, the warp and the woof (weft). In "plaited" or "hand-woven" basketry there is interlacing of the two, as in loom-weaving; but the plaiter's elements are not soft and narrow threads, which might easily get entangled, but comparatively stiff and wide splints of, say, coconut and pandanus leaves, acacia twigs, conifer roots. A second type, "coiled" basketry, is really sewing, a foundation of splints or grass, corresponding to the warp, being stitched together (*Pl. 18, fig.* 5) with the aid of a bone awl, the usual primitive substitute for a needle.

Each of these main types has numerous subdivisions, but only a few forms of the hand-woven type need be considered here. If each element of the woof set alternately crosses over and under one element of the warp, "checkerwork" results (*Pl. 18, fig. 4*) and it is impossible to tell from a finished sample which has been warp and which woof. "Wickerwork" differs only in having a rigid warp (*Pl. 18, fig. 1*). If more than one element is regularly crossed, the technique is "twilling", which readily leads to decorative designs (*Pl. 18, fig. 3*). Finally, "twined" basketry has two or more intertwining weft elements holding together the rigid warp (*Pl. 18, fig. 2*).

These techniques have definite distributions, some peoples using only a limited number. The Ona know a single form of coiling. In Samoa coiled basketry was originally unknown, but checker and twilling abound. Twining flourishes in northern California to the exclusion of coiling, which is equally typical of the southern part of the state. Elsewhere, however, various processes are used

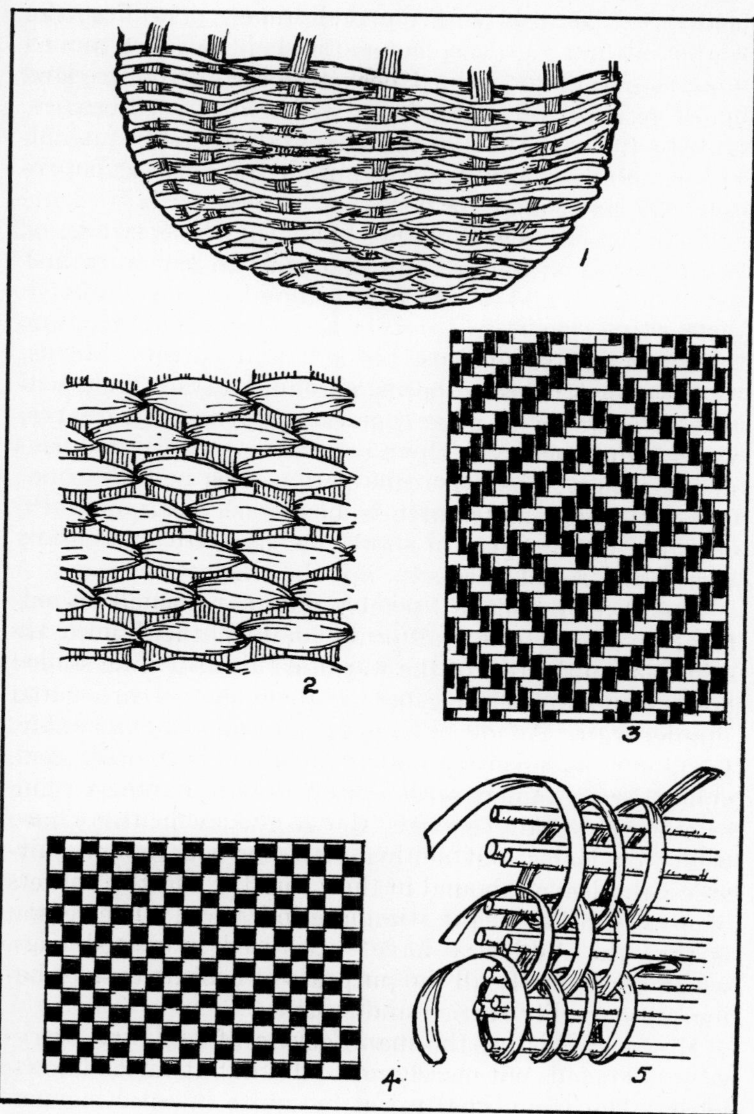

Plate 18: TECHNIQUES OF BASKETRY.

1. Wicker Weave [Kroeber (18) p. 289] 2. Twining [Kroeber (18) p. 292] 3. Twilling [Roth (33) p. 318] 4. Checker Weave [Roth (33) p. 344] 5. Coiling [Kroeber (18) p. 302]

simultaneously and with equal deftness. The Pomo of central California, conspicuous for their basketry among American Indians, twined baskets for stone-boiling and coiled ornamental ware, have wickerwork seed-beaters, and sundry variations of fundamental processes. A culture generally reserves one technique for a particular object: the Havasupai, for instance, twine water bottles and burden baskets. On the other hand, they both twine and coil their trays; and a Hopi mat may be partly twilled, partly wicker, and bordered in coiling.

The basketry technique yields a great variety of objects. The Havasupai use burden baskets, water bottles, shallow bowls, cooking-bowls, parching trays. Their bottles are coated with pitch, but various tribes can produce watertight basketry. There are stiff basket-work shields in the Congo; basketry caps and cradles in California; fans, knapsacks, mats, satchels, boxes, fish creels, in northern South America. In short, the uses are indefinitely varied and so, of necessity, are the shapes and sizes.

The development of basketry does not depend on cultural level. Simple California hunters, the Pomo, are said to excel the rest of the world in this art, while skilled potters and weavers lag behind them in the earlier and simpler craft. Adequate substitutes explain the anomaly. Earthenware vessels are better for cooking than baskets, and other containers serve equally well for stone-boiling or storage. Oddly enough, the Ashluslay in the Chaco weave on looms, but neither plait nor coil though suitable palm leaves abound in their country and the baskets of nearby tribes might stimulate imitation. The reason is that the Ashluslay have specialized in netted bags, which serve nearly all the purposes of baskets besides being more readily carried and stored.

However this be, the manufacture of basketry everywhere demands not merely manual skill but varied knowledge. The Havasupai reject mesquite in selecting material for warp and weft, treat cottonwood and willow twigs as inferior, and prize "cat's-claw" acacia twigs as the best. But these are not simply used as nature offers them. If dry, they are soaked; in any case the leaves are stripped, and the butts of the twigs trimmed off to yield two different sizes. The longer twigs are split in three by the use of the teeth and the hands, the central third being discarded; and the two outside strips are scraped to uniform thickness with a knife. There is a definite beginning for twined baskets—two pairs of long twigs crossing each other at right angles—and as she proceeds the maker constantly moistens the wefts to keep them pliable. When coating a water bottle, she must first apply an appreciable body of empirical information. She rubs the surface with a dry corncob to fill the interstices, sprays water over the basket, smears and rubs soapweed paste on it, adds a mixture of pulverized paint and water, then allows the vessel to dry in the sun. Only then is the boiled piñon pitch poured inside the bottle, which is continuously turned over near a bed of coals so the heat will prevent the pitch from coagulating before the interstices are filled. A coating with the same material follows. Once hardened, the pitch does not melt appreciably in the sun. Ability to use the heat effectively on the highly inflammable pitch implies considerable rule-of-thumb knowledge of physics.

Weaving. True weaving, like basketry, differs from felt in having interlaced materials, and from basketry in the softer and narrower nature of the materials, which require a loom for manipulation. In other words, weavers use *spun* material, string or thread. Spinning is thus preliminary to loom work.

While weaving is lacking among Australians and Polynesians, as well as many African and American tribes, spinning is universal. Its function is to lengthen and strengthen such natural fibers as wool, cotton, silk, hair, bast. This is frequently done without any implement whatsoever. Ashluslay women scrape and dry the fibers of Bromelia leaves, then twirl them with their hands on their thighs. In New Guinea the string for bags is commonly made of the shredded bast of certain trees by a similar maneuver. The Paviotso of northeastern California rolled two strands of sagebrush bark on the thigh separately on the downward stroke and combined on the upward stroke, thus producing the usual California two-ply string.

Old World peoples anciently invented a spindle with a whorl, the latter acting as a flywheel when the spindle was dropped with a twirl and thus giving twist and tension to the loose threads of linen or wool. American Indian cotton-growers discovered that cotton can not be effectively spun on the thigh like other fibers, hence twisted it between the fingers and then wound it on a shaft, which also bore a whorl-like disk (*Pl. 20, fig. 4*). But apparently this was a mere guard for keeping the thread from slipping off, for there is no evidence of the natives' ever dropping the shaft; in Peru, where textiles were most highly developed, the whorls were too small to make effective flywheels. This makes the American spindle essentially a bobbin or reel.

Spun thread is the material for loom-weaving. A loom is a frame in which the warp is stretched so that each woof thread can regularly pass over and under the warp elements (*Pl. 19, fig. 1*). At each thrust those warp threads must be above the woof which in the preceding and succeeding thrusts lie below. In other words, weaving is a development from plaiting with threads hung over a frame substituted for splints. Yet even that is not the basic difference. There is a form of plaiting in which threads are also hung from a frame, as in making the blankets of the Alaskan Tlingit or the Maori. This is not weaving, because the worker pulls the woof threads singly through the warp. In a true loom the woof yarn is wound on a shuttle and unwinds itself as the shuttle is shot across a warp prearranged by means of a "heddle" so that all warp threads meant to lie above the new woof element can be raised as a unit. That is, at the first thrust all the odd warp elements are raised together, at

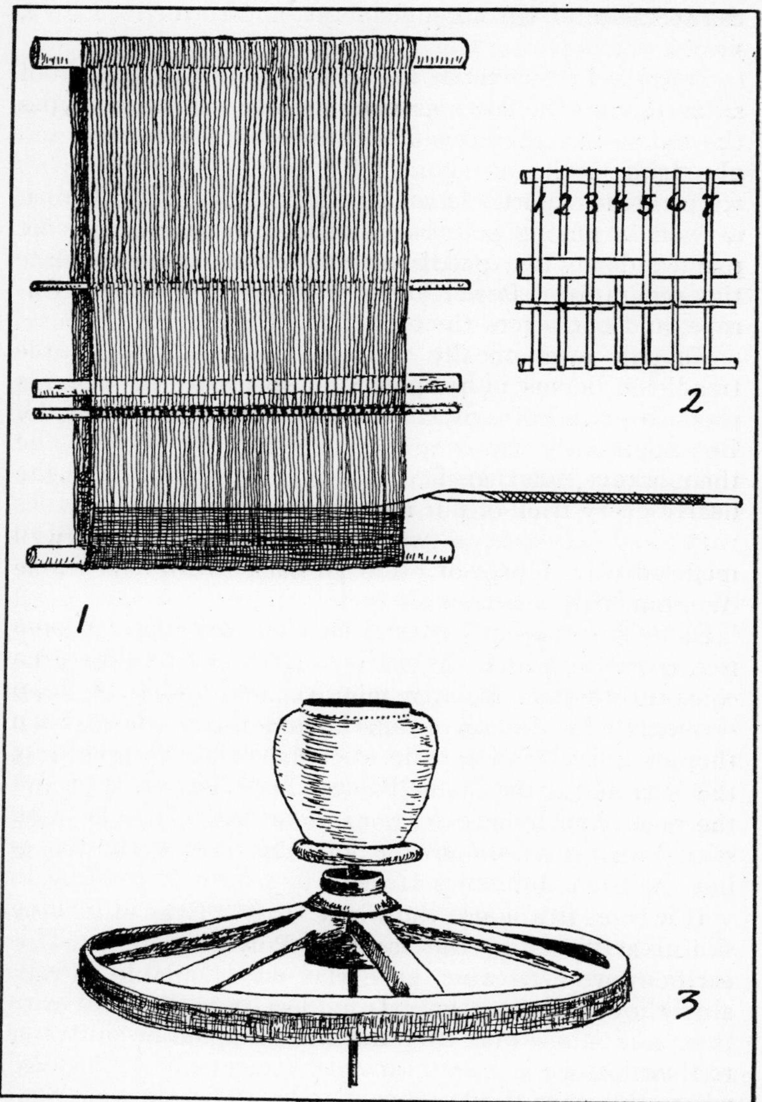

Plate 19: True Weaving and Pottery.

1. A Simple Hand Loom from Assam and Indonesia [Ephraim (6) p. 40] 2. Detail of same, showing Position of Loom-Stick and Heddle. 3. A Potter's Wheel from Brittany [Horwitz (14) p. 754]

the second all even warp elements, and so forth (*Pl. 19, fig. 2*).

Progress in technique lies in relieving the worker of as much manual labor as possible. In all earlier types the hands had to throw the shuttle with the woof and also tend to the mechanism for keeping odd and even warp threads apart. In ancient Egypt, India and China, as well as among peoples influenced by them, the feet pressed down two pedals alternately so as to regulate this separation. Power looms arose only in western Europe, and not before the end of the Eighteenth Century.

Though mechanically inferior, however, the simple treadleless looms of peoples who specialize in weaving produce extraordinarily fine work. The rugs woven by Central Asiatic Turks are famous for the closeness of their weave, and ancient Peruvian textiles duplicate nearly every trick of our modern factories.

Pottery. Pottery is work in fired clay. Some well modeled clay figures of bison go back to the Old Stone Age, but fired earthenware is not positively known until later. One reason is clear. Old Stone Age men were roving hunters, and pottery vessels would inevitably be constantly broken on their migrations. In historic times several Plains Indian groups abandoned pottery when they gave up farming to hunt buffalo. Hunters such as the Ona and Australians likewise lack earthenware, and the much higher pastoral nomads of Asia generally substitute leather containers for pots. In short, a wandering life tends to eliminate pottery.

However, this is not the whole story. Even such very skilful artificers as the farming Polynesians made no earthenware even when good clay was available. Probably they once had the art but lost it in the course of their migrations over the South Seas, for in order to get to their historic homes they must have passed Melanesia, where there are fairly many potters. The question here would be why they did not reinvent it, and a partial answer is that they had taken so largely to earth ovens as

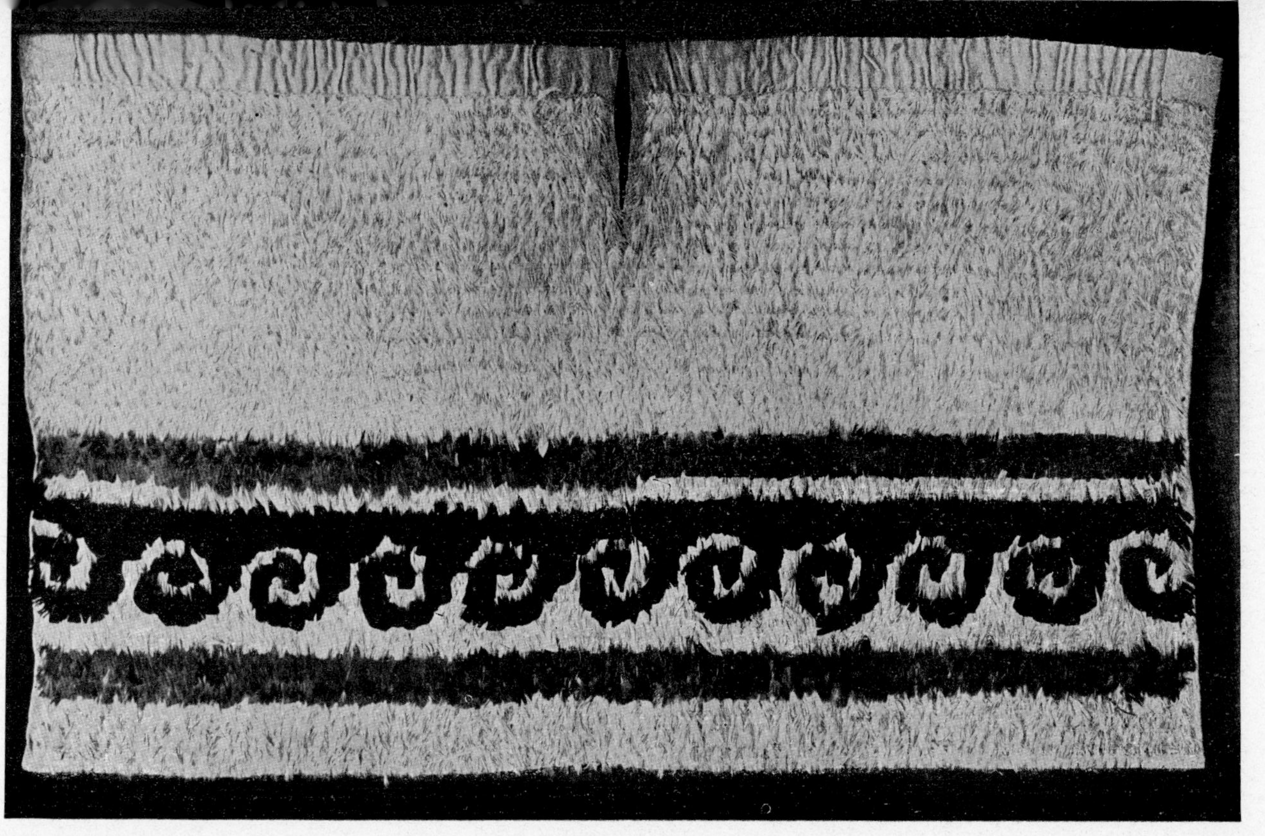

Plate 19A.

Feather-decorated Woven Poncho from Peru. (Courtesy of American Museum of Natural History.)

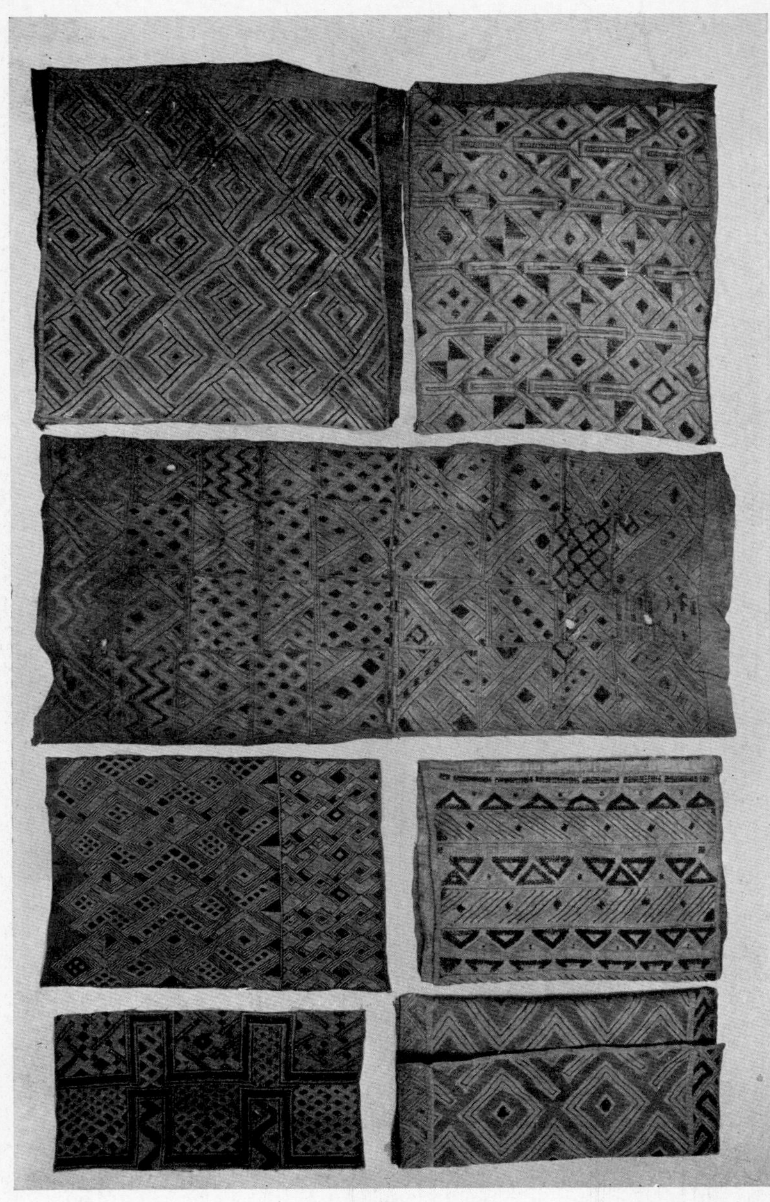

Plate 19B.

Pile Cloth of the Bakuba Negroes, Congo. (Courtesy of American Museum of Natural History.)

not to require earthenware vessels for cooking, while their artistic sense expressed itself in other ways. This, however, does not adequately explain the facts. The British Columbia Indians boiled food with stones, so certainly could have used pots to advantage; yet with all their progress in other lines, they were not potters.

The point is that true pottery represents a technical achievement that is not likely to be often duplicated. First of all, not every kind of clay will do. It is not from mere fussiness that native experts insist on getting their material from particular spots. Potter's clay consists largely of silica and aluminum oxide, but their proportions vary greatly; in two South American samples from different tribes the ratio was 45.60:37.00 and 57.75:22.56, respectively. In the latter case the potters compensated for the excess of silica by adding a large percentage of fusible substances. Clay must be readily molded when wet, and if it is oversupplied with sand, something must be added to make it more plastic. On the other hand, it is equally fatal to have clay that sticks to the worker's hands and cracks in drying or under heat. That is why potters, taught by experience, get their material from tried localities. But good clay is not everywhere to be found, hence long trips must be made to secure it. That, however, is not always practicable, and the alternative is to improve upon nature by adding suitable ingredients. Thus, the ancient Egyptians added quartz, the Chinese feldspar, the Greeks lime. Similarly, South American Indians tempered unplastic clay with mica, and overplastic clay with pounded potsherds, shell, sponges, or other substances. Nigerian Negroes similarly mix sand or crushed pieces of old pots with their clay. In other words, successful pottery means a certain knowledge of applied physics and chemistry, and this holds not only for the shaping but also for the firing of the vessel, which alone makes it durable. Failure to heat uniformly, an unexpected rain shower during firing, the unpredictable kick of a vagrant domestic beast against a drying pot, will destroy hours of arduous work. The surroundings of Indian huts north of Lake Titicaca are thus strewn with fragments of pots marred in the making.

In short, the invention, like the practice, is very difficult. That is why many peoples failed to produce earthenware, and why its invention can not have occurred frequently. Indeed, many scholars believe that in America it originated only once, somewhere between Mexico and Peru, and traveled from these higher centers to simpler peoples. That would explain why the peoples of British Columbia made no earthenware: they were too far from the starting-point of the invention to be influenced from that source, and the rise of pottery depends on so many favorable circumstances that they failed to duplicate the technique.

Pottery is either molded by hand or mechanically on a wheel (*Pl. 19, fig. 3*). The potter's wheel was invented in Egypt about 3,000 B.C. and spread from there to other Old World civilizations. Very gradually it also reached less civilized peoples of Europe. In the early Middle Ages the Germanic peoples still made most of their pottery by hand, and this held for the Slavs until about 1,000 A.D. In the New World no tribe either borrowed or invented the potter's wheel. In other words, all primitive and all American pottery are classed as hand-made.

Hand-made pottery uses essentially one of two processes: either a lump of clay is shaped with the hands into the desired form; or the body of the vessel is built up by coiling, that is by adding one sausage of clay to another in a spiral formation. Coiled pottery is extremely common throughout the world, but its manufacturers often shape the base in a lump and coil the rest of the vessel. Also the same people, as in southern Yucatan, have been known to shape small pots directly and to coil larger ones.

In south-central California, a Mono or Yokuts woman starts with a handful of clay, which she rolls into a ball of even consistency, then flattens the ball into a disk

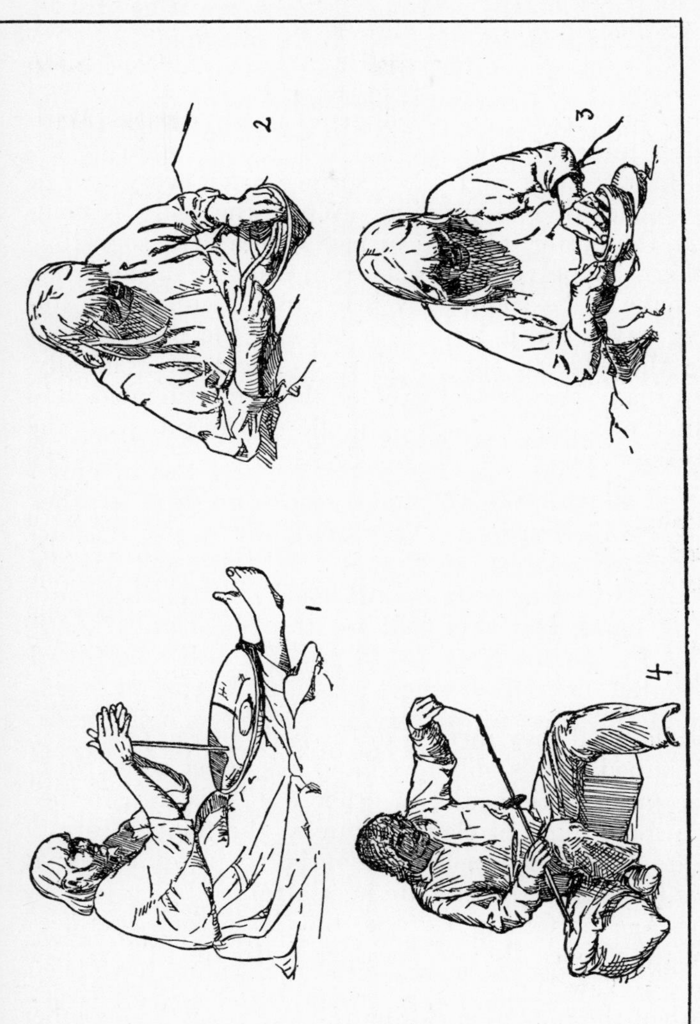

Plate 20: Pottery and Spinning.

1. Making the clay "sausage." Mono, California [Gayton (8) *Plate 95b*] 2. Laying the coils in place, Mono, California [Gayton (8) *Plate 96a*] 3. Smoothing the pot before firing, Mono, California [Gayton (8) *Plate 97a*] 4. Hopi man spinning (From a photograph by Lowie)

and turns up the edge as a base for the first coil. This bottom is set in the middle of a round basketry tray (*Pl. 20, fig. 1*), and from now on the pot grows by successive rolls of clay fitted to the circumference (*Pl. 20, fig. 2*), the junction between two coils being smoothed out by the worker's wetted fingers (*Pl. 20, fig. 3*). With a small piece of wood or part of an acorn husk she smooths the inner and outer surface after every two or three inches of coil-building. When the body is completed, the potter rubs the surface with a little soapstone polisher. To prevent the pots from cracking in the firing, they have to be completely dried in the sun. The following day a fire is built in a pit and the pots are put along the edge to subject them to the heat gradually. When ready they are shoved to the fire with poles and set in the hot ashes in the middle of the pit, with the fire reassembled about them. Cooking-pots were exposed to the heat for at least twenty-four hours, often twice that long. Toward the end they are sharply tapped with a hard stick, a clear metallic sound being proof of adequate baking. If deemed fit, they were again set along the edge to make them cool off by degrees. Maricopa potters also followed the coiling process but combined with it the widespread device of holding a stone or pottery anvil inside the vessel while beating the coils with a paddle until they merged in the body of the pot.

If shaped clay is only dried and has water added to it, it becomes plastic again, in other words, is transformed into a mere lump of clay. Firing at the temperature of at least 400° Centigrade is essential to prevent this; it seems to be the approximate heat attained by early New Stone Age potters in Europe, but later they produced more than twice that temperature. In the Old as well as in the New World firing progressed from open-air exposure of the pots to enclosing them in a heated chamber —a kiln or furnace.

Pots may have all sorts of attachments, such as lugs, rims, legs, ring bases. But these are not at all essential.

The pots of the upper Nile lack all handles, though transverse decorative stripes roughen the surface and thus yield a somewhat better grip.

Apart from pure decoration, pottery may have technical refinements in the form of coatings. Glaze is a glassy coating melted on the surface of a pot to make it waterproof, for even well-fired pottery remains porous. Some of the extinct natives of New Mexico used a coating that resembled glaze in appearance, but it was neither of glass nor did it serve to prevent porosity since it was only applied to portions of the body, hence was mere decoration. Glass and glaze originated in ancient Egypt and traveled to other high cultures, but did not reach central Europe until after 800 A.D. The simpler peoples made their vessels less porous, perhaps unintentionally, by smoking them and smearing them with fat. South American Indians of the tropical lowlands applied a varnish of melted resin, partly to prevent the water from oozing out, partly for decoration. In the higher cultures the vessels received a surface coat of clay finer than the body of the vessel in order to have painted decoration applied to it. This conceivably also serves a practical purpose, since the finer, more homogeneous "slip" is less permeable to water and can be more effectively polished and hardened. Technically, this is a great achievement, for the coating and the foundation must have a common coefficient of evaporation and react similarly in firing.

The most remarkable development of glazed ware is porcelain. The Chinese had coiled pottery in their New Stone Age and later adopted the wheel from civilizations to the west. When they ultimately learned about glass they at first used it sparingly. Finally, however, during the Han dynasty (206 B.C.-220 A.D.), they began to glaze earthenware. Soon a period of experimentation set in, and by the Seventh Century the Chinese achieved true white porcelain, i.e. that form of earthenware in which the glaze is not a mere coating but evenly penetrates the entire vessel. This invention was not duplicated in Europe until the Eighteenth Century. Here we see again how several divisions of mankind collaborate to bring about a supreme result. Pottery in general is the achievement of some New Stone Age people; glass, glaze, and the potter's wheel must be credited to the Bronze Age of Egypt; and porcelain, an original combination and further development of these ideas, is the undisputed creation of the Chinese.

The pottery technique has had many applications, and correspondingly there is as much variation in shape and size as with basketry (*Pl. 21*). There are not only earthenware cooking-pots, water jars and cups, but also ladles, parching pans, ceremonial vessels, figurines, funerary urns, and tobacco pipes. In the northern Chaco a woman stores the family ornaments in a treasure jar, and in Guiana there were burial urns over five feet in height. In regard to shape, some pots are pointed, others round-bottomed; some are spherical, others have a collar or shoulder or flaring mouth. The decoration of pottery belongs under the head of art. It may consist in incised marks, in painted design or sculptural effects.

Wood-carving. Some form of shaping wood into pails, weapons, drums or dolls is common; but as a well-defined craft wood-carving is more limited. Excellent potters, for example the Pueblo Indians, are indifferent carvers. And in the Plains, where skin-dressing flourishes, there is very little woodwork. Abundance of good timber and suitable tools accompany the high development of the art. In the northeastern Congo the Mangbettu excel in woodwork partly because, unlike surrounding tribes, they have not two-edged but one-edged iron knives (*Pl. 23, fig. 5*) and are able to control finer movements of the blade by holding the blunt edge with the forefinger. This process is preceded by rough-hewing with an adze (*Pl. 23, fig. 1*). In ancient Egypt, it has been suggested, ground axes were common in the Badarian period (p. 9) because at that time the climate was more humid and supported timber which carpentry could

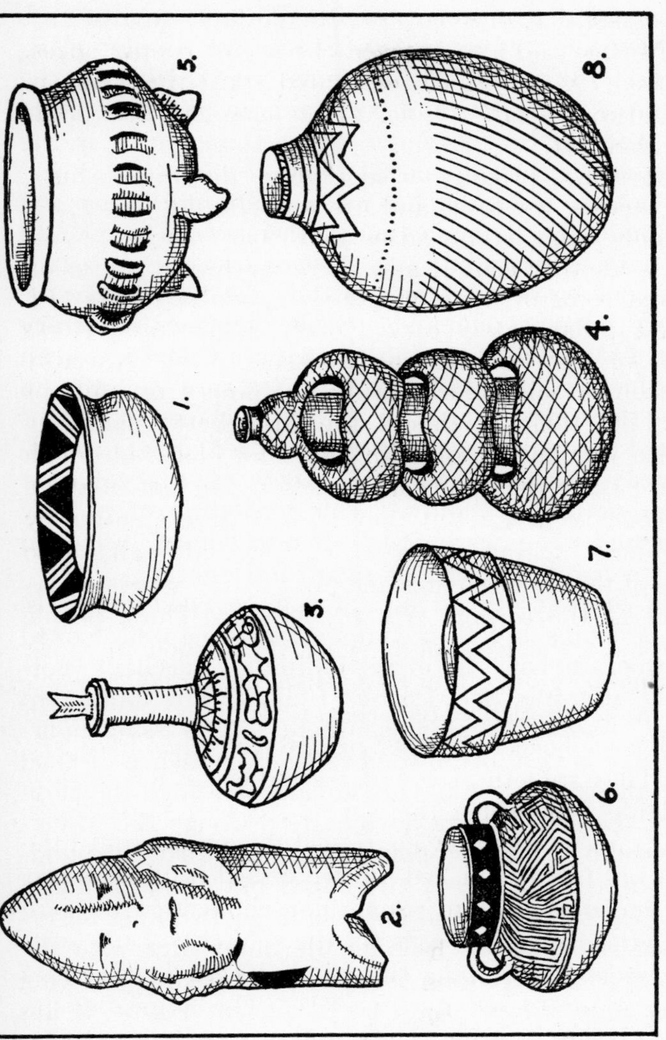

Plate 21: SAMPLES OF POTTERY.

1. Cherokee [Harrington (12) p. 191] 2. Chaco [Nordenskiöld (29) p. 200] 3. Guiana [Roth (33) *Plate 86B*] 4. Mangbettu Water Bottle [Schweinfurth (37) *Plate XVI, No. 4*] 5. Chaco [Nordenskiöld (29) p. 45] 6. Guiana [Roth (33) *Plate 87a*] 7. New Guiana [Finsch (7) *Plate IV, No. 6*] 8. Dinka, Upper Nile [Schweinfurth (37) *Plate I, No. 6*]

exploit; when the wood disappeared, the tools and the art, too, vanished. The Aztec carvers were favored by the dense forests that once covered the environs of the Valley of Mexico and also enjoyed the use of copper adzes. Tomtoms (*Pl. 22, fig.* 5), decorated spear-throwers (p. 214), and masks (*Pl. 22, fig. 4*) are characteristic products of their art.

Melanesians produce remarkably decorated huts, canoes, masks, weapons, and utensils (*Pl. 22, figs. 1, 6*), their tools being stone adzes and boars' tusks. West Africa is another center, and there we find a profusion of figures, some of them grotesquely shaped, masks (*Pl. 22, fig. 2*), elaborately carved doors, chests, and stools (*Pl. 22, fig. 3*). African woodworkers almost invariably carve from a solid block, using no joinery or nails or glue. Like their neighbors the Mangbettu carve an elaborate woman's stool from one solid block, although there are three distinguishable sections: a foot, a stem, and a concave disk. But they also produce a settee by true joinery, fitting strips of raphia leaf stalks into grooves of the frame shanks and pegging the several parts together at the corners (*Pl. 15, fig. 8*). These people further have the trick of burying their wood in moist earth, thereby giving it an ebony-like blackening.

But it is probably the coastal Indians of British Columbia who excel all other primitives in manipulating wood. They split the wood of the red cedar and work it into planks, smoothing them with stone or bone adzes. For extra fine effects they continued this process until the surface was highly finished, then polished it off with grit stones and dogfish skin. Some household utensils were made by heating the boards till they could be bent, sewing the sides and calking the joints. Thus boxes could be made into stone-boiling vessels. The large dugouts hollowed from a cedar trunk and worked to an even thickness, then steamed and spread, were among the most noteworthy results of the industry.

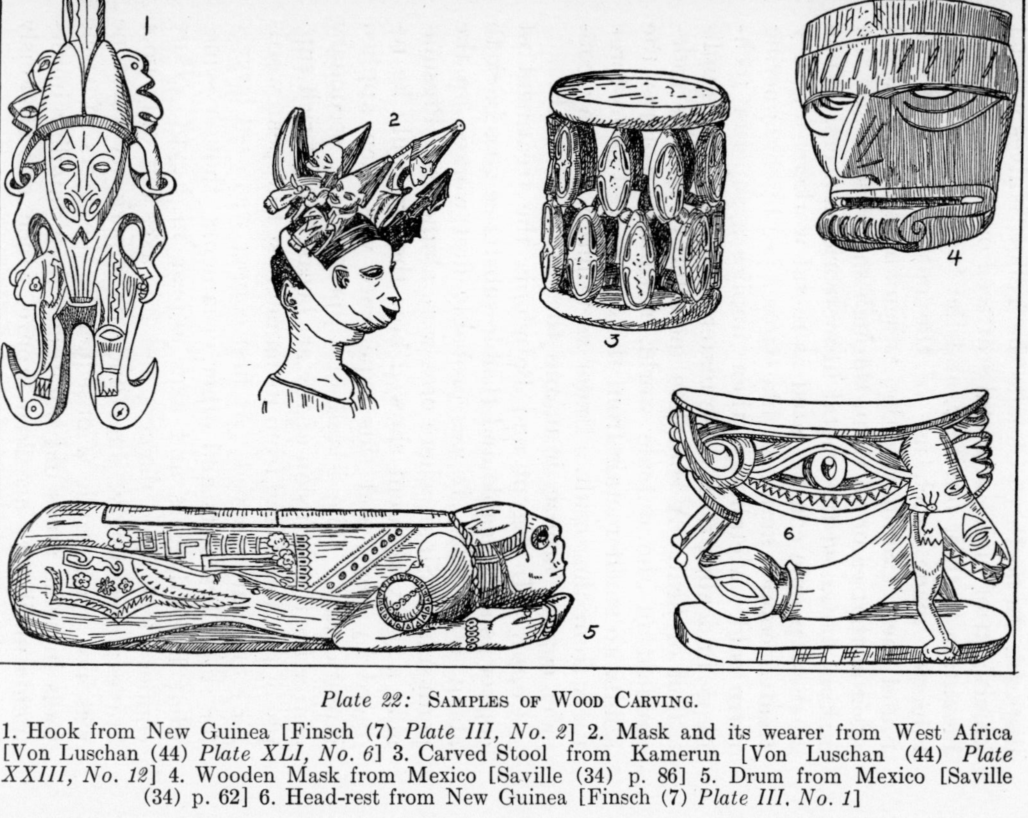

Plate 22: Samples of Wood Carving.

1. Hook from New Guinea [Finsch (7) *Plate III, No. 2*] 2. Mask and its wearer from West Africa [Von Luschan (44) *Plate XLI, No. 6*] 3. Carved Stool from Kamerun [Von Luschan (44) *Plate XXIII, No. 12*] 4. Wooden Mask from Mexico [Saville (34) p. 86] 5. Drum from Mexico [Saville (34) p. 62] 6. Head-rest from New Guinea [Finsch (7) *Plate III, No. 1*]

Metallurgy. Metallurgy does not mean merely the use of metals which some fortunate chance places at one's disposal. In northern Canada the Yellow Knives worked knives out of pieces of metal scattered on the slopes of a mountain in their territory, and the Indians about Lake Superior made much use of the native copper to be found there. Similarly, the Andaman Islanders picked up iron that came to them through shipwrecks, and the Eskimo obtained this metal in meteoric showers. None of these people can be rated as metal workers, for they treated copper and iron like stone, i.e. by hammering them cold. Metallurgy, then, implies a superior technique in dealing with these materials, notably the application of heat. A complete metallurgy, i.e. one independent of the outside world, naturally requires the ability to smelt metals from the ore as well as to forge tools from the result. Under metallurgy we may consider copper, bronze, iron, and the precious metals.

Copper. In Egypt and Babylonia the treatment of copper as a malleable and fusible substance goes back to about 4,000 B.C. It was probably first worked on the peninsula of Sinai, where ores were abundant. Presumably a lucky accident showed how the ore could be reduced by heat, and this experience was then applied intentionally. The island of Cyprus was a secondary center for the diffusion of the art because of its rich supply of the metal, and from its name most European words for copper are derived. At first copper was used largely for rings, bracelets and other ornaments, though somewhat later daggers and axes appear in Egypt. Pure copper yields good daggers and fair axes but only poor knives; accordingly, sometimes its superiority to stone was not recognized. Consequently the users of stone tools in some areas did not reject their familiar implements until they acquired bronze, which was obviously better than stone.

Copper is taken from the furnace in the act of solidifying, broken up, and then remelted in crucibles, the contents being poured into molds. In order to increase its hardness, the edge of a casting may be hammered.

Bronze. Bronze is an alloy of copper and tin. At first men doubtless happened to use copper ore containing certain impurities; they noted that chance impurities gave better results and then tried to produce them at will. When this was achieved, the Bronze Age began. However, there is an important geographical factor to be considered. Tin is relatively rare, hence the invention must have occurred where a copper-using people lived near supplies of this metal (see p. 109). This condition holds for the Babylonians in the Old World and the highland Peruvians in the New; the former were more advantageously situated than the Egyptians, the latter than their brethren of the coast. In Babylonia the Bronze Age probably began about 3,000 B.C., in Peru about 1000 or 500 A.D. Both countries became centers for the spread of bronze casting; but since it was so much more recent in America and means of transportation were inferior, it never extended very far there. The Peruvians had bronze knives, chisels and club heads; but among the Aztec such articles were inferior and rarer. In Yucatan, where virtually no ores existed, the Maya Indians of 1492 were still in the Stone Age. Indeed, even the Aztec still used stone so largely that they were rather in a state of transition to a Metal Age than full-fledged representatives of such a stage.

The ratio of 90% copper and 10% tin is regarded as ideal, but this was by no means uniform even in the highest Old World civilizations. In early Egyptian times the percentage of tin did not rise above 2. Also, there often are other materials in the bronze which characterize certain areas: Chinese and Siberian bronzes, for instance, are rich in zinc. In late Peruvian times the coastal bronzes contained from 3% to 6% tin. A somewhat greater proportion of tin, say 10% instead of 5%, does not necessarily imply greater hardness, for the Peruvians made up for the difference by hammering.

In the Renaissance a widely used bronze process was the "lost wax" technique. It was practiced also in Peru and on the west coast of Africa, where the Negroes may or may not have been stimulated by European influence. This ingenious method consists in making a clay figure, covering it with wax, and this with a clay coat, air holes being left to pour in the metal later. The figure is heated and the wax melted out, then the molten bronze prepared meanwhile is poured in and the mold is destroyed when the alloy has cooled.

Iron. Iron is still harder than bronze and far more widely found than tin. These qualities make it the most desirable material for tools and weapons. However, its earliest use was for ornament.

Some very early iron beads occur in Egyptian graves, but the metal has turned out to be meteoric in origin so that its occurrence is no more significant than the use of meteoric iron by the Eskimo. Deliberate smelting of iron probably began some time between 2,000 B.C. and 1,500 B.C., south of the Black Sea, in a region with rich ore deposits and a civilization high enough to profit by them. Actual proof of iron tools is several centuries later—about 1,300 B.C. we hear of a shipment to Egypt. Egyptians, indeed, were slow to use the new material, and apparently the Assyrians were the first to arm troops wholesale with iron weapons. Again, there was diffusion, but at a fairly slow rate. At the time of Homer, that is, about 900 B.C., the Greeks were still partly using bronze implements, and the Chinese did not pass into their Iron Age much before 500 B.C. Outlying parts of Europe, such as Scandinavia, lagged behind; and the simplest Asiatic and African peoples, as well as the Oceanians, Australians and American Indians, never either borrowed or invented the technique of iron-smelting. A curiously intermediate position was taken by various Indonesian peoples. They learned to work iron tools and even perfected a distinct form of bellows; but they imported the

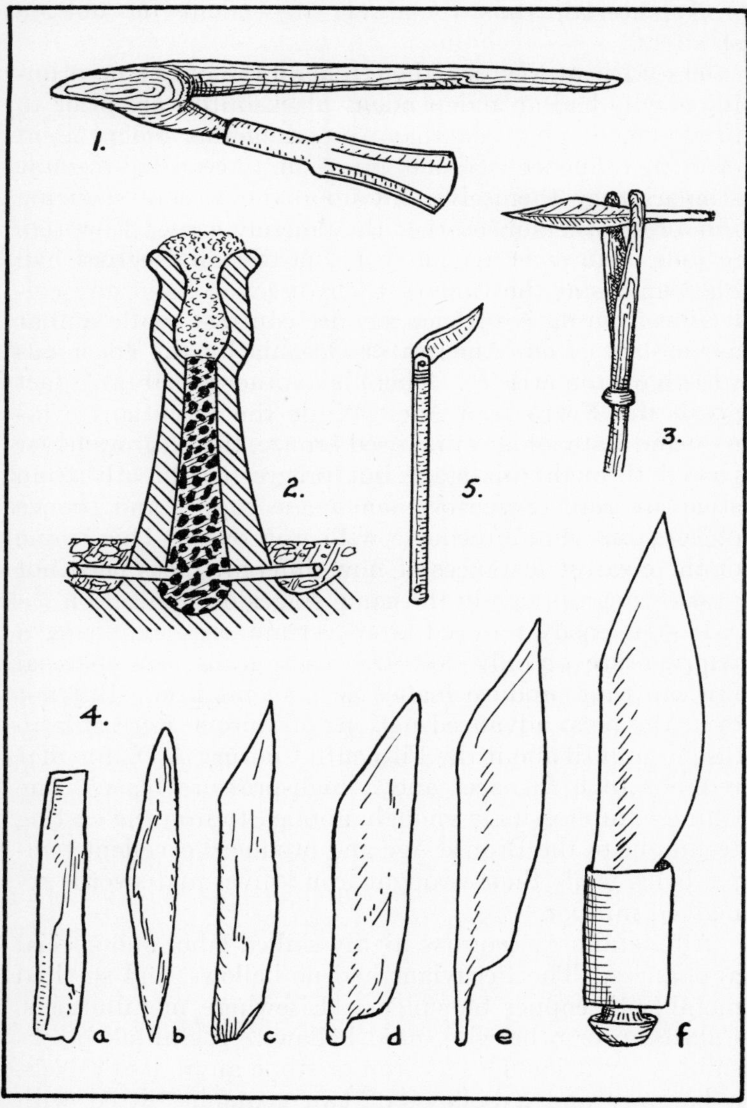

Plate 23: Blacksmithing.

1. Adze from the Mangbettu [Schweinfurth (37) *Plate XVIII, No. 11*] 2. Cross-section of Smelting Furnace, Jur, Upper Nile [Schweinfurth (37) *Plate II, No. 20*] 3. Blacksmith's Tongs, Bongo, Upper Nile [Schweinfurth (37) *Plate V, No. 8*] 4. Steps in hammering a knife blade from a metal strip, Lobi [Labouret (21) *Plate IV*] 5. Single-edged Knife for Wood-carving, Mangbettu [Schweinfurth (37) *Plate XVIII, No. 13*]

iron material, thus remaining dependent on outside smelters.

The African Negroes, then, remain the only true primitives who had an independent blacksmith's art prior to recent times. How far they were altogether independent of white influence is a moot question. According to some scholars they themselves hit upon the idea of reducing iron ores; others insist that they merely copied Egyptian models. However this may be, nearly all Negroes had blacksmiths at the time of their discovery, and any collection from native Africa at once contrasts with similar assemblages from America or Oceania by the enormous wealth of iron articles. There is another remarkable fact about the Negro Iron Age. While the Egyptians, Chinese and Babylonians first used bronze, the Negroes never passed through this stage but progressed directly from stone to iron. Some of them made copper and bronze objects, but simultaneously with iron ones. This is one of the clearest instances of how different races need not pass through precisely the same stages of civilization.

Iron is easily reduced from certain ores, requiring a temperature of only 700-800° Centigrade. A charcoal fire can thus produce malleable *wrought* iron. But not even the most advanced nations of Europe were able to fuse iron until about the Fifteenth Century A.D., for that requires high furnaces and a high-pressure blast. The Chinese, interestingly enough, applied to iron the casting technique of the Bronze Age and produced excellent temple bells, while their wrought iron knives and swords remained inferior.

All metallurgy requires highly skilled labor and special appliances. The Peruvians had no bellows, and smelted metal with copper blowpipes. Elsewhere metallurgists, Caucasian or otherwise, used bellows. A Shilluk blacksmith's outfit includes an iron or stone anvil, two chisels, a hammer and a bellows of two goatskins fitted with handles at the top (*Pl. 24, fig. 5*). The far end merges into a wooden tube with an iron continuation, and that into a clay pipe in contact with the fire. An apprentice raises a goatskin to admit air and alternately presses down the two skins, driving the air into the tubes. Another common African form occurs among other tribes of the upper Nile area (*Pl. 24, fig. 1*). Here the forger gets his blast by alternately pressing down the hides stretched over two earthen vessels placed side by side and opening into a tube that leads to the fire. When smelting he allows four of these bellows to connect by as many tubes with the clay furnace, which rises to a height of 5 feet. The rest of his equipment is simple: he wields an unhafted rock for a hammer over an anvil of the same material (or a slab of iron) and handles the red-hot metal with a split stick for tongs (*Pl. 23, fig. 3*). The successive steps by which a West African smith forges a knife are shown in *Plate 23, fig. 4*.

The Tanala of Madagascar, the western outpost of the Malay stock, use the typical bellows of their brethren in Java and Sumatra. It consists of two wooden cylinders 3 to 5 feet high with a 6-inch bore (*Pl. 24, fig. 2*). Each has a piston worked by a long handle and a wooden head with a cloth ring loosely tied to its lower side (*Pl. 24, fig. 3*). On the up-stroke the ring falls away from the head so that the air enters; on the down-stroke the friction of the cylinder wall forces the ring up against the head and compresses the air below. Two bamboo pipes, each inserted near the bottom of one cylinder, converge toward a clay tube and conduct the blast into the fire as the operator alternately pushes his pistons up and down (*Pl. 24, fig. 4*).

Precious Metals. Gold was among the very earliest metals to be worked, and while it could not assume the place of copper or iron in practical life, its use stimulated the metallurgical arts. In Mexico it was found in nuggets on the surface, but mainly in the sands of river beds. It was kept in dust form in cane tubes, or melted in pots with hollow reed blowpipes and cast in bars. The goldsmiths, who ranked as an honored profession, beat the

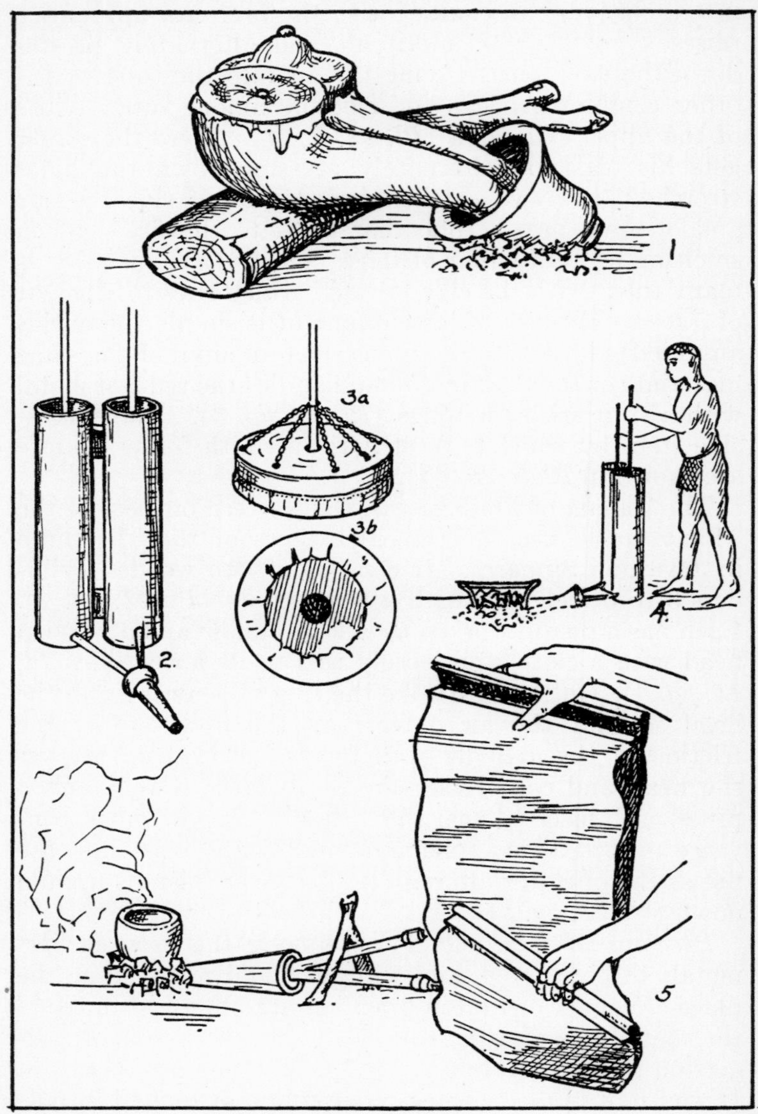

Plate 24: Types of Bellows.

1. Clay Bellows of the Bongo, Upper Nile [Schweinfurth (37) *Plate V, No. 6*] 2. Piston Bellows of the Tanala, Madagascar [Linton (24) p. 81] 3a and 3b. Details of same, showing inside of cylinder [Linton (24) p. 81] 4. Use of same [Linton (24) p. 81] 5. Hand Bellows of the Shilluk [Hofmayr (13) Fig. 22b]

metal with stones and embossed it with a pointed tool. The Peruvians made bowls, saucers, drinking-cups and ear-ornaments of both gold and silver, and fashioned hollow silver figures of llamas and alpacas. In Colombia the Indians had no bronze but made an extraordinary alloy of copper, gold and silver called tumbaga. An awl of this material proved to contain 55%, 33% and 12%, respectively, of these metals, and tests prove the chisels, hoes, and awls of tumbaga to be quite on a par with bronze in point of hardness. Here we have again a proof of an ingenious specialized invention by American Indians.

Metal Work as a Criterion of Culture. If a tribe practices metallurgy it is clearly not on the plane of savagery: only stock-breeders and farmers forge metals. But cultures can no more be graded by this than by any other single trait. In the Near Orient the Bronze Age is linked with the plough, political organization, the wheel, and writing; and a combination of all these certainly represents civilization. But, as noted, bronze at first spread without these accompanying features, and by itself it does not suffice to lift its possessors to a higher level. The same applies to iron; whether the Negroes learned its use from Egypt, or invented the blacksmith's art themselves, they lacked stone masonry, writing, the plough, and the wheel. It would be absurd to rate them higher than the Bronze Age Egyptians. Similarly, the Maya, though still in the Stone Age in 1492, can not for that reason alone be placed below the Shilluk, the Aztec, or the Tanala. Any one trait is only a rough marker as to cultural grade; we must compare cultures by at least half a dozen such significant characteristics.

IX

TRADE AND TRANSPORTATION

Trade

Motives for Trade; Antiquity. As shown (p. 108), natural and cultural reasons make trading necessary. Raw materials, such as Australian diorite, are limited to a few localities. The lucky residents, being monopolists, insist on getting skin bags in return for allowing strangers to exploit the quarries. A ceremonial article, say, red ocher, is often regarded as a necessity, and Australians will go 300 miles to get it. The same holds for specialized manufactures. One West African village devotes itself to weaving, another to ironwork; and in Guiana one Indian group spins the cotton which a neighboring tribe weaves into hammocks. Throughout the Orinoco country manioc is grated, but two tribes supply the rest with the instrument used, every hut being a factory with piles of graters hanging from the roof ready for export.

This is not a recent development. Even paleolithic Belgian cave-dwellers used flint peculiar to districts of France, whose residents surely exacted some compensation. Much later tinless Sweden imported bronze and was thus enabled to pass into a Metal Age. Babylonians got gold from Egypt, iron from the Hittites, cedars from Lebanon, spices and camels from Arabia; while Egypt imported Syrian timber. In the United States native copper from Lake Superior was carried far and wide; and obsidian, nowhere found naturally east of Yellowstone Park, turns up in Ohio mounds. Travel in search of metal resources or artifacts is thus very ancient and must often have been tied up with trade.

Forms of Trade. Trade may be carried on by barter or by purchase and sale, which implies a standard medium of exchange. It may occur within or without the community, between single individuals or groups, privately or at regular markets. Also, compensation may be rendered immediately or may be delayed if credit is granted.

Silent trade is reported for the Mountain Vedda of Ceylon in their relations with Sinhalese blacksmiths. They put game before the smith's hut at night and without any exchange of words expect to find arrowpoints placed there in return. This custom obviously implies some previous communication, otherwise neither party would know what to expect.

A deep-seated social principle among many peoples is that of reciprocity. Except from his kin a person expects no out-and-out gift or free service. A Plains Indian woman who accepted a neighbor's offer to tan skins was morally obliged to grant a subsequent request of her helper's or appear ungracious. In Lesu, New Ireland, a man is loath to accept a present if he sees no prospect of requital.

On the other hand, there is also compulsory acceptance of "gifts" with the understanding that they must be repaid within a reasonable time. On the coast of British Columbia this form of trading is bound up with ideas of prestige, credit, and even something like life insurance. At a "potlatch" festival a prominent man tries to add to his social standing by publicly giving away property to his guests. They must accept and return the property with 100 per cent. interest or admit their inferiority to the donor. In this manner enormous quantities of goods change hands. Since a man acts not merely on his own behalf but as a representative of his family or major group, the return gift need not be made to him personally, and he is thus laying up a nest egg for his heirs.

The craving for prestige colors primitive commerce in manifold ways. In Lesu, for instance, there is never any bargaining and never an urge for profit. In order to display his wealth, a rich man willingly pays more for a pig than does a poor neighbor. Similarly, a seller disposes of his objects for less than he gave for them, never for more. Such transactions, like the potlatches, are witnessed by impartial outsiders, whose presence makes them matters of public record.

Melanesian intertribal trading is often organized on a major scale, involving voyages consuming several months. The pottery made in a few villages in New Guinea is thus widely disseminated. But in addition to commercial traveling some Melanesians exchange such ceremonial articles as rings and necklaces, which must circulate in a definite direction among the trading groups. The articles do not remain in the possession of one person for more than a year, so that no permanent advantage accrues. The whole procedure again revolves about the prestige gained by properly taking part in the exchange. No motive is more conspicuous among primitives than this emphasis on social standing.

Markets develop out of more or less periodic gatherings for the exchange or sale of goods. They occur even among fairly simple societies. The Wishram Indians, fishermen living several miles above the present town of Dalles on the Columbia River, were privileged middlemen who amassed products from as far as California and the Plains. In their markets an Indian could buy shells from the coast, horses from the Plains, fish, canoes, furs, slaves, Hudson's Bay blankets. In Melanesia, off the coast of Malaita, Solomon Islands, live the Auki islanders, manufacturers of shell money, which they trade for food at markets regularly held in Malaita.

In several areas of Africa literally thousands of buyers and sellers congregate on fixed days. In the southwestern Congo the Bakuba hold markets every three days, this regular recurrence creating a sort of week. Among the Lobi of the Upper Volta District a priest founds a market and puts it under the protection of deities. It becomes a sanctuary for criminals, and while it lasts peace has to be preserved, on pain of heavy penalties. Women are especially prone to attend, and most comers bring stones to sit on under the shade of trees. A Lobi market may hold as many as 100 female hucksters and up to 700 buyers. The wares sold include beans, millet, peppers, cattle, goats, salt, copper and hatchets. The founder of a market makes a levy on the sellers, using the proceeds either for religious rituals or for his personal profit. In Uganda the chiefs strictly supervised markets, fixed the price of commodities and exacted a ten per cent. sales tax.

Money. Money is a standard of value that serves as a medium of exchange. It assumes many forms, the general course of evolution being from useful, and therefore intrinsically valuable objects, to symbols of value such as our paper currency.

Even before they have a definite standard, traders roughly gauge the value of goods in terms of other goods. The Southern Siouans, for instance, considered a beaverskin more or less equivalent to two otters, or to from ten to twelve raccoons. When people set the same store by one particular commodity, it may become the general norm and thus evolve into money. This holds for domestic beasts, shells, mats, or other commodities such as African hoes or spades (*Pl. 6, fig. 4*). Stock-breeders naturally think of values in terms of their live-stock. Our word "fee" originally meant "cattle", like the German *Vieh,* which is pronounced the same and has retained the old meaning. It suggests how compensation was conceived or measured by earlier speakers of English. Similarly, our "pecuniary" comes from the Latin *pecunia,* money, which in turn is derived from *pecus,* stock. The Kirghiz pay a fine and the bride-price with so many head of live-stock, as do South African Negroes. Plains Indians, who in earlier times compensated with arrows or other commodities, no sooner acquired horses than they used them as a convenient standard.

Shells, originally used for decoration, readily pass into

money. The Northwestern Californians prized dentalium shells of 5 distinct sizes, ranging from about 1⅞ to 2½ inches, and, so far as possible, strung together those of one size. Strings were folded back and forth and enclosed in a purse of elk antler covered by a lid. Each size of shell and the corresponding string bore a distinctive name. In the early days 11 of the largest shells made a string roughly estimated at $50, while the string of smallest shells was worth only $2.50. This currency involved some clumsy reckoning. The size of the shells being too irregular for exact estimates of value by strings, the dentalia were gauged individually. The shells on a string were matched against each other and then laid against the fingers from crease to crease of the joints, the largest from the farther crease of the little finger to the fold in the palm below. Naturally these distances varied with every person. Measurement by fives more nearly approached a standard, for then the distance was that between the end of the thumb-nail to a series of lines tattooed across the forearm, these marks being made from standard quintettes and thus independent of the individual Indian's measurements. In central California the Pomo were the chief manufacturers of money. They used, however, another kind of shell, which was broken up, ground round on sandstone, perforated, strung, and then rolled on a slab. The value differed according to diameter, thickness and polish. The major unit was a string of 400 beads, originally set at $2.50 by the Indians. Instead of measuring lengths of string, however, the Pomo counted the beads, thus developing a much better sense of high numbers than their neighbors.

Melanesians also had shell money and usually strung it in fathoms, i.e. lengths corresponding to the distance between the fingertips of a man's outstretched arms. But in Santa Cruz purely symbolic money occurred—coils of parrot feathers which had been gummed on pigeon feathers; for, while the shells retain a decorative function besides their service as money, the feathers in question are never anything but currency.

The cowrie shell has for some time been the favorite minor unit of exchange over a large part of Africa, but its home is in the Maldive Islands, southwest of India.

The uneconomic ideas primitive people attach to business transactions naturally affect their notions of money too. The potlatch-making Indians of the coast of British Columbia have as a lesser unit a blanket replacing the older elk skins. But copper plaques of definite shape loomed as bills of higher denomination, worth thousands of blankets apiece. A chief offered a copper to some rival, who had to buy it or lose standing. Its value automatically grew in proportion to the property distributed at the festival in which it changed hands; and the oftener this happened, the more highly was it prized. To add luster to his name, a chief sometimes deliberately destroyed a copper of the utmost value, thus proving how great a man he was. Here again the element of prestige was all-important.

Equally odd is a phenomenon in Yap, a Micronesian island. The natives have shell money but set greater store by limestone wheels from 25 to 75 inches in diameter, the larger ones being made to rest outdoors against house walls or coconut palms. Though used in buying and selling, these curious "banknotes" are mainly for show and social aggrandizement. The islanders are very particular about them and do not like to see foreigners so much as touch them. Strangest of all, limestone does not occur in Yap, so the natives are obliged to make a dangerous trip of 240 miles to another island and go to the trouble of loading and unloading the material. All this, however, is cheerfully borne, showing that primitive man is not afraid of work when he is interested.

Coins appear relatively late in history and at an advanced stage. The Babylonians had lumps of silver of a given weight and used so many of these "shekels" in buying, say, an ox. But about 700 B.C. the kings of

Lydia, in western Asia, stamped lumps of fixed weight with the royal symbol and thus created the earliest coins.

Paper money was invented by the Chinese about the Ninth Century of our era. Under the Mongol dynasty Friar Rubruck noted its use in China, and a little later the famous Venetian traveler, Marco Polo (1254-1324), marveled at its effective circulation in the empire. Sheets of paper were made out of the bark of the mulberry in different sizes and of different value, and forgery was severely punished.

Some Correlates of Trade. Trade fosters peaceful relations, at least for the time of the transaction. Brawlers at an African market, we noted, were severely dealt with. Still more important is the spread of ideas made possible by such commercial intercourse. To be sure, particular handicrafts may not be imitated because people rely on the outside source; but other features, say, of dress or custom, are spontaneously noted and may be copied. So culture comes to diffuse even without wholesale wanderings of peoples.

A business relationship, however, depends on certain social factors. It implies a certain equality of position and power on the part of the negotiators. The Samoan architects are able to defy a chief employing them because they are so well organized as to dominate the situation. Where men are ruled by autocrats, the monarch simply imposes his will, appropriates whatever property he covets, and forces subjects to work for him. In parts of Polynesia, where a chief could make a canoe his own by putting his sacred foot on it, the property rights of the subjects would be too insecure to promote trade among them.

Another noteworthy point is the kinds of commodities transferred by trade. Localized natural resources and artifacts by specialized craftsmen have been mentioned. Luxuries and objects of religious or prestige value also loom very large. Thus, bundles of sacred articles were sold at enormous prices among Plains Indians, both within and outside a particular tribe. They are what our law calls "incorporeal property", for the buyer obtains not merely the tangible objects but the privilege of using them, a sort of patent (see p. 281). Such prerogatives are greatly prized in many parts of the world: the right to perform a certain dance is bought in New Ireland; in the Banks Islands, another Melanesian group, the right to sing a song is paid for with a fathom of shells; and Pueblo Indians likewise pay for instruction in prayers.

On the other hand, many practical things are not purchasable. Thus, with the rarest exceptions, primitive peoples consider land inalienable. Again, food is often liberally shared gratis but is not sold. The Melanesians of Lesu typically never sell taro, bananas, or coconuts in normal circumstances, but generously give them away to strangers. Similarly, a successful Ona hunter at once sends his wife to neighboring households with complimentary portions of guanaco; and a stranded whale is not claimed by the owners of the territory but distributed among members of all the thirty-nine hordes. Extreme specialization forces some Melanesian potters and makers of shell money to import all their food, but such instances are rare. Even when foodstuffs are regularly on sale at African markets, as among the Lobi, no one expects to cover his wants by his purchases; the native invariably farms his own plot and depends mainly on his harvest.

Transportation

Carrying Devices. A trader of material goods needs carrying devices. Savages of the Old Stone Age lacked domestic beasts, and many recent peoples were no better off. Polynesians could not ride pigs, chickens, and dogs, or load them with baggage. But they and others have contrivances to help them transport themselves and their goods. The part of footgear (p. 71) and sledges (p. 39) (*Pl. 25, fig. 5*) in travel has already been indicated. We now turn to methods of carrying loads on the person.

A Maricopa woman as a rule took a burden on her head, using no prop except a willow-bark head ring for pots. Sometimes she wrapped the burden in a blanket, tied the corners together and rested it on her forehead; or she tied the blanket around her waist so the pack was supported by the small of her back.

In Polynesia the men carry burdens from either end of a pole balanced on one shoulder, a custom that gives many Samoans lumps there. Even with a single light basket a man would rather sling it over his back on a pole than take it in his hand. Unlike their congeners, the Maori, however, always packed on the back with the aid of shoulder straps. The carrying-pole is typical of China, and crops up also in Mexico and Panama. But the common South American way is to convey heavy weights on the back, whether on the Ona and Andean principle of holding them by a strap that passes over the chest, or by the use of a tump-line over the forehead, a method also popular in North America.

Children are carried about in various ways. In a Shilluk village an infant straddles his mother's hip; on longer trips he is wrapped in skins and hung from her neck in front of her breasts. An Ona child is borne astride his mother's back, covered by her cloak and held firmly by a leather strap passing over her head. A baby is wrapped in a skin and tied to an upright ladder frame leaned against a tree or hut. There he is kept away from the wet soil and dogs, while his mother attends to her daily chores; at night she takes him down to sleep by her side. In Guiana and Bolivia there are cotton baby slings made after the pattern of the native hammocks (*Pl. 11, fig. 1*); they are worn slung over the right shoulder and passed under the opposite armpit, the corresponding arm steadying the child within. North American Indians commonly use cradles, which vary considerably in material, shape, and even use. Most mothers bear the cradle on their backs, but Pueblo and Havasupai women more commonly carry it in their arms. The

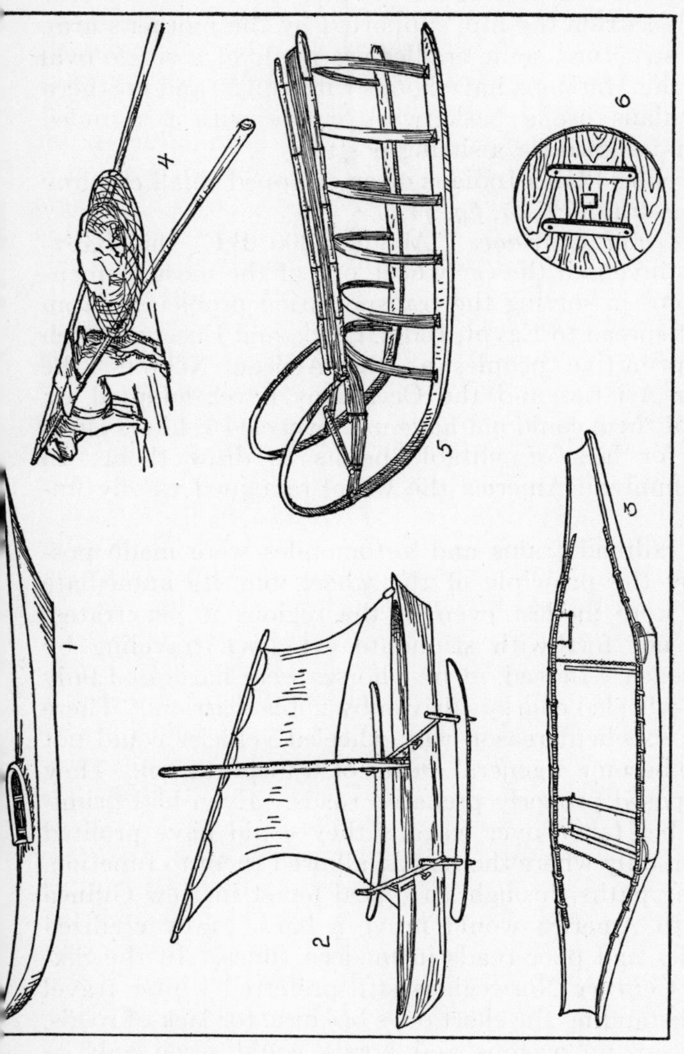

Plate 25: METHODS OF TRAVEL.

1. Eskimo Kayak [Mathiassen (28) p. 92] 2. Outrigger Canoe from East Africa [Von Luschan (44) *Plate XXVII, No. 2*] 3. Bark Boat from Guiana [Roth (33) p. 616] 4. Dog Travois of the Assiniboine [Lowie (26) *Plate 2*] 5. Yukaghir Dog Sledge [Jochelson (17) p. 353] 6. Wooden Wheel from Formosa [Horwitz (14) p. 737]

Maricopa often balanced the cradle on the head or held it under the arm resting on the hip. A baby over a year old rode astride the hip, supported by the mother's arm. As for structure, some cradles are made of a single oval board, the Maricopa have hoops with rungs, and northern Californians use a basketwork cradle with a rounded bottom designed for a sitting posture.

Traveling Plains Indians often strapped small children to a dog-dray (*Pl. 25, fig. 4*).

Carts and Carriages. About 3,300 B.C. the Babylonians invented the cartwheel, one of the most momentous steps in solving the transportation problem. From them it spread to Egypt, India, China and Europe. Such truly primitive peoples as the African Negroes, the simpler Asiatics and the Oceanians never adopted it; many of them could not have used wheeled vehicles effectively for lack of suitable beasts to draw them. In pre-Columbian America the wheel remained wholly unknown.

Our railroad trains and automobiles were made possible by the principle of the wheel, but its immediate effects were modest even in the regions it penetrated. It did not forthwith stimulate extensive traveling by stage-coach. Indeed, at first horses were harnessed only to two-wheeled chariots driven by noble warriors. There was an excellent reason why wheeled vehicles could not at once become a general means of transportation. They presupposed properly prepared roads. Even had primitive tribes taken over wagons they could have profited by them only where the terrain allowed them to function. Winding paths through a tropical forest in New Guinea or South America would prove a bar. Many civilized countries had poor roads in modern times. In the Sixteenth Century Norwegians still preferred winter travel notwithstanding the short days because, for lack of roads, there were no wagons and horses could serve only as mounts. In Denmark one main road was passable only in good summer weather, for the people tried to make tolerable bridle paths without further improvements serve as wagon roads. Eighteenth Century novels frequently refer to the trials of traveling by coach in England.

The oldest Babylonian type of wheel was disk-shaped and predominated until 2,300 B.C. But such spokeless forms survive in a number of regions—in Formosa (*Pl. 25, fig. 6*), in the Caucasus, and even among the Spanish Basques. Thus we have another evidence of human conservatism.

In general, very little basic progress was made in locomotion for several thousand years. The Romans organized splendid highways, but invented no new principle. Even they were unable to regulate urban traffic satisfactorily, for streets were too narrow to permit wheeled transportation in the daytime. Wagons with iron springs seem to have remained unnoted in Europe until 1615. A marked advance came only after Watt's steam engine, patented in 1769. It led to a steam locomotive in 1804, followed by Stephenson's improved form, which pulled a train at four miles an hour in 1814. Fast travel is thus an extremely recent achievement.

Bridges. In many regions the obstacle of streams is overcome by some sort of bridge. Narrow watercourses are easily spanned by logs. In Guiana the Indians sometimes chopped down a tree of appropriate size so it would fall across the stream. They even propped up such a log and added a handrail. At the time of Cortés the Aztec capital was half water, and the Conquerors noted many solid bridges of long, broad beams, some big and strong enough to carry ten horsemen abreast. In Peru chasms were spanned by suspension bridges, which occur also in New Guinea and Africa. The cane suspension bridges of the Ekoi of Southern Nigeria are strong enough to bear a dozen porters, are over fifty yards in length, and so closely constructed that a dog can safely cross them. In the Congo forests the Pygmies are especially apt at bridge construction, interlacing vines from the giant trees and connecting these cables with sticks to walk on.

Water Travel. The Hopi in arid Arizona have no need for boats, and the Bolivians south of Santa Cruz lack them because their rivers are not navigable. In other cases the absence of any sort of craft is not so easily understood. The Ona, like some of their neighbors, could use boats to advantage, but at most they wade clumsily through shallow streams, displaying a horror of anything more ambitious. That, however, is an extreme case; more commonly men have some contrivance for crossing water too deep for fording. There are rafts, skin and bark boats, and dugouts; they are punted, paddled, or rowed; and may or may not bear sails.

Cigar-shaped tied bundles of rushes are known as "balsas". Even the Tasmanians had them, as did the Peruvians of Lake Titicaca and tribes in southern Arizona, California and Nevada. A balsa, like a raft, floats by specific gravity but is not watertight. However, it served Indians to cross San Francisco Bay, and with no better craft the Tasmanians ventured out considerable distances from shore. The balsa was generally punted but sometimes propelled with paddles. The type of raft familiar to us also occurs in simple societies: the Maricopa, for instance, merely used two logs side by side, with sticks tied across, and either paddled them with their hands or pushed them with long poles.

Rafts are fine for rapid streams but can not take the place of canoes for long trips or against the current. Men of a South American tribe in Bolivia go downstream in rafts, which they discard at their goal, returning afoot. The defects of rafts suggest that certain tracts of the earth's surface could have been settled rapidly only by people in possession of true boats, since others would have found big rivers an obstacle to their advance. A people's wanderings are thus the result of environment and also of their equipment. As Arabia and the Sahara are habitable only for camel-breeders, so parts of South America are open only to canoe Indians.

For crossing the Missouri the Hidatsa and other tribes put a buffalo-skin cover over a frame of twigs resembling an open inverted umbrella, whence the name "bull-boat". A similar contrivance is, or was until lately, in vogue in Wales, Scotland and Ireland. More complex are the Eskimo skin boats, one type used in hunting, the other for travel. Their kayak (*Pl. 25, fig. 1*) has a light framework of wood or bone covered so completely with skin that there is only a central hole for the hunter, who sits there propelling his craft with a double-bladed paddle, keeping harpoons and lines in front on the deck, and tying his game aft. The traveling boat is a flat-bottomed affair, open on top but otherwise covered with seal or walrus hide. In contrast to the kayak and almost all other primitive craft, this boat is rowed, the oars being held in place by locks; there is also a big steering-paddle.

Bark canoes are so light as to be easily carried around cataracts. The Canadian form north of Lake Superior is typical. Its 16-foot cedar frame with 5 thwarts was covered with birchbark stitched with spruce root and gummed with pitch. Less well known is the Guiana "woodskin", made from a single piece of tough bark of the purpleheart tree. After cutting away a wedge-shaped piece from the outer layer, the maker folds the inner layer upon itself, so as to prevent water from coming in, and raises the bow and stern ends at an angle from the water. After several days' weathering, seats are forced in, or are hung from a rod sewn along inside the gunwale edge by some tribes (*Pl. 25, fig. 3*). The slightest motion is likely to upset a woodskin, which then sinks immediately because of its great specific gravity. The smaller specimens are 14 feet long, others measure as much as 30 feet. They frequently accommodate three passengers with their belongings.

Probably the most widespread of all primitive boats, however, is the dugout, hollowed out from a log with the aid of an adze and fire, as noted for the British Columbia Indians (p. 54). It dates back to the New Stone Age of Switzerland and was common in Africa, both Americas, and Oceania.

A dugout is practicable only if there is suitable timber. In the islands off southern California this was not to be had except in the mountains, and there were no streams large enough for floating logs. Hence the canoes there are built up of lashed planks. But the argument can not be reversed: people with a good supply of wood sometimes fail to make the most of their opportunities. North of Point Concepcion the California coast-dwellers were quite boatless, notwithstanding the excellent redwood forests at hand.

In Oceania some boats were dugouts, others plank canoes—the latter possibly having evolved on coral atolls, where big timber was lacking. Still others were dugouts enlarged by planks, or double canoes, separable or permanently united. Samoans used both main types; their small dugout is still considered indispensable for fishing inside the reef. Melanesians generally paddle simple dugouts on the rivers, but their seaworthy craft are furnished with a balancing pole parallel to the boat known as an "outrigger". Outrigger canoes are also characteristic of Polynesia and Indonesia, whence the type was carried to Madagascar and in exceptional cases to East Africa (*Pl. 25, fig. 2*). Another device common in Oceania was a sail, usually of palm matting.

The more pretentious Oceanian boats measured 100 feet and more in length. The double canoe of Fiji accommodated 100 passengers and several tons of cargo. Of all primitive races the Polynesians are supreme as mariners. Their homeland must have been in southern Asia, and in the course of time they have literally spread over thousands of miles in the Pacific, their outpost in Easter Island being much nearer to the coast of Chile than to the Asiatic starting-point. In the higher civilizations of the Old World the Egyptians about 2,700 B.C.

were the first to construct sea-going vessels, but their actual achievements as seafarers are completely dwarfed by those of Polynesians, nor did they surpass them in any basic principle of navigation. The same holds for the Greeks and Romans. The wanderings of Odysseus are like trips in a teapot compared with the 2,300 miles involved in a voyage from Hawaii to Tahiti. It was only after the introduction of the mariner's compass, adapted from a Chinese invention, that Europeans in the Fifteenth Century A.D. began to equal these records by the discovery of America and the circumnavigation of the globe. The application of steam and motor power belong to the most recent part of history.

X

AMUSEMENTS

Man is nowhere content with a humdrum existence. He craves entertainment and is willing to sacrifice practical things on behalf of his pastimes. Even religious ceremonials minister to this need; whatever other purpose they serve, they break the everyday routine and often afford beautiful or soul-stirring pageants. Indeed, definite portions of them are clearly designed for no other end. The same may be said for art, which can not be clearly divided from amusement. Folktales, for instance, are told to while away the time but also represent an important part of unwritten literature (see p. 198).

Because of the deep urge for recreation man has invented hundreds of pastimes in the narrower sense. Some of our own come from foreign lands. Dominoes, checkers, cards and kites go back to China; dice to India; polo to Persia. Amusements may thus travel over immense distances. On the other hand, they often show great tenacity: in the Caucasus Professor Von Luschan learned about a modern dice game played with a single astragalus die, partly of lead and with a wooden spine. This model was exactly duplicated by a Hittite find dating back to the Ninth Century B.C.

We can distinguish children's games, sports, other games of skill, games of chance, social games, dances, and buffoonery.

Children's Games. Everywhere children mimic their elders and thus get painlessly educated for adult tasks. Ona girls put up miniature screens or huts in imitation of their mothers, while the boys hurl slingshots and organize archery contests. Similarly, Plains Indian girls pitched and broke camp, cooked food, transported their tents on the march, while their brothers hunted rabbits, shot at targets, and imitated the men's military clubs. In Ceylon, Vedda men encourage the boys to play at honey-getting as a sort of vocational training; South African lads are experts at making traps; and Maori boys construct models of fortified villages.

Apart from these educational pastimes there are toys. Ona infants play with rattles of mollusk shells, and girls carry about crude images of women as dolls. Queensland girls fix a forked stick on their necks to suggest a baby's limbs dangling over the mother's shoulders. In Arizona the Maricopa mounted disks of clay on a 6-inch stick to be twirled between their palms for a top. The Plains Indian equivalent was a wooden cylinder tapering to a cone; a boy lashed it on the ice in competition with others to see whose top would spin longest. Similarly, Guiana boys spun their tops (*Pl. 26, fig. 3*) into a square tray to see which would knock the others out. Maori children had jumping-jacks: a well-carved human figure had its arms loosely fixed by means of cords; when these were pulled and the image shaken it was supposed to perform a dance. Samoan girls tossed a jackstone, executing various figures while it was in the air. Many of their tricks had to be gone through in proper order or the player lost her chance to an opponent. The first act was to hold one stone in the hand while four others were on the floor, toss it up, pick up another stone and catch the first. Transferring one stone to the left hand, the girl repeated the performance with each of the remainder until all had been picked up separately.

Often primitive children merely exhibit their animal spirits. Ona girls get a great thrill by tickling one another and swinging on thongs between trees. Chaco lasses will stand up one behind another with legs apart, and the last one in line then crawls on all fours between the legs of her mates. Nor is sheer deviltry lacking, as when Plains Indian boys stole the meat hanging on the racks in camp and took to their heels for a picnic by themselves.

Sports. Wrestling is probably universal. It is the Ona's favorite sport: bystanders watch with bated breath, shout words of praise and criticism, and discuss the merits of the combatants for weeks after the event. Sometimes there are pitched encounters between groups, but definite rules are upheld; it is a foul to trip up an opponent, and a wrestler who pushes his adversary across an arrow marker scores a point. Boxing seems to have been much less common, though we read of a legendary Hawaiian hero who slew an opponent with a single blow of his fist. Such contests are fashionable among the Eskimo: one man strikes his antagonist with his fist either on the temple or on the bare left shoulder, the winner being of course the one who can longest stand this trial of strength, in which men are occasionally killed.

Races are far more common. Companies of Ona often run in friendly competition from two to six miles; the Hopi have established long-distance records; and relays are known among the Maricopa. Southwestern Indians usually select a spot, run to it, and then return to the starting-point as the goal. The Asiatic Turks naturally race on mounts, and so do the Plains Indians since the introduction of horses.

Ball games are also widespread, but vary greatly in type. The Euahlayi of Australia sew up a kangaroo-skin and throw it into the air; the catcher goes with his side into the middle, the opponents forming an outer circle. When the ball is again thrown up, they have a chance to catch it and get into the middle of the ring. And so the game proceeds, that group winning which keeps the ball longest. Among the Chané of the northern Argentine a player throws a solid rubber ball, which his opponents must throw back with their heads. Touching it with the hand is forbidden, and the side that misses five or ten times, according to agreement, loses the game.

On the Orinoco the Indians similarly had to parry a thrown ball with the right shoulder.

Frequently ball games are played in a more elaborate way. Chaco Indians bat wooden balls toward either of two goals from three to six hundred feet apart—in other words, they play shinny or hockey, as do many North American Indians. A feminine variant, "double-ball shinny", was popular in the West. The Maricopa women used a strip of leather or willow heavily knotted at each end and tried to strike it with sticks until it fell over the opponents' goal. In the eastern United States a lacrosse game was an affair of state played by village against village or tribe against tribe and watched by throngs of hundreds or even thousands. Among the Choctaw each side performed ceremonies to gain success by supernatural means and every one bet heavily on the result, even staking the clothes he wore. Each player had two rackets for catching the ball, which was beaten back and forth until it touched a goal post. Twelve goals settled the game. There were violent scrimmages, from which many emerged with dislocated joints, bloody noses, or broken limbs. This tribe also played hand-ball with equal ceremony and excitement. A kind of football frequent in our Southwestern states was even played intertribally, say, between Pima and Maricopa. Each side selected its best runner and his assistant, who ran ahead with a stick. One man kicked the ball, possibly into the bushes, then the helper struck it back into the path. The idea was to bring the ball to a selected spot, then back to the starting-point. Here, too, there was ample betting and free recourse to magic.

In the Plains and Southwest of our country the "hoop and pole" game enjoyed great popularity (*Pl. 26, figs. 1, 2*). The Maricopa hoop was 6 inches in diameter and made of a bundle of straw. It was rolled along the course, and the two contestants threw 6-foot poles after it so it would fall on one of the poles. The owner scored and had the right of rolling the hoop next. The precise way in which the pole and hoop came together determined the score, which was differently counted by different tribes. Some of them netted the hoop or made it of larger size. "Chunkey", as played in the Southeast, falls under the same head, though here a smooth round stone was the object rolled; the Choctaw allowed both men to hurl their poles, one aiming at the disk, the other at the first pole to divert it from the intended course.

Compared with such sports rope-skipping seems simple, but the Australian Euahlayi make an art of it. A man at each end swings a long rope at an even pace, then the performer goes in and takes thorns out of his feet, jumps like a frog, dances, runs out for a moment to snatch up a child with which to skip, or measures his length on the ground while letting the rope slip under him. Oddly enough, men over 70 years of age excel at this exercise.

Polynesians lead in aquatic sports. Maori learned the native side-stroke at a very early age and as they grew older delighted in both swimming and canoe races. They had the knack of crossing swift rivers by treading water, practically walking upright to the opposite bank in a slanting downstream direction. They would also fearlessly jump into the water, feet foremost, from great heights, sometimes running up an oblique beam for a proper diving place. Riding the surf on boards was practiced from Hawaii to New Zealand.

Maori stilt-walkers raced one another across streams and also tried to upset one another's balance as their fellow Polynesians do in side streets of Papeete, Tahiti. In America stilts are sporadically found as toys from Montana to the Chaco, while French shepherds walk on them the better to overlook their flocks. But the oddest use of stilts is in West Africa; though occasionally toys, they more frequently go with men's secret societies there, no women being allowed under any circumstances to know about them.

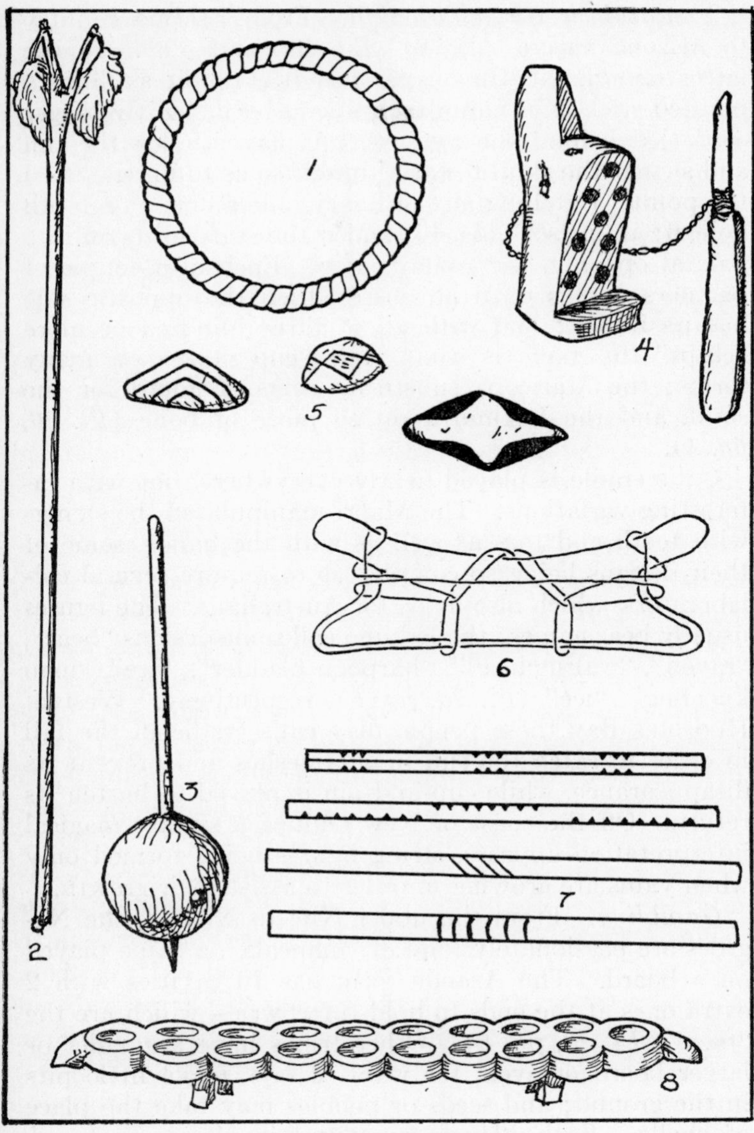

Plate 26: GAMES.

1 and 2. Hoop and Dart, Crow Indians [Lowie (27) p. 241] 3. Top from Guiana [Roth (33) p. 496] 4. Cup and Pin Game, Eskimo [Mathiassen (28) p. 220] 5. Bone Dice used by Crow Women [Lowie (27) p. 238] 6. A Cat's Cradle from the Eskimo [Birket-Smith (3) p. 278] 7. Stick Dice used by Crow Men [Lowie (27) p. 239] 8. Gaming Table used by the Azande, Northeast Congo [Schweinfurth (37) *Plate XIV, No. 11*]

Non-athletic Games of Skill. From Eskimo country to Arizona natives play at "the cup and pin". In the latter region, the Havasupai fasten a rabbit skull to a pointed stick less than 4 inches long by a slightly longer cord tied behind the incisors. A player holds the pin and swings the skull toward himself so as to impale it on the point. Catching any ordinary hole scores 1; a tooth hole, 6; an incisor hole, 40; and if the stick splits off in a palatal opening, the game is won. Each of a couple of partners swings until he misses, then the opposite side has its inning; and with all of three hundred or more "chips" the game is won. The "cup" takes on many forms; the Maricopa substitute rings of gourd for the skull, and the Eskimo a pitted piece of bone (*Pl. 26, fig. 4*).

Cat's cradle is played nearly everywhere, but with interesting variations. The Maori manipulated the strings with teeth and toes as well as with the hands, some of their designs being so complex as to require several collaborators, which also holds for Australians. The figures usually bear names; the Eskimo call some designs "bear", "raven", "walrus head", "harpoon bladder", "fire", "man kneeling", "ice" (*Pl. 26, fig. 6*), respectively. West of Hudson's Bay these people play cat's cradle in the fall in order to catch the sun in the meshes and prevent its disappearance, while cup-and-pin is played to hasten its return. Off the coast of New Guinea a similar magical interpretation appears, string figures being formed only when yams are growing in order to assist their growth.

Gambling. From the upper Nile to Nigeria, the Negroes are passionately fond of "mancala", a game played on a board. The Azande form has 16 cavities with 2 extra ones at the ends to hold the cowries, which are the "men" (*Pl. 26, fig. 8*). Other tribes have a smaller or larger board or even, for want of one, make little pits in the ground; and seeds or pebbles may take the place of shells. Each player transfers his pieces from one cavity to another according to fixed rules, paying attention to their number. Thus, in Nigeria a person tries to drop his last piece opposite the hole in which his opponent has 1 or 3, capturing them if he succeeds.

No civilized nation has more inveterate gamblers than the American Indians. Sports contests were associated with wagers, and in certain games of pure chance men would lose not only all their property but, according to tradition, even their wives and their scalps. Foremost among these pastimes is the hand-game, an aboriginal parallel of our "Button, button, who's got the button?" In California a public assembly or even mourning ceremony was hardly complete without this amusement. To illustrate the procedure, the Maidu start with an equal pile of sticks for counters on each side, the aim being to win 8 "chips". One marked and one plain bone are hidden behind a player's back or under a mat, and the opponent has to guess the hand with the unmarked bone. Usually there are two players on each side, thus multiplying the possible combinations. A doubly wrong guess forfeits 2 chips, a wholly right one wins the game. To discover 1 bone gains a single counter, and the loser's partner shuffles next. If he, too, fails to deceive the guessers, they get the lead. The concealer sings songs, rhythmically swaying his body and trying to mislead his opponents by his facial expression. Details vary: some tribes play with sticks instead of bones, start with a neutral pile of chips, have a preliminary guess for the right to hide first, and so forth. But essentials remain the same, and everywhere the hold of the game on the Indians is almost inconceivable. The Maricopa men used to play it every evening, and the Idaho Shoshone spent whole nights at it when entertaining guests.

Dice need not be of cubical shape; in America sticks are common (*Pl. 26, fig. 7*). A Maricopa set consisted of 4 flattened sections of mesquite root, about seven inches long, each with distinctive patterns burned into it—a longitudinal zigzag, a central token, two lines crossed with an oblique one, and a pair of horizontal lines at each end. These scored, respectively, 25, 15, 6, and 4. A player held the set clenched in his right hand and struck it from below with a stone in his left. If one marked face turned up alone, it scored its face value; but two marked faces scored 2, three up, 3. With 4 plain dice up, the set went to the opponent. Each player sat by a row of twenty-five shallow pits and passed a stick or stone tally along them to indicate his score. After twenty-five he began anew, since fifty points won the game. Frequently our Indians use billets flat on one side and convex on the other, a form also found in the Chaco. There, too, a row of pits serves as a counting-board, while the more sophisticated Peruvians played with an actual wooden board or flat stone, using differently colored beans as markers.

Another American form of this pastime, especially used by women, consists in throwing wild-plum seeds with distinctive faces or equivalents of some other material (*Pl. 26, fig. 5*) by placing them on a bowl or basket, which is struck against the ground. The scoring was wholly conventional. In Montana the Crow have a set of three circular and three triangular bones: 6 plain or marked dice scored 6; 3 marked disks with 2 marked triangles, 1; 1 marked disk with 1 marked triangle, 4; 1 marked disk, 2; 3 marked disks, 3; 2 marked disks with 1 triangle, 3.

Strange as it may seem to us, however, dice are sometimes connected with serious purposes. In India they were thrown in order to predict the future, and this use is prominent among African Negroes. The Thonga, for example, have elaborate sets of astragalus bones with other objects and have elaborated a science of divination, every conceivable occurrence of their lives being somehow linked with the combinations of their bones, which are considered too sacred to be sold.

Social Entertainments. Many pastimes, like some of our parlor games, have a verbal basis. The Crow have tongue-twisters like our "She sells sea-shells by the seaside", which are to be recited at breakneck speed without error. The most popular is basakapupe′cdec akapupapa′-patdetk (My people who went to the Nez Percé are not wearing their belts Nez Percé fashion). In Australia riddles play a considerable part in social life, and a connoisseur is esteemed. They are propounded as little songs describing the thing to be guessed, the singer also acting its peculiarities in pantomime. A Euahlayi sample is the following: "The strongest man can not stand against me. I can knock him down, yet I do not hurt him. He feels better for my having knocked him down. What am I?" Answer: "Sleep." Such conundrums are in vogue among many Asiatics and Africans. Indeed, they may be said to form a branch of Negro literature; a collection of riddles from a single tribe fills two dozen pages. A Shilluk ushers in his riddle with a stock phrase; if his audience fails to guess the answer he proceeds triumphantly, his opponents humbly admitting their defeat. In South Africa conundrums are equally popular. A typical example from the Thonga asks for the animal whose leg is so heavy that it could not be carried to town, the answer being "The mosquito." In one form played here the answers are now quite meaningless and must accordingly be learned by rote. Thus the starter may ask, "The people against the wall?" Answer: "Ah, if only I should die!" Probably in course of time the proper responses have been shuffled so they no longer fit rationally. Here, too, the leader always begins with an obscure traditional phrase: "Son of the moon, shadows."

Dances. Dances are often ceremonies and will be considered from that angle (p. 316). But many of them are first of all amusements. And if they are linked up with religion, that is only because simpler peoples tie up their beliefs with *any* everyday activity, whether it be eating or hunting, gambling or house-building. Besides, all dancing, whether profane or sacred, has a formal pattern that allies it with art. Thus, dancing can be viewed in its recreational, religious, or aesthetic phases, these not always being sharply distinguishable. For example, the Hawaiians originally took their hula very seriously; it was patronized by the chiefs and taught by priests in a sacred hall. The apprentices observed many strict rules, abstaining from certain kinds of food. Nevertheless, the hula *was* a definite set of movements, hence an art, and a form of exercise, hence a recreation. Similarly with the Maori haka. It accompanied mourning rituals; and in its special form as a war dance any error in the steps was fraught with peril. Nevertheless there could be no haka without rhythmic movements of the body and limbs to the accompaniment of singing. Tongues were protruded, eyes assumed a ferocious glare, the hands vibrated rapidly or were clapped to the thighs, the right foot was stamped at the leader's signal. All this was entertainment for performers and audience alike.

There may be solo performances, as when an African king dances alone before his subjects, or by a group in unison. The sexes may join or dance apart; either sex may be barred or have a special function, such as chanting or drumming for the dancers. A particular step is often the property of an organization; each military club of the Plains Indians had its own dance as well as its peculiar badges. Figures vary even among the same tribe, according to the type of dance held. Indeed, the hula included both agile capers by the younger dancers and mere swaying of arms and bodies by sitting or kneeling performers. Posture dancing was popular in Micronesia and Polynesia; and in the Tobacco ceremony of the Crow movement was reduced to a minimum, a performer standing in the same spot while moving his clenched hands forward and backward. At the other end of the scale is the violence of the Maori haka. The coordination of joint dancers is another point of interest. In Nevada and Utah both sexes perform a round dance, neighbors interlocking fingers, with a sidewise step. In the same area partners of opposite sex sometimes face and hold each other for a sort of one-step back and forth

On the other hand, Shilluk men and women never touch each other in dancing; they either move in separate circles around a drum or each faces the other with alternate raising and dropping of the hands. Pueblo masqueraders are all male, stand in Indian file, and merely stamp their right feet while shaking the arms of the same side. Among the Yakut and Yukaghir of northern Siberia men and women circle around arm in arm without definite order, first moving the left foot along the ground toward the left, then bringing the right foot near it, then stamping twice with both heels held together, standing without changing positions on their toes. They bend and unbend their knees, sway their bodies to and fro, raise and lower the shoulders and bend their heads first to one side, then to the other. Thus they whirl about all day to the point of intoxication and exhaustion.

Australians regard social dances as their greatest amusement; in effect, they are their operas and ballets. Euahlayi songs and steps for such entertainments are sometimes said to be inspired by spirits, being composed in a state of ecstasy; others travel from tribe to tribe over enormous distances. Large fires serve as footlights, and the women comprise the orchestra, beating rolled-up rugs and clicking boomerangs together. The men paint their bodies and decorate their heads with feathers before entering from the dark brush and beginning to dance. Several features are especially admired, such as an in-and-out movement of the knees while the feet are close together, and a display of arm and leg muscles. Such performances merge in drama—the imitation of birds, for example, with their movements and cries.

A community festival of the South African Thonga falls roughly in the same category. The chief orders the boys to take part, and they drill in the bush for weeks, organizing their ballet and the several unrelated scenes. For a beginning the adults may betake themselves to the bush, then return limping and singing a song in which they complain of their lumbago. There follows a tune by a soloist, who threatens to oust his mother-in-law because she is suffering from the small-pox. In response to this cruelty all the other performers in a body express the wife's objections and pity. Such farcical scenes are relieved by a dialogue and dance and by a choral song eulogizing the chief and his ancestors.

For the Shilluk, too, dancing is the foremost recreation, and he takes every opportunity to practice of an evening. Often the young of both sexes meet to dance without drums, the spectators clapping their palms to their thighs. Two girls rise and invite their partners, then both pairs circle about as already described. One pair relieves another until every one present has had his fill. But dancing is more than a juvenile amusement. Not to speak of religious performances, a youth is reckoned of age whenever permitted to join the warriors' dance; and a chief can make a proclamation to the people at large only by summoning them to a public dance. Then, according to an eyewitness, all the Negro's unhappiness seems blotted out: "his face beams with pleasure, his eyes glisten, his teeth shine from inside a joyous mouth, his body drips with fat, and all his muscles twitch with excitement and enthusiasm." Many of the figures simulate battle: the actors rattle shield and spear, play at sneaking up to the foe, dodging missiles, dashing for an attack. Such acts merge into animal mimicry: with or without masks giraffes are shown breaking off twigs, or elephants represented rummaging about with their trunks. There are also pantomimes of everyday events of life, say the harpooning of a hippopotamus; and nowadays the white man is exhibited in characteristic poses, such as peering through a field-glass or writing a letter.

Buffoonery. Either with or without sacred ceremonials primitive folk are given to organized buffoonery. The Arapaho of Wyoming had a military club called the Crazy Lodge, whose members acted as foolishly as possible during their public appearance and annoyed every one in camp. One of them would climb a tent pole, pretending to be a bird; the rest shot at him, and he would feign death. On such occasions they acted and spoke by contraries. Any one inviting them to a feast must bid them stay away; if they carried a heavy load they pretended it weighed nothing, and vice versa. Yet other activities of this society are important and serious.

Similarly, the Zuñi of New Mexico have two distinct groups of clowns, both playing a significant part in magic and religion. One group forms a fraternity of powerful wizards especially famous for their love magic; the other is constituted by men wearing quaint knobbed masks who are supposed to transmit prayers for rain, for which they are liberally compensated. Notwithstanding this all-important function they play ridiculous games, burlesque serious dances, and expose their naked bodies, the excuse being that they are mere children. As they pass through the village the women drench them with water from the housetops. At a Hopi ceremony clowns mimic the priests, steal food, annoy bystanders, and act ridicu lously when any one resents their behavior.

The initiation festival of the Ona includes comparable scenes. Two masked clowns appear tottering about in the guise of decrepit hunchbacked dotards. One of them stumbles and falls while the women giggle and make fun of them. Then one buffoon seizes the other by the hair, drags him about, beats and kicks him until a third clown enters and is promptly maltreated by the two others, who somersault over his body. Such scenes are repeated at intervals of about six days. As a variation the clowns frighten the women and drag off their wind-screen covers.

Such performances are probably meant to relieve the monotony and tension of a long and solemn ceremony spun out over weeks.

Conclusion. The above is only a meager assortment of aboriginal pastimes. Clearly enough, we can hardly overemphasize the rôle of amusement in human history.

Man has never lived by bread alone. In the dark winter hours an Eskimo family would die of boredom if they could not while away the hours with games and story-telling. Other peoples need relief from their drab every-day existence. Even the Australian and the Ona relish entertainment, seeking it at the expense of much toil and trouble; and this holds for all ages and all levels of culture. Religion is often coupled with amusements because it enters all phases of life, but also because amusements are so important that they are deemed proper in a sacred setting.

XI

ART

General Considerations

Universality and Age of Art. The desire for beauty is a deep-seated human urge. Everywhere men have taken trouble to embellish themselves and their implements. Baskets, pots (*Pl. 21*), and moccasins (*Pl. 30, fig. 4*) not only serve a practical purpose but give pleasure by their form and decoration. Eskimo needle cases are engraved with a circle and dot design (*Pl. 29, fig. 2*); Plains Indian rawhide bags for storing dry buffalo meat were painted with angular patterns (*Pl. 27, fig. 3*); in the Philippines geometrical figures were incised in regular zones on bamboo lime holders (*Pl. 27, fig. 2*). A Bali in the Kamerun molds on his clay pipe-bowl a Negro head, certainly not to make smoking more pleasurable but to exhibit his potter's skill (*Pl. 29, fig. 6*). The Azande of the Nile-Uelle watershed consider twin effects beautiful and so spend otherwise needless labor to put two spires on a hut and two bowls on a pipe. Such endeavor is not always for show; sometimes the ornament is hidden from view, so it must have been wrought to delight only the maker.

This craving for beauty is extremely ancient. Generally the birth of art is set back to the latter part of the Old Stone Age because incised tools, ivory carvings and clever animal paintings (*Pl. 28*) date back to about 20,000 years ago. Actually art is still older. In the earlier Old Stone Age, possibly between 50,000 and 100,000 years ago, craftsmen had already begun shaping their fist-hatchet more gracefully. Symmetry did not make it a better cleaver, but did enhance its appearance.

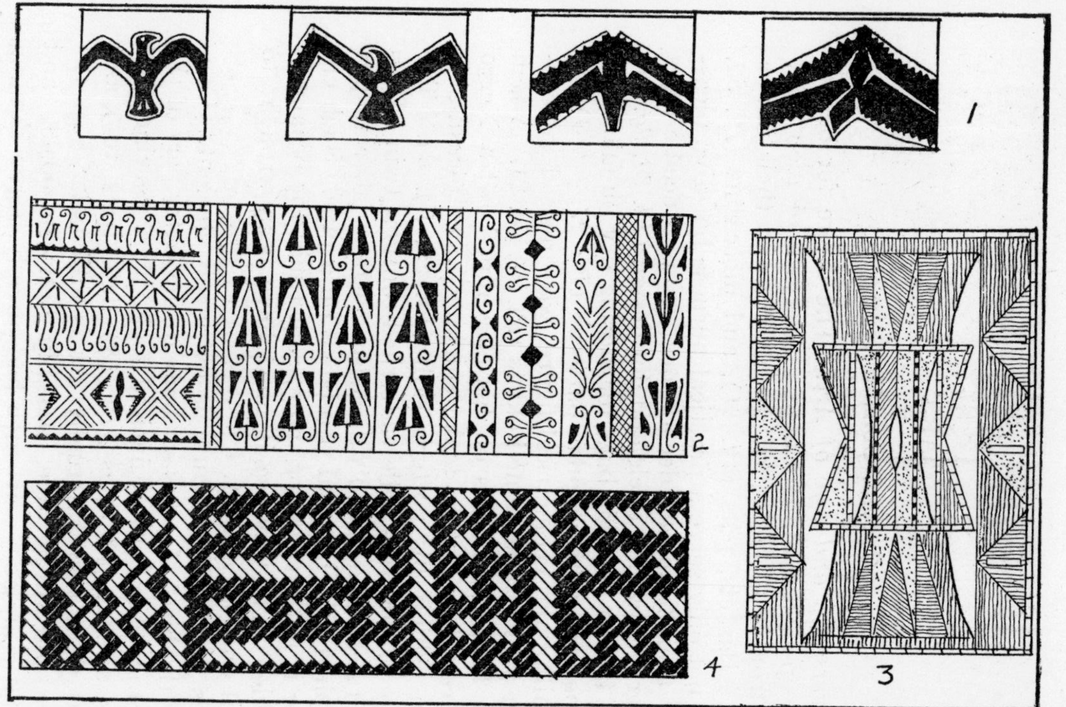

Plate 27: Designs.

1. Conventionalizing of a Design, Bismarck Archipelago, Melanesia [Von Luschan (44) *Plate XXXVII, Nos. 9-12*] 2. Incised Design on a Bamboo Lime Holder, Mandaya, Philippines [Cole (5) p. 198] 3.

Plate 27A: PERU.
Examples of Tapestry Weaving from Ancon and Pachacamac. (Courtesy of American Museum of Natural History.)

Plate 27B.
Maori Carved Prows. (Courtesy of American Museum of Natural History.)

Tribal Differences. Universal as this longing for art is, peoples vary greatly in the ways they manifest it. All have music in the form of song, and literature in the way of folk-tales; but such arts as sculpture are very unevenly distributed. The Ona, for instance, never model or carve. They paint their bodies and utensils, and particularly at the boys' initiation festival they smear their chests and legs with intricate designs (*Pl. 37, fig. 2*). On that occasion they also impersonate mythical beings of the earth and sky and perform difficult dances. The masquerader (*Pl. 37, fig. 1*) who plays the part of a benevolent sky spirit constantly leaps sidewise without turning his head. Thus, apart from song and tale, Ona art expresses itself in decorative painting, drama, and dancing. Californian Indians as a rule are similarly disinclined to plastic work; only the Santa Catalina Islanders with their abundant soapstone carve recognizable sea mammals in this easily shaped material. Such limitation is not due to the rudeness of Ona and Californian culture. The Bushmen are no higher in the scale, but produce first-rate realistic rock-paintings (*Pl. 4, fig. 1*), and the Northeast Siberian Koryak make excellent carvings for the sheer love of the art (*Pl. 29, figs. 3, 4*), vastly excelling their more advanced neighbors. We must assume that in some tribes a genius with a particular gift gave direction to later effort, creating a special development of one art rather than another.

Art and Craft. Every art has its own medium, with peculiar virtues and limitations. Language, the medium of literature, can never give so clear a picture of a person as painting or carving, but has a wider range of subject matter. Even within a particular art the special form or material chosen or available determines the result. Stone is not so easily decorated as earthenware, hence Australians deserve credit for the accurate circles they draw on stone with opossum teeth. The quality of the stone is also significant: the Greek sculptors had fine marble, much superior to anything accessible in Mexico.

Plate 28: Prehistoric Paintings.

1 and 2. Paintings from the Cave of Altamira, Spain [Cartailhac and Breuil (4) pp. 95 and 92] 3. Ancient Spanish Painting of a Deer Hunt [Obermaier (30) *Plate III*]

Again, a sonnet is ill adapted for telling a story; and twilling can not but distort curves since it rests on the interlacing of straight elements. The tools used are also important: it is their one-edged knives (*Pl. 23, fig. 5*) that help make the Mangbettu superior carvers in their part of Africa. However great an artist's genius, he can only go so far and no further with certain implements and materials. The greatest medieval mosaic workers could not rival a mediocre oil painter as regards shades of color; and a Chinese artist could not shade when he put unalterable strokes of ink on silk material.

Thus, art is rooted in craft; and that is why art thrives where craft has developed. When a craftsman controls his technique, its difficulties no longer cramp him, hence he can allow free play to his imagination. If he has none, he may indeed remain a mere technician, but without mastery of his processes he is not an artist at all. Accordingly, the art of West Africa, Melanesia, and British Columbia is displayed in woodwork, that of California in basketry, that of Pueblo Indians in pottery.

In these areas artists teem with original ideas. For hanging utensils in New Guinea they devise double hooks shaped like inverted birds' heads, which in turn merge in the legs of a native who dominates the whole appliance (*Pl. 22, fig. 1*). Headrests are carved with a great variety of props, including acrobatically distorted human figures (*Pl. 22, fig. 6*); and a throwing-board has fanciful openwork carving to hold the dart (*Pl. 34, fig. 6*). African stools show the same range of imagination. Among the Mangbettu the concave seat is uniform, and the polygonal or circular foot very nearly so, but the connecting stem is infinitely varied: it rises in spiral grooves, is formed of two parallel rings, or is worked into truncate octahedra, and so forth (*Pl. 15, fig. 2*). In West Africa the stem also shows geometrical diversity (*Pl. 22, fig. 3*) but often consists of animal and human props. In this region a carver will not content himself with making a mask but feels impelled to top it with figurines (*Pl. 22, fig. 2*).

Technical Influences. Craft techniques may even go further and directly produce art. Checkerwork basketry is bound to present a chessboard pattern, especially if the two sets of interlaced elements happen to vary in shade (*Pl. 18, fig. 4*). A twiller similarly produces diagonal strips willy-nilly, and these are brought out sharply by any color contrast of warp and weft. Such diagonals are readily combined into diamonds and other simple figures in the course of twilling (*Pl. 18, fig. 3; Pl. 27, fig. 4*). In other words, the basketmaker unintentionally becomes a decorator. But as soon as such patterns strike the eye they may be sought deliberately. Other technical processes are equally capable of stimulating design. The coiling of a basket may suggest a spiral; twining, the guilloche; and so forth. What is more, when these geometrical figures have once been grasped as decorative, they need not remain riveted to the craft in which they arose. A potter may paint a twilled design on his vase, a carver may imitate it on his wooden goblet. In other words, unintended geometrical ornaments sometimes develop into well-defined elements of art.

Conventionalization and Reading In of Meanings. This, however, is not the whole story. Geometrical designs can arise from simple copying of natural forms; any one trying to draw the moon in its characteristic phases will make a circle and a crescent. Beyond this there may be conventionalization. Artists, beginning with a faithful rendering of some living form, gradually reduce the picture until nothing remains but an ornamental design. A series of decorations on spear shafts from the Admiralty Islands, Melanesia, can be arranged so as forcibly to suggest this process (*Pl. 27, fig. 1*). The first sample is the plain picture of a bird; the next seems to be a slightly less realistic representation of the same model, with the wings losing their curved shape; the third specimen would not be identified as a bird unless connected with the preceding one; and in the fourth what meets the eye is a geometrical pattern.

Plate 28A: Copan, Honduras.
Limestone Figure. (Courtesy of American Museum of Natural History.)

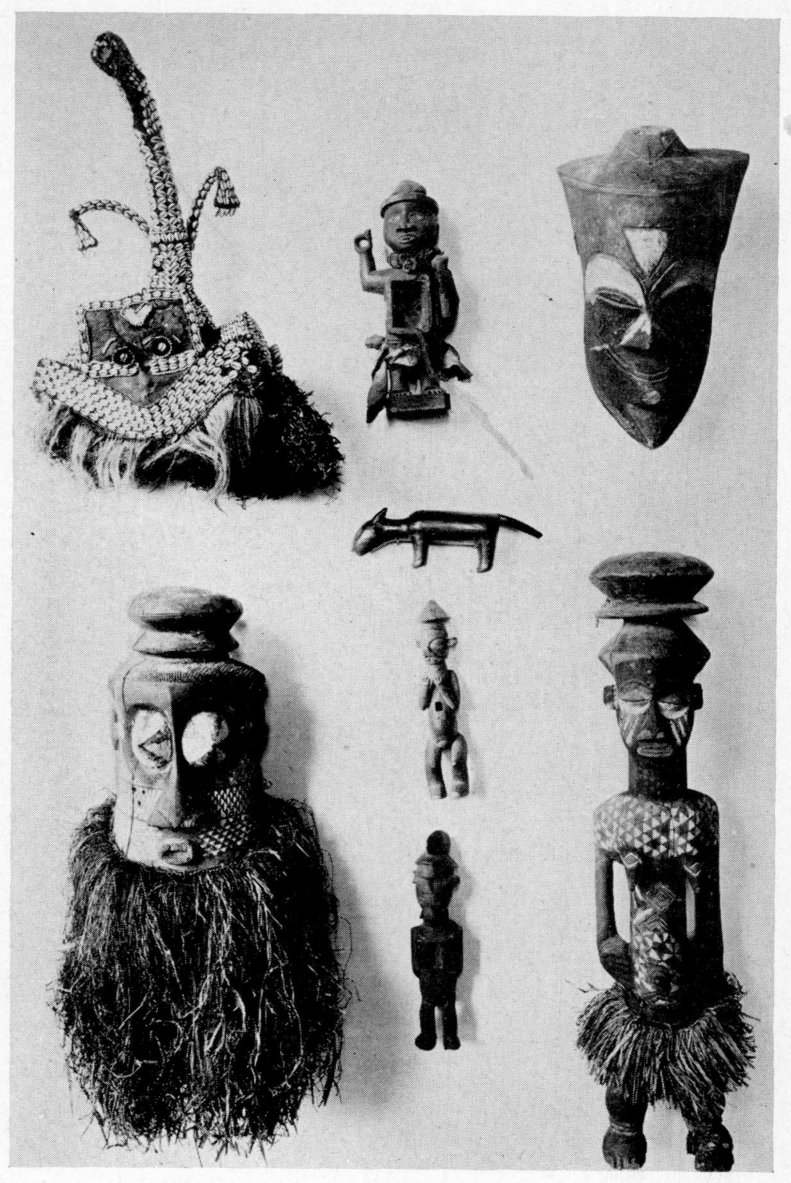

Plate 28B: AFRICA.
Images and Masks. (Courtesy of American Museum of Natural History.)

The Mandaya of the southern Philippines often weave a crocodile figure into their skirts. A series can be constructed, beginning with a clear picture of a man eaten by a crocodile and ending with weird patterns of hooks, polygons, and other unrealistic shapes. This, like the Melanesian case, certainly illustrates conventionalization if the first picture is the oldest of the set. Of that, however, we can not be sure. The Mandaya incise intricate patterns on bamboo, sometimes identifying them as crocodiles, sometimes treating them (*Pl. 27, fig. 2*) as nothing but embellishment. For all we know, the order must be reversed. Though conventionalization is one process that has occurred in art, there is another which works in the opposite direction, namely the reading of meanings into geometrical designs. Just as a particular cloud may remind us of a camel and a stalagmite in a cave of Shakespeare, so a simple figure may suggest a possibly fanciful resemblance to a real object. No sooner, however, would an artist's mind be seized with the idea than he might add features to lend force to his interpretation. The Plains Indians often called the isosceles triangle they commonly painted or embroidered a "tipi", and nothing was more natural than for them to add a door to the figure. The name given to a design is therefore no safe clue to its origin. It may be a label stuck on because of some sudden inspiration that it looked like this or that object. The Central Australians affect curved decorations, sometimes using them in religious settings and sometimes in ordinary drawing. On one sacred article spirals or circles stand for a man, on another for a frog or tree or even a water hole. We might suppose that, say, a frog was once drawn realistically and then dwindled away into a set of circles, but it is inconceivable that four or more utterly diverse motives all ultimately became such circles. Evidently this favorite Australian pattern is the basic thing, and varying meanings are read into it according to the religious interests of the persons concerned. Similarly, among Plains Indians, a diamond will sometimes be called a navel, at other times a person, a lake, an eye, a turtle, a tent interior—even such an abstract thing as "life and abundance." Indeed, Dakota men will identify as enemies the same rectangles which their wives, who execute the designs, call boxes—the clearest conceivable case of a secondary association.

In short, geometrical forms have more than a single origin. Some are due to techniques such as twilling; others may be conventionalized life forms. Some bear deceptive names in suggesting conventionalization; but these names are often merely afterthoughts, based on fanciful or real resemblances.

Representative Art

Naturalism. Strictly speaking, art is never naturalistic in the sense of being an exact copy of reality. The artist always differs from a photographer in giving values which nature does not supply, in stressing this or that part of his canvas, because either he individually or his school considers such emphasis essential. This is as true of the drama as it is of painting or sculpture. Shakespeare was more realistic than the French dramatists in making the rabble speak like common folk; but he, too, made Greeks and Romans converse in English and crowded a quite unusual series of events within the scope of an evening's entertainment. Realism, therefore, is a relative term, never to be taken absolutely. We speak of a style as realistic when it recognizably pictures something real, but it is always a matter of tradition which part of reality the artist insists on showing and which he ignores.

In Old Stone Age carvings the female figure is usually shown with exaggerated hips and thighs, without features or feet, but with some sort of coiffure. The Indians of British Columbia are often content to mark a beaver merely by showing his tail or his incisors (*Pl. 30, fig. 3*).

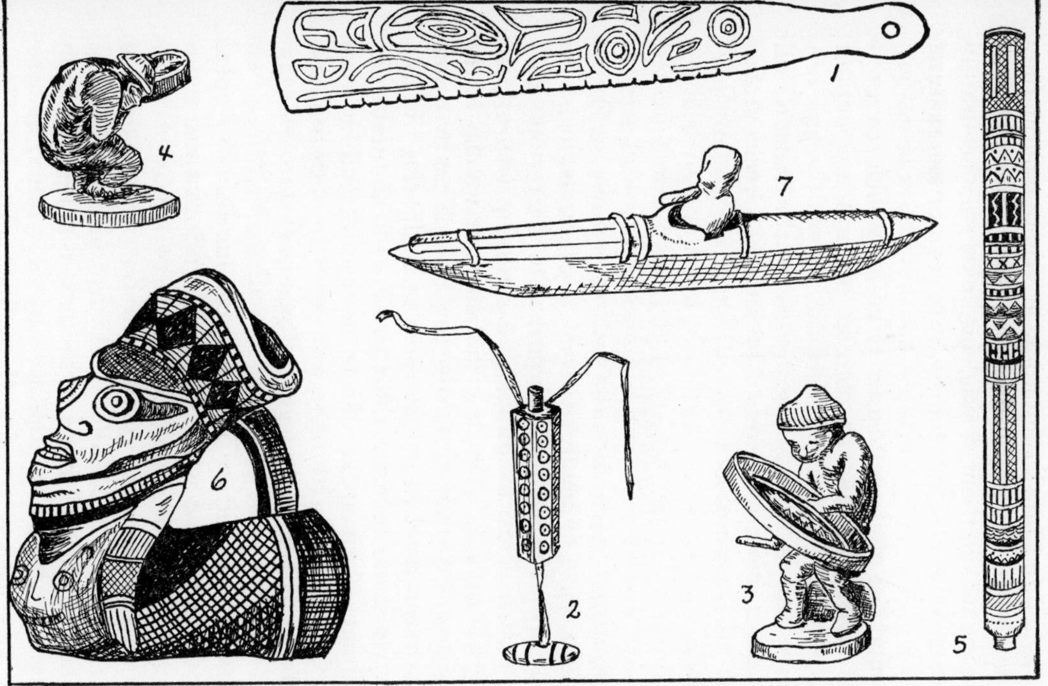

Plate 29: Decorative and Representative Art.

1. Bone War Club with Carving, British Columbia [Smith (38) p. 77] 2. Eskimo Needle Case [Birket-Smith (3) p. 248] 3 and 4. Ivory Statuettes, Koryak [Jochelson (15) 653-655] 5. Incised Tobacco Tube, Bagobo, Philippines [Cole (5) p. 71] 6. Decorative Clay Pipe from Kamerun [Von Luschan (44) p. 52] 7. Figure of man in kayak carved in ivory, Eskimo [Mathiassen (28) p. 217]

The Alaskan Eskimo silhouette their figures; the Blackfoot Indians give us X-ray pictures of an animal, drawing the heart and lungs they know are there even if they can not be seen. Again, in northern Spain, the artists of the Old Stone Age painted single animals very accurately (*Pl. 28, figs. 1, 2*) but hardly ever combined distinct figures into one picture; while their colleagues in eastern Spain (and the modern Bushmen) painted such scenes as hunters chasing game (*Pl. 28, fig. 3*) and a group of dancers.

Representative art must be judged by the artist's skill in relation to his intentions. The ancient Greeks strove to show the live form as it actually appeared in any possible position. But the technique for doing so was acquired only during several hundred years of concentrated effort. At first figures were sculptured in a stiff frontal position, in harmony with the still more ancient Egyptian tradition. Typically, the arms remained close to the sides, with the left foot forward. Only after 500 B.C. did the Greeks learn to draw and carve men naturally as seen from any angle. In view of their aims we can fairly say that they *progressed* to this goal, which many other peoples never reached. Strangely enough, the humble Koryak hunters independently achieved this result in their miniature carvings in ivory or wood, for they were able to show distorted bodies of wrestlers, drummers, fire-drillers, with a high degree of accuracy (*Pl. 29, figs. 3, 4*).

However, it would be unfair to blame other peoples or ages for not doing what they never tried to do. The Chinese, for instance, do not pretend to draw human bodies with anatomical correctness but try to express moods. In the early Middle Ages European painters had not mastered the technique of realism, but neither were they striving to picture things as they were: it was enough to *suggest* objects and their space relations. Thus, in an Italian mosaic the Virgin sits in the same plane with the Christ child and all the figures are presented in

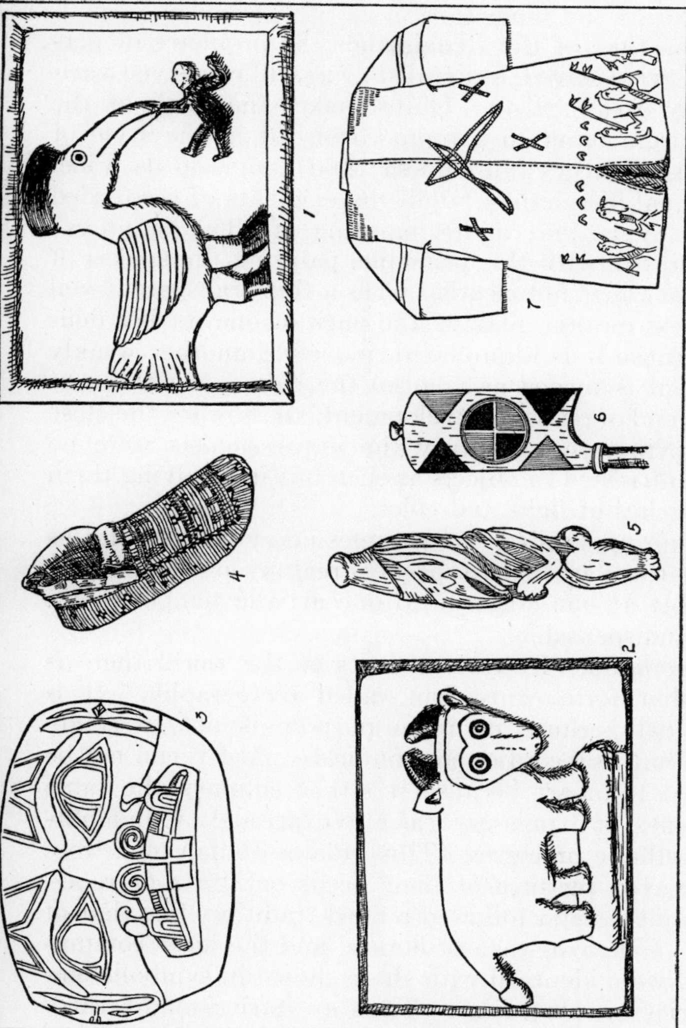

Plate 30: DECORATIVE AND REPRESENTATIVE ART.

1 and 2. Clay Bas-reliefs from the Dahomi, West Africa [Waterlot (45) Figs. 10a and 17a] 3. Stone Mortar Carved in Conventionalized Figure of Beaver [Smith (38) p. 29] 4. Arapaho Moccasin [Kroeber (20) p. 42] 5. Carved Wooden Figure from New Guinea [Finsch (7) *Plate XV, No. 6*] 6. Decorated Handle of a Ceremonial Ax, Bismarck Archipelago, Melanesia [Von Luschan (44) *Plate XXXIV, No. 6*] 7. Back of a Decorated Coat, Sioux [Wissler (47) p. 268]

a front view. But then these mosaics were conceived as wall decorations, not as independent paintings of human forms.

By the time of the Renaissance the problems of perspective were solved, but realism was still conceived variously by great artists. Dürer makes the birth of the Holy Virgin occur in a room furnished in the style of Sixteenth Century Nuremberg; and Leonardo da Vinci gives equal distinctness to all the elements of a crowded canvas. Velazquez in his painting of "The Spinners" (1657) broke with this principle, painting the spokes of a moving wheel not clearly but as a thin transparent veil to suggest motion, making the back of one worker definite because it is illuminated, modeling another weakly because it is turned away from the light. Yet this was not the end of realistic development, and toward the close of the Nineteenth Century the impressionists were no longer interested in objects as such but in resolving them into patches of light and color.

To sum up, realistic art assumes many different forms because there are many aspects of reality, some appearing negligible at one stage or to one artistic temperament, others indispensable.

Pictography. In various parts of the world there is a peculiar form of realism called pictography. It is hardly art because its main purpose is not to create beauty but to record or communicate. Yet it can not be divorced from art because it either employs the same techniques, or expresses ideas also expressed by undoubtedly aesthetic processes. Thus, Plains Indian men wore or displayed pictures of their deeds on shirts or robes. Such a pictograph followed a fixed tradition, like that of an art, in showing men or horses; and the ideas communicated were identical with those shown in symbolic embroideries on moccasins. Thus a warrior might carry about with him a pictorial history of his deeds painted on his robe, possibly showing himself on horseback striking an unhorsed enemy or stealing up to a hostile camp;

Plate 30A.
Totem Poles and Other Carvings from Bismarck Archipelago, Melanesia. (Courtesy of American Museum of Natural History.)

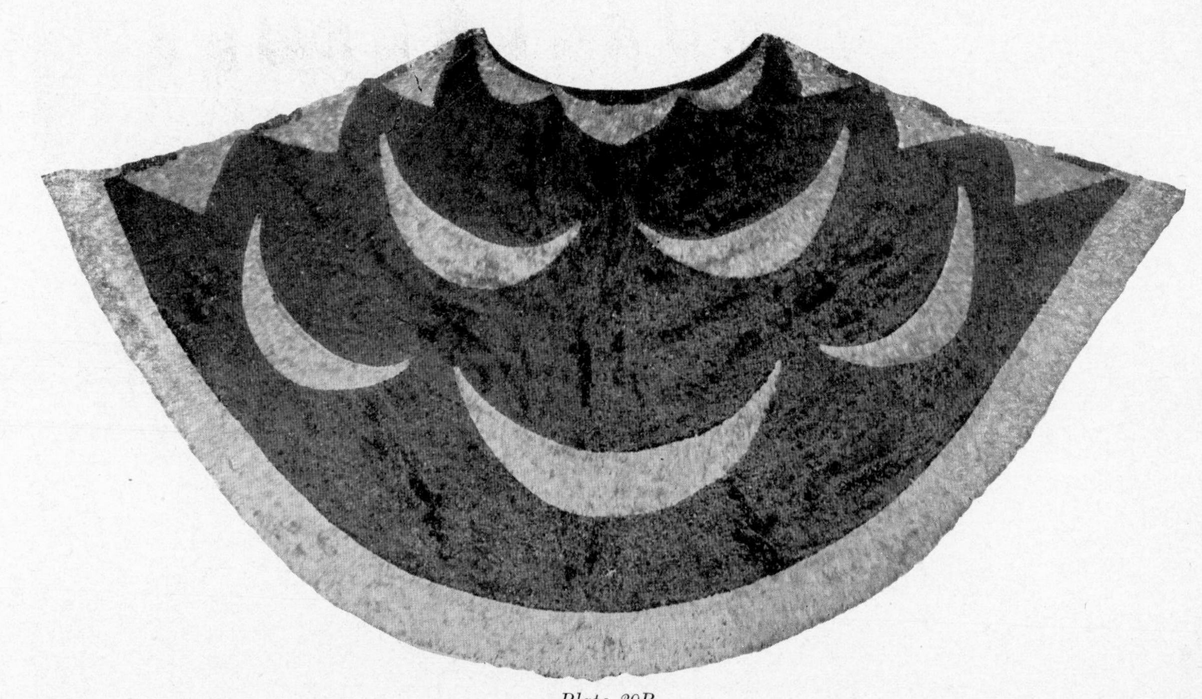

Plate 30B.

Hawaiian Feather Cape. (Courtesy of American Museum of Natural History.)

and this would serve not only as a pleasant souvenir for himself but as an advertisement to the world at large. A Dakota coat (*Pl. 30, fig. 7*) shows a mingling of realism and symbolism. The men are Crow enemies encountered by the wearer; the curves stand for the tracks of stolen horses; the bows represent a hand-to-hand fight with these weapons; and the crosses symbolize the rescuing of a friend.

Every king of Dahomey in West Africa had his palace walls decorated with colored clay bas-reliefs which commemorated events in his or a predecessor's reign, or even some noteworthy sayings dropped from royal lips. One bas-relief shows a Dahomean warrior cutting an enemy's leg; in another a brave carries his doll-like prisoner on his shoulder; in a third a hostile chief's head appears in a trap. Very commonly a ruler had himself represented symbolically as a powerful animal—as a buffalo (*Pl. 30, fig. 2*), shark, elephant, or fabulous giant bird with a beak so strong and powerful that it could seize any one (*Pl. 30, fig. 1*). One king had said with reference to a rival people, "It is easy to land a fish that takes the bait." This aboriginal utterance was immortalized by the picture of a hooked fish.

North Siberians sometimes scratch messages on birchbark. In one case the "writer" drew the course of two streams, three tents, some boats and canoes to indicate the movements of two families (*Pl. 31, fig. 1*). Indians around Lake Superior also incised figures on birchbark to remind them of sacred songs.

In many parts of the world there are rock-paintings and engravings. Though recent natives generally disclaim any knowledge of their meaning, some of them come properly under the head of picture writing. Thus, the Indians in the interior of British Columbia identify certain paintings on a bowlder as a girl's lodge (*Pl. 31, fig. 2*), as a dog (*Pl. 31, fig. 4*), and as a crossing of trails with a fir branch put up for a sacrifice (*Pl. 31, fig. 3*). These Canadian pictures are definitely less realistic than

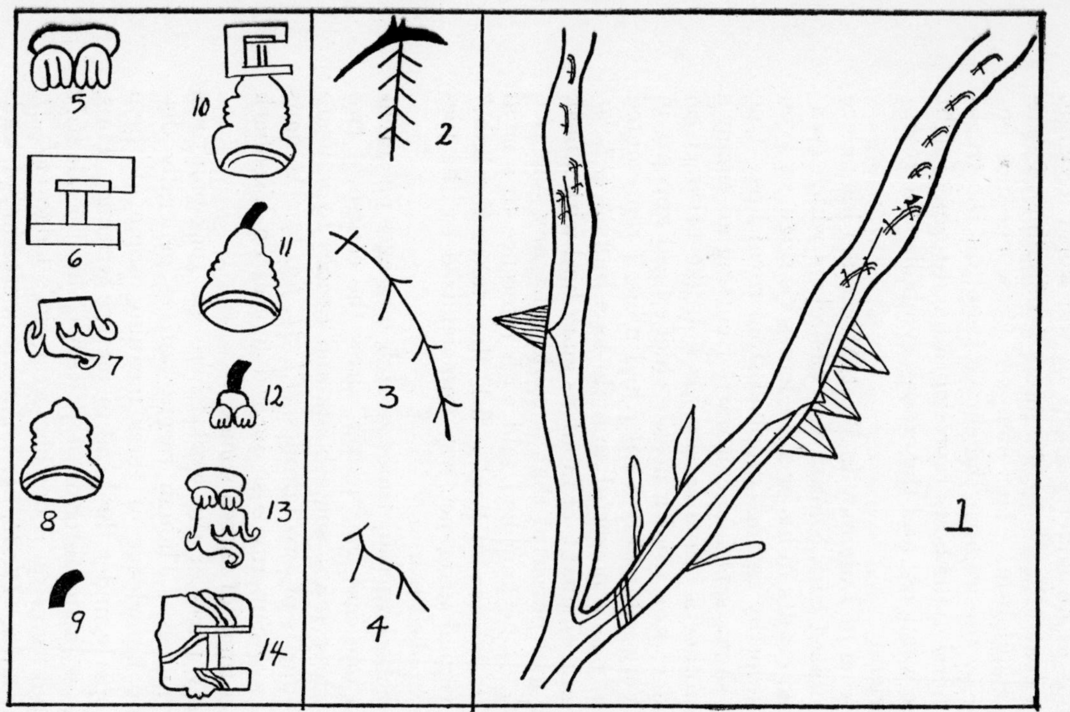

Plate 31: Pictograph Writing.

1. Pictograph Account of a Fishing Trip [Jochelson (17) p. 435] 2, 3, and 4. Pictographs of a Woman's Lodge, a Cross-Road, and a Dog, British Columbia [Smith (38) p. 99] 5, 6, 7, 8, and 9. Mexican Symbols: "tlan" from word for "teeth"; symbol "cal" from word for "house"; symbol "miz" from word for "cloud"; symbol "tepec" from word for "hill"; symbol "itz" from word for "dog" [Spinden (39) p. 198] 10, 11, 12, and 13. Rebuses for the proper names "Caltepec", "Itztepec", "miztlan" and "Itzlan"

the West African or Plains Indian pictographs. The "dog" might be taken for some sort of beast, but the two other figures are unintelligible unless one happens to know the system.

However, this is largely true even of the realistic pictographs, and therein lies the difference between them and true writing as a means of communication. Script is unambiguous and expresses every possible utterance precisely. But even the less allegorical bas-reliefs of Dahomey at best show only a warrior wounding or carrying another. They can not explain when the event took place. Similarly, the Siberian picture mentioned does not show beyond the possibility of misunderstanding which stream the wanderers started from. As for abstract ideas, pictures can express them only if there is a previous agreement as to their symbols. A cross might thus stand for Christianity, but even so it would not always be easy to tell at once whether the abstract notion was intended rather than some concrete idea, such as a forked road or an actual cross.

Writing

Nevertheless picture writing was the beginning of every complete script. The Mexican Indians got started on the road to true writing but stopped short with a very partial rendering of their language—mostly of proper names—by the "rebus" principle. A rebus is a puzzle in which a picture represents not only the object it indicates but also any object bearing the same or a similar name. Thus, in an English rebus the drawing of a foot from below would stand for "sole" in all its meanings and also for "soul". "Isinglass" might be pictured by drawings of a cake of ice, an inn, and a glass. If, then, a word can be broken up into parts, each of which can be drawn, it is capable of *phonetic* expression. This clears the deck, then, for expressing any and every part of the language, no matter how abstract. The Aztec, for instance, analyzed the proper name Caltepec into two parts, "cal" and "tepec". The first sufficiently resembled their word calli, "house" (*Pl. 31, fig. 6*); the second, the word tepec, approximated tepetl, "mountain" (*Pl. 31, fig. 8*). Accordingly, a house on a mountain was the sign of the entire word (*Pl. 31, fig. 10*).

Similarly, Miztlan (*Pl. 31, fig. 13*) was represented by a combination of the symbol for cloud, miztli (*Pl. 31, fig. 7*) with that for tlantli, teeth (*Pl. 31, fig. 5*). The signs for Itztepec (*Pl. 31, figs. 9, 11*) and Itztlan (*Pl. 31, fig. 12*) show the common first syllable; those for Itztepec and Caltepec (*Pl. 31, figs. 10, 11*) the common terminal syllables. Evidently, the Aztec signs are only partly pictures; some are purely conventional, whatever they may have been originally.

The Egyptians and the Sumerians of Babylonia, also starting from pictography, evolved complete scripts between 4,000 and 3,000 B.C. Both conventionalized their pictures, especially the Babylonians, whose marks, made with blunt reed styli on soft clay tablets, grew wedge-shaped so that they ceased to bear any resemblance to material objects. Both peoples split up their languages into the existing syllables and had a symbol for each so that they were able to denote any word without ambiguity. The Egyptians went further, analyzing the sounds of their tongue until they had symbols for twenty-four consonants, the vowels being supplied by the reader, as they commonly are in shorthand. Thus, the Egyptians came close to a complete alphabet without quite attaining it. Actually, they continued to add a picture after they had spelled the consonants of a word, as though they could not wholly trust the legibility of a phonetic rendering.

However, the great step of phonetic writing had been made, and when the Phoenicians in about 1,000 B.C. learned to write from the Egyptians they discarded pictography altogether and wrote only by the consonantic signs. The Greeks, in turn, borrowed the Phoenician script, which included marks for consonants the Greek language lacked. By turning them to use for their vowels, the Greeks accomplished the first complete alphabet. This was adopted by the Romans, who passed it on to other Europeans.

Chinese writing evolved at first along the same lines, that is, from realistic pictures to conventionalized forms. But they made only a partial use of the phonetic principle, expressing words not by their sound but by an arbitrary symbol, such as clasped hands for "friendship". Accordingly, they never developed an alphabet. Their script has thus remained very cumbersome and difficult to learn because of the number of symbols, but there are compensations. All languages change in pronunciation in the course of time. Spelling is likely to be conservative, so that English spelling today very inadequately represents the sound of words. The Chinese, whose speech has split up into a number of mutually unintelligible languages, are thus held together by the fact that all literate people can still understand one another's writing precisely because it represents, not the changing sounds of words, but the unalterable ideas they express.

All systems of writing in the world are derived from the Egyptian, Babylonian and Chinese. Going back to the Bronze Age, they mark an epoch in human civilization. They were much more than a means of communication between acquaintances unable to converse. Writing meant that any fruitful idea, instead of having to be transmitted by word of mouth, could be conveyed to future ages by a more precise and safer method and to a far larger circle of people in both present and future.

Literature

Language as a Medium. Literature is that art which uses language for its medium. This medium differs from the painter's pigments and musician's sounds in that everybody puts it to another purpose, namely, communication with fellow-men. But it is only the use of speech for delighting and stirring an audience that creates literature. As for the medium itself, it is everywhere adequate to express the thoughts and emotions of the speakers. The vocabularies of all primitive peoples are remarkably rich in words for concrete experiences, so that on that score aboriginal authors are not handicapped. Here, as in other arts, the creator is one who controls his technique. Every group has set phrases which belong to the common stock. In Crow prayer the seasons are described as "when the leaves turn yellow", "when the cherries are ripe", and so forth. A word artist not only has such expressions at his fingertips, but wields them with originality and adds to them. Even in recent years the Crow praise certain men who in council use words never heard before, yet at once understood. Such in any age and on any plane are the masters who have grasped the genius of their mother tongue.

Literary Devices. But style involves more than diction. Every group prizes certain tricks and rigidly insists upon them. Ancient Greek and Roman poetry lacked rhyme but imposed regular meters resting not on accent, as in English, but on the quantity of syllables. Arab poetry uses not only rhyme but also assonance, which is the same as rhyme except that only the vowels count, as if two lines ended with the words "baby" and "chary", respectively. Assonance, still characteristic of Spanish poetry, has never become popular in English; on the other hand, it is found among the Mongols, Turks and Finno-Ugrians. Alliteration is another device of these Asiatics and was much in vogue in early Germanic verse. It is illustrated in Tennyson's "Fly o'er waste fens and windy fields" and carried to extremes in Wagner's operas.

Repetition for literary effect is a widespread trick. The ancient Egyptians and Hebrews used "parallelism", repeating lines completely or with variations. This also occurs constantly in Navaho and Eskimo poetry, the

Greenlanders further employing a refrain of nonsense syllables with one intelligible word. Such parallel lines provide a framework and a rhythmic effect. Repetition of thought with change of phrase is popular in Hawaii. "Linger not, delay not your going" is a typical example. The Crow are similarly verbose: "His mother died, then he had no mother"; "he divorced his wife, he was wifeless"; "all the Crow, the whole camp, mourned." Folktales of all natives have the same episode recurring not merely for rhythmic effect but for climax. If four brothers go out to conquer a monster, the first three are slain after identical adventures, but the fourth triumphs, the number of repetitions commonly depending on the number held sacred (p. 320). Sometimes primitive taste relishes what we should consider a surfeit of repetitions. In a Shoshone story a boy going to visit his grandfather crosses a fire. "One of his feet burned off. He went home. He stood in his lodge on one foot. The people heard about it." Setting out again he successively loses his other foot, his legs, thighs, waist, trunk, arms, stomach, intestines, liver, heart, head, neck, cheeks, tongue, eyes, ears, teeth, and brains; and each time the stock phrase recurs after his return.

Balance of structure is often sought for rhetorical effect. In high-flown style a Hawaiian will not say, "My four children are dead", but "Four children are mine, four are dead." So in a Crow myth the hero does not simply tell water fowl to dive for a soft object but couches his instruction in these words: "When you get there, if you get to something hard, that is not it; if you get to something soft, put it into your bill." Lavish antithesis, however, grows directly out of the ordinary speech of these people, who employ it in the interest of clearness. The Dakota, neighbors and relatives of the Crow, regularly direct people in this fashion: "You will go on for awhile, and soon there will be a road branching off to the left; but that's not it. Farther on, there will be another; but that's not it. Soon after there will be a third;

and that's it." Instead of a hard and fast line between common and literary speech, there is here a healthy bond between them; the artist develops trends already current.

Certain features shared by primitive literatures grow out of the natives' illiteracy. Among ourselves a man does not speak publicly in the style he uses when writing. Facing an audience introduces a personal note; and repetition unnecessary for a reader may be essential to impress points made by the spoken word. A primitive author, being always in the position of our orators, uses their technique: he uses nearby objects for illustration and repeats statements to let them sink in.

Literary Types. Every people and age has not only its peculiar style but its own literary types, such as sonnets, odes, lyrics, essays, romances. Incredible as it seems today, the novel became popular only in the Eighteenth Century, while mystery tales and short stories are still younger. Old World peoples have a host of proverbs and riddles, while neither form was developed in America. An African orator peppers his plea with adages, quoting them as our lawyers cite precedents; and Tibetans yield a moot-point if confronted with an apt saying. Riddles have been noted as an Australian game (p. 171), and they figure conspicuously in Polynesian romances, where a villain will thrust sphinx-like conundrums at the hero. Preferences for one type or another can not be predicted on general principles. Epics might be expected only on higher levels. But though really not found among the simplest Siberians, they are also lacking in China; on the other hand, these elaborate poetical narratives loom large in the literature of Europe and the Asiatic nomads.

The literary types of South Africa include proverbs, riddles, lyric poems, dirges, songs in praise of the king, poems of the chase and war, satires, religious songs, the communal plays already described (p. 173), and a wealth of folk-tales, many of them revolving about animal characters. The Eskimo sing songs when berrying or traveling by kayak, when petting children and when trying to confound an enemy in a singing contest; they also tell tales with mainly human characters. The Polynesians have elaborate stories about the origin of the universe and tribal migrations; lyrics and panegyrics on the chiefs also figure largely. They often improvise: the Tahitians celebrated Darwin's arrival in verse and more recently waxed lyrical over the European War. The Tongans pay unusual attention to scenery, and the Hawaiians produced the tale of Laieikawai, a full-fledged novel with some 40 named characters.

Literature and Culture. Literature is intimately bound up with other features of life. Hence, where conditions are parallel in simpler and more complex societies they yield similar results. In Polynesia and Africa there were monarchs and also poets laureate charged with eulogizing their patrons. A Hawaiian poet had to recite his chief's pedigree letter-perfect on pain of death. Professionalism led to complexity, as in the above-mentioned romance, and to an ornate grandiloquent style. Similarly, the priestly caste evolved elaborate tales and chants about the creation of the universe (p. 305). Among the Greenland Eskimo other correlations occur. A poem is considered the property of its author, as it would be by our copyright law; on the other hand, no one can become immortal because a dead person's name is taboo. Morality and etiquette still affect art. The most realistic dramatist dare not reproduce billingsgate quite as it occurs in life, and in Voltaire's time the French stage would not even tolerate the innocent "thou" of familiar address. Thus, political, social and moral ideas influence all literary practice. Primitive authors are affected merely by linkages other than ours. Thus, we dissociate poetry from music; but most primitive poems are sung, so that the total effect is due to a blending of two arts.

Drama. Drama is especially hard to classify because it is often involved with religion (p. 323). Ona actors impersonate spirits, and the mock-fighting of Plains Indians was part of their greatest ceremonies. On the other hand, dramatic scenes may be performed as a communal entertainment (p. 173) or as unpretentious farces, as when a Tahitian pantomime showed the theft of a basket of food from a sleeping servant. Simple and groping efforts of this order occasionally blossom out into full-fledged dramas.

Such are the open-air comedies of the Mandingo in West Africa. Performed in the village square at night after the harvest season, they are attended gratuitously by the residents. After a ballet and a prologue the troupe is presented, whereupon follows the drama itself. Men play feminine as well as masculine rôles, but the women stand on both sides of the four drums of the orchestra and respond to the chanting of the actors, who include the anonymous authors. The eternal triangle and the ridiculousness of a braggart or coward are favorite Mandingo themes.

Narrative Prose. Narratives are as difficult to place as primitive plays. Many explain the origin of the world and thus belong to primitive philosophy or science, turning into history insofar as they describe the tribe's fortunes; and if linked with holy things, such as rituals, they fall under religion. Yet in all cases a narrative unfolds a sequence of events, and this can be done with greater or less skill and power. Thus, whatever else a story may be, it can be viewed as literature.

Narratives include sacred or philosophical myths, fiction of the novel type, stories of recent and possibly trivial happenings. For two reasons we can not draw a sharp line between myths and tales. As just stated, a myth is a particular kind of narrative, hence has a purely literary aspect. Secondly, the same people or neighboring tribes often tell a story in both a popular and an esoteric version. The Indians around the Great Lakes, for instance, if members of a secret society, use a deluge episode to explain the origin of their cult, while the uninitiated hand it down as a mere folk-tale In the same way a plot may or may not be tied up with a quasi-scientific explanation. A Navaho story accounts for the eye color of the coyote by the pine gum he stuck into his sockets when blinded. He had lost his eyes for disregarding the caution of those who had taught him to send his eyes out and then recall them. But this biological theory is an afterthought; other tribes couple no explanation with the plot, and the Arapaho Indians give a new twist to the tale. *Their* blinded eye-juggler falls in with a mole, cheats him of his eyes, and thus causes his dupe's blindness. The quaint plot is thus basic, the explanations may or may not be tacked on; and it would be absurd to call the same story a mere tale or a myth according to whether it lacks or includes the incidental frill.

Treating, then, fiction in a lump, we note certain widespread features. Much of it is laid in a prehistoric era in which no one died, when birds and beasts talked, when men made shift without fire and tools, when the sun was close to the earth, and so on. The stories explain how this topsy-turvydom was changed to present conditions. In Crow myth, Old Man Coyote bids birds dive to the bottom of a primeval ocean for mud so he can shape the earth from it, creates men, and teaches them how to work and live. Another hero, Old Woman's Grandson, later conquers the monsters which infest the world. Thus, a man used to burn up Indians by pointing his moccasins at them, a witch drew people into her tilted caldron, snakes crawled into persons' bodies, a huge buffalo swallowed those who approached him. Old Woman's Grandson killed all these evil beings and then turned into a star. He is thus a savior and shares the honor of transforming the world with Old Man Coyote, who in addition is a "culture-hero", i.e. teacher.

The Ona picture animals, rocks and mountains as once human; earthly existence was arranged mainly by God's deputy, but the work was shared by other mythical personages. Another ancestor killed the woman then hoarding all the water, squirted it here and there, and thus filled the beds of streams and lakes.

Leaving aside the philosophical value of these figments, they bear witness to considerable imagination. The trick of reversing the condition of things may seem obvious, but not so the variety of characters and situations. Diving to the bottom of a sea and meeting ogres of the kind described are not parts of actual experience. Some motives may have been suggested by actual phenomena: for instance, primitives might conceive the disappearing of the sun as his being swallowed by a monster. But it is a far cry from this to the episode as it actually appears. To take the Crow version, Grandson is scented by the swallowing buffalo, which sucks him in. Inside are plenty of people, some already dead, others alive but pining away, still others of recent date and in good condition. Grandson upbraids these for not liberating themselves. He examines the buffalo, pokes his heart and kidneys, stabs them, and cuts a way out for himself and the rest. The author, it is evident, has clearly visualized a whole sequence of scenes and invested them with human interest.

In addition to the savior-transformer type there often appears a trickster, as in the European cycle of Reynard, the Fox. In South Africa it is the Hare whose cunning worsts bigger but duller-witted animals, in North America the part is assigned to Coyote, to Raven, to Rabbit, or to a human being. Oddly enough, the Indians frequently conceive a Dr. Jekyll-Mr. Hyde character: he confers benefits on man, yet acts as a greedy and lecherous reprobate, who is not even uniformly supreme in cunning. Old Man Coyote of Crow mythology represents this curious blend. Having created the world and man, he roams about constantly cheating others to get food, is himself tricked at times, and flouts even the most sacred laws of the tribe. His consistent cunning and ribaldry is an unending source of amusement.

Another category of fiction may or may not be laid in

the prehistoric period. It comprises imaginative stories of adventure, true novelettes, thoroughly realistic according to aboriginal standards, which do not balk at marvelous happenings. A frequent theme is the exaltation of the worthy but humble—a favorite topic of our own juvenile literature. A poor Crow boy is abused by a tyrannical chief, gets aid from a supernatural being, turns the tables on his enemy, and himself becomes a chief. So a South African heroine, despised for her barrenness, magically conceives by swallowing a pea and ultimately becomes the favorite wife. All men seem to appreciate the contrast between a lowly start and final success.

Generally speaking, primitive fiction is rich in fanciful incidents and picturesque detail. A talented narrator expands a familiar tale by incidents from another cycle, elaborates particular episodes, attempts graphic description, and enhances it by pantomime. A South African mimics the rough voice of the elephant, then shifts to mincing tones for the chameleon's speeches. Judged by modern standards, primitives fail to shade individual characters: a trickster is a trickster, a hero a hero. But we must remember that even Molière's characters are largely personified single qualities. A second fault lies in the flimsiness of the construction. The story-teller does not push the thread of his story to the conclusion but loses himself in attractive details. A Plains Indian lingers over the butchering of a buffalo, a South African lovingly dwells on the details of cookery. In the otherwise remarkable Hawaiian romance of Laieikawai characters disappear and reappear in a manner we should consider intolerable. Here, too, we must note that a closely knit plot is a very recent achievement of Western authors; even some modern readers do not treat irrelevancies as blemishes if they consider them intrinsically worthwhile.

African Negroes are fond of explicitly moral stories differing from the foregoing in having a very simple plot.

Thus, a Thonga mother warns her children against certain fruits on their way; one of them disobeys and promptly perishes.

Drolls constitute another primitive prose type well illustrated by the following specimen from the Caucasus. Three men from the district of Auch went traveling and came to a cave. They supposed it to be inhabited by a fox, so one of them crawled in. But it was occupied by a bear, who with a single blow tore off the intruder's head. When the man gave no sign of life at all, his two companions pulled him out and discussed his headless state, but neither could recall whether he had ever had a head. Then one of them ran to the village and asked the widow whether her husband had really at one time had a head. She answered, "I can not recollect for certain, but I do know that every year I made him a new cap". Such funny stories are not necessarily fictitious. Crow wags seize upon some recent incident of local interest and deftly play it up with the help of gestures.

Finally must be cited true stories devoted to matters of tribal moment or serious personal experiences, for all these are capable of literary flavor.

Primitive and Civilized Literatures Compared. On the whole, primitive literature is much more varied than might be assumed and can produce powerful aesthetic effects. Both in literary devices and types it prefigures civilized man's. The richness of modern literature must be understood as due to a complex culture that has powerful aids lacking in simpler communities, especially for the dissemination of ideas. In literature primitive peoples, too, have borrowed from one another and thus enriched themselves. Stories like that of the earth-diver (p. 199) are found among Atlantic and Pacific Coast Indians, as well as in Siberia, and must thus have traveled over wide areas; and this holds for many other tales. The diffusion was aided by intertribal marriages, contacts at ceremonies, and trade relations. Australians and Plains Indians had a gesture language which enabled people of diverse speech to communicate freely, and perhaps some stories were spread by this means. But at best these processes were very slow compared to our diffusion of printed matter, including translation from many foreign languages. A modern American author, whatever his native talent, has access not only to the riches of English literature but to the combined literary legacy of all the ages. Considering further that there are more individuals in most modern countries than in any illiterate people, it is easy to see why the joint output should be different in scope and quantity.

Music

General Features. Music is not only a universal human achievement, but one which man does not share with any animal. Birds produce sounds that may be agreeable, but only man grasps the relationship between sounds. While a parrot mechanically learns a tune without being able to alter its absolute pitch, all human groups hear notes as series with set intervals. By us a melody is felt to be the same, whether in a tenor or bass register. South Sea Islanders have been tested and proved able to transpose a set of sounds as a unit.

Even civilized nations differ in their scales; our 7-tone scale has come down to us from the Greeks, but the Chinese equivalent has 5 tones. The greatest difference, however, that divides musical systems is that between melody and harmony. Harmony arose in Europe between 1300 and 1600 A.D. and is found nowhere else. African Negroes do produce something comparable to medieval effects when a solo singer alternates with a chorus.

Though otherwise simpler, primitive music may claim more complex rhythms than ours or the Chinese. In West Africa a tune may be accompanied by a set of drums, each with a rhythm of its own, while hands are clapped to still another.

Classification of Instruments. Instruments are classed as idiophones, aerophones, membranophones, and chordophones according to the way the vibrations are produced. Idiophones include tomtoms, xylophones, rattles, and bells because in all of these the player produces the vibrations in the substance of the instrument itself. If it is the air that is primarily made to vibrate, we have aerophones—our common wind instruments, such as trumpets, pan-pipes and flutes. If the sound is made by a membrane stretched over an opening the instrument is a membranophone; this class comprises all true drums. Finally, chordophones are instruments with stretched strings. Their simplest form is the musical bow, in shape similar to the weapon. This occurs even among the simplest African natives. In an old form the wood of the bow is held against the teeth and the tapped or plucked string thus vibrates into the cavity of the mouth, for which some tribes substitute a gourd as resonator. By hollowing a wooden back the ancient Egyptians developed a bow-harp before 2,000 B.C.; and later they played the lyre, in which the body is a skin-covered trough, with strings diverging to the cross-bar of a yoke. The modern harp is a development of the early Egyptian form, and our piano is really a harp laid in a case on one side, with strings struck indirectly through a keyboard.

Associations of Instruments. Instruments, like literary forms, often enter into association with phases of life that seem at first unrelated to art. We have church organs and military bands, thus associating music with religion and warfare. In primitive life such combinations are manifold. In Australia and New Guinea the natives produce a booming noise by whirling "bull-roarers", i.e. oval pieces of wood tapering to both ends and swung from a string so as to rotate around the long axis. The deafening sound is said to be the voice of spirits. It is used especially when youths are raised to the status of adults and gives warning to women and uninitiated

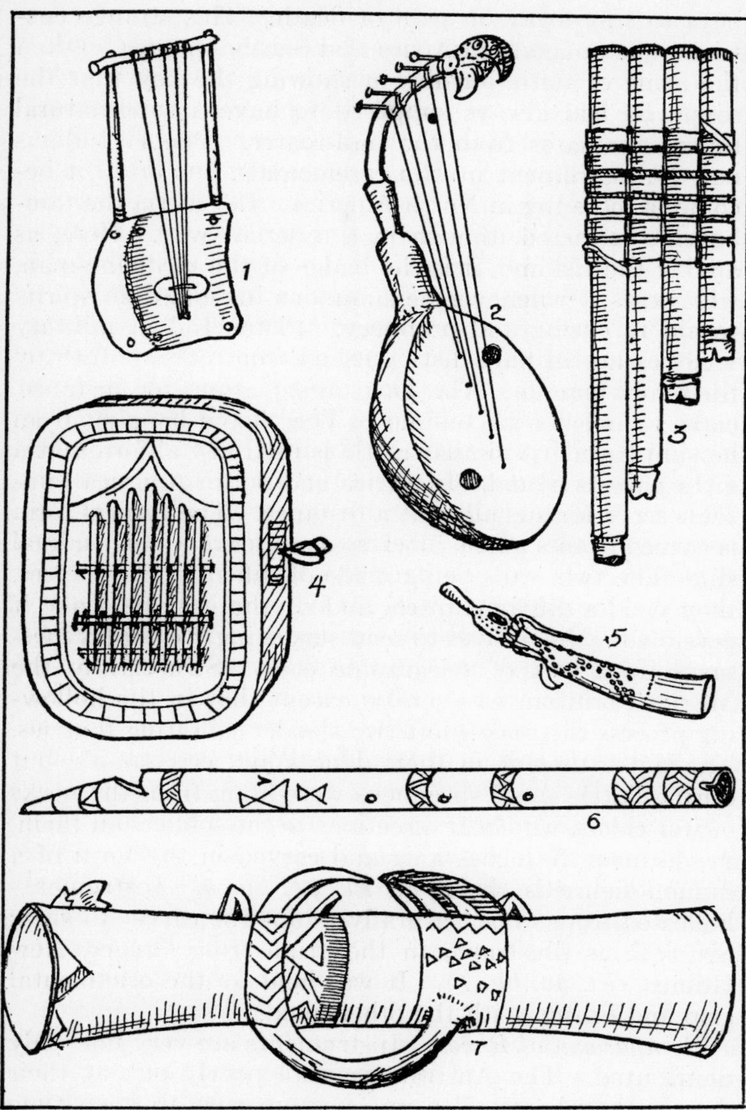

Plate 32: MUSICAL INSTRUMENTS.

1. Lyre from the Mittu, Upper Nile [Schweinfurth (37) *Plate IX, No. 4*] 2. Harp from the Azande, Northeast Congo [Schweinfurth (37) *Plate XIV, No. 5*] 3. Pan Pipes from the Yuracare, South America [Nordenskiöld (29) p. 62] 4. Sansa from the Banjangi, Kamerun [Staschewski (40) Fig. 82] 5. Horn from the Mangbettu [Baumann (1) p. 87] 6. Flute from Guiana [Roth (33) Fig. 236b] 7. Drum from New Guinea [Finsch (7) *Plate XIII, No. 2*]

boys to stay away on pain of death. This strange custom crops up again in Africa and South America. Often the acme of initiation lies in showing the boy that the sound he had always supposed to have a supernatural source emanates from the bull-roarer. Pueblo Indians use the instrument in rain ceremonials, but often it becomes a mere toy in North America. In Siberia the tambourine is sacred, though in a different way. Here, as among the Eskimo, it is the badge of the medicine-man, who beats it whenever he summons his guardian spirits to aid in curing and prophecy. Plains Indian military societies are in part distinguished from one another by their instruments. The Dog organization, for instance, carries a stick with buffalo or deer hoofs hanging from its skin cover. A similar rattle is used in California at a girl's puberty ritual. In Africa and South America tomtoms serve for signaling at a distance. The typical form is carved from a single block so as to leave a longitudinal slit. The two walls being made of different thicknesses, they yield a different pitch, and rhythmic beats make it possible for the natives to send surprisingly complex messages by a sort of telegraphic code. Structurally the Mexican tomtom was similar except that in the hollowing process the maker left two slender vibrating tongues. The Aztec used it in their dances and ceremonies, but during battle small specimens were hung from the necks of war chiefs, who beat directions to the soldiers on them. A specimen 27 inches long and carved in the form of a human figure is shown in *Pl. 22, fig. 5.* Instruments hollowed from wood naturally tempt the carver to show his skill, as illustrated in the drum from Grager, New Guinea (*Pl. 32, fig. 7*). It was held by the ornamental grip and beaten with the other hand.

Comparison of Races. Instruments are very unevenly distributed. The Australians were poorly off; at their dances they beat rolled-up opossum rugs to keep time or clicked two boomerangs together. American Indians had a richer equipment. Their idiophones include the above-mentioned tomtom of Mexico and South America, gourd and rawhide rattles, and a curious notched stick scraped with a plain piece of wood over a resonator. Among aerophones they had the bull-roarer, flutes (*Pl. 32, fig. 6*), trumpets in Mexico and southward, pan-pipes in Peru, Bolivia, and Brazil (*Pl. 32, fig. 3*). The pan-pipes from Brazil prove to be remarkably similar in type of scale and absolute pitch to Melanesian specimens from the Solomons. As for membranophones, in North America the Siberian tambourine was widely distributed, with or without ceremonial associations, and so was a double-headed drum. The great deficiency was in chordophones. Except for musical bows that may have been introduced by whites or Negroes the American aborigines wholly lacked stringed instruments. Since no one tribe had all the forms characteristic of the New World, Indian music thus remained predominantly vocal.

In this respect the Negroes unquestionably excel all other primitive groups, so that kings of Uganda and other countries maintained veritable orchestras. In addition to the simpler idiophones of other areas we find the "sansa", a set of rattan or metal keys fastened to a board over a bridge and plucked at the free end (*Pl. 32, fig. 4*). Still more complex is the xylophone, with wooden keys fastened in a portable frame and a corresponding set of gourd resonators. Aerophones include trumpets (*Pl. 32, fig. 5*), and not only ordinary flutes but also a type shared by the South Seas which is blown with the nose. There are drums of various kinds, and above all chordophones—a harp-guitar (*Pl. 32, fig. 2*) and a lyre (*Pl. 32, fig. 1*).

Racial Theory Applied to Music. The wealth of African instruments suggests the problem whether it is due to an exceptional native capacity for music. Plausible as this theory seems at first blush, it is untenable. The chordophones (and especially the lyre) which raise the Negro above other primitives have a limited distribution in Africa and go back to Egyptian models—i.e. can not be credited to the Negro race. The xylophone, which remarkably resembles the form found in Java, Burma and Siam, is traced to this area by the students of comparative music. With these instruments eliminated, the African array becomes unimpressive. In other words, in this department of culture, as in others, contacts with other groups are significant: African music excels because of the Negro contacts with Egypt, India and Indonesia. The Negro deserves credit for adopting and using his instruments, but not for creating them.

The racial theory also breaks down when applied to modern nations. In the last hundred and fifty years the Germans have been supreme as composers, but this period is too brief for any biological change to have occurred in the German population. Further, since Germans are a mixture of the Alpine and the Nordic race, their progress would be due to the qualities of either or both stocks. But Alpines and Nordics occur in France as well, and Nordics are at least as prominent in Sweden and the British Isles as in Germany. Nevertheless, these countries have produced no composers to rival the greatest Germans. The obvious reason is that, say, about 200 years ago the Germans began to concentrate on music and to foster whatever talents appeared. Native *individual* ability was a prerequisite, but its encouragement was a matter of cultural preference. The Germans thus excel in music for the same reasons the Peruvians excelled in weaving—because of specialization.

XII

WAR

Weapons

Weapons can not be sharply separated from other implements. A fist-hatchet can cleave an enemy's skull as well as a game animal's. A sling hurls stones in battle, in hunting, in games, and against birds that threaten the crops. A staff serves for fencing, but also as a cane or a symbol of office; clubs, shields and lances are all dance regalia as well as weapons. However, in the present section the emphasis is on military uses. We can distinguish offensive and defensive equipment; and the former includes weapons held for hand-to-hand encounters and missiles.

Weapons for Hand-to-hand Fighting. Men of the Old Stone Age wielded fist-hatchets and doubtless also suitable pieces of wood. The Indian tomahawk combined a spherical or pointed stone head with a wooden handle sheathed in a skin cover holding the head, which either hung loose from the haft or was rigidly fixed to it. Many peoples used clubs without stone axes. Thus the Havasupai delivered crushing blows with a round-headed piece of heavy wood. Their relatives, the Mohave, had two kinds of clubs, a straight type and one with a mallet for crushing the enemy's face with an upward thrust. Samoan clubs were of the heavy, smashing variety, each combatant digging himself a permanent foothold from which to wield his weapon. Other Polynesians used more delicate weapons allowing quicker strokes, parrying and footwork. The Maori progressed furthest, developing nimble feints with quarterstaffs and a backhanded thrust with light double-ended clubs. On the upper Nile the Shilluk and their neighbors use a knobbed stick of heavy wood with an iron point (*Pl. 33, fig. 3*). They also fence with long sticks, aiming at each other's heads, which is also a favorite Australian trick.

Metallurgy added weapons for smashing and hacking. Iron battle-axes are common in the Congo; and the Mangbettu sickle-shaped chopper with a wooden butt for parrying is a noteworthy type (*Pl. 33, fig. 6*).

Daggers are of many forms. Those of New Guinea are often of cassowary bone (*Pl. 34, fig. 5*). An ugly Micronesian weapon, also found in Matty Island, north of New Guinea (*Pl. 33, fig. 2*), has a handle edged with shark's teeth. Of the same order was the favorite Mexican weapon—a wooden board with a row of razor-like obsidian blades in each edge. These saw-swords enabled the Aztec to kill Spanish horses.

Here, too, the blacksmith's art produced remarkable novelties. The Azande dirk has a pierced iron blade with blood-gutter (*Pl. 33, fig. 1*); and the Indonesian blades are often highly tempered, inlaid with silver, and twisted in sinuous lines. Swords could develop only with metallurgy. While a stone spearhead easily turns into a dagger, it becomes too brittle if considerably lengthened. Hence blades did not evolve into swords before the Bronze Age. Then Italy developed a short stabbing rapier, and Northern peoples a long slashing weapon. Recent Azande blacksmiths made wooden-hilted iron scimitars from 20 to 30 inches long (*Pl. 33, fig. 8*).

Spears are often thrust but will be treated under missiles.

Missiles. Almost any weapon can be converted into a projectile, but special inventions were required for effectiveness. Under this head come throwing-sticks, slings, spears and spear-throwers, blow-guns, and bows.

Arizona Indians and Southern Californians threw curved flat sticks at rabbits. The Australian boomerang is of similar shape; contrary to popular ideas, the form

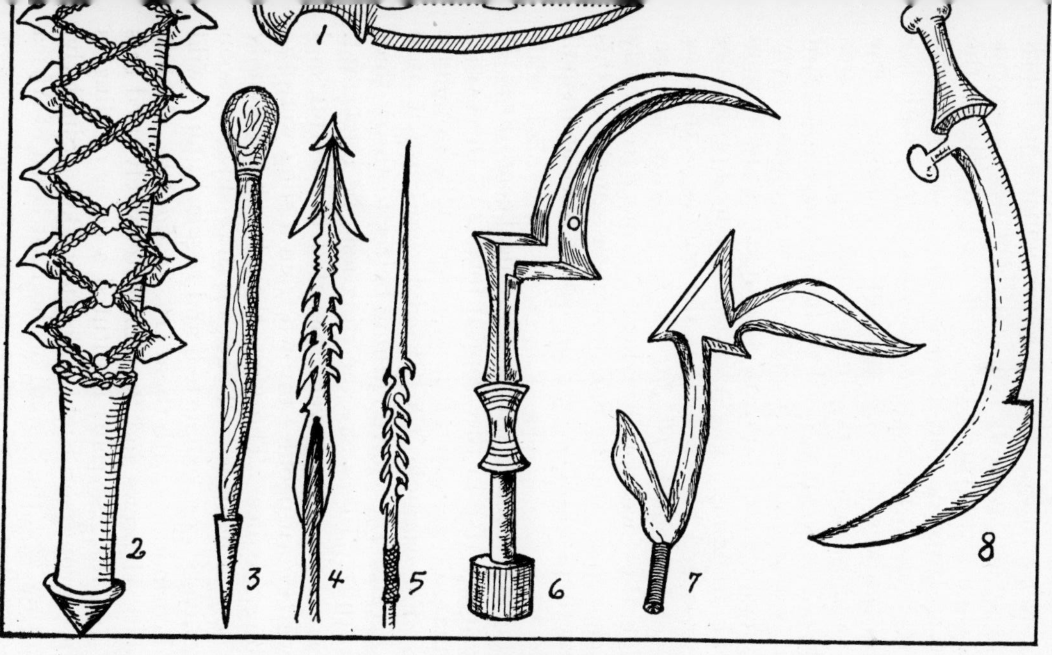

Plate 33: WEAPONS.

1. Azande Dagger, Northeast Congo [Schweinfurth (37) *Plate XII, No. 6*] 2. Sharks' Teeth Club from Matty-Island, near New Guinea [Von Luschan (44) *Plate XXXIII, No. 12*] 3. War Club used by the Dinka, Upper Nile [Schweinfurth (37) *Plate I, No. 18*] 4. Azande Spear-head, Northeast Congo [Schweinfurth (37) *Plate XIII, No. 3*] 5. Mittu Arrowhead, Upper Nile [Schweinfurth (37) *Plate X, No. 16*] 6. Saber-like Weapon from the Mangbettu [Schweinfurth (37) *Plate XVIII, No. 1*] 7. Three-bladed Projectile of the Azande, Northeast Congo [Schweinfurth (37) *Plate XII, No. 2*] 8. Azande Sword, Northeast Congo [Schweinfurth (37) *Plate XII, No. 16*]

returning to the thrower who misses his goal is relatively rare, often a mere toy. A boomerang has a curved upper and flat lower surface. The thrower imparts as much rotation as he can, possibly ten or fifteen turns a second. After the first fifty yards or so of upright flight, the weapon turns over on the flat side, curves away to the left and then rises; the rest of its course varies with the individual thrower and the type of boomerang. The ordinary war form strikes the ground some 20 yards ahead, then flying some 80 yards farther at a height of 4 feet; it will cut clean through the soft parts. Very large boomerangs are swung at close quarters and require the use of both hands. The Azande shape iron projectiles with 3 two-edged blades so that the chance of striking one's target is trebled (*Pl. 33, fig. 7*). Owing to their great value, these weapons are, however, more frequently used for chopping. In the Sudan simpler samples of this type, sometimes of wood, are hurled at fowl and small mammals.

The sling is correlated with geographical conditions. It would be ineffective in the tropical forests of the Congo or the Amazon region, and it is excluded by lack of stone for shot. For example, the Chaco Indians use it only as a toy because they have nothing better to throw than clay and fruits. Elsewhere the sling may be important. In Samoa, where arrows were relegated to hunting and fishing, waterworn pebbles thrown from a sling were the outstanding missiles. The Ona, though relying mainly on their bow in fighting, fell back on their slings as soon as their quivers were exhausted, and regularly hunt wild geese and cormorants with them (*Pl. 34, fig. 10*). Among the ancients, Hebrews and Persians extensively used this weapon, and the Assyrians instituted a corps of slingers about the Seventh or Eighth Century B.C. Similarly, half a century ago, the Somali of the East Horn of Africa had slingers flanking an army of lancers and archers. Around Lake Victoria the explorer Stanley was repeatedly attacked by slung stones.

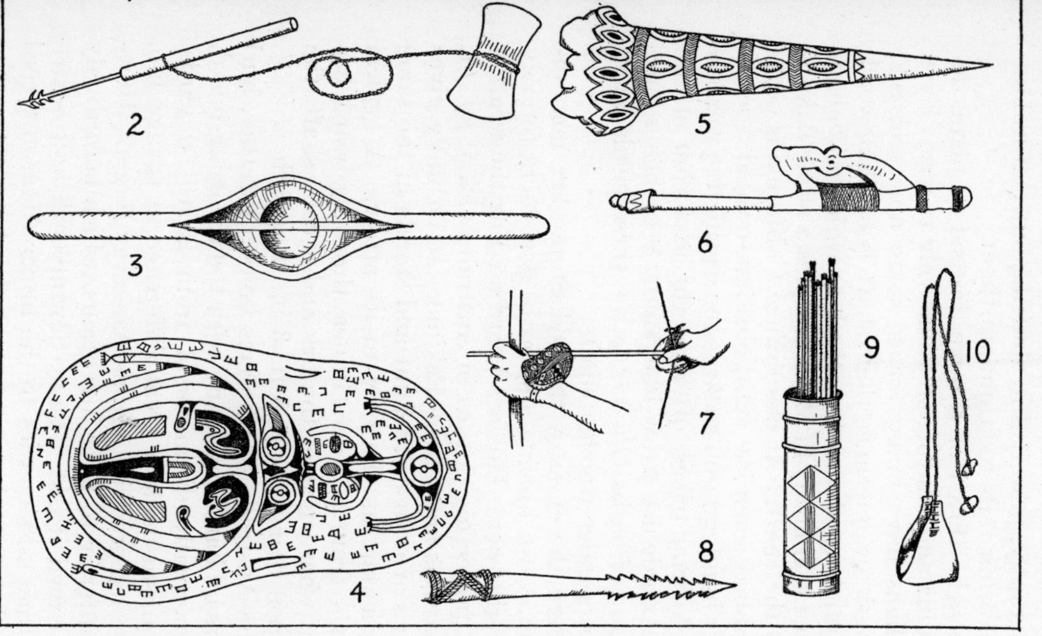

Plate 34: WEAPONS.

1. Blowgun, Malay Peninsula [Schebesta * (35) p. 57] 2. Harpoon, Victoria Nile [Lindblom (23) p. 51] 3. Shilluk Parrying Shield [Hofmayr (13) *Plate II, No. 5*] 4. Shield from New Guinea [Finsch (7) *Plate XII, No. 2*] 5. Dagger of Cassowary Bone, New Guinea [Finsch (7) *Plate XI, No. 7*] 6. Spear Thrower, New Guinea [Finsch (7) *Plate XI, No. 3*] 7. Arrow Release used in Kamerun [Von Luschan (44) *Plate XXIV, No. 1*] 8. Spearhead, New Guinea [Finsch (7) *Plate XI, No. 2*] 9. Quiver and Poisoned Darts for Use with Blowgun, Malay Peninsula [Schebesta * (35) p. 64] 10. Ona Sling [Gusinde (9) p. 244]

** The writer is indebted to F. A. Brockhaus, Leipzig, for permission to reproduce these items.*

In Africa the sling is strangely lacking south of the Zambesi, even where the terrain seems eminently suited for it. Geography, powerful in shutting out cultural developments, often fails to stimulate them.

Spears may be thrust or thrown, barbed or plain, devoted to fishing and hunting or exclusively to war. Even the Australians have many forms, some nine feet and more in length. Sometimes their shaft is of light wood, carefully straightened and smoothed, to which a blade of another piece is spliced; in other samples a stone flake is attached to the shaft. At close range Californians occasionally stabbed enemies with obsidian-headed spears. On the other hand, an iron spear is the distinctive weapon of warlike African tribes, often to the exclusion of the bow. The Azande use arrow-like points, 8-19 inches long, with two rows of barbs (*Pl. 33, fig. 4*), these heads being mounted on slender wooden shafts.

Even before the close of the Old Stone Age man invented a device for hurling a spear or dart more forcibly —the spear-thrower. This is a board holding the weapon either by a projecting peg, as in Australia (*Pl. 5, fig. 1*), or in a groove as among the Eskimo. It virtually gives the thrower's arm an extra joint and stands in the same relation to a dart as the bow to its arrow. A typical spear thrown from a New Guinea throwing-board has a wooden tip hardened in the fire and a cane shaft, the entire weapon being about 5 ft. 3 in. in length (*Pl. 34, fig. 8*). The Australians, who lack bows altogether, hurl many spears by hand and many with the throwing-board, achieving normally distances of from 25 to 60 yards. This mechanism made a great difference in savage life, since it afforded precision against far-away targets. However, it is inferior to later inventions, which accordingly tended to crowd it out. Thus, Seventeenth and Eighteenth Century missionaries to the upper Amazon record the spear-thrower there, but South Americans who learned about the blowgun from other aborigines adopted it in place of the older weapon, while other South Americans substituted the bow. The Australians presumably separated from the rest of mankind before any human group had hit upon the bow, and so remained without it. However, the spear-thrower may persist even after superior projectiles become known. The Eskimo continued its use for bird-hunting, while employing bows for other purposes; and the Mexicans fought with both weapons. Indeed, they still shoot fish and aquatic birds with the aid of the spear-thrower.

Tropical South America and Indonesia are the centers for the blowgun. It is efficient in warfare if long reeds with uniform bore are available and if there is a poison for the darts blown through the tube. This double limitation restricts the distribution of the weapon. It diffused widely in South America only as native trade spread the deadly curare and suitable cane for the pipe. The Huanyam, a Brazilian people, substitute a kind of bamboo, inferior because of uneven thickness; also its bore is double the usual size, requiring darts more than twice as long and much heavier than the Guiana type, which averages about 1½ inches in length. The Semang of the Malay Peninsula blow palm rib darts resembling knitting-needles. Being thoroughly unwarlike, the people blow the tiny weapons only at monkeys and other game animals. A particular species of bamboo growing only at certain altitudes, provides the tube (*Pl. 34, fig. 1*), which is 6 feet and more in length, hence made of two natural lengths. A wooden mouthpiece is fitted on, and for protection the barrel is encased in an outer bamboo. A bamboo quiver for the darts (*Pl. 34, fig. 9*) and the poison-case completes the outfit. In Borneo the natives make blowguns by drilling long pieces of hard wood with a straight iron rod.

The bow, popularly considered the typical weapon of early times, actually came somewhat later than the spear-thrower. It was entirely unknown to the Tasmanians and Australians, while the Shilluk degrade it to a toy and the Samoans excluded it from use in fighting. On the other hand, it is the favorite weapon of Pygmy tribes and occurs among the rude Ona. In some regions, such as coastal Peru, the dearth of good wood explains the lack of bows. But timber was plentiful in New Zealand, and a specimen unearthed in a swamp there proves the Maori to have once known the weapon. They must have given it up because they specialized in other methods of fighting.

Bows vary greatly in length and structure. Even within California and Lower California different tribes make bows averaging 3 and 6 feet, respectively; and structurally there are both simple and compound bows in this area.

The simple or self-bow is made of a single piece of wood. The compound bow probably originated where tough wood was scarce so that several pieces had to be fastened together with glue and sinews, a technique also applied to bits of horn. A well-made compound bow is more powerful than a self-bow, which, however, often survives beside its rival for use against small game and as a toy. In Egypt and the higher Asiatic civilizations the compound bow dates back to before 2,000 B.C. In Asia it spread so that only such isolated peoples as the Andaman Islanders retained the simple type. In America the composite bow occurred only north of the Rio Grande and generally west of the Mississippi, the idea probably coming from Asia and stopping short at certain points simply because time was not sufficient to carry it further. Actually the usual American equivalent of the compound form is a self-bow backed with sinews. In northwestern California the yew bow was so weak that it would have broken without such strengthening.

Bowstrings are of vegetable material such as twined bast or of animal substance, such as sinews, tendons, or strips of skin. Among the problems primitive man solved were fastening the string so it would not slip and preventing injury of the left wrist from the recoil of the string. Many primitive archers wore a protective bracelet like the little leather cushions of the Wute Negroes in Kamerun (*Pl. 34, fig. 7*).

Arrows, like bows, demanded superior craftsmanship if they were to work. An Ona had to split the wood for his shaft, round and straighten it by heat, rub it back and forth in the grooves of a smoothing stone, split and attach feathers, shape a stone head by pressure, and then tie it on with sinew. Feathers aid the flight of the missile but are not indispensable; they are lacking in the South Seas and on the fish arrows of several South American groups who feather war and hunting arrows. Quivers are also common but not universal.

Tribes differed in the technique of archery and also in their skill at long range. Ona marksmen often shot arrows over 500 feet, and experts scored 200 yards. The feeblest method of discharge is that of an untutored boy among ourselves, who will hold the arrow between thumb and index finger, pulling it back together with the string. Nevertheless, this way is occasionally met among the Ainu and some American Indians. Other tribes lightly press the arrow against the sinew while they stretch the string with the index and middle finger. The Chinese and Persians held the arrow with the index, stretching the string with the thumb, which thus required a protective ring. Different again was the technique of the Egyptians, Greeks, and the ancient Mediterraneans in general; the sinew was stretched with the tips of the three middle digits, while the arrow rested between the index and middle fingers. This technique often goes with leather thimbles. Extraordinarily powerful is the release achieved by the Wute of Kamerun with a hooked stretching-ring (*Pl. 34, fig. 7*). The four fingers grasp the ring so that its broad surface lies on the back of the hand, while the hook on the thumb side grips the string and stretches it with the power of the whole arm.

Thus, a host of primitive inventions rendered the bow a more effective implement. They include the use of poison, which could be equally well smeared on arrows and blowgun darts, and the application of barbs, which already appear on Old Stone Age harpoons. Negro blacksmiths of the upper Nile twist arrowheads in serpentine lines while the iron is red-hot and produce downward pointing barbs to prevent extraction of the bolt from a wound (*Pl. 33, fig. 5*).

The Roman crossbow was a bow mounted on a stock with a trigger releasing the arrow, a mechanism thus superseding brute strength. Roman catapults were the beginning of artillery: the missile was placed in front of a bowstring connecting two bundles of stretched sinews. A reconstructed ancient engine of this order hurled arrows well over 1,000 feet and 1-pound weights a distance of 900 feet.

Firearms go back to the Chinese, who as early as the Sixth Century A.D. used gunpowder in religious ceremonies for firecrackers, and about 600 years later with projectiles. These were fully developed under the Mongols of the Thirteenth and Fourteenth Centuries. The Arabs, who exported saltpeter from China, mention firearms as early as 1312 and introduced them into Spain.

Defensive Equipment. Most commonly shields and armor serve for protection. A simple device, little more than a parrying stick, is that used by the Shilluk in their fencing contests (*Pl. 34, fig. 3*), though for other purposes they carry heavy shields of hippopotamus or elephant hide. Skin shields are general among African cattle-breeders, such as the Zulu and Masai. Round buffalo-hide shields were part of the Plains Indian's equipment, while in Mexico shields as well as helmets were of wood. In the northern Congo basketry shields are adequate to catch the throwing-knives (*Pl. 33, fig. 7*) and lances used in the region.

Shields are often ornamental objects. The finest Aztec ones were embellished with feather work or mosaic; and in the Trobriand Islands, New Guinea, the surface was covered with elaborate red and black patterns on white (*Pl. 34, fig. 4*).

Two widespread forms of primitive armor occurred in northern California. The natives wore a waistcoat of rods tied together or an elk-hide jacket. Some primitive tribes, such as the Maricopa, shifted without defensive equipment; and the Ona simply warded off arrows with their guanaco-skin cloaks. On the other hand, the Gilbert Islanders of Micronesia, facing not only daggers (*Pl. 33, fig. 2*) but long spears edged with shark's teeth, appropriately covered themselves with a sinnet suit and a stiff cuirass of coconut fiber over it. The head was protected by a helmet, the entire outfit weighing as much as 20 pounds.

Military Purposes and Means

Motives. Warfare is bound up with the ideals and social structure of a people. In the history of Western civilization peoples have fought for economic gain, for national prestige, for gratifying a ruler's whims. These motives exist among primitive peoples only insofar as there were comparable institutions. When the Zulu were ruled by a ruthless autocrat they, too, fought wars to augment his dominions. Since pastoral tribes of Central Asia and southern Siberia required large pastures for their herds, they had economic conflicts over them among themselves and with settled peasants. Similarly, East African stock-breeders subjected farming populations, whose lands they appropriated at their pleasure for grazing. Chaco Indians also fight for economic reasons. One tribe will dam a stream and prevent fish from ascending to the territory of its neighbors. The latter attempt to destroy the dam, possibly killing a fisherman, and then a feud is on.

But many peoples in the world have no national consciousness, no monarchs or even chiefs; and often practical motives for warfare are lacking or insignificant. The Yurok of northwestern California, bound together primarily by kinship, were without formal government.

There were fights between Yurok settlements or between a Yurok and an alien village without other Yurok taking the slightest interest. A war sprang up to avenge some imaginary or real grievance, never from a desire for plunder. Indeed, the peculiar notions of these natives made the victors the economic losers, for with ultimate peace indemnities had to be paid for losses precisely as in a private quarrel.

In the discussion of trade it was pointed out that land is often considered inalienable (p. 153). Some tribes maintain this principle even in war. The Ona, believing that a mythical ancestor had divided up their island among their local subdivisions, never coveted the territory of another horde. So Australian bands are bound to their ancestral areas and never lust for alien territory. With them, as with the Yurok and Ona, revenge for real or imaginary grievances was the outstanding motive. Of 70 recorded battles, the Murngin of Northern Australia fought 50 to avenge a slain kinsman; 5 for what to them is the same reason, namely, punishment of sorcerers supposed to have killed tribesmen by black magic; 10 because of kidnaped women; the remainder being prompted by a sacrilegious deed that both affronted and imperiled a clan. The Ona similarly sought revenge for murder, overt or magical; hence their object was not loot but the maximum destruction of life and property. They also resented trespass as a deliberate challenge.

In some regions motives of a different order enter. Over a wide area, from southeastern Asia through Indonesia to parts of Melanesia, men fight in order to get human heads. Often these are considered essential for the head-hunters' ceremonies; sometimes a man must capture a head before he can hope to get married. To the Bagobo of Mindanao these trophies, however, are less significant than a killing as proof of prowess. Here a man's chief aim in life is to slay at least 2 persons, for that places him at once in a social class wearing a chocolate kerchief and under the protection of 2 great spirits. An additional couple of victims entitles the brave to blood-red trousers, while a score of 6 is indicated by a full suit of that color, a mark of prominence. Such a one leads war parties and assists at annual ceremonies. It is the craving for these honors that makes men brave. But their bravery conforms to curious standards. To ambush a passing foe, to slay sleeping enemies of either sex, perfectly satisfies the native code. A man may even add to his score the murder of a faithless wife and her lover.

The Northern Plains Indians also emphasize prestige and define valor in conventional terms. Though the desire for loot and revenge played their part, the outstanding goal of these tribes was glory. To attain it a man risked his neck; on the other hand, he was normally glad to save his hide if he could score by technicalities. Thus, a deed highly esteemed throughout the area was that called "coup" by the French Canadians—a tap delivered on the enemy's body with the hand or any object held in it. But the "first coup" went not to the warrior who had shot down a foeman, but to the first tribesman who, no matter by what chance, managed to "tag" the body. A good runner was thus at an advantage and gained credit which we should deny him. Like the Bagobo, these Indians recognized badges of valor. A Dakota who was first to strike wore an eagle feather upright in the back of his hair, the second striker wore a feather with an upward slant, pointing to the right; and so on. These Plains tribes set great store by the stealing of horses. The Crow, however, did not reckon mere theft as a feat; the horse had to be cut loose from its picket in the middle of the hostile camp, one such deed far outweighing the capture of a dozen head grazing on the outskirts. While these people desired spoils, they thus subordinated economic motives to a conventional set of values.

In short, the motives of primitive warfare rather seldom coincided with those familiar to us. Revenge, religious motives, and the longing for personal prestige, generally appear as more potent.

Only the purposes of primitive warfare explain phenomena unintelligible from our point of view. The typical Plains Indian enterprise was a raid organized to gratify the ambition of a leader. He gained glory if he killed an enemy or brought back loot *without loss of a man.* Hence operations were designed to that end. There being as a rule no national aim such as the extinction of a hostile tribe, there was never a strategic sacrifice of men for bigger objectives. There were indeed daredevils and officers pledged to foolhardy conduct, but such were given a wide berth by the common run of warriors on the other side. All were eager to tag such a man but hardly to risk death in dashing against one determined to sell his life dearly. These tribes thus manifest contradictory urges. Their whole notion of social standing centered in valor. Yet the rank and file tempered their ardor with an instinct of self-preservation, trying, like most human beings, to get as much for as little effort as they could. Hence, apart from untoward surprises, even men in good standing among these eminently warlike tribes usually managed to escape with their lives, and the total of casualties was proportionately small.

Plains Indian warfare, from another angle, loomed as an exciting pastime played according to established rules, the danger lending zest to the game. The primary goal was to score, only the loss of kindred prompting reprisals on a major scale. Wherever men fight for glory, practical ends are bound to recede. There is a story of a Maori engagement with the British in which the latter suspended fighting for lack of cartridges. The Maori chief then sent word to the British commander that it was not necessary to stop since the Maori had plenty of ammunition and would send the enemies half of their own supply! If the tale is not true, it is well feigned to illustrate the unpractical chivalry possible among primitive tribes.

Organization of Fighting. Simpler tribes have a minimum of organization. Lacking chiefs, the Ona informally chose as leader a relative of the man whose death was to be avenged, stealthily approached the enemy, let fly a sudden volley of arrows, and either killed their opponents or put them to flight. Slings hurled stones when arrows were exhausted, and stubborn resistance led to hand-to-hand wrestling. Maricopa operations were more elaborate. They made surprise attacks against marauding tribes from the mountains and fought pitched battles with the Colorado River peoples. Club-bearers marched in front, archers behind. Every party, led by the one contemporary who had the proper religious dreams for leadership, was accompanied by a clairvoyant, who went into a trance to discover the position and numbers of the enemy. At least one standard-bearer took a front position and was obliged to stand his ground irrespective of danger. Even when others retreated he would recklessly dash into the thick of the fray, seize an enemy by the hair, and club him to death. Pitched battles were begun by hurling formal insults at the enemies, who were compared to women, then every one rushed against a foeman, trying to beat him down with a club. Sometimes a ruse was used in surprise attacks: a party divided into several groups, which approached from different directions, a single section decoying the enemy to a spot where he could be easily overwhelmed by the whole troop.

Since most Plains Indian fighting was an individual undertaking, the organizer was automatically the leader who recruited followers from those believing in his competence. He dispatched one or more scouts with wolf-skin emblems, they reported to him, and guided by their observations he issued orders for the attack. Such enterprises were prevented by the camp police when the tribal chief considered an expedition too dangerous, but young hotheads were likely to steal away in spite of this precaution. Much more rarely a whole band or tribe might be embroiled in a major battle. Then fighting became the concern of the chief, aided by experienced councilors. He would issue orders through a herald and assign special duties to men of noted prowess and to the several special military clubs (see below).

Such remote peoples as the Plains tribes and the Torres Straits Islanders shared the custom of a surprise attack at dawn, when sleep is reckoned deepest. Some primitives shun night attacks from fear of the dark.

The Murngin Australians, like the Maricopa, practice both surprise attacks and pitched battles. The latter, involving relatively large numbers and heavy casualties, only follow a protracted series of killings. After a formal challenge, the two sides stand some 50 feet apart and hurl short spears at each other. Though there is no leadership, ruses are sometimes employed to lure opponents where warriors whose presence they do not suspect can fall upon them. The "death-adder" maneuver consists in surrounding a camp and destroying the inmates.

Treatment of Enemies. Even the same people treated enemies differently according to circumstances. When inflamed with revenge, victors might utterly destroy a hostile camp regardless of the victims' age or sex. Most Californians killed all the men and rather slaughtered than enslaved women and children. The Ona killed men but spared children and connived at the escape of women captives; with the Ona economic system an extra wife meant only another mouth to feed. On the other hand, Plains Indians often married captive women, who could make themselves useful in skin-dressing and other industries and whose lot was a fairly easy one.

In some areas prisoners were systematically tortured. The Creek and other Indians of our Southeastern states usually stripped their captives, barbarously lashed them, and burned them to death, after which the corpses were mutilated. These tribes shared a widespread form of cannibalism: like the Bagobo of the Philippines, for instance, they ate the heart of a courageous foe in order to acquire his courage.

Head-hunting, though tinged with religious notions in Indonesia and Melanesia (p. 220), aimed elsewhere merely at getting a trophy. This held in California, where a victor decapitated a fallen foe if time allowed the operation, and brought home the head. Otherwise he contented himself with the skin from the skull extending to the eyes and nose and including the ears. But while people made merry with a scalp, a man did not earn distinction by securing one. In marked contrast, the Southeastern Indians sought above all to scalp an enemy. They took a much smaller portion than Californians, namely the skin round the top of the skull, which they stretched in a small hoop, painted red, and brought out from time to time as a reminder of their valor. No one was esteemed without at least one scalp to his credit. Northern Plains Indians also scalped extensively, but the trophy ranked below other honors (p. 221); a Crow would publicly brag of his coups, successful leadership, and picketed horses, but never of scalps. South American aborigines commonly take heads, but the Chaco is the one main center for scalping. These scalps are hung up outdoors in honor of the victor and play a part at festive carousals, for which occasions villages without trophies borrow their neighbors'.

While many primitive customs revolt us, the psychology underlying them is sometimes less shocking than appears at first blush. As noted above, cannibalism may be nothing more than a naïve magical rite, and head-hunting is sometimes considered essential for ceremony, i.e. for the good of one's tribe. The Marquesas Islanders ate human flesh to enhance the spiritual power of their own tribe and to destroy that of the enemy. Human sacrifice is thus practiced as a rule not from sheer ferocity but to conciliate deities. When a Maori priest ate the heart of the first foe slain in battle, it was really the gods who were supposed to partake of it through their servant.

Defense Mechanisms. As noted previously (p. 103), the Maori sometimes palisaded their villages, a practice common among sedentary aborigines, such as the Iroquois and other Indians near the Atlantic. The Hopi sought safety from marauding neighbors by building on steep eminences. While the Maricopa used neither of these devices, they did post sentries when suspecting forays. Boundary guards were stationed in central California and Ceylon to prevent trespass. Samoans often protected their settlements with stone walls, and to impede approach set sharp stakes at strategic points so as to pierce the feet of would-be attackers. This latter was also a Bagobo trick; naturally the knife-like bamboos put up to confound enemies had to be carefully picked up before giving pursuit to a retreating foe.

Training. Training was generally informal among the simpler peoples. Nevertheless, here and there certain agencies definitely promoted military efficiency. The Masai of East Africa have virtually a standing army composed of the bachelors of the settlement. The initiated but as yet unmarried men live in a camp of their own and are responsible for military operations, looting the cattle of nearby peasant tribes, and slaughtering their owners. Spies, recruited from a subject tribe dwelling among the Masai, aid them in planning raids. Each company of bachelors has a spokesman with a club for badge of authority, several officers called "Bulls" wear bracelets or bells in token of their bravery, and still others rank as "benefactors" because they generously slaughter cattle to feast their mates.

The Plains Indians had a system of societies which included every adult man and was copied by the boys in play. These organizations also had other than military functions; they were social clubs, with distinctive dances and regalia, policed the camp, and sometimes performed religious ceremonies. But above all they fostered the military spirit. Among the Crow two clubs, the Foxes and Lumpwoods, were rivals, each striving to precede in striking the first enemy during a particular season. Certain officers bearing lances as emblems, like the Maricopa standard-bearers, were pledged to die rather than retreat. In the Dakota "No-flight" society all members were required to fall or stand together. This tribe also had intense competition between different organizations. Each tried to be first in killing an enemy, and returning members of rival bodies would assemble to boast of their respective deeds, each eager to outdo and shame the other.

Among firmly governed peoples a real army became possible. About the beginning of the Nineteenth Century, Chaka made the Zulu, then a petty tribe, the greatest South African power by improving both native military tactics and military organization. Until his time these Negroes had hurled reed javelins from a distance. He substituted thrusting-spears and made his troops advance in solid formation, which completely upset his enemies. Apart from these innovations in tactics, Chaka built up a standing army, huge for aboriginal conditions. It was partly recruited from conquered tribes, their boys entering on terms of equality with the Zulu, while adult captives were killed. Those who distinguished themselves had their heads shaved as the sign of manhood. In this way possibly 15,000 warriors were organized, each regiment of 600 to 1,000 occupying a separate camp for barracks. The king supported these soldiers, liberally supplied them with cattle, and allowed them a share in the booty. This freedom from work and the social prestige of warriors attracted volunteers, notwithstanding the iron discipline. Chaka allowed no soldier to marry without special permission, exacted absolute obedience, and executed hundreds of soldiers for real or supposed cowardice in order to impress his men with the duty of bravery.

War Ritual. As already intimated, primitive peoples did not treat fighting as a mere practical matter, but made it into a strict ritual. A Plains Indian war party followed a fixed procedure at every stage. Returning scouts had to signal from afar according to an established code and reported only after first kicking over a pile of buffalo droppings put up by their waiting fellows. Nor did the party as a whole directly enter the camp when they got back. If they had suffered losses a messenger would signal the extent of the casualties from afar. If they had killed an enemy, all braves blackened their faces as a sign of victory and organized a parade through camp. To such features must be added strictly religious elements. No Crow dared recruit followers without the sanction of a vision in which a spirit had precisely explained where and when he was to strike and with what results. The leader always carried his sacred bundle and every warrior if possible brought some equivalent. The very shields were considered helpful as much because of the revelation which had authorized them as because of their tough buffalo hide. The Maricopa were led and counseled by dreamers to whom success had been promised in their dreams. Before an expedition the entire settlement joined in ceremonial songs and dancing, and a person with special dreams sped the warriors with four set speeches. Further, the Maricopa looked upon contact with the enemy as a defiling source of disease, hence every member of a returning party had to undergo a 16-day purification, during which he ate sparingly and was made to vomit. Scalpers had to wash their trophies every morning to purge them of their dangerous character. After the period of purification the tribal scalp keeper mounted a scalp on a pole, old women danced around it during the daytime, and at night old men joined them in chanting. Finally, the scalps were turned over to the official custodian. This intense feeling of pollution was shared by other Arizona tribes and made it hard to use them as scouts in the United States Army since they insisted on a period of ceremonial retirement after every killing. Similar ideas held sway in Polynesia: homecoming Marquesan warriors had to live apart from others for 10 days for they were both exposed to danger themselves and a source of peril to others.

Peace-making was also often a matter of elaborate ritual. In Australia an injured Murngin group invites the enemy to assemble with them. Both companies appear in ceremonial paint and stand at a safe distance from each other, then the hosts dance over to their guests and informally walk back. The opposite side respond in the same way. The men accused of instigating the murder that caused the late unpleasantness then run in a zigzag across the middle of the field. Every member of the aggrieved clan hurls a headless spear at these miscreants, and those feeling most intensely throw several spears while their fellows roundly curse the enemy. To this there must be no reply lest peace be again jeopardized. Next the actual murderers must run the gauntlet in the same way, except that they are exposed to spears with stone heads. However, the old men of both groups walk about as moderators, cautioning the throwers against actually hurting their targets and the other side against answering their revilers. Finally, one of the hosts thrusts his spear through the thighs of the murderers. This signifies atonement for the injury, removes fear of further trouble, and is followed by a joint dance to express the harmonious relationship of the former combatants. But a *slight* wound suggests a mental reservation, hence only a truce, while a mere scratch serves as a direct notice of vengeance to come. Even apart from this contingency the peace negotiations may easily merge into another battle if one of the participants gets excited. In any case, however, there is a standard technique for closing hostilities.

Influences of War. Notwithstanding its atrocities, war must be recognized as achieving certain positive results. It creates the same type of organization as a communal hunt—in other words, fosters subordination to a common goal and stimulates such qualities as bravery and loyalty. Its practice is so deeply anchored that it can not be uprooted without throwing the entire structure of a warlike society into chaos. Murngin men of standing acquire as many wives as they can, with the result that young men are obliged to remain single. Unless a relatively large portion of the younger men were killed off, as they are, in the interminable feuds, polygyny could not be maintained. This may seem a desirable result; but since Murngin society rests on the institution, it would suffer in strength if suddenly deprived of this prop. Again, in Plains or Southeastern Indian societies war was the be-all and end-all of masculine life. To weed it out would have meant destroying what to the natives were the most powerful goads to heroic effort. Thus, eliminating war in war-minded societies can be successful only by substituting what William James called some "moral equivalent".

XIII

MARRIAGE AND THE FAMILY

General Biological and Social Aspects

The Sex Instinct. Man shares with other animals the sexual urge, but differs in discriminating between proper, less proper, and improper relations resting on it. Human societies thus treat the intercourse of the sexes not as an individual or biological, but also as a social or ethical, matter. Every community regards as superior a relatively permanent bond between permissible mates, and this is marriage; on the other hand, it condemns other forms of relationship as vicious. In between lie various degrees of approval and objection. The ideal type can not always be realized: weaklings fall short of ethical standards, outlaws actively defy them.

Promiscuity in the scientific sense is not mere looseness but a hypothetical condition in which society is indifferent as to the mating habits of its members. If prohibited degrees were lacking so that parents might mate with children, there would be promiscuity. Such license, however, occurs nowhere, and there is no evidence of its former existence on the human level. Societies differ in the restrictions they impose, but all of them somehow limit choice of mates.

Status and Individuality. Modern civilized societies notably differ from primitive man's in their attitude toward the individual. In the last generation or two, Western civilization has stressed the rights of the individual. Earlier periods and primitive communities never ignored individuality, but they subordinated it to social status. A person was treated not as a being with such and such natural gifts, but as a member of a class, sex, or family. This attitude affected marriage arrangements until the most recent times. Just as a European prince marries for reasons of state, so every one was expected to marry less from personal inclination than in the interests of his family. This was not unreasonable in the circumstances. Sex life is biologically indicated long before there is maturity of judgment; specifically, the primitive girl was normally married at puberty, possibly at thirteen or fourteen. It was thus not cruel for elders to direct her choice in the light of what seemed best for her kin as a whole. Moreover, life was often such that parents had to consider the desirability of a child-in-law from their point of view. This included such personal traits as bravery, skill as a hunter or skin-dresser, but also very decidedly his or her social connections.

Determination of Mates

Incest Feelings. Almost all societies recoil from the idea of parents mating with their offspring, and brothers with their sisters. The latter kind of union was favored for Peruvian and Hawaiian royalty because their rulers could find no other mate of equal rank, but these are most exceptional instances. Such exceptions, however, like the breach of these rules by hardened sinners in modern civilization, suggest that the horror of incest is not inborn, though it is doubtless a very ancient cultural feature.

Beyond the closest kin the circle of prohibited relatives varies greatly. Many peoples actually prefer marriages of certain kinsfolk; while others, like the Maricopa, guard against any such unions. The Blackfoot and Ona went so far as to discountenance marriage within one's band lest otherwise some remote blood tie might be overlooked. The rule forcing a person to marry outside of his group is called "exogamy". It may apply either to one's local unit, or to one's kin; but often local exogamy, as in the cases cited, rests at bottom on kinship exogamy. The incest horror may, however, be extended very widely. Some peoples assume a bond between persons of the same clan (p. 254) even when no blood relationship exists; Australians will not mate with members of similarly named clans living a hundred miles away; and the Chinese forbid marriage between individuals of the same surname.

Endogamy. The reverse of exogamy is endogamy, the rule that persons must marry *within* their own class. Peruvian and Hawaiian incest rested on this principle, a person of lofty rank requiring a peer for a spouse. Elsewhere endogamy did not require such close interbreeding. European princes married princesses, often cousins but not closer kinswomen. In India the caste system involved strict endogamy, and the Masai blacksmiths (p. 107) also illustrate an endogamous occupational class. Those of our states which prohibit marriages of whites and Negroes legalize racial endogamy.

Preferential Mating. Many primitive societies are not content with general rules as to the group outside or within which individuals must marry, but particularize what persons should be married. In Australia all individuals with whom one has social intercourse at all are classed and treated as relatives. Brothers and sisters being excluded, first cousins are thus the nearest marriageable kin in one's own generation. Actually, Australian tribes fall into two categories: those prescribing marriage with a first cousin, and those which bar such marriages, allowing them only with more remote cousins.

However, Australians and the majority of primitive peoples do not group together all first cousins but generally divide them into two classes; and this distinction goes with a corresponding one as to uncles and aunts. Not recognizing these distinctions, we have no current words for them and special terms have been coined by anthropologists to express the native ideas. The father's brother is called a "parallel" uncle, the mother's sister

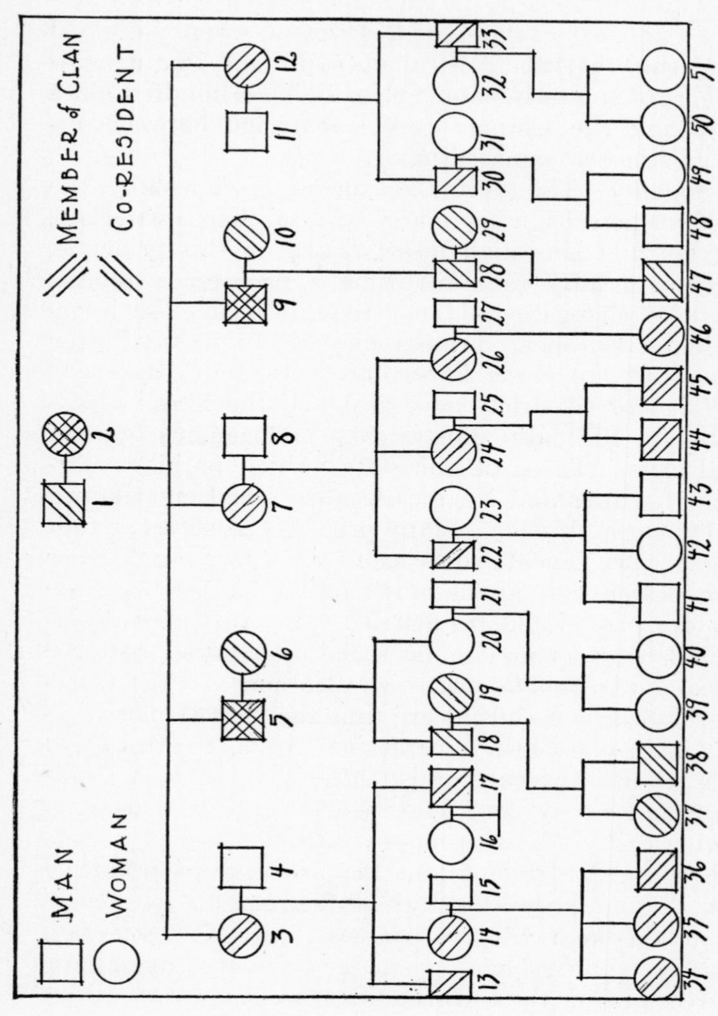

Plate 35: Matrilineal Descent and Matrilocal Residence.

The descendants for three generations from a married couple, the third generation being still in its childhood. Showing (a) the clan members and (b) the co-residents.

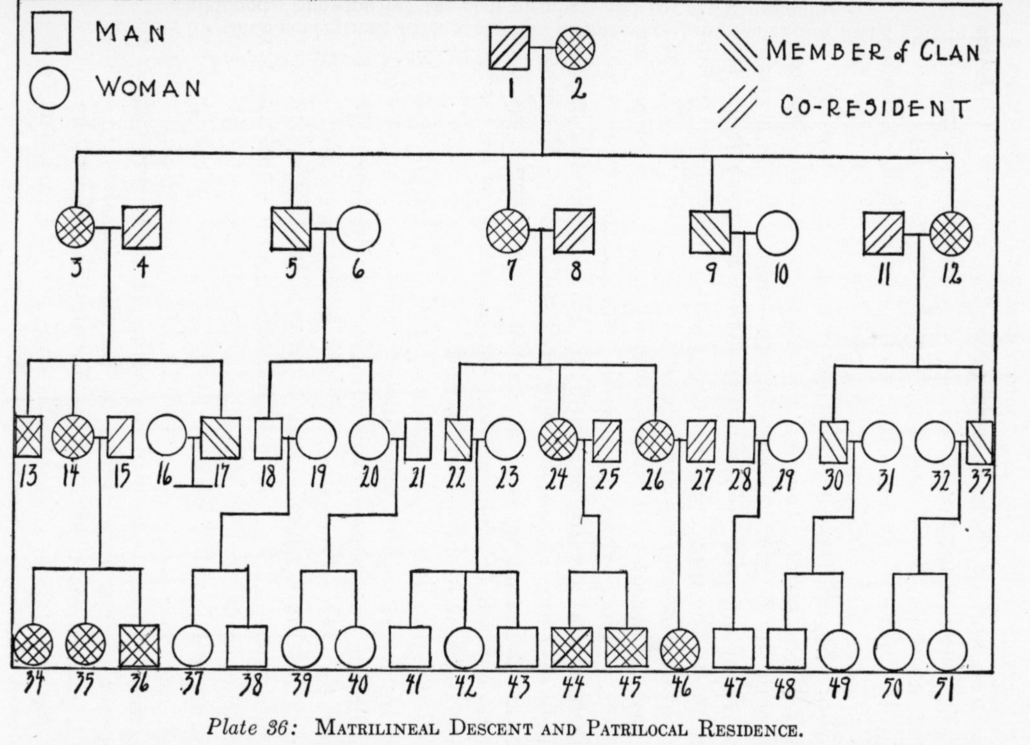

Plate 36: Matrilineal Descent and Patrilocal Residence.

The descendants for three generations from a married couple, the third generation being still in its childhood. Showing (a) the clan members and (b) the co-residents.

a "parallel" aunt; the mother's brother is a "cross"-uncle, the father's sister a "cross"-aunt. In Plate *35*, individuals *3* and *12* are parallel aunts of each other's children and of their sister's (No. *7's*) children. Thus, *3* is parallel aunt to *22, 24, 26, 30,* and *33;* and she is cross-aunt to *18, 20,* and *28*. Her brothers, *5* and *9,* are parallel uncles to each other's children and cross-uncles to their sisters' children. "Parallel" here means that the sex of the relative in question, e.g. father's brother, is that of the parent through whom he becomes a relative, namely the father. "Cross" means that there is a crossing from one sex to the other when we pass from the parent to the uncle or aunt considered. Obviously parallel and cross-uncles are equally close relatives, yet an amazing number of tribes regard parallel kindred as closer. They thus frequently call a paternal uncle "father" and a maternal aunt "mother", reserving special uncle and aunt terms for the cross-relatives. Naturally these uncles addressed as father called their parallel nephews "sons", their cross-nephews or nieces by a separate nephew or niece term; and similarly for aunts.

Corresponding to this grouping, the children of parallel uncles or aunts are called "brothers" and "sisters", while the children of cross-relatives of the uncle generation are "cross"-cousins. These latter, accordingly, include father's sister's and mother's brother's children, while father's brother's and mother's sister's children are parallel cousins. In Plate *35,* individuals *13, 14,* and *17* are all parallel cousins of *22, 24,* and *26;* and they are cross-cousins of *18* and *20*. The Arabs prefer a man to marry the daughter of his paternal uncle, but very few peoples favor any union of parallel cousins. On the other hand, Australians and Melanesians, as well as some American, Asiatic, and African peoples regard cross cousin marriage as eminently fit.

Here further differences appear. Some tribes have no preference as between letting a man take his mother's brother's or his father's sister's daughter. This type is called "symmetrical" cross-cousin marriage. But the Murngin of Australia and the Miwok of California insist that a man may marry only the daughter of his maternal uncle, not of the paternal aunt; and in the Trobriand Islands, New Guinea, there is precisely the reverse rule. These, then, are forms of "asymmetrical" cross-cousin marriage.

In typical cases the aim is to marry an actual first cousin of the preferred kind. But obviously this may be impossible because a young man's mother has no brother or because the maternal uncle has only sons. Hence the natives permit substitutions. A "sibling" in biological nomenclature is a brother *or* a sister. As explained, parallel cousins are commonly called "brothers" or "sisters". Now it is a widespread principle to treat two such siblings of the same sex as socially equivalent, and since a parallel male cousin is considered a kind of brother he may take the place of a real brother. In other words, a young man is allowed to marry his mother's male parallel cousin's daughter if she has no brother. Similarly, if the maternal uncle or his equivalent has no daughter, a niece whom either of them *calls* "daughter" may take her place.

Even much more widely distributed than the cross-cousin marriage are two institutions known as the levirate (Latin *levir,* brother-in-law) and the sororate (Latin *soror,* sister), both providing for the remarriage of widowed persons. The levirate is the practice of a man's marrying his brother's—usually his older brother's—widow. It is a right but also an obligation: a North Siberian woman may be too old to fulfil wifely duties, yet her brother-in-law is obligated to provide for her after her husband's decease. On the other hand, in many societies young men find it difficult to get a wife. In Australia seniority gives a man higher status and he acquires as many spouses as he can; in Africa there is usually a bride-price, which a youngster can not readily get together. In such conditions a young man is only too glad to obtain a wife by inheritance. The sororate is a similar replacing of a dead wife by her younger sister.

To both institutions may be applied the rule of substitutions explained for cross-cousin marriage. Lacking a brother, a deceased man's parallel cousin or even more remote kinsman is allowed to step into his place; similarly, the sororate may involve marriage of the widower with his wife's cousin. Further, both institutions illustrate the importance of status (p. 231). Marriage being a bond between two *families,* the tie is not allowed to snap with the death of an individual partner; instead a substitute is forthcoming from the same social unit so that the alliance persists. Another way of strengthening the union of two groups is to allow a man to marry two or more sisters or cousins at the same time. In many Indian tribes a man established something of a lien on his first wife's younger sisters or kinswomen, and he would consummate marriage with them as soon as they reached maturity This custom is known as "sororal polygyny" (see p. 244).

In some tribes the substitute for a dead spouse, or an additional wife, may belong either to a younger or older generation than the predecessor. The Omaha practice sororal polygyny, but also marriage with the wife's paternal aunt or with her cross-niece, namely, her brother's daughter. Thus, a man might marry into three generations: his own, the one above, and the one below. In the Banks Islands, Melanesia, and in northwestern British Columbia a young man inherited the wife of his maternal uncle. In many Negro tribes there is "filial inheritance", a son inheriting his father's wives with the exception of his own mother, a custom also reported for the Indians of the Orinoco and for the medieval Mongols.

Preferential marriages with younger or older persons are not limited to cases of inheritance. In various tribes of the tropical South American forest area and coastal Brazil a man claimed his sister's daughter as a wife. The Tlingit of southern Alaska and the Trobriand Islanders off the coast of New Guinea favored marriage with a paternal aunt, her daughter—a cross-cousin—being reckoned a substitute if no aunt was available. In addition, Tlingit men often married their elder brother's daughters.

As this last instance suggests, the same tribe may regard several forms of marriage as orthodox, even though one may be preëminently so. The Tamanak, an extinct tribe of the Orinoco region, practiced the levirate, filial widow-inheritance, the sororate, cross-cousin marriage, as well as marriage with one's sister's daughter and wife's parallel niece (her sister's daughter).

Methods of Acquiring a Wife

Primitive tribes rarely consecrate marriage by religious ritual, but secular formalities are common. A Maricopa bride was supposed to be adept at supplying water, at cooking and grinding corn; unless she passed a formal test in these accomplishments, the groom's family rejected her. In view of the useful work done by a young woman for her household, it was natural not to surrender her gratis. In some tribes, such as the Maricopa, to be sure, parents demanded nothing in return; and often the bride's and the groom's kin merely exchanged gifts of about equal value to add dignity to the transaction. But compensation was very common, taking the form of exchange, service, or purchase. This practice contrasts with the dowry accompanying the wife of middle or upper-class European society. Since she was not a breadwinner but an economic burden, her husband naturally required assistance in order to support her "in the style to which she was accustomed".

Exchange. The simplest way of arranging marriage without loss on either side was to exchange girls. That is, two families with a son and a daughter in each would allow the young men to marry the girls. This was a favorite method in Australia and Melanesia, but it had its limitations. Obviously, the ratio of male and female children would not permit all unions to be of this type. Further, the preferential marriage forms might or might not harmonize with exchange. Where cross-cousin marriage was symmetrical, a man's sister was given to his wife's brother in return for the latter's sister. But with the Murngin this is barred, for a man may marry only his maternal uncle's daughter, not his father's sister's daughter; and since that is the relationship in which a groom's sister stands to his brother-in-law there can not be an exchange.

Service. Service for a bride looms large in the Old Testament as an ancient Hebrew custom. It appears fairly often among recent primitives. Naturally it implies that the groom must reside with or near his connections by marriage. The service may be temporary, possibly for a year's time, or permanent. The Tamanak and other South American Indians developed this custom in typical fashion. A son-in-law brought his hammock and other possessions to his wife's parents' home and stayed there, fishing, hunting, felling trees, and generally acting as their servant. This institution is connected with an uncle's claim to his sister's daughter (see above). When the man serving for his wife in her family's settlement gives his daughter to her maternal uncle, he is relieved of part of his chores; on the other hand, his brother-in-law gets a wife without having to render any service at all. This illustrates primitive reciprocity. It also shows how apparently diverse social practices may be interwoven, and how a deeply rooted institution such as wife-service may be abrogated in particular cases without overthrowing the system.

Purchase. Bride-purchase is never degrading to the girl. The Crow and Dakota consider it the most honorable form of marriage. A man pays only for a competent bride of good character, and unions of this sort are regarded as more stable than mere love-matches. In northern California liberal payment for a bride enhanced the prestige of every one concerned; a person's standing varied with the amount offered for his mother; and the children of a man obliged to serve for his wife were at the bottom of society. Purchase was highly developed in Africa, where chiefs and wealthy men quite commonly bought 6 wives and more, whence the dearth of women for others. Consequently, the levirate and filial widow-inheritance were a boon to the young and poor; and some sought illicit relations with the wives of older tribesmen. Full payment for a wife generally entitled the Negro husband not only to her person and services but to all her offspring, whether begotten by the lawful husband or not. Purchase generally implies the right to take the wife to one's home or settlement. But even in Africa it does not degrade women to the status of a chattel that might be sold to another man at will.

Unorthodox Means. In all societies individuals will depart from ideal sex standards. Some of these deviations are strongly condemned, and here and there even punished with death; others are condoned, or the unions may become permanent, finally to be recognized as marriages rather than mere escapades. Crow lovers who eloped without formality might arouse criticism at first, but after a while their irregularity would not be resented, though their union would not rank with one based on purchase. Among the Murngin, runaway matches and other irregular arrangements cause no end of trouble and are heartily disapproved at first, but may be ultimately accepted if the lovers keep outside the prohibited degrees of kinship.

Residence

The residence of a newly married couple has important consequences for the position of both sexes and for the social relations of their children. Two contradictory types are recognized: residence is matrilocal if the groom settles with his wife's kin; patrilocal, if the bride goes to the husband's family. However, these are not the only forms. Some primitive tribes, like ourselves, practice neither, a couple starting an independent household. Frequently, too, the husband settles with his wife only temporarily and then sets up an establishment of his own. Moreover, moving to a spouse's dwelling in the same community is one thing; being taken to a different settlement, quite another. Finally, some tribes may favor either arrangement, yet depart from it in special conditions.

Matrilocal Residence. Matrilocal residence has already been described in correlation with South American bride-service. Some of the tribes of the tropical forest zone make the arrangement permanent, others limit it to a one-year period, several allow chiefs' sons to take their wives to their own settlement. On the coast of Brazil a young man of prominent family began matrimony like ordinary folk, but lavish gifts to his parents-in-law released the husband from further obligations and he was finally allowed to move to his own home. Among the Hopi the women own the houses, and residence is strictly matrilocal. In consequence, a typical household embraces an old woman (*Pl. 35, No. 2*), her husband (*1*), her daughters (*3, 7, 12*) with their husbands (*4, 8, 11*) her unmarried sons, her daughters' daughters (*14, 24, 26*) with their husbands (*15, 25, 27*), and her daughters' sons (*13*) so long as they remain single.

A matrilocal arrangement places the husband among his wife's relatives and inevitably limits his authority. He is less likely to abuse his wife, and the children owe obedience first of all to the masters of the home, their maternal grandparents and mother's brothers. This applies especially when the husband moves to the village of his parents-in-law, where his own kin are not near enough to maintain the balance of power. Then his children are also bound to develop more intimate sentimental ties with their maternal than with equally close paternal relatives.

Patrilocal Residence. Where patrilocal residence is consistently followed along with local exogamy, the results are the direct reverse of the matrilocal case. Australian tribes are patrilocal in this sense, so that a particular territory is always inhabited by an old man (*Pl. 36, No. 1*), his wives (*No. 2*), his sons (*5, 9*) with their wives (*6, 10*), his sons' sons (*18, 28*) and their wives (*19, 29*), and his sons' daughters as yet unmarried. The men thus play a dominant rôle in an area which demands detailed knowledge of a district if its inhabitants are to survive. The women, coming from other regions, are ignorant of these details, so that the men with their geographical information must direct their wives' search of vegetable food. Here the woman is wrested from her kin and familiar surroundings and is correspondingly at a disadvantage.

Number of Mates

The number of male and female births is approximately the same in every human group. That is, the ratio rarely exceeds 100:110 in favor of either sex. This indicates monogamy as a natural condition. However, the natural ratio can be disturbed. If many young men are killed in fighting, as among the Murngin and the Plains Indians, the women of marriageable age will predominate. If, on the other hand, the hardships of life or superstition should cause men to kill a percentage of girl infants, marriageable youths will exceed young women. In both cases polygamy—plural marriage—becomes possible; if adult men are outnumbered, there will be polygyny—two or more wives to a husband; the reverse leads to polyandry—two or more husbands to a wife.

Monogamy. Monogamy is the rule of some primitive tribes. The Hopi insist upon it, so do various Pygmy groups. More frequently it is not compulsory but actually prevalent. Among early Greenlanders there was no taboo against plural wives, but only one Eskimo in twenty had as many as two wives. Similarly the Ona mostly contented themselves with a single woman, and though preëminent men might have several, more than two aroused unfavorable comment.

Polygyny. Polygyny depends not only on the ratio of adult men and women but also on economic and social factors. An Ona man has difficulty in supporting more than one wife since he is the food provider. Mohammedans have religious sanction for four wives, but very few Kirghiz are able to pay for more than one. On the other hand, when the women farm, as often happens in Africa, every additional wife adds to the larder. In Africa, moreover, absolute monarchs take an unlimited number of women by royal prerogative, and wealthy stock-breeders can buy many wives. While neither of these conditions holds in Australia, the old men are masters there and to the detriment of their juniors arrogate to themselves more than their normal share of women.

Polygyny is neither primarily due to masculine lust nor is it considered degrading for women. Primitive men have opportunity for sex relations outside of matrimony and without its duties. They may marry additional wives in order to provide for a kinsman's widow, because more wives add to their social standing, or because of their actual economic value. It is often the first wife who demands that her husband get another mate to assist her and reproaches him for stinginess if he fails to buy her what is virtually a lady's maid, for usually the first wife remains the principal one. This naturally limits the jealousy that might otherwise be felt. In general, the several wives of a primitive family get along with surprising harmony, especially when there is sororal polygyny.

Polyandry. As an established institution polyandry is very rare. It is true that many primitive tribes permit a wife to consort with more than one man. This simply means plural sex relations, not plural marriage. Thus, an Eskimo may oblige a visitor by surrendering his wife temporarily, and a man coming from one Masai settlement to another expects to be similarly treated by a member of his own age-grade. Again, with the levirate fully established, a younger brother unable to secure a wife may anticipate his rights in Australia. In Polynesia the Marquesas Islanders not only permitted brothers access to their wives, but extended the privilege to male assistant workers. None of these customs constitutes polyandry because marriage implies not mere sexual intercourse but a fixed bond with mutual duties. In the cases cited the temporary mates were under no such obligations, nor did society consider the men husbands. The true husband might for a time yield his privileges, but maintained his status, and other men enjoyed them by his consent or by stealth at their peril.

In Tibet and among the Toda of southern India, however, a woman is legally espoused by two or more men. The Toda situation, which is best known, becomes possible from the native practice of killing off a number of female infants. In some cases several brothers jointly live with a woman, all being socially on a par both as husbands and as fathers of all her offspring. When the husbands are unrelated to one another, they may live in different villages, and the woman usually spends a month with each in turn. They enjoy equal marital rights, but the official status of "father" to the children is established by a ritual. By agreement one husband performs it, thereby becoming legal parent of all the woman's children born before one of the other men goes through the same ceremony. This means that certain children are heirs of one man, others of another, not because they are begotten by him but by a purely arbitrary criterion. The rule illustrates the absence of a paternal instinct. Given the circumstances, husbands can not be sure as to paternity and are not interested in it; they disregard the concept of father as procreator and substitute the concept of a *legal* father.

Group Marriage. Marriage being a permanent bond with fixed mutual rights and obligations, there is no such thing as group *marriage* anywhere. Temporary looseness, no matter on what scale, is not to be confused with group marriage, a purely hypothetical condition. For example, the Masai warriors (p. 226) live together with the girls of the settlement. This involves no further obligation and is carefully distinguished from the fixed marriage relationship after the warrior leaves the bachelors and settles down with his wife.

The Family

The family is the social unit based on marriage. It includes the parents and their children. These terms, however, as the Toda example teaches, must be understood in a social, not a biological, sense. When a younger man inherits his brother's widow he becomes legally the children's father and is usually so designated by them. On the other hand, a child may be adopted, as often happens in Oceania, and thereafter be treated exactly as an own child. In some of the islands of this region adopted children divide their time between two homes so that their social relationship can not be precisely determined. In such instances, then, it would be difficult to define a family group. Apart from these highly exceptional instances, the unit formed by parents and children is universal.

Family relations thus imply those between husband and wife; between parents and children; between siblings of the same and opposite sex. Those between the several wives and several husbands in polygynous and polyandrous communities, respectively, have already been discussed.

Husband and Wife. The bond between spouses emphatically differs from that of lovers in implying mutual obligations apart from sex life. Largely they rest on the division of labor: an Australian wife gathers roots, while her husband hunts and fishes; a Bantu woman in Uganda raises bananas, her husband provides her with bark cloth; a Maricopa man planted corn, hunted, wove cloth, his wife did the harvesting and grinding, picked wild mesquite beans, prepared the cotton, and shaped pottery. This arrangement generally imposes no undue burden on either sex. Generally speaking, women are more continuously employed, while men's work is more strenuous while it lasts.

As a rule women own what they produce and freely dispose of their manufactures, while a husband has no right to give away or sell his wife's property. On the other hand, the kind of property a woman holds may be limited by convention. Among southern Siberian nomads only men are allowed to control the live-stock. However, in certain regions women enjoy remarkable property rights: a Pueblo house invariably belongs to the woman, so that a divorced husband is simply banished from the home and has to seek shelter with his mother or sister.

Fidelity is an important factor in the treatment of primitive women. Many societies permit maltreatment of an unfaithful wife. Beating is common, a Blackfoot might cut off her nose, and an Australian would sometimes kill her with impunity. A woman—especially in Africa—was expected to produce offspring, failing which her purchaser considered himself cheated. He might abuse and divorce her, or demand a substitute from her kin. Superstitions also affect woman's position. While twins are reckoned auspicious by some tribes, others regard them as a source of danger and do away with at least one of the infants. An East African tribe looks with horror upon a mother who has given birth to twins.

Disloyalty, barrenness, twin births may thus cause harshness and even cruelty. But apart from social standards the intimate relationship of marriage is largely shaped by the individual temperament and character of the partners. An Australian attached to an erring wife will condone repeated offences; and henpecked husbands exist among Mohammedans and Chinese even though their philosophy teaches the inferiority of woman. In all human societies, regardless of theories, prolonged association and joint interest in the children foster a strong mutual bond with affection. Under favorable circumstances there is self-sacrifice and romantic devotion even among Australians.

To what extent husband and wife become spiritual mates depends on the conventions of a society. In Australia woman is excluded from much of the sacred ritual that occupies masculine minds; in parts of Melanesia the men sleep, work, and eat apart in their club house. Some of the most civilized countries have standardized a similar division of the sexes; the ancient Greeks and modern Latin nations have restricted woman's sphere to the hearth in contrast to modern Anglo-Saxon and Scandinavian trends. Participation in vital concerns of the tribe is nevertheless often granted to women. Plains Indians often expect wives and husbands to coöperate in ritual; the Iroquois allowed women to nominate and impeach chiefs; among the Khasi of Assam there are high-priestesses and women chiefs; in the Philippines the spirit world is generally approached by female mediums, and this holds also for northern California.

It is thus hard to generalize as to woman's position in the home and society. To Americans or Swedes, a Spanish or French girl seems hemmed in by inhibitions of which she herself is rarely aware. Similarly, restrictions, odd to us, on primitive women are not resented by them and are not felt as impediments to a healthy conjugal life. By and large, throughout the world the majority of women lead lives that are not unduly hard compared to man's, and social restrictions rarely, if ever, preclude sentimental relations of husband and wife.

Marriage, being usually a purely secular affair, is readily dissolved by simpler peoples. Since cumbrous legal machinery is lacking, the greater frequency of divorce as compared with civilized countries is not surprising. Further, personal inclination will assert itself; and a boy who is a mere puppet in his elders' hands at fourteen will have ideas of his own about a mate when he has once made his mark. Considering all the circumstances favoring divorce, it is remarkable how many primitive couples remain together for long periods. Among the Murngin, for instance, lifelong marriage is not at all abnormal.

Parents and Children. Love of adults for children is a universal human trait. It is not limited to one's own physiological offspring, which, as in the Toda case, can not always be known. In South Africa the purchaser of a woman becomes legal father of all her offspring and insists on claiming them even when he knows they were begotten by a lover. The craving for children leads to divorce of a sterile wife and prompts adoption. This has also other sources. Marquesas Islanders underwent an adoption ritual from the same motive that commonly underlies primitive marriage arrangements—the cementing of friendship between two families. They also felt safer about the fate of their souls after death if there were more children to make offerings on their behalf.

Almost uniformly, primitives treat children with great indulgence. Corporal punishment is inconceivable to many peoples and strikes them as fiendish brutality. Education is partly by example, partly by precept. Lengthy formal speeches to boys and girls were frequent among American and African tribes. Maricopa and Plains Indian fathers admonished their boys to be brave in battle and decried the evils of old age, saying it was a good thing to die young. In order to promote fortitude, youngsters were occasionally subjected to severe tests: Maricopa elders pinched and beat boys or thrust them into ant hills and bees' nests. Australian girls learn from their mothers how to collect vegetable food, build huts, and make nets.

However, outside agencies often supplement the education by parents. An Australian boy of about 7 years is likely to join the bachelors' camp, thus coming mainly under the influence of older lads. In Melanesia the club house of the Banks Islands not only separated husbands from wives, but sons from both parents; for the dormitory was divided into graded compartments, and the boy would normally occupy a lower grade than his father. Southern Nigerian tribes are split into age-classes, sometimes starting at 4 to 7 years of age, and these are virtually clubs disciplining their memberships. Each class has its special tasks: one will look after the roads, another fell trees, and so forth. The boys' military societies among the Plains tribes have already been noted (p. 163).

Conspicuous in the child's development are puberty rituals, which may be roughly compared to confirmation. Some of them belong rather to magic and religion (p. 317), but an educational aspect is common. Thus, in West Africa the adolescents of each sex are secluded under strict supervision for months and get training in the arts of life, as well as sex instruction. In Australia the ceremonial of girls is relatively trivial, while the boys' initiation occupies months, involving instruction in the sacred lore and vocational activities, as well as the severe trial of circumcision or other disfigurements (p. 318). Not all puberty rituals sever the ties between parent and child. Sometimes they even stress the bond, as when a Dakota father honors a beloved daughter by such a performance, at the same time advertising that she is now marriageable. Educational training of the same type may, of course, be imparted whether or not the ceremony is directed by the parents. The point is that societies frequently separate boys or girls, or both, at or before puberty and to that extent automatically limit the influence of the parents. The bond persists but it is modified.

The deep love felt by primitive parents for their children, real and adopted, is not disproved by the occasional exposure and killing of infants. Apart from unnatural individuals, who may occur in every grade of culture, not cruelty but superstition is likely to be the cause, as in the case of twins (p. 247). Another reason is grim necessity. Eskimo and Murngin have been known to kill newborn infants simply because there was no one to suckle them; either the mother had died or she had no milk for the new addition to the family.

Where it is in vogue the rigid separation of the sexes naturally affects the relations of parents and children as it does that of husband and wife. But here, too, it fails to abolish the sense of kinship. A Murngin mother is separated from her boy when he is circumcised, but she is keenly interested in his social advancement, celebrates his first kangaroo killing, and offers gifts to the man who paints him for his initiation ceremony.

In certain societies the tie between father and child is seriously affected by the part assigned to the maternal uncle. As noted, a husband taking up his abode in his wife's settlement is in a peculiar position, and his wife's brothers may control his children and influence them more than he himself. A preponderant position of the mother's brother may occur even without matrilocal residence and is termed "avunculate" (Latin *avunculus,* maternal uncle). Among the Hopi a maternal uncle gives religious instruction to his sister's sons, and his priestly office is inherited by them rather than by his own sons. In some parts of Melanesia a man is similarly obliged to pass on his magical lore to his sister's son. Such conditions certainly alter the legal relationship of a father to his children, real or adopted; but they do not diminish the sentimental attachment nor do they imply ignoring the father. Frequently the same tribes that stress avuncular privileges give equal weight to another relative, the paternal aunt, who often plays so important a part that we can speak of an "amitate" (Latin, *amita,* father's sister) balancing the avunculate. What is more, in the very tribes of British Columbia and Melanesia where the mother's brother seems supreme, a father is constantly found striving to benefit his son, even circumventing his legal obligations to his cross-nephew.

Thus, other social factors may and do modify the nature and scope of the parent-child tie, but they can not abolish it because it is rooted in the universal family unit.

Siblings. Siblings, if of the same sex, may generally take one another's place, as exemplified by the levirate and sororate. The most general feature of the sibling relationship is that of mutual helpfulness, which lapses only where an intense lust for wealth or power sets brother against brother, as happens among African and European pretenders to the throne. A Murngin man who claims ceremonial rights is aided by his next older brother and confers with him. Brothers coöperate in making a canoe and all of them, whether so employed or not, have an interest in its disposal to aliens; a spear or club may belong preëminently to one individual, but his brothers would be allowed to use it and have a secondary claim to it. Similarly, sisters are companions and help each other; an older sister may teach and discipline a younger one. Many tribes contend in favor of sororal polygyny that a man's wives are not likely to quarrel if they are sisters.

Among many people brother and sister, though aiding each other, are under strict taboos in mutual intercourse. A Crow woman makes moccasins for her brother, presents his wife with fancy dresses, and watches a suspected sister-in-law's movements, but she does not chat with her brother after childhood, speaking only for an important communication, and avoids meeting him alone. The rule is far more rigid in Melanesia and Australia. A Murngin never sleeps in the same camp as his sister—indeed, they are separated at an early age; nor may either address the other.

The Family Unit. The total of sentimental, economic and legal ties between spouses, parents and children, and between siblings, makes the family a very strong social unit. Some simple societies resemble our own in expressing this closeness in speech. That is, they distinguish between members of the family and all outsiders, no matter how closely related. Thus, the Southern Maidu of central California, like ourselves, have a word for "father" different from the words for "uncle" and a word for "mother" that differs from the words for "aunt".

We have already seen that many other tribes fail to draw the line in this way. Treating siblings of one sex as equivalent, the Australians call the father's brother by the same term as the father himself, and the mother's sister by the same term as the mother. Logically enough, the children of this uncle and aunt—the parallel cousins—are then addressed as children of the speaker's parents, i.e. as siblings. But these natives do not fail to set the immediate family off from more remote kin. The social father—the man who watched over a child's infancy, whether his begetter or not—is distinguished from his brothers, the mother from her sisters. Where there is cross-cousin marriage, for instance, the man's aim is, if possible, to marry the *nearest* kinswoman of this order—his true mother's own brother's daughter.

In other words, when as in Australia relatives are grouped in large classes, each class being ticketed by a single term, the natives still discriminate and treat the remoter kin as mere substitutes for the closer.

Notwithstanding the strength of the family while it lasts, it is, in the nature of things, a loose unit. Children grow up and found new families. If residence is matrilocal, men are lost to their households or even villages; with patrilocal residence the same holds for the women. If, as among ourselves, the couple set up an establishment of their own, neither partner can be any longer so intimately related to his old family as he was before. In this lack of stability the family contrasts with another type of unit to be considered.

XIV

THE CLAN[1]

Clan and Lineage

By blood an individual is equally related to both parents. In general our society recognizes this fact, but not as to the family name, since children bear only the father's. However, girls drop it on marriage in favor of the husband's name. If they retained the paternal name for life, we should be practicing paternal descent like the primitive peoples organized into patrilineal clans. A patrilineal clan is a unit composed of an ancestor, his children, and the children of his male descendants through males. Given such a system, a person is of his father's and his paternal grandfather's clan. However, while a man passes on his name to his children, a woman keeps hers during her lifetime but never transmits it. Actually, the essential thing is transmitting *membership,* which can be symbolized otherwise than by name; but the name is the simplest of symbols.

In theory a paternal clan originates from a single ancestor. A clan including only descendants of a single ancestor is a "lineage". Commonly it includes members of two or more lineages, but the concept remains the same. A paternal clan, then, is a group of actual blood-relatives, or of actual and assumed blood-relatives, tracing their descent from a single ancestor through males.

Many tribes, following maternal descent, are organized into matrilineal clans. A matrilineal clan is a group of actual or of actual and supposed blood-relatives, tracing their descent from a single ancestress through females.

[1] Also called "sib."

Here a person belongs to the same clan as his mother and mother's mother; a woman transmits the name to her descendants, a man retains it himself but does not pass it on. Matrilineal clans composed only of blood-kin are also known as lineages. Some Hopi clans are lineages, others consist each of several lineages.

Clans become extinct if in a certain generation the children all belong to the sex that does not transmit the clan name. In a small community this is likely to happen frequently. When a primitive lineage begins to dwindle, the members tend to attach themselves to another, as has happened among Pueblo Indians. This is doubtless why clans frequently include fictitious as well as real members. After a while their diverse origin is forgotten, and a common descent is inferred from the common name; or the differences in pedigree are simply ignored.

The Clan and the Family

The clan and the family thus both rest on a blood-tie, which in both cases can be extended by adoption. The important difference is that the clan counts only relatives on either the father's or the mother's side while the family includes both parents. On the other hand, the clan includes all the relatives on the favored side, the family only the parents and children. There is a further difference. The family, we discovered, is a brittle unit. The clan is not only larger but more stable. The most remote kinsman on the side weighted is labeled as such by his name or other symbol, and among primitives there is a great deal in a symbol. He is probably called "brother" and aided like a brother, even if not with quite the same ardor.

If a people recognized only clan units, an individual would have no social tie with his father under maternal descent and no tie with his mother under paternal descent. This never occurs because the family unit, which includes both parents, is universal. Just as we do not ignore the mother in the home even though children fail to take her name, so in primitive clan systems neither parent is ever disregarded in relation to the child, but either may be *for particular purposes.* The clan thus never supplants the family; it is simply one unit more and may complicate social relations by dividing a man's loyalties. Thus, the avunculate of some matrilineal Melanesians, part of a clan system (p. 251), imposes the obligation to aid one's sister's son, ignoring the son-father tie. But *society* does not ignore it, because the family unit coexisting with the clan stresses it.

Where clans exist, the side that does not determine membership is always recognized in one way or another. The Maricopa have exogamous paternal clans. If only clan kinship mattered, a man might marry his mother; actually he may not even marry any of her blood relatives. Hopi clans are matrilineal and coupled with the avunculate; nevertheless it is the father's kinswomen who give the child a personal name. Among the Crow descent is maternal, yet gifts are always presented to paternal kinsfolk.

While no people lacks the family, many societies are without clans. The simplest Asiatic tribes, such as Chukchi and Andaman Islanders, and the simplest American tribes, say, the Mackenzie River tribes and Paiute, lack clans, while many farming populations are organized into them. They also fail to occur in Western civilization, though simpler European nations such as the Albanians are still credited with clans, as are the ancient Romans, Greeks, and Chinese. Clans do not arise in the very earliest stage of society, but on somewhat higher levels play their part for long periods, ultimately disappearing under a strong centralized government.

Clan Functions

Certain social and political clan functions are widespread. Being related, clan members do not intermarry.

In Queensland breaches of the rule were punished with death; among the Crow, the culprits were publicly derided, a grave penalty for primitive people. Frequently clansfolk address members of their own generation as brothers and sisters; always there is an obligation to help a fellow-member not only in economic and industrial tasks but in legal and political relations.

Sometimes property is inherited within the clan, the lineage of the deceased being favored if there is more than one. As a consequence, husband and wife rarely inherit from each other. In patrilineal societies the sons are a man's heirs; in matrilineal societies, the sister's sons; in either case property might go to siblings, who are always clan mates. The rules of passing on possessions may be a compromise between clan *and* family affiliations: in a matrilineal group certain kinds of property may cleave to the clan while others go to the sons. At times the clan as a corporation owns property so that an individual possessor figures only as a trustee and may not sell without the consent of his fellows.

Outstanding in primitive law is the principle of collective responsibility when, according to our ideas, a single individual is concerned. Given a clan system, a murdered man's kin seek revenge, but are content to slay any of the criminal's clansmen. Here once more status ranks above individuality (p. 231). On the other hand, the culprit's kin, irrespective of his guilt, shield him and if one of them dies, the feud goes on.

Politically, then, the clan unites a much larger group than a family unit. On the other hand, it prevents national unity because the clan regards the interests of its members as paramount.

More rarely the clan serves religious or magical purposes. The Hopi fraternities performing sacred ceremonies include members of several clans, but a particular one—or one of its lineages—is responsible and provides the priests.

The most common phenomenon of this order is "totemism". A totem is generally an animal, more rarely a plant, still more rarely a cosmic body or force like the sun or wind, which gives its name to a clan and may be otherwise associated with it. Often the linkage has no deeper meaning. The Seneca Iroquois clans were called Turtle, Bear, Wolf, Hawk, etc., and carved representations of these animals over the doors of their houses. But this was like the use of an elephant as a symbol of the Republican party. On the other hand, most totemic peoples observe totemic taboos. In Ruanda, for instance, the Buffalo people will not eat buffalo; other clans prohibit the use of the dwarf antelope, weasel, and so forth. The natives often explain their abstinence as due to descent from the species they are named for; belief in such ancestry seems quite plausible to primitives, who do not sharply distinguish between animals and man. Though actual worship of the totem is rare, Australians usually go through elaborate rites at sacred spots supposedly hallowed by their totemic ancestors, the object being to increase the animal or plant species. Totemism thus ranges from the simple heraldic use of convenient symbols to a complex system of religious and magical observances.

Totemic ideas may originate from pondering the clan names and explaining them by actual kinship with the species. However, not all clans bear such appellations. In Africa some are named after human chiefs, and in the northwestern Plains of America they bear such nicknames as Sore-Lips, Tied-in-a-Knot, Greasy-inside-their-Mouths.

The Clan and the Political Unit

A matrilineal society that consistently practices matrilocal residence with local exogamy can not achieve a maximum of political solidarity. Its fighting strength is made up largely of men from without, possibly from a dozen clans, hence potentially at loggerheads with one another. In *Plate 35,* if *1* belongs to clan *a,* his sons

(*5* and *9*) are of his wife's clan, not his own; his sons-in-law may be of three distinct clans.

The reverse condition exists typically among the Diegueño of southern California. These Indians live in bands, each owning and controlling a definitely bounded district. There is patrilineal descent of band membership and patrilocal residence. Thus, a girl is born into the band of her father and father's father, but passes out of it in marriage, while the men remain anchored to their paternal line. Band and clan loyalties thus merge into a single concept for them. Wherever a patrilocal clan is thus localized, it forms a miniature state, i.e. an independent political group. But socially it must lean on other groups, because exogamy demands women from elsewhere. With matrilineal descent and patrilocal residence, a man's male descendants are united with him territorially but clan obligations may offset the local bond. In *Plate 36,* if *1* is of clan *a* and his wife is *b*, their sons (*5, 9*) are his co-residents but belong to *b;* and *their* sons may be *c* and *d*. Thus, clan dissension might array the descendants of a man against one another.

More commonly a single clan does not hold a distinct area, which rather belongs to a major unit, the "tribe". This is divided into two, three, or a dozen clans which jointly exploit the tribal territory. A tribe may thus unite far greater numbers than a clan, but because of clan sentiment (p. 257), tribal solidarity remains fragile.

Moieties

When only two intermarrying clans dwell together, each is a "moiety" (French *moitié,* half). In the southwest corner of Australia were exogamous matrilineal moieties named White Cockatoo and Crow; in the extreme north the Murngin have patrilineal moieties with untranslatable names. The Choctaw of Mississippi were divided into two great exogamous clans with maternal descent and names of uncertain meaning. All these were moieties subdivided into lesser clans. On the other hand, the patrilineal moieties of the central Californian Miwok linked with Water and Land, respectively, are not divided into minor groups.

Exogamous moieties are common in Australia and Melanesia, fairly so in North America, but virtually lacking in Africa.

Where the entire tribe is split up into two hereditary and intermarrying groups, certain peculiarities enter the clan system. For one thing, every person in the tribe is bound to every other as belonging either to his father's or his mother's moiety. Since definite obligations are usual toward relatives of either side, reciprocal functions of the moieties arise. Some Australians performed totemic rites only when requested by the opposite moiety; among the Choctaw, members of one great clan buried those of the complementary clan; and similarly the Miwok halves aided each other at funerals and other ceremonies. Moreover, a moiety system offers a line of cleavage in athletic games. A Winnebago (Wisconsin) did not have to choose partners for a lacrosse game, he joined the players of his hereditary tribal half.

An exogamous moiety system limits a person in the choice of a mate more than a multiple clan organization does. If there are a dozen clans, a man may—other things being equal—marry in any of 11 groups, and with polygyny he may marry into several. With only two clans, he is limited to the one opposite his own. Actually, of course, the difference may not be so great. The moiety is likely to be a larger unit than a single clan; and limitations may go with the multiple clan system, such as the preference of two clans for marriage with each other.

A dual clan organization fixes the position of all relatives. If I am in moiety A and descent is paternal, my mother and her brother are B, my father and his sister are A; my maternal uncle may marry my father's sister and their children will be doubly my cross-cousins. Further, in such a system I may marry my cross-cousins but never my parallel cousins because the former inevitably belong to the opposite moiety, the latter to my own, whether descent is maternal or paternal. Thus, keeping the same assumptions, my father's sister's daughter must be B because her mother (my father's sister) is A and has a B husband, who passes on his moiety affiliation to his children.

However, cross-cousin marriage, while consistent with the moiety system, does not directly follow from it. In the first place, in such an organization the cross-cousin is only *one* of a large number of possible mates, while often the aim in cross-cousin marriage is to marry a real first cousin (p. 237). Secondly, the moiety system can not explain why the Murngin and Miwok permit only one kind of cross-cousin to be married, when both belong to the proper moiety. Thirdly, the cross-cousin marriage exists without moieties.

Moieties may antedate multiple clans in some regions and be later in others. Small clan units have a tendency to dwindle and become extinct so that, say, five original clans may be reduced to two. On the other hand, the reverse process is equally possible: an overgrown moiety may split up into lesser clans. If the members retain a sense of their origin, they found subdivisions of a moiety organization; otherwise a multiple clan system develops. Both processes probably occurred in different areas and periods.

When a moiety is subdivided, its rule of exogamy may weaken and be limited to the lesser groups. According to the Iroquois this happened in several of their tribes in recent times, the moieties retaining other characteristics of a dual organization but the clans alone insisting on exogamy.

Except where there is such positive historical information, mere non-exogamous halves of a tribe should not be treated as equivalents of moieties. For instance, the Toda are divided into two *endo*gamous units. And some of our eastern Algonkian tribes more or less arbitrarily assign one child in a family to one half, another to another half of the tribe. A moiety is one of two exogamous clans in a tribe. Hence, neither a unit that forces members to marry among themselves nor a unit without a definite rule of descent belongs in the same category.

Phratries

Where there are many clans, some may develop more intimate relations with each other than with the remainder. The Maricopa and related tribes have about 16 paternal clans, each with at least 1 totem. Some of the clans share totems and recognize a bond due to this common element, but no consolidation took place. The Crow went further. Their 13 clans are linked in 5 pairs and a trio, the members of each major group considering themselves as especially friendly and associating in various activities. Such brotherhoods of clans are called "phratries" (Greek *phratēr,* brother). Subdivided moieties are thus also phratries, but a phratry need not be a moiety, it is simply a union, possibly very loose yet recognized by the natives, of two or more clans. Hence a tribe may have moieties *and* phratries. The Kansas Indians had exogamous moieties and also grouped their clans in 7 phratries.

The Origin of the Clan

The clan must have originated in conditions of clanless tribes that enlarged the family on only one side. Two things must be explained: how persons of different families came to unite, and why certain individuals are shut out from these larger groupings.

One way of enlargement occurs among the Macusi, a tribe of Guiana. Matrilocal residence draws a newly married man into his father-in-law's village and house, where he and his wife have their own fireplace and hammocks. The new couple plant and harvest their own plot, but in preparing the farm products the women of the several families join, using the major implements that are open to all. Hunting and fishing occasionally bring together all the men of a settlement under the headman's leadership. These arrangements do not make for a firmly knit unit because temporary co-residence is the only bond that holds people together. With these people a man does not need to settle permanently with his wife's kin, so that a child born in her native village may or may not grow up there. In other words, some of the children whom a matrilineal clan would unite remain together, others separate. The men of a village represent different lines of descent, coming as they do from various alien settlements. Conversely, starting from a single family, adult brothers who normally would support one another through thick and thin may be scattered over half a dozen localities. In other words, while the Macusi have a working combination of individuals beyond the family, this larger unit is equally brittle.

If matrilocal residence were permanent, the result would be quite different. Then children born in village A would grow up to maturity there; and the girls would remain, forming the female core of a possible matrilineal clan. In order to complete the clan group it is only necessary to bring the boys as well as the girls into the picture. If *all* the children born in a settlement or house were labeled by a common name or other symbol, a maternal lineage would arise.

In Guiana this is uncommon, because most of the tribes apply the matrilocal principle temporarily and inconsistently. It is the first wife alone that usually draws her husband to her own home, additional wives being brought there, too, so that the children of the several women represent not one but several diverse maternal lines. Further, these Indians frequently except the son of a chief from the matrilocal rule. In consequence, two conflicting rules of residence militate against a uniform grouping of kin either patrilineally or matrilineally.

Not all matrilineal peoples in the world are now matrilocal, but the origin of a matrilineal clan is most easily understood from such cases as that of the Hopi, i.e. from tribes with rigid matrilocal residence. For there all the women who make up a maternal lineage are actually brought together in daily life and all female outsiders are excluded. It remains to bring in the appropriate males so that they shall not be lost to the matrilocal group by marriage. This can be done by giving them, as well as the girls, a fixed group name on birth. Among the Hopi they are also linked together by joint rituals and sacred property.

The reverse condition of patrilineal clans has been foreshadowed in varying measure in different parts of the world. The clanless Havasupai begin matrimony with matrilocal residence, but later take up residence on the land of the husband's family—the tract jointly inherited by brothers, women rarely controlling any land. Typically, a man and his sons form an economic unit in charge of an unparceled section until division becomes desirable. Among the Algonkians of eastern Canada, hunting territories were uniformly held by men and transmitted to their male descendants; residence being patrilocal, there is here a closer approach to the typical alignment of kin in a patrilineal system. While women share in the Havasupai farming operations and occasionally plant independently, only men hunt, hence these Canadians segregate the male core of a paternal lineage. The Ona carry this process a step further. Each of their 39 named and strictly delimited hunting territories belongs to a distinct patrilineal group, numbering from 40 to 120 persons with a sense of kinship, who join in athletic contests and resent poaching. Residence is patrilocal, and the fear of overlooking remote blood ties leads men to seek women from a considerable distance. This yields true localized paternal lineages and at the same time political and social units, provided the individual's bond with the group is fixed, for women as much as for men. This condition may not have been completely realized because a man was not prohibited from settling in an alien district with the owners' permission; and it is not clear to what extent a woman was associated with her native tract. However, the overwhelming majority of men clung to their hereditary hunting territory; and a woman did not lose her affiliation by marriage, for as a widow she was equally at liberty to stay with her husband's kin or to return to her old home. The Ona organization thus represents a borderline case and may be considered a clan system at the very point of birth.

Australia illustrates both stages of development. Normally a tract of land is held by a local horde composed of a permanent core of males and a changing assortment of wives brought from without, daughters leaving as soon as married. But there is likewise another type of unit, by which females, though lost to the horde, remain permanently associated with the men of the horde—the paternal clan, which they leave only by death.

In the northwest Amazon country strict patrilocal residence is worked out into an unquestionable clan system: the men born in a village remain permanently together, usually occupying a single huge house with their wives, sons and unmarried daughters, the number of occupants rising to 200 and more; all those born in the settlement bear the same name and all co-residents regard one another as kin. They thus constitute a patrilineal clan.

So, both simple hunters such as the Ona or Australians and more advanced tillers—the South Americans of the tropical forest zone—live in conditions that naturally group together certain relatives of one sex and exclude others. Sometimes factors operate against the development of a full clan system. At other times conditions not only segregate a clan core but weld to it the siblings of the opposite sex, thereby creating a clan.

Maternal and Paternal Descent

Maternal descent does not imply a dominant position of women. In Australia their status is no better in matrilineal than in patrilineal tribes. That women are less liable to abuse under *matrilocal residence* is obvious, but this practice may exist without any fixed form of descent, as in most of Guiana; and control there belongs to the men of the settlement, not their wives.

Among primitive peoples a difference in descent can not be mechanically correlated with levels of culture. Australians present both forms and are very uniform in culture. In North America north of the Rio Grande the more advanced Pueblo and Southeastern tribes have matrilineal clans, but the matrilineal Crow hunters are not superior to the semi-sedentary Omaha; and the Peruvians, highest in South America, had paternal descent.

What holds true is that the most highly centralized governments in history, including the illiterate Africans, favor paternal descent, even where there is no clear-cut clan system. The reason has already been suggested. Maternal descent and the elements that often accompany it separate men who might otherwise form a body with naturally strong solidarity. Brothers go to different settlements to serve for their wives, and fathers are rent by conflicting sentiments of love and duty when a son's interests have to be weighed against a cross-nephew's. These disturbing features are forestalled by paternal descent with its correlates. While it does not create solidarity, it favors consolidation into major political units.

XV

RANK, ETIQUETTE, AND PROPERTY

Rank

Informal Ranking. Even democratic groups recognize individual differences and judge them according to the current standards. The Ona and Canadian Indians esteem good hunters; Plains Indians, warriors; the Maricopa, men with dream experiences; the Siberians, persons inspired by spirits; stock-breeders, the owners of large herds. Such appraisal grants no authority, but prestige; and tribesmen do defer to the people they admire. Among ourselves Theodore Roosevelt, even as a private citizen, was a power to be reckoned with.

Contrariwise, every society has its misfits, tolerated perhaps, but without influence. Such would be a regularly unsuccessful hunter among the Ona, or a Plains Indian without a single feat at arms to his credit.

Many tribes designate individuals according to their position in the cycle of life. The words used may be vaguely descriptive, such as our "baby" or "youth". Often, however, they indicate social standing in the community. Thus an Australian boy is a nobody until he is initiated, and different terms describe him before and after. An "old woman" may eat food and take liberties forbidden to a younger matron. The designations do not pave the way for aristocracy because in due time every member of the community attains each status grade. Nor does it always happen that the older groups dominate. Among the Masai the bachelors representing the fighting strength of their people were the most important element of society. Status grading is thus transitional to other forms of ranking.

Non-hereditary Class Ranking. The Crow admired bravery, but those who had achieved four standard feats were set apart as "chiefs". In matrilocal Guiana the word for son-in-law took on the meaning of servant; the sons-in-law of a settlement were vassals of the old residents. The money-mad Yurok of northwestern California divided the tribe into class-conscious groups of "rich" and "poor". Such divisions readily pass into hereditary castes when property is inherited, but where mere wealth underlies rank a lucky upstart can achieve both. Melanesians and West Africans combine differences in wealth with club grading. In the Banks Islands, a rich boy does not have to begin at the bottom of the scale, and only the exceptionally well-to-do ever reach the top.

Similarly the Ibo of Southern Nigeria buy rank in societies which exclude slaves and usually aliens. Enormous fees, £50 and even £200, are paid in order to enter the highest clubs, but the compensations are proportionate. All are mutual benefit organizations, and members draw interest from their investment by getting their share of all subsequent admission dues. Each degree has its emblem, such as scarified patterns on the forehead, white cloths round the head, or cotton anklets. Members of the highest organization are exempt from public labors and entitled to food gifts from others; sometimes they are safeguarded from assault. The member of a society may also be a chief, so that prestige blends with political office. In other instances religious features are stressed: the novice's ancestors receive sacrifices, and initiates are put under taboos, such as not being henceforth allowed to eat outside their own dwelling.

Hereditary Classes. Wealth often fails to create hereditary classes, because it can be easily won and lost. Among nomads, who stress large herds, an ambitious youth will loot the stock of neighboring bands. On the other hand, a cattle plague can reduce the wealthiest men to poverty. But other distinctions can be made to hinge on birth. Among these are occupational differences. Though often individual, they tend to be transmitted from father to son even in simpler European communities and in those primitive groups sufficiently advanced to have specialized trades. Tanners and blacksmiths are despised hereditary groups among several African peoples; nor can a Masai blacksmith better his plight by renouncing the trade, he still remains an outcast. The rigid caste system of India is bound up with such occupations, barbers and carpenters being graded with reference to the Brahman class.

In Polynesia the house-builders, tattooers, and canoe-builders were honored experts comparable to an upper middle class or petty nobility. In Samoa the builders' guild ranked still higher; connected with the great god Tangaloa, they were called "the companions of kings". In theory, they are all descended from the founder of the organization, but the blood tie has largely become lost and been replaced by legal fiction, a fully trained apprentice being formally admitted to the guild.

Occupational lines sometimes coincide with racial or national ones. In Ruanda the ruling class embraces cattle-breeders of mixed Negro and Caucasian stock; the common people are Negro peasants; the hunters are Pygmies. Where membership in a caste is at once indicated by a person's appearance, the social cleavage naturally tends to persist. In modern civilization the correlation of calling and nationality is not perfect as in the Ruanda case, yet certain trades are still followed more extensively by one group than another. Chinese laundrymen, colored Pullman porters, and Scandinavian sailors illustrate the point.

Apart from occupation, certain primitives are as aristocratically minded as any medieval European country. The Indians on the coast of British Columbia were organized into three castes—noblemen, commoners, and slaves. The slaves were captives from other tribes, well treated under ordinary circumstances but at any time liable to death at their master's pleasure. The common people differed from the aristocrats mainly in lacking certain prized privileges. By exceptional good luck a plebeian might acquire the incorporeal wealth that conferred nobility, but he was always regarded with suspicion and rarely accepted as a peer by the older bluebloods. These were themselves not equals but active rivals, their elaborate potlatches (see p. 151) being given for superior prestige. As in most caste systems, endogamy was stressed.

This class spirit had its counterpart in Polynesia. The Samoans still confer chiefly honors, and use intrigue to secure them. Prominent chiefs enjoy special titles to be called out at ceremonial occasions, when using their ordinary names would be a grave breach of etiquette. Kava is served in a definite order, which advertises the relative rank of the noblemen attending.

In general Polynesian aristocracy rested on divine right; noblemen were descended from the gods, or at least more directly so than others. This idea underlies the stress on pedigrees (see p. 197). Polynesians differed like European nations as to the inheritance of titles. Those of Samoa were conferred by family vote, but the Maori, like the British, limited them to the eldest son.

In most tribes organized into clans all the clans of one system are on a par. However, this is not universal. In Uganda only certain clans could present candidates for the throne. In North America such distinctions did not cut deep because of the prevalent democratic tendencies. However, certain honorary functions were often associated with clans. The Winnebago chief was invariably of the Thunderbird clan, while the police were recruited from the Bear clan.

Rank and Power. To rank is not necessarily to dominate. The proverbial power behind the throne appears also on primitive levels, and a man with a higher title may enjoy no practical advantages. Polynesia presents all possible variations. In Tahiti the loftiest rank was that of the king, who automatically made an object his own by touching it, for it thus became too holy for a lesser man's use. But in Tonga about 100 years ago the political ruler had to do obeisance to the "tuitonga" as his superior in rank, much as a medieval monarch showed deference to a pope. In Samoa power is vested in the gentry as a body, and such a well-organized group as the builders can defy the chief; yet a title handed down from a mythical past is still socially prized, as is a duke's in England. The Marquesan chiefs lost both the halo of divinity and political power.

In short, rank may imply political privilege, but it may merely be an expression of human vanity.

Etiquette

Etiquette partly flows from distinctions in rank, is partly bound up with kinship customs, and partly belongs to the daily routine.

Rank and Etiquette. Title-hunting breeds etiquette. A man prompted to outshine his fellows demands a maximum of outward recognition. Religious sanctions increase formality. The Hawaiian subjects prostrated themselves before a king, Tahitians stripped themselves to the waist in his presence. Lest he surcharge the ground with his divinity, a Tahitian ruler was carried on the shoulders of attendants. The Samoans not only serve kava in a definite order, calling out the guests' ceremonial titles, but standardize even so minute a detail as the receiving of a cup. A high chief takes it by hooking his forefinger over the rim, a "talking chief" must receive it in his open palm.

Etiquette may impose obligations on a title-bearer as well as work to his advantage. A Samoan chief must lay in a large stock of kava for ceremonial use or suffer in prestige. Plains Indian chiefs had to be lavishly generous, a "wealthy" Yurok must be self-restrained while a "poor" man is unhampered by the code of his betters.

In the United States many resent evening clothes, for which people without social pretensions have no use; and a European prince attends many formal functions in which he takes not the slightest interest.

Kinship Usages. The behavior of the closest kin has been discussed (p. 249). Civilized societies also have relevant rules. Parents care for their children, and siblings of opposite sex are somewhat circumspect in each other's presence even if there is no approach to Melanesian taboos. But apart from a few regulations for the immediate family, ours are remarkably vague. We pay some deference, perhaps, to seniors, but we do not distinguish between a paternal or maternal uncle or aunt or between parallel and cross-cousins. For an Australian such discrimination is vital. Indeed, he puts all persons with whom social intercourse is maintained into some class of blood-relatives, which determines behavior toward them. Similarly, a Dakota can not act with propriety until another's kinship status is determined; in a myth when 4 young men encounter an unknown woman their first concern is how to classify her, and when they decide on her being an "elder sister" mutual conduct follows from this relationship. A Murngin girl sees in any father's sister her possible mother-in-law; a boy expects food from his paternal aunt and gives presents to his maternal uncle as a prospective father-in-law; a father's father claims his grandson's canoe; a mother's father feeds his daughter's son; and so forth.

Including under this head connections by marriage, we may recognize three great groups of conduct—avoidance, privileged familiarity, obligations and rights of a practical order.

Among the Murngin a mother-in-law and son-in-law completely avoid each other. If they met accidentally, they would turn aside with averted eyes. The penalty for a breach of this custom is supposed to be a large swelling in the groin. Such parent-in-law taboos are found widely in Siberia, America, Africa and Melanesia.

In Guiana a Lokono son-in-law is prevented from seeing his mother-in-law by a partition; and if they must travel together by boat, she enters first so as to be able to turn her back to him. Usually the rule is stronger between persons of opposite sex, and there is generally no restriction between mother-in-law and daughter-in-law. In both respects the Ona depart from the norm. With them a man refrains from addressing his wife's father, never looks at him, and gets out of his path. Any questions have to be asked through his wife. If the older man wants some service he requests it in a soliloquy audible to his son-in-law. For mother-in-law and daughter-in-law the same rules apply for the first year of marriage, but after that they are relaxed to some extent, though the two women never chat. Here, as with all primitives, the motive for avoidance is never animosity, but respect verging on awe. The Siberian Turks taboo social intercourse of a woman and her father-in-law. They, like the Plains Indians, forbid the use of any word that is part of the tabooed parent-in-law's name, a custom leading to clumsy circumlocution.

The Lesu of Melanesia impose taboos on cross-cousins of opposite sex, who do not approach each other within 20 feet, or refer to each other by personal name, or exchange food except through a go-between. The custom seems a direct corollary of the parent-in-law rule, since these natives prohibit marriage between cross-cousins but prescribe it beween a man and his cross-cousin's daughter.

Less extreme restrictions on conduct occur. Owens Valley Paviotso brothers-in-law were restrained in conversation about sex and did not philander in each other's presence. The Crow observed the same rule, though allowing brothers-in-law to joke each other about their war deeds.

At the opposite pole stands privileged familiarity. Crow and Blackfoot allow a man to romp with his sister-in-law, both indulging in ribald language to each other.

Somewhat less extreme liberties are indulged by corresponding persons in Melanesia. A Banks Islander may abuse and mock his father's sister's husband, while in Fiji a nephew treats his maternal uncle's property as his own and even wantonly destroys it with impunity. Among the Dakota two brothers-in-law were preëminently "joking relatives".

Practical duties and rights form an important category. Some go with the avunculate (p. 251). Among Melanesians the maternal uncle often assumes responsibilities for his nephew, paying for a boy's admission into the men's club, or for the rites of infancy. By way of reciprocity nephews aid their uncles in various enterprises. Among the Tlingit of southern Alaska a boy of 10 years was taken to the house of his maternal uncle to be raised there. As the amitate suggests (p. 251), the relation to paternal relatives is equally significant. With the Crow any distribution of gifts implied first of all consideration of the father's brothers and sisters. On the other hand, paternal kin were the advertisers of any meritorious deed.

The significant thing about all such rules is the definiteness with which primitive communities determine the social behavior between given relatives.

Daily Etiquette. Primitive peoples often omit forms of courtesy we consider essential, but impose others that seem strange to us, as the Havasupai rule of smacking one's lips to show enjoyment of a meal. Even after a long absence the Ona neither use any special verbal salutation, nor do they kiss or embrace or shake hands. But a decorous visitor remains standing until a place is pointed out for him; he never plunges into the conversation, nor does he display curiosity about his surroundings. He finally speaks of trivial occurrences in his home and on his journey, painfully avoiding any criticism of his hosts, their ancestors, or their territory, and postpones bad news until he is ready to go away. In the meantime the woman of the house has cooked the best morsels available and set them before the visitor, but he holds back until repeatedly urged to fall to. It would be churlish to bid him leave before he is ready; rather will the whole family postpone a hunting trip and beg meat from neighbors.

A constantly recurring feature among simpler tribes is the reluctance to hurry matters of business. When a Shilluk delegation comes to a neighboring settlement with an offer of marriage, they seek out the elders gathered in the shade of the village tree (*Pl. 13, fig. 1*), silently deposit their lances, and squat down. At last the headman calls the name of the oldest visitor, and each resident follows suit, saluting all the guests. Then a roundabout conversation ensues, for coming to the point would be highly impolite. Instead the speakers scoff at masculine foppishness, criticise the indecencies of young women, and describe their own hunting trophies. At last the newcomers' spokesman pulls out a package with rods of different size to indicate his client's live-stock.

When two Shilluk meet, the older says, "Are you alive?" or "God has brought you"; the younger responds in the same phraseology. With these formulas the maximum number of names are uttered—the more, the greater the compliment. In speaking to an elder a Shilluk employs a polite word corresponding to the German "Sie".

The peoples of the world, civilized and illiterate, vary in their attitude toward kissing. Anglo-Saxons indulge in it more sparingly than Latins and find the double-cheek kiss of adult Frenchmen funny. American Indians tend to restrict kissing to lovers and children; the Maori and Eskimo touch noses as an equivalent. Some South Americans and the Andamanese oddly salute friends by weeping.

Names are handled in gingerly fashion, even when the observances are social rather than religious. The Choctaw, Mohave, and many other American Indians, were averse to mentioning their names, and it was bad manners to ask for them pointblank. But among New and Old World natives husband and wife, instead of calling each other by name, will substitute "So-and-so's father (mother)"; this is constant Hopi practice, for instance. Others than spouses use the same mode of speech: a Lesu man refers to his wife's brother, and a woman to her husband's sister, as the parent of So-and-so. The custom, known as teknonymy (Greek, *teknon,* child), in a way recognizes status, the person addressed being thus set in a grade higher than one merely married.

Many aborigines taboo mentioning the names of the dead. Choctaw claimants, knowing that they thereby lost title to extra land, refused to enumerate their deceased children; and the Yurok fined a person two or three strings of shell money for referring directly to a man no longer living. To avoid offence Mohave delicately designate the father's settlement or kin as "on the right", the mother's as "on the left". In this same spirit of sparing the feelings of a survivor a Crow will speak of "the one who is not here".

Countless rules define the proper behavior of the sexes in daily speech and apparently indifferent activities. A Dakota woman uses an imperative form and exclamations different from a man's, sits with both legs flexed to the right, never crosslegged, and must play the coy maiden when courted by a suitor snatching at her blanket.

Among the most striking points of primitive etiquette is the regard for other persons' feelings. Except for relatives with license to be familiar, or for outbursts of anger, nothing will be said to hurt another's self-respect.

Property

Property is movable, real, or incorporeal. It may be private or communal; it may or may not be inherited, and if so, according to different principles; and these possibilities are interwoven with social, political and moral ideas. Some of the last-mentioned require special treatment.

Moral and Legal Claims; Communism and Individualism. Hospitality is commonly carried by primitive peoples far beyond our practice. Most of them feel that food must be shared, while the idea of selling it is intolerable or at least degrading. When a whale is stranded, the Ona relax their strict law against trespass and permit every inhabitant of the island to fetch his share. A self-respecting Dakota hunter feasted old men after a successful trip; a Crow was said to earn long life by regularly inviting his father's clansmen. Thus, a primitive will not starve so long as there is food in the community; and the sense of this moral obligation marks a difference between such uncivilized and civilized peoples.

This, however, does not necessarily imply a *legal* or equal claim to food. A Caribou Eskimo who neglects his family from laziness is likely to lose his wife and has to wander from settlement to settlement as an unwelcome visitor. He will not be allowed to starve, but falls to the level of a pariah. The Dakota have two distinct words for "visiting". One denotes a social call made with the understanding that the incidental favor of a meal will be reciprocated. The other suggests a deliberate food sponger, who is dreaded and ridiculed unless he has the excuse of old age. Again, in Lesu the good-for-nothing idler is in no danger of starving so long as there is no general famine. But he loses standing, fails to get a wife, and is publicly derided for his shiftlessness.

Thus, the concept of poverty may be quite different from ours. It does not imply want of a roof and food; it means lack of those possessions, material or immaterial, which make life worth living for a man of pride. From this angle we must qualify the view that status overshadows individuality among simpler peoples. Siblings *are* in a sense equivalent; but no society reckons the alert master craftsman or tracker on the same plane with his bungling or lazy brother. And though a parasite may appropriate his kinsman's food, clothing and chattels generally, no one feels that he has the same *right* to them.

A flavor of communism does not thus exclude preeminent individual claims. The Caribou Eskimo allow any one to hunt anywhere over their land, or to use means of production that would otherwise lie fallow, such as traps or salmon weirs; a finder may retain lost articles, a borrower need not replace a borrowed article destroyed in use. Nevertheless, even within one household, a kayak belongs to the husband, a pot to the wife, and neither sells the other's property; the very children must individually consent to a sale of their possessions. What is more, even Eskimo communism as to food is invaded by legal in contrast to moral claims. Of two hunters, the killer takes an animal's forepart, the companion the hind part. If many are present, those who have taken no active part in the chase receive no share but merely a subsequent present of meat. In short, individual ownership appears even where superficially it seems absent.

Quite different from communism, with its denial of all specialized property, is joint ownership, which may be vested in a family, a man and his eldest son, a club, a community, or any other association of individuals. Such collective ownership is common and can easily coexist with individual property rights concerning other objects.

Movable Property. Movable property includes dress, utensils, weapons, and also live-stock. To some of these chattels property rights are attached by the act of creating them. Thus a woman is undisputed owner of her pot, a man of his bow. However, this would not hold in all stratified societies, because there a superior sometimes expropriates the manufacturer or forces him to work for little, if any, compensation. It is not even always a case of coercion; if the chief is considered divine, sacrifices are willingly made.

Live-stock is often branded to advertise ownership.

Cattle are useless without pasturage, hence presuppose access to grazing land. This condition has been a fertile source of strife between diverse nomadic peoples, as well as between nomads and farmers (p. 53).

In Ruanda the king is in theory owner of all the livestock in the country, the individual nobleman being merely a feudal holder of his herds. However, in practice the ruler no more dispossessed any member of the upper class than the king of England in recent centuries asserted his theoretical title to all land.

Slaves are a special form of chattel. Though liable to abuse on occasion, they are often treated as members of the family. Not all slaves were prisoners of war. In northwest California, indeed, no captives were ever taken, but men unable to pay their debts became slaves, making string and nets or catching fish for their masters. West African debtors regularly surrendered themselves or their children's persons to a creditor, but such pawn slaves were always well treated and redeemed as soon as the debt was paid off.

Real Estate. Land tenure varies with a people's economic technique, but many other considerations enter. For one thing, land is usually inalienable among primitives (p. 153), so that their whole concept of ownership is distinct from ours. As noted, the Ona and the Australians have never thought of acquiring land by conquest. On the other hand, the Maori, who did recognize this principle, permitted one family to own a tract for root-digging and another for rat-hunting. Again, in New Guinea and West Africa the trees on a plantation may be owned independently of the soil.

Some hunters (e.g. the Plains Indians) do not limit land tenure within the political unit, the entire tribal territory being free to any member for exploitation. This holds for the Ona and the Australians, but with important differences. While a Plains tribe numbered possibly several thousand, the Ona or Australian horde was a group of barely more than 100. More important still, the territories of the smaller units were definitely bounded, while those of the Plains tribes were not. In eastern Canada the Algonkians hold hereditary hunting territories within family groups, poaching being strictly punished. The Owens Valley Paviotso held title communally, all the residents of a district sharing the right to hunt, fish and gather seeds within their territory; but among the Washo east of the California Sierras, families own clumps of pine-nut trees. In Queensland, too, land belongs to families, usually to blood-brothers or fathers and sons, and in one instance to a woman and her daughters. It is thus a grave error to assume communal land tenure for all hunting peoples.

Pastoral nomads generally own the grazing land in common, but the Kirghiz depart from this rule *in winter,* when suitable pastures are scarce. Practical considerations thus led to seasonal differences. Further, since the size of a herd vacillates, a man with dwindling live-stock tries to dispose of his winter quarters. In other words, land becomes alienable.

Farm holdings also depend on specific circumstances. Havasupai brothers, we noted, jointly shared a tract until practically driven to make a division (p. 264). In this tribe effective use gives possession, as it does among the Eskimo (p. 278); unless a man cultivated his plot, his title lapsed and another cultivator took his place. Another factor often enters to nullify ownership: after a few years' tenure the soil is exhausted so that a new clearing becomes necessary. This, however, does not always imply a lapse of ownership.

In Africa, political conditions affected real estate law. As absolute monarchs the kings of Dahomey and Uganda claimed all the land. In Uganda the chiefs received feudal grants, which they allotted in smaller plots to the peasants in return for menial and military duties. Where African chiefs have little power, as in Togo, each kin group holds joint title to lands within the village. Here, then, there is no individual real estate, the head of a group being merely a manager while any member has the right to till a part of the common domain. In contrast to the Havasupai rule, title is not forfeited by failure to cultivate. Similarly, among the Lobi an abandoned lot can be farmed only by permission of the former tiller, who furthermore reserves the future use of any trees growing on the field. The hereditary owner, accompanied by a priest, must offer a sacrifice to the local gods and give them formal notice of the transfer. In Ruanda the subject peasantry have no rights; the dominant stock-breeders destroy crops whenever it is convenient for grazing purposes.

To sum up, under democratic conditions, effective use created land titles; but the nature of primitive farming often prevented these from becoming permanent so that, strictly, the farmer possessed rather than owned the land. The Havasupai case is typical of an indefinite number of tribes. So long as a Choctaw stayed on his premises, raising corn and beans, his rights were generally respected. As soon as he moved, his title was forfeited without claim to compensation; and Chaco Indians followed the same plan. This principle was abolished mainly by the right of eminent domain asserted by monarchs and noblemen; or by religious sentiments that made a particular tract sacred to its occupants.

Incorporeal Property. Most primitives acknowledge an exclusive right to songs, myths, designs, and so forth. Even when tangible objects were involved, as in the case of a Plains Indian sacred bundle, the proprietor was not conceived as owning these particular birdskins, tobacco pipes, etc., but as having the *right* to assemble these articles. In this case the ultimate sanction for the patent came from a supernatural revelation. But commonly the god empowered his beneficiary to sell the privilege at a price consistent with its dignity. Similarly, the Siberian Koryak, who know incantations that help in the emergencies of life, sell them at a goodly price.

Not all incorporeal property is sacred, yet everywhere

its rights are respected. No Greenlander or Andaman Islander ventures to sing the song of another without his permission.

Notwithstanding its frequently fanciful origin, incorporeal property may prove the most important form of wealth, being readily convertible into tangible property. Lesu natives can not become rich by selling pigs because the code forbids selling at a profit. But the magical knowledge hoarded by a few wise men is an ample source of income, because their clients consider spells essential in sickness, war, love, and all vital economic pursuits. No wonder such information is secret; if it leaked out, fees would be abolished.

Like other forms of property these prerogatives, too, are sometimes held by groups, at other times individually. A Plains Indian vision generally conferred an individual right that could not be transferred even to a son without a formal sale. But in matrilineal Melanesian tribes the spells *had* to be taught to a sister's son, in other words, the individual using them was not absolute proprietor but shared them with his maternal kin.

Inheritance. In some of the simplest societies material property is not inherited but destroyed at death, as among many Californians. The Ona similarly wrap up a dead man in his clothes for burial, then burn his hut and all his other belongings; only dogs are turned over to some kinsman.

When property accumulates, an aversion to such summary sacrifice leads to fairly fixed rules of disposal, the guiding principles usually coinciding with the social structure. In harmony with the basic fact that spouses are members of different kin groups, they hardly ever inherit from each other. From expediency women generally inherit feminine utensils; boys get whatever goes with masculine pursuits. When a rule of descent exists, it affects inheritance, as in matrilineal Melanesia (see above). The conflict of avuncular and paternal sentiment (p. 251) sometimes introduces contradictory motives; especially do we find that a chief's son may succeed to his office—virtually a form of incorporeal property—in a matrilineal society. A correlation of inheritance and descent appears in the disposal of widows (p. 237). Filial inheritance rather marks patrilineal peoples, such as the Mongols and certain Africans; nephews acquire the widows of their maternal uncles among the matrilineal Banks Islanders and British Columbian tribes.

Extreme primogeniture as to possessions in general is not common among primitives, the eldest son being often, as in South Africa, a trustee or administrator rather than the sole heir. Sometimes it is the younger brothers who successively assume control of the estate. Sporadically, as among the Kirghiz and some Eskimo tribes, there is ultimogeniture or junior right, i.e. the youngest son takes the lion's share because the older sons tend to leave the parental roof as they grow up.

It is in harmony with primitive emphasis on status that individuals are rarely free to will their property at pleasure. An eldest son has supreme claims if primogeniture is in vogue, a nephew under the avunculate, and so forth.

Summary. Property reflects social and political institutions, but also reacts upon them, creating prestige, classes, and superior political power. Private property is nowhere absent, but it may be restricted to special things. It tends to be weakest as to bare necessities, but this comes rather from the strength of a moral obligation than from recognition of a legal claim.

XVI

GOVERNMENT AND LAW

Informal Control

Public Opinion. Some simple societies appear anarchistic because they lack chiefs, courts and officers of the law. They are thus at one time led by a physical bully, at another by a man credited with supernatural favor. Actually, there is never complete anarchy because public opinion universally curbs individual action. In the rudest community sexual offenses are condemned (p. 231), and in the worst autocracies the ruler can not afford to go beyond a certain point. He may safely assert traditional privileges, but he meets opposition if he runs counter to established beliefs. The strength of a Polynesian monarch lay in his acceptance by the people as a divine personage.

Public opinion checks the individual because he craves praise and hates to "lose face". Fearing ridicule, he abstains from what he may secretly long to do, and coveting praise he gives away his treasured possessions at potlatches (p. 151) or sacrifices his life (p. 221). In the Trobriand Islands men commit suicide when publicly insulted for marrying within the clan. The powerful urges of sex, acquisitiveness, and self-preservation are constantly repressed by the still more powerful wish to be appreciated by one's fellows. Among the Crow each individual's "joking relatives", the children of his father's clansmen, were privileged to mock him for cowardice or any breach of social law, and fear of being put to shame before all his people was an abiding safeguard against unsocial behavior.

Supernatural Sanctions. Customary law is obeyed willingly if people believe in automatic punishment of a breach by some supernatural power. Thus, many Eskimo believe that when any one breaks a food taboo a goddess is infuriated and keeps the seals away, causing a famine. The Yokuts of south-central California were largely deterred from cheating, neglecting their ceremonial duties, and so forth, by fear of sorcery. The chief, having no coercive authority, hired a medicine-man to make an antisocial tribesman fall sick. If the allies went too far, the medicine-man might be killed by the enraged relatives and the chief would lose prestige, possibly even his office. But normally the combination succeeded in maintaining peace and a fair amount of interest in the general good.

Crime and Tort. Crime is an offence against the community, a tort is a wrong against an individual. Primitive groups regard many of the crimes in our law as mere torts but they always consider certain actions intolerable and punish them collectively, which is the test of "crime". The Caribou Eskimo do not treat theft as a serious matter, and murder is not necessarily criminal; but witchcraft *is* a crime, looming as an insidious attempt at murder. If a man repeatedly makes himself a nuisance by such antisocial behavior, he is put out of the way. Many Eskimo tribes also regard as criminal the eating of seal and caribou at a single meal because breach of the taboo is supposed to endanger the food supply (see above). Among Plains tribes murder was a greatly regretted occurrence, but only a tort against the victim's kin; on the other hand, premature startling of a buffalo herd was a crime punished by the tribal police. In parts of South Africa theft is a private grievance for which the injured party was indemnified. But hurting or killing a subject was a crime, and the indemnity went to the chief, not to the victim or his family.

Unwritten Codes. Public opinion can create a definite code. Even in the absence of constituted authority the

Yurok of northwestern California and the Ifugao of the Philippines have organized a complex system of law. The Yurok assess every possession, privilege, and injury in terms of property, the status of the parties as "rich" and "poor" affecting the amounts due. An adulterer paid the aggrieved husband from 1 to 5 strings of shell money; for the killing of a poor man the price was 10 strings, for a wealthy man 15; the utterance of a dead man's name called for 2 strings, if he was rich, for 3. In a dispute each party naturally pressed its claims as forcibly as possible, the weaker in wealth and in kin being at an obvious disadvantage. Nevertheless, the traditional rules, however twisted in a special case, were informally recognized by all as a basis for their negotiations.

An interesting feature of Yurok law, widely shared on the primitive plane, is the complete neglect of the actor's intentions. Damage was damage and had to be atoned for, whether due to malice, chance, or ignorance. This disregard for moral aspects appears also in primitive supernatural relations, where an accidental error in uttering a prayer or spell may cause disaster not only to the reciter but to quite innocent associates.

Another typical Yurok element is the possibility of compensation for the killing or injury of a person. This payment, technically known as weregild, persisted even into European history. It is a useful mechanism for stopping an otherwise endless feud. But some primitive tribes regard blood vengeance as a sacred duty that can not be obviated by a consideration. The Caribou Eskimo do, however, tend to exempt a man who has thus punished a murderer from further trouble.

The Blood Tie and the Local Tie

Crime implies a disinterested third party equivalent to our State. This is represented by a whole Eskimo settlement outlawing a sorcerer, or by a Negro king claiming his fees for mayhem. The outstanding difference between most primitive communities and ours is the weakness of the State, which is correlated with the strength of the blood tie as against local bonds. Typical primitives respond to a given occurrence in terms, not of abstract justice or the common good, but of personal relations. There is a collective solidarity and responsibility of kin. If a person is killed, his family or clan clamor for revenge, and the culprit's kin protect him irrespective of his guilt or innocence. The aggrieved party holds the offender's kin responsible as a body and may be content to kill any member of that group. Thus reprisals back and forth may last for years.

Such an attitude prevents national unity, and if logically carried out makes of each family or clan a separate political unit. Killing a tribesman of another kin would be exactly like killing an enemy. Actually this principle is never consistently carried out because the local tie, though weak, is never absent. In other words, a Crow felt differently toward an unrelated Crow and toward a Dakota. When a Dakota was killed every one rejoiced; the death of a fellow-Crow was a grave matter for all clans, not merely for the parties immediately involved. To be sure, there was no official *punishment* for murder. But official action could be taken to minimize trouble. The Crow Indians could not afford a feud in their midst, hence the chief and his police labored as go-betweens to bring about a reconciliation. The aggrieved kinsmen finally consented to accept weregild, which the murderers' kin were only too glad to pay. There was thus a machinery for preventing rupture even though without coercion. Above all there was a sense of obligation beyond the clan, a quasi-national sentiment, though a weak one, resting on co-residence. Similarly, among the Ifugao of Luzon, superficially one of the most anarchistic peoples in the world, a thief from another family was merely fined, while if from another *district* he was killed.

The weakest political aggregates are thus held together

not merely by blood but also by a weak sense of local solidarity. This germ has been developed to its extreme in the modern State, which takes over all the business of government within its area and in theory does not tolerate any other agencies that profess to make and execute laws or to set themselves up as judges. A revolution implies that such agencies have been organized illegally until they are powerful enough to set themselves up as a new State.

Very early human groups were doubtless as loosely organized as the Yurok or Ona. Several factors helped in different areas to pave the way for larger aggregates than tiny units of kin. Exogamy brings one or more alien kin groups into the same settlement and allies even those members who are not actual co-residents. The principle can be developed further. In Australia a youth about to be initiated is sent on a tour to distant districts, where his sacred character renders him safe even if the groups are otherwise hostile. They remain friendly for the rest of his life, and he may get a wife from one of them. Thus his children become related to a remote band; and since other youths travel different routes their horde as a whole develops friendly contacts within a wide swath of territory.

Aside from marriage, men of different kin groups may be united by joint initiation to manhood, which establishes a permanent tie among the Masai, or by membership in the same religious fraternity or club. All these may not weld large groups together, but they do associate persons on principles other than mere blood relationship. Modern types of government are doubtless most expeditiously created by a military and organizing genius. African history shows different stages of this process. Some tribes are split up into minute groups with headmen lacking real authority. Others are ruled by constitutional monarchs, the chiefs being checked by a council of elders. In still other instances conquest brought hundreds of thousands under the control of an autocrat, who embodies the State. Where the ruler is absolute, the kin group may persist but it has lost its ancient governmental power. An African king can not tolerate a feud between clans, and unlike a Crow chief he has means to suppress it. Thus, over a large part of Africa, the blood feud, which elsewhere plays a large part, is eliminated in favor of court procedure. When a man is answerable only to the chief for injury to another subject's person, the blood tie has been superseded by the local tie, by obligations to the supreme sovereign of one's territorial unit. Nevertheless here, as in civilized countries, this principle is not always carried out with complete consistency. The Shilluk lynch poisoners caught in the act and carry on blood feuds, which the king turns to his advantage by claiming the indemnity for each life taken.

Legal Formalities

Evidence. Where the kinship tie predominates and disputes are settled on a personal basis, evidence is irrelevant. But ordeals of various forms occur even in the absence of regular courts. The Chukchi of northeastern Siberia settled a difference by a wrestling-match. The Mohave had a tug-of-war over disputed farm holdings, each side trying to shove one of their number across the land of their opponents. Dissatisfaction with the issue led to a brawl with cudgels, each group again trying to drive the other back. Victory meant definitely establishing title to the property.

Ordeals usually have a supernatural aspect and are coupled with oaths. When two Crow warriors claimed the same honor, one might challenge the other to an ordeal. Each impaled some meat on an arrow, touched it with his lips, then raised it aloft, and called upon the Sun as a witness, saying that if he lied he was to die. Then, if shortly afterward the oath-taker died or lost a close relative, the tribe regarded him as the perjuror, the honor in litigation going to his rival.

Oaths and ordeals are highly characteristic of Old World peoples, especially among African Negroes, and survived beyond medieval times in Europe. Various tests were employed, usually with religious sanction. In old Benin, Nigeria, the priest greased a cock's feather and pierced the tongue of the accused: if it passed easily through, the man accused was adjudged innocent, otherwise he was guilty. Another common test was to spurt a corrosive juice into the defendant's eyes, which were supposed to remain unhurt if he was innocent. In the same area a decoction was administered for capital offences: if a person vomited it, he was free, otherwise he was condemned to death. Here, as in some other ordeals, everything depended on the officiating priest: if he gave an overdose he could produce vomiting and save the accused. Another procedure was to pour boiling palm oil over a man's hands. Often a mere oath sufficed in Nigeria, the defendant invoking a god to smite him with death or misfortune if he lied. If nothing happened within a year, the accusation was dismissed and the accuser punished.

Trials. Practically absent among other primitives, court sittings are highly typical of Africa. There even loosely organized tribes such as the Lobi hold lengthy sessions, which give an opportunity for forensic eloquence and serve as general entertainment. At one open air Lobi trial for larceny the defendant was asked by the presiding elder to express his side of the case. He admitted the theft of several chickens belonging to relatives in order to get money for gambling. The plaintiffs were then heard, whereupon the judges discussed the matter among themselves and decided on severely reprimanding the offender. During the proceedings villagers of both sexes attended and several times questioned the magistrates and the defendant.

In the more complex African societies the chief combines executive and judicial functions, and appeal is possible from the petty to the paramount chiefs, and from them to the king. Among the Shilluk, cases are first tried before the village or provincial officials and discussed at enormous length. But great crimes may be brought directly to the king's attention. The king has numerous spies, who report even trivial occurrences throughout his dominions. He is thus completely informed before sitting in court and accordingly all speeches are succinct in contrast to the diffuseness permitted in the lower courts. In doubtful cases there was an ordeal. Condemning a man to death was part of the royal prerogative.

Penalties and Execution of Judgment. The overwhelming number of primitive peoples know two main forms of punishment, fines and death. Imprisonment was rare, but in Uganda and some other African countries a condemned man was sometimes placed in the stocks. In New Zealand plundering the fields of the offender and his kin was an established institution. Corporal punishment, apart from death, was repulsive to some natives, but freely indulged by others. A recalcitrant Shilluk debtor was flogged with whips of hippopotamus hide and pilloried.

Judgments were sometimes executed in informal manner. Among the chiefless Lobi there was no coercive force, but from fear of supernatural disfavor the defendant's relatives made him submit to the elders' verdict. On the other hand, the Shilluk monarch had warriors bring in a fugitive defendant, while his bodyguard levied taxes and saw to the payment of fines. Capital punishment was inflicted secretly by a special royal appointee.

American Indians rarely concentrated executive power, but at the time of a communal buffalo hunt the police were in supreme control. Whoever disobeyed their orders was liable to be whipped and to have his tent demolished; and if he resisted he might even be killed. This extreme severity is remarkable because of the normal freedom enjoyed by the individual in these tribes; it is due to the economic danger to which a hunter "playing a lone hand" might expose all of his people. Some West African secret organizations assumed juridical and constabulary functions. Among the Yoruba, for instance, the Ogboni society passed judgment and left the execution of criminals to a subordinate organization.

Rulers

As already shown, many primitive communities are governed by public opinion rather than by constituted authority. Even in parts of Africa and Polynesia the power is held by a body of prominent men rather than by individual rulers. In Queensland all the elder males made up an informal council that settled affairs of state, received visitors, demanded satisfaction for the murder of a member, and punished by death a breach of exogamy. The North American Indians had "chiefs" but often these were mere advisors and virtually never dictators. Except in emergencies they had no power over the lives and property of their fellows. Naturally a man of strong personality could assert himself, but his influence was not rooted in office, so that it died with himself. This holds also for many South American tribes. In the Chaco a headman of the Ashluslay Indians works exactly like his fellows and has neither a special hut nor a place of honor at feasts. An Ona group is guided by a venerable patriarch, whose competence and character all respect, though he is in no sense an official. Even among the Indians of British Columbia, where caste played so important a part, the chief was not a despot. For instance, the head of a Haida clan could not compel obedience even within his group and had no real authority outside it; while a Tsimshian chief, far from being an Oriental potentate, was responsible for losses in war.

Religious sanction sometimes gave absolute power in Polynesia and Micronesia (p. 270). To defy a chief was sacrilege, to obey him unqualifiedly the highest duty. Strangely enough, this advantage was not used for consolidating major groups. Even large islands like those of New Zealand were split up among innumerable tribelets. Thus, especially in Hawaii and Tahiti, Polynesians illustrate supreme power vested in a divine chief but, owing to the separatism of the natives, no large population was ever anciently brought under a common head.

In striking contrast the African natives have again and again founded pretentious kingdoms with a population and area comparable to those of smaller European countries. A little over a century ago Chaka rapidly changed the government of the Zulu from a limited monarchy into a despotism and made his tribe a first-rate power in native South Africa (p. 227). His example shows that autocracies are unstable, for under his less able and ferocious successors much of his ascendancy was again lost. The monarchies of Africa present probably all the variations found in the history of civilized countries. In Ruanda there is a strictly stratified society based on the subordination of racially diverse groups: possibly a million and a half Bantu farmers are the plebeians ruled by pastoral patricians of mixed race, while Pygmy hunters form the pariah class. Here the chief of the invading stock-breeders is the feudal lord (p. 279) of his own people and king of the country as a whole. The Bantu of this region happened to be split up into minor groups, which the conquerors deftly played against one another.

Uganda presents a different picture. There is no aristocracy, but a vast number of officials including the king's ministers, governors of the 10 provinces, and various grades of chiefs, who are not in any sense bluebloods. The State organization has been worked out on a surviving clan basis, many clans rendering special services to the king. In the southern Congo the Bakuba king, treated with the utmost marks of outward respect, is a mere figurehead dominated by his ministers.

In West Africa the secret societies typically influenced kingly powers. Among the Kuyu of the Congo basin the chief confers membership, conducts the initiation, and terrorizes his subjects by his supposed mystic association with the leopard. Here the fraternity is merely an extra tool for exploitation in the chief's hands. But among the Kpelle of Liberia the men's tribal society is headed by a "grand master" credited with the power to kill and resuscitate by magic. He is an independent counterbalance to the king in ordinary times, and during the 4-years period of an initiation ceremony he takes over a large part of administration, summons councils, and attends to the maintenance of bridges and roads. The secret society and its grand master thus seriously curtail the royal power. Again, among the Ekoi of the Kamerun region a secret organization punished theft, collected debts for its members, and flogged outsiders. In short, it made all the difference in the world whether a monarch used the secret society for his purposes or whether it was partly or even mainly independent of him.

As in Polynesia, the king was sometimes considered divine and hedged about with ceremony and restrictions that might prove galling at times. Thus, except at a certain festival, the ruler of Benin was not permitted to leave his palace. Not even his nobles were allowed to look him in the face, and they had to retire from his presence crawling backward. Altogether, there was an elaborate and in part whimsical court etiquette. The queen dowager had 17 villages placed at her disposal, held court in a palace of her own, and was consulted on all important affairs, but she and her reigning son must never see each other. Each grade of office had its own emblems, such as swords, brass anklets, and coral necklaces.

While in simpler conditions brothers characteristically aid each other, the craving for power makes for strife among princes in many sections of Africa. This was further stimulated by a curious indecisiveness as to the succession. Instead of having a fixed rule, some countries had the dying king clandestinely announce his successor from among his sons. In Benin the confidant in due time passed on the information to the field marshal and after various formalities the new monarch was brought to the capital to reign supreme. Since the dispossessed princes often plotted against his life, the ruler had them slaughtered when convenient. In the early Eighteenth Century, however, a king abrogated the old principle in favor of primogeniture.

The political structure of the Shilluk presents some distinctive features. The kingdom is divided into 4 major and 2 lesser provinces, the governors of the former being chief electors in the choice of a new king. There are many districts and villages, and as usual all the executive officers of different grade are also judges. The king chooses wives from all over his realm and is rather expected to marry one of his half-sisters. He lives in Fashoda, the capital, which he enters for general recognition by his subjects, first remaining secluded for a month in order to commune with the Shilluk god and culture hero, Nyikang. On the day of his coronation his subjects are privileged to scold him and spit at him.

Henceforth, the king is not only a ruler but high-priest. Lesser offerings may be made by others, but the king personally kills a sacrificial beast to bring rain and orders a human sacrifice for extreme drought and in a difficult war. He inherits his father's property, gets a part of every hippopotamus killed by the Shilluk, as well as all elephant tusks, leopard skins and giraffe tails. All booty from raids belongs to him, and his income is increased by his judgments in court. In addition, it is his subjects' duty to build huts for their monarch and to supply him with the finest dugouts.

Though the king lives in less splendor than some other African monarchs, he also follows a strict etiquette. Some of the huts in the capital are reserved for consultations with chiefs, others for eating, still others for drinking. The ruler sleeps in the daytime and walks about at night, heavily armed. A special vocabulary used at court is supposed to surround the king and his retinue with a halo.

Both the accession and the close of a Shilluk reign are distinctive. The king succeeds neither by fixed rule nor is he chosen by his dying father. Instead there is a secret election by the provincial governors, who, however, are amenable to sundry influences. Unless imbecile, disfigured and left-handed, all sons of the late king are eligible. Each prince makes a point of traveling about in his youth in order to become popular with the electors and those who influence them. Pebbles symbolizing the several candidates are thrown into the fire at the secret conclave, and a pebble that assumes certain colors marks the heir, who is secretly challenged to a duel and after a brave defense receives the news of his election.

No Shilluk monarch dies a natural death. As soon as he is sick, he is suffocated, for weakness is not consistent with the sacredness of Nyikang, who is believed to possess the king. A royal weakling would be a calamity to the country. If he is unpopular, a cold may be sufficient pretext for strangling him. The deed is done by remote relatives of the king with the consent of the princes, the corpse is furtively wrapped in a leopard skin and carried into a hut outside the capital. An ox is sacrificed, then a young wife of the dead ruler is placed at his feet to be walled up in the hut. The Shilluk commoners only learn about the event some two months later. Then the skeletal remains are taken to the temple hut sacred to the deceased. For a year one of the governors acts as a regent, then the successor is elected.

Theory and Reality

In many phases of culture things are really different from what they purport to be. In theory, marriage within the clan is impossible, but not every one follows the rule. In theory, slaves are mere chattels, but actually in ancient Greece and among recent Negroes they are treated as members of the family. Nowhere is this distinction more important than in the field of politics. Apparent anarchy unmasks as strict control by public opinion. On the other hand, chiefs may merely bear an honorary title, while decisions are made by all the men as a body; and even kings are often mere puppets, real authority being in the hands of their cabinets or an independent secret society. The Shilluk example shows that even when royalty is sacred there are methods of putting a ruler out of the way. The theory of a people's government is important as showing their ideals, past or present; more important is it to know how they are actually governed, which means, what forces make and execute their laws.

XVII

RELIGION AND MAGIC

Motives of Supernaturalism

Life is full of hazards. Disease, enemies and starvation are always menacing primitive man. Experience teaches him that medicinal herbs, valor, the most strenuous labor, often come to naught, yet normally he wants to survive and enjoy the good things of existence. Faced with this problem, he takes to any method that seems adapted to his ends. Often his ways appear inconceivably crude to us moderns until we remember how our next-door neighbor acts in like emergencies. When medical science pronounces him incurable, he will not resign himself to fate but runs to the nearest quack who holds out hope of recovery. His urge for self-preservation will not down, nor will that of the illiterate peoples of the world, and in that overpowering will to live is anchored the belief in supernaturalism, which is absolutely universal among known peoples, past and present. What particular form it will take varies locally, yet some of its features are all but universal.

Impersonal Supernaturalism

Imitative and Contagious Magic. One of these widespread notions is the belief in being able to fulfil your wish by imitating the event you long for. An Australian wants rain to fall, so he fills his mouth with water and squirts it out in different directions; and a Hopi for the same reason draws the picture of clouds and dropping rain. When game was scarce, a Crow magician once turned a buffalo skull with its nose toward camp, and presently a large herd came. After the Indians had slaughtered their fill, the skull was turned in the opposite direction and the buffalo disappeared. Such imitative magic takes a more complex form: a Maori shapes an effigy of his enemy and strikes it, thereby supposing himself to injure the real person. So a Crow chief once drew an image of his rival on the ground, punctured its heart, blew smoke over it, and blotted it out with a curse. This practice has not been restricted to savages, but flourished in Europe throughout the Middle Ages and is still popular among the peasantry of less accessible districts there. Sometimes primitive folk couple the idea with another: they can wreak havoc best by working on something in intimate contact with a person's body. A hair from the enemy's head, a bit of his cloak, or a nail paring, is enough for an Ona sorcerer. He puts it into a little bag, which he kneads and pulls, tramples underfoot, and slowly exposes to a flame or submerges under water. All this maltreatment, he imagines, is transferred to the victim, who will perish within half a month. The people at large believe so firmly in such "contagious magic" that they carefully conceal their clipped hair and nail parings to avoid magical arts against them. No wonder Dr. Gusinde had the greatest trouble to persuade his Ona friends to let him have samples of their hair for his collection.

Spells. Spells—mere words, recited or sung for their supernatural value—represent another type of magic. In northeastern Siberia some Koryak and Chukchi have spells for any emergency—for curing illness, improving the weather, or hunting reindeer. Naturally enough, whoever has inherited such magical formulae does not part with them gratis but sells them at a stiff price: they are his "incorporeal" property (see p. 281). In New Zealand magical incantations virtually usurped the place of prayer. Every phase of life had its proper charm. There were chants to aid in childish games;

a fisherman could not succeed without saying his formula; every stage in farming, house-building, tree-felling and warfare had to be inaugurated with spells, the more important being known only to the higher priests. But the recital must be letter-perfect: "any break in the continuous flow, or error in recital, was an omen of failure and disaster." These spells were not mere words that produced results as mechanically as the recipes of a cook-book or the directions of a chemical laboratory text. So when a Hawaiian declaimed his temple chant, absolute silence was imperative: the barking of a dog or hoot of an owl nullified the whole procedure. The atmosphere surrounding these formulae was one of holiness and awe. That is why primitive magic can not be rated as a lowly form of science but must be considered the psychological equivalent of religion, whether or not it is linked with gods and spirits.

Divination. Men use occult techniques not only to shape the future but to pry into it, and from early times to the present they have resorted to divination. Siberians and Mongols hold the shoulderblade of a reindeer or sheep over a fire and interpret the kind of crack produced as foreboding good or ill. An Eskimo diagnoses a man's chances of recovery by binding his head with a string tied to a stick: if lifting the head seems easy, all is well; if it feels heavy, the augury is unfavorable. So in West Africa an Ewe diviner spits on an egg and throws it on his roof, and if it fails to break the omen is good. In South Africa, as in ancient India, dice are thrown, and the manner of their disposal on the ground is interpreted by an intricate code. Here, too, the use of such procedure is not profane; a native refused to surrender his set to a missionary on the ground that they were *his* Bible! Still other methods have been popular over wide areas. Hawaiians read the future from the position of the entrails of sacrificed pigs, and some Negro tribes keep poultry exclusively for similar uses.

Taboos. Taboos are considered a negative type of magic: people believe that unless they refrain from doing certain things dire catastrophes will befall them. Some things were in their nature perilous or polluting, and the result of contact with them was automatic punishment. For example, Maricopa and Polynesian warriors returning from battle had been contaminated and had to submit to a purifying rite (see p. 228). A Crow informant was under a personal taboo not to permit the young of any animal in his tipi, and he explained his rheumatism for the past eleven years by some one taking such a beast there in his absence. The Eskimo sentiment against eating seal and venison at the same time (p. 285) falls under this head. A similarly quaint taboo holds in the Andaman Islands, where the Pygmies never burn bees' wax lest a deity named Biliku cause a storm.

The last examples are doubly instructive. They show that magic may be tied up with supernatural beings, who either lay down prohibitions or prescribe a positive line of conduct. But they also show that primitive supernaturalism may be oddly unethical: its laws are often whimsical, need not bear any relation to social welfare, and completely ignore the idea of a transgressor's intentions. When the rule is once broken, even the greatest power in the universe may be unable to stave off disaster.

Amulets and Fetiches. Often trees, rivers, even objects made by man are considered holy and mysteriously powerful because a nymph, sprite, or other being, dwells in them. But that association is not essential. Spells, we have seen, need not emanate from a deity; they are potent in their own right and sometimes superior to the greatest of the gods. So it is with objects used for protection on the body or in the village—what we call amulets or talismans. Fetiches, too, are material things revered because of their mysterious power. The word itself comes from the Portuguese explorers, who first applied it to the wooden images of the West African

Negroes. But the essential thing is not that they are artifacts: a leaf or stone of unusual shape may be treasured and adored in exactly the same way as a carved figure. On the other hand, in the very area where the phenomenon was first observed the most elaborate image is merely a work of art until a magician has "consecrated" it—say, by thrusting a particular kind of paint into an opening or crooning a spell over it. That is to say, here, too, the source of power may be *im*personal, vested in an unintelligible way in the paints, words, or techniques used.

Animation of Nature. Practically, it is not always easy to distinguish where the impersonal ends and the personal begins. Primitive folk are often illogical from our point of view. A Plains Indian will meet a supernatural bird-man, who blesses him and gives him the right to wear a certain feather in battle. He escapes injury and ever after cherishes his feather as a holy of holies. Is it merely a symbol to him of his divine protector? Does he pray to it only because of its connection, or does it seem charged with power of its own? We can not be sure. For here another feature enters. Primitive people do not always draw the distinction between animate and inanimate, and tend to personify both. Near the boundary of Mexico and Arizona an old Akwa'ala Indian was seen talking to rain clouds and shooing them away as though they were a flock of geese; and the Crow Indians firmly believe that a certain rock can give birth to little ones. Further, as the savage merges the mineral and the animal kingdoms, so he recognizes no absolute barrier between beast and man (see p. 258): snakes, buffalo, crocodiles, even insects, he assumes, may converse and act like human beings; and in his myths men marry animals and are descended from them. Primitive men are capable of seeing the difference between dead and living matter and in their everyday lives do not mistake a mosquito for a fellow-Indian. Nevertheless, when emotionally wrought up, an Indian or Negro will for the time being invoke a pebble, a bit of charcoal, or a lizard; though as soon as his excitement passes he sees the same object realistically. Hence primitive man does not dogmatize that everything in the universe is animate. His world-view simply does not, on principle, make it absurd to invest *anything* with life or personality, so that under proper conditions anything *may* temporarily appear as a person. The Maori of recent times did not expect to observe their hills wandering about the land under their eyes, but they did believe that Mounts Kakaramea and Maungapohatu were once husband and wife, quarreled, separated, and became fixed in position. So our own fundamentalists do not hope for a span of 969 years, but they accept as consistent with their notion of possibility that Methuselah did once attain that ripe old age.

Mana. The South Sea Islanders evolved an abstract concept for all forms of supernatural power. They called it *mana* and applied it alike to personal and impersonal things; our Algonkian Indians had a similar notion under the head of *manitou;* and, more or less consistently elaborated, the basic idea is very widespread. To the Polynesian *mana* was like an electrical fluid that could charge persons and things and be diverted from one to another. Any conspicuous success was due to mana, failure to its absence or loss. A Marquesan youth who could not memorize native traditions was said to lack mana; a master of such lore, if worsted in a contest of wits, had lost his mana. A warrior absorbed the mana of all enemies he had killed and thus increased his own. Certain localities had this power, hence a fugitive had only to get there in order to be safe. Clubs had it if they had always been wielded in victory, and so did exceptional adzes. In short, good luck, efficiency, outstanding wisdom, were the outer signs of mana as the operative cause. Some Maori priests, striving for a consistency by no means essential to all their compatriots, conceived all mana as primarily held by Io, the Supreme

Being, and the greater gods had somehow to reach out for it. Even among such philosophically minded people as these New Zealanders, we can not be certain whether personal or impersonal force is primary. Io created the universe by using the very formula by which a magician overcame barrenness. Now since the Maori were presumably not taken into the Creator's confidence, the spell must have been *their* product to begin with and they secondarily ascribed it to Io, hence Io's creation is at bottom due to his knowledge of an incantation, and this impersonal set of words lies at the basis of his creative act.

Personal Supernaturalism

Religion and Philosophy. The personal and impersonal aspects of supernaturalism are, then, often inextricably interwoven. But, undeniably, personal supernatural beings—deities and spirits—have played an enormous part throughout history. A pitfall we must avoid in this connection is to confuse religion and philosophy. Their subject matter often coincides, but their attitude is distinct. Our acid test is man's behavior in a crisis. What he does when stirred to the depths of his being, when he is racked with pain, when his crops fail, when he is ground under the heel of a foreign tyrant—that constitutes his religion. Anything else may be connected with it, as all things human somehow hang together, but religion it is not. For example, whether or not a certain god created the universe may be a matter of no significance whatsoever from the point of view of faith. The ancient Greeks regarded Zeus as their foremost deity, but he was emphatically not the originator of the world; to put Oceanos at the head of Greek belief because Homer puts him first in time would be to outrage the facts. So in viewing Polynesian religion we must not be hypnotized by the high-sounding concoctions of the native priests. These were specialists, and like all specialists tended to become virtuosos, who ostentatiously exhibited their skill in handling and amplifying traditional lore. A favorite device of theirs was to picture the gradual unfolding of the world in successive generations marked by distinct entities. For example, some Maori cosmogonists started with the Root, which was followed by the Taproot; the Rootlets; the Creeper; the Growth; the Great Wood; the Conception; the Sound; the Chaos; the Darkness; the Sky; and the Earth. More esoteric, but even less intelligible, is another version according to which gods and men appear only in the Sixth Era, the predecessors of which are characterized in such terms as these:

The first period. . . .

From the conception the increase,
From the increase the swelling,
From the swelling the thought,
From the thought the remembrance,
From the remembrance the consciousness, the desire.

Whether we regard this as profound wisdom or pretentious and meaningless verbiage, will depend on our metaphysical taste. But no one can seriously believe that any one, the priesthood included, turned to such phraseology for a solution of life's problems. Unquestionably it is among the world's literary and intellectual curiosities, but its relation to religion is precisely nil. This is not to say that all great gods and all noble conceptions of the supernatural are divorced from religion, but merely that for each people it remains to be separately investigated how important a part they play in the individual's consciousness. Indeed, on this point there is often much diversity even in the same tribe. Especially where a sharp cleavage of castes separated society, as in Polynesia, the cult of the aristocracy is usually distinct from the popular faith. Nothing warrants us in sharing the native patrician's conceited notion that *his* is the national system par excellence. Among the Maori, Io, the Supreme Being of the upper crust, was wholly unknown to the vast bulk of the population; and below him ranked several major deities, among them Tu, who presided over warfare. Yet a fighting force would rely not so much upon him as upon a mere district god, or even the shades of their recent ancestors. Any of the warriors might make a forebear into a special protector by performing certain rites. Thenceforth the spirit would use him as a medium, watch over him, warn him of danger; and we can be quite sure that to the medium this familiar spirit meant more than all the ornate pantheon of the elect. Possession by spirits and ancestor-worship, like the magical spells, are veritably basic ideas of Polynesian supernaturalism.

Animism. Although religion is not essentially a matter of intellect, it necessarily involves intellectual processes. Possession and ancestor worship imply the idea of spirit. All peoples the world over believe in a kind of existence less material than that of solid bodies. All, for instance, credit men with a soul that survives his body. The soul is pictured as shadowy or film-like and often compared to a reflection in the water. Very commonly the view is held that such a soul wanders about in sleep, that it can go astray or be captured by enemies. The primitive belief in spirits, technically known as "animism", does not imply what our philosophers and religious teachers describe as immaterial existence. A shadow is not a rock, but neither is it beyond the realm of physical nature. Hence continued life after death is not equivalent to immortality. A soul can be destroyed by its kidnaper; even ghosts are mortal according to West African theory, and if a Jagga in East Africa fails to feed his deceased ancestors they dwindle and perish. The Ojibwa around Lake Superior gave circumstantial accounts of the soul's journey to the hereafter and told how some souls died from eating alluring but poisonous wild strawberries by the wayside.

The Hereafter. Though all peoples are animists, they give different weight to the same features of their belief and altogether work out their doctrines on varying principles. Thus, the ancient Egyptians were vitally concerned with the hereafter, on which the Greeks lavished little thought; and while the Ojibwa have a secret order to render the path of the soul less perilous, the Crow have no coherent theory of life after death and merely accept its continuance from the sporadic experiences of men supposed to have come back. In other words, faith in a hereafter is not an essential ingredient of religion. Still less so is any notion of future reward or punishment. Even when souls of the dead separate into different camps, their division proceeds on other than ethical principles. Thus, Aztec warriors slain in battle or women dying in delivery went to the sun; persons drowned or struck by lightning joined the rain gods; while those who died a natural death were condemned to a perilous journey to the underworld. The Maori recognized an earthly and a celestial abode, but retribution for good and evil deeds was foreign to their scheme: those who sympathized with the Earth descended, while those who sympathized with the Sky were carried thither by a whirlwind.

Animism and Religion. Animism and religion largely overlap, but they are not identical. Supernatural persons need not be of the shadowy nature of souls. The gods of ancient Greece, for instance, have been aptly described as magnified men. When a starving Crow hunter meets a butchering dwarf whose muscles stand out in lumps, there is nothing to show that this manifestly supernatural being was ever human, that he controls any object as a soul directs its body, or that the picture formed of him is in any way patterned on the soul. On the other hand, primitive folk sometimes conceive of spirits as part of their universe without bringing them into contact with their religious life. They may imagine a film-like being in the mist or rainbow, a spirit in the dawn or cloud, without ever invoking them or trying to relate them to their needs, or even without crediting them with any powers beyond the normal.

The trolls of the Ona form a good illustration. Soul-like in essence, but with the qualification noted for all primitive conceptions of the spiritual, these ogres form a lewd and exclusively male society of their own, inhabiting the woods, where they pounce upon stray Indians, stun them with stones and specialize in ravishing either sex, though preferably women. Naturally such monsters are shunned. But the natives display not the slightest reverential awe toward them, and even consider it possible to worst them with an arrow shot. These forest demons are therefore not in any sense divine; they are a distinct species of persons, a part of Ona folk-anthropology, not of Ona religion.

Ancestor Worship. Frequently, however, this association of ideas does occur, and ancestor-worship is one form it takes. As noted, a Jagga ancestor requires sustenance, hence he insists on sacrifices and afflicts neglectful descendants. One of the most typical African procedures in case of illness is to divine which ancestor is offended, to discover what he wants, and to offer him the bull or goats he demands. Commonly such sacrifices are coupled with a convenient extension of the animistic doctrine. As man has a soul, so the sacrificial flesh is said to have a more spiritual essence, and this alone is the food proper for the supernaturals, so that the substance of the offering may be devoured by the worshipers themselves. Ancestor-cults are highly characteristic of the Old World, but are rarely typical of American Indians, hence they are not an inevitable stage in religious evolution. Even in Africa and Asia they figure quite differently in different settings. Bantu ancestor-worship often lies at the very root of religion, but in West Africa major deities loom as more important. Among Central Asiatic Turks, as in New Zealand, it was the spirit of a forebear that took possession of a medium. Again, since primitive folk often fail to draw the line between man and beast they may trace their lineage to an animal founder, who occasionally is actually reverenced. In totemism, however (see p. 258), the religious element is generally slight: the clansmen abstain from eating or injuring the animal or plant with which they are associated but perform no acts of devotion. But, to cite still another form of the institution, the members of an ancient Chinese clan worshiped the human ancestor, or supposed ancestor, of their group as a powerful protector. They erected crude stone or wooden statues of him, consulted him by divination, prayed for his assistance, and rewarded him with sacrifices. The modern Chinese practice of general ancestor-worship grew out of this simple idea.

Other Spirits. Ancestor-worship, however, is only one form of animistic faith, for spirits never supposed to have inhabited a human body are also invoked. As shown, any natural phenomenon may be personified or considered the seat of a spirit directing it, and so there are tree and water spirits, rulers of thunder, residents of the sun, moon and stars. All of these may in a given case lack religious quality and, like the Ona trolls, be nothing more than elements of aboriginal folk-science; but one of them may assume divine virtues and become the object of an elaborate cult. It would be artificial to draw a sharp line between gods and spirits of the religious category; the latter have aptly been called "godlets", and the natives themselves usually fail to distinguish classes of supernaturals. To a Maori the humble wood-elf is an "atua" just as much as Sky and Earth. Moreover, whether an outsider considers the Sky god greater or not, the humblest familiar spirit of a philosophical scheme may mean infinitely more to its possessor than a Supreme Being.

For what counts from the consumer's point of view, so to speak, is whether he gets what he craves of life's values. Hence, satisfactory relations with powers that can fulfil his wishes is far more important than to put these powers in their respective niches. He requires a technique comparable to that of magic, but adjusted to relations with supernatural *persons*. Persons can be influenced by prayer and offerings, and accordingly the most complicated ceremonials belong at bottom to either or both of these categories.

Priests and Shamans. In some cultures every one can approach gods on an equal footing with his fellows, but many peoples insist on a go-between. Priests, as exemplified by the Polynesians, are masters of ritual. As in the recital of spells, so in supplication and sacrifice absolute precision was considered essential by primitive men; an error might not only bring a complicated tribal performance to naught, it might bring down the inescapable wrath of the deities. Hence specialists were needed to shoulder the responsibility, men who had somehow learned exactly how to go through a given ceremony. Such were the temple priests of Hawaii, Tahiti and the Marquesas. It is not necessary that such an adept at ceremonial should meet his gods face to face, get oral instructions from them, or be temporarily possessed by them as their medium. An individual who does enjoy such intimate relationship is called a "shaman", the Siberian name for this phenomenon; and as the priest requires no direct revelation in order to go about his rite, so a shaman need not have the slightest connection with ritual. In Uganda the functions of these two intermediaries between man and god are nicely divided. There every temple has its medium, who is at times possessed by a particular god. In this condition he is in a frenzy, and his utterances, which are accepted as oracular, must be interpreted by the priest —an appointee of his clan. Here the shaman, nothing but a temporary vehicle used by a god, is definitely subordinated to the priest, who is alone empowered to make offerings. The Pueblo Indians, on the other hand, have priests but no shamans. However, in many regions there is a personal union of these two duties. Among the Siberian Turks it is the medium who offers sacrifices and conducts the lingering soul of a dead man to the spirit world.

Shamans are often nervously unstable persons and even epileptics. Hence they work themselves into a frenzy during their professional labors, and this condition is interpreted as possession by a spirit. An early traveler describes a Tahitian medium with convulsed muscles, distorted features, and strained eyes. "In this state he often rolled on the earth, foaming at the mouth, as if laboring under the influence of the divinity by whom he was possessed, and, in shrill cries, and violent and often indistinct sounds, revealed the will of the gods", the priests interpreting the mysterious message. Similarly, when a Siberian Turk receives his first summons from the spirit world, he has a fit, trembles and yawns, utters inarticulate sounds, leaps about madly, seizes and swallows pins, and at last falls to the ground twitching and covered with perspiration. Often a Siberian fears the spirit and tries to evade the relationship foisted on him, but the spirit threatens him with death and cows him into submission. An Ona shaman, when treating a patient, at once begins to sing in order to summon his familiar—the soul of a dead shaman—through whom he hopes to extract the cause of the illness. Suddenly the doctor is seized with a tremor, he sings louder and faster: the spirit has entered his body and merged with his soul. The doctor wildly shakes and distorts his torso. In a state of the utmost excitement, "as though mad", he begins to suck out the disease-causing agent, stares at it with glassy eyes, and topples over completely exhausted. From Africa and Oceania, from Siberia and Tierra del Fuego we thus have evidence that shamans are either abnormal or at least temporarily capable of passing into abnormal mental states. In such a condition they are likely to give amazing proof of the divine power within them. A Polynesian medium could then eat as much as four men. An Eskimo makes his drum rock and jump on his forehead. A Siberian uses ventriloquism to imitate the calls of visiting animal spirits, has himself tied hand and foot, yet releases himself unaided.

Dreams and Visions. North American Indians were rarely possessed. To them revelation came in vivid dreams and visions. A Paviotso of Owens Valley, California, would dream of an eagle, a rattlesnake, a bear, even a personified mountain. Each of these might speak to him and grant him a special form of power. As a result some tribesmen became skilful hunters, others could make themselves invisible, still others were bullet-proof or learned to be doctors. A woman befriended by an eagle acquired speed and could gather a sevenfold harvest of pine-nuts by using the feathers symbolic of her protector. But here, as among neighboring and related tribes as far as southern Mexico, the revelation was not left wholly to chance. The natives knew the narcotic properties of jimsonweed (*Datura meteloides*) and some deliberately partook of the plant in order to stimulate visions. By eating the seed a Paviotso would come to see his dead kin, while a Nevada Paiute could discover lost goods. Polynesians, by the way, sometimes drank kava to induce possession.

Eastern and Plains Indians democratized shamanism by making the quest of a vision a general standardized institution. In Wisconsin a Menomini boy or girl withdrew at puberty, fasting and thirsting in a secluded spot and praying for a visitation. Their elders would see them daily and inquire as to their success. Sun, Moon, or Thunder might come to a youth and make him a great hunter or bless a maiden with long life. The visionary had to offer tobacco to his familiar and to keep on his person some token of his guardian. In return the spirit promised his assistance. The Crow did not limit the search for a tutelary to adolescence, but allowed any person to try for a vision whenever he craved a desirable end. In order to arouse supernatural pity more effectively they generally tortured themselves not only by fasting but by chopping off a finger-joint or dragging buffalo skulls attached by skewers to their perforated backs. Thus, some went out to gain glory or horses in warfare, others in order to revenge themselves, still others wished to become ceremonial leaders. A man's career was determined by his experience, for if he was promised long life his implicit confidence in the vision made him a reckless warrior; if he was told how to treat wounds, he set up as a doctor.

Visions grew so dominant in Crow consciousness that all success was ascribed to them, all failure to lack of them; hence, in theory, every war raid was prompted by a special revelation (see p. 228). Although normally a Crow looked for a vision, he might gain one unsought, sometimes in a dream, but that only came by exceptional good luck or when he faced an emergency, such as starvation or capture. The Indians were quite sincere in their quest, and some admitted failure in spite of all their efforts to be adopted by a tutelary. These had, however, a chance to get some supernatural power by buying it of more successful god-seekers. Nevertheless, in each generation a goodly number of men and women believed they had met supernatural beings and received their blessing, so that in contrast to other areas the tribe would, by definition, harbor dozens of shamans at one time. But the Crow were wise enough to know that *conspicuous* power could not be so common, hence they informally distinguished as "holy men" only those who gave marked demonstration of their gifts. If an Indian could bring buffalo when the camp was starving, if he sent out warriors on a raid and they returned with plenty of loot, if he could make berries and wild plums grow in midwinter, or cure a patient given up by other doctors, his fame as a "holy man" would be secure. This was not to deny power from revelations to others, but simply applying a commonsense test for distinguishing among the many tribesmen who could lay claim to supernatural relations of a sort.

As for the supernaturals who appeared in the Crow visions, they ranged from the Sun and Thunderbird to all manner of beasts and birds. As a rule, a man relied implicitly on the support of his familiar, whom he regarded as his "father", and this bond was the central part of an individual's faith. But the spirit was a capricious martinet, who withdrew protection as soon as his rules were broken. If he had forbidden his ward to eat birds' eggs and the Indian disobeyed, however unwittingly, he inevitably lost his claim to supernatural aid.

Treatment of Disease. Sickness and death constantly recur in human life and men everywhere try to ward them off as effectively as they can. On the primitive level of knowledge this commonly means resorting to supernatural aid. Thus, priests and shamans, though not at all essentially "medicine-men", actually are often called upon as doctors. Two widespread theories of disease are coupled by savages with corresponding methods of treatment. Either some foreign body has entered the patient and must be taken out; or the soul has been lost, possibly kidnaped, and must be recovered. The Ona procedure (p. 311) conforms to the first theory, which is shared by many American, African and Australian tribes. By suction the Ona shaman brings to light an arrow-head, a piece of sinew, or some other small object, which he blows away. In other regions the extract is destroyed. The intrusion theory does not need to exclude its rival. Some Far Western American and some Siberian natives apply either according to circumstances. In Owens Valley, California, a shaman sucks at the ailing part, or he sends his own soul on a journey to retrieve his patient's, which he then restores to the body. The shaman may give a picturesque account of the trip, retailing how he or his familiar spirit grappled with a soul-snatching demon before the sick person's soul could be returned. In Polynesia intrusion was conceived as possession by a demon, whom priests tried to exorcise by their spells.

In many cases such procedure produces a veritable cure. Often the patient has worried himself sick simply from fear of being bewitched; as soon as his doctor pulls out the arrowpoint or pebble supposedly shot by the sorcerer, the disease, being at bottom a mental disturbance, disappears. This explains also why the faith in shamans persists: unsophisticated people want results, and if they get well they do not ponder the problems of scientific pathology. As for the shamans, with all their tricks, they are rarely humbugs. They, too, are saturated with a world-view that allows of miraculous happenings; they have been deeply affected by the sights and voices that guide their professional conduct; and their cures by an unconscious psychiatry impress them no less than their employers. If they fail, something has gone wrong. A hostile shaman or a malevolent deity has thwarted them. The general sincerity of native practitioners is proved by the risk they run. Repeated failure might mean not merely loss of standing but death. Since doctors were often credited with power to cause as well as to remove sickness, a shaman who lost several patients in succession was readily set down as a sorcerer, so that in and near California even quite recently such men have been killed by enraged relatives of the dead Indians. When tribal custom barred such behavior, perils of another order remained. If a Siberian shrank from accepting intimacy with a familiar spirit, it was because his blessings were linked with taboos and the capricious helper might at any time turn in wrath upon his ward. Similarly, a mistake in reciting his incantation could recoil with deadly effect upon a Polynesian doctor-priest. As against such hazards there were indeed at times heavy fees, but in some tribes, say, of central Australia and Tierra del Fuego, even these were wanting, and the doctor's sole reward was added prestige.

Ceremonialism

Main Forms. Ritual or ceremonial is a fixed set of solemn observances. It need not be tied up with religion but develops wherever behavior is taken seriously, as in court etiquette. But because men attach such tremendous importance to all relations with the supernatural, ceremonial thrives especially in that connection. If one error in a single word of a spell nullifies a complex festival and brings disaster to the celebrants, every minute feature in a performance must loom as significant. In this context, then, ritual is the external side of religion. Everywhere important, it sometimes dwarfs the inwardness of faith. A Pueblo Indian, for instance, is so bent on making his prayer-stick offerings, on reciting the appropriate formulas, on puffing smoke the approved number of times, that he seems to lose the sense of addressing personal beings at all. His gods, too, figure only as so many counters in an intricate magical procedure. All of this does not deprive his observances of the high-seriousness and awesomeness peculiar to supernaturalism, but in quality they differ enormously from the fervent prayer of a votary throwing himself on divine compassion. Supernatural ceremonialism branches out in all directions, so that social life, war activities, poetical and dramatic developments are all intertwined with it. Yet its basic forms are few: there are magical ceremonies in which supernatural persons play, if any, a subordinate rôle; and there are vows, prayers, offerings, and thanksgivings by which appeals for similar ends are made to personal beings. Any one of these may be charged with any degree of emotional intensity. A magical rite is to an Australian the holiest of acts. On the other hand, a Tibetan who inscribes his prayers on slips, encloses them in a cylinder, and has them revolved by a wind-mill because the more frequent the revolutions the more effective the invocation, is evidently going through a mechanical performance.

The example teaches us that the boundaries between magic and religion in the narrower sense are often blurred. What is in form a supplication may be in substance a spell. Similarly, Winnebago Indians offer tobacco to spirits because acceptance coerces these beings to grant the favors sought. Here, the semblance of worship is in reality a compulsory magical rite.

Puberty Rituals. Rituals are commonly linked with puberty and death, while primitive folk rarely treat marriage as anything but a civil affair. But these observances may be quite as solemn when divorced from supernatural beings as when intimately connected with them. In southern Oregon, a Klamath girl at the first signs of maturity sleeps in the bush for 5 days, unwashed and unkempt. She has to dance facing eastward and supported on each side by an attendant. Three rules are imposed: she must not scratch herself with her fingers but with a special stick; she is not allowed to eat meat or fish; and every morning she must run toward the dawn. After the 5-day period she bathes and her clothes are burned. There is no suggestion here of gods or spirits; a magical set of acts and taboos ensures the girl's safety and wards off harm from her community, which otherwise might suffer from contact with a person in that condition. Now a Navaho girl, too, must refrain from meat and scratching herself; moreover, she is to run in order to become strong, a purely magical idea. However, a clearly religious note enters: a priest paints the adolescent's face, and in songs refers to the principal deity. Much more dominantly this motive figures in the boys' initiation festivals of Australia and New Guinea. The Euahlayi, for instance, believe that these mysteries were instituted by their hero and creator and erect earthen figures of him and various totem animals. These Australian ceremonies mingle features of amusement, social regulation, and belief. In a sense they make of all men a secret society as against their wives and sisters, since every male must be initiated while all women are barred. Every woman must leave as soon as she hears the bull-roarer (p. 204). Boys, on the other hand, are progressively instructed in the tribal lore, virtually passing through several degrees. Their elders frighten, scratch, and generally haze the boys, each of whom has a front tooth knocked out. In return the youngsters get a new name, sacred stones, the right to marry and eat all kinds of food—in short, they ultimately gain full-fledged citizenship. And all these solemnities are combined with dancing, sham fights and wrestling, secular and sacred elements characteristically fusing in major festivals of simple peoples.

Mortuary Rites. The mortuary rites of these Australians are equally instructive. The mourners wail and intone a dirge enumerating the dead person's totems. Since death is attributed to sorcery, the corpse may be asked for the murderer, one name being uttered after another until the body seems to give a knock. The survivors put the corpse with the personal belongings into a bark coffin, the soul is commended to the creator-hero, the bereaved relatives wail and gash their bodies with sharp stones, for etiquette demands blood, while the widow covers herself with mud, remains speechless for 3 days, daubs her face white and plasters her head for months. A smoky fire is designed to ward off spirits and to disinfect those present. Here the ceremonial is largely social, yet the questioning of the dead brings in the belief in sorcery and the address to the creator adds an indubitably religious element.

Several funeral customs are surprisingly similar in remote areas. In America tribes as distant from each other and the Australians as the Crow of Montana and the Ona of Tierra del Fuego lacerate themselves profusely to show their grief. The Crow crop their hair, while the Ona practice tonsure comparable to a Franciscan monk's. Ona and Owens Valley Californians both burned the dead man's possessions to remove painful memories, and at least for a time carefully refrained from uttering his name. Tahitians begged the deceased not to look back to the world; and the Crow said, "You have gone, do not turn back, we wish to fare well." Very common, too, are deposits of property, often deliberately made to serve the deceased. That is why the Paviotso sprinkled pine-nuts and killed dogs over a grave, and also why slaves were killed for Maori chiefs and African kings.

Notwithstanding such resemblances death also evokes great differences in attitude, and the admixture of religion varies considerably. In the abstract, for example, the Ona trace all deaths to their Supreme Being, and a grief-stricken mourner may occasionally rebel against his cruelty. But apart from this they proceed in a matter-of-fact way to inter the corpse and blot out all unnecessary reminders of the deceased, without the slightest regard to either his or any other spirit. At the opposite extreme stand the West African Lobi, who consult the gods even before beginning to wail, sacrifice oxen and sheep, and ask the corpse for its consent to burial. Here, too, there is not only provender hung up for the spirit, but cowries are thrown down for its payment of toll in crossing a river and for posthumous purchases en route.

Prayer and Offerings. Prayer is one of the basic religious acts directed to a personal deity. On the primitive level it is naïvely and undisguisedly egotistical. This appears especially when, as usually happens, an offering accompanies the invocation. Indeed, these two features can rarely be separated. A Crow chops off his finger-joint as an offering to the Sun, or gives him an albino buffalo-skin for a robe; in return he asks for long life and success on the warpath. A votive offering implies a thanksgiving ceremony. A Crow often invoked a supernatural being in some such fashion as this: "If I live till the fall (or 'bring loot'), I'll put up a sweat-lodge for you." In other words, the idea of a contract underlies the relationship; the supplicant performs acts which he supposes please the supernatural and expects compensation; or he makes his acts of devotion contingent on specified favors. Yet the essence of the matter is not always so baldly presented or felt. In a Fox prayer to the Thunder gods the supplicant's humility is manifest: "O my grandfathers! I burn this tobacco to you as an offering in the hope that you will grant me your blessing. Long may I live, I humbly beseech of you."

Prayer and offering are not purely spontaneous outpourings of the votary's heart: what he does or says, and how, are things just as much predetermined by the tribal pattern as the Crow's method of seeking a revelation. Every Crow sooner or later prays in stereotyped phrases to be allowed to see the seasons of the next year: "May I reach the ripening of the chokecherries, the falling of the leaves, the first snow, the sprouting of the grass." No Crow ever dreamed of sacrificing a dog or horse, while Siberians, Africans, and Oceanians constantly offer the carcasses of their domestic beasts. Human sacrifices, again, are highly typical of the Aztec of Mexico, of Polynesians, and African Negroes; but over wide areas of the New World they were quite unknown. For some tribes particular procedures are so important that they become essential in any vital situation. Thus, kava, the general Polynesian stimulant, which could induce possession or serve as a libation to the gods, was stressed so much in Samoa that "nothing of any importance can be commenced . . . without a preliminary bowl of kava." Among some of our Plains Indians the vapor bath attained a similar position, and other tribes regularly employ incense or smoking of tobacco.

Complex Ceremonies. Many primitive ceremonials seem incredibly intricate and built up of discordant elements. They certainly are not so unified as a closely knit modern drama, but both their length and their incongruity can be largely explained. Their duration is partly due to the influence of a mystic number. Most North Americans hold, tacitly or explicitly, that the universe naturally runs by fours, hence every significant

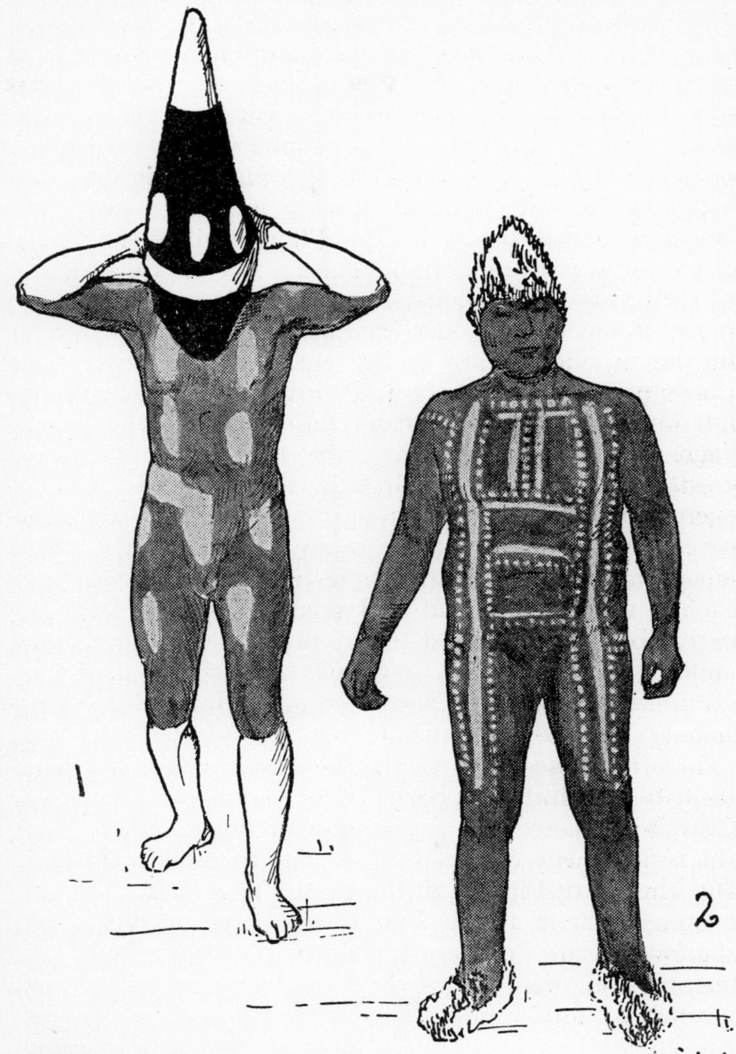

Plate 37: Ceremonial Dress.

1. Ona Dancer [Gusinde (10) Fig. 100] 2. Ona Man ready to take part in Ceremony [Gusinde (10) Fig. 98]

song will be repeated three times, every act must be quadruplicate; and other tribes substitute five, seven, nine, or what not. As for the disharmony of constituent parts of a performance, the natives are not bent on solving a mathematical problem with maximum elegance, but try to follow the customary cues of a given setting. For a major ceremony people are invited from near and far. That automatically inaugurates the etiquette of hospitality. But, for Plains Indians, any large gathering was the inevitable cue for everybody formally to recite his war exploits, from which it was but a step to act them out. A performance designed as a prayer for the public welfare or the curing of the sick might thus embody features not at all involved in that purpose but obviously following from the nature of the assemblage. Australian initiation rites thus come to involve wrestling and dancing, while in New Guinea they are even coupled with a pig market, for these traders par excellence naturally clutch at any opportunity to hold one. Similarly, the firstfruits festivals of Polynesia were such a medley of social and sacred activities that one early observer compared them with the Olympic games, another with a Bartholomew fair. Apart from its bloody sacrifices, one West African ceremony reminded a missionary of a German picnic.

In other cases a particular idea once conceived lends itself to indefinite but perfectly logical elaboration. The Crow Sun Dance was a prayer for revenge amplified by the irrelevancies due to the throwing together of Indians. But the central idea quite naturally suggested details in keeping with it, to wit, acts of imitative magic to foreshadow the desired result. Hence a tree figured as an enemy and was struck by the warriors. A woman pointed an antler prong at it with the wish of piercing the enemy's eye. Because black symbolized a killing, various articles used in the ceremony were painted black. Similarly, wherever initiation is conceived as a rebirth, a number of ideas logically follow and may be realized with quaint effects. Thus, the Lobi of West Africa treat novices as infants, name them anew, and make them profess complete ignorance. The boys put food into their ears, are unable to speak, hold a quiver by the wrong side; and the girls spill water and pour millet on the ground.

Drama and Ceremonial. Often these major performances have dramatic elements, and at one time it was believed that a ceremony was merely a dramatized myth. We now know that when myth and ritual are linked, the myth, whether older or younger than the ritual, has often been added as an afterthought. For example, there is a popular American tale about the perennial feud of Thunderbirds and a water-monster, and in one variant the birds get an Indian marksman to help them. The Hidatsa have a ritual connected with their sacred "Bird bundle", which they derive from this hunter's experiences. But since the observances in no way represent his adventures, the bond between the rites and the story is of the loosest; some ingenious native evidently sought to give more plausibility to the religious claims of the bundle by tracing it back to generally known mythical incidents. Nevertheless, true dramatization of mythological figures and episodes is not by any means unknown among the simpler peoples. To give a few examples: A great annual festival of the Mandan, next-door neighbors of the Hidatsa, was in part the memorial of a great flood. Some of the principal ceremonies of the Australians represent the traditional wanderings of their totemic ancestors. Again, the firstfruits ritual of Hawaii largely dramatized the myth of a god who had killed his wife and traveled about fighting every one he met in his grief. The king himself impersonated the god, landing in a canoe, and suffered a mock-attack by spearsmen. In short, primitive ceremonial may be more than mere pageantry and rise to true theatrical performance.

Ceremonial Organizations. But ritualism may take still another line of development. Initiation in Oceania serves to set off men from women, who are doomed to be outsiders; and African Negroes have separate initiation rites for boys and girls. By special ceremonies of admission, however, one may just as well discriminate among members of the same sex or among tribesfolk regardless of sex. In this way the population can be split up into age-grades, clubs, fraternities and sororities of limited membership. The cleavage may be social in character, but often a religious aspect is stressed. Some Plains tribes had organizations formed by all those who shared a revelation by the same being, say, a buffalo. The Crow, with their notion that a visionary might sell part of his blessing had a Tobacco society divided into many chapters. In return for compensation the founder of each branch had adopted new members, who in turn had taken in others, so that there evolved sects of a common cult, each empowered to plant the sacred weed according to the specific rules of its own branch. A Hopi fraternity had the public duty of producing rain by a biennial "Snake dance". The priests conducting it inherited office in the maternal line, the rank and file being recruited from tribesmen cured of snake bites by the priests. West Africa is dotted with secular and religious societies, many of which stress sorcery, perform mysteries, terrorize the outsiders, and in fact sometimes arrogate to themselves the supreme power of government (p. 294). In point of religion they use the ideas general throughout the area, such as ancestor or fetich worship, sacrifices of domestic animals, and food taboos.

Altogether, ceremonialism displays an amazing blend of religious, social, political and aesthetic strains.

Primitive and Civilized Religions

Survivals. At one time "paganism" was opposed to "revealed religion". The antithesis no longer holds since Indians, Negroes and Polynesians all claim revelations no less than did Moses and Mohammed. If primitive supernaturalism ranks as inferior, it must then be because of the *nature* of the revelation. Primitive supernaturalism revolts us, intellectually because it is incoherent, and morally because it seems selfish in aim and gross in method. Yet the inconsistencies and brutalities are not all on the side of the "savages". Christianity proclaims the brotherhood of man, yet modern war demands more victims than all the human sacrifices of all the primitive peoples who ever lived. The world-view of the Stone Ages has not yet disappeared. It is only yesterday that the last witch was burned in Switzerland; her judges were contemporaries of Hume and the prerevolutionary philosophers of France, but they believed in the powers of a sorcerer. Today European peasants wear amulets and practice imitative magic, while educated Americans consult mediums and attend séances, sharing—rightly or wrongly—the primitive conviction that possession and personal intercourse with spirits are realities. Throughout history the votaries of the "higher" faiths have blended lofty and crude conceptions. Islam stresses the oneness of God, but its followers largely accept a host of genii. So, in a calamity, the Chinese, who have long had the notion of an omnipotent heavenly deity, try to appease spirits or to thwart them by ritual and amulet. In India fine-spun doctrines of reincarnation go hand in hand with the crudest animism. In short, the supernaturalism of savages has an amazing vitality and gives continuity to the faiths of all peoples.

Nascent Coördination. But this continuity rests not only on what we now reckon the inferior attributes of savage belief. On both the intellectual and the ethical side even the simplest tribes display nobler conceptions. Their religious notions are not a mere medley of unrelated absurdities, but imply some effort toward ordering the data of reality. When sun and moon are conceived as brother and sister, or as husband and wife, two phenomena of the universe are brought into association. And this ranging of facts may go much further. West

Africans and Polynesians arrived at two major deities, a dualism of Sky and Earth. Even the hunters of California and Nevada recognized two antithetical beings, Wolf and Coyote, the one benevolently eager to save mankind from trouble and death, the other a marplot intent on making them labor and die. Here the faint foreshadowing of a good and an evil principle is unmistakable.

Monotheistic Notions. But the philosophical type of coördination would evidently be one that brings *all* powers in the universe under one head. As shown above (p. 305), some of the Polynesian priests actually achieved the idea, even though it never became the popular faith and may have been with them, too, more of a metaphysical speculation than a live religious conviction. Yet when one deity is intellectually conceived as the overlord of the universe, religious emotion, too, may be directed toward him. The Ewe of West Africa regard their spirits as so many messengers of a wise, potent and benevolent Sky god, who sends them out to kill evil men; and priests regularly address prayers to him. Since many primitive peoples recognize chiefs, they naturally transfer the idea to their spirits and consider one of them as outstanding in power. But even that is not essential, for tribes without a strong government have also sometimes evolved the notion of a Supreme Being. Thus, the Negrito hunters of Luzon differ from their rice-growing Malay neighbors in holding the conception of a great creator who provides them with sustenance and in return receives the "firstfruits" of the chase. We may assume that on every plane of culture some individuals, at least, are able to ponder the mysteries of existence and to reduce them to a single personal origin. When this philosophical idea fuses with an ethical one, a true monotheism evolves, even though it never ousts ruder conceptions among savages any more than among civilized peoples.

The usual fate of such a primitive Supreme Being is

to be accepted in the abstract but condemned to a relatively passive part; or, he passes into folklore, is identified with one of its figures, and acquires a character wholly inconsistent with that of a dignified God. So, the Crow revere the Sun as their greatest deity, pray to him, and make definite offerings to him. Yet they do not explicitly subordinate to him the spirits that bless men, so these visitants may exercise a greater influence on individual faith. What is more, the Sun is not the shaper of the earth and the creator of Crow custom and arts unless identified, as in some versions he is, with Old Man Coyote, the principal figure of the folk-tales. But this character is a curious contradiction (p. 199): on the one hand, a teacher of established usage, he sporadically defies the most sacred of Crow laws, playing the trickster, the craven, the lecher, as fancy seizes him. Hence, the Sun either remains a rather cloudy if immaculate and powerful figure, who has nothing to do with creation or the institutions of the Crow; or he becomes an all too fleshly bundle of contradictions.

The Ona equivalent, Temaukel, is kept clear of such entanglements, but by that very fact recedes into the background. The most powerful of beings, he is pictured as living wifeless and childless in the sky, where the souls of ordinary mortals join him; and he punishes with death those who flout his laws. As for creation, he originated the sky when it was yet without stars and the first amorphous earth. Virtually everything else was left to his deputy, Kenos, ultimately a star, who raised the sky, transformed the world, created human beings, and taught them Temaukel's code. Nevertheless, Temaukel is not a mere abstraction remaining outside the religious consciousness. He is invoked to grant good weather and on behalf of sick children, and receives small offerings of meat. However, these are meager manifestations. Temaukel is no more the center of Ona cosmology than Oceanos was the center of Greek myth. Neither the goblins of the woods nor the spirits of the great initiation festival have the slightest connection with the Supreme Being. What is more, the shamans, who largely control the daily routine, cause sickness and recovery, good and bad weather, success or failure on the hunt, never derive their power from Temaukel but solely from the souls of dead shamans related to them. And, unlike the souls of common folk, those of shamans never join Temaukel but merely wait to possess an apt successor to their office. In short, the Ona are not supermen who have attained a purity of religion superior to that of the most enlightened peoples. Their faith in Temaukel is theoretically and practically limited by other beliefs not brought into unison with it. Nevertheless, theirs is a highly instructive case. Monotheism in essence is possible even among the simplest of tribes. It may be accompanied by other beliefs and overshadowed by them; it may be a mere figment of the poetical or metaphysical fancy. Yet at least the religious genius of the community may be able to seize upon the idea and mold it into a religious reality by relating it to human behavior and needs.

XVIII

KNOWLEDGE AND SCIENCE

Primitive Knowledge

Superficially considered, primitive man lacks science altogether. His treatment of man and beast as peers, his picturing stars as transformed persons, seem travesties of zoölogy and astronomy. Still more does his reliance on a magical spell to alter the course of events fly in the face of any sound philosophy of nature. Yet if he is without science as we know it, he has the knowledge that alone made science possible. He is weak in philosophizing about reality but admirable in his grasp of concrete detail. His deficiencies are manifest, his strength requires exposition.

Physics and Chemistry. In flaking an arrowpoint, twirling a fire-drill, felling a tree, carrying weights at the ends of a balancing pole, boiling water and firing pottery, primitive man applies physical principles. He could not state them in words, but he grasps them by intuition. So when he puts brains on a hide or steeps it in urine, he is inducing chemical changes even though unable to formulate what happens. All tools and handicrafts imply a host of physical principles; for example, the Maori applied the wedge, the lever, the inclined plane, and the skid; and similarly, cooking is largely applied chemistry.

Mathematics. Uncivilized peoples know little mathematics, but all can count. This means that all are able to think of numbers in an abstract way, but the need for this is not uniform throughout the primitive world. The highest Ona number is 5; to express 8 a native first showed the digits of one hand, then three fingers of the other, simultaneously uttering the words for 5 and 3, respectively. Such relationship of counting with the hands, or the hands and feet, is general. A Lobi in West Africa and a Creek in Alabama begin by doubling the little finger, then the ring finger, and so forth, the Negro clenching his fist for 5. Being connected with the digits, the counting systems of the world are preponderantly quinary, decimal, or vigesimal according to whether a single hand, both hands, or hands and feet suggested a major unit. All three methods occur in California, where the Yuki Indians hit upon an original variation by counting, not the digits, but the four spaces between them.

The Ona evidently can add 5 and 3 even if they have no word for the sum. Many counting systems directly prove arithmetical operations. In Crow 20 is "twice 10"; 9 is expressed as 1 less than 10, as it is by the Lobi. Fractions are a weak spot in primitive numeration. A term for one-half is general, but whether with a clear notion of the exact ratio remains doubtful; and though the Lobi also designate a quarter, that exhausts their interest.

Systems of numeration are meager, not from racial incapacity to *conceive* larger numbers, but from lack of cultural need for them in aboriginal conditions. The Australians, who did not go beyond 5 before white contact, readily learned to count larger numbers of sheep. The Pomo of California were of the same race as their neighbors but excelled them arithmetically because they preferred counting to measuring shell money (p. 150).

The acme of non-Caucasian mathematics is the notation of the Maya Indians of Yucatan. They devised symbols from zero to 19 along with a position system and expressed numbers above a million in connection with their calendar system, which in turn depended on their astronomy (p. 332). This achievement eclipses the Greeks and Romans, who for lack of a zero used a cumbersome notation, while the Maya philosophically conceived abstract nothingness and fixed it by a symbol. Any one who tries to do long division by the Roman system will recognize the triumph of principle involved in the Maya notation.

Very commonly certain numbers are the object of emotion. In German folklore all good things are 3. According to many North American Indians everything in the universe goes by fours, so that songs and dances are repeated in quartettes. This notion crops up in other continents: a newly elected Shilluk chief or king is secluded 4 days, and a major festival lasts for the same period. The Paviotso of Nevada substitute 5, while in the Near Orient mystic value clung to 7. The belief in sacred numbers looms large in early Greek mathematics and continued to influence European science at least as late as 1600 A.D. A professor at Padua argued against Galileo that there could not possibly be more than 7 planets.

Measurements. In early stages of knowledge measurement remains inaccurate. Development grows out of actual needs. At first parts of the body furnish rough-and-ready standards, as our Anglo-Saxon "foot" reminds us. The Havasupai do not measure by feet, but do step off houses, gauge arrow foreshafts with the finger span from the tip of the thumb to that of the middle finger or with the length of the hand from this tip to the wrist. The arm span or fathom (p. 150), eked out by finger spans, is applied to buckskins. On similar principles the Hopi compare the length of ears of corn with the forearm. Californians and Melanesians measured shell-money by distances marked on the hand and by fathoms (p. 150). Among the Maori various standards had special designations: "maro" was the arm-span; half of it, i.e. one arm length plus half the width of the body, figured as the "hau"; "konui" denoted the length of the first joint of the thumb; and so forth. The Lobi measured length by the foot, palm, or hand, but also with a cord held by two persons.

Capacity was rarely of moment. The Maori spoke of so many baskets of sweet potatoes, the Lobi and South Nigerian Negroes sold grain by the gourd. Still less was there any use for weighing. A Nigerian might mention as a crude standard the load commonly carried on a man's or woman's head, but only sophisticated people such as the Peruvians had regular scales and weights. In the Old World they were first fully developed in Babylonia.

Time Measurement and Astronomy. The reckoning of time is inseparable from elementary observations of the heavens and recurrent natural phenomena. All men recognize the difference between day and night, note the waxing, waning, and disappearance of the moon, distinguish between a cold and a hot, or a rainy and a dry, season. Precision is usually lacking. An old-fashioned American Indian's noon was "when the sun arrives in the middle". He pointed at the sky to show time of day by the position of the sun, the very method in vogue in West Africa. In Crow the finer divisions of the year are designated by figurative expressions (p. 194). The Maricopa begin their year with the budding of the trees, late in January or thereabouts. They reckon twelve lunar months, bearing clan names, but take no interest in their exact duration.

Prominent stars are universally noted. They were the Polynesians' compass on their lengthy voyages and everywhere figure in myth. Even the Ona distinguish Sirius, Procyon, and Betelgeuse. Primitive man's interest is practical rather than abstract, and nothing is more practical to him than supernatural favor. Thus, the association of stars with gods and rituals was doubtless a powerful goad to accurate observation. Hence astronomy developed as part of religious lore, and the alliance flourished not only in Babylonia and Egypt but in the modern period of European science. Two of the greatest astronomers of all times, Tycho de Brahe and Kepler, were stirred by an interest in astrology.

The Pleiades often play an important part. Chaco Indians and the West African Lobi sow as soon as the constellation first becomes visible at dawn. The Maori started their year with the first new moon after the rising of the Pleiades, and observed other stars to regulate their farming. Tribes of hunters had equivalent interests: the Ona watched for Betelgeuse, because its appearance foreboded a lengthening of the Antarctic day.

Relatively systematic observations are taken by various peoples. The Havasupai stand at a definite place to observe the solstices at sunrise, apparently without the ritualistic interest which stimulated their Hopi neighbors to do likewise. Every day the Haida of British Columbia mark the spot on the wall opposite to where a ray from the rising sun enters a hole in the eastern wall of the house. At each solstice the sun shines several successive days at one end of the line, then starts back toward the other. The new year starts on the second day of the first new moon after the winter solstice. With such precision naturally comes a wish to adjust the lunar to the solar year. If the new moon on which the 1st or the 7th month is due to begin precedes the solstice, the old month is stretched over two months. The palm, however, goes once more to the Maya. They used four systems to mark the passage of time,—a year of 365 days, a year of 360 days, a "tzolkin" of 260 days based on an artificial 20-day month, and a lunar year. With their calendar they evolved the extraordinary mathematical notation that allowed them to think in terms of cycles of 144,000 days. Astronomically, they closely observed several planets and correctly determined the revolution of Venus as taking slightly less than 584 days.

Geography. Geographical knowledge is a matter of life and death to primitive man. To be ignorant of water holes in arid Australia or South Africa is fatal. Equally important is information about the correlation of woods and steppes with fauna and flora. Consequently, primitive men have an incomparable familiarity with their habitat. An Ona clearly visualizes the details of his island and has a proper name for every prominent feature of the landscape. Lobi hunters draw charts in the sand, indicating with fair accuracy houses and watercourses passed on their travels. Eskimo aptitude in this direction has aroused the admiration of every explorer. In the summer an Eskimo rover notes every feature of his monotonous country, for in the cold season he must not only himself find hidden stores of provisions but be able to describe their location to others. He rarely fails to recover his bearings even after temporary discomfiture in a blizzard. He draws or carves maps with astonishing precision, indicating bays, points, islands, or lakes. He may exaggerate the size of the districts familiar to him, but the best of these charts are superior to those of a civilized traveler unaided by instruments.

Biology. Primitive man's acquaintance with his flora and fauna is incomparably better than practically any civilized man's. Naturally, utility determines which phase of his environment he knows best. The Ona, being hunters, are more interested in zoölogy than in botany. They know how the rodent they eat constructs his burrow, when guanacos give birth, how each species can be most easily ambushed. They note every peculiarity of shape and coloring on an animal, and have taught their normally yelping dogs to move in absolute silence on the hunt. Butchering a guanaco, with the discarding of the undesired spleen and entrails, amounts to a laboratory course in anatomy. The flora, too meager to be equally important, is not neglected. Punk is gathered for tinder, the properties of timber are carefully noted in bowmaking, and every child rejects canelo for firewood because of the stifling smoke it yields.

Where plant life provides much of the fare, natives are experts on the regional botany. In desert California they distinguished by name and used for food at least

60 species; and from Northern Queensland have been listed some 240 plants used by the aborigines. Correspondingly, Polynesians know the habits of fish, the Eskimo those of their sea-mammals.

Medicine. So much of primitive medicine is superstition that its positive qualities are easily underrated. Even shamanistic treatment has something to recommend it. A believing patient gets from his medicine-man the mental reassurance that often yields results (p. 315). Apart from this, some primitive procedures are potentially or absolutely valuable, even if their associations are fantastic. Thus, a Crow vapor bath is an offering to the Sun, but that does not make it less useful. With or without supernatural ideas, as a medicinal or mere purifying device, sweating is practiced in North America, South Africa, Hawaii, and among the Euahlayi; it flourished in Sixteenth Century Scandinavia and is still extremely popular in Finland.

The Havasupai cut boils and squeeze out the pus; bathe a bleeding nose in cold water; set a fractured arm, bandage it and bind it between thin splints tied close to the body. An Ona suffering from indigestion calls a neighbor to massage him, a procedure used everywhere and applied to other ills. The Lesu cure inflammation and swellings by heating ginger leaves and then pressing them on the affected parts. This serves the purpose of a counter-irritant like our mustard plasters. Melanesians and Peruvians skilfully cut out broken bones of the skull to relieve pressure on the brain. In this delicate operation known as "trephining" they were more successful than European physicians of the Eighteenth Century.

The materia medica of aborigines is imperfectly known as to its curative value. But *all* our medicines come from substances once used without rigorous scientific sanction; and no aboriginal remedies are more absurd than those prescribed in Europe by the best physicians of the Seventeenth Century. As late as 1691 a famous

French doctor, Charas, backed by the medical faculty of Paris, recommended the oil of ants against deafness and peacock droppings against epilepsy. The herbs and roots employed by Queenslanders and Melanesians partly coincide with those of India, a country of much higher culture, so that some of them may well be effective. For example, in Lesu the leaf of a Ficus species is administered to babies for diarrhoea, and at least the same genus serves a similar purpose in India. Again, Australians use the leaves, bark and gums of various Eucalyptus species, which furnish some of our own medicines. Our Southeastern Indians had an enormous pharmacopoeia. Their angelica roots, chewed for disorders of the stomach, were prized by their white neighbors, and a scientific observer of the late Eighteenth Century credits several of the native remedies with strong cathartic virtues. What is absolutely certain is that our local anesthetics go back to the Peruvian Indian's coca leaves, whence our cocaine.

Science in Civilization

Primitive and Present Science. Primitives, then, accumulated a vast body of empirical knowledge. How, then, did it differ from our science of today?

In the first place, differences in diffusion again enter. The total of aboriginal knowledge was great, but it was never combined in any one culture. The Ona did not know what the Samoans or Kirghiz had discovered. Ignorance of writing was partly to blame. A literate Maori today can put himself in touch with all the knowledge contained in books; an illiterate Maori remained ignorant even of developments in Hawaii. Since writing diffuses in time as well as in space, the primitives were once more at a disadvantage; they could and did lose knowledge because oral tradition, however developed, can not vie with writing. In short, modern science commands all the knowledge recorded anywhere and at any time.

Secondly, modern science has a type of specialist never known before. Advancement in any line comes from concentrated effort, as in Samoan architecture and Peruvian textiles. But primitive men had no such adepts for advancing pure knowledge. The Maori had "priestly experts," but their duty was to transmit the sacred lore as handed down to them. Doubtless new observations were made from time to time, as when priests had to watch the stars. But instead of being a goal, such discoveries were mere incidents of more important business. Training, accordingly, was not in the interest of expanding but of preserving knowledge; and if new observations ran palpably counter to the old, they were not treasured but discarded. The conscious striving by trained workers to increase knowledge regardless of past convictions is unknown in primitive and early cultures.

Thirdly, our experts are not merely prompted by practical considerations, but also by sheer intellectual curiosity. This doubtless appeared also on lower planes but more rarely and less self-consciously. In civilization it has perfected pure mathematics and other branches of science. Often, too, what seemed sterile abstractions were later turned to eminently practical use. Dearth of intellectual interests kept men from borrowing knowledge they could have assimilated. Seeing no immediate utility, they spurned the chance, thus barring further development.

Fourth, trained workers in a field are not merely willing to learn by diffusion and able to do so through printed records, but they consciously promote diffusion. There are local and national societies in every important science, as well as international congresses. Colleagues correspond, meet for discussion, circulate their publications, and criticize one another.

Fifth, modern science controls instruments of precision unparalleled in earlier times. Astronomy advanced by leaps and bounds when Galileo turned a telescope to the skies, and the microscope created a new biology. This implies a point of much greater importance. Telescopes and microscopes are not made by astronomers and biologists but by skilled craftsmen who apply the principles of physics. Not only do the several sciences interchange favors, but there is coöperation between scientists and skilled mechanics. A slight error in an instrument of precision may be fatal to a navigator and give wrong clues to a theoretical physicist. Hence, modern science depends on craftsmanship, but further one craftsman depends on another. In making a large refracting telescope an optician depends on the glass founder, and unless he gets the desired size of disk of glass uniform throughout, he is helpless; a patch of density greater than the rest spoils everything.

This leads to a still broader correlation. A science depends not only on other sciences and on skilled mechanics but on the whole organization of society. If all makers of photographic plates went out of business and computers could no longer be hired, the work of great observatories would be crippled; and a prolonged printers' strike would affect all science. In our complex modern society division of labor is essential, which means that one part of society hinges on others.

Basic to all other questions is the economic one. Without adequate resources much of modern research is impossible. A large telescope is immensely costly to make and to install. The depths of the ocean can not be explored from the shore; there must be equipment for a trained student *and* for a whole ship's crew. Whether a private patron or a state can spare the means is a question independent of whether there are competent investigators. Still more fundamental is another problem. An Ona constantly roaming after guanacos, as every Ona must, could neither get the time for the training preliminary to modern research nor later find leisure for investigation. In other words, a scientist can exist only if his society produces a surplus of food from which he and all the other specialists, skilled laborers, etc., can draw for their needs.

Thus, modern science is rooted in modern culture and inconceivable in other settings. But the gap between the primitive and the civilized world is not absolute, and in order to see both in proper perspective a brief historical survey is needed.

Historical Development of Modern Science

Modern science rests on our inheritance from the Greeks and Romans, who in turn borrowed from the Near Orient. Hence a survey must begin with Babylonia and Egypt.

Since Babylonians and Egyptians were metal-working farmers by 3,000 B.C., their science, reflecting and affecting the general level of culture, was bound to surpass that of simple hunters. Both peoples achieved feats of engineering, the handling of huge stone blocks by the Egyptians being especially remarkable. But contrary to what is usually taught, the Near Orient also made some steps in pure science. About 2,000 B.C. the Babylonians, apart from astronomical observations, had tables of cubes and squares. The Egyptians, on the other hand, learned how to handle fractions. They discussed such problems as how to divide 100 loaves among 5 men so that the shares should be in arithmetical progression, and that 1/7 of the sum of the largest 3 shares should be equal to the sum of the smallest two. While they did not command a theory of simultaneous equations, they secured equivalent results by methods of their own. Another problem was to find a quantity such that it and its fifth would sum up to 21. The Egyptians solved this by assuming 5 as a first wrong guess to be corrected. Substituted, it gives of course 6 instead of 21. Thus, the argument ran, 5 must be multiplied by the same number which, multiplied by 6, would yield 21. This idea of ratio and proportion was dominant in Egyptian solutions.

In geometry the Babylonians empirically established a number of rules, such as that for computing the area of a rectangle, and assumed *pi* equal to 3. In this latter result they were excelled by contemporary Egyptians, who evolved an approximation of 3.16. About 1,850 B.C. the Egyptians further evolved a formula for the volume of a frustum of a square pyramid, and correctly calculated the area of a hemisphere about 1,600 years earlier than the Greeks.

It is thus clear that the Greeks had worthy predecessors. Thales (640-546 B.C.), who ushers in Greek philosophy, and his followers were greatly indebted to Babylonian astronomy and to both Babylonian and Egyptian mathematics. The Greeks were not supermen, but they did lift science to a much higher plane. Their forerunners, notwithstanding some of the notable results mentioned, were on the whole content with rule of thumb approximations. The Greeks proved general propositions by rigid logic and welded them into a system. They were not free from mysticism, for Pythagoras (582-500 B.C.) stressed mystic numbers; and they were not fanatics of intellectual freedom, as shown by the trial of Socrates. But on both scores they mark a great advance. In arithmetic they were hampered by their awkward notation, which remained inferior to that of the Maya, and from lack of interest they were deficient in applied science and experiment. This, however, like most sweeping statements about nations is not wholly true. For instance, Archimedes (287-212 B.C.) was both a deductive philosopher of science and an experimentalist. He gave the first mathematical proofs in mechanics and also devised engines for the defense of his native city. The Romans supplemented Greek science by remarkable practical applications in architecture, bridge and road building. The Hindus made their contribution in the field of pure mathematics, to which they added the concept of negative numbers. Whether they also invented the numeral and position system that came to us directly from the Arabs does not seem to be certain. We do know that through the conquests of Alexander the Great (330 B.C.) the civilization of India and of the Mediterranean peoples came to blend. The Arabs, after becoming civilized in the Eighth Century of our era, best preserved this joint heritage and left a deep impression on European culture. Their schoods at Cordoba, Toledo and Seville were famous centers of learning, and their books on algebra were the standard texts in Europe. Our words for algebra, zenith, nadir, and alcohol, are of Arab origin.

Thus, European science at the dawn of modern times was a crazy-quilt of Babylonian, Egyptian, Hindu, Greek, Roman and Arab patches. But the ample empirical knowledge of illiterate peoples proves that the Near Orient does not represent an absolute beginning. It, too, built on a foundation laid by others. If it is the first step that counts, the discoverers of fire-making and the simplest tools tens of thousands of years ago were the real creators. From this angle science, like all of culture, is not the work of one or two favored nations or races but of humanity as a whole.

XIX

LANGUAGE

Definition

Language falls under the definition of culture because it is invariably acquired by an individual through his fellowship in a social group. A Negro born in the United States does not naturally, i.e., instinctively, speak a Bantu or Sudanese language, such as his ancestors spoke in Africa five centuries ago; he treats English as his one and only mother tongue. In other words, his language is not a racial but a cultural characteristic (p. 3). For that reason it is not surprising that the fundamental principles of growth which hold for food-getting, dwellings, social life, and religion may be equally well illustrated by the facts of speech.

Language is primarily and essentially a matter of the *spoken* word, for adequate writing (p. 192) had not developed anywhere some five or six thousand years ago, and, until compulsory education was established in the Nineteenth Century, the overwhelming majority of people in the most enlightened countries remained illiterate. A given language is thus, above all, a system of sounds. It differs from mere cries uttered automatically in pain in that the linguistic utterance is voluntary and generally strives to convey ideas and emotions to a fellow-being.

There are means of communication besides writing which dispense with auditory symbols. Deaf-mutes converse through motions of the hands, as do Plains Indians and Australians in special situations (pp. 202f.). Such systems, though never rivaling speech, may be fairly complex. But signs cannot be considered the parent of language because everything suggests that they are a mere makeshift for it or a dispensable frill on ordinary discourse. The Plains Indians all have elaborate languages of their own, for which they substitute gesticulation mainly when encountering a foreigner—just as they used to wave robes in order to convey a message to a tribesman beyond reach of the voice.

Universality; Diversity; Age

Language is absolutely universal in the human species and at the same time is extraordinarily diverse. Often within a small area, as in New Guinea or California, several languages appear with totally different vocabularies; and even extremists trying to connect the languages of remote areas are obliged to leave a large residue of families so different from one another that no relationship can be assumed. This indicates the great antiquity of speech, for such differentiation takes time. Notwithstanding the influence of the Normans on British speech, the English grammar and vocabulary remain unmistakably Germanic after nine hundred years. Yet the Old French that mingled with British German after the conquest did not itself represent a wholly distinct pattern: French, German, Greek, even Russian and Sanskrit each merely exemplify one branch of the great Indo-European family; i.e., they all have in common certain word stems and features of grammar. If after nearly a thousand years English and German remain demonstrably not only members of the same stock but even of the same branch within that stock, we can imagine how long it would take to efface *every* vestige of relationship. To be sure, we can not directly argue from one instance to another, for different languages vary greatly in their rate of change; some have a greater intrinsic tendency to alter; others happen to be more powerfully affected from without. Nevertheless, if the Indo-European stock took several thousand years to develop its various ramifications, we must evidently reckon with a far greater span of time to account for *all* the families in the world that we are unable to connect with another.

Evolution of Language

Because of this immense antiquity it is idle to speculate about the origins of language. But we may make one or two useful general points, on the development of language.

Imitation of Natural Sounds. Negatively, we must dismiss the idea that speech evolved from an attempt to represent phenomena by sounds that intrinsically suggest them. Words like our "cuckoo", which echoes the bird's call, form only a small fraction of the total vocabulary of any language. Further, a language is never made up of isolated words: it always has a grammar. Usually variations in basic meaning are expressed by modifying the stem of a word, as when we change "house" to "houses", "housing", "housed." Evidently the final "d" sound has no intrinsic connection with the idea of past time, nor the "s" with plural number. Still more important, the grammar of every language fixes the relations of different words to one another. In English the subject must come before the object, because otherwise a simple statement like "The man killed the bear" would leave the listener guessing as to who killed whom. But in Latin, where the actor and the one acted upon are distinguished by different endings, the word order is immaterial. Here it is obvious that nature could not suggest one rule in one case and its exact opposite in the other; and sounds are not in any sense involved as models. In short, the theory explains very few words and does not account for grammar at all.

Grading of Languages. Another significant fact is that languages can not be rated according to any conceivable scale. The size of a vocabulary is in itself no test of superior merit. English has a huge store of words because it mingled French and German stems, but this is an advantage only when it enables us to express differences in meaning with greater nicety: we could get along quite well without "commence" as a synonym for "begin." On the other hand, primitive languages often draw very fine distinctions in regard to concrete situations; they not only have special words for the plants and animals that figure in their daily life, but also for relatives we do not recognize (p. 233) and for modes of action we fail to distinguish. Thus a tribe may have one word for breaking by pressure, quite another for breaking by rending asunder. By way of compensation it has sometimes been alleged that primitive peoples fail to have abstract words because they are inferior in abstract thought. The fact is that our own abstract words at bottom rest on very concrete images: to "comprehend" is simply to "grasp." Primitive peoples have the same capacity to expand and delimit the meaning of words whenever the need for abstraction arises. The Crow originally had a single domestic animal, the dog, micgyé; when they became acquainted with cats they called the new creature icbí-micgyé, i.e., mountain-lion canine. That is to say, they recognized the affinity of the cat with its wild relative, putting both under the head of icbí; and they qualified the innovation as not wild by generalizing the concept "dog" to embrace other domestic beasts. Every language seems to have precisely this intrinsic ability to adapt itself to novel conditions, and from that angle, therefore, none can be rated higher than another.

Still less can we treat a complex grammar as a sign of superiority; otherwise we should have to regard English as one of the lowest forms of human speech. Indeed, the history of English from the Anglo-Saxon to the present period demonstrates the significant point that development may be from the complex to the simple. While some Indo-European languages, like Lithuanian, have preserved most of the ancient forms, English has gradually sloughed them off until its grammar has become quite attenuated as compared with, say, German. Chinese, whose history can likewise be traced through many centuries, has similarly acquired a simpler grammar.

It would be a mistake simply to invert the statement and to consider the simplest as the highest grammar. The true conclusion is that neither simplicity nor complexity is a criterion of greater or lesser worth, seeing that all languages are able to achieve the primary function of speech, irrespective of what kind of grammar they possess. It remains, however, a most remarkable fact that in two of the largest speech groups, English and Chinese, the development of the last thousand years or so has been from the complex to the simple.

Language, Cultural Relationships, and Race

The great family of which English is a member illustrates another noteworthy fact. Peoples who speak related languages are not necessarily similar to one another in other respects. Thus, not only English and French belong to the Indo-European stock but so do Russian, Albanian, and Armenian. The speakers represent great qualitative differences in their institutions, and the Albanians clearly represent a much simpler mode of life than most other Europeans (Chapter XXIX). Similarly, the Finns at the summit of Western civilization and the reindeer-breeding Lapps belong linguistically to the same stock, the Finno-Ugrian. In America the seed-gathering nomadic Ute and the Aztec of Mexico with their well-knit political organization, architecture, and calendar were both of the Uto-Aztecan family.

Furthermore, since a particular language is easily learned in infancy, there is no close correlation between race and language. American Negroes are linguistically as Indo-European as American whites; the Lapps as Finno-Ugrian as the Finns. The Northern Albanians are of the same subrace (p. 6) as their Yugoslav neighbors, but their speech forms a distinct branch of the same family. Most of the Pygmy tribes of the world share the speech of adjoining peoples of quite distinct racial affiliation, as in the case of the Philippine Negritoes, who speak a Malay tongue; and the Malays themselves speak a language related to that of Polynesians and Melanesians, both of the Malayo-Polynesian language family, though widely different in race (pp. 5f).

It would be a mistake to assume that the cases just cited represent the only type known, i.e., that it is always the ascendant people that imposes its tongue on an alien race. Actually, there are not a few instances of other processes. In a part of the Solomon Islands, the conquering Melanesians adopted the Papuan tongue of their subjects (Chapter XXIV); the overlords of Ruanda (p. 293) dropped their original speech in favor of the Bantu dialect of the peasants they subjugated; and the Normans, though injecting innumerable new words into it, failed to eradicate Anglo-Saxon. Even when the language of the conquerors prevails, it does not usually remain unmodified. Why do the several branches of the great Indo-European family, which has made itself dominant in Europe, diverge so widely? The reason is that they have borrowed features from the languages they displaced. Peoples who come into contact may exchange not only goods and crafts, but also take over one another's words and even subtler aspects of speech. The Southwest German dialects resemble French in using nasal vowels otherwise unknown in German; and similarly Armenian, an Indo-European tongue, shares sounds of Georgian, a language of the near-by Caucasus that is totally unconnected with it. In other words, in this as in other spheres of culture, we have to reckon with diffusion.

Diffusion

Simple Loans. To what extent diffusion operates in language—whether, for instance, it affects grammar as well as phonetics and vocabulary—is a moot problem that we may ignore. Even apart from such possibilities, the total amount of linguistic borrowing in the past has been enormous. Taking English, we find any number of words traceable to foreign vocabularies. Often new cultural items are introduced with the term of the people from whom the trait itself is derived. "Coffee" corresponds to the Arabic "qahweh", and the Abyssinian province from which it originally comes is called Kaffa (p. 32). "Tea" was introduced from China with the beverage itself. "Spinach", unknown in England until the sixteenth century, is the equivalent of Spanish "espinaca", Arabic "isfenah", Persian "aspanah." More recently the idea of a kindergarten was adopted from Germany, as was the designation. In other cases, a word comes from the area where the thing it denotes is especially developed, as in the Polynesian "taboo" and "tattoo."

New Coinage. However, a certain capriciousness must be noted here. Not all languages simply take over new words for new things. Often the novelty—as in the case of the cat introduced to the Crow—is compared with things already known and classified accordingly. An Australian group called the first horse they saw "male kangaroo from the land of spirits",—kangaroo because that seemed the nearest equivalent among the few mammals they knew; "from the land of spirits" because the white rider was interpreted as a spirit returning from the hereafter. The Dakota Indians correspondingly called the horse "big-dog", while the Shoshone classified it as a kind of deer. The Crow readily saw that cattle were a kind of buffalo and so designated them, distinguishing the native form as "genuine buffalo." To cite a few other examples, in Australian scissors are "two-teeth"; in Crow, "two-knives"; the Quechua of Peru conceived firearms as "thunder"; for the Crow a gun was an "iron bow." The Crow calls a railroad station "where they tap metal", i.e., he picks out the telegraph operator ticking away and lets a part stand for the whole.

Loan with Alteration. These examples show, then, that there is an alternative to simple word-borrowing, viz., a definition of the new phenomenon in wholly native terms. However, even when the word is taken over, the process is not so simple as it seems. That is, the word is generally not pronounced as in its original form, but with such alterations as make it fit better into the phonetic scheme of the borrowers. "Coffee" is not *identical* with the Arabic word to which it is traced, because English lacks some of the characteristic Arabic sounds. Northwest Australians have no "p", hence our "pipe" becomes "bibe", and for lack of the "st" combination "steamer" turns into "deemer." Our "boulevard" looks like a typical French word, and from France we got it; but the French themselves borrowed it from German "Bollwerk", (our "bulwark"), transmogrifying it in the borrowing.

These changes may go much further than pronunciation. Because German has three genders and an article for each, any noun borrowed from another language must have *der, die,* or *das* associated with it to indicate whether the word is masculine, feminine, or neuter. English "bar" happened to be made into "die Bar", hence drinks in German are served at *her.* Especially instructive is the case of "das Girl" for a show girl; here the analogy with the German word "Mädchen", a diminutive and hence illogically a neuter word, made the new word similarly neuter. A somewhat different case is that of Hottentot "hahs" for "horse": because a final "s" in Hottentot classifies a noun as feminine, the loan word is applied only to a mare; and an entirely new word "hahb" is made to designate a stallion because "b" is the masculine suffix.

Diffusion Not Automatic. To sum up, diffusion operates on a large scale in language, but not mechanically. While some languages readily take over new vocables for imported ideas, others have a knack at using their own resources for designating the novelty. And here, too, borrowing may involve rejecting part of what is offered and remolding the rest to fit into the old tribal speech pattern.

Patterns

How the patterns of any particular language have arisen we do not know because they date back too far; nor are the underlying processes at all clear. In English we form the plural of nouns by adding "s", but such words as "men", "geese", "oxen", "feet" are survivals from the period when there were several distinct ways of pluralizing. There is no obvious superiority in the addition of an "s." What we do constantly note is that a pattern, once established, dominates the scene. Thus, practically any new word, e.g., "gas", "volt", "bus", is pluralized in consonance with the ruling pattern. Because this holds for phonetics as well as grammar, we find the typical changes in borrowing mentioned above. The French do not aspirate their stops (k, t, p), consequently when they take over a word from English the loan word loses its aspiration in order to fit into the phonetic pattern.

Origins Generally

It should not be surprising that ultimate origins in language are impossible to ascertain, for we are even unable to explain how very recent words came into being. Thus, no one knows how "sundae" came to be applied to a mixture of ice cream with crushed fruit, or why a tramp figures as a "hobo" in the United States. As a matter of fact, outside of technical nomenclature, few words are consciously invented; some one happens to coin a vocable that for obscure reasons gains currency and at last may even be admitted into dictionaries. What holds for words holds still more definitely for grammatical processes. No one deliberately decides to drop the subjunctive or to use "shall" with the first person; these things just happen, and it is centuries or even millennia later before a philologist takes conscious note of them.

Linguistic Affinity

Method of Proof. Just what do we mean when we say that English and Russian are related languages? Obviously it does not mean that they are mutually intelligible: we cannot even understand so close a language as Dutch without specially learning it. When we say, then, that English and Russian both belong to the Indo-European family, we simply mean that in these languages so many words for similar ideas resemble each other that the resemblance can be due neither to borrowing nor to accident. Moreover, the grammars also share some features that set the related languages off from others.

For elementary purposes the point is best illustrated by starting with closely related languages and limiting the comparison to words. The Crow and Hidatsa Indians live in Montana and North Dakota, respectively, and belong to the Siouan family. Here are a few common words with English translations:

English	*Crow*	*Hidatsa*
buffalo bull	tsī′rupe	kī′rupe
tent	ací	atí
head	acū′	atu′
who	sapé	tapé
woman	wía	wía
to join	atsí	akí
to climb	úa	úa

The words are clearly either identical or vary according to a definite scheme: a "ts" in Crow corresponds to a "k" in Hidatsa; a "c" or "s" in Crow is equivalent to Hidatsa "t." There has been a "phonetic shift" similar to what we find between two related European languages, as when Italian has "otto" (eight) against Spanish "ocho", and "notte" (night) against Spanish "noche."

If we extend comparison from Crow to Dakota, we still find words that are very much alike, e.g., Dakota "u" against Crow "hu", "he comes"; where the similarity is not apparent the Hidatsa form may be a connecting link. For instance,

English	*Crow*	*Hidatsa*	*Dakota*
heart	dās	dáta	tcánte
to eat	dúci	dúti	yúta
to seize	dútsi	dútsi	yúza
buffalo	bicé	mité	pte
tent	ací	atí	ti

The fact that one sound is again and again substituted for a particular other sound can not be explained by accident; it can be due only to variation from the same ancient form. On the other hand, we can not expect complete regularity because in course of time many changes occur to blur the relationship. If we merely knew the common German word for dog, "Hund", it would not suggest affinity with English; the German "Dogge" and the English "hound" have each been specialized in meaning so that they would not appear on a general word list. A fair number of definitely equivalent words is thus adequate to suggest linguistic affinity.

This is naturally strengthened when important grammatical features are shared. Thus the three Siouan languages all use prefixes to denote the part of the body with which an action is performed. In Crow, seizing with the hand would be "dútsi", while seizing with the mouth becomes "dátsi"; and Dakota, as well as more remote Siouan tongues, uses equivalent or identical prefixes.

Practical Import of Affinity. Theoretically the proof that two groups speak related languages may be of the utmost significance. The Athabaskan family embraces

Indians of three separate and remote regions: a solid block of tribes extending from Alaska and British Columbia southeastward to Hudson Bay; a smaller number of groups in northwestern California; and the Navaho and Apache of Arizona and New Mexico. In all these cases the resemblances in speech are so marked as to demonstrate original unity beyond any doubt whatsoever. This means, then, that in not too remote a period extensive migrations brought people from the extreme north of the continent to our Southwestern States. In custom and general mode of life the Californian and Southwestern Athabaskans are so different from their Northern congeners, as well as from one another, that except for the testimony of language no one would have dreamed of these major wanderings.

Still more remarkable is the light that philology sheds on the history of Europe, where its results in part rest on ancient literary documents. In 1786 Sir William Jones pointed out that Sanskrit, Greek, and Latin were offshoots of a single prehistoric tongue. This at once revealed an affinity between the speech of certain ancient Asiatic and European groups, whence the name Indo-European for the whole family, which subsequently turned out to embrace also the Germanic, Romance, Slavic, and other languages. In short, wherever may have been the home of the folk speaking the ancestral tongue of the family, its descendants spread over an enormous area, from India over the greater part of Europe. What is more, in Europe the speakers of Indo-European languages came to crowd out those of other families who at one time held the field. Thus inscriptions of the Sixth Century B.C. show that the Etruscans once occupied part of Italy; about two hundred years later the Cretans spoke neither Greek nor any related tongue; and in the Pyrenees the Basques remain as a quite distinct group surrounded by French and Spaniards.

But, however interesting these data are in unfolding

the past, linguistic affinity must be of the closest possible kind—must approach identity—before it becomes a potent social factor. Thus the fact that the Russians, the French, and the British are all of Indo-European stock did not prevent the Crimean and the Hundred Years' wars. Even membership in the same branch of the family is not enough, as events in Europe attest.

Still more remarkable is the fact that within the same country there are often intense feelings of animosity coupled with minor differences of pronunciation. The Bavarians and Prussians are a notable example. Even between average Americans or between British of different sections the consciousness of kind suffers whenever there is a perceptible difference in speech. The curious psychological basis of these sentiments seems to be that language in the particular form in which it is learned in infancy acquires early and extremely intense associations. Thus, it becomes a symbol of home, family, class, country, whence comes resentment of any appreciable departure from the accustomed norm. A marked Southern accent may evoke ridicule in New York or California, a dropped "h" puts the English speaker into a lower level of education, and so forth. Nowhere is the difference between tweedledum and tweedledee a more powerful barrier than in language. In Norway the two forms of speech now officially recognized are most closely allied from a linguistic point of view; yet the most violent conflicts have raged there in order to place the synthetized peasant dialects on a level with the traditional literary Dano-Norwegian. When infinitesimal variations of this type can become matters of life and death, it is clear that *practically* people can not spontaneously respond to the call of uniting under a common Pan-Slavic, or Pan-Teutonic, let alone, a Pan-Indo-European slogan.

In this connection we must also recall that all the major language groups of the world are artificial units. In, say, 600 B.C. each tiny Hellenic commonwealth had its own separate tongue, though its citizens were probably able to converse with those of the other Greek states. Only from the Fourth Century B.C. did the local dialects yield to a common speech based on Attic, which became dominant because of the superior culture of its speakers. In such great modern states as France, Italy, Germany, for example, there are likewise many natural local variants which sometimes diverge beyond the limits of intelligibility: what binds the people of one of these countries together linguistically is the common language *artificially* imposed upon them by compulsory education. But the fact that Germans learn the standard grammar and pronunciation in school never completely effaces the influence of the deep-rooted local speech. Variation in speech is not, indeed, the only factor in human life that militates against the consolidation of large numbers of people, but it is one of the most persistent causes of social, if not of political, separatism.

XX

THEORY OF CULTURE

A complete theory of culture must explain why the same people have a different social heritage at different points of time; in other words, why cultures change. Further, it must account for the differences and for the resemblances between the cultures of distinct peoples, whether these are contemporaries or not. We are very far from this goal of being able to interpret the entire inventory of all societies past and present, but we have made considerable headway in barring simple but false solutions in biological and geographical terms.

Geography and Race

These solutions are logically inadequate because the same biological equipment and the identical geographical environment are consistent with totally different cultures, while the same traits reappear in the most diverse races and environments. Arab and Nordic civilizations have undergone radical changes within the last few thousand years without a corresponding change in the physical type of the culture bearers (p. 9). On the other hand, such distinct racial stocks as Europeans, Negroes, American Indians, and Australians share the fire-drill (p. 55); some Negroes, the Arabs, many Australians circumcise (p. 82f.); the Chinese, like the Europeans and Negroes, freely bandy proverbs generally unknown to American Indians though they are racially much closer to the Chinese (p. 196). Such instances may be cited to infinity.

Similarly, the same geographical environment may

support utterly divergent forms of life. In Ruanda there are herders, peasants, and hunters (pp. 108f.); in Arizona and New Mexico intense agriculturists have lived in close proximity to hunters who did a minimum of farming or none at all; and California presents today a very different civilization from that of the seed-gathering fishermen and hunters who occupied it only a century ago. And here, too, the same elements crop up in totally diverse geographical settings. Matrilocal residence is as likely to appear in arid Arizona as in the humid forests of South America (p. 242); moieties are typical of tropical as well as of desert Australia and the humid northern coast of British Columbia (p. 260); the couvade thrives in bleak Fuegia no less than in the South American tropics (p. 400).

In short, *simple* racial and environmental explanations are worthless.

Nevertheless, it is possible to embody biological and geographical considerations in a theory of culture *if* we make appropriate qualifications. In the first place, it is undisputed that only human societies possess a full-fledged social heritage, which is thus at present correlated only with the human level, i.e., with the biological constitution peculiar to modern man (*Homo sapiens*). But the fossil remains that have come down to us from the earlier periods of the Old Stone Age (p. 11) suggest a more primitive brain and anatomical organization than that of living races; it is thus conceivable—though not proved—that their crude arts were correlated with their lack of inborn capacity. So long as psychologists fail to devise satisfactory tests for all living racial stocks, inborn differences among them must also be considered conceivable, even though they may explain at best only a very minute fragment of the totality of phenomena to be accounted for (p. 9).

A special form of the racial theory that has recently become popular must also be considered. According to Professor Eugen Fischer and his disciples, the colored races are not inferior to the white race *on the average,* but rather because of their failure to produce a comparable number of outstanding personalities. Progress, however, is said to be due wholly or mainly to such geniuses, heroes, and prophets; hence failure of a race to give rise to such extreme variations explains its backwardness.

This contention is valuable in so far as it prompts a new line of inquiry, viz., into the relative variability of distinct races. Unfortunately its advocates assume that a difference in variability actually exists, whereas we have so far no knowledge whatsoever on this subject. Secondly, they accept the Carlylean theory of the "great man" as the prime mover in civilization, another disputable assumption that can not be brushed aside but that is to date undemonstrated and in part improbable.

It is thus necessary to reiterate that at the present moment the racial doctrine has nothing useful to offer for an explanation of culture, though conceivably—but only conceivably—some phases of the theory may ultimately turn out to be fruitful.

From this angle the geographical factor has at the present time far greater explanatory value. To be sure, it does not account for origins but it does explain the absence of a trait and, on certain further assumptions, its presence (pp. 13, 87f., 98f., 103, 109, 146, 160, 212, 214, 216). This is especially true if geography is not conceived too narrowly; thus the backwardness of the Tasmanians cannot be explained by their climate, which is ideal, but by their location with reference to other peoples, which barred them from a chance to borrow new inventions (p. 38). This, however, evidently brings in another type of factor, viz., the historical one: the habitat of the Tasmanians is important not by itself but because it was unfavorable to contact with other groups. For a satisfactory analysis we always must consider determinants of *both* types. As shown (p. 146), the natural resources of Sweden would have excluded the natives from developing a Bronze Age; yet because they had intercourse with alien groups who had bronze and because the world had reached the stage of navigation, they were able to overcome the geographical difficulty.

Why is it that a student of culture must consider environment while he can largely ignore biological equipment? As shown, he does not really ignore biology, but has simply discovered that, granted the plane of modern man, inborn differences are negligible for his purposes. On the other hand, the environment is never negligible, however limited its influence may *seem* to be from a particular angle. The Fuegians are a star example of insufficient adaptation as regards dress (p. 70); but in a hundred other ways—say, in their guanaco hunting (p. 16)—their adaptation is admirable. Every society in the world has had to make some adjustment to surrounding nature; hence none can be fully understood without taking environment into account. All we have to guard against is the oversimplified, hence misleading, notion that geography automatically evokes an intelligent response. This is a serious fallacy because man is not a logical machine but reaches appropriate conclusions only after prolonged striving and bungling (see e.g. pp. 105f.).

Typology

After registering our data the first task in any science is to classify them, but that is often far from easy. Yet a wrong classification leads to endless confusion. The point is, of course, to group together what is alike in essentials and not to be captivated by outward appearance. The untutored observer regards the whale as a fish; the scientist, probing deeper, sees its relationship to mammals.

The proper botanical determination of a plant may seriously affect special parts of culture history. Thus, botanists regard the sweet potato as a South American species in origin. If this holds true, the use of this tuber by the Maori, Hawaiians, and Easter Islanders in pre-Columbian times could be explained only by Polynesian voyages to the New World, whence the navigators must have imported it into Oceania; transportation by American Indians is excluded because they were not seafarers on a large scale. But this conclusion has important corollaries: if the Polynesians were able to borrow one thing from the Indians, they could have borrowed a dozen; and, on the other hand, such contact would make it possible for the Indians to acquire new ideas from their visitors. However, doubts have been raised whether the old Maori plant called "sweet potato" is really the same as the American tuber; and this matter has not been settled once and for all. What interests us in this setting is the importance of accurate classification for anthropology even when the determination has to be made by another science.

In a study of the history of bronze (p. 139) everything hinges on a proper definition of the alloy. An accidental admixture of tin means nothing; the Peruvians are credited with having achieved "bronze" because of the proof that they deliberately sought the advantage of adding tin to copper.

Sham problems abound because scholars, when first confronted with a new phenomenon, are frequently misled by spurious analogies. Thus, at first they confused animal worship with totemism (p. 309) and sought a common origin for these diverse phenomena; and even nowadays some writers speak glibly of the origin of "plant cultivation" as though the sowing of cereals and the planting of banana shoots were the same process (p. 36).

Because new facts continue to come to our notice our classifications must be constantly revised. A *perfect* typology can not therefore be expected until research itself has reached its final goal. But the closer we approach that ideal, the less shall we be retarded by false problems, and the more fruitfully are we able to attack real ones.

Distribution and History

Basic to the understanding of our phenomena is their distribution. If the Andaman Islanders and Ona had an arithmetical position system, we should not marvel at its presence among the Maya (pp. 330, 340); its occurrence there, along with its lack in ancient Greece and Rome, is what gives the fact its significance.

As in zoology or botany, the way in which features are spread over the face of the globe inevitably gives rise to problems in anthropology also, particularly to the question of whether a trait found in remote areas is due to independent development or to dispersal from a common center (see e.g. pp. 49ff.).

In many cases we know definitely that there has been diffusion because the appearance of the trait in the region concerned is a matter of record. Thus Chinese writings tell us about the introduction of the grapevine and alfalfa (p. 34); and we know that neither Asia nor Europe knew the potato before the discovery of America. In other instances we are not less certain that a feature has been diffused even though we may not give an exact or even an approximate date. Thus for botanical reasons maize can not have been domesticated independently in North Dakota because no wild species exists there from which it could conceivably have been developed.

There are still other cases in which diffusion may be inferred with complete assurance. If we chance upon a group of Negroes in Bermuda conversing in English, we know that they or their ancestors must have learnt the language by contact with English-speaking whites. It is utterly inconceivable that any human society could duplicate the vocabulary and grammar of a tongue spoken elsewhere. The point is that human minds can not recreate the enormous number of parallels that would be implied in the assumption of an independent origin for Bermudan Negro English.

Folk-tales and myths often present equally convincing evidence. Thus, the Lapps tell in virtually identical words the story known from the Caucasus as "The Man without a Head in the Bear's Den" (p. 202). The only difference is that one of the companions solves the puzzle by recalling the victim's beard instead of his cap. What underlies our judgment that these are mere variants of a single tale? First, there is not mere coincidence as to a single feature but with reference to a whole series of motifs—the existence of a society of nincompoops, the presence of three of them in the story, the adventure in the bear's den, the extraordinary, boobyish reasoning. Second, the point in both versions is so grotesquely far-fetched that it is hard to imagine its independent conception by distinct peoples. Third, it is easy to understand the path by which the story spread. The Lapps are, indeed, unrelated to the Caucasians, but they speak a Finnic language and live in immediate contact with the Finns, among whom the identical narrative has been recorded; and while Finland seems a long way off from the Caucasus, Finnic tribes live on the Volga, whose mouth is within striking distance of this area.

In short, diffusion is convincingly demonstrated when: (a) the resemblances are numerous; (b) the similarities compared are highly distinctive or unusual; (c) the course of diffusion is clear, either by a continuous distribution or by its equivalent, several steppingstones suggesting such a distribution in the past.

However, though the union of all three conditions is always desirable for a satisfactory proof, most scholars are willing to assume diffusion on lesser grounds. Regardless of the occurrence of other parallels or of a discontinuous distribution, a single trait may strike them as so extraordinary that they must explain its presence in two distinct places by a spread from one center. Or they may be content with assuming diffusion when the two phenomena or whole cultures compared share several, though not necessarily very distinctive, elements. The latter procedure is of doubtful value unless there is at least one decisive link in the chain of evidence. But the indubitably true parallels with intermittent distribution merit attention, for sometimes they indicate facts not otherwise discoverable.

Intermittent Distribution. A good illustration is furnished by hockey (p. 165). It is played from Alaska to Arizona, being practically universal among the Indians of the United States, and again turns up in the Gran Chaco. The game may be reasonably regarded as sufficiently distinctive to be derived from a single invention. If so, the Indians of the Chaco must once have had contacts with North American tribes which other South American natives lacked or whose influence has been lost among them. A similar argument has been advanced with regard to the mythologies on the Asiatic and the American side of Bering Strait. The stories of the Eskimo, it is contended, resemble the Northeast Siberian ones far less than the latter resemble the tales of the Indians south of the Eskimo, hence Northwest Indians and Northeast Siberians must once have been in close proximity, being later wedged apart by an Eskimo migration into Alaska.

What concerns us here is not the correctness of the conclusions, but the logic involved, which is perfect. *If* hockey is a game that is not readily duplicated, *if* the Siberian-Indian parallels decisively outweigh the resemblances between the Eskimo and either of the other groups, then migrations of the nature inferred must have taken place.

Here two factors must always be taken into account, viz., whether independent invention is really out of the question, and whether the distribution is adequately known. The former point is often subject to doubt; as to the latter, earlier information is often corrected by later research. Thus it was once stated that in the New

World coiled basketry (p. 122) occurred nowhere south of Mexico except in Fuegia. This assumption might easily have led to erroneous conclusions, for we now know that the technique is or was found in most major areas of South America, including Panama, Colombia, Ecuador, northeastern Brazil, Peru, Bolivia, the Argentine, and Chile.

Center of Diffusion. Unless there are extraneous facts to guide us, as in the case of maize, it is much more difficult to prove the direction than the mere reality of diffusion. There are, indeed, some useful common-sense criteria, but in many instances they leave us in the lurch.

Possibly the most satisfactory pointer is a linguistic one. Peoples quite generally have a rich vocabulary for the deeply rooted traits of their social life; when, therefore, they apply a foreign term to some beast, plant, custom, or dance, the probability is overwhelming that they borrowed simultaneously the trait and the term given to it by the lenders. Thus, there is botanical evidence that the banana is post-Columbian in the New World; and we find accordingly that many South American Indians have taken over either the Spanish "plátano" or the Portuguese "banana" for the plant. To take examples from our own civilization, the words "soufflé", "kindergarten", "andante" show that in cookery, pedagogy, and music the British learnt from French, German, and Italian models, respectively. There is no conceivable reason why the British should have given a French name to a native dish; hence the provenience of the dish itself is obvious.

Unfortunately, as we have seen, some peoples prefer to coin new phrases of their own for innovations rather than to adopt the alien words for them. Nevertheless, in a great many cases the criterion is applicable and hardly ever deceptive.

Sometimes the descriptive phrase by which people designate some element of their social life indicates whence it came to them. When the Chinese designated the cultivated walnut as "the Iranian peach", they thereby gave a clue as to its derivation. Similarly, the Dakota would hardly have called an indigenous ceremony "Mandan dance"; they evidently adopted it from this fellow-Siouan tribe. Naturally a phrase of this sort need not reveal the *ultimate* place of origin: if the French and Germans at one time called our Indian corn "Turkish wheat", this merely shows the direction from which the cereal reached *them*.

A much less satisfactory criterion is that of intensity of development. A priori, to be sure, it seems very convincing that of two peoples who share a trait, the lenders, having had it for a longer period of time, also had a chance to elaborate it to a greater extent. Actually, many historic examples can be found of a feature that is highly complex at or near its original center and fades out towards the margin of its range of distribution. The British parliamentary system evidently is far less significant for social life in the South American and Balkan countries that copied it than in the United Kingdom. There are illustrations for whole complexes of linked traits. Several thousand years ago Egypt and Babylonia had an urban civilization, with metallurgists and other artisans, resting on intensive husbandry; these features spread to the north and west, gradually thinning out, so that the Danubian contemporaries of these near-Oriental plough-farmers were migratory peasants who merely hoed the ground and had to shift their tiny settlements at brief intervals because of soil exhaustion (p. 25).

However, it is impossible to generalize from such unquestionable facts because there is a formidable array of contrary instances. Nothing is more certain than that Buddhism started in India, where Buddha was born in about 560 B.C. Yet today continental India is without the faith that was born there, a faith which plays in somewhat varying forms an important part in Burma and Siam, China and Japan, Tibet and Mongolia. The fervor with which the modern Mongolians follow their Lamaistic version (p. 502) might utterly deceive a naïve observer as to its relative antiquity. Again, we know that tobacco, coffee, and tea are extremely recent acquisitions of Western civilization; nevertheless, they have come to color our daily life to such an extent that without recorded history no one would guess that they were anything but deep-rooted ingredients of Euro-American culture.

A closely related argument must likewise be treated with the utmost caution. When a complex and a simpler culture come into contact, it does not follow—as is sometimes alleged—that culture flows in an irreversible stream from the higher to the lower. Of course, by definition the more advanced people have more to offer, but they may also benefit very considerably from their intercourse with lowlier neighbors. The cultivated plants our ancestors obtained from American aborigines represent a most striking illustration. The Chinese, to cite another, did spread their learning and institutions far and wide, but they adopted felt and boots from northern nomads, seafaring from Malays to the south.

In this connection it is important to note also that many traits that may be shared by higher and lower cultures do not rest on a special refinement of technique or involve the prestige of the dominant group. Accordingly, in such matters—say, in games, folk-tales, folk-beliefs—the feature that is common may just as well be borrowed in one direction as in the other; or it may go back in both cases to a dim past in which no notable distinction of cultural plane existed.

To sum up, the proof of diffusion does not imply evidence of its course; unless there are special considerations, linguistic or geographical, for example, we can not safely infer the direction of diffusion.

Age and Range. Frequently the distribution of two features is compared, and an inference is drawn from their respective range to their comparative antiquity.

The underlying assumptions are that it takes time for a trait to spread; and that the time is proportionate to the distance traversed.

This principle has been bitterly assailed; yet some of its sharpest critics concede some measure of validity to it. In other words, it must be used with discrimination. In the first place, no one supposes that there is a direct ratio between the area covered by a feature and its antiquity. All that is implied is a *rough* correspondence; and the question is not one of square mileage, but of range of distribution. It is more important that a trait crops up in such remote marginal districts as Fuegia and Tasmania than that it covers an immense area in a central region. Secondly, the rate of dispersal is very different for different phases of culture. Cultivated plants often spread with amazing rapidity; nevertheless, Christianity did not reach Poland until the Tenth Century, and the Negroes never adopted writing or the wheel from Egypt. Hence comparison should be restricted to features belonging to the same department of life. Thirdly, the degree of variation which the same basic trait has undergone is significant. It not only took time for maize to travel from Central America to North Dakota, but the techniques used in growing it are so different that they must have required a period of adaptation. In the case of religion a cult may sweep spectacularly over thousands of miles within a short time, but well-marked variations—as in the case of Buddhism—suggest greater antiquity.

Admittedly, cultural happenings may be so complex that with all our precautions we may go wrong in our relative chronological estimates. Nevertheless, several impressive facts stand out sharply. By the incontrovertible evidence of prehistory the dog is the oldest of domestic beasts (p. 37); it is also far more widely distributed than cattle, sheep, goats, horses, all of which are confined to portions of the Old World. Similarly, there is direct archaeological proof that stone tools precede metallurgy, and here again the range-age principle is borne out. Thus signs of fire occur in extremely ancient sites; and all modern groups of humanity use fire, nearly all of them being capable of making it at will (p. 55). Again, such marginal peoples as the Australians, Fuegians, the Siberians, Eskimo, and Northern Indians are hunters; and agriculture demonstrably represents a later as well as a less expanded phenomenon.

We may safely conclude, then, that the principle is a worthy one, provided it is not applied mechanically, but with a due regard for factors tending to interfere with its normal operation.

Reconstruction of the Past. Except for the relatively recent written records of literate peoples the anthropologist has no direct evidence as to the past of human societies apart from that supplied by archaeology. This resembles the evidence of the geologist and paleontologist both in its definiteness and its limitations. When one undisturbed stratum is found above another with distinctive implements, then obviously there has been a change and the lower layer represents an earlier stage. Thus it has been definitely proved that stone tools preceded metallurgy; that hunting was earlier than farming; that basketry preceded pottery. Such stratigraphic findings are among the most precious results we have, since they provide a trustworthy framework for the course of man's development along material lines.

In one respect the anthropologist is worse off than the paleontologist: he is concerned not only with arts that leave tangible remains but with such imponderables as marriage customs, religious beliefs, ethical notions. Indeed, even of material products only the durable ones will survive through thousands of years, so that it is usually impossible to answer directly even such a question as whether a particular ancient people used bows. If a certain tribe specializes in woodcraft but makes no pottery and little stonework, even its technical accomplishments will be very imperfectly disclosed to the future excavator of its sites.

Because of the uncertainty of reconstructing the past some scholars reject all efforts in this direction and would confine study to the observable present. This view is extreme and willfully overlooks certain considerations. As just pointed out, the range of distribution is not negligible, and its import may be reinforced by other considerations. Thus all peoples tell stories, but only a strictly limited number of them have epics (p. 196). It requires no proof that a people like the Tasmanians could not have evolved so complicated a literary form as the *Iliad*. Similarly, when a site reveals a food-gathering culture devoid of any earthenware, we safely infer that its bearers were not advanced in stone architecture or mathematics. Whence comes our assurance? From the tacit conviction, based on an indefinite number of observations, that instead of being unconnected certain items which we must separate in describing a people for purposes of exposition are organically related. The bond between them may be such that trait A always goes with trait B; or A may exclude B; or A may render B more (or less) likely. In short, we are dealing with the problem of correlation, which is thus seen to be very important in the reconstruction of the past, as it will be shown to be important for other reasons.

To take a concrete instance, we are quite safe in denying to paleolithic man an elaborate political system with large populations under the sway of a single autocrat. The realization of what is involved in gaining a livelihood as a roaming hunter of the Ona type is enough to explode any such assumption and to suggest instead a loose body of kin and neighbors as the only probable form of political association (p. 288). Much less satisfactory is the determination of paleolithic beliefs. The form which religious notions assume can not be so readily correlated with an economic basis as can government. Comparing all the unequivocally simplest hunting tribes of today in order to extract common elements, we meet the difficulty that each group has had a long history during which most of them have been liable to influences from without, as well as to internal development. Nevertheless, some tentative conclusions, negative and positive, are permissible. Certain phenomena that clearly hinge on economic and technical advancement, such as temples and an organized priesthood, may be ruled out for the earliest stages. On the other hand, it may be significant that the Negritos of Luzon have a monotheistic belief *not* shared by their Malay neighbors but similar to the notions of the simpler African tribes, beliefs which again are lacking or subordinate among superior Negro populations. In this field a further aid lies in the amazing tenacity with which human beings cling to their traditional supernaturalism, which lingers on long after a more rational philosophy of the universe has become official. The universality of imitative magic and its persistence to the present day (p. 325) warrant the assumption that it is an extremely ancient part of human tradition.

For an inferential chronology, too, linguistic facts may prove of significance. Simple, unanalyzable words are, as a rule, demonstrably symbols of more ancient cultural phenomena than are descriptive phrases: American Indian cultivators have simple terms for plants like maize, not such revelatory phrases as "Turkish wheat"; on the other hand, Sioux has a simple word for dog but calls the imported horse "big dog" or "mysterious dog". On the coast of British Columbia, the Kwakiutl have a short one-syllable word for the attendant at a feast, while their Nootka neighbors speak of him as "the one who walks about in the house". It is highly probable that this ceremonial feature is older among the Kwakiutl. Even the relative period of occupation of a certain area may be illuminated in this fashion. In northern California Mt. Shasta is known to many tribes; the Yana designate it by an unanalyzable word, while the Hupa call it "white mountain"; and here the linguistic evidence is borne out by other facts about the Hupa as relative newcomers.

Laws of Sequence. The fact that we can draw reasonable inferences as to the nature of the past and the comparative age of different phenomena does not mean that we are able to reconstruct the entire history of human civilization in all its details. That would be possible only if culture developed uniformly according to a fixed law. This, however, is contrary to experience. Certain events do, indeed, presuppose others, but frequently we can not reverse the proposition and infer that a certain consequence is bound to follow a particular antecedent. Thus, bronze work is inconceivable except after experience with stone and other materials; but a Bronze Age is not an inevitable step, as shown by the instance of the Negroes who passed directly from stone to iron (p. 142). This example is easily explained by contact with a people of blacksmiths who taught the stone-using Negroes to forge iron tools.

Here we have the typical sort of disturbance which plays havoc with any longe-range scheme of sequence. Human societies have learnt from one another since very early times. As a result, even if there were a natural tendency for culture to pass through the same stages everywhere, that tendency would be constantly deflected by intrusive influences. To take a hackneyed example, only through contact with more southerly peoples could the Indians of North Dakota have come to raise maize. Again, the Japanese may ultimately have developed along the same lines as Westerners, but there is no proof whatsoever that they would have done so. All we know is that their modern progress is due to intercourse with Europe and America.

It is particularly dangerous to infer a law of sequence from the events of a brief period. Thus during the Nineteenth Century the literate nations of the world seemed to be evolving towards a greater measure of democracy and internationalism. This was, of course, largely due to the example of certain Western nations whose prestige impressed a similar pattern on others. But, even assuming that there was a general democratic trend, we see today in many countries the most violent reaction against the principles of democracy and cosmopolitanism.

Because of the extraordinary complexity of the relevant phenomena, regularities in culture history are very limited, and accordingly prediction becomes extremely hazardous.

Progress and Retrogression. The question of historical laws merges into that of progress. In how far are we warranted in recognizing an upward trend in human history? In order to answer this question we must first understand the crucial term. We rightly say that farming is superior to hunting because the purpose of an economic system is to provide a secure and ample food supply, and agriculture is potentially able to do that, while hunting is not. Similarly, an iron ax chops down a tree more effectively than a stone hatchet does (p. 10). Again, our control of nature has expanded through the accumulation of knowledge. Summarizing, we may say that in the strictly rational sphere of existence man has advanced because there the aims envisaged are clear and he has succeeded in accomplishing them, on the whole, more effectively with the lapse of time. An outstanding factor in such development has been the possibility of specialization (pp. 336ff.), which itself rests on an economic organization that permits some men to devote less time than their fellows to the production of food and other necessaries.

But while it holds true that as a whole humanity has progressed from the early Old Stone Age in the rational phases of culture, particular eras and areas have experienced a decline. Impoverished Lapp herders have had to turn back to fishing, some Plains Indians have given up farming completely in favor of more intensive hunting. Sometimes there is only partial loss, with compensatory gains, as when South American Indians who migrate into a stoneless area lose the art of chipping but substitute others; or when Polynesians discard the bow for warfare while developing a series of other weapons.

Such instances of decadence, complete or partial, once more militate against the acceptance of a uniform law of development. All we can say is that mankind as a unit has in the long run progressed in technology and knowledge, but that geographical or other factors may arrest advancement and even cause actual loss in particular cases.

Far more debatable is the question of progress in art, social organization, religion, and morality. In these important fields there is no ascertainable norm that would be accepted by all men. Everything hinges on whether the purpose of a feature is defined once and for all time. The purpose of an ax is to fell trees; but what is the purpose of art, communal life, belief, marriage? No tree chopper prefers a stone to an iron blade if he wants to accomplish his task as quickly and painlessly as possible; but whether a picture of living forms should aim at anatomical accuracy or ignore that for other kinds of aesthetic effect is a matter of taste (p. 186). Similarly, thinkers of equal prominence have written for and against democracy, while religious and ethical preferences are notoriously colored by personal attitudes. For example, the doctrine of the greatest good for the greatest number is spurned by philosophers with an aristocratic bias.

One curious fact, however, may be noted with regard to religion and ethics. If we judge by those standards which are at least common among ourselves, there has not been a steady approach to them from their antithesis. On the contrary, the simplest tribes often come closer to our norms than do peoples of intermediate complexity. The Pygmy hunters of Africa, for instance, are monogamous and have monotheistic leanings, while their economically and technologically superior Negro neighbors practice polygamy and ancestor-worship.

To sum up, progress can be objectively established only for the rational aspects of culture. In these fields the backward developments of particular epochs and peoples are outweighed by the advancement of mankind as a whole. In the non-rational departments subjective estimates alone are possible; and if our norms are treated as definitive, there still is no regular sequence through earlier stages.

Psychological Problems

In the immediately preceding sections the historical aspects of culture have been stressed, but actually every one of its phenomena is at the same time historical inasmuch as it is placed in time, and psychological because it is accompanied by mental processes of human beings. The very topics often treated as wholly historical may just as well receive attention with psychological emphasis.

Diffusion. Diffusion is not automatic when two groups come together, but selective: hundreds of features might be borrowed, but only some are chosen. The Japanese have taken over our science, not our ethics or our art, for their ancient equivalents were too deeply rooted. In general, if it fully meets their needs people prefer their indigenous feature to an innovation. The difference in reaction to the same possible loan often lies in the native equivalents. The Maori eagerly substituted the potato for their sweet potato as a manifestly superior crop, while the Chinese clung to rice as a more palatable and nutritious diet.

The failure to adopt a trait may be due to sheer inability. While friction matches have been readily taken over by primitive peoples, they can not, of course, borrow the match industry, which requires a much higher technological plane. On the other hand, people borrow an item if they can readily assimilate it to prior notions.

Because the Polynesians reveled in pedigrees (p. 305), the Hawaiians, to the astonishment of early missionaries, committed to memory the genealogical tables in the Bible "and delight to repeat them as some of the choicest passages in Scripture." The Quechua of Bolivia assimilate the Holy Virgin to their old female Earth deity, and credit her with the invention of coca-chewing, while Brazilian aborigines identify Christ and St. Peter with Sun and Moon, respectively.

Such assimilation is never wholly passive and may involve considerable originality. The loan of the idea of riding a mount leads to experimentation (pp. 49f.) and novel results; some Siberian varieties of reindeer are weak-backed, hence must be ridden by straddling the shoulders. Glazing spread to China from the West, but on this basis Chinese artificers created their wholly original porcelain (pp. 133f.). In about 1888 Wovoka, a Paviotso prophet, promised his tribe a reunion with their dead and for that purpose organized the Ghost Dance; by 1890 his restive and warlike disciples on the Plains had converted the message into a gospel for the destruction of the whites. In contemporary politics, the Germans have copied Mussolini's Fascist principles but have fused them with a race creed originally lacking in their model. Thus diffusion often implies a creative synthesis.

Psychic Unity. If diffusion is unintelligible without the mental processes of the recipients, the same holds for a uniform law of sequence. Only if human groups are at least roughly similar in psychology would similar results flow from the same causes. On the other hand, a certain "psychic unity of mankind" is quite as essential for diffusion, for the borrowers must grasp to some extent what they are to receive.

Psychic unity is thus a presupposition on either theory; and precisely because it underlies all cultural happenings it cannot explain *particular* phenomena, such as the sporadic occurrence of similar features in remote areas. If cross-cousin marriage in Fiji and in central

California is due to psychic unity, we should have to suppose that these Californians are mentally nearer to the Fijians than to Northern Californians, an absurd assumption. Thus psychic unity is useless for interpreting specific facts of culture history, being rather a general postulate for all of them.

Parallelism versus Diffusion. Some scholars try to explain all resemblances between peoples by diffusion; they assume that man is basically so uninventive that he advances only by a lucky fluke that is most unlikely to be duplicated elsewhere.

The dogma of human uninventiveness monstrously exaggerates the correct view that men do not spontaneously and everywhere achieve adequate adjustments to their environment. The solitary instance of the bitter manioc (p. 31) suffices to disprove it, but there are many similar cases in which particular tribes must be hailed as the inventors because the trait in question occurs nowhere else on the face of the globe. Thus, in pre-Columbian times, though similar trees occurred also in Africa and Asia, only certain South Americans knew the properties of rubber, making balls and syringes from this material.

In addition, we have seen that borrowing may precipitate a truly creative process.

What the dogmatists overlook completely is that into many parallels the question of originality does not enter at all. Moieties, for instance (p. 259), result simply when the clans of a tribe are reduced to two; and this is bound to happen if the original number of clans is small, so that a resemblance may evolve in remote areas without any creative act of the imagination.

Language provides convincing instances. The Greeks and the Shoshone Indians had a dual number, though no possible connection can be traced between their tongues; and when rice came to the notice of the Tsimshian (British Columbia) and the Crow (Montana), tribes in no way related, they independently labeled the new food "looking like maggots." But such analogies are precisely the essence of mythological concepts: if two remote peoples can each hit on such a simile as the one just quoted, they are also able independently to compare the disappearance of the sun in an eclipse to that of a hero in a monster's maw.

The primitive Messianic cults of the historic period yield incontrovertible evidence. Springing up in the most remote parts of the world, they display a welding of Christian and native beliefs, with remarkable resemblances in detail. Thus Wovoka was identified with Christ, as had been a South American counterpart on the upper Rio Negro in about 1850, and a South African Messiah. The return of the dead loomed large in the Papuan movement of 1919 no less than in the North American uprising of 1890; and so forth. These several cults did not spread from one continent to another; they represent incontrovertibly independent developments with independent assimilation of Christian ideas.

The sane position, then, with reference to the general moot problem is to shun a uniform explanation and to judge each case on its merits. There has been plenty of diffusion in the history of culture; but there are likewise unchallengeable instances of independent development. Accordingly, in any concrete instance either alternative is equally respectable until special evidence inclines the balance.

Stability and Change. The strong conservatism of human societies has for its counterpart the indubitable fact that changes have occurred. To ask why these antagonistic principles exist is to face a psychological question.

One of the contributions made by anthropology to psychology is the proof that individual behavior is largely determined by the tribal norms. In modern slang, a culture "conditions" its participants so that they react not merely as they would by virtue of their congenital make-up, but according to the dictates of the social standards. A Plains Indian, whether naturally foolhardy or not, risks his life to gain glory; a Northwest Californian, even if not a congenital miser, craves wealth as the means to prestige; and so forth. Much that was once reckoned part of the original nature of man is now seen to be socially determined. Thus the Toda exhibit no "parental instinct", ignoring any consideration of who the actual progenitor might be in favor of a ceremony for determining legal fatherhood (p. 245).

Behavior, then, can not be satisfactorily understood either from what is instinctive in the whole of mankind or from the individual's mental character; we must also take into account the society that has molded him.

But mere emphasis on this point is insufficient, for it would overlook two obvious considerations. First, the norms did not exist from the beginning of the universe; hence there was a time when they were unable to influence individuals. Secondly, the norms do change, which would be impossible if they merely rubber-stamped the several members of a community. We are thus led to the question of individual variability.

Individual Variability. In regard to its population a primitive tribe exhibits as many differences among its members as a civilized country. Even so rude a people as the Ona, without professional artisans, have bunglers and recognized masters at arrow-chipping (p. 107); and the Crow know very well which storytellers are supreme in the control of style and plot (p. 194).

As a matter of fact, without such individual variations no culture would long continue as a going concern, for the conditions of life are such that automatic repetition can not go on forever. Assume a community prescribing marriage with the daughter of a mother's brother. What happens, then, if a young man's mother has only sisters? The "rubber-stamped" citizen would be utterly stumped by such a contingency, while a bolder spirit finds an easy solution: if the mother has no brother, she has at least a kinsman in the same generation, who by legal fiction can be counted as a brother. Thus, he extricates his family from a dilemma while still bowing to the established rules of matrimony. Actually, the Hopi treat particular clans as the trustees of particular ceremonials, so that when a clan passes out of existence, then, the ceremonial might also be supposed to lapse. But being unwilling to forego their sacred performances, the Hopi consolidate diminishing clans or hit upon other makeshifts. Such devices, however, are possible only if there is an Indian of superior ingenuity to conceive them and at the same time of sufficient force of character to impress his ideas upon his tribesmen.

With reference to its code any fair-sized community is bound to have its martinets and its outlaws. The average member neither flouts tradition at all costs nor follows its guidance through thick and thin: he compromises, rendering obeisance to fine principles in the abstract and finding excellent excuses for doing as he pleases in concrete circumstances. The Burmese are Buddhists, hence must not take the life of animals. Fishermen are threatened with dire punishment for their murderous occupation, but they find a loophole by not literally killing the fish. "These are merely put out on the bank to dry, after their long soaking in the river, and if they are foolish and ill-judged enough to die while undergoing the process it is their own fault." Such sophistry is evidently the product of a mind of more than common subtlety. It represents the acme of what psychiatrists call "rationalization", i.e., a *secondary* justification for behavior whose real motives are of a far less creditable character. When so convenient a theory had once been expounded, it naturally became the apology of the whole guild of fishermen.

In this case the importance of individual variations is inferred; in other instances the evidence is direct. Theoretically, a Crow Indian ought to die young, fighting against the enemy; and old age was constantly represented to boys as a burdensome condition. But bravery, though universally exalted, was of course distributed like any other human trait in this tribe: there were madcaps and cravens, along with a majority of average men eager to be as brave as they dared without risking their necks. The tales of adventure recounted by the Crow warriors themselves strikingly display the whole gamut of possible values: some men attained the ideal, others shrank from its implications.

Among the same people visions were considered all-important (pp. 313f.); but while some individuals by virtue of their mental make-up were repeatedly blessed, others were congenitally unsuited for such revelations notwithstanding repeated trials. Clearly the vision-seeking norm had been established by individuals naturally disposed to enjoy such intercourse with the supernatural and possessed of such prestige that their example set the style. That is to say, an idiosyncrasy grew into a tribal pattern. In recent times the Crow are known to have changed ritual because some influential tribesman had been so directed in a revelation. Here there is direct evidence not only of individual differences, but of an alteration in the social legacy due to such deviation.

Another type of deviant may flavor culture and, in special circumstances, exert an influence. Even in the simpler tribes there are skeptics, men who not merely circumvent the norms of their community, but at least secretly challenge them. Some Caribou Eskimo confided to Rasmussen that they considered certain of their shamans humbugs; indeed one informant who had vainly undergone suffering to gain a revelation rejected the whole of the shamanistic system.

Whenever there is ample evidence on a major religious movement, such as the Ghost Dance, we get glimpses of all possible forms of temperament—the enthusiastic leader, the fervent disciple, the lukewarm opportunist, and the unbeliever. It is the interaction of these several types of personality that makes a cultural system a live reality. Individual variability is thus of genuine importance for the maintenance as well as the modification of social life.

Leadership. In discussing leadership it is essential to distinguish between several disparate ideas. The "leader" is a reality; that is, in any society certain individuals possess characteristics which make others follow their guidance. Furthermore, such personalities may powerfully affect human welfare. To take a miniature society, hundreds of Crow Indians must have died for glory because certain leaders at one time set up the ideology characteristic of the Plains as congenial to their own temperament. The influence of a Negro king, such as Chaka (pp. 227, 293), is far greater and in turn pales before that of a contemporary dictator.

But to recognize the immense practical importance of the leader is one thing; it is quite another (a) to determine the inborn traits of the leader, and (b) to assess his role in the advancement of civilization.

As for the leader's personality, it naturally does not conform to a single type, but by a rational scale his rating is frequently very *low* either intellectually or in point of character, or in both respects. The most conspicuous traits are a self-assurance often degenerating into a complete lack of self-criticism; and a callous disregard for the interests of others. These attributes may, as in Chaka's case, be coupled with truly extraordinary talent for organization, but the Zulu—let alone humanity—drew small profit from his genius.

If Chaka typifies the "hero" of romantic historians, the shaman represents a more common form of primitive leadership. That his intellectual powers are frequently inferior can not be doubted: our best authorities describe the Siberian shaman as typically pathological (p. 311), frequently an epileptic, a maniac, even a pervert. Wovoka was doubtless less able and less forceful than the Plains Indian disciples who reinterpreted his message but continued to reverence him as the fountainhead of a new dispensation. In South America the Guarani, obsessed with the fear of a world catastrophe, have again and again migrated from one region to another as directed by medicine-men, who in turn were inspired in visions to seek a secure haven. In South Africa a prophet of the last century ordered his people to slay all their cattle, which he promised to resuscitate by his magic. Considering the Negroes' idolatrous attitude towards livestock (p. 43), their obedience to this command is a marvelous testimony to the power of leadership. But what a rude awakening there was when the beasts did not come to life again! Similarly, the Guarani were doubtless lulled into security by confidence in their several prophets, but was this temporary benefit compensation for their disappointment when the promised earthly paradise faded into thin air? Surely these misguided people would have fared better without false saviors.

There are fortunately potential leaders of real worth, but often circumstances limit the scope of their activities. In an aristocratic society of the Polynesian type, a plebeian of the greatest capacities would be condemned to fruitless imaginings. In contemporary politics the statesman of a small country is inevitably restricted. Fridtjof Nansen (1861-1930), the Norwegian explorer, was also a cultivated philanthropist, an ardent patriot, and a statesman of cosmic vision. But his native land was not one of the great powers and he could never make history in the manner of Herr Hitler, the shaman who sways Germany and with her the civilized world.

Leaders, then, are necessary because without them there can be no change. But the changes they inaugurate are frequently harmful, and the influence they exert bears no ratio to their powers of mind and character, which are frequently below par, so that their acceptance at face value looms as one of the heaviest indictments against the human species.

Of course, there have been benevolent despots. At a time when the thatched roofs of city houses were responsible for the devastating conflagrations that constantly consumed the towns of neighboring Denmark, a Swedish king was able to make his capital fireproof by enforcing strict building laws (p. 91). In days of scarcity Frederick the Great (1744) bullied his Pomeranians into planting potatoes. Charlemagne, another outstanding example, encouraged education and disseminated Christianity.

But here a doubt obtrudes itself. Granted the benign effects of these rulers' policies, how important were they *in the long run?* The immediate result in saving human life, precluding famine, spreading literacy and a nobler faith was notable. But did these great men deflect or materially accelerate the course of history? This seems extremely unlikely. By 1800 even the tardy Danes had proscribed thatched roofs in their towns. By 1744, as a result of earlier famines, Germans all around Prussia had already begun favoring potatoes, so that an expansion of the idea was a mere matter of time. Christianity, which got even to Poland and Russia within two hundred years of Charlemagne's death, would assuredly have reached the Saxons earlier than that.

In the practical sphere, then, the leader is immensely potent, but his ability to mold culture in a way to confer lasting benefits upon mankind can not be rated very high; and his influence is frequently baneful rather than constructive, even when his endowment is superior. In science the role of the leader is so intimately related to the character of our contemporary Western civilization that he is best discussed in that context (Chapter XXX).

Laws and Correlations

In some of its branches natural science has established regularities of such scope that they have been called "laws." But a very large part of science—much of zoology, botany, and geology, for instance—makes no such pretensions. Indeed, critical physicists have a growing aversion to taking their "laws" for more than what they are, viz., shorthand summaries of experience; they are content to speak of greater and lesser degrees of probability. The facts of society are far more complex than those of physics, hence no laws have hitherto been discovered. However, the search for regularities is always legitimate, and we are certainly warranted in determining how our phenomena are interrelated.

This quest has not been fruitless, for certain cultural traits appear to be organically linked, so that one of them renders the presence of another more probable or, on the contrary, may tend to exclude it. In some instances the nature of the correlation is clear to us; in others we merely recognize its reality and suspect that some intermediate link eludes us. Thus we readily see why pigs do not go with pastoral nomadism (pp. 40f.) and why pottery accompanies a sedentary life (p. 128). But if the association of epics with dairying (p. 196) is not due to sheer chance, the reason for the coupling remains obscure.

In culture one phenomenon is hardly ever determined by one particular cause; there is rather a functional relationship between them and, it may be, an indefinite number of other features. Unless this fact is realized we are likely to get a distorted picture. For example, offhand it seems very reasonable that the avunculate (pp. 251, 257, 274) should be linked with matrilineal clans; but the real crux of the matter may be common residence of uncle and nephew, irrespective of rule of descent.

Of course, the determination of such correlations is not the sole concern of anthropology, but it is one of its important aims.

The Proper View of Cultural Elements

The general goal of anthropological study is to understand the whole of culture in all periods and ages, and to see each humblest fragment in relation to that totality. To grasp one such tiny element from all possible angles would be to gain an insight into the processes and factors of all culture. Let us use the cultivated potato for illustration.

Our cultivated potatoes are all of the species *Solanum tuberosum* and form a most important gift of the American Indian to world economy. Indeed, all the tuber-bearing species of this genus are confined to the New World. But here a puzzle arises. At the present such states as Maine, Minnesota, and Idaho stand out for their potato crops, but in pre-Columbian times cultivation never spread beyond the Andes. This is all the more curious because wild species occur in Mexico and our Southwest; indeed, Navaho as well as Zuñi eat the small tubers nature provides, yet even the Pueblos have never made an effort at planting. Why this failure on the part of such skilled farmers? Perhaps, it has been plausibly suggested, because agriculture reached the Southwest with maize and this plant was "well enough adapted to local climatic conditions so that there was no necessity of experimenting with local wild starch foods." Scientists agree that the center for the cultivation of the potato was in the Andes, a conclusion supported by direct proof of its antiquity in this region, for dried specimens were recovered from ancient graves at Arica in northern Chile, and ancient Peruvian earthenware displays unmistakable representations of the tuber. It is, then, certainly odd that a trait native to the Andes should not have been transported directly thence to the many suitable places where it might have been—and later actually was—easily acclimatized further north. Yet its appearance in North America is wholly due to Europeans: in 1613 a British ship brought potatoes from England to Bermuda, whose governor in 1621 sent a cargo of potatoes and other vegetable produce to Virginia. Whence in America the British derived their specimens remains obscure (notwithstanding popular tales about

Sir Walter Raleigh and Virginia), but according to the specialists it must have been somewhere between 1586 and 1590. About twenty years before, the tuber had reached the Italians, who had derived it, of course, from the Spaniards, who, in turn, had noted its importance in Peru.

Without going much further it is obvious that the simple potato brings us face to face with the perennial questions of invention and diffusion. The precise history of its spread is clearly a strangely tortuous one. But besides the strictly historical aspects of the case there are various psychological problems linked with them at every point. How did the notion of raising this tuber arise? Was it an extension of the idea of cultivation (p. 35) as already practiced with some other species, such as possibly the sweet potato? Or was it a literally independent conception, which, on the contrary, may have stimulated the growing of other tubers? The matter of racial achievement enters, for this trait is an indisputable contribution of the American Indian; on the other hand, geography has its bearings: the origin of the potato was inevitably restricted to the area of its wild ancestors, and its Andean home suggests that it is likely to thrive in comparable climates.

Extending our survey, we find that generally this assumption is borne out. The potato is of little economic significance in the tropics except where the latitude is compensated by the altitude, as in the Arfak Mountains of western New Guinea. It is a striking fact in this connection that the only Polynesians who have become vigorous potato-growers are the Maori of temperate New Zealand.

More interesting because more puzzling is the neglect of the tuber in regions to which it is admirably suited. Notably the Chinese, except in certain highland districts, have failed to be deeply affected by the potato, which ranks as an inferior article of the poor. Since these people have readily adopted the sweet potato and maize, their attitude toward the potato can not be due to their inborn conservatism, as has sometimes been alleged. The real reason is similar to that for the failure of the Pueblos to domesticate their wild tubers, viz., the presence of a previous staple of great value. As the Southwestern Indians already had maize and hence saw no great object in experimenting with the cultivation of an available *Solanum* species, so the Chinese, who had long looked upon rice as an adequate staple, had no motive for an economic revolution when confronted with the potato. They were the less inclined to favor it even as a secondary crop because it had been preceded in their country by the sweet potato and various kinds of yams (*Dioscorea*).

This selective fastidiousness contrasts instructively with the position of the Maori, who prized the potato above all other introduced forms of food and substituted it for their native *kumara*. When they migrated to New Zealand, these Polynesians had been compelled to drop the yam except in the northernmost part and to abandon all farming in the south (p. 33); hence they eagerly cultivated the potato even in the South Island. The reason for the sharp difference between the Chinese and the Maori is clear. In northern New Zealand the previous crop—unlike the Chinese rice—was indisputably inferior to the innovation; in the South Island there was no competitor whatsoever.

But the Maori case illustrates additional points. For one thing, the natives did not take over potato culture mechanically, but devised new techniques unknown to the European settlers. For example, they succeeded in preventing exposure to frosts while still obtaining very early crops. Again, the potato became so dominant a feature of their life that without historic records one would never guess its recent introduction: as early as 1839 a European traveler found "wild" potatoes growing everywhere and the Maori themselves evolved the tradition that the plant had been known to them before the coming of the whites.

Turning back to Europe, we find still other principles exemplified. In a way the history of the potato there is an epitome of the advent of all agriculture. As explained (p. 25), cultivation in general was not particularly significant in its immediate results, but in its ultimate possibilities. So the potato was at first merely an oddity of no economic importance whatsoever. The great French botanist Clusius, who in 1601 first described it in scientific terms, had obtained two samples in 1588 brought into Belgium by the papal legate, who "ate these tubers, prepared like chestnuts or carrots, in order to gain strength, as he was of delicate health." At that time the Italian peasants boiled potatoes with mutton and fed them to pigs, but in Spain (whence the Italians must have acquired their original supply) the tubers were not grown before 1800.

As a matter of fact, no one at first had the intuition to detect in the newcomer a plant of revolutionary value. In 1822 its consumption on the Continent was still small in comparison with that of the United Kingdom, where it had overcome violent prejudice. The Scotch deprecated its use because it was not mentioned in the Bible; elsewhere it was denounced as unwholesome or even as positively poisonous because it belonged to the nightshade family. As late as 1805 it was still associated in British minds mainly with Ireland and the north of England. It was in Ireland, where natural and social conditions were peculiarly favorable to its reception, that the potato was first recognized as a field crop of importance for human beings—prior to the starvation year of 1663.

Periods of dearth, indeed, affected the cultivation of the potato as it previously had influenced the adoption of rye as a staple (p. 35). It was urged as a famine antidote in England in 1662 and in France at various times during the Eighteenth Century. During the terrible dearth of 1770 the Academy of Besançon offered a prize for the demonstration of plants that might supply food to famine sufferers. It was awarded to the farmer-chemist Parmentier, whose experiments proved that the potato flourished even in unpromising soil and that its chemical analysis revealed no poisonous substances. Thus he destroyed the prejudices of his countrymen. In Germany, as already explained, the misery of the Thirty Years' War fostered the extension of potato-growing.

In all these developments the strictly psychological element is never in abeyance. We find popular resentment of novelty, however useful, and even unexpectedly religious irrationalism. On the other hand, apart from the initial steps in Chile or Peru, there are the bolder spirits who were ready to test the tuber, to adapt it to new conditions (Maori), to use it for forage and even as a staple for human food. Yet we do not anywhere discover a creation out of nothing by one outstanding genius. Parmentier stands forth prominently, but closer study shows that his ideas were stimulated by the potato diet he became familiar with during his captivity in Germany as a prisoner of war, and that, however sporadically and unintensively, the potato had been grown in France before him. Indeed, about 1755 another Frenchman, Duhamel du Monceau, had also insisted on the value of potatoes in times of scarcity. This does not minimize the rigorous scientific contribution of Parmentier but exhibits it in proper perspective, as the culminating point in the line of development.

Thus the potato instructively shows how any element of culture should be approached. It is not an isolated atom apart from the rest of the social inventory but is vitally interwoven with every other fact of human civilization. If we knew literally *everything* about the potato —how it came to be deliberately raised in South America, what were the initial responses of the community to its introduction, how it evolved to its position in the Andean highlands, what phases of supernaturalism were interwoven with its cultivation, and all the subsequent steps of diffusion of which we literally know only the bare outline—we should know a great deal about man and culture.

PART II

ILLUSTRATIVE CULTURES

XXI

THE FUEGIANS

Tribes and Habitat

In the Isla Grande de Tierra del Fuego and the Cape Horn Archipelago live the Ona and Yaghan, the two southernmost peoples of the world (*Pl. 38*). Yet they live not nearly so far from the equator as the Eskimo in the northern hemisphere, since even the tip of South America corresponds in latitude only to central British Columbia or southern Scotland. Nevertheless, the climate is disproportionately severe because of the antarctic currents. The temperature, it is true, never drops to extremes, but there is little seasonal variation, so that snow may fall in mid-summer. Constant cloudiness, heavy precipitation, and terrific squalls make this one of the most forbidding regions of the globe, though the magnificence of its glacial scenery dwarfs that of Norway. Indeed, there are many contrasts in Fuegia. Thus despite a dearth of plant species, heavy beechwoods characterize part of the area, which stands out sharply from the northern parkland just south of the Strait of Magellan. The fauna also varies. In the northern section of the Isla Grande edible rodents are a main part in the native's bill of fare, while to the south the guanaco is his mainstay; although this dwarf camel has even swum across the Beagle Canal, it never reached most of the Cape Horn Archipelago.

The Ona and Yaghan speak utterly unrelated languages and also differ noticeably in physique, the Ona, who roughly equal North American whites in stature, towering half a foot above their southern neighbors. Several centuries ago there were possibly 3,500 Ona and

2,500 Yaghan; now they are reduced to considerably less than a hundred each. Their lives present hundreds of common items, as well as radical contrasts. Though both are "hunters", even their economies are largely distinct. A third tribe, the Alakaluf, lives to the west and northwest. Though very little known, they resemble the Yaghan in essential aspects of their life, but

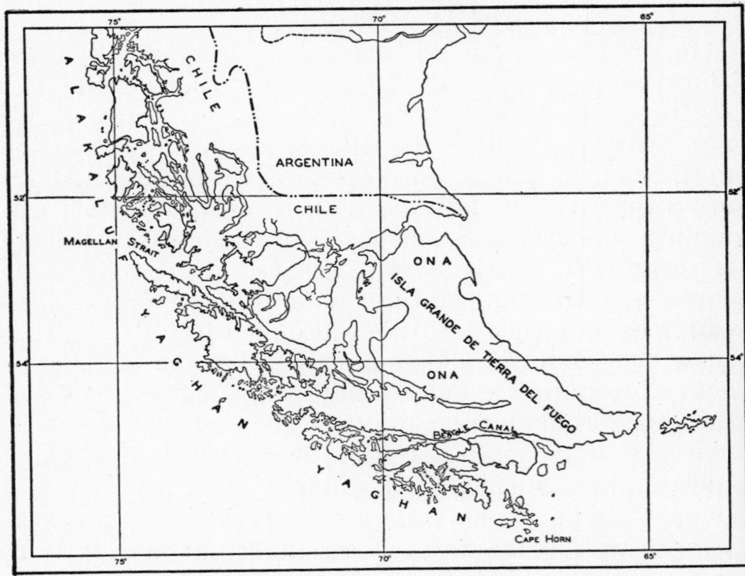

Plate 38: ISLA GRANDE DE TIERRA DEL FUEGO AND CAPE HORN ARCHIPELAGO.

in language they are distinct from both of their neighbors.

Ecology

Food. The Ona, ignorant of navigation and even of swimming, have a horror of travel by water and gain their subsistence chasing guanaco herds or digging rodents out of their burrows. The Yaghan, averse to cross-country marches, spend most of their time in fragile bark canoes, harpoon seals and whales, and collect quantities of mussels. Both are thus mainly "flesh eaters" and "nomads", but these catchwords are evidently merely blanket terms covering great diversity of existence.

Division of Labor. The diversity appears also in the part played by women. Although the Yaghan man makes the canoe, his wife paddles it within range of his quarry, catches fish, spits crabs, pries loose the mytilus shellfish which often form the staff of life. She is likewise the family swimmer: when the boat cannot be secured on the landing place, her husband and children disembark while she steers it to a bunch of kelp some distance away and dog-paddles back in the icy waters. She is thus strictly indispensable in the food quest. On the other hand, her Ona sister, who neither shoots guanacos nor ferrets out edible rodents, only supplies a few berries, which are a mere luxury. To be sure, she cooks, fetches firewood and water, carries the baggage on the march, makes baskets, and scrapes skins, but she is not even remotely the economic asset represented by a Yaghan wife.

It is easy to understand why a Yaghan spurns Ona girls in marriage. In his migrations a canoe is his house; it may last him a year, while his huts are necessarily abandoned every week when the resources of a site are exhausted. To him a non-paddling, non-swimming wife would be a luxury he could not afford. One may fairly ask how far the status of women in the two tribes hinges on her economic importance, for though even among the Yaghan there is no question of a matriarchate the social position of their women seems definitely better.

Fire and Shelter. Fire is an absolute necessity for both tribes, more important than their dwellings, which with some exaggeration have been said to be shelters for the fire rather than for the inmates. It remains true that a hut is dispensable whereas fire is not. Even in his canoe the Yaghan carries it with him, the children feeding and tending it so as to guard against a conflagration. The Ona on their overland marches through a less humid habitat are not so constantly dependent on artificial heat, but must kindle a fire when camping at night. Strangely enough, neither tribe drilled fire in the almost universal aboriginal American fashion, both striking flint against pyrites and catching the spark in tinder. Since the requisite materials were limited to special localities, this stimulated trade between different bands.

The Fuegian dwellings afford very imperfect protection, and no comfort, but the nomads have no use for substantial houses and furniture. Notwithstanding the crudity of the shelter, the several local types reflect geographical differences. In the pampas of the main island there is a mere windbreak (p. 97; *Pl. 14, fig. 1*); in the timbered country the Ona erect conical huts. These are also typical in the more tempestuous part of Yaghan territory, where the Indians can get thick and smooth beech stems, which offer better resistance to the terrific gusts of wind. In the west, where the weather is comparatively calm, the Yaghan have a beehive-shaped hut, which allows the heat to expand more evenly and is favored by the thinner beech stems accessible there, which are easily interlaced.

However, the matter is not one of sheer geography. The beehive hut is shared by the Alakaluf directly north of the Yaghan on the Pacific Coast; while the introduction of the white man's ax has greatly extended the range of the conical hut because thicker trunks are now more generally available throughout the region. In short, *someone* made an adaptation to environment, but the Yaghan may have merely brought the convenient dome structure with them when they came from the adjoining Alakaluf habitat; and either they or the Ona may have borrowed the conical type from whichever of the two first used it. Here, as in other cases, the full explanation of why this or that people do thus or so at a given time is not purely environmental, but a combination of geographical and historical factors.

Dress. That man does not automatically respond to his physical surroundings is proved by Fuegian dress. The guanaco hunters wear a long cloak of guanaco skin, which, like the shorter sea-lion skin cape of the Yaghan, mainly shields its wearer from the wind rather than from the cold. Against that our Fuegians depend on their fire and a mixture of earth and grease which they smear over their bodies. Their scant clothing is at the opposite extreme from the ample tailored suits of the Siberians and the Eskimo (pp. 68 ff.). Still there is not a complete lack of adjustment to physical conditions: if the Yaghan have generally failed to adopt the long Ona garment, it is because it would impede the free movement of the canoer's arms; and if the Ona applies a less profuse coating of fat, we must remember that he remains on the whole less exposed.

Weapons and Trade. The double effect of geography and history is also reflected in Fuegian weapons. Bows, clubs, slings, and harpoons are common to the two tribes, but with a somewhat different role. A canoer finds harpoons, clubs and slings more useful than archery, which is most effective against guanacos. Actually, the bow is mainly used by the Yaghan in the narrow strip of their country roamed over by these animals; and there they commonly get bows, arrows, and quivers from the Ona in exchange for sealskins, whalebone spearheads, and pigments.

Natural resources are reflected in other ways, too. For their bows not only the Yaghan but also the northern Ona of the pampas must trade with the Indians of the timbered zone; and because a slaty stone from a special district is deemed preferable for the arrowhead, there is a further motive for trade relations.

Tools. All Fuegians are properly classed as Stone Age men in the sense that they were without metals. But actually their only true stone-working technique was in pressure-flaking arrow points, dagger- and lance-heads with little bone rods (p. 112). The meagerness of their tool kit is remarkable. There were no axes: the Ona had to pull down tree trunks with lassoes; when a Yaghan split up firewood, the mauls with which he drove whalebone wedges into his logs were wholly unworked rocks picked up at need and discarded after use. In old Yaghan refuse heaps chipped blades turn up which may have served as knives, but the historic Yaghan had merely shells that made incisions in bone, bark, or leather but did not cut through anything hard. Their most generally useful tool was a shell blade set on a stone handle with a moss or barberry buffer to prevent breakage. With this implement they scraped skins, cut up meat, or notched wood. When dulled, its blade could easily be sharpened on available whetstones. Pumice stone was also abundant and served for polishing wooden shafts. Very striking, indeed, is the lack of a drill. Fuegian awls of bone or sharpened wood can pierce skin but cannot make a hole even in wood. Because of this deficiency artifacts remained simpler than in the Upper Stone Age of Western Europe. What borers meant in the history of invention becomes clear on passing from a Yaghan collection to a set of Eskimo specimens. Diverse ways of fastening objects that are matters of daily routine for a Greenlander are impossible for the Fuegian without a drill: ivory buckles, antler arrow-straighteners, or perforated belt buttons of musk-ox horn are simply beyond him.

Containers. Containers are few in Fuegia, and, though suitable clay is not wholly wanting, there is no trace of pottery at any period. For want of proper vessels, food was never boiled in the old days, only roasted over a fire or baked in the ashes. The people were not altogether ignorant of stone-boiling but never used it in cookery. They did resort to it when they needed a little warm water, which they heated by dropping hot pebbles into a large shell holding the fluid. The

Ona stored objects in bags of fox or guanaco skin, and in one type of basket, possibly borrowed from one of the Yaghan forms. The Yaghan themselves also made several kinds of skin pouches and constantly used a bark bucket in bailing out their boats.

Dogs. To the guanaco-hunters of Fuegia the dog is indispensable; among the Ona, accordingly, it must be an ancient acquisition. Not so among the Yaghan, who used it mainly in hunting otters for their furs and hence could do very well without it. Indeed, the earliest travelers never mention Yaghan dogs.

Society

Families and Hordes. Since all Fuegians had to wander continually or starve, there could never be any large aggregation of people in one spot except through some lucky fluke. That is why an assembly of possibly two hundred people for the initiation of boys generally became possible only through the stranding of a whale, whose flesh would help feed people for weeks. Thus the single family remained the main economic and social unit; and notwithstanding some political solidarity among the families of one locality, the tie was not strengthened by a common chief. The Ona, more land-minded than the neighboring water nomads, more definitely split up their country in hereditary districts, resenting trespass except for the blessed event of a stranded whale, which let down all barriers. A person was born into his father's horde and, if a male, remained there for life, bringing his wife into his own group. The women were less rigorously tied to their natal district, but even so the Ona had something like unilateral lineages or clans (p. 264).

Marriage. Owing to their dread of inadvertently marrying blood-kin, the Ona liked to take girls from as remote a district as possible; the Yaghan shared the horror of incest but did not on principle seek brides from far away. Most unions were monogamous, as dictated by the mode of life. The levirate, the sororate (p. 237), the special mutual avoidance of a man and his *father-in-law,* and graduation from the tribal initiation school as a preliminary to the man's marriage are common to the Ona and Yaghan. As for the girls, the Ona, who do not initiate theirs, at least insist on some ritual at puberty, when both tribes impose definite rules, secluding the adolescent, making her abstain from food and speech, and giving her moral instruction.

Couvade. At childbirth the Ona limit both parents' diet for some time after the delivery, and the Yaghan besides make the father lie in and refrain from work while his wife resumes her normal chores a few hours after the birth. Thus, the Yaghan, the southernmost people of the New World, preserve the full-fledged "couvade", that widespread South American custom by which a father is confined lest his exertions injure the newborn infant.

Initiation. From an early age boys are separated from girls in Fuegian society, but though the Yaghan keep them apart even in their small canoes, it is the Ona who stress sex cleavage by rigidly barring women from initiation. This, indeed, has the dual purpose of training the boys and bullying the uninitiated, the women attending on the periphery of the dance ground mainly so that they can be intimidated by men masquerading as spirits (p. 321; *Pl. 37, fig. 1*). The Yaghan initiate both sexes, haranguing the adolescents on their moral duties and subjecting them to a strict discipline reserved by the Ona for their boys. During their several months' seclusion the youngsters are allowed to sleep and eat as little as possible, must maintain difficult postures, and suffer other forms of discomfort. They also receive a little stick to take the place of their fingernails when they scratch themselves. This curious implement is one of the most widespread features in American cultures: it occurs in Brazil, Arizona, California, Wisconsin, and even in British Columbia, not necessarily at puberty but always at some critical stage in the individual's life.

Since women gain Yaghan "citizenship" on equal terms, the misogynist tendencies of the Ona are lacking from their neighbors' initiation. Nevertheless, the Yaghan practice the Ona custom of cowing women through mummery but embody it in a separate festival held by a men's secret organization. The usage evidently has a single origin, for all sorts of details are identical. For example, in both instances the women learn that the masqueraders are spirits who are terrorizing the members as well as the outsiders; and to lend probability to the tale the men deliberately make themselves bleed, smearing the blood all over themselves to prove to their wives how cruelly their supernatural visitors are abusing them. It is also clear that the Yaghan have borrowed the idea and attenuated it in the borrowing. They themselves trace the custom to the north; they use the Ona, not their own, form of ceremonial lodge for the mummers' performance; moreover, an anti-feminist tendency is so foreign to the spirit of Yaghan culture that actually the bars are let down for a few "trustworthy" women, who are allowed to view the performances of what is in principle a society for keeping their sex in place.

Ceremonial and Religion

Spirits and God. The spirits represented in this festival have absolutely no religious or philosophical value in either tribe. Apart from their social aspect they satisfy Fuegian aesthetic needs. These people, who neither carve nor attempt realistic drawing, exercise their fancy by creating a host of imaginary characters with distinctive masks for dramatic entertainment, but it never occurs to them to render these figments of their imagination any kind of worship or to connect them with the shaping of the world they know. The Fuegian world-view is compounded of two ingredients unrelated to the spirits of the dramatic impersonations—shamanism and belief in a Supreme Being called Watauinewa, The Ancient One, by the Yaghan, and Temaukel by the Ona (p. 327).

This high-god concept must be considered aboriginal, because it lacks any distinctively Christian ideas, such as vicarious atonement or retribution in a hereafter. The Ona god is not a true creator, for it is his deputy who brings the earth into its present condition, while the stars are transformed ancestors. And among the Yaghan the Ancient One fashions beasts, but neither mankind nor the universe.

The Yaghan deity is less remote from human affairs than Temaukel; hence he is much more frequently addressed in prayer; and while the Ona supplicate their god in phrases dictated at the spur of the moment, the Yaghan employ set formulae. But they are not uniformly reverent; ascribing all deaths to the Ancient One, they roundly abuse him as a murderer when in an ecstasy of grief over a lost relative.

Shamans. Shamans of both tribes get their power from spirits who appear in dreams and teach them songs. A shaman in action lures his tutelary by his chants and works himself into a frenzy until his soul recedes before the spirit, who takes over the singing. Cures are effected largely by sucking out the cause of illness, which is then displayed to the patient (p. 314). Sleight-of-hand tricks are naturally in vogue, but the acme of power is demonstrated by stranding a whale.

Notwithstanding these resemblances there is an expectable difference. Important as the Yaghan shaman is, he does not enjoy quite the prestige of his Ona colleague nor are the relevant beliefs equally elaborated. The reason is obviously the relatively greater significance of the Yaghan high-god. Ona shamans are absolutely independent of Temaukel: their souls do not join him, and a tribesman afflicted by a shaman's enmity appeals not to his high-god, but to another medicine-man. But among the Yaghan there is no such absolute divorce. To be sure, they are inconsistent in theoretically tracing all deaths to the Ancient One, yet imputing particular instances to malevolent shamans. On the other hand, in difficult cases a Yaghan medicine-man does directly implore the Ancient One to remove the disease.

Myth. Fuegian mythology recognizes an ancient era definitely set apart from the recent period. The pre-human beings largely bore animal names and because of certain events, say, a deluge, assumed their present guise of beasts, birds, rocks, and heavenly bodies. There was also a great revolution by which an earlier matriarchate, which rested on the terrorizing of men by female mummers, was overthrown, the men henceforth appropriating the disguises used. Still more important for humanity was the origin of death, for in the mythological period senile persons could be restored.

Here appears one of the most interesting divergences. Ona myth has Temaukel's deputy rejuvenate the ancestors by washing; his successor is thwarted by an evil sorcerer who sings against his own brother's recovery. The Yaghan substitute two brothers quite unrelated to the high god. The elder plans to make things easy for man, e.g., by never letting fires go out, while his junior persistently urges the necessity of hard labor for humanity. When their mother grows old and feeble, passing into a stupor, the older hero eagerly resuscitates her, but once more the younger carries the day, introducing death into the world. This dualism is virtually identical with that of Californian tribes thousands of miles to the north.

Conclusion

In their totality the Fuegian cultures, simple as they are, offer an epitome of civilization. There is an inevitable adaptation to physical environment, for notwithstanding the wretchedness of native dress and habitation, other phases of life show a great sensitiveness to geographical conditions: in the timbered part of their area the Ona substitute huts for mere wind-screens; in the north abundant rodents take the place of guanacos for food and skins; in the southeastern littoral mollusks and sea mammals become more important. Yaghan utilization of thicker beeches for a distinct type of hut reveals similar responsiveness. But here we note at once that it is not a mere question of geography, for as soon as white men brought axes the natives chopped down timber unusable with only aboriginal equipment and extended the range of the conical house type.

Since the Fuegians live at the very margins of the New World, the question arises whether they have preserved typical features of other Indians. The answer is strongly affirmative. To mention only features that are not technological, they practice the typically South American couvade, hold the same theory of disease as most Indians, ascribe magical power to songs, and tell stories reminiscent of California and the Basin. Some of these elements are probably part of a very old layer of American culture.

Some scholars have suggested that the Fuegians have kept elements brought from the north simply because they traversed the length of South America with uncanny speed. This assumption seems improbable, however, in view of the difficulty of travel and the lack of adequate means of transportation. But even if their southward migration had been rapid, we should have to allow a long period of occupancy in the new environment for, as shown, the Fuegians evolved two radically different modes of adjustment to their southern habitat.

A fair degree of antiquity in or near Fuegia is also indicated more directly by archaeological finds. In the Cape Horn Archipelago there are large and numerous shell heaps; and though the artifacts in them show no basic differences at the bottom and the top, their number and size argue for a deposition during centuries of occupancy. Still more convincing are the finds made by Mr. Junius Bird in a cave near the Strait of Magellan, virtually in Ona territory. Here there are five distinct strata set off by the nature of their implements, the uppermost with small arrow points of modern Ona type, the lowest with spear points accompanied by bones of extinct horses and sloths. Five changes in material culture and remains of extinct species indicate a historically, even though not necessarily geologically, old residence.

Thus both in Yaghan and Ona territory occupation dates back to a considerable period; and though particular traits doubtless trickled southward by normal processes of diffusion, some elements of Fuegian culture may be extremely ancient.

Apart from such historical points, there are stimulating parallels with other continents. The anti-feminist bias of the great Ona festival recalls Oceanian and African initiations, a resemblance of psychological interest. On the other hand, the cure of disease by suction is so widespread that it may be a veritably ancient human conception. On that assumption its retention by the Fuegians shows how stable certain phases of belief can be. Finally, the resemblance between Ona and Australian hordes (pp. 264f.) is probably merely the result of independent development from similar antecedents.

XXII

THE MURNGIN

Political Units; Habitat

In Arnhem Land, a part of northernmost Australia west of the Gulf of Carpentaria (*Pl. 39*), there live eight groups collectively called "Murngin". Being without a sense of political unity, they are hardly so many tribes, let alone a single nation; but they do share essentially identical institutions, arts, and beliefs. The patrilineal, exogamous, landowning clan of not more than forty or

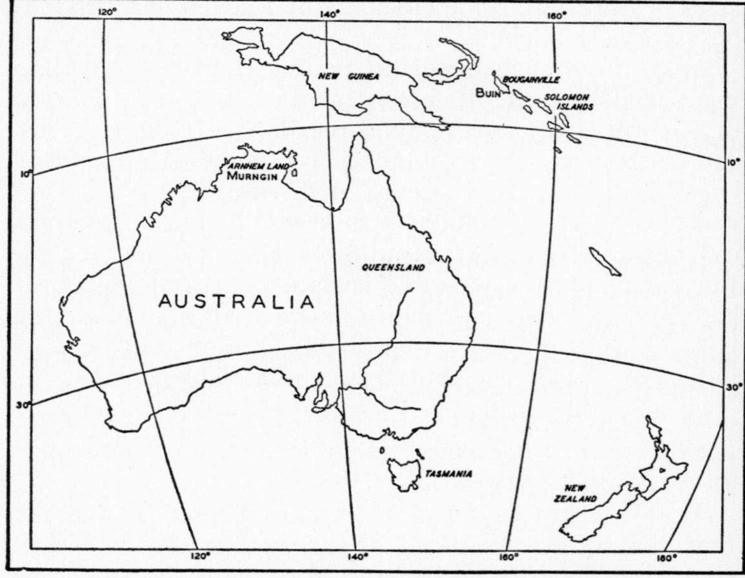

Plate 39: AUSTRALIA.

fifty persons on the average is extremely important here (p. 265). It may make war and it maintains peace within its borders, but above all the members are welded together by their relationship to the clan totems; in so far as headmen exist they are the leaders of ceremonial, most of which revolves about these totems.

Geographically, the country harbors the typical Australian fauna and flora—kangaroo and emu, eucalyptus trees and spear grass. But the Murngin differ from two-thirds of their congeners in occupying a tropical area, from about 12° to 15° S. Lat. This likewise brings them closer to the more advanced inhabitants of Indonesia and New Guinea. Moreover, their closeness to the sea gives them an advantage over the aborigines of the interior in making possible the exploitation of marine animals. The climate is characterized by a dry season with plentiful food and a lean wet season that brings from fifty to sixty inches of rain within the space of several months.

Material Culture

Before Malay traders supplied them with iron tomahawks the Murngin completely lacked metal implements. On the coast they did not even manufacture their own stone knives and spear-heads, importing characteristic Australian forms from the interior (pp. 113f.). On the other hand, the ground stone axe is not only a local product but dates back a fairly long time, for it turns up in an early archaeological level.

The Murngin are not only hunters but nomads—a fact that inevitably prevented the accumulation of wealth since they have to carry their possessions by their own power. For though they have dingoes, it never occurred to them to make these dogs transport goods in Plains Indian fashion (p. 155); moreover, both their ancient bark canoes and the more recent Malay dugout are linked in their minds not with transportation of goods but with turtling and other foraging expeditions. The

Australians as a whole have been greatly influenced by considerations of carriage in accepting or rejecting innovations from foreigners. So long as they cling to a roving life they must forego heavy articles irrespective of utility. Although they themselves manufacture impressive emblems and regalia for ritual purposes, these articles are either destroyed after use or hidden in secret spots. Otherwise they could not be carried about without being seen by the uninitiated, to whom they are taboo.

A single clan roams, on the average, over some 360 square miles, the women digging up wild yams and roots while the men hunt game. In the rainy season the economic unit shrinks to a few brothers with their families; but when the drying of the land opens up larger tracts, several such groups combine into a major band in which several friendly clans are represented. In short, the clan is not so jealous of its property rights to land as the otherwise similar Ona lineage (p. 264). Still larger bodies of people unite in times of abundance for the great communal festivals.

Like other Australians the Murngin lack bows and arrows, but they hurl spears at their game from spear-throwers (p. 21), harpoon turtles, and take fish by drugging, trapping, or netting. Very much like the Bushmen (p. 19), they sneak up to their quarry in a disguise so as to get within close range. The boomerang, which many other Australians hurl as a hunting weapon, never serves that purpose among the Murngin, who merely beat time with it at ceremonies.

In preparing food, the Murngin grind seeds on a quern (p. 61), drill fire (p. 55), steam big animals in earth ovens (p. 59), and cook fish directly on an open fire or in a bark wrapper. They cannot boil food because they lack both earthenware and any other solid containers. The twined baskets of fairly close weave serve only for transporting food.

A Murngin does not depend on dress to protect him

during a cold night, but if caught unawares he will set up a windbreak and build a fire in front of it. For the sake of decoration and modesty a pubic apron of fur string is hung from a belt of human hair, material saved whenever cut from the head and spun on a spindle in two strands. The natives wear many decorative and ceremonial articles, such as plaited armlets, bracelets, and anklets, necklaces of grass fiber or fish vertebrae, and forehead bands. In the absence of pockets the women loop their food bags over their foreheads, letting them hang down the back, and the men sling their equivalent baskets over the shoulder and under one arm.

Even in the dry season the windbreak is not the only shelter, there being more substantial dwellings with a ridgepole resting on two forked posts and an arch of bark laid over this frame. In the rainy season the women bend and tie together six-foot sticks into a dome, which they cover with paper bark. In one district the natives go so far as to erect a gable-roofed pile house. Conceivably adopted from the Malays, this may be a mere elaboration of the ridgepole structure which the blackfellows often use for suspending objects.

Malay Contacts

Intercourse with Malays was amicable and lasted for several centuries. Yet except for their boats, possible fragments of Indonesian folklore, and the practice of mast-raising, which was oddly imitated in funeral ceremonies, the foreigners diffused very little of their superior culture. Murngin men took over some Malay words, adopted iron tomahawks necessarily as finished products without knowledge of how to make them, and imitated the cut of the mariners' beards. The Malays made a trifling contribution to the dietary habits of the Murngin since the rejected seeds of the tamarinds they themselves ate sprouted all over the region. Although the natives learnt to use a new fruit, no one dreamt of actually planting the seeds.

Thus the only significant innovation due to the Malays was their dugout canoe with sails and mast, though oddly enough the outrigger did not find favor in Murngin eyes. The solid dugout proved clearly superior to the frail aboriginal bark canoe on turtling trips, but the easily manufactured ancient craft persists for ordinary travel.

Society

Law and Government. The ceremonial leader comes as close as any person to being a headman but exercises very little authority except when conducting a ritual. It is the old men as a body that govern, for they alone know all the mysteries and control, step by step, the initiation of their juniors.

Warfare never aims at dispossessing a clan, for its association with its hereditary district is accepted as too intimate to be broken. The Murngin, then, fight mainly to revenge a death, whether actually due to an enemy or supposedly to a sorcerer, and also to punish sacrilegious acts (pp. 220, 229, 230).

Under normal circumstances human intercourse follows the principle that all persons without exception fall into some category of blood relationship; when that is once determined, behavior of a definite type is prescribed. Thus a visitor to a distant horde would first of all establish the nature of his relationship to every one of his hosts. If he called a particular man his maternal uncle, he would have to treat him like other possible fathers-in-law because of the cousin marriages practiced by the Murngin; from the father of that "uncle" he would expect food, as from a real maternal grandfather, and so forth (p. 272).

Because the clan is exogamous, the persons inhabiting its territory can never be of a single clan; and because the Murngin practice patrilocal residence it is the male clan membership that remains fixed while the adult women come from other clans (p. 243). The kinship tie and the local tie are thus indissoluble for the male portion of the population.

Marriage Rules. Actually, marriage must conform to other rules than patrilocal residence and clan exogamy. The several clans scattered over the country are all classed as either Dua or Yiritja, and the totality of either forms an exogamous patrilineal moiety (p. 259). In other words, a Murngin youth is not only barred from marrying a clanswoman but is prohibited from taking a wife from any clan in his half of the Murngin people.

The moieties have nothing to do with political alignment; in fact, most fights are between clans of the same moiety. But, apart from regulating marriage, they are important in native ritual and philosophy. Thus, at certain stages in a festival the Yiritja men will dance jointly while the Dua watch, and vice versa. Also the Murngin apportion every cosmic phenomenon to one or the other of the moieties: e.g., they consider the shark and the red parrot Dua, while the black duck and the Caucasian are Yiritja. In this respect their moieties are like the non-exogamous divisions that serve as racing teams among the Canella during the rainy season (p. 431).

To revert to marriage, the Murngin still further restrict a young man's choice: they halve the moieties, splitting up the population into quarters, so that a young man must wed a girl from one particular fourth of the tribe. Thus if we call these four sections Dua I, Dua II, Yiritja I, Yiritja II, a man from Dua I may not marry into Yiritja II even though she is of the right moiety, but may marry only a Yiritja I, who is of the one and only possible section for him. Still odder is the rule of putting the offspring of such unions into sections. For, though Dua and Yiritja are patrilineal moieties, the child of a Dua I man and a Yiritja I woman is, indeed,

Dua (like his father), but Dua II (unlike his father). That is, he is in the section of neither parent.

This seems arbitrary, but can be readily explained. The Murngin simply recognize both named patrilineal moieties *and* unnamed matrilineal moieties and prohibit marriage within either. To make the matter plainer, let us name the anonymous matrilineal moieties "Mary" and "Ellen", respectively, so that every Murngin shall bear a double name. The possible combinations of maternal and paternal names are, of course, four: Dua Mary, Dua Ellen, Yiritja Mary, Yiritja Ellen. These are our four sections. Now a Dua Mary must not marry *any* Dua because of patrilineal moiety exogamy; but neither may he marry a Yiritja Mary because *she* shares his mother's moiety name. Accordingly, he is limited to Yiritja Ellen, who is not in the same moiety by either rule of descent. As for the children of a Dua Mary man and a Yiritja Ellen woman, they must be Dua if the patrilineal moiety is to count, but they cannot be Dua Mary for that would obliterate any suggestion of their mother. Hence they are bound to be Dua Ellen.

As a matter of fact, the Murngin arrange only their marriages on this quartering plan, but for classifying the children they further bisect the sections, making eight "subsections" in all, four in each moiety. They then put a man's children into a particular half of the section, depending on the mother's subsection though of course never coinciding with it.

There is still another peculiarity of the Murngin system. Most Australians practice marriage by exchange: a boy from one family weds a girl from another, and in return his sister marries his brother-in-law (pp. 237, 240). Where cross-cousins marry, this implies that a man may take *either* his maternal uncle's or his paternal aunt's daughter. For, if he is represented by number 13 in Plate 35 (p. 234) and marries 20 (his mother's brother's daughter), then his sister, 14, is his brother-in-law's (18's) father's sister's daughter. The Murngin, however, prohibit marriage with the paternal aunt's daughter and thereby likewise preclude an exchange of brides.

By this asymmetrical arrangement a Murngin inevitably looks to his mother's native horde (clan) to provide him with a wife; and if she is to be of his own generation, she is bound to be a mother's brother's daughter, for in the mother's clan the men of *her* generation are her brothers, either real brothers or more remote kinsmen so reckoned.

Life Cycle. Because sex cleavage goes far beyond the customary division of labor, the life cycles of men and women differ radically. Murngin philosophy emphasizes esoteric observances yet rigorously excludes women from them. Typically, they receive sacred names but never know what they are. In the great festivals, again, women attend, but only in the capacity of a foil, setting off by their very existence as outsiders the superiority of the other sex. They are barred from the men's ceremonial ground and gain the acme of distinction within their reach when in old age they are able to direct the ceremonial procedure of younger women. A woman who accidentally stumbles on a sacred emblem would be killed by her own clan.

A boy, on the other hand, rises above the feminine level when about six or eight years of age. He is then initiated into his first age grade by circumcision and henceforth lives with other single males in a bachelors' camp supervised by a widowed elder. In the succeeding years he must observe food restrictions, which drop off when he becomes a father. In the meantime he learns more of the sacred lore, being introduced at successive ceremonies to the lower totems and finally, as a mature man, to the highest totems. Some of the intermediate stages are optional but confer dignity on a volunteer, as when he offers his arm to be gashed at a ceremony in order to supply blood for gluing bird's down on the performers' bodies.

Even in death the treatment of the sexes is different,

as is their form of participation in the funeral rites. The Murngin first bury a corpse at a depth of some four feet, but exhume the bones several months later, clean them, and finally lay them to rest in a hollow log planted upright in the camp. It is customary to erect several grave posts for a man of consequence, but a woman would ordinarily have but a single one in her honor. Again, women are allowed to carry about the bones of the deceased, but at the exhumation they must be screened from what is going on.

To the native, however, the life cycle is far more than a series of temporal events, being intimately tied up with his animistic and totemic ideas.

Supernaturalism

Animism, Totemism, and Mana. Each person is credited with two souls, one identified with the heart, the other with the shadow. After the death of the body, the shadow soul goes to the jungle and turns into a trickster spirit, but the heart soul is of vital significance throughout the individual's career. Before birth the infant's soul resides as a little fish in the sacred well of its clan. It appears in a dream to its prospective father, who directs it to one of his wives as its proper mother. At death the survivors paint a design symbolic of the deceased person's totem on his body, which aids the ancestral spirits in conducting the heart soul to its own well. There it meets both its clan forebears and the great totemic figures of yore.

Native ritual is predominantly interwoven with these notions. A dying man imitates the motions of his totem animal. The songs then sung help unite him in native belief with his ancestors, preventing his abduction by trickster spirits when he is on the way to his well. The distinctively totemic festivals extend over months of the dry season, during which all ceremonies are performed. A boy or youth rises in the social scale in proportion as he is initiated into the lower and the higher totemic lore; for the highest totemic emblems, being eminently sacrosanct, are reserved for the sight of the older men. And while these beliefs thus serve for an age-grading of males, the overtly initiatory ceremonies teem with songs and dances relating to the emu, snake, iguana, and so forth.

While the Murngin use other terms for mana (p. 303), such as "dal" and "mariin", the underlying concept is akin. A qualified elder may invest a common object with extraordinary power by giving it a sacred name. Some things, like the great totems, may be mysteriously powerful in their own right, others may become so by contact with either the totems or the dead generically. Thus the blood from a bewitched man's heart gives luck on the hunt or in battle and naturally finds its place in a magician's kit. Songs, too, have supernatural potency, as when chanted about two creator women intimately connected with the origin of ceremony. Marvelous, indeed, is the effect of such music in myth, forcing a ghost woman to surrender the morning star to a human visitor, or changing a man's sex. Indeed, even today certain chants loom as the deadliest weapons against an enemy.

Magic and Doctoring. Magic is not altogether the prerogative of professionals. In rainmaking, particularly, a layman may resort to imitative ritual, such as singing, to approximate the sound of rain and splashing water as though drops were falling. But the more impressive forms of magic belong to specialists.

While image magic (p. 299) occurs, the typical form of witchcraft is to steal a man's soul. Fantastic notions are associated with the practice. The sorcerer supposedly sneaks into the victim's camp with an accomplice, slips a rope around the poor man's neck, and drags him to the jungle. There he cuts open his body to expose the heart, into which he thrusts a magic stick, and collects the blood in a container. Having thus kidnaped the soul, he closes the opening made in the body, effaces from his enemy's memory all that has happened, and bids him die so many days hence.

In such cases of soul-loss a doctor cannot restore health, but he is able to identify the murderer by inspection of the corpse. He may then either kill him by retaliatory magic or point him out for the vengeance of the dead man's kin. Besides being a diagnostician the doctor can cure people sick from intrusion of a foreign object, which he then sucks out (p. 314) even though it may have been injected by an evil spirit.

The Murngin doctor derives his power from two or three child spirits who appear to him in a vision. He differs from his Siberian equivalent (p. 311) mainly in not being actually possessed by his familiars and in being a normal not a morbid specimen of his group. Like American Indian shamans, he loses his power by breaking, even unintentionally, the rules laid down by his spirit helpers, and he must receive a fee for his services. Curiously enough, his familiars die if he gets covered with salt water.

Ceremonialism. While totemic ideas pervade ritual, it may also be regarded from other angles. The great festivals, which often spread over months, are uniformly held in the dry season of plenty. In all of them women and the uninitiated play a subordinate role. The participants paint themselves and use feather ornamentation in traditional styles. Irrespective of the festival celebrated, there are cycles of songs and dances. Further, whether ostensibly the emphasis is on the totemic wells and emblems or on promotion to a higher status, the dances mimic particular animal species. Thus the performers, painted to resemble turkeys, dance through fires that represent those actually built on a bird hunt, one man playing the part of a brush turkey out on the plains. Again, in accompaniment to the wallaby chant, two men posture to simulate the animal's front legs and jump sideways as it does when alarmed. Major festivals, moreover, conclude with a purificatory brushing of the participants and the communal eating of ceremonial palm-nut bread. In short, a definite pattern of behavior is considered essential in the greater ceremonials.

Equally remarkable is the subjective view the Murngin take of these activities. Going beyond most aborigines, they not only find sanction for their doings in myth but connect every important aspect of their ritual with two tales of the dim past. According to one, the Wawilak sisters with their offspring wandered over the land and committed clan incest, the older woman also accidentally profaning the Python's pool. Because of this sacrilege the snake caused a terrific rainstorm which the sisters vainly tried to halt by ritualistic chants and dances. Python bit and swallowed them, then stood up erect, thereby flooding the earth. Later he regurgitated them, but swallowed them once more. When he ultimately spat them out they turned to stone. By his interference he had prevented them from circumcising their sons, but the spirits of the women appeared to men in dreams, ordering them to inaugurate the several initiation ceremonies. The other myth, purporting to account for distinctively totemic performances, is not unlike the first. The two Djunkgao sisters first paddled, then walked over the Arnhem Land region, creating totem wells and naming clan districts, as well as the animals they met. The younger was incestuously ravished by a member of her moiety; finally they lost their totemic emblems, which were stolen by men who anciently had played the outsiders' part in ceremonial. Both myths recall the more dramatic Fuegian tale of a masculine revolution by which women were dispossessed of the masks they had hitherto used to dominate men.

What is characteristic of the Murngin is their resolute attempt to justify all sorts of ritual details by reference to these myths of origin. Thus, the three principal initiation festivals use a trumpet, a bull-roarer, and a tom-tom, respectively; but each of these instruments is a symbol of the snake himself. Thus the triangular dance-ground pictures the Python's body enclosing the woman he devoured, with the base line representing his head. A particular dance merely duplicates that of the Wawilak pair when trying to stop the rain. When men are gashed to furnish blood for gluing birds' down on the performers' bodies, the Murngin think of the blood that profaned the sacred pool or that drawn by the snake in biting the sisters. Similarly, in another festival the men handle their spears as canes because the Djunkgao so used their digging sticks; and a dance back and forth in a line mimicking the tides of the ocean is accompanied by a parrot call because such a bird watched the movements of the mythical sisters along the beach.

Obviously the Murngin conceive their ceremonial largely as a drama of mythical happenings (p. 323). That, however, is not the whole story, for other Australians practice elaborate initiation performances with partly similar activities yet with different supernatural sanctions (pp. 317f.). The initiation procedure itself includes elements not only of general Australian character, but found in other areas where boys are segregated before puberty as incipient members of the male community. Thus, the Murngin women wail in commiseration with the boys about to undergo circumcision. The novices are at first carried like infants on the shoulders, receive their first pubic covering as a badge of a new status, and begin carrying a man's basket in masculine fashion. In short, the Murngin, like a host of other aborigines, stress the transition from infancy to years of discretion, from the tutelage of women to manhood, an idea which clearly cannot be derived from the Wawilak story. Further, initiation, as elsewhere, is disciplinary: the tyro is put on a strict diet; he must observe a taboo of silence; he is enjoined to respect his elders, to adhere to the marriage laws, and on pain of death to keep the rituals secret from the uninitiated. So the segregation of the boys from the main camp and the older men's efforts to terrify them are widespread phenomena not to be derived from the myths of origin any more than the occasional buffoonery presumably serving its usual purpose (p. 175).

In historical perspective, then, Murngin ceremonials might be represented as follows. They spring from a widespread Australian basis, psychologically paralleled elsewhere, that includes the schooling of segregated boys before puberty; the sharp division of the tribe by sex and age; the use of the bull-roarer or equivalents as signals; the elaboration of ritual by multiplication of simple ideas (animal dances) and the inclusion of amusement features (buffoonery). On this foundation the Murngin developed in an individual way by correlating their ritual practice with myths of origin and then integrating myth and ritual by specific dramatizations and elaborate symbolical interpretations in terms of the tale.

Mythology. The principal ritualistic tales have been summarized above. Oddly enough, there is also a quite trifling story that traces circumcision back to two flying foxes, which thus set an example to mankind. In general, there is a clear conception of a mythic period in which animals talk, women make sacred rites, and fire is lacking; the stories explain how these conditions contrary to the present were overcome and how the world of experience and established usage came about. Thus Lizard teaches Crocodile to make fire; emus now walk because of a fight that broke their ancestor's arms; Opossum's wives throw hot coals on him so that his legs shrivel and he turns into his present shape. Equally prominent is a cycle about a lecherous and foolish trickster whose exploits are an unending source of amusement.

Summary

The Murngin illustrate, first of all, the extraordinary complexity in social usage and ceremonial that may accompany the simplest material equipment. Compared with other nomadic hunters, such as the Ona, the contrast is marked. Technologically, the two tribes are roughly on a plane: neither manufactures pottery or weaves on a loom; and if the Murngin have stone axes absent from Fuegia, the Ona in turn make bows and arrows. But the ceremonials of the Australians are even more complex than the Ona initiation festivals; and Murngin moieties, sections, and subsections have nothing to parallel them among the Ona.

On the other hand, certain phenomena in Arnhem Land are strikingly similar to those found in other areas. The resemblances are not all assignable to the same causes. Since the spear-thrower was known in Europe before the close of the Old Stone Age (p. 214), it is quite possible that the remote ancestors of the Australians brought the device with them from the mainland of Asia. Similarly, the theory that disease is due to a foreign body which must be sucked out is so widespread (p. 314) that it, too, may date back to the earliest immigrants into Australia. But other parallels suggest merely an independent origin from like antecedents. If the Murngin and Canella (p. 431) both divide up all the phenomena of the universe between two moieties and two racing teams respectively, it is because the notion of a dual division has become an obsession with these peoples. Again, the Murngin horde recalls the Ona lineage, but the common features are most satisfactorily explained by a similar economic system by which males in one line of descent become attached to a definite tract of country.

The distribution of other traits suggests a more complex explanation. Thus the rigid separation of the sexes or at least the banning of women from sacred ritual is a marked feature of both Ona and Murngin society. But it does not occur so commonly among very rude tribes as to indicate Paleolithic antiquity, being absent from most American societies and even lacking among the Yaghan, next-door neighbors of the Ona. On the other hand, the trait is not restricted to the Australians, let alone the

Murngin, but is equally distinctive of Melanesians and some Polynesians. We must compare, then, the Ona with a very large part of Oceania. In these two remote regions development was doubtless independent and may have resulted from some common factor yet to be ascertained. But the Murngin and other Oceanian occurrences within one continuous area must go back to a single source within the Oceanian area, whether the Australians borrowed from the Melanesians or vice versa.

Much simpler is the case of the dugout, which (with a few other elements) can be definitely traced to recent Malay contact. The Malay loans, however, despite their paucity, illustrate the diverse ways in which diffusion operates. The dugout demonstrates *selective* diffusion since the Murngin failed to take over the outrigger; the tamarind exemplifies the wholly passive borrowing of a cultural feature; while the idea of raising a mast, independently incorporated into the Murngin funeral ceremonies, represents a creative effort of the Australian mind.

In comparing the Murngin with the blackfellows further south, the value of geographical *position* is thrust into relief. It is most obvious in the case of their water craft, vastly superior to what is found in the temperate regions of the continent and a direct result of outside contacts that the South Australians did not enjoy. Such enrichment is not limited to the Murngin, but shared with other North Australians, who alone possess ceremonial masks and sacred musical instruments. A favorable location is thus seen to contribute at least as effectively as a favorable environment.

Curious is the specialization of the boomerang, virtually restricted to musical use. It illustrates the frequent change of function despite the preservation of form. Another significant point is the extraordinary amount of time and energy lavished on the ceremonies, which must be interpreted as diversions no less than as sacred performances. Finally—though almost every phase of

Murngin life offers some food for reflection—the anonymous matrilineal moieties beside the named patrilineal ones teach us that the apparently one-sided emphasis on one side of the family is actually often balanced by recognition, even though less obvious, of the other side (p. 256).

XXIII

THE CANELLA: A TIMBIRA PEOPLE

The People and the Country

In the interior of northeastern Brazil three small tribes are known as "Canella". The best known, the Ramkókamekra,[1] until recently occupied a village 48 miles southeast of the town of Barro do Corda in the State of Maranhão (*Pl. 40*). In 1934 the residents emigrated because of lack of timber, and after several epidemics split up into two groups, which were reunited two years later. In recent times the population has been approximately three hundred.

Our Canella are but one of about fifteen tribelets which jointly constitute the Timbira, one of the branches of the widespread Gê family. The total area of this branch extends from 3° to 9° south latitude and from 42° to 49° west longitude. Although a few of its minor groups occupy tropical forest country, most of the Timbira, including the Canella, live in steppe country, with true timber only along the watercourses.

Though there are no real droughts, there is a definite dry season from July to December, which also coincides with the ceremonial half of the Canella year. The low latitudes imply hot days, but after midnight there is a rapid drop in the temperature, so that one is not comfortable outdoors except by a fire. However, the natives of both sexes, unless influenced by civilization, go stark naked except for decorative bands and emblems of status.

[1] The term "Canella" in this chapter refers to this tribe; the Brazilians, in addition, include the Kenkateye and Apanyekra. "Timbira" includes these three groups as well as other members of the same branch of the Gê family.

Ecology

Decoration. Two features in their appearance are characteristic of the Canella and their closest relatives. Both sexes have their hair cut so as to leave a character-

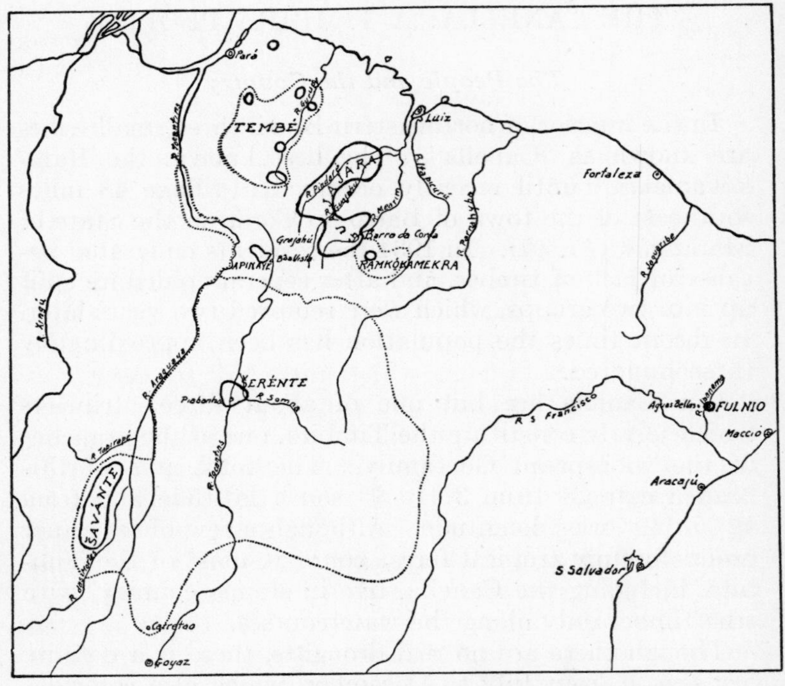

Plate 40: MAP SHOWING THE LOCATION OF THE CANELLA.

istic furrow; hence, when the unoiled coarse and stiff Indian hair stands on end, the effect is that of a cap. Secondly, boys have their ear lobes pierced; the ornamental wooden disks inserted into the holes are the pride of the wearers and the delight of the women.

For the decoration of their bodies, as well as of any utensils, the Canella use a red pigment, urucú, taken from the seeds of the *Bixa orellana* shrub. It also serves as an antiseptic and insures hunting luck. For blackening they employ the latex of a low steppe tree, mixed with powdered charcoal. For a bluish-black paint, very rare except for certain ceremonies, the Indians apply the juice of the heated genipapo fruit (*Genipa americana*), which may defy obliteration for a fortnight. Urucú and genipa are very widespread in tropical South America, the former sometimes being obtained by bartering where the shrub does not grow.

Food Quest. The brooks of the area are stocked with only moderate quantities of small fish; accordingly fishing is a negligible pursuit, though the Indians shot fish with bows and arrows and drugged them with a narcotic root. Fishhooks were originally unknown.

During the last twenty years Canella economy has been completely modified by two factors: the whites taught them to plant rice, a non-American species, and to prepare manioc flour, which the civilized Brazilians themselves had learned from the Tupi, more advanced Indian agriculturists. But the Canella were by no means ignorant of farming in earlier times. Probably they even raised manioc, baking the tubers in earth ovens instead of grating and squeezing them. The main difference between Timbira and Tupi agriculture is simply that while both groups raise manioc and maize, these were originally less important for the Timbira, who rather stressed the cultivation of sweet potatoes and yams, their "daily bread". Most interesting is the cultivation of a *Cissus* species, a creeper with thick, starchy tendrils, which the Canella and their kin bake in earth ovens. This plant is a typical native of dry lands and is wholly unknown either to the Tupi or the civilized Brazilians. Thus the Timbira cannot have taken its care over from their neighbors, but must receive the credit for independently domesticating a food plant.

With tobacco the Canella were familiar prior to white contacts, but even today they fail to cultivate it. Cotton-raising, on the other hand, seems to be of long standing, for despite the absence of loom work, cotton is used for baby carrying-slings and for all sorts of ceremonial articles.

Altogether Canella agriculture exhibits a suggestive interplay of geography, history, and culture. Although primarily a steppe people, they can farm only in the galeria forests, for their hardwood dibbles are unfit to cope with the arid regions of their country. That is why they were bound to be migratory and not permanently settled farmers, oscillating between one stream and another, returning after possibly a decade when natural afforestation had once more taken place. That was the cause of the migration of 1934. But historical factors have also been operative. The invasion of Brazilian colonists did, indeed, bring rice and new technical equipment, but it also reduced the Canella habitat to one-twentieth of its former extent. Any considerable dependence on hunting has thus become impossible, especially since firearms greatly diminished the game supply. Thus, if the Canella were to survive at all, grim necessity would make them more intensive farmers.

The ancient life of the Canella was that of a few contemporary Timbira groups inhabiting uncolonized territory. That is, they did some farming but subsisted largely on game and wild fruits. For the latter the galeria trees are still significant, especially the babassú palm and the buriti, the latter also providing leaves that are the main materials for basketry. Even wars were fought by Timbira tribes for the possession of clumps of babassú. The collection of wild vegetable fare is still practiced by bevies of women and girls sallying forth for days in search of edible fruits gathered into gourd bowls. Men stalked such game as deer, tapirs, and wild pigs or lay in ambush for them, but in the grand tribal hunt—still kept up as a ceremonial act—the beasts were surrounded by a grass fire and dispatched with arrows and clubs in their flight from the flames. The principal weapon, only gradually superseded by muzzle-loaders nowadays, is a six-foot bow with a string of tucum palm fiber; the cane arrows are little, if any, shorter. Dogs were unknown in pre-Columbian times and, being untrained, are little used in the chase even at present. Thus the Canella have not a single aboriginal domestic beast; and even nowadays the few hogs, horses, and chickens adopted from civilization are of negligible importance. On the other hand, like other South American Indians, they like to keep pets, particularly wild pigs (*Dicotyles labiatus*), on which they confer human names.

Settlement and Houses. The Canella always settle near some watercourse and galeria forests; because of their passion for daily dancing they choose for a site some clayey ground, since rocks or sand would be hard on naked feet. A typical village is about nine hundred feet in diameter, with the houses arranged along the circumference. A ring-like boulevard, uniformly over twenty feet in width, runs along the inner side of the house circle, widening at two spots into a dance ground. Since the residents are forever dancing and racing there, not a blade of grass is to be seen growing on the boulevard. In the center of the village is a circular plaza about one hundred and fifty feet in diameter, with which each house is connected by a path kept clear for festive occasions, while between these radii the grass grows undisturbed. The total aspect of the settlement thus suggests a giant wheel with its spokes (*Pl. 41*).

The dwellings are substantial rectangular, gable-roofed structures, thatched with palm foliage, as are the walls. Though there are no windows, the house type seems to be modeled on that of Neo-Brazilian ranchos. For temporary camps or ceremonial use the Canella still put up the old-fashioned beehive form of hut about six feet in height (*Pl. 41*) and sometimes carefully thatched to shut out rain. Although the men erect the permanent houses and the women put up the beehive huts, it is a

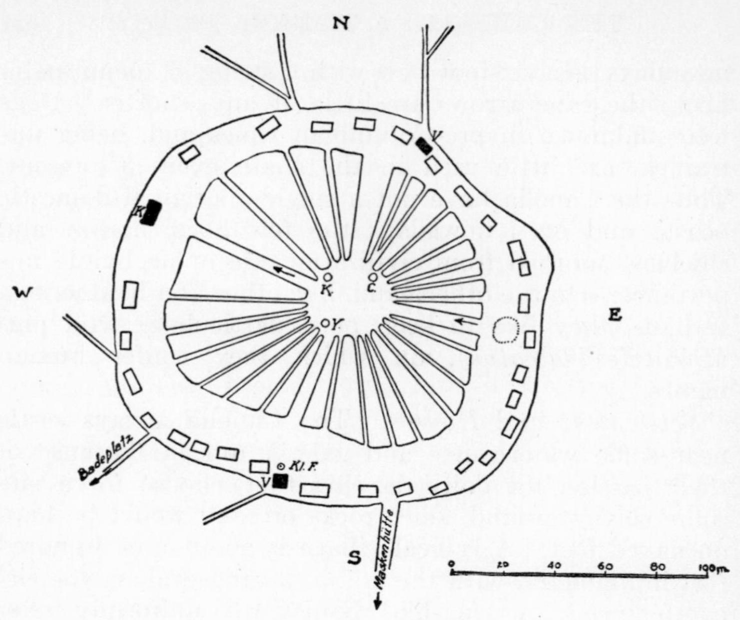

Plate 41: PLAN OF A CANELLA VILLAGE; A CANELLA HUT.

basic principle of Timbira law that the dwelling of either form should belong to the women.

In all probability these Indians anciently had some other, larger type of house than the modest beehive form, which was far too small for ceremonial assemblies of sometimes over fifty participants. But the nature of this major structure remains an enigma.

In contrast to the Indians of the tropical forests, the Canella do not sleep in cotton hammocks (p. 100), but on settees that also serve as tables and are the most conspicuous part of the furniture. These beds are simply grates of buriti leaf-stalks resting on four forked posts at some twenty inches above the floor. They are from five feet, seven inches to six feet, seven inches long, the width varying with the number of bedfellows, each individual family having a bed of its own. Young women, however, put their beds up near the roof, at the level of some six and a half feet above the floor, partitioning them off with mats and climbing up on a notched pole; and the older boys and youths, unless driven indoors by rain, sleep outdoors in the plaza. Mats take the place of bedsheets and blankets, but the feet remain uncovered and are kept warm at night by a fire burning at the foot of the bed.

Whenever possible the Canella keep a fire alight, but if it should go out and there is no neighbor from whom a brand can be borrowed they use a flint-and-steel strike-a-light. This naturally is a loan from Brazilian neighbors that supplanted the native fire-drill, which, however, has by no means dropped from memory.

The Canella have no earthenware pottery and accordingly cook food by broiling on a spit, roasting in the ashes, or baking in an earth oven. A particular kind of fruit is stone-boiled in a pit lined with leaves (p. 60). The oven is situated some distance back of the house, toward the open steppe. While the men kept fires in the plaza, they used them only for heat, not for preparing food.

Society

Men and Women. Socially, feminine house ownership is linked with a whole series of significant traits. Residence is as strictly matrilocal as among the Hopi (p. 242). A husband, having no legal claim to his wife's dwelling, retains an interest in his mother's; there is a close bond between him and its inmates, including his sisters' offspring, whom he constantly meets there (p. 251). After the official evening session of the village council an elder, before going to his wife, pauses at his matrilineal home, where his mother, if still living, his sister, or her daughter will regale him with a snack. He is responsible for the support of these nephews and nieces in case of need, takes an active part in his niece's marriage arrangements, and was formerly accompanied by his nephews in raids against the enemy. Further, personal names loom large in Canella consciousness; while girls get theirs by transfer from a paternal aunt or other patrilineal kinswoman, the boys obtain their names from a maternal uncle or a matrilineal substitute; and these titles—for that is what they virtually are—qualify a youth as a member of certain ceremonial groups and also put him into one of two opposing teams that figure in athletic contests or otherwise during the rainy season.

As might be expected from the domiciliary arrangements, a Canella woman is not abused by her husband. Altogether, while there is not female dominance, the sexes enjoy roughly equal status. A wife does the domestic chores, gathers fruits, weeds, and harvests; and she is the undisputed owner of the farm, even though her husband has made the clearing and shared in the planting. Men not only hunt, but also manufacture the mats and much of the basketwork, so that there is a rather equitable division of labor. Socially it is true that there are no exclusively women's organizations, but each of the several men's clubs has two girls as associate members. Moreover, in the daily dances held in the plaza during the dry season the young women take part on equal terms with the young men.

Dual Organization. As regards the children, they are always of the mother's group, for the Canella are divided into matrilineal exogamous moieties. These are linked with the east and west, respectively, the women of one moiety having their houses on the east part of the village circle, while the other moiety is associated with the western half of the settlement.

Indeed, a dual arrangement is an outstanding trait of Canella society. A set of names acquired by a boy or girl puts the youngster into one of two rival teams, distinguished by black and red body paint, which are pitted against each other in the racing contests of the rainy season. These teams have nothing to do with marriage, but in the minds of the Indians they are linked with contrasted parts of nature: one embraces the east, the sun, the daytime, earth, red, and so on, while the other includes the west, the moon, the night, water, black, and so forth.

But not content with splitting up the entire tribe into paired groups on two different principles, the Canella apply two further modes of bisection to the male population exclusively. A second set of names puts a boy into one of six groups with definite stations in the plaza; these six are ranged in another contrasted pair, one on the east, the other on the west of the ceremonial center of the village. This division yields opposing teams of racers during the dry season and figures prominently during phases of the boys' initiation, where all offices are double, so that a functionary of the eastern half of the plaza regularly has a western mate. Finally, the Canella have an indefinite number of male age-classes, each including those who were jointly initiated; but of these classes only the four youngest are active in sport, and these are again ranged in two opposed parties with eastern and western assembly places in the plaza.

Age-Classes. Initiation is absolutely essential for

boys, who are not allowed to marry before twice going through the two ceremonies involved in full-fledged admission to manhood. The novice, about five to ten years old, is secluded for three months for the first degree; after an interval of two or three years, he passes through a different seclusion for the second degree; and these identical performances are repeated with two- to three-year intermissions, so that all together the process of initiation is spread over a decade.

The age-classes are so deep rooted a part of the social system that even the little boys organize and imitate the older groups. It is the council of chiefs and elders—the rulers of the village—who decide when this unofficial grade is fit to start on the initiation cycle. When such a new company is recognized it always takes up a position on the north side of the plaza, northeast if the preceding body of novices entered on the northwest, and vice versa. Thereby it ousts the class hitherto assembled there, which moves south, pushing out in turn the oldest of the four active classes, which now retires from the sports association to pass into the very center of the plaza, being thus promoted to the status of councilors (*Pl. 42*).

Anciently an active age-class would organize joint hunts and war raids; nowadays they build houses for persons engaged in public business and aid in harvesting when so ordered by the council. But essentially they are and have been sport and ceremonial clubs.

Ceremonial. Ceremonial, however, among the Canella is predominantly secular, largely serving for entertainment. Not a year passes without either an initiation or some other major festival that consumes weeks and months, but strictly religious features are generally absent, though magical elements are more common. In the first phase of initiation, for instance, singing lures the souls of the dead into the novices' bodies, which then act like the dead themselves until purged by ablution and flogging. But this is the only specifically religious

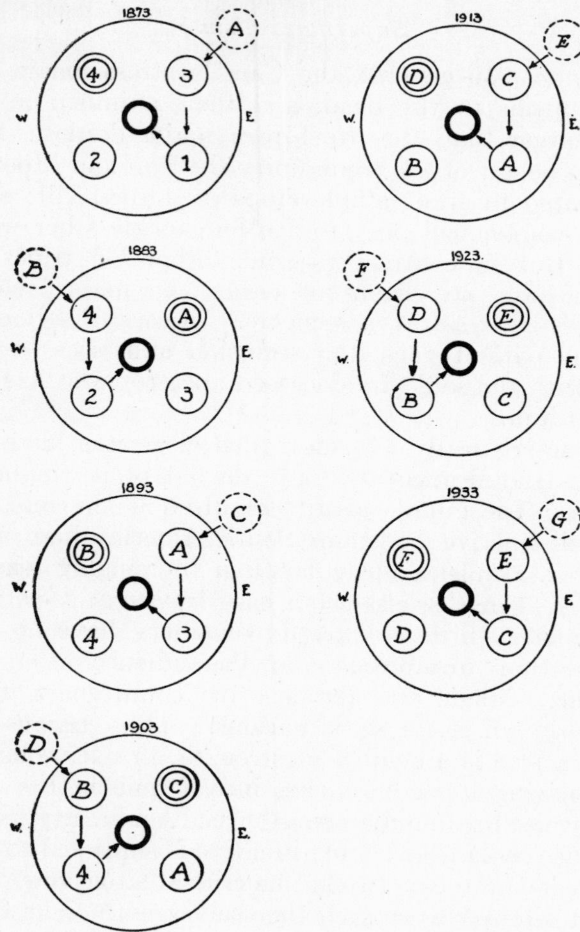

Plate 42: Age Classes in a Canella Community.

element of this festival. On the other hand, there are various magical features: the whole second-degree ritual purports to promote the rapid growth of the initiates; and in the first phase an old man will rub his hand against his armpit and then stroke the boys' faces in order to transfer to them his own longevity.

Supernaturalism

Religion. In general, the Canella stress magic more than appeals to the dead, and their animism in turn looms larger than the worship of major deities. However, on behalf of the community the Sun and Moon are supplicated to grant ample crops or a good kill; and a barren woman will pray to the Sun to bless her with a child. But in contrast to some other Gê tribes, the Canella have no visions of either the major celestial bodies or their astral messengers. In case of serious illness the patient goes into seclusion and tries to commune with the soul of a deceased ancestor who has been close to him.

Characteristically, objects which elsewhere have high religious significance are quite devoid of it among the Canella. The gourd rattle that often is the medicineman's distinctive badge in South America here serves merely as a musical instrument in the singing teacher's hands; and masks, elsewhere used by secret societies to impersonate spirits and terrify outsiders, have no other purpose than to amuse a Canella audience.

Magic. Magic and its negative counterpart, taboo, appear in all sorts of situations. Thus because the sucupira tree is a symbol of strength, in native belief a child placing its navel string into a hole in the trunk thereby acquires similar resistance. Again, a grasshopper dance by lads squatting in a line is supposed to ripen the sweet potatoes. In various critical situations people are not allowed to scratch themselves with their fingernails, but must use a little scratching stick. This taboo holds for boy initiates, for girls at puberty, for the parents of a newborn infant. The latter are, indeed, subject to all sorts of rules from the beginning of conception. They must not gnaw leg bones, or kill snakes, or eat armadilloes or parrots. In case of difficult delivery the husband must walk around the house outside. After the birth both parents remain rigidly secluded for a short time on their partitioned bed-settee, less strictly for over a month; neither may eat anything but vegetable fare. The man must not perform any difficult work or otherwise exert himself; his wife also abstains from her usual domestic chores. All these regulations of the couvade pattern are designed to prevent injury to the child.

Amusements

The comparatively weak development of personal religion is doubtless a result of the dominant concern with such entertainments as dancing, drama, and sport, all three being combined in the major festivals.

Races. The most popular sport is a relay race with heavy logs, usually from the place of manufacture to the village. For this purpose the Canella construct lengthy tracks, some of them miles long, which lead out from the house circle toward the cardinal directions. Whenever the Indians return from a common enterprise, they are likely to stage an impromptu log race. More regularly, definite social units compete: during the rainy season the rivals are the teams entitled to black and red paint, respectively; and on other occasions still other fixed units are pitted against each other. More rarely women and girls also race, though of course with lighter logs. Characteristically, there are no wagers. The Canella race from sheer sportsmanship, and the victors merely enjoy the prestige that accompanies athletic prowess.

Ceremonialism for the sake of ceremonial is a keynote of Canella behavior. Few important events fail to be conducted according to a fixed sequence of procedures. The very organization of a log race may be ritualized: The challengers assemble by the manufactured logs, followed after a while by their slowly advancing opponents. When the first team catches sight of the newcomers, they begin to sing and clap their hands, which are raised to the stamping of their feet as the other party approaches. Similarly the ceremonial dry season is formally opened and closed by a series of prescribed performances.

Men's Societies. In these entertainments there figure six men's societies, the Falcons, Jaguars, Ducks, Agoutis, Masqueraders, and Clowns. Only a talent for buffoonery makes a man a Clown, but membership in pairs of the others—Duck and Agouti, Falcon and Jaguar, or Jaguar and Masquerader—hinges on one's personal names. The antagonism of certain of these organizations creates dramatic scenes in some of the spectacles of the major ceremonies. Thus, in the Masqueraders' festival, the Agoutis badger the Jaguars, who try to catch their tormentors.

Ceremonial Decoration. In all the festivals great importance is attached to the celebrants' ceremonial dress and other paraphernalia. Some actors always have falcon down stuck on their bodies; the leaders of the age-classes wear at the back of the head a fan of towering macaw feathers; before the novices come out of their seclusion at initiation they are painted with genipapo and urucú, the design varying according to their plaza group; and so forth.

Comparisons and Conclusion

The Canella thus illustrate several important principles. Their material culture reveals many efficient adaptations to physical environment. On the other hand, it is clear that only a limited number of them are due to local invention. Compared with their Tupi neighbors, the Canella lack pottery, weaving, cotton hammocks, and boats, proving that they have not borrowed everything that came to their notice. But the Canella did not borrow their coiled baskets, which the Tupi lack; or the cultivation of Cissus from *any* other group, Indian or white, since it is restricted to themselves and a few related groups. Similarly, their matrilineal moieties and most of their elaborate socio-ceremonial organization were certainly not taken over from the Tupi, who have nothing of the sort.

Canella culture, regarded by itself, illustrates strikingly how a few leading ideas may become obsessions, affecting or overriding behavior based on rational grounds. Thus the very choice of a village site hinges not only on the proximity of water and timber, but on whether the soil is suitable for barefoot dancing. Similarly, log races and ceremonial performances not even purporting to have any serious object consume months of the natives' time. Again, dualism is a constantly recurring notion: there are two exogamous moieties; the teams of the rainy season, the pairs of active age-classes, the two trios of plaza groups all represent a type of moiety organization, even though not affecting marriage. In mythology, Moon is a simpleton who serves as a foil and butt for his cleverer companion, Sun, whose efforts he sometimes thwarts by sheer folly. In fact, the entire universe is divided up between the two rainy-season moieties.

When we compare the Canella with the Apinayé or Western Timbira, who live a little further inland, between the Tocantins and Araguaya Rivers, other points emerge. Both share all the essentials of economic adjustment and a host of other traits, such as matrilineal moieties, matrilocal residence, female house ownership, log races. But supernaturalism assumes a very different aspect. For one thing, among the Western Timbira Sun and Moon, playing similar parts in myth, bear a more vital relation to human beings and to the moieties, which here are linked not with east and west, but with north and south. The Sun, in particular, appears in visions. Equally distinctive are the ideas on disease. The Western Timbira, like the Canella, may seek help from the dead, but they also attribute illness to the souls of plants or animals eaten by the patient, which sometimes set up disturbances and must be sucked out by the doctor.

Such differences prove, first, that even closely allied

tribes tend to diverge from a common basis of belief; and, secondly, that the economic factors *common* to the two groups cannot account for their *divergences* in the field of supernaturalism. Similarly, the dual organization of the Western Timbira, despite its similarities, differs radically in not being exogamous, for they regulate marriage by an altogether peculiar system. The tribe is quartered, and a person of one quarter may marry into only one of the other three units; moreover, membership is not fixed on the clan principle but is ordered so that sons follow their father and daughters their mother. Thus, unit A comprises the sons of A men and of B women; and the daughters of D men and A women. For an A man may marry only a B woman; a B man a C woman; a C man a D woman; a D man an A woman. Reversely, an A woman marries a D man, and so forth. This unique scheme again proves the tendency to evolve divergently from a common social tradition; it also illustrates the fact that while economic conditions may account for a good deal, they cannot explain everything.

Finally, it is worth while to make comparisons further afield. Somewhat further south on the Tocantins River than the Western Timbira are the Šerénte, also of the Gê stock, but representing another branch. As might be guessed from their location, they resemble the Western Timbira more than the Canella, but all three tribes have many features in common, such as some sort of dual division, log races, and ceremonial correlates of personal names. However, in one vital respect the Šerénte differ from both Timbira tribes: their moieties are not matrilineal, but patrilineal; and this feature goes with other differences since the Šerénte men own houses and farms and make their wives reside with them. Matrilineal descent may not cause the affiliated Timbira traits, but some of the associated traits do seem to bear to one another more than a chance relationship. This impression is strongly corroborated when we turn to the Hopi of the Shoshonean branch of the Uto-Aztecan family.

Here is a tribe thousands of miles away and bearing no relationship to the Gê, yet it resembles the Canella and the Western Timbira in sharing feminine house ownership, matrilocal residence, and matrilineal descent. Furthermore, this set of Hopi traits does not occur among such near-by Shoshoneans as the Ute or Paiute. Why do the remote and unconnected Hopi and Timbira share these traits, which sharply set them off from close relatives? There can be but one answer: some one of the traits—it may be matrilocal residence—is crucial in rendering certain others probable. Assume that the ancestors of the Hopi and of the Timbira for some reason both evolved matrilocal residence, and some other resemblances thereby became far more probable. In other words, cultural elements are not merely related fragments, but are in some measure organically linked. This means that *to a limited extent* it is possible for remote peoples to duplicate their development. The qualification is essential, for we have seen how even very closely related tribes, like the Canella and the Western Timbira, fail to take an identical course.

XXIV

THE BUIN (SOLOMON ISLANDS)

History

In the fertile, densely wooded district of Buin on Bougainville, one of the northwesternmost Solomon Islands (*Pl. 39*), there live some 7,800 natives speaking a Papuan tongue. This fact is noteworthy, for geographically the Solomons form part of Melanesia, and the Shortland Islanders, directly to the south of Buin, speak a Melanesian dialect, i.e., belong to the great Malayo-Polynesian speech family which, irrespective of race affinity, embraces Malays, Melanesians, and Polynesians. The occurrence of a Papuan language here is further remarkable because it is that of a subject population adopted by a conquering group. For the Buin of today are not a homogeneous people: only several centuries ago the indigenous population, short and broad-skulled, came to be periodically raided by the taller, long-headed Shortland Island head-hunters, who enslaved the women and children and killed any men who offered resistance. Some of the pirates settled in Buin, rallied around them bands of the terrorized natives, and thus founded stratified societies with chiefs and bondmen. That no such class distinction existed in earlier times here is shown by conditions still found in neighboring districts of Bougainville.

In the course of time the sharpness of the cleavage was lessened. The conquerors had brought only a few women with them; hence their descendants were largely obliged to marry the daughters of the indigenous population. Because women of the higher class were so rare, endogamy (p. 233) could be enforced only for the successor to the chieftaincy, and broke down as a hard and fast principle. It continued to be applied to the first-born daughter but not necessarily to other aristocrats: a chief's widow might espouse a commoner, her second daughter a half-caste, and so forth. Naturally, the sons of such mixed marriages were favored above the common herd. Closely related to the chiefs, they were called their "pillars" and came to constitute an intermediate class of freemen, whose life and property were respected by the overlords. The contrast of ruling and subject class was thus materially lessened, so that we find no parallel here to the extravagant caste spirit of Polynesia (p. 270).

Economic System

Food. Even before their conquest the indigenous people had been dibble farmers, their wives raising taro while the men fished and hunted. But the invaders added to the resources of the country by introducing swine and various cultivated plants, such as bananas, sugar cane, and coconuts. Taro, however, remained the staff of life; and pigs do not contribute much to general subsistence, being rather symbols of wealth and distinction at banquets (p. 41). Women rarely eat pork, and then only as a special mark of their husbands' favor, though one of their most important duties is to raise pigs. In addition they plant and tend the tubers that furnish the staple food—taro, yams, and sweet potatoes—gathering taro in intervals of several days, according to the needs of the household, for, unlike the yam, this tuber does not permit storage. Men still fish and hunt but are not completely dissociated from farming. They regularly make clearings for their wives, usually three or four gardens to ensure an ample supply of taro; they also put up and repair fences to keep out marauding pigs. Men likewise plant and tend most of the fruit trees, including the banana and the coconut.

Persons unable to raise enough taro are never allowed

to starve, but they lose the respect of the community. Beyond this attitude must be noted another social feature due to the stratification of Buin society. The invaders who settled as chiefs claimed the land of the conquered, but permitted them to cultivate and use it in return for serf-like services. While the economic basis of life—farming—thus remained unaltered, a family could no longer freely consume the economic goods they produced. However, the yoke imposed was relatively mild. Fortunately, there was ample land for everybody. The chiefs were thus quite willing to let their younger brothers or vassals own property and even allowed commoners to hold plots in return for a tribute of first fruits.

Settlement. The food-producing unit consists of a single family or at most of several closely related families occupying from one to four rectangular, gable-roofed dormitories on lofty piles which serve to protect the sleepers against hostile attacks. Cooking sheds, workshops, and storehouses rest directly on the ground. Such a homestead is always in a clearing in the forest, being connected by trails with the main road. On the other hand, the chief governing a number of such hamlets, with anywhere from six to fifty subjects, builds his towering hall on the highway. The size of this structure, the number of its wooden tomtoms—formerly adzed with stone blades out of heavy logs—and the painted carvings on both tomtoms and house posts are symbols of the chief's power. In front of the main pillar the Buin imagine the standing figure of the ruler's personal war god, whose face reaches up into the clouds, thus remaining invisible. In order to appease this divine patron the chief was accustomed until recently to offer him human skulls.

Industries. Pottery is the only genuinely specialized craft, but its manufacturers practice the art in addition to farming, not as a trade enabling them to dispense with cultivation. For the most part they live on the slopes of mountains, near suitable deposits of clay. In return for their vessels, which are sold at some chief's hall, possibly a three or four hours' walk from home, they receive shell money, which is used mainly for purchasing pigs.

In some settlements the potters are women; in others, men. The women also plait carrying baskets, make small fish nets, and sew pandanus leaves into sleeping mats and rain mats. Their husbands carve weapons, plait the decorative wrappings of spears, clubs, bows, and arrows, make sundry netted bags, and plait taro baskets and fish traps.

Society

Chiefs. As already indicated the marked class system did not make the chief an autocrat. He cannot oppress his inferiors at will, for an offended subject will retire into the bush or join another chief, thus weakening his own lord's power and possibly even becoming a traitor. Such eventualities are staved off as far as possible by gifts. In Buin, rank is thus rather coupled with prestige than with coercive authority. Accordingly, very much as in British Columbia (p. 151), every chief tries to outdo the other. He tries to build the most magnificent hall, which, however, is impossible without the full-hearted collaboration of his people. Thus strictly forced labor is softened into a reciprocity of favors: the men of the district drag heavy tree trunks through the woods and adze them into tomtoms or posts, and the lord indemnifies them with presents and lavish entertainment.

Feasts. Feasts are essentially pork banquets, whence the extraordinary place of the pig in Buin life despite its negligible value for daily meals. Because prestige rests on the liberal distribution of pork, a chief will farm out his sucklings to the commoners, who receive a small compensation for their trouble. The importance attached to the feasts also explains why the feminine accomplishment prized above all others is skill in raising pigs.

Pigs and Money. The preparations for these entertainments are influenced by sentiment: a chief can not bring himself to slaughter his own pigs. Simple exchange between hog-breeding homesteads might overcome this difficulty as in fact it does in neighboring parts of Bougainville. But the Buin complicate matters by introducing as a necessary feature the use of shell money: it is an axiom of theirs that swine should be compensated by an equivalent in this currency and vice versa. Thus, after a chief's death his successor distributes part of the inherited shell money among his vassals and commoners; these take pride in providing him at some future time with a sizable porker, whose quality adds to the donor's social distinction. Contrariwise, the pigs in the legacy go to other chiefs and kinsmen, who must indemnify the kin with shell money, which the heir will apply to the purchase of pigs. By such devices he can accumulate up to fifty pigs for the memorial feast that follows nine or ten months after his predecessor's cremation.

The Buin currency merits some attention. It is true money in the sense that the shells no longer serve decorative ends but merely symbolize value (p. 150). Further, it is not manufactured in Buin, but imported from Alu, one of the Shortland Islands, whence its comparative rarity. At first it was probably only the chiefs who exchanged the two honorific types of value—pigs and shell currency. But as the cleavage between conquerors and conquered narrowed, pigs and currency came to represent values independently of their connection with the overlords, so that their possession conferred eminence irrespective of class. However, the bulk of the currency, which, unlike pigs, cannot multiply, and as an import remains rare, is still in the hands of the chiefs, each of whom serves as his community's banker. When a vassal or commoner requires money in order to get a wife, he borrows currency from the chief and is obliged to pay interest, possibly a total of 50 fathom on a loan of 100 fathom. Here again the native's aim is not to get a maximum equivalent for a minimum outlay, but rather to remain in his superior's good graces and thus pave the way for loans in the future. When a chief repays the loan advanced by one of his peers, the prestige factor is dominant. The debtor makes an extra payment as a gesture of liberality, and the creditor in return offers a gift, if possible exceeding the value of the increment. This is but another sample of the emulation of the upper caste springing from the desire for prestige. Sometimes, especially in aristocratic marriages, the ambitious father of the bride deliberately returns more pigs than correspond to the proffered shell money. The groom's father, if similarly minded, will send back more currency or pigs; and this may continue until the resources of one competitor are exhausted, so that his rival remains the victor. This closely parallels the potlatches of British Columbia (p. 151).

Effect of Class Distinction. Class distinctions, even though not carried to extremes in Buin, affect daily life in diverse ways. As might be expected, the eldest daughter of a great chief receives far more of a bride-gift than a vassal's daughter, possibly three hundred or even four hundred against two hundred fathom of currency. An overlord jealously keeps his wives from the gaze of commoners, who once were punished with death if they met these women on their trails. On the other hand, a chief may appropriate the commoners' daughters for concubinage not only with himself but with his guests at major banquets. But the caste spirit has also wrought subtler effects on the very core of family life.

This appears most clearly when we compare the Buin with those of their neighbors who remained unconquered and unstratified. Thus the Nagavisi are divided into exogamous totemic clans and practice matrilocal residence with the usual guarantees for the wife's security from maltreatment (p. 242). What is more, in this society domestic though not political power is largely vested in the women. A marriage is arranged by the mothers of the bride and groom. Characteristically, it is the latter's prospective mother-in-law that takes the initiative. When she is satisfied that a certain young man would prove an efficient gardener, she makes an initial gift to his mother, who in return contributes pigs for the wedding feast if the marriage occurs. Most marriages are monogamous; in the exceptional instances a man goes to live with his several wives in turn, successively on each estate. Naturally in divorce the children remain with the mother and her clan, which is their own.

This represents roughly the ancient situation in Buin. A generation ago this district still had exogamous matrilineal clans bearing the names of bird totems. But the circumstances of the original conquest had led to a stressing of the paternal rather than the maternal side. Because necessarily the majority of the women were of the subjugated population, descent through the father was rated higher than through the mother, and succession to office thus became patrilineal. The example of the tone-setting aristocracy was widely followed and led to an emphasis on rank, wealth, and political expediency. A rich commoner, for example, is eager to have his son marry into a family of distinction; according to the aboriginal rule, theoretically still considered ideal, the boy should wed his cross-cousin (p. 236), but nowadays the quest of prestige often overrides the older principle.

The patrilineal conception, linked with that of social eminence, is today manifested in many ways. When the bride's father receives shell money from the groom's father, he distributes most of it among his brothers, brothers' sons, and other patrilineal kin. When a widow remarries and her father once more receives a bride-price, this is at once claimed by the deceased man's oldest son; the theory is that her dead husband had acquired her services, now to be lost by the second marriage, and his kin are entitled to an indemnity. This is paid by turning the bride-price over to the son, who shares it with his brothers and other relatives through his father. This illustrates a complete reversal of the conditions found among the matrilocal neighbors of the Buin, where the wife is never conceived as the husband's property. In Buin, on the other hand, even the pottery made by a woman is sold by her husband, who adds the profit to his hoard for future pig-buying or for the discharge of sundry ceremonial obligations. In short, the female sex is under definite disabilities, which are overcome solely by exceptional individuals practicing as medicine-women. Only such a woman would even today dare to enter a men's hall, for only twenty years ago any ordinary woman venturing there would probably have forfeited her life.

Leagues and Head-hunting. Although no despot, a capable chief still exerts considerable authority. Partly through their belief in his patron deity, Oromrui, his subjects have been generally willing to support his interests, not only by gratuitous labor but also until recently in warfare. For, as already hinted, overlords of Buin often turned into ambitious, proud, and sensitive competitors who readily took umbrage at one another's actions and precipitated feuds at their vassals' expense. On the other hand, two chiefs might celebrate a great feast in order to cement an alliance for mutual protection which would also be binding for their immediate successors. These leagues, among other things, often involved a secret pact, by which for a consideration one lord surrendered the life of one of his subjects. A henchman of his ally's, bearing the honorific title of "slayer", would lie in ambush to club or spear the victim, whose skull was then laid with earlier offerings of the same order before the pillar sacred to Oromrui. A lord prided himself on the extent of such offerings, whose number in his great hall ranged anywhere from three to sixty. Naturally not all of them were acquired in the same way: the chief might send his slayer against a hostile rival's subjects or even against a commoner of his own if suspected of treason or of an intrigue with the lord's women. Head-hunting on a major scale was thus a feature added to the aboriginal cults.

Supernaturalism

Underlying Buin supernaturalism are widespread animistic and magical ideas. In a sense the latter flourish more than ever, for since colonial administrators have prohibited official or non-official slaying, vengeance resorts to poisoning by sorcery, which must be combated by shamans. An older shaman trains a promising youngster, who during his novitiate repeatedly passes into a trance and learns to see both ancestral spirit helpers and demons. Buin animism recognizes three souls in every person, associated respectively with the heart and dreams, the shadow, and the reflection. When a demon kidnaps the reflection, its owner must die unless it is restored. After death this soul, if its owner was a distinguished man, not only enters the hereafter but turns into an ancestral spirit, who then goes back to his native village. There he either protects and augments a descendant's pigs, money, or taro; or he may possess a prospective shaman (p. 310) and aid him to recover the stolen reflections of living people. Other ancestral helpers merely hover near the practicing medicine-man, some of them wandering about in order to bring him information from the vicinity.

During a treatment one of these helpers whispers his diagnosis into the ear of the meditating shaman, who announces that the soul has been kidnapped and must be fetched by a patron spirit lest the patient die. Hereupon the fee is paid in shell money, and the doctor washes and rubs the patient's skin. Finally the spirit returns from his journey, perches on the doctor's shoulder, and whispers that he has brought back the lost reflection, which the shaman pretends to seize and introduce into the sick person's head, stroking it downward toward the neck and back. But this reincorporation does not suffice: recovery hinges on whether the patient can recognize his reflection in a little coconut oil poured out on a banana leaf. Not always does the patron spirit succeed in his quest; sometimes the ruler of the hereafter has hidden the reflection, or a demon outwits the rescuer, in which case there is no hope.

Instead of stealing the soul the demon may have entered the patient's body, a fact likewise revealed by the shaman's tutelary. In such an event the doctor massages out of the sick man some small bit of betel nut or pork which is supposed to harbor the evil spirit, who is thought to be held fast by the spittle expectorated into the bowl with the extracted objects. The shaman may remove one demon after another; then he takes the bowl to a river and throws the demons into it, thus at last rendering them harmless.

Although shamanism and sorcery may be practiced by members of all three classes, they influence to a large extent not only a person's social eminence and authority but also his wealth, which in turn lays a foundation for distinction. A conspicuously successful medicine-woman could even gain access to the men's hall, otherwise closed to her sex; and a noted shaman quickly becomes rich through his fees.

This is only one way in which the more recent ideas of rank and wealth have affected the fundamental faith of the Buin, which centers in an ancestor cult with burnt offerings. The soul of a cremated man must buy entrance into the hereafter with the essence of a pig and fathoms of currency contributed and burnt by the survivors. The underworld, situated in the mountains to the north, is ruled by the spirit of a one-time chief. Oromrui is at the same time the god of thunder and lightning and the living ruler's protector who craves skull offerings.

Summary

Buin culture is instructive from various points of view. Above all, it exemplifies the results of conquest even when no essentially new food-getting techniques are introduced. Because the conquerors brought few of their own women with them, most of them inevitably had to marry native women, creating a middle class; and the yoke of the commoners remained relatively light because an abused subject could always flee to the overlord of a near-by district. Nevertheless, the differences in rank created by the invaders radically altered many aboriginal customs. The earlier natives had been matrilineal; but since the women were overwhelmingly of the subjugated group, prestige hinged on the father's status, which gave a violent twist in the direction of patrilineal reckoning. Prestige, however, came to be a general watchword. The chiefs vie with one another in lavish pork banquets to their peers and followers; the subjects try to distinguish themselves by providing their overlord with large pigs; women can best please their husbands by skill in pig-raising.

The role of pigs is especially significant, for pork is served exclusively at feasts, not as the daily food of any class; yet social life largely revolves about this animal. A further sophistication appears in that the beasts can be paid for only in shell money and vice versa. What might be treated as a wholly rational economic factor is interwoven with fanciful ideas of sentiment, vanity, and what not. As in British Columbia, social emulation may lead to bitter rivalry and neglect of the profit motive.

The stratification of society has further affected social life. The great chief takes the commoners' daughters as his concubines, jealously guards his wives from prying subjects, and exacts a much greater bride-price than other fathers. Moreover, the spread of prestige motives has abolished the older cross-cousin marriage since nowadays a wealthy commoner is eager to have his children marry into families of rank. Altogether woman's status has become inferior, so that she is no longer free to dispose at will even of the pottery she has manufactured. Religion has been remolded by the conquest of the original occupants of Buin. The overlord's patron god came to loom large for all the people; and because the chief wished to appease the deity with offerings of skulls he would send out "slayers" to kill victims to be laid before the sacred pillar of the chief's house. Thus, head-hunting was added to the native cults.

XXV

THE HOPI

History and Affinities

In arid northern Arizona some three thousand Hopi occupy seven villages and their outposts. Their settlements are situated on three flat eminences (mesas), but until about 1700, when the people sought refuge from Spanish and nomad Indian attacks, all but a single Hopi village were in the valley.

As to speech, the Hopi are of the Uto-Aztecan family, which embraces the Ute, Paiute, and Shoshone of Utah, Nevada, Idaho, and Wyoming, as well as the Aztec of southern Mexico. With the former tribes—simple hunters and gatherers—the Hopi contrast sharply, being skillful farmers who live in stone houses and have an intricate socio-ceremonial organization. On the other hand, they did not attain the Aztec plane, for they remained without a knowledge of metals or incipient writing (p. 191), their architecture is still very crude, and they have ever been intense separatists without the germs of a national spirit. By and large, however, they mark the acme of aboriginal achievement north of the Rio Grande. This level, however, they shared with the other Southwestern villagers or "Pueblos", people of three alien linguistic families, viz., the Zuñi, the Keresan, and the Tanoan. On the First Mesa one village is occupied by the descendants of Tanoan immigrants, who have intermarried with Hopi and are bilingual.

Subsistence and Arts

Economic Life. The pre-Columbian Hopi were already primarily farmers, growing maize, beans, squashes, and cotton. Maize, their mainstay from time immemorial, came from the south, but the Hopi have clearly adapted its cultivation to their dry climate, planting the seeds twelve inches or more below the surface so that they may catch the moisture in the soil and develop roots to protect them against wind and flood. As a safeguard against destructive storms and animal pests the farmer drops a number of seeds into each of the holes dug with his dibble. His other tools are equally simple —a paddle for digging up weeds and sagebrush, and a rake of juniper for removing this debris. The main fields remain unirrigated, but small gardens are supplied with water stored in tanks.

The most essential article of furniture in every house is a frame enclosing a set of sloping stone querns, on which the women grind corn kernels into meal (*Pl. 43, fig. 1*). Many maize dishes are in vogue, among them wafer bread (p. 61).

Domestic animals have never been of outstanding importance here. Dogs serve to guard their owners against strangers and witches; occasionally used in the chase, they were eaten only in times of dearth. As for turkeys, they have always been raised for their feathers, not for food. The white man's horses, donkeys, and wagons do, of course, facilitate farming at greater distances than before. Sheep must also be reckoned an addition, but their presence has not stimulated the use of manure and their utility lies mainly in providing wool. In short, white contact failed to revolutionize Pueblo economy, and that accounts for the Hopi's exceptional success in salvaging his aboriginal mode of life.

Notwithstanding its dependence on corn, the tribe has continued to draw on the wild flora, such as onions and potatoes, for supplementary articles of food or for ritualistic necessities, such as tobacco—never cultivated by this people—and the yucca plant, whose pounded root takes the place of our soap in ceremonial head-washing. Other wild species furnish basketry materials, and alder bark serves for tanning skins. For lack of timber in the immediate vicinity the men had to get fuel from the Black Mesa forests, a day's journey or more, some of the wood thus procured being also suitable for carving.

Hunting, too, has diverse aims. Buckskin is made into moccasins and kilts, and from various animals the Indians could get material for shields, rattles, bowstrings, drums, and pouches. However, the chase also lent variety to their mainly vegetarian diet and offered more excitement than the agricultural routine. In the old days hunters ran down deer and antelope on foot till they could shoot them with bow and arrow. Some Hopi drove antelope into a pound (p. 17), but the practice seems to be a loan from the Navaho. On the other hand, a communal rabbit drive with boomerang-like clubs (p. 210) is still a general practice, interwoven with the ceremonial calendar.

Settlement and Houses. Town sites have been determined largely by the proximity of water and the desire for security. The latter motive has been strong enough for the survival of mesa residence at considerable inconvenience long after all danger had disappeared (p. 103).

The old-fashioned dwelling unit is a rectangular room with clay floor and sandstone walls plastered with mud, while the beams for the flat roof are covered with sticks and mud. An upper story was set back from its predecessor, yielding a terraced effect (p. 96ff.; *Pl. 14, fig. 5*). Only in modern times have doors and windowpanes come in; the earlier Hopi entered the ground floor by a hatchway and ladder from the second story, and small openings high in the wall had selenite instead of glass panes. Houses are put up one alongside of another according to convenience, resulting in an irregular street or court with a ceremonial plaza (*Pl. 43, fig. 2*). Besides the dwellings there are also oblong subterranean chambers for masculine labors and sacred dances (*Pl. 44, fig. 1*).

Plate 43.

1. Hopi Woman Grinding Corn in Walpi House. 2. Houses in Hopi Village of Walpi. Note Notched Log Used as Ladder.

Plate 44.
1. Walpi on Bench in Subterranean Chamber. Note the altar piece.
2. Hopi Woman Climbing First Mesa.

The house looms large in Hopi life. Economically, its inmates form a mutual benefit group, each collaborating according to his status. Socially, it reflects the bonds of lineage and clan, the rules of marriage and property. Only women own houses, and matrilocal residence brings together the matrilineal kin (p. 242). Further, sacred objects are stored in particular dwellings to be fed by the women there.

Although the Hopi occupy a restricted area, speak a single tongue, and share essentials of their social heritage, they are emphatically not welded into a single political unit. Each village is a wee "state" distinct from the rest, and even within one of these tiny units solidarity is strongest within the kin groups.

Notwithstanding their skill as farmers, the Hopi thus have not the stability to be inferred from their intensive husbandry. They have migrated not only because of famines and fear of enemies, but also in consequence of internal feuds, as when in 1906 the conservative faction of Oraibi village emigrated to found a new settlement.

Crafts. Loom work and painted pottery, as well as stone houses and intensive farming, make the Hopi appear outposts of the higher Mexican civilizations. On the other hand, their basketry does not approach the best Californian samples, many specimens seen in a Hopi dwelling being imports from simpler tribes. Nevertheless, the Hopi surpass other Pueblos in this craft, for they do produce flat plaques, food trays, and large coiled jar-like containers. Within the tribe there is local specialization: The Oraibi women make only square wicker trays, while coiled yucca trays are restricted to the Second Mesa. Sometimes the Hopi color their materials, the dyes being derived from sunflower seeds, iron ochre, limestone, or various other mineral and vegetable substances.

Since the introduction of sheep, wool has become the principal textile material, but until some decades ago the Hopi wove blankets, dresses, belts, and kilts from native cotton grown by themselves. However, part of the dress, such as moccasins and the women's leggings, was prepared from skins.

Pottery is coiled (p. 130), the finer pieces being variously decorated. Besides the cooking vessels, there were shallow bowls with incurved rim, canteens flat on one side, dippers, spherical jars, and other forms. The industry centers in the First Mesa.

Interestingly enough, the excavations made by archaeologists on old Hopi sites led to a great artistic renaissance, for one of the women in the village of Hano was stimulated by the ancient ware into reproducing designs long extinct. Many of these are bird forms; the basketry also displays realistic motifs, such as birds, butterflies, antelopes, or snakes, though some of them appear strongly conventionalized.

Division of Labor. In none of the above-mentioned crafts is there full-fledged professionalism, but individuals are recognized as excelling others in certain skills, and there is a sexual division of labor. This in part contrasts with non-Pueblo usage in the United States. As further south, the men, not the women, do most of the farming. Moreover, they spin (*Pl. 45, fig. 1*) and weave, tan skins, and prepare clothing for themselves and their wives, who, however, did formerly make rabbit-fur rugs. In housebuilding both sexes collaborate, floors and walls being plastered by women. In harmony with general primitive usage, women make all the pottery and men all the carvings.

On the whole, there is less rigidity about the sexual allotment of labors than often holds among primitive peoples. For instance, winnowing trays are made by men, even though women manufacture basket plaques; and though the heavy farm work is masculine, the women keep vegetable gardens.

Trade. The craving for salt has led to expeditions into the vicinity of the Grand Canyon, and nowadays to a salt lake forty-two miles south of Zuñi, New Mexico; but generally the Hopi have been stay-at-homes acquiring objects brought to them by alien Indians and passing them on as middlemen according to their convenience.

Open-air markets held in a dance court give opportunity for bartering among neighbors as well as with outsiders. First Mesa potters exchange their ware for baskets from the Middle Mesa, ten small sacks of unhusked corn will be offered for timber a Navaho brings in suitable for roof beams, formerly cotton kilts would buy buffalo skins from the Plains, and so forth. In this way Hopi artifacts find their way east and west, while their makers profit from the industry and resources of other Pueblo and of Paiute, Apache, Havasupai, Navaho. The trade routes thus established have demonstrably paved the way for elements of quite a different order, such as dances and ceremonials (p. 152). They explain in large measure a certain general similarity among the more sedentary Southwesterners and the spread of at least some elements from nomad to Pueblo and vice versa.

Society

Lineage and Clan. The Hopi offer typical examples of matrilocal residence (p. 247) and matrilineal descent. A chief who is actually three-quarters Navaho is, from the native angle, wholly Hopi because his mother's mother was Hopi. Houses are invariably owned by women, so that a husband takes up his abode with his wife's mother along with the husbands of his wife's married sisters. Strictly speaking, the home belongs to all the matrilineally related women, from an aged crony and her sisters down to their youngest female descendants through females. A divorced husband thus has to leave the house, in which he is really in a sense a guest. Yet he does not become homeless, for so long as he has matrilineal kinswomen of his own he may claim a domicile with them.

Feminine house ownership and matrilocal residence, then, underlie the clan system found here. Some of the clans are composed wholly of blood-kin through the mother so that they correspond to lineages (pp. 254f., 264); others, rated on a par with them, embrace two or more lineages. The all-important ceremonials are primarily associated with the maternal lineage, the fetich vitally bound up with a particular ceremony being fed by the women who own the home housing it. It descends from elder to younger brother or from an uncle to his eldest sister's eldest son. Its home is also the rallying place for the whole clan.

Despite differences in detail, all the villages share the same social scheme. The clans are exogamous and bear totemic names, such as Snake, Corn, Bear, Badger, but there is no belief in descent from the totem, and the emotional tie with it is weak. Thus, the Bear people kill bears and the Rabbits do not scruple to hunt the animal from which they derive their name. Moieties are lacking.

But there is nothing like complete uniformity. Precisely because everywhere an attenuated lineage or clan tends to merge with another and because the fortunes of a group in one village cannot be exactly duplicated in another, variations are bound to occur. That is to say, a clan X may dwindle in one settlement through the absence of female children and prosper in another, or special relations may develop with a second clan in one locality only. At Walpi Corn and Cloud are regarded as merely synonyms for the same clan; on the Second Mesa the names are emphatically declared to represent distinct units.

The Hopi system has been under the scrutiny of scientific observers for fifty years, during which it has not altered its basic principles. It is thus invaluable in showing what kind of changes do and must occur in a primitive organization without a decay of the social structure.

Family and Clan. Notwithstanding the importance of the matrilineal tie, the father and his kin are far from negligible. It is a paternal aunt that gives the newborn infant a name suggesting her own and her brother's clan, not the child's; and the paternal grandmother makes the cradle. A boy accompanies his father to the cornfields and is likely to learn from him how to farm, herd, and make moccasins. Certain ritual rights and duties may pass on at least temporarily to a son, even though they ultimately revert to the original trustee's matrilineal nephews. In old age, on the other hand, a man may be supported by his son or his brother's son. Against these bonds stands the avuncular tie. The mother's brother must be consulted in all important matters and picks out a suitable nephew for his apprentice and ultimate successor in sacred functions. Thus there is a nice balancing of the attachments to the two sides of the family.

Government. Although a village has for its chief the head of the Flute ceremony, the real power is vested in a hierarchical council composed of the headmen of various ceremonial organizations. These elders in turn harangue the people at large at general gatherings, telling them how to behave. However, the councilors are responsible to the community; the people resent any defection from the traditionally proper official conduct and by incessant gossiping about misbehavior may force a headman to resign.

Since all strife is considered harmful socially and fatal to the efficacy of prayers, the town chief should be a peaceable and patient man apt at learning long ceremonial chants. Although he is properly the predecessor's nephew, the succession does not go automatically to the oldest sister's oldest son, but to the matrilineal junior most acceptable to the hierarchy. In one historic instance, after much reluctance on his part, a mild young man was chosen as most nearly embodying the ideal, which thus markedly contrasts with the picture of forceful leadership found in many other societies.

There is a strong sentiment of reciprocity between village chief and people. He prays effectively for the common good, and in requital the people fetch firewood, plant and harvest in his behalf, and plaster his house for him.

Supernaturalism

Pantheon and Mythology. According to Hopi myth the ancestors of long ago lived in the underworld, whence they escaped from a flood by coming up out of a hole often symbolized in ceremonial. The first emissary of the Indians to the earth above surprised a deity named Masauwü, who befriended him, giving him squashes and other vegetables. When all the people had got out, they found it was quite dark, so they first made the stars, then the moon and the sun. By himself dying and not returning, Coyote introduced death and retired to the underworld. The Twin Boys shot their lightnings, thereby creating canyons into which the waters of the flood drained, and also made the mountains.

This tale, which comes as close to a cosmogony as any told by these Indians, introduces several significant characters of Hopi supernaturalism. Coyote is the typical trickster (pp. 200, 326) and a teacher of witchcraft, but also a patron of hunters. Far more important is Masauwü, the first housebuilder, the protector of the Coyote-Firewood clan, a god invoked by farmers and travelers. He is also associated, however, with fire, war, and death. The Twins are likewise war gods, and their grandmother Spider figures as the mother of all beings.

These are but a few of the innumerable deities that appear in ritual, some being represented in effigy, others by masqueraders, while still others are at least symbolically referred to. Nearly every supernatural being may be impersonated by a mummer and is then referred to as a "kachina". The basic idea of kachinas, however, is that they dwell on mountaintops and promote precipitation, thereby safeguarding the all-important crops.

Visions are not typical of the Hopi, as they are among most non-Pueblo Indians in the United States (pp. 312f.). This implies a less intensive subjective sentiment toward particular deities. By way of compensation there is an extraordinary development of ceremonial, in which prayers for rain blend with stirring theatrical performances and a profusion of ritualistic acts. On the social side, ceremonial is interwoven with secret organizations and the clan system.

Secret Societies. Every boy must be initiated into one of four societies during a festival held in November, at which new fire is ceremonially drilled. Altogether there are at least a dozen organizations, in part concerned with treating specific diseases, in part with rainmaking. In native theory animals and certain spirits bring particular forms of sickness that can be cured by special societies. The control of an organization belongs to its hereditary head assisted by a small group, the rank and file being recruited from cured patients or otherwise. Thus in the Snake society the chief priest has inherited his office from an elder matrilineal kinsman and all men of the Snake clan are potential members; but entrance is granted to those outsiders whom the priest has cured of snake bite.

Although the majority of the societies are masculine, there are three comparable women's organizations (*Pl. 45*).

Calendar. The major festivals succeed each other in a definite order except that the Flute and Snake dances are biennial, alternating in any one village. As in the ancient civilizations of the Near Orient, religion stimulated astronomical knowledge, the proper time for a celebration resting on solar or lunar observation. Roughly, the year may be divided into two ceremonial periods—the interval between the winter and summer solstices, and the remaining months. It is only during the earlier half of the twelvemonth that mummers impersonating the kachinas appear in ceremonial and their season terminates with their formal Farewell festival. Though this difference constitutes a well-defined cleavage, the Hopi themselves start the year with the November ceremony of the four boy-initiating organizations. As a matter of fact, this performance does affect other ceremonies, for if novices have actually been admitted during it this fact automatically lengthens a number of subsequent festivals.

Ritualism. Observances connected with the life cycle are not unlike those of other Indians (p. 317). On attaining her maturity a girl grinds corn for four days in a paternal aunt's house, a rug shielding her and her querns from the sunlight; she abstains from salt or flesh, uses a head-scratcher, has her hair washed, and prays to the Sun for strong arms and legs so that she may grind well and fetch water efficiently. But among the Hopi such celebrations are eclipsed by bewilderingly elaborate festivals, even though these, at bottom, rest on relatively few and simple ideas (pp. 320, 322).

Thus prayer and offerings are dominant conceptions here as elsewhere (p. 319), but with the Pueblo they have become standardized with a wealth of ritual detail. Feathers, supposedly desirable in the eyes of spirits, are commonly offered to them, either loose, or tied together, or tied to a stick. Hours, however, must be devoted to the proper preparation of "prayer sticks", which are generally barked, painted with pigment, fastened together in pairs, smoked, and finally deposited in some sacred spot. Yet, despite all these technicalities, the fundamental purpose is simple: the feathers are either yielded by a bargainer paying in advance for blessings he demands, or are presented by a supplicant in the humbler mood of begging for pity.

Similarly, impersonal supernaturalism bears familiar forms. Downy feathers are placed over the face of the dead to impart their own lightness for the journey before him. More particularly, a Hopi has innumerable ways of compelling, or at least suggesting, rainfall by imitative magic (p. 298). One magical reason for smoking tobacco is to make clouds. When celebrants pour out water it is expressly to stimulate a like dropping of rain; and the bull-roarer (p. 204) is swung because it makes a noise like thunder, thus helping to bring storms and the good lightning that fertilizes. Similarly, a design representing clouds with rain falling from them appears on the walls of ceremonial chambers (*Pl. 44*), and the runners of ceremonial races are setting an example for the spirits who are to fill the watercourses with rushing torrents.

However, by no means all magic is mimetic; songs, for example, also have a coercive power if properly chanted (p. 299). And as music and words may be potent in their own right, so there are various sacred objects charged with holiness, whether they are directly and permanently connected with spirits or not. Foremost among these fetiches (p. 301) rank ears of corn that are either flattened out at the tip or perfectly kerneled. The head of a society is trustee and custodian of such an ear for his matrilineal kin and will carry it in processions and have it set out at the altar.

In a major performance the observances referred to and many others are combined into an impressive whole. To mention a few features, the celebrants go into a four or eight days' retreat in their ceremonial chamber, where they abstain from salt and meat, devoting themselves to sacred duties, manufacturing prayer sticks, arranging the altar, chanting, and smoking. The preparation of the altar involves painted cloths or wooden slabs set upright, the fetiches proper to the occasion, and a mosaic made by sifting or pouring different colored sands from finger and thumb. There are offerings and ritual acts, usually repeated four times in correspondence with the mystic number (p. 320); and at the end it is necessary to exorcise the performers lest prolonged contact with holy things prove dangerous to them. Typically, the esoteric part of the major ceremonies extends over eight days, being followed by a public performance on the ninth.

Festivals. There is thus an infinitude of ritualistic detail, each executed rigidly according to the tribal norms. But in the assemblage of these elements and their combination with other cultural traits there is considerable latitude, which in part accounts for there being different festivals at all, since the avowed aim of all is identical—to bring rain and to ward off disease. Yet even apart from the use or non-use of masks there is, within the general scheme, considerable variation, depending upon the traits that are to receive emphasis and the mythical notions and features of entertainment that are interwoven. A few examples must suffice.

The Winter Solstice festival, so important that any settlement lacking it is considered a mere suburb or colony, stresses the dramatization of the sun's annual course. Hence, in addition to elements common to other solemnities, a performer who impersonates the Sun-god postures and stamps on a board, while the singers shout at him, repel him when he rushes at them, and thus force him to pursue his customary path.

The Powámu ceremony, held in the following month, derives part of its character from its calendric position. Its purpose is to melt the snow and get omens as to the next crops from the forced growth of beans. Here buffoonery (p. 175) looms large, with clowns tumbling over one another pell-mell, stealing meat, and being chased by a man who recovers their booty (*Pl. 46*).

In the Horned Water Serpent Dance the snake that figures in myth as the flood-maker appeased by human sacrifices is represented in a puppet show. The image, up to forty-four inches in length, is formed of ten hoops tapering from twelve to four inches in diameter and covered with a painted cotton cloth. The operators, stationed behind a curtain with six openings, thrust as many effigies through them and enact the suckling of the young snakes by their mother. Naturally the Hopi link the

Plate 45.

1. Hopi Spinner, Village of Mishongnovi. 2. Women's Society Dance in Plaza of Mishongnovi.

Plate 46.

1. Kachina Dancers, First Mesa. 2. Clowns Sprinkling Corn Meal on Kachina Dancers in Imitation of Priests, First Mesa.

mythical beast with their favorite motif: the Horned Serpent, as one of Cloud's pet animals, is invoked to intercede for lightning and rain. The idea also figures in other ways in this ceremony; masqueraders shoot a lattice of jointed sticks into the underground chambers, beat drums, and whirl bull-roarers to imitate thunder.

The Snake festival, once more, is a prayer for rain, but in part it dramatizes the myth of a youth who explores the river on which the Hopi once lived, actors playing the part of the hero and the maiden he married. Further, there are reminiscences of an originally military facet: two secret societies must collaborate in this ceremony, the Snake organization, which represents braves on the warpath, while the old men of the Antelope fraternity make "medicine" on their behalf. Finally, in the terminal public dance the performers carry live snakes between their teeth as they circle round the plaza.

Thus each major ceremony, notwithstanding the pervasive tribal pattern as to ritual detail and ultimate purpose, has both for the actors and for the spectators a sharply defined individuality.

General Character of Supernaturalism. Hopi supernaturalism has been aptly characterized as instrumental. That is to say, it envisages practical values and proceeds to attain them by techniques assumed to be efficacious. Thus it sharply contrasts with any faith that stresses the votary's inward exaltation. Because of the extreme ritualism of the Hopi, outward observance often seems the essential thing, existing for its own sake, with the subjective attitude of the worshipper receding into the distance. Yet this is not wholly so, for it is a cardinal principle that harmony in a village is prerequisite to efficient ritual behavior: Cloud shuns towns rent by internal feuds. However, the emphases of Hopi religion inevitably eliminate mysticism and with it the close bond between the individual and a particular patron deity, while they throw into relief the impersonal or magical phase of supernaturalism.

Summary

The character of Hopi religion thoroughly harmonizes with the tenor of their culture as a whole. Its spirit prescribes a harmonious, tranquil, coöperative social life and deprecates aggressiveness or self-aggrandizement. The boastful Bagobo or Plains Indian warrior (p. 225) would appear as a churl in a Pueblo setting. The Hopi thus illustrate one very clearly definable type of primitive ideology.

Historically they are equally noteworthy. Their rising above such kindred tribes as the Paiute must have been due to impulses received, directly or through other Pueblos, from the south, whence alone maize could have reached them. As a matter of fact, they share various specific features of belief and cult with Mexican peoples. Like the Zapotec, they believe in a flood-causing Horned Serpent. Like the Aztec, they associate rain gods with the cardinal directions, ceremonially drill new fire every year, with a more elaborate quadrennial performance, and have novices carried on the backs of their sponsors.

But however much they may have been stimulated by others, the Hopi did not remain mere copyists. Their clan system is quite distinct from any Mexican social organization; their method of growing corn in an untoward environment is an original achievement that can hardly be overestimated; even their ceremonial and mythological scheme includes many distinctive features. We must further remember that a feature common to Aztec and Hopi need not have been borrowed by the Hopi, but may have been part of the ancient ancestral culture shared by the early Uto-Aztecans. The Mexicans are demonstrable or probable donors only with regard to such traits as maize-planting or technological accomplishments like masonry.

But Hopi culture must be reconstructed also with reference to those more recent neighbors with whom they have maintained such lively trade relations. These account for much of the basketry encountered in a Hopi household; and scholars ascribe both the impounding of deer and the girl's puberty ritual to Navaho example. Even in so distinctive a performance as the Snake Dance there are sacred songs in a Keresan tongue, which can mean only that the ceremony itself comes in part from an alien Pueblo village.

Quite apart from such considerations, the Hopi represent one of the very best instances in the world of a well-knit matrilineal society; and they likewise exemplify in ideal form the indissoluble bond between economic, social, and religious sides of culture.

XXVI

THE BAGOBO

Habitat and Affiliations

In the southern part of Mindanao, west of the Gulf of Davao, lives a tribe of some ten thousand people known as the Bagobo (*Pl. 47*). Its wilder members occupy the eastern and southern slopes of Mt. Apo, the highest peak in the Philippines, rising about 10,000 feet above sea level.[1] Like all natives of these islands, the Bagobo belong to the far-flung Malayo-Polynesian family of languages and share certain traits typical of more westerly Malay populations and, indeed, of Southeastern Asiatics generally. Because they have resisted the lure of Islam, to which some of their neighbors succumbed, they illustrate the pre-Mohammedan faiths of the archipelago.

Material Culture

Metallurgical Stage. Living on the periphery of the areas of higher Asiatic civilization, the Bagobo occupy the intermediate status of most Indonesians: they have completely outgrown the Stone Age in depending on homemade iron tools, though they import the raw iron smelted elsewhere (p. 140). Their blacksmiths, who enjoy the highest esteem and are under the protection of a great spirit, use precisely the same implement—the piston-bellows of Madagascar (pp. 143f.)—which Malay metal workers apparently carried wherever they happened to voyage. Copper- and brass-casters form an-

[1] The account here given describes the conditions found about thirty years ago.

other class of skilled artisans, manufacturing bells, bracelets, and betel boxes by the "lost wax" process (p. 140).

Economic Life. As outposts of Southeastern Asia the Bagobo have horses and buffalo (p. 44); but since they live beyond the dairying area and have clung to the dibble as their sole farming implement, their domestic beasts are not of fundamental importance. They do serve for transportation but are not numerous enough

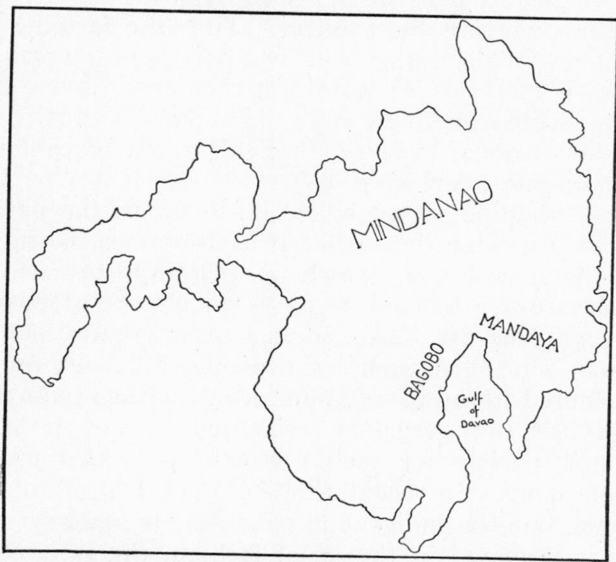

Plate 47: MINDANAO.

for regular slaughter; hence for flesh the natives must rely on hunting and fishing. They spear or harpoon deer and wild pigs, snaring or netting wild fowls and other birds, which are also shot down with bows and arrows. Boys kill them with darts projected from a blowgun (p. 215), but the missiles are not poisoned and are ineffective beyond a range of twenty feet. Fishermen drug fish (p. 20) and commonly trap them in a bamboo funnel into which they are guided by stone conduits.

However, the diet is largely vegetarian, with rice as the main crop. Next in importance as food are the sweet potato, maize, bananas, sago, and the coconut. Of these, the first two are post-Columbian importations brought by the Spaniards. Rice, however, is predominant, and its cultivation is intertwined with much ritual. There is no irrigation. The fields are made in clearings along the mountain side and abandoned for new plots when the struggle becomes hopeless against the rank cogon grass that overruns the country. Thus the farming has to be done farther away from home each year until the distance is too great for comfort; then the entire settlement is shifted to a new site. The Bagobo thus exemplify the migratory type of agriculture so often found among simpler peoples (p. 25).

Before yielding a plot to cogon, however, the natives first substitute for rice either sweet potatoes or the so-called Manila hemp, which is actually an inedible banana, *Musa textilis,* that plays an important part in native weaving (p. 32). Several other plants are important. During droughts the people fall back on the flour secured from the soft interior of the sago palm, and at festivities they serve the fermented juice of the sugar cane stored away for such occasions in sealed jars or bamboo tubes. In recent times a good deal of tobacco is grown, but the indigenous stimulant is betel (p. 32), which is prepared in the usual fashion, the areca palm nut being chewed with lime in a pepper leaf wrapper. This practice lends a deep red color to the saliva, which the chewer freely expectorates on the floor, walls, and furniture of the dwelling.

Fire is commonly struck with flint and steel, but the typical Malay method of sawing one bamboo with another survives (p. 57). Food is mainly boiled in earthenware, though offerings have to be cooked in bamboo tubes (p. 60), probably the original process since ceremonial generally preserves ancient custom.

Dwellings. The typical dwelling is a variation of the

gable-roofed oblong house found in Indonesia (p. 96). The floor of its single room is raised on piles, some of which extend above the floor to support the beams. Access is by means of a notched log or a bamboo ladder. The roof is always made first and then raised to the desired height. It is covered with several layers, the topmost being of flattened bamboo, a material which also forms the sides of the room. The floor merges in a platform at one end, used by some of the inmates for a bed.

Close to the door is the fireplace, a bed of ashes with three stones to support pots or jars. Near by rises a wooden pedestal for the rice mortar and pestle; against the wall is a bamboo rack for half-coconut dishes and Chinese plates; and always there is a copper gong, usually along with boxes and jars of Chinese origin. Every dwelling harbors a receptacle for offerings; it consists of a bamboo rod split into several branches at one end, where shorter horizontal strips are interwoven to form the container.

With nothing but tiny peep-holes for windows and with the smoke from the open fire such a home is a rather gloomy place. However, it protects the inmates from the sun and the mosquitoes, and the light entering by cracks in the floor and walls allows the women to perform their daily tasks. Resinous nuts are burned for illumination after dark.

Much more pretentious than the ordinary dwelling is the chief's home, which also serves as the ceremonial center and the place of refuge in case of danger. It accommodates up to several hundred guests and may be forty-four by twenty feet. Yet in general structure it closely resembles the humbler homes.

Dress and Adornment. Garments are woven of "hemp" (p. 470). The men's dress includes an undershirt, a coat decorated with beads or embroidery, and knee breeches, the lower leg being covered with a decorative band; one belt holds up the breeches, while another supports the knife indispensable for working and fighting. A woman wears a "hemp" skirt held in place by a cloth or belt, with a jacket above it so that the upper part of the body is fully covered.

These essentials are eked out by a variety of ornamental features, notably brass bracelets and ivory ear plugs (pp. 77, 81; *Pl. 11, fig. 4; Pl. 12, figs. 6, 8*). There is no tattooing, but both sexes file and blacken the teeth at puberty (p. 75; *Pl. 10, fig. 3*).

Division of Labor; Industries. In farming men and women collaborate: the man, digging holes with a dibble, is followed by his wife, who drops seeds into the holes and pushes the soil over them with her feet. It is also she that cuts the rice with a small knife at harvest time.

Apart from their household chores, the women make baskets and earthenware, but pottery is poorly developed and has even become a lost art in some districts. The outstanding feminine craft is the weaving and dyeing of "hemp" fiber. In arranging her threads the operator carefully wraps or ties with waxed threads those parts of the warp which she wishes to remain white, so that when the material is later dipped into the liquid dye the covered portions remain unaltered. This elaborate technique is of great interest, being ancient in Turkestan and India, and highly developed in other parts of Indonesia. As already explained, the most esteemed masculine occupation is metal work, but more generally men are the housebuilders and manufacture such domestic utensils as spoons and mortars.

Art. The Bagobo satisfy their aesthetic impulses only along special channels. There is next to no realistic woodwork, and the homes lack all effort at embellishment by painting or carving. Pottery and most of the household utensils are also plain. On the other hand, the articles worn on the person or constantly carried about display a profusion of ornamental design. This is intelligible since art and industry so often go hand in hand (p. 179). Moreover, Bagobo clothing is the peak of feminine craftsmanship, while the brass bracelets and betel-nut boxes represent the most specialized masculine industry. The metal castings frequently show scroll designs (p. 81; *Pl. 12, fig. 6*) ultimately derived from the Mohammedan Malays to the south but modified in an original way. Equally characteristic are the bamboo tubes for lime and tobacco (p. 185; *Pl. 29, fig. 5*), with zones of incised geometrical patterns, a feature also common in other tribes of Mindanao (p. 178; *Pl. 27, fig. 2*).

Although the Bagobo tend to regard certain designs as crocodile symbols and attach protective value to them, the overwhelming number of patterns have no meaning but serve solely to embellish the decorative field.

Travel and Trade. Geographical conditions have precluded any kind of boat (p. 158). The Bagobo have mostly lived far from the sea, and the watercourses of their habitat are quite unnavigable, changing overnight from tiny rivulets into rushing torrents. Anciently regular land trails were also unknown, a traveler merely hacking his way through the underbrush to his destination; but the American government insisted on the building of roads, by which the natives now transport themselves and their goods on the backs of their horses and buffalo. Thus they obtain various goods from the coast.

The chief export is "hemp", for which the Bagobo receive trade cloth, iron pots, copper gongs, bells, and beads. Other surplus articles carried to the outside world include betel boxes, knives, and knife guards. Among the vital imports are things of no practical value, but reckoned indispensable by the natives, such as the ivory from Borneo that is fashioned into ear plugs. Still more important are the Chinese-made gongs imported into the Philippines from Singapore. The gong has become the standard of value in major transactions, such as calculating marriage dowries or large debts. For a festival the giver requires a series of these percussion instruments, which are hung from a bamboo rod by loops of rattan.

Society

Warfare. Bows and arrows are of little moment in fighting. At long range the Bagobo rely on spears and for hand-to-hand combats on knives. For protection they cover themselves with many strips of "hemp" cloth and crouch behind circular or oblong shields. To hold back an enemy they set sharp pieces of bamboo into the ground on the probability that they will pierce the attackers' feet (p. 226).

Local feuds were a constant feature before American intervention. Though they seriously interfered with travel and trade, these hostilities were bound up with notions of prestige. A man who had never slain an enemy was a nobody; the killer of at least two men gained the social status of a "brave", marked by a special head-covering; thereafter every additional foe to his credit enhanced his influence (pp. 220f). The military ideology thus affects the structure of society.

Social Organization. There are no clans. Each district has its headman, and until some decades ago there was a paramount chief at Cibolan who traced his pedigree back through ten generations. The chief has real power, for he may fine men and have a follower stealthily kill a recalcitrant tribesman. On the other hand, he owes his people entertainment and protection in his house. While as likely as his subjects to work at the forge or in the rice fields, he eats all by himself, even his immediate family taking their meals at a respectful distance. He is both the civil and the ecclesiastic head, in which latter capacity he offers sacrifices. In secular and religious activities he may be assisted by a council of old men and women.

People may become enslaved through capture or through inability to pay fines, but they are leniently treated and readily merge in the general population.

Even a slave woman may marry a chief, whom her son might succeed in office. The freemen are not grouped into rigid castes. Men, we have seen, rise to distinction if they demonstrate bravery according to the conventional standards of their people; and it is honorable to ply the blacksmith's or copper-caster's trade. Women can gain prestige as spirit mediums, a calling in which they greatly outnumber the men.

In general the women enjoy a favorable position, having definite ceremonial privileges and unchallengeable rights of ownership to utensils and other chattels. Though a bride-price is paid, the girl's father returns gifts amounting to half the value of what he receives lest he appear to sell his daughter like a slave. As a matter of fact, there is usually an initial period of bride-service which to a certain extent continues for several years.

There is no legal limit to the number of wives, but a man may not take a second spouse until his first has borne a child or has been proved barren beyond all doubt. Moreover, he is not only obliged to pay the bride-price to the new parents-in-law, but he must also give an equal amount to his first wife, who passes it on to her father.

Though no clan bond exists, the blood-kin assume equivalent obligations in avenging a relative's murder. There is also a marked feeling of comradeship in a settlement: personal possessions are freely borrowed, and for housebuilding or making a clearing, a man's friends assist him without thought of pay, feeling equally free to call on his aid in comparable situations.

Religion

Animism. Bagobo psychology postulates two souls, identified with the shadows cast on the right and left side, respectively. The right-hand soul is good and never leaves its owner during his lifetime, while its left counterpart often departs in sleep or trances, when it may incur grave dangers for itself and the dreamer. If a demon should catch it during its wanderings, the sleeper would run the risk of pain, illness, and death. This left-hand soul is identified with the reflection in the water (p. 306). After a person's death it joins the corpse-devouring demons, haunting graves and other lonely spots.

The right-hand soul resembles the living Bagobo, but is of flimsier substance. It is really the life principle, hence passes out of the head of a dead person. At first it assumes the shape of an insect, visiting every house in the world before the burial and chirping cricket-fashion to announce the death. After the disposal of the body these visits cease, for the soul has then departed for good; a rainfall directly after interment represents its tears.

A traveling outfit accompanies a burial; the rice, betel box, and other objects included are each supposed to have a soul of its own to accompany the dead person's on its journey to the hereafter, which is laid in the underworld. In other words, inanimate things are also credited with having a spiritual essence. Before the liberated soul of the person reaches its goal it must pass through the "Black River", where a priestess washes it. Then it proceeds to the land of the dead, where its occupations exactly duplicate those of a living Bagobo. Only the time order is reversed, for the sun stays below while it is dark above the ground, so that the spirits work and play while mortals sleep.

This basic conception of the hereafter may be modified in detail when dreamers and delirious people report what they have seen on supposed visits to the underworld. There is virtually no idea of retribution for good and evil deeds, but the mode of death is significant, people slain by sword or spear going to a district of their own (p. 307), though they live like the rest. There is another distinction that has nothing to do with ethics but rests on age: the souls of deceased nurslings remain with the priestess of the Black River, who gives them suck until they are old enough to join the souls of their kin.

A soul is ascribed to artifacts, small birds, and bees, while fowls, as well as large birds and beasts, are credited with two souls each.

Supernatural Beings. On this animistic basis the Bagobo have worked out an elaborate pantheon. However, some of these deities, though endowed with impressive attributes, are properly not religious figures at all but literary characters. This holds particularly for "the gods of the nine heavens"; their adventures are related in songs and romances, but since they pay no attention to human affairs, they are neither prayed to nor conciliated by offerings. They are probably taken over from the Hindu pantheon.

On the other hand, the natives have a warm regard for Pamulak Manobo, the creator of earth, sky, and man. They address him at ceremonies and invite him as an honored guest to their festivals, but being uniformly benevolent he requires no appeasement or bloody sacrifice. Foremost in the affections of the Bagobo stands another deity, the Divine Man at the Source of the Waters, who with a string strangles every disease that is sent to him at his spring. Never sleeping, he always hears prayers, and as a consequence is the most frequently invoked of all supernatural beings.

A host of deities presides over special departments of nature. One grants an abundant rice crop if the relevant ritual is properly performed; another protects the bees, whose wax is required in metal-casting; a third helps the Bagobo hunt deer and boar in return for an offering of arrows. A female deity concerns herself with weaving and other feminine occupations, while the chief of war gods fills men with pugnacity and specially protects the successful killers of enemies. He eats human flesh, but unlike the demons, consumes only the corpses of slain warriors or sacrificial victims.

In contrast to these and many other benign gods, the demons send disease, intent only on somehow getting corpses to devour. Largely, but not altogether, this malevolent crew is recruited from the evil left-hand souls of the deceased. Much of Bagobo supernaturalism centers in these beings, but the attitude towards them differs radically from that towards the gods. For instance, it is not the evil spirits but the benevolent deities that possess mediums, answering questions and giving advice. Again, both categories of supernatural beings have altars, but the demons' altars are never within the ceremonial house; and words addressed to them are protective spells rather than true prayers. The gods, too, may cause illness, but only for some breach of a religious rule; the demons enter a human body and torture it with disease merely to kill it and increase their stock of edible bodies. Fortunately, the worst demons are a stupid lot and can be easily duped.

The measures against demons include magical formulae, the erection of wooden images of living men, the wearing of amulets, as well as the carving, painting, or weaving of crocodile designs.

Ceremonial. Foremost among the various ceremonies performed by the Bagobo is the annual Drinking Festival. The time for its celebration is set by observation of the moon or other heavenly bodies. There are no temples or any organized sacred order or secret society, priestly functions simply devolving on the chief or old people of either sex. In contrast to some areas, women play a prominent part in ritual, and even the young members of the community have definite functions.

Regardless of other purposes, all ceremonial aims at driving away sickness. This, as already explained, may be due to the breach of a taboo, or possession by a demon, or the dream adventures of the left-hand soul. Remedies vary widely—from the use of drugs to magic and devotional acts. In the ceremonies the priest sprinkles people with leaves and twigs supposedly having medicinal virtue, a procedure that also brings wealth. Moreover, every ceremony combines several of the features that make up the tribal pattern, which is completely represented in the Drinking Festival. This includes offerings of food, always boiled in bamboo, and of sacred liquor made from sugar-cane syrup; the offering of betel and of garments or other valuables, which must never thereafter be sold; and the recitation of ritualistic formulae, with the names of the gods worshipped, a list of the offerings, and the favors sought. Music supplied by sets of Chinese gongs and dances by both sexes in full-dress costume add to the entertainment. Towards the close of every ceremony there is a great feast, and either immediately before or after the festival there is usually a séance. Advice from the spirits is also sought before a new house is erected or a journey is undertaken, and during epidemics and earthquakes. The medium, usually an old woman, officiates in a darkened room, where she goes into a typical shamanistic trance (p. 311), shivering, shouting, chanting, and delivering the oracles granted by the deities who successively possess her.

In the Drinking Festival all these rituals are combined with the sacrifice of a slave to several gods, including the chief war deity, who drink the victim's blood. During the four days of this celebration the warriors, in turn, recite their exploits in killing enemies. Another characteristic feature is the display of beautiful embroidered dresses made by women on the theory that the spirits present enjoy the spiritual essence of these products, still another sample of Bagobo animism.

Conclusion

Bagobo culture exemplifies many interesting principles. The Tasmanians were destined to remain on a low level, not from any environmental difficulty, but because their position separated them from the rest of mankind; the Bagobo have been favored by their habitat not because it offers unusual advantages, but because its location led to contacts with technically advanced populations. In this way their culture, which in its outlines suggests the mode of life of sedentary Stone Age people, actually assimilated the metallurgical techniques of southern Asia. Rice cultivation, tie-dyeing, and elements of their mythology are traceable to the same source. Curious, indeed, is the present indispensableness of the Chinese gongs, for which the natives are wholly dependent on foreign trade. Equally interesting is the preservation of many traits distinctive of the Indonesian region of which Mindanao forms a part—the fire-saw and bamboo cooking-vessels, the blowgun and the gable-roof house.

While features such as these demonstrate the force of geographical nearness and cultural affinity, others prove that remote and unconnected peoples may develop rather similar attitudes. Bagobo ideology of warfare strikingly resembles that of the North American Plains (p. 225), with its emphasis on bravery as the source of prestige, its conventional definition of honorific acts, and their formal recital in ceremonial situations.

Finally, Bagobo ceremonialism instructively exemplifies a definite tribal pattern (p. 320); the extreme complexity that results from combining a number of simple elements, and the mingling of the most serious religious aspects with aesthetic features (pp. 320-324).

XXVII

THE SHILLUK

Habitat

The Shilluk are Nilotes—Nile-dwellers—of the Anglo-Egyptian Sudan. Superficially, they inhabit country not unlike that of the Canella (Chapter XXIII). Living on the White Nile and the lower Sobat, these Negroes are not much farther north of the equator than the Timbira dwell to the south. Both regions are marked by grassy tracts of little elevation; and in both a wet and a dry season are sharply contrasted.

Material Culture

Live-stock. But even ignoring differences between the wild fauna and flora of these two tropical areas, we find a great contrast in their economic life rooted in the two peoples' past history. The Brazilian steppe could support live-stock and, in fact, does so for the white settlers today, but before Columbus the Indian natives neither had wild beasts suitable for domestication nor enjoyed contacts with the Old World populations that might have introduced them. On the other hand, the Shilluk have been close enough to the centers of higher civilization to own plenty of cattle (pp. 42f.), sheep, and goats. That the Shilluk and their neighbors derived from Egypt some of the cattle to which they are so passionately devoted is suggested by the peculiar way in which they distort the left horn, which can be exactly matched from a picture of the Pyramid Age dating back to about 2700 B.C.

Farming. Agriculturally the difference between the

Nilotes and the Indians is less vital. The main crop of the Shilluk is, indeed, sorghum, a typically Old World plant that is practically, if not botanically, grouped with millet; but whether one's vegetable fare consists of sorghum rather than sweet potatoes seems unessential. More important is the contrast in farming implements, for inconvenient as is the short handle of the Shilluk hoe (p. 29), its iron blade (*Pl. 48, fig. 3*) is more effective than the wooden dibble of the Timbira. Furthermore, it epitomizes the superior technical level of the Negroes. Lacking iron ore in their country, they were nevertheless able to import it from neighboring natives and thus to develop a full-fledged blacksmith's art (pp. 142f.).

Crafts. An ample supply of milk and sorghum, eked out with fish and wild game (p. 20ff.), enabled the Shilluk to crowd an amazingly large population within a limited area (p. 13), where hamlet succeeds hamlet in rapid succession along the Nile "like beads on a string". This wealth of human material, as usual, goes with some advancement in craftsmanship (p. 107). Apart from the blacksmith's spears (*Pl. 2, fig. 1*)—the principal weapons—and other iron implements, there are pots (*Pl. 48, fig. 4*) and fancy mats made by the women, while men plait coarser mats, build houses (p. 93), carve headrests (*Pl. 48, fig. 1*) in animal shape to preserve their beautiful hairdresses (p. 76), and construct reed rafts exactly like those of the ancient Egyptians. In this largely timberless region a canoe requires months of labor, for there is not merely the usual shaping by adze and fire (pp. 54, 159f.), but also the need for uniting and calking separate parts. The boatwright is thus a specialist in woodwork, and as such he also makes the big cowskin-headed drums of acacia wood.

However, the Shilluk have not carried artisanship so far as have some other Africans. Accordingly trade remains limited and has not led to the development of either markets or true money (pp. 148f.). Values are

Plate 48: SHILLUK.

1. Three Shilluk with painted faces and with headrests. 2. Shilluk minstrel with guitar. 3. Shilluk women with short-handled weeding implements. 4. Shilluk utensils.

reckoned in terms of live-stock, a canoe-builder receiving a cow for his boat.

Society

Family and Clan. The sexual division of labor accompanies a certain social separation of men and women, but the idea is not carried to extremes. Men always eat apart from their wives, and women must not milk or tend cattle; but in the dance, foremost of Shilluk diversions, youths and maidens freely join (p. 174), and there is no segregation of brothers and sisters.

Socially the patrilineal clan and polygyny are important features reflected in the mode of settlement itself. For the householders of any one hamlet (p. 93, *Pl. 13, fig. 1*) are clansmen, often close blood-relatives, and each of the several wives of a man occupies her own hut. The clans are linked with animals, such as the crane, ostrich, and crocodile, which are tabooed as food though some of them may be killed. There is thus a form of totemism (p. 258), but it does not affect the lives of the people very deeply.

The rules of residence necessarily permit the children of brothers to see more of each other than do other cousins, who grow up in distant settlements. On the other hand, notwithstanding patrilineal descent, the mother's brother plays an important part: he gives a boy his first spear, has something to say about his niece's choice of a husband, and is entitled to part of the cattle given for a girl, even though inheritance is strictly patrilineal and nephews and nieces get nothing from their maternal uncle except as a free gift. But this bond is in a measure balanced by the amitate (p. 251), for the father's sister regularly contributes two head of cattle to her nephew's bride-price.

Marriage. Marriage is barred with all clansmen and all individuals related on the mother's side. In typical African fashion (p. 241), payment for a bride entitles the husband to the wife's children, irrespective of whether they are his own offspring or the result of adulterous intercourse. This notion appears also in the rule that a woman's family must return her bride-price if she dies childless. The basic idea that wealth must be offered for a wife involves a series of important consequences. A young man can not raise the required number of live-stock unaided, but looks to his father and his paternal aunts to provide the payment. These head of cattle, however, come in large part from the wealth received by the youth's father in return for a daughter; in other words, any bachelor is vitally interested in having his sisters married off, since that enhances his own chance of securing a wife. The difficulties of a young man in acquiring the requisite wealth explain his privilege of having sex relations with the wife of his brother by another mother or with the wives of clansmen in his generation; indeed, he may even consort with his father's wives except his own mother.

Familiarity and Avoidance. The in-law relationships likewise assume typical forms among the Shilluk. A wife's sister is treated familiarly and may be taken as a second wife on payment of the full price. A woman must show great respect to her husband's parents; conversely, her father-in-law shuns sex relations with her. Again, between a man and his wife's parents there is avoidance which is only relaxed with the lapse of years; and he must never speak to his wife's maternal uncle.

Monarchy and Religion

Royal Privileges and Duties. But all these customs, like the whole of Shilluk life, are affected by the political structure, with its absolute, divinely inspired monarch and his subordinate governors and chiefs (p. 295). Thus the king's dignity is inconsistent with haggling over the price of a desired wife; consequently he chooses the mates he wishes and himself fixes each father-in-law's compensation. Similarly, a king can not stoop to take cattle for his daughters, hence they may indulge in amours, but can not be legally married. Furthermore, the rules of avoidance are abrogated for the ruler, whose parents-in-law offer him the general reverence, while he has no obligation to treat them with the respect normally due to such connections.

The political system restricts the individual subject's personal and property rights: for example, some objects, such as leopard skins, may be owned only by the king; and even his closest relatives must approach the ruler with conventional marks of awe, averting the face. High chiefs likewise wield great authority, though they have duties as well as privileges, being expected to feed the hungry, to leave the wives of their subjects in peace, and to refrain from vituperation. Indeed, the king himself—supreme as he remains during his prime—is regularly killed for the good of the people as soon as he shows signs of debility.

This feature illustrates the intimate connection between monarchy and supernaturalism among the Shilluk. For it is a firm article of native faith that if the king falls ill or grows senile, the live-stock of the country would sicken, its crops would fail, and its men would die off. Thus his supremacy rests on his supposed public services, which are possible because the king is possessed by the mythical culture-hero, Nyikang; but since weakness is a contradiction in terms for one so favored, he must be put out of the way as soon as his strength diminishes (p. 296). Who, however, is to determine what constitutes "weakness"? In the case of an unpopular ruler a cold may be used as a pretext for eliminating him. Thus the theoretically absolute autocrat really owes definite duties to his subjects and is in the long run dependent on his immediate attendants for continued existence itself.

Monarchy and Ancestor Worship. Monarchy, moreover, is not merely tied up with supernaturalism but lends it a distinctive flavor. Ancestor worship, with propitiation of particular forebears by offerings of livestock, is typical of African Negroes (p. 308) and occurs among the Shilluk. But here it is eclipsed by the regard paid to *royal* ancestors, to whom special temples and attendants are dedicated. A native facing some difficulty first prays and makes offerings at the near-by grave shrine of a former king, perhaps subsequently going through similar procedures at his own forefather's grave, though he would resort there immediately if the royal shrine were too far away. The acme of this cult is the worship of Nyikang, the legendary founder of the realm, whose spirit is venerated at certain cenotaphs. Foremost among the festivals in his honor are the annual rain-making, where the king himself acts as priest (p. 295), and the harvest ceremony.

Theory of Disease. Spirit possession (p. 310), another typical trait of Old World culture, is correspondingly tinctured. Disease, which in many regions is attributed to any demon intruding into the patient's body, is here generally imputed to the spirit of one of the early kings; and again it is the immanence of these royal spirits that makes shamans of ordinary tribesmen. On the other hand, evil sorcerers are not inspired but are congenitally depraved men who work harm by imitative and contagious magic (pp. 298f.).

Supreme God. In addition to ancestor worship, however, there is also adoration of a Supreme Being, Juok. He is, at least in theory, far above Nyikang, who is considered an intermediary between him and mankind. Juok, the creator of the universe and humanity, is described as invisible and as living on or under the earth rather than in the sky. While he has exercised Shilluk imagination much less than has Nyikang, Juok does receive first fruits and also offerings in case of illness; and the natives address him in simple prayers. He may be profitably compared with the high-gods of Tierra del Fuego (p. 402 f.).

Art

In sharp contrast with the Negroes of the western Sudan, the Shilluk are markedly weak on the artistic side. Representative painting is confined to crude figures of animals; and domestic designs comprise only a few plain geometrical patterns on mats and temple walls. Wood-carving, so elaborate in West Africa (p. 137), is virtually lacking. Literature, however, conforms to general Negro patterns. The abundant folklore includes the familiar motif of a weak beast, like the hare, duping bigger animals (p. 200); and there are both proverbs and riddles (p. 196). Poetry may describe martial events, embody prayers, celebrate kings, or lampoon foreigners and undomestic maidens. Gifted minstrels will (*Pl. 48, fig. 2*) eulogize the ruler or a nobleman in lengthy songs and receive presents for their pains.

Summary

While the Buin illustrate the consequences of conquest by a group that grows into an upper caste, the Shilluk rather demonstrate the pervasiveness of the monarchical principle and its combination with religion. The ruler enjoys special privileges and theoretically absolute power, his forebears take precedence over the commoners in the typical Negro ancestral worship, he himself is supposed to be inspired by Nyikang, the legendary founder of the Shilluk kingdom. Yet actually the sovereign is less autocratic than would appear from a superficial view. The general welfare depends upon his well-being, hence a comparatively slight ailment is a sign that Nyikang no longer favors him. Thus the more powerful of his subjects come to challenge the authority of a hated monarch and have him suffocated. Irrespective of this contingency, the king draws great economic benefits from his sacred office and is surrounded by a special code of etiquette.

On the material side the Shilluk have profited from their proximity to the higher Old World civilizations. As craftsmen and artists, it is true, they do not rival the West African Negroes. But they have iron tools and their economic life rests on intensive farming and live-stock breeding. Yet it must be noted that here again borrowing has not been wholesale; the Shilluk never adopted the plough or the wheel; and while their cattle are of practical utility they do not by any means exploit them to the fullest extent, since they slaughter only for religious sacrifices, use oxen normally for nothing at all, and get only a comparatively meager amount of milk out of their numerous, but small cows (p. 43). On the other hand, the fantastic love they display for their beasts is typically primitive and irrational.

Inferior to many other Negroes in wood-carving and lacking such economic institutions as markets, the Shilluk are otherwise highly typical of the higher African states. With all its deficiencies their economy supported an exceptionally dense population; they had a common form of Negro bride-purchase, with its usual social involvements; their oral literature conforms to type; and their complex political system makes some advance toward the modern conception of a civilized state pattern. It certainly implies stronger centralization of power than characterized independent Albania (p. 506).

XXVIII

THE MONGOLS

History

The Mongoloids form one of the great races of mankind, a population of several hundred million people (p. 5). But of these only some 4,000,000 are "Mongolic" in the sense of speaking a language akin to that of the Eastern Mongols or Mongols proper, who occupy the region west of Manchuria and north of China. Just to the north of Mongolia, near Lake Baikal, live the Siberian Mongols, called Buryat; the Western Mongols. among whom the Kalmuk are best known, can be found in Turkestan and well within Europe, on and westward of the lower Volga.

The Mongols affected the history of both Eastern Asia and Europe; on the other hand, their own development has been profoundly influenced by relations with China and India. In the Twelfth Century the true Mongols were simply a series of ununified pastoral tribes sharing the general mode of life of their Turkic and Tungusic neighbors and, like them, able to harass the weakened Chinese monarchy (p. 47). Genghis Khan (born ca. 1160, died 1227), who as a boy inherited the leadership of several Mongol groups, successively conquered one neighboring people after another, thus making himself supreme lord of all the Mongols in 1206. By that time he had already overcome the Turks on the southern slopes of the Altai, and in 1209 he subjected the Uigur, another Turkic people. These had adopted a Semitic alphabet from the Nestorian Christians, which they passed on to their new masters, who thus turned literate and in some measure learned to write even before the definite conquest of their teachers. A little later Chinese characters were used, but only in communications to the Chinese court. A third script was introduced by a Tibetan lama who adapted it to Mongol speech on the basis of Tibetan letters. This became the only official writing by an imperial decree in 1269, but since it proved too cumbersome, the present Mongol script was evolved by a modification of the Uigur (1307-11).

Not content with dominating Mongols and Turks, Genghis Khan attacked the Tungusic rulers of northern China, took Peking, overran the Mohammedan dominions in southern Turkestan, and advanced as far as Bokhara. Under his son Ogotai's sovereignty, the Mongol general Batu terrified all Christendom, occupying Moscow in 1235 and Kiev in 1240. He invaded Hungary, Poland, and Silesia, crushing the Polish and German forces at Liegnitz in 1241. Europe stood aghast, but Batu did not follow up his victory, turning southeast toward the Russian steppes, where he founded the kingdom of the Golden Horde. In the same year Ogotai died and was succeeded by his first wife, then by her son Kuyuk. To him Pope Innocent IV sent the Franciscan monk Plano Carpini to offer a treaty of peace and baptism. But the Mongol sovereign declined conversion and stipulated that before any further negotiations the Pope and the rulers of Europe must do homage to him in his capital, Karakorum. Embassies to the Mongol empire were also equipped by King Louis IX of France. One of his envoys was the famous Franciscan Rubruck, who left Constantinople in 1253 and after a brief stop in southern Russia was sent by one Mongol governor after another to the next superior in rank until he reached Mangu Khan, Genghis Khan's grandson and since 1251 supreme ruler, in Karakorum. He returned to France in 1255. In the preceding year the Polo brothers, two Venetian merchants, had started toward Karakorum, where they remained till 1269. In 1271 they returned with Nicolo Polo's son, Marco (p. 152), who remained in China for many years under the Mongol dynasty, filled a subordinate office there, and left an impressive picture of the great Kublai Khan's court.

However, Mongol glory was short-lived. It was the creation of a few daring political and military geniuses who strove for world empire before their subjects had attained the stage of national solidarity. Accordingly, separatism soon developed; the Mongol governors of Russia, for example, became independent rulers. In China, Kublai's descendants were unable to maintain their ascendancy and were ousted by the purely Chinese Ming dynasty in 1368. Further west the Mongols for a while contended with Turkic people till the Turk Tamerlane in 1365 gained control. Since then the Mongols have in the main retreated to their ancient haunts and present the appearance of primitive pastoralists. Yet in the midst of their country industrial centers, extensive highways, magnificent temples and monasteries with printing establishments and ample libraries bear testimony to the influence of higher civilizations. On the other hand, quite possibly it was through the Mongol invasion that printing and other traits reached Europe, directly or indirectly.

Nevertheless, the memory of ancient power outlived the reality and from time to time a supposed descendant of Genghis would try to reunite the Mongols, as did Dajan (ca. 1500) and his son Altan, who invaded China and in 1550 burnt the suburbs of Peking. In part to further the consolidation of his people, Altan summoned a diet in 1577, at which Lamaism became the official Mongol religion. However, these and subsequent efforts proved futile, for the Eastern Mongols were more suspicious of their Western brethren than of the Manchu, who cleverly used the Mongols to dominate China. They definitely delimited the territories of the several Mongol princes and made them mere officials of the Manchu dynasty. Tracts of pasture land that had formerly been tribal property now passed into the hands of nobles and monasteries or wealthy stock-breeders, while the common Mongols were expropriated. At the same time Chinese farmers came trickling into the old Mongol domain, ousting the natives or furthering their impoverishment, for the perseverance of the Chinese and their experience in business transactions put the Mongols at a great handicap. Thus, a merchant would sell the Mongol a little inferior flour for a few newborn calves, "generously" allowing the former owner to keep the live-stock for a year or two, and later collecting the grown animals, for which the former owner could then obtain a vastly greater equivalent.

Economy

Forest and Steppe. Within Mongol territory there is a sharp regional contrast: a traveler passing from Kalgan, northwest of Peking, to Lake Baikal traverses a great treeless plain until he reaches the town of Urga, where he finds mountains covered with timber and crossed by streams flowing through fertile valleys. In about 1100 A.D. this difference in habitat was coupled with an economic division of the people. The forest-dwellers living from Lake Baikal to the upper Irtysh and Yenisei hunted and fished but had some knowledge of herding; the steppe people south of them, between the Great Wall of China and the Altai, did a good deal of hunting but were above all horse-breeders. In the immediately succeeding period, pastoralism extended northward, gaining followers among the woodland tribes. The Mongols predominantly given to the chase dwelt in wooden huts, while the pastoral nomads had felt tents with dome-shaped tops (pp. 95, 97).

Tents. The dwellings noted by Rubruck north of the Crimea in 1253 are virtually identical with those photographed by Professor Ferdinand Lessing north of Kalgan in 1931. Evidently the felt-covered tent, now carried on a camel's back in wanderings, was eminently suitable for Mongol needs. But though collapsible tents were similarly packed on beasts in the Middle Ages, there was also a more impressive method of transport for the more pretentious type. Rubruck saw a complete tent set on an enormous wagon drawn by twenty-two oxen in two rows, all of them guided by a man standing in the entrance of the tent (*Pl. 49*). Utensils and valuables were stored in high rectangular chests also covered with felt and put on carts drawn by camels. A tent always faced south, with the owner's seat in the rear and his wife's on the east side, while any men took their places in the western half of the dwelling. Batu, the great general, had twenty-six wives and a large tent for each; and his encampment was like a sizable town with an inconsiderable male population. Sartach, a lesser governor, had six wives, each of them with a tent of her own, and possibly two hundred carts.

Food; Herds. The Mongols of the Don did not know how to catch fish, but were willing to eat them "if large enough to be consumable like mutton." But hunting remained important among these pastoralists, who would surround herds of large game in great communal drives. Like some of their neighbors, they practiced falconry, also a favorite sport among their European contemporaries, of whom Emperor Frederick II composed a treatise on this sophisticated form of the chase. Through intercourse with various farming populations the medieval Mongols already had access to rice, millet, and wheat, all of which were fermented into beverages in the winter. But their native and chief drink—their main sustenance in summer—was fermented mare's milk (pp. 46f.). Their large dependence on herds of horses, cattle, goats, sheep, and camels is distinctive of Mongols and Kirghiz, who milk the females of all these species. In the Thirteenth Century they do not seem to have regularly slaughtered their stock, but when an ox or horse happened to die, its flesh was cut into thin slices for drying

Plate 49: MEDIEVAL MONGOL TRAVEL.

[Yule's Marco Polo, 1: p. 254 and Herbst's Rubruck, frontispiece.]

in the sun and preserved for winter use, while the entrails of a horse were made into sausages for immediate consumption. Mutton soup was likewise a favorite dish.

Because the Mongols did not store fodder or put their live-stock into stables during the winter, migration towards sheltered pastures became necessary with the cold season. The wanderings forced upon them by the needs of their beasts naturally varied from region to region. These normal shiftings must be kept distinct from the great medieval expeditions of conquest; in recent times they do not seem to average annually above 100 miles.

In the bleak timberless steppe the dung of cattle and horses formed an indispensable substitute for firewood.

Dress. Even in the Thirteenth Century these people freely used Chinese silk for summer clothing, while pelts for winter wear were imported from Siberian and Turkic tribes. The winter dress consisted of an inner coat with the hairy side towards the wearer's skin, and a wolf or fox skin coat with the hair on the outside; for the latter garment the poor substituted dog or goat hides; raincoats were of felt.

Felt. Felting was—and is—a basic industry since it enters into all vital phases of life (p. 119). The natives wetted sheep's wool, beat it with sticks, pressed it, and tied the rough strips of wool to grazing horses to be dragged across the smooth grass of the steppe. Dwellings, as well as the booths erected over treasure chests transported on carts, were covered with felt, which for the latter purpose was soaked in tallow or ewe's milk to make it rainproof. The Mongols sat on felt rugs and at a king's coronation ceremony placed the king on a mat of white felt to extend to him their good wishes. For similar reasons a bride is seated on white felt, as is a wayfarer about to start on a long journey. Oddly enough, every tent had its felt idols—a doll on the north side over the owner's head, another above his wife's, a third between the two others. On the women's side of the dwelling still another doll was provided with a cow's udder to symbolize the feminine task of milking cows, while on the opposite side a counterpart had a mare's udder, correspondingly referring to the masculine duty of securing the material for kumyss. At a meal the inmates first made an offering of drink to the images or greased the idols' mouths with fat.

Sexual Division of Labor. In the division of labor, men tended camels and horses, milked mares, fermented the yield into kumyss, and made bags for storing it. They made the wagons and tent frames, horsegear, and naturally bows and arrows, which formed their principal weapons. Women drove the carts, churned the butter, dressed skins, and sewed them with sinew. Sheep and goats were herded together, and either sex might milk the females.

Society

Marriage. By analogy with surrounding tribes the Mongols may reasonably be credited with patrilineal exogamous clans or lineages, all fellow members being descended from a single ancestor. Certainly close blood-relatives—within the second degree, according to Rubruck—were prohibited mates, which presumably means that cousins did not marry. On the other hand, polygyny was proper and a man might marry his wife's sisters simultaneously or in succession (p. 252); moreover, a son would inherit his stepmothers and was in any case obliged to support his father's wives (p. 238). Marco Polo, who likewise reports filial widow-inheritance, adds the levirate (p. 237) as a proper form of marriage. According to our medieval sources, men bought their wives, but after the contract had been made the girl fled and there was a mock abduction by the groom. In polygynous families the first wife was held supreme.

Property. Every major subdivision owned its own territory, prized as pasture land. Live-stock was owned individually, the sheep and goats being tended by herders, while the larger beasts grazed at large, each bearing its master's mark. Property was inherited by the youngest son, as among neighboring Turks (p. 283). Anciently some at least of the live-stock and slaves were killed at their owner's death, a custom not abrogated until 1577, when Lamaism substituted an equivalent offering to the clergy as a fee for their prayers.

Political Development. In the Thirteenth Century the Mongols were already far removed from the status of a simple organization of sundry autonomous clans. On the one hand, economic pressure or sheer adventurousness would make men secede from their own group and found independent units; on the other, successful founders of such new branches would attract poorer folk of alien clans as their vassals and might even reduce a conquered group to servitude. At the height of Mongol power a particular clan was thus no longer a democratic body of kin but embraced the dominant core of the group, their poor dependents, and the slaves. Nevertheless, all these people would be called by the master's clan name.

The more powerful clans as thus constituted tended to form larger bodies by temporary confederacies, governed by a tribal council in which the influential clan leaders dominated. For great communal hunts and warfare this council elected a "khan", who might succeed in prolonging his authority. Before the establishment of the empire there were local and frequently rival khans of varying power, and the wealthy stock-breeders might shift their allegiance according to their interests. Very important were aristocratic soldiers of fortune, who freely offered some khan their military services, taking an oath of loyalty. Coming from alien groups, they further broke down the solidarity based on clan kinship; and as the khan's personal bodyguard they were predestined to become generals and governors directly responsible to him while independent of the old clan aristocracy. At the time of Genghis' accession, however, centralization of authority was not yet absolute: the aristocrats who elected him did not offer absolute obedience except in war and the chase; and at first he ranked supreme only as the representative of his immediate kin.

Genghis revolutionized the old system by feudalizing it. That is, he apportioned his dominions partly among his family, partly among personal retainers, each of these feudal lords controlling the movements of the people allotted to him and exacting tributes from them. Thus, in 1253 Batu had thirty attendants within a day's march of his camp, and each had to furnish him daily the milk of a hundred mares. While such taxes had not been unknown previously, they now became a regular institution. But this civil organization was fused with a military division, the realm being divided into units capable of furnishing ten, a hundred, a thousand, and ten thousand soldiers, and each of these groups being made to coincide with a feudal fief. Since the military units were composed of various clans and even tribes, the old political system was thus destroyed in favor of a feudal military monarchy. But, as shown above, the separatist tendencies proved too strong, and the great state created by Genghis did not last for more than a century and a half. Indeed, dissension set in soon after his death, leading to a partition of the realm.

Cultural Effects of Empire

The conquests of the Mongols brought them into contact with many unrelated peoples of higher, urban civilization. Thus they came to enjoy the results of foreign craftsmanship and at least became aware of quite novel idea systems. From the Alani, expert blacksmiths, they acquired armor; from the Persians, iron shields and helmets. Nonagricultural, they easily obtained from subject farmers what millet, wheat, or rice they wanted. Indeed, with the trade routes opened by political unification, all sorts of products became available—costly furs from Siberia and Russia, silk from China, cotton from Persia.

As a result of their predatory expeditions the Mongols were able to command the services of expert foreign craftsmen from all over the known world. At the capital Rubruck made friends with a Parisian master metallurgist taken prisoner in Hungary. This skilled artisan constructed for the emperor an ornamental silver tree with four lions at its roots spewing forth mare's milk and received a thousand marks for his reward. Indeed, anything more cosmopolitan than Mangu's court is not easily conceived. There was a woman from Lorraine married to a Russian housebuilder; there was an Englishman's son born in Hungary and able to understand French; there were Hungarians, Georgians, Armenians, Turks, as well as Chinese artisans and herbalists.

Most remarkable of all, in view of contemporary conditions in the world of Islam and Christendom, there was great religious tolerance. Karakorum had twelve temples for "idolaters", two mosques, and a Christian church; indeed, Nestorian monks were swarming over the capital. During Rubruck's visit Mangu arranged a public disputation of Christians, Mohammedans, and idolaters about the merits of their respective faiths. He was evidently not convinced by Rubruck's fervor, for he summarized the situation from his own point of view as follows: "God gave you Holy Writ, which you fail to live up to. To us he gave diviners; we do what they say and live in peace."

Religion

Medieval Beliefs. From the medieval reports it is, indeed, clear that the basic beliefs of the Mongols were still largely those of the surrounding illiterate peoples. When Genghis in his earlier period escaped from his enemies, he loosened his belt and doffed his cap in token of humility before the mountain that had protected him, and made a libation of kumyss to it. And throughout his life he invoked the Everlasting Blue Sky. Rubruck's "diviners" were obviously shamans of the Siberian pattern, who beat tambourines, sang magical chants, and worked themselves into an ecstasy when summoning spirits in order to question them. They consecrated white mares, poured out a libation when the new kumyss of the year was ready to be drunk, foretold the fate of a newborn boy, and doctored the sick.

Almost equally prominent was shoulderblade divination. Mangu would not engage in any enterprise before noting the form of crack on a sheep's scapula held over a fire (p. 300). The felt idols in every tent have already been noted. Quite as typical of primitive thought was the taboo against touching the threshold of a dwelling with one's feet; for unwittingly transgressing this rule Rubruck's companion was ever after excluded from the khan's palace. There was also great fear of storms, and stones were worn on the person as amulets against thunder and lightning.

In 1253 the Mongols were already acquainted with Buddhists; Rubruck describes the tonsure of their priests, their monastic communities, the recital of magically potent words over rosaries. From his Parisian goldsmith he even heard of a three-year-old Chinese boy who ranked as a "living buddha", i.e., as the reincarnation of a deity or prelate. Kublai Khan became a votary of Buddhism, but it was not until 1577, long after the peak of Mongol power, that Buddhism in the Tibetan form of Lamaism became the state religion.

Buddha and Lamaism. Siddhartha Gautama, later known as the Buddha, founder of the faith, was born of a princely family in northern India about 560 B.C. The essence of his philosophy is its emphasis on the vanity of existence: salvation lies in meditation, by which the devotee ultimately strips himself of all human striving and emotion, thus attaining through loss of individuality "a sacred calm, unmoved by any feeling whatever, in lifeless, timeless bliss." Buddha, however, renounced the temptation to throw off suffering for himself alone and turned Messiah by vowing to remain in existence until all mankind was saved. He never stressed the worship of God; believing, like his compatriots, in a host of deities, he held that they, too, required salvation. Among the earlier Indian notions preserved by Buddha and sometimes carried to ridiculous extremes by his disciples was the commandment against killing any living being.

This abstract creed, running contrary to the human urge for self-preservation, was bound to be modified and combined with less abstruse beliefs before it could gain a large following. In any case, Buddhism did not enter Tibet until 642 A.D., over a thousand years after the founder's death, and by that time had already undergone changes in India itself. In Tibet it assumed the form called Lamaism, which throws all the religious responsibility on the lamas or priests. Only the lama understands the religious doctrines and ritual, only he may experience a daily mystic thrill; he may then allow spiritual blessings to trickle through to the laity. Through his esoteric lore he can verily create the deity; by prolonged concentration he himself turns into a god. Not all lamas can be expected to share the fullest knowledge of ritual, which is limited to the duly tested and ordained pupils of monastic schools. The abbots and other superior prelates, graded in a hierarchical series, are thus of the utmost importance, the supreme head being the Dalai Lama or pope-king of Lhasa, the capital of Tibet. Because of the tremendous prestige attaching to the religious order incredible numbers of Tibetans enter monasteries and nunneries.

It is this Tibetan form of the cult, then, that became established in Mongolia, with its stress on monasticism and belief in reincarnation of deities in living lamas. Accordingly, Buddhistic works translated from the Tibetan form the greatest part of Mongol printed literature; and the reputation of having studied at Lhasa raises a Mongol lama to a pinnacle of glory. But notwithstanding their servility to the Tibetan model, the Mongols inevitably departed from it, partly because of the frailty of human nature, partly because indigenous beliefs can never be simply abolished by designating some more sophisticated system as the official religion.

Survivals and Reinterpretations. Thus, we find that a modern votary will not scruple to slaughter a ram, excusing himself on the ground of not being able to live without its flesh in so forbidding a habitat as Mongolia. By way of a compromise he will put together the bones and read a holy text over them, thus ensuring for the beast a more advantageous rebirth. On the other hand, shoulderblade divination is as much in vogue nowadays as it was in Rubruck's time; and contemporary visitors to a tent are warned against turning their feet towards the fire lest they offend the fire-god. This regard for a "lord of fire" is doubtless very ancient, for it is found among those Buryat who have accepted neither Islam nor Lamaism.

In other cases, an aboriginal observance is overlaid, if not smothered, by Buddhistic conceptions. Thus, the ancient Mongols had cairns to which passersby added rocks, rags, and other offerings to the supernatural lord of the site as a thanksgiving for a safe journey and a prayer for future protection. These sacred piles have been retained but are combined with ideas imported from India. The central heap of rocks now has four rows of smaller stones radiating from it to symbolize the cardinal directions; the cairn is dedicated to the Indian snake demons to ward off plagues and drought; appurtenances of Lamaistic cult are introduced; a drum made from a skullcap, a statuette of Buddha placed on the altar, and so forth.

Similarly, the Mongols still have the shaman, as in the Thirteenth Century, but with Lamaistic frills. Like his Siberian colleagues, he wears a special costume, allows himself to be tied during a séance, and, possessed by his guardian spirit (pp. 311f.), goes into a trance amid the beating of drums. The shaman, however, in emulation of Buddha, pretends to have vowed to remain in existence till he has redeemed all living beings; he carries the thunderbolt emblem of Tibet in order to destroy demons; and his pupils recite passages from the Lamaistic scriptures.

Oral Literature

Far more interesting than their largely borrowed religious writings are the folk-tales and poems orally handed down by the common folk and equally illiterate itinerant minstrels. The Mongols have their great epics, whole cycles centering about the legendary exploits of Genghis, transfigured into a heavenly being who overcomes the monsters of this world. Formally, as well as in content, these poems correspond to a type found among the ancient Turks, Finns, Hungarians, Tungus, and Indo-Europeans, all of whom shared alliteration and assonance (p. 194). Lyric poetry is well developed, but here foreign influences are perceptible. A Chinese tang appears in a recent sample when the duck is introduced as a symbol of conjugal fidelity; and a love chant gets a religious trimming when it closes with a hope for the Dalai Lama's benediction. Humorous poems are very popular and continue to be improvised. Some of them lampoon the conduct of the lamas, proving that the folk are well aware of the frequent contrast between the actual behavior of their clergy and their theoretical purity.

In prose there are likewise amusing narratives, some about a trickster capable of duping the lord of hell himself, others satirizing the stupidity or cowardice of the Chinese. Riddles (p. 171) are also common and are used in a competitive "parlor game", each team trying to solve the conundrums propounded by their opponents.

Finally, some of the elaborate Lamaistic festivals, replete with priestly symbols and mysticism, are for most of the lay spectators nothing more than a magnificent dramatic spectacle with thrilling spirit impersonations by masqueraders mingling, it may be, with the buffoonery of a clown. Other ceremonies are combined with horse races and wrestling matches (pp. 320-23).

Summary

The Mongols prove in striking fashion that a people's culture may be profoundly affected by their historical relations. Unaided they might conceivably have achieved literacy, but except for their intercourse with Uigurs, Chinese, and Tibetans they certainly would not have dallied with the three types of script actually once used by them. Nor is it at all thinkable that they would have evolved from shamanism to Lamaism without Tibetan contacts. On the other hand, the tenacity with which the Mongols have clung to various features of material and spiritual existence is no less remarkable, indicating that conservatism and readiness to take over innovations are not mutually exclusive phenomena. In such cases it is most interesting to ascertain precisely what is retained and what is adopted, and why.

The short-lived glory of the Mongol empire looms as one of the curiosities of history but is not unintelligible in a general way. Had China been in a less hazardous state at the time, even Genghis Khan's outstanding gifts would have found only local scope for their display. Given both the weakness of the civilized nations and Genghis' organizing ability, the creation of the Mongol realm becomes conceivable. Its fall is equally intelligible when we recall the inadequate preparation of the medieval Mongols for a major international role. They had been long accustomed to relatively small political units, and this separatism reasserted itself as soon as the pressure toward union exerted by a few dominant personalities vanished. When Chinese and Turkish resistance became strong, the Mongols simply receded.

XXIX

THE ALBANIANS

History and Geography

Political Past. Albania lies to the east of the Adriatic Sea, with Yugoslavia on the north and east and Greece on the south and east. From the heel of Italy it is separated only by the narrow Strait of Otranto. The natives have been identified with the Illyrians, who inhabited part of the prefecture of Illyricum established by the Roman emperors Diocletian (284-304) and Constantine (324-37). Their location inevitably brought contacts with Romans, Slavs, the Byzantine Empire, the Turks, and the Italians. For several centuries the country was in part actually, as a whole nominally, under Turkish rule, from which it was not freed until 1912. At that time a German prince became king, but he left at the outbreak of the World War. For a period Albania had no official government, but ultimately proclaimed itself an independent republic. Ahmed Zog, its first elected president, assumed the royal title in 1928, which he retained until the annexation of his country by Italy in 1939.

Tribalism.—These statements, however, give a purely formal picture, for one of the outstanding facts about the Albanians is their lack of national solidarity. This is precisely one of the points that render them most instructive for anthropological study. Here, within Europe, is a population of about a million that never achieved a national state in the modern sense, for even under King Zog this remained a pious wish rather than a reality. First of all, there are two speech groups, the Ghegs of the north (*Pl. 50*) and the Toscs of the south, speaking dialects of the same language but sufficiently apart to render free communication difficult. With this distinction goes a difference in physical traits: the Ghegs

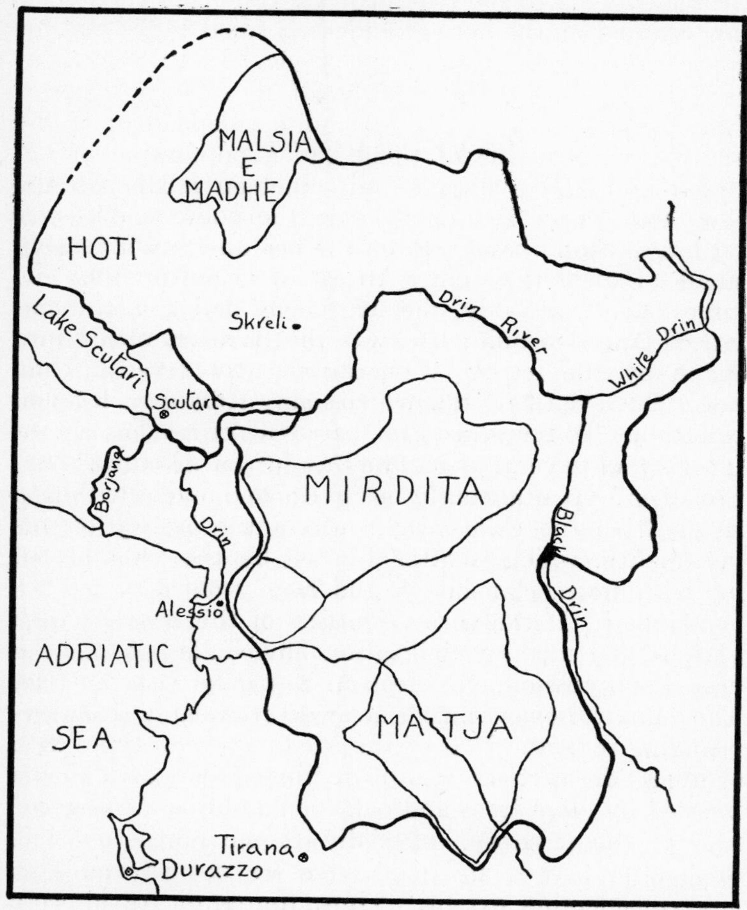

Plate 50: Northern Albania.

are considerably taller, typical Dinarics, while the Toscs correspond to the Alpine subrace (p. 6). But though there has been a traditional cleavage between Gheg and

Tosc, Albanian separatism goes much farther. In the remote northern highlands neither Turkish rule nor Slavish influence has abolished ancient tribalism, the people clinging to the two medieval canons of customary law codified by the hero Skanderbeg (died 1467) and his contemporary Dukagjini, respectively. In 1918 an accurate statistical inquiry established fully seventy tribes of Gheg speech, for the most part quite independent of one another; twenty-one of them had a population of between four and five thousand, nineteen fell below the thousand mark. In other words, the political unit was no larger than that of Indian tribes and incomparably smaller than that of many African Negro countries. The largest coherent body, the Matja, by actual count embraced 23,643 people; this was the tribe organized into shape by the leader who subsequently became King Zog. But even he remained to many Albanians a tribal chieftain. To recognize the "kapidan" or head of a confederacy of several tribes was as far as Albanian "nationalism" spontaneously aspired; and even within a single tribe the chief's influence hinges largely on his personality, which is often limited by the assembly of local headmen, clan heads, and family elders.

Isolation. If the varied contacts of this country with ancient and modern civilization have failed to make a deeper impression, the reason is partly geographical. The climate, however, does not vary noticeably from surrounding regions. It is of the Mediterranean type, with summer drought and winter frosts, the flora being marked by olive trees and oak forests. But the ruggedness of the territory, especially in the north, made it difficult of access, and the rivers are not navigable to any considerable extent. Thus, routes of travel were restricted to a minimum and as late as 1931 the first railroad line, connecting the capital, Tirana, with its port, Durazzo—a distance of twenty-two miles—was as yet only under construction. In fact, travel by airplane preceded transportation by rail. In the middle of the last century communication by land was such that if the crops miscarried in some southern district its inhabitants imported provisions by sea from Trieste instead of over the rough roads from central Albania.

Foreign Relations. Isolation, however, is never absolute for human groups. Accordingly, even in this inaccessible country many foreign influences are demonstrable. First, we may note the language. To be sure, its structure is so distinct that philologists class it as a separate branch of the Indo-European family—coördinate with the Romance, Slavic, and Germanic branches. Nevertheless, Albanian is full of loan words from Italian, Slavic, Greek, and Turkish. Similarly, alien contacts led to the Mohammedanization of seventy per cent. of the natives, the remainder professing either Greek Orthodoxy or Catholicism.

As regards material culture, the Albanians have been as eager as any nonindustrialized primitive people to obtain factory products that answered their needs. About ninety years ago, when their women still did a good deal of textile work for domestic use, the Toscs were already importing English cotton goods on a large scale. At that time Great Britain and Austria, which then still embraced Venice as well as Trieste, sold quantities of raw iron to the Albanians, who themselves forged it into ploughs, horseshoes, and nails. Thus their metallurgical status resembles that of certain African Negroes who, lacking ore, import iron from neighboring tribes, but depend on their own blacksmiths for finished tools and weapons. The fez, or truncate tasseled cap of Turkish pattern, was at one time imported from Tunis, but the North African manufacturers were unable to compete with Viennese merchants. Finally, the warlike highlanders, who could not conceive going about unarmed, got their guns and ammunition wherever they could, often smuggling them in from a considerable distance in evasion of Turkish attempts to disarm them. Many flintlocks used about the beginning of the Twentieth Century have been traced to a gunsmith in Constantinople; and though powder was sometimes produced locally, the saltpeter required had to be brought secretly from Italy. These are only a few instances of foreign trade relations.

Material Culture

Live-stock. In 1308 a French ecclesiastic described the Albanians as migratory herders living largely on milk and cheese. Even in quite recent times whole tribes depend on their flocks, migrating each fall to the winter pastures in the plains and in summer returning to the pastures at higher altitudes. Stall-feeding is of correspondingly little moment. The most important stock animals for herders and farmers both are sheep and goats, for which there is an ample nomenclature, with special words for ewe, ram, barren females, and so on. Meat is generally regarded as a luxury, the people's main food consisting still, as in medieval times, of milk and cheese. Oxen and buffalo (p. 44) are used to draw ploughs, as well as the creaking two-wheeled carts that serve as vehicles where the terrain permits. Horses, donkeys, and mules are ridden and packed. Only the Christian minority keep pigs, which are taboo to the Mohammedans.

Farming. Farming remains on a simple level and is largely determined by local conditions, since large sections are not arable. Thus in one area the soil may favor vineyards rather than the old Albanian food crop, wheat, which in post-Columbian times has been overshadowed by maize. Another originally American product, tobacco, is widely raised and even exported; in the swamp lands the people grow rice. A plough and a harrow represent the farming implements, whose simplicity contrasts with the extensive irrigation works. In this dry country these assume such great importance that water rights are jealously guarded and the men who repair aqueducts stand outside clan feuds.

Crafts. Herding and farming, however, do not exhaust Albanian occupations. In some districts the able-bodied men ply hereditary trades, such as weaving, not in their native villages but at a considerable distance, leaving to the women and the elders the care of cultivated plots and vineyards. At one time the masons, wood choppers, and house carpenters of Turkey and Greece largely came from Albania, whither they returned only for brief visits in the summer. Commonly they banded together in unions, led by a headman, who made all requisite contracts for the membership.

Artisans who thus absent themselves from their native village for the greater part of the year are not peculiar to the Albanians, but are a widespread Balkan phenomenon. For instance, the Vlachs of Thessaly and Macedonia, people speaking a Rumanian dialect, follow the same custom: though regarding certain hill villages as their true home, they will wander off as far as Athens in the winter while their wives and mothers, aided by the older men, tend to the settlement. Similarly, as late as 1932 Mr. Adamic found near the boundaries of Greece and Albania the Yugoslav village of Galichnik, whose adult men return home for only a few summer weeks annually. In consequence there are wholesale weddings in July.

About a hundred to a hundred and fifty years ago the itinerant absentees of South Albania frequently were not engaged in useful occupations at all, but as the core of the Turkish mercenary troops were as likely as not to see service in the Barbary states and in Egypt, returning with rich spoils from these remote countries, which they helped to keep in subjugation.

Dwellings. The mode of settlement, as well as the type of the dwelling itself, is affected by geography. In the warmest coastal belt people live at an altitude of 3,000 feet; otherwise the majority remain between 750 and 2,000 feet above sea level. In the Gheg highlands each estate, comprising one or two structures, is isolated from the rest; at the foot of the mountains there are serried house-groups with gardens and olive groves. The natives of the malarial coast belts escape the mosquitoes either by building their dwellings at a height of sixty to ninety feet along the slope of the hills rising from the plains, or by erecting summer arbors on lofty piles. In the coastal northern plains, for lack of stone, only the wealthiest can afford anything but wooden dwellings. Where easily split rocks such as limestone are available, everyone lives in a stone house. Owing to local variation and the lack of roads, in an hour a traveler may find a total change of house type.

Because of regional differences in raw material and the variety of historic relations, the Albanian dwellings are of great diversity. The traditionally oldest form is a one-celled structure with gable roof. In earlier times the roof was more commonly thatched because wheat straw lends itself to this purpose more readily than do maize stalks. In timbered regions herders inhabit log cabins about four and a half feet in height; elsewhere they put up equally low stone hovels having a door but no windows and a roof of loose boards, weighted down with rocks. Among the peasants one finds the simple wattled hut, a larger one-room stone dwelling, with a pillared porch, and impressive stone forts several stories high. In the cruder type there is neither ceiling nor window; other structures are divided into the women's and children's compartment with the fireplace, and the space for the men and their guests. When there is an upper story, the ground floor is divided into the stable and the storeroom, but otherwise the same roof may shelter the master and his live-stock. The type of house in a measure depends on the security its occupants enjoy. Where conditions are safe, verandahs appear; in the feud-ridden districts houses with verandahs would invite attack, hence are reserved for women, whose lives are spared

Plate 51: Albania.

1. Fortified Albanian house with loop-holes for windows. 2. Albanian andirons. 3. Albanian interior. Top of table rests against wall when not in use.

according to the rules, but whose husbands remain in lofty stone forts with loopholes, easily stopped overnight, instead of windows (*Pl. 51, fig. 1*).

The furniture of a rural home is of the simplest type: an open fireplace takes the place of a stove; chimneys are lacking; in the absence of closets utensils are hung from nails on the walls, put on shelves, stowed away in chests or barrels. A circular wooden slab serves as a table; it is set up—at a height of about eight inches above the floor—immediately before a meal; when not in use it rests against a wall so that it may be kept clean. No higher than the table are the three-legged stools, some of which, by addition of a back rest, evolve into very low chairs. In a more pretentious house there will be a comfortable chair as the place of honor for distinguished guests.

Dress. Dress is at least as variable as the dwellings. Notwithstanding all manner of imported materials and goods, the influence of the basic sheep-herding economy still reveals itself in the mountain districts. Thus in Malsia e Madhe the highlanders wear a jacket of white woolen cloth, topped by a very short-sleeved jacket of black wool or a sheepskin vest. Their trousers are of thick, white woolen cloth and their hooded cloak, which extends to the knees, is of black wool. The women wear a one-piece woolen suit that is coatlike in its upper half and expands into a conical or bell-shaped skirt; their apron is made of the same material. Styles vary in detail from region to region, and sometimes within a district among members of different faith. As in other primitive groups, status differences crop up (p. 80): a Skreli girl's dress is white, a married woman's black. The fact that, notwithstanding Albanian conservatism, foreign trade has for a long time influenced the type of clothing has already been pointed out. At one time the hides for Albanian sandals were of Argentine origin, though imported by the Albanians from England.

Travel. The primitiveness of travel has already been

mentioned. Important rivers, too deep to be forded, remain unspanned at crucial points; and until 1914 bridges that would have passed muster in Western Europe or

Plate 52: ALBANIAN BRIDGE AND FORDS.
1. Albanian swimmers' float and baggage crate. 2. Albanian ferry. 3. Bridge at Skala Madhe.

the United States simply did not exist. Typically, the natives avoided both true arches and pillars resting in the river bed, since these are liable to be carried away by an inundation. In the best-known sample, tiers of successively longer beams jutted out from the stone props on the banks corbel-fashion (p. 99) until these inverted wooden stairways could be joined by available logs (*Pl. 52, fig. 3*). Where even these contrivances are lacking the Albanians swim across, holding on to inflated sheepskins, or pushing along goods in a framework of withies (*Pl. 52, fig. 1*). Crude dugouts occur and are sometimes steadied either by simple log outriggers or by coupling boats (*Pl. 52, fig. 2*). In the latter case, horses are ferried with their front legs in one dugout and their hind legs in the other. The only indigenous vehicle for land transportation is a horribly creaking springless cart with two wheels nearly six and a half feet in diameter, this height being designed to cope with the mud of the plains. The driver, sitting on the floor of the frame or standing up, does not whip his oxen or buffalo, but urges them on with a pointed goad such as is used in Asia Minor, the Caucasus, and the Mediterranean area.

Society

Fraternities. The social institutions almost at every step reveal parallels to "savage" customs. In central Albania, as in Africa and among the Plains Indians (p. 250), there are boys' companies that develop into permanent organizations. They include about twenty-five to thirty members of the same age and following the same occupation. Each contributes a certain sum to a common purse administered by a chosen headman, who uses the proceeds for two or three major banquets a year. Each organization has two attendants who are unable to pay the fee, substituting services as cook and waiter, respectively. Every society has its own rules and fines members for a breach. The sense of solidarity is intense: fellow members are obliged to aid and protect one another in any human situation. At times there are rival societies, which on occasion fight. The tie continues for many years and in some instances is not dissolved until the members are fifty years of age.

Marriage and Woman's Status. Matrimonial customs and the relations of the sexes as a whole depart widely from Western European norms. While there is much local variation, the very fact that here and there parallels to savage usage have survived is of the utmost interest. Thus, the levirate (p. 237), locally prescribed, may lead to bigamy since even a married man must take to wife his deceased brother's widow. Even apart from widow-inheritance, polygyny was found only twenty years ago among both Greek Orthodox and Catholic natives, the usual motive being the first wife's barrenness or the need for additional labor in the household. From two districts is reported the couvade (p. 400), with a special term for "the man whose wife has been delivered of a child and who himself lies in bed like a woman in confinement, receiving visitors." Infant betrothal is common and so is bride-purchase even among nominal Christians. Wife and husband take their meals separately, especially when there are guests. As in some Indian tribes, a wife—particularly a newly wedded one—must not call her husband by name, but designates him as "that one". Altogether women are regarded as inferior; for example, male progeny is preferred, and if there are any sons in the family, all their sisters are barred from the legacy. Even if male issue is lacking, daughters inherit only chattels while the real estate goes to the dead father's nearest kinsman, however remote his relationship may be.

House Community. Locally there is furthermore the patriarchal house community that unites under a single roof a father with his sons and sons' sons, the wives being brought from without. Up to fifty persons have been found living in this way in a single house. However, this is not a distinctively Albanian practice, being more particularly associated in historic times with the Southern Slavs. Even in 1932 Mr. Adamic found a Serbian unit of this type, composed of eleven single families dwelling in one twenty-room house.

Clans. The Northern Albanians have not consistently adhered to this mode of residence, but they alone seem to have maintained until the present the full-fledged concept of the exogamous patrilineal clan. What is more, they exhibit this unit in a variety of instructive forms. Thus the clan may coincide with the tribe, but in 1918 the Shala tribe embraced mainly two clans which intermarried, thus forming to all intents and purposes moieties (p. 259). One of them represents the ancient indigenous population, which thus was at one time a localized clan presumably marrying into any outside group; the other is composed of later immigrants who settled in the district. But it also happens that a clan embraces several tribes. Thus three tribes of the region known as Mirdita trace their descent to a common ancestor who lived in the Fifteenth Century. They even extend the sense of kinship to the Shoshi tribe, which is supposedly descended from the brother of the three tribes' ancestor. On the other hand, the reverse process has also been noted, members of a clan splitting off to found units of the same type; and in such cases it may happen that people still cognizant of a common origin no longer respect the exogamous rule outside the new subdivision, which thus becomes a full-fledged independent clan.

About the middle of the last century such incipient segregation could still be observed. In the village of Lyabóvo about twenty-seven out of one hundred houses belonged to the Dodats—the clan descended from the legendary Dodo. But within this group several branches were recognized, one of them already called Mexats after its founder Mexis, who was also no longer remembered as a historic figure. Quite distinct clans in the same village were the Kiliats (descended from Kilo) with twenty houses; and the Michanchulyat with thirty-three. These latter had for their ancestor a certain Michel, who originally came from the neighboring village of Chulyat. Thus these highlanders illustrate the secession of a subdivision that grows into a distinct clan, the affiliation of particular clans with particular settlements, but also the reshuffling of clans as a result of migration.

One mark of a true clan system is the permanence of the tie that binds an individual to his unit. Because this is not clearly established for the Ona, we are not absolutely certain whether they have genuine paternal clans or are only approaching that condition (p. 265). But among the Albanians in the episcopate of Scutari there is no doubt on this vital point. Even the women who by patrilineal residence come to live away from their kin are indubitably affiliated with the clan into which they were born. This is demonstrated by the application of the principle of blood vengeance. It is not her husband and her connections by marriage but her own clansmen who avenge an injury to her person. This is given as one reason why warring clans spared each other's wives: it would bring the transgressing side into difficulty with still another clan. It also tended to prevent a husband in this patriarchal society from excessively abusing his wife since such conduct might embroil him with all of her kin.

Feuds. This leads us to the political aspects of the system. The entire clan exacts satisfaction for harm suffered by any one member; conversely, they are jointly responsible for any of his misdeeds. Thus a feud involves whole clans, is inherited and may lead to endless bloodshed, for with these proud and warlike people retribution for a wrong is a matter of honor. The shooting of a dog may precipitate murder. Within the historic period the several tribes developed somewhat different rules in this matter, some accepting weregild while others spurned it as ignominious (p. 286). In about 1850 the Selitza held a council, which decreed that henceforth vengeance should be limited to those kinsmen who shared the criminal's roof. Nevertheless, decades later the mortality from feuds amounted to twenty-eight and even thirty-two per cent. of all deaths in certain districts. It may take years of negotiations before the aggrieved clan consents to end a feud, and then only after the murderer has publicly humiliated himself, surrendering himself helpless into their hands. Characteristically, the principle holds that "a family cannot owe itself blood" with the result that if a cousin of the same clan kills another he goes scot-free, however much his act may be deplored: a clan *cannot* proceed against a member, and it is no other clan's business. In this respect the Albanian attitude exactly corresponds to that of the Ifugao of Luzon, who are clanless but apply the identical axiom within the family unit (p. 287).

Religion

Magic and Animism. If Albanian social life is shot through with ideas characteristic of the illiterate peoples of other continents, this holds at least equally true for religion. Nominally, all the people are Christians or Mohammedans, that is, strict monotheists. But in practice they mingle magic and animism with the rites and beliefs of their respective denominations. Down to the very present they prophesy from the appearance of a sheep's shoulderblade, as the Mongols do and did seven hundred years ago (p. 300). When a new house is put up, a Mohammedan owner puts a Koran into the unoccupied structure to drive away evil influence, thus using the sacred book as a wonder-working object. In one district the houseowner would undress and shoot off his pistol at the fireplace in order to scare away evil spirits. In such circumstances bloody sacrifices were until recently very popular. In 1850 a new bridge across a torrential river was dedicated by slaughtering a dozen sheep and putting their heads under the foundation. Tradition even has it that formerly human beings were sacrificed to ensure the safety of such structures. The Albanians likewise share the belief in the evil eye so common in Southern Europe and Western Asia: certain persons, sometimes without so willing, inflict harm on others by glancing at them. Little children and beasts are especially susceptible, so the former are provided with amulets or garlic, the latter ranking as an excellent preventive. Mystic numbers are not lacking: fire, which is credited with beneficent powers, must be maintained for forty days in the room of a woman after her delivery; and mourners keep up their dirges for forty days after a death.

Burial Customs. Burial customs in Rissa show a strange blend of Greek Orthodox and pagan ideas. No sooner does a man breathe his last than the women present set up a terrific howling and shrieking. His sisters, sisters-in-law, wife, and daughters cut their hair, lacerate their cheeks, beat their breasts, butt their heads against the walls—in short, behave like their Fuegian or Australian sisters (p. 318). The corpse is undressed and swathed in cloth, then the female relatives sit round it and begin the formal lament, in which their friends join. If possible, the body is buried on the same day. The procession forms amid the tolling of bells, the priest leading it, followed successively by the men, generally the bearers of the bier, and the women, the mourners among them shrieking pitiably while their friends comfort them. Only the men enter the church, the women continuing their wailing outside. Their grief reaches its acme as the body is interred and covered with stone slabs and earth. Then there is a sudden calm as boiled wheat is served to all from large platters, for it would be sinful to mourn while partaking of this dish, of which everyone eats a handful while uttering the words, "May he be forgiven." On the third day after the burial there is another lament at the grave, and in the home of the deceased the dirges are kept up for forty days. However, the chief mourning is that of the first three days, during which there must be a constant succession of consolatory visits. The guests bring food for the mourners, for whom cooking is tabooed during this period. When a native of Rissa has died at a distance, the rites in his village are the same except that a pretzel carried by a boy on the platter with boiled wheat symbolizes the corpse and is finally presented to the priest. Under normal circumstances the body is disinterred after three years, the bones are cleaned, washed with wine, put into a bag, blessed in church, and finally deposited in a bone house or some other special locality.

Calendric Notions. It is equally odd to find the same people mingling animistic and magical notions with the Orthodox calendar. Thus they believe that during the period between November 15 and Epiphany evil spirits are especially dangerous; hence nobody goes outdoors at night unless he absolutely must. Again, on New Year's Day poultry is slaughtered, for it brings good luck to shed blood in the house on this day.

Folk-Lore. Such conceptions abound in folk-lore. The highlanders believe in man-eating witches whose souls ride on andirons (*Pl. 51, fig. 2*) at night, enter houses by the smoke vent, tap the blood of their victims' hearts and drink it, or roast his heart before devouring it. After the dread deed the soul returns to its body. Witches are especially dangerous on the night of Ash Wednesday. On the other hand, anyone who saves a bit of pork on Shrove Tuesday and strokes the crosses of the church door with it during Easter Sunday mass thereby imprisons whatever witches are inside.

The characters of folk-tales are often considered actual beings by the narrators and their audience. This holds for the female ogre known as Kulshedra, and her inveterate enemies, the Drangues, for every thunderstorm is conceived as a conflict between these opposing forces. In 1913 the Drangues of a particular region were believed to have annihilated the local Kulshedra by piling trees and boulders on her and then drowning the stupefied monster in the Shkumbi River. A Drangue is represented as so powerful that he can tear trees out of the ground. He is born wearing a shirt and a felt cap, with wings at his armpits.

Oral Literature

Varied Influences. The stories told are also interesting in other respects. In addition to the mythical characters of the type just described there is the widespread trickster (p. 200), often represented with a scalp disease; even among the devils a scald head appears as supreme in cunning. There are also such common European elements as dragon-slaying heroes; animal helpers; the treacherous young men who cut the rope on which their younger brother tries to climb up from the underworld, and his escape on a bird's back; a hero's magic birth and the tests to which he must submit. Nowhere else do we find clearer indications of the checkered history of the Albanians. Thus they have taken over a whole cycle of funny Turkish stories centering in one Nasreddin, who appears sometimes as a trickster, at other times as a simpleton. Very odd is the blend of Christian and Mohammedan ideas in the beginning of a tale: "St. George went into the mountains to hunt one day. He met two people named St. Peter and St. Paul. And he said to them, 'Allah be with you!' " Again there are motives that seem to have been handed down from Greek antiquity. There is a perfect version of the one-eyed giant story: the hero blinds him with a red-hot spit, then escapes under his hands in a sheepskin disguise. Another tale suggests Ixion, punished for his affront to Zeus' wife Hera; the fairy Mauthi has been identified with Amalthea, the goat that suckled Zeus and who was anciently especially sacred in Dodona, a region close to Albanian territory.

Formal Features. Formally, these tales likewise offer characteristic features. They usually begin and close in a stereotyped fashion. The South Albanian opening, "There was, there was not", is equally suggestive for its quaint wording and because it exactly parallels a favorite formula of raconteurs in the Caucasus. An old Albanian ending is to banish the fanciful images of the tale to some remote spot while wishing the audience good health. Aged herders are credited with a special gift for story-telling, but tales are circulated by both sexes and must be told by each guest in turn at a wedding party.

Riddles and Proverbs. However, prose fiction forms but one part, though a very important one, of folk literature. Women and girls will get together of a winter evening around the fireplace to beguile their spinning with conundrums similar to those associated with Africa or Australia (p. 171). Proverbs also conform to Old World patterns (p. 196). As a sample may be cited: "He who looks, finds." "A drowned man is not afraid of getting wet." "An empty belly does not jump well, a full one does not jump at all."

Poetry. Poetry is equally well developed. Sometimes the themes of folk-tales appear in metrical ballad form, and there are epic rhapsodies about the exploits of valiant heroes. Dirges are chanted by women at funerals, a solo singer alternating with the chorus and possibly sketching the life of the deceased. Young men like to serenade the girls with topical songs of a humorous or teasing character. On the other hand, the Ghegs reserve the extravagances of erotic poetry for Platonic love of boys, another possible reminiscence of ancient Greece.

Summary

Albanian culture is thus instructive from many different points of view. Its bearers, partly of Alpine, partly of Dinaric stock (p. 6) cannot have been held back in development from biological causes, since these would have similarly affected other members of these subracial divisions. For corresponding reasons geography figures only in so far as it has impeded the steady effect of progressive development elsewhere, that is, in so far as it has delayed intensive intercourse with the outside world. But, as the data show, the isolation has been strictly limited, so that in practically every phase of their life varied relations with alien peoples come to the fore. In short, the Albanians clearly demonstrate that the present culture of a people remains largely unintelligible without a knowledge of their past.

At the same time the Albanians exemplify the tenacity with which deep-rooted customs live on alongside of apparently contradictory principles. Even Christian Albanians of the last century have been known to practise bride purchase. Most conspicuous of all is the preservation of the clan system in part of the country, with its primitive correlate, collective responsibility. To the very end of Albania's history as an independent country this particular survival has militated against the establishment of a modern state, the natural aspiration of the more progressive Albanian spirits who had imbibed the ideals of western Europe. Their failure, or at best very partial success, illustrates the difficulty encountered in imposing a new idea-system upon a population unprepared for it. The notion of belonging to a modern state, which at first blush might be thought to flatter the vanity of even the backward Gheg, was bound to clash with their most inveterate sentiments as soon as its implications became clear in concrete instances. For, since a civilized state could not tolerate the blood-feud and the underlying sentiment of loyalty on the basis of kinship (pp. 286ff.), it ran counter to the deepest feelings of the mountaineers.

Here lies in principle the difficulty of all "acculturation", that is, assimilation to an alien culture. To take over the outward trappings is easy enough, but the core may long remain unaltered. On the other hand, it is no less true that because of the largely unknown ways in which different parts of culture are organically linked, a seemingly harmless innovation may ultimately come to revolutionize social life. The invention of a laboratory scientist may affect modes of communication (telephone, radio) and warfare. So, the migratory habits of many Albanian tradesmen (p. 511) would in the long run tend to affect all sorts of matters not directly connected with their economic life. The break in the continuity of family life is obvious. In addition, however, the temporary emigrant is liberated from the supervision of his elders, hence free to indulge his personal wishes so far as they are not opposed to his hosts; and, further, he is exposed to whatever new ideas are brought to his notice in a strange environment. This is by no means a process peculiar to the Balkans, but can be studied in any typical group of foreign immigrants into the United States. So long as the group clings together *as* a group, it remains largely an alien society transplanted to American soil. But, as individuals break away, that society crumbles so far as the seceders are concerned, and the way is paved for their acculturation to the American scene.

XXX

OUR WESTERN CIVILIZATION

Advanced Contemporary Cultures

Albania serves as a foil for our contemporary civilization in the United States and Western Europe. Instead of a clan organization we have a sovereign state; instead of a law based on blood-relationship, we have courts dispensing abstract justice regardless of personalities. Our economic life rests not on herding and farming, but on industry; even our agriculture is industrialized, for it depends on factory-made implements and produces not merely for home consumption and local markets but for the world at large. Again, the machinery used to make farming appliances, the means of transportation for distributing both the implements and the farm produce, the telephone and telegraph which aid us in ordering and transmitting the necessaries of modern life rest on the advanced state of our scientific knowledge. Some of these technological advantages are, of course, to be found in the larger Albanian towns, but in Western Europe and North America they have been so generally diffused as to affect the life of the countryside. With all this goes compulsory education, made necessary because in the complex modern world a person ignorant of the elements of school learning is at a hopeless disadvantage. A farmer in the United States, who gets his daily paper by mail or absorbs the news by radio, who periodically drives his Ford to the nearest town and sends his children to the state university is in a very different position from that of a Gheg mountaineer. He may be a rustic by residence, but at least potentially he is in touch with all that urban civilization has to offer.

The Rural Lag

Rural Conservatism. Nevertheless, these possibilities are only imperfectly realized, and remoteness from the cities which in Europe and America are centers of advancement implies in varying degree an approach to the older rural standards. This has been true in all periods and all countries that could boast an urban civilization. In the latter half of the Eighteenth Century the British Isles and France were in the vanguard of progress; but Dr. Samuel Johnson describes a dwelling in the Hebrides lighted by a hole that was alternately opened and plugged with a lump of turf, and at the outbreak of the Revolution even sizable provincial French towns had whole streets without a glass windowpane (p. 92). In southern Sweden, the naturalist Linnaeus found houses without chimneys, the door alone serving as a smoke vent.

Even in recent decades—even at the present time—Albania is by no means the sole example of a pre-industrial economy and a pre-rationalistic philosophy. Individualism and an up-to-date world view no more govern the untutored Pole or Irishman or American backwoodsman than the Melanesian. A few illustrations will drive the point home.

Primitive Social Conceptions. The Polish peasant, like the savage, treats marriage as a contract between kin groups (p. 232), with little concern for the couple's personal wishes. As in Africa, so in Poland the "heir" to an estate is its trustee rather than its owner outright and is expected to manage it for the good of the family. As among the Ifugao (p. 287), there is no possibility of theft between kinsmen; and in both cases family solidarity implies joint responsibility for all fellow members (p. 257). Western Ireland displays the same attitude. In County Clare the farmer turns over his homestead to a marrying son, only reserving the west room for his own future use. He is, indeed, indemnified with his daughter-in-law's dowry, but here again he is not an absolute owner: the amount received should provide for his daughter's dowry. There is thus a close psychological parallel to the African custom by which the payment for a girl is used by her father to buy a wife for his son.

Nothing could be further from modern individualism than the sentimental notions that in both Poland and Eire blend with the attitude towards economic goods. Like the Indian or Melanesian (p. 277) the Polish peasant recoils from selling food; and the rustic from County Clare who goes shopping in his market town is impelled by "no frantic search for better qualities at lower prices". He gives his custom to a friend or relative who in turn is willing to extend credit and feels hurt when the entire debt is paid off: *that* is interpreted as a notice that the customer is planning to buy elsewhere.

Various details of peasant usage parallel savage custom. In northwestern California (p. 241) the bride normally goes to the groom's kin, as she does in Poland; and in both areas the unusual form of matrilocal residence is detrimental to the husband's standing. More striking is an Irish analogy to the Australian age-grade system: as the blackfellow attained status only by a ceremonial initiation (p. 250), without which he would remain a "boy" for life, so in County Clare the man of fifty whose parents had not yet turned over the homestead to him still ranked only as a boy.

Animistic Survivals. Strange, indeed, are glimpses afforded of rural belief below the surface. Let us recall that Christianity dates back even in Poland and Russia to the Tenth Century. Yet the country folk everywhere persist in clinging to pagan survivals that combine oddly with a monotheistic faith. The Polish peasants recognize kings of serpents, wolves, deer, and owls, precisely as the Indians of Labrador postulate an overlord of the caribou; and, like the Fuegians, they avoid speaking ill of winds and weather lest some vengeance overtake the impious utterance. In true animistic fashion they assign spirits to the house and the water, believe that the soul leaves a dreamer's body and may find it difficult to reenter it. Such a mentality is apt to give a quaint twist to Christianity. In 1910-12 impoverished Polish tillers emigrated to southern Brazil. Forthwith there sprang up the legend that the State of Paraná, hitherto hidden by a mist, had been unveiled by the Virgin Mary as a haven for the miserable peasants. According to one variant, the rulers of the earth drew lots for the ownership of the new territory, the pope won three times in succession, and at the behest of the Virgin threw it open to Polish emigrants.

Magic and Witchcraft. Witchcraft lingers on, not only in Eastern but also in Western Europe, and in the United States as well. In the seventies of the last century a Basque confessed to having attended a witches' Sabbath; another, regarding a black cat as a witch transformed, one night cut off its ear, which he found the next morning turned into a woman's ear, decorated with a ring. The isolated sections of our own country yield similar instances. There is the case of white parents in rural Louisiana whose child suffered from shingles: for a remedy they docked a black cat's tail and with the blood made the sign of a cross over the patient's chest. Again, in recent years the people of a village in Illinois—of predominantly British descent—were found carrying potatoes in their pockets as an antidote for rheumatism. These people also feared a cloudy life ahead for couples that got married on a cloudy day.

Not even in rural America, then, has the modern spirit gained complete sway.

The Urban Lag

Urban Superstitions. But our urban population is of rural origin, much of it only recently transplanted; hence except in externals it is not noticeably different from the country folk. The superstitions that are so deeply rooted in our simpler communities thus have an excellent chance of surviving in a metropolis. New York hotels generally lack a room numbered 13, and in many office buildings the astonished passenger leaps directly from the twelfth to the "fourteenth" floor. This attempt to secure safety by giving reality a different label is a typical savage reaction.

Lag in Town Planning. In a more practical way, the entire history of modern city life has been a more or less bungling effort to cope with the implications, usually unforeseen, of progressive techniques. What is, in the abstract, an improvement may upset the social equilibrium so as to spell disaster for the supposed beneficiaries.

Because urban life did not automatically produce measures to safeguard the safety and health of large congregations of people, conflagrations and epidemics wrought untold havoc (pp. 105f.). This is the phenomenon the sociologist Ogburn has called "cultural lag"; and before him Tylor had pointed out numerous "survivals", i.e., items of custom or belief that once fitted perfectly into their setting but are utterly out of keeping with their present context.

The growth of towns, along with the rise of inventions, has been an endless source of problems, by no means all of which have been satisfactorily settled. The automobile parking situation in metropolitan centers is a minor annoyance but a real one. The transportation of men over large distances from homes and to workshops has its serious aspect. Grave, indeed, are the problems of hygiene. Roving nomads are in that respect far better off than were medieval European burghers. In fact, a rational disposal of waste matter is one of the most recent concerns of advanced Western countries. In London it took the cholera epidemic of 1848 to force upon the residents a Metropolitan Commission of Sewers; corresponding sanitary measures in the United States date back to about the same time. These, however, were mere beginnings, and the ideal disposal of sludge is a thing for the future.

From another angle the problem of the slums as a breeding ground of crime is another challenge to rational city governments.

Social Ideals. The reason for this painfully slow groping toward livable conditions in an urban setting is obvious. Man had been accustomed for millennia to existence in minute groups; he could not forthwith sprout a new center in the cortex of his brain to take care of the altered urban circumstances; hence he bungled and continues to bungle, improving only by the gradual method of trial and error.

Now, what applies to the mere outward arrangements of modern life holds with tenfold force for social ideology. The common run of modern man still sees social life from the standpoint of the horse-and-buggy era, if not from that of the paleolithic trudger over the world's surface. In *theory* he may accept an ideal of justice transcending personal ends; but in practice he favors his kin, family, or party in defiance of the merits of the case —exactly as would a Crow or a Solomon Islander. A lofty national policy may be the slogan of election platforms, but parliaments run by compromise between narrow local interests, and politicians—despite the anathemas of the moralist—follow the principle: "To the victor belong the spoils."

In Albanian law nothing revolts us more than the notion of collective responsibility (p. 257). It seems nothing less than monstrous that a person should suffer for a deed he has not himself committed or designed. But every modern state has relapsed into this savage principle in wartime, starving and bombing the civil population, thus doubtless causing more destruction than can be laid to the charge of Albanians or of all the savage tribes of the world from the dawn of history. The contemporary totalitarian states have gone farther and in times of peace gloatingly punish the kin or even fellow nationals of persons who happen to have offended them.

The Puzzle. But if present-day Westerners are at bottom no different from Albanians or savages, whence can we derive those distinctive features that so sharply set off industrial civilization from its predecessors and contemporaries? An effect surely cannot exist without an adequate cause.

Race and Variability

Modified Racialist Theory. At this point the racial theory, dismissed in its general form (p. 9), again rears its head in a new guise. Its saner champions concede the facts cited against a direct ratio between cultural achievement and racial endowment (pp. 7-9, 206-208, 330, 341). Shifting their ground, they admit that not only an Albanian, but even a Negro or American Indian may drive a taxi and clerk as competently as the average white. What they contend is (a) that certain races are more variable than others, hence within comparable populations produce a larger number of leaders; and (b) that all progress in social organization, science, art, and religion starts with such great men. The colored races, then—or, in Europe, the non-Nordic subraces—may not be inferior in the mass; they *are* inferior, however, it is asserted, in producing only few, if any, outstanding personalities and are thus incapable of advancing civilization.

In this extreme form the allegation is certainly wrong, for the Maya who hit upon the idea of the position system must be reckoned an intellectual prodigy (p. 330f.), and the history of American Indians or African Negroes is full of warriors or rulers whose gifts have aroused the admiration of white observers. Yet in the qualified form—that some races are more variable than others and are hence more productive of raw material for great achievement—the idea is useful, *but only as a provisional guess awaiting careful scrutiny.* So far not one tittle of evidence has been adduced in its support. If it ever shall be proved, all honest students of culture will at once proclaim the fact from the housetops.

The "Hero" as Statesman. But the second proposition of the hypothesis is as vital to the racialist philosophy as the first. What is the place of the "hero", as Thomas Carlyle called him, in human history? From a general point of view the matter has already been treated (p. 381). Let us merely insist once more on the necessity for discriminating between the reality of the leader's influence and its *value,* which sometimes is a moot question. We must also ask how important it may be for mankind to have results attained at a particular point of time. In the sphere of government, judgment of these matters is peculiarly difficult because of subjective bias. Charlemagne is doubtless one of the towering figures in European history; but twelve hundred years after him scholars are not yet in accord as to the measure of his success and the importance of his achievements. To take a single aspect of them, his tenacity of purpose certainly imposed Christianity on the Saxons, but would they not have become converted before long in any case? And contemporary German pagans even deny that they ought to have been converted at all.

The "Hero" in Science. In the sphere of science, pure and applied, the question of value need not disturb us, but another problem remains. Granted that individual differences are significant, what is the nature of the socially valuable differences, and how important are they in the long run? To the racial romanticist the great scientist is a "hero" who unravels the mysteries of reality as the Sherlock Holmes of a detective story solves the perfect crime. A realistic view substitutes the picture of a number of trained investigators groping toward a solution on the basis of past knowledge and with the aid of skilled artisans (pp. 336-39). Rarely can one thinker be credited with the total achievement in an intellectual sense; never is his success conceivable without the co-operation of cultural factors beyond his control.

One of the pitfalls to be evaded in this question is that of primitive romanticism. As pointed out (p. 199), illiterate societies generally ascribe their arts and customs wholesale to a mythical character, the "culture hero", who is said to have stolen, imported, or created them for the benefit of his people. There is not a single case on record that any major part of a culture was so derived, yet more advanced peoples have spun similar fantasies. The Greeks traced the knowledge of fire to Prometheus; and Chang Kieng, who actually brought to the Chinese the grapevine and alfalfa (p. 34) when returning from Persia, was subsequently credited with introducing all sorts of other species which were not even known during his lifetime either in Persia or China. This tendency to fanciful exaggeration survives among us because the critical faculty is still little developed in any society.

A correct approach to the subject is to compare the status before and after the appearance of historic great men and to determine what distinguishes their contribution from that of other people. The history of science furnishes helpful material. The typical situation it reveals is not that of *one* creator out of nothing. In the extreme case of Sir Isaac Newton (1642-1726), often rated as the supreme intellect of natural science, we still find that he was the foremost of a number of remarkable investigators. His theory of universal gravitation rested on the foundation laid by Galileo (1564-1642) and Kepler (1571-1630); and Kepler's laws in turn were based on the astronomical observations of Tycho de Brahe (1546-1601). The sober view of scientific progress explodes the romanticizing myth of a culture hero, preventing distortion of the facts with malicious unfairness to the lesser, but equally essential, contributors.

To take another example, in 1609 Galileo made startling astronomical discoveries by means of a telescope; however he had not invented it, but had merely constructed such an instrument from the description of a toy in vogue in Holland. Its invention there was undoubtedly a lucky fluke. As the great physicist Huygens remarked, only a superhuman mind could have conceived a telescope on purely theoretical grounds, whereas the frequent use of lenses by opticians during the three preceding centuries rendered it highly probable that some one of them should put a concave and a convex lens into juxtaposition and note the effect. Without opticians, in short, no telescope would have been possible; and we may add that nowadays, when instruments of precision have grown infinitely more complex, not even the genius of a Galileo could unaided reconstruct a telescope from a description.

"The origins of the majority of technically improved inventions are still a mystery," says Feldhaus, the historian of technology. The explanation is that a particular achievement was normally the end result of minor adjustments by skilled craftsmen. Individual variability clearly enters: each innovator must necessarily have possessed more than average sensitiveness in mechanical matters, but he need not be a solitary prodigy.

In some cases the psychology of the process is historically documented. The ophthalmoscope, an instrument for inspecting the retina, had long been desired by eye specialists, but for lack of the physical knowledge they were unable to devise one. In the mind of Hermann Helmholtz—physician by his father's decree, physicist by choice—the two lines of requisite knowledge coalesced: he saw the quandary of the ophthalmologist, but he also had the knowledge of optics to solve the problem (in 1851). Helmholtz was a great scientist, and his solution certainly would not have occurred to a moron. But from his own report a lesser man might have achieved it if only he had had the prerequisite double training.

Again, our modern matches represent an incalculable

advance over previous methods of fire-making (p. 58). But even a brief account of the beginnings presents a whole series of men who played a vital part in the developments. Brand discovered yellow phosphorus in 1673, Haukwitz the ignition of sulphur and phosphorus by friction. In 1827 the druggist Walker rubbed along sandpaper a bit of wood dipped into a mixture of chlorate of potash—itself a discovery of Berthollet's in 1786—with sulphide of antimony. In the next decade we hear of one Sauria and later of Kammerer substituting phosphorus for this mixture; in 1844 Pasch of Stockholm made the first safety match, and Lundström opened the first Swedish match factory. These were all able men, no doubt, but not one of them was an intellect of the first order; and it is difficult to suppose that progress would have been long delayed if one of them had devoted himself to other interests.

These unchallengeable facts do not, then, disprove the importance of great ability; but they reduce to its proper proportions the significance of the "leader" in the one field where objective appraisal is feasible. In specific situations it is conceivable that only the intuition of a single genius could achieve the desired result; but even here the question recurs whether a deferred solution vitally affects human interests. The case of Mendelism is in point. In 1865 Gregor Mendel presented his laws of inheritance to so obscure a scientific organization that they were lost to his fellow workers. Nevertheless, equivalent results were obtained a generation later by three independent workers, who unearthed the recondite source. And today the universally cultivated science of genetics cannot be said to be suffering from this period of arrested development.

Primitive Parallels. Primitive man's contrivances present innumerable evidences of precisely such mental processes as characterize the history of modern technology. Our Nineteenth Century experimenters muddled along with dangerous forms of the friction match until finally a safer substitute was hit upon. Siberians imitated equestrian neighbors in mounting reindeer; and where the variety of the beast proved too weak-backed to support them they straddled his shoulders instead of his back. That South American aborigines could have transformed the deadly manioc into a staple supporting thousands of people (p. 31) seems almost miraculous, but it is not a unique accomplishment. On a lower plane Californian gatherers (p. 22) learned not merely to rid their acorns of the bitter tannic acid, but came to pulverize and leach the fruits so as to render them at once edible instead of having to wait for months until the slower process by burial or immersion took effect. Felting (p. 119) and pottery (p. 129)—in fact, all the native handicrafts—imply for their evolution the identical combination of dexterity with mechanical intuition, the creative synthesis of ideas and processes that underlies the rise of modern technology.

Rejection of Racialist Theory. Without, then, prejudging the problem of racial differences in variability, we may reasonably guess that it has slight bearing on the puzzle of Western contemporary civilization. Even if, say, the Australians should turn out to be innately deficient in this regard, Negroes and American Indians have demonstrably had a large number of outstanding personalities and have shown those particular traits of mind on which the criteria of modern culture rest.

But there is a more decisive argument. The criteria in question separate us not only from the savage and the Albanian, but also from the Nordic of 1800 A.D. The hypothesis would therefore have as its corollary that the Nordic organism altered within the last one hundred and fifty years in such a way as to yield a larger number of geniuses per million than it was capable of producing in previous periods. There is not even the faintest suggestion of evidence for any such mutation. Equally improbable is it that our differentiae are explainable by a greater variability than that of the urban civilization of Greece in the heyday of Athens.

The Solution

If we take the outburst of technological innovations as the basic factor, our era may be compared with other periods that witnessed a similarly spectacular spurt in other lines, such as the age of Pericles and the Renaissance. Francis Galton gave the proper explanation for the Renaissance, expressly spurning the suggestion that its generation experienced a change in hereditary quality. "These sudden eras of great intellectual progress," he wrote, "cannot be due to any alteration in the natural faculties of the race, because there has not been time for that, but to their being directed in productive channels."

There lies the rub. The ancient Greeks were not lacking in inventiveness, but for at least two reasons they were not generally interested in practical applications. First of all, there was the cultural tradition that abstract thought ranked above manual operations, which were rather looked down upon. Then the tone-setting class had no need for laborsaving devices since there were always plenty of slaves, whose comfort was not a primary consideration. Accordingly, when a scholar stooped to invent something, it was likely to be an ingenious, but utterly useless contraption, the means for beguiling an idle hour. In striking contrast to this attitude, our age has consistently set a premium on useful contrivances, with the result that a host of able men seek a career in satisfying this demand. Although nothing indicates that the proportion of superior ability has risen, the absolute number is naturally greater among the thirty-two million who resided in England and Wales in 1900 than among the nine million that constituted their population a hundred years earlier. There is thus a considerably greater number of men willing to undergo a rigorous training for the purpose of deliberately coping with clearly defined problems (pp. 336-39). It is not surprising that the total result is a spectacular development of science, pure and applied, corresponding to the marked rise in the arts during the Renaissance.

However, these achievements, noteworthy in themselves, have been linked with other phenomena that are less desirable from a human point of view. The difficulties of urban living have been singled out as conspicuous and indisputable, but there are even more fundamental disharmonies in an industrialized world. The interests of the producer are not those of the consumer, the capitalist's may clash with the laborer's, the workingman's are not identical with the farmer's. These economic conflicts may be unnecessary, but so long as they are felt as necessary by the parties involved, they are a sinister social reality. The same applies to the clash of national interests; how to reconcile these with a humanitarian outlook so as to prevent war is one of the outstanding tasks for contemporary statesmen. In a general way all such problems may be reduced to a simple formula. Man was primarily and has been for thousands of years accustomed to live in tiny political units with a correspondingly narrow sense of moral obligation. In the Western world Christianity and the internationalism of science have been attempts to enlarge his ethical sense; it is a question how far Western man is capable of assimilating their message.

APPENDIX

ADDENDA

Lapps (p. 5). More recent studies do not class the Lapps as Mongoloid, but treat them as distinct from both true Mongoloids and true Caucasians, i.e., as representing originally "a stage in the evolution of both the Upper Palaeolithic Europeans and the Mongoloids". See Carleton S. Coon, *The Races of Europe* (New York, 1939), 305.

Origin of Plough (p. 28). Some scholars regard the spade rather than the hoe as the prototype of the plough. See J. B. Leighly, review of Leser, "Entstehung und Verbreitung des Pfluges," AA 34: 517*sq.*, 1932.

Maize (p. 34). Recently botanists also consider South America, say, Colombia or Peru, as a possible center for maize cultivation. See A. V. Kidder, "Speculations on New World Prehistory," *Essays in Anthropology presented to A. L. Kroeber* (Berkeley, 1936), 150f. and Carl Sauer, "American Agricultural Origins," *ibid.*, 289. According to the very latest researches the Indians of the Bolivian and Paraguayan lowlands were the first to domesticate maize, but its intensive cultivation began in the Peruvian highlands. See P. C. Mangelsdorf and R. G. Reeves, *The Origin of Indian Corn and Its Relatives,* Texas Agricultural Experiment Station, Bulletin No. 574 (College Station, Texas, 1939).

The Horse (p. 45). Recent discussions suggest the possibility that in Western Asia, though not in Egypt, the domesticated horse may be considerably earlier. Moreover, about 3000 B.C. the Sumerians of Babylonia seem to have used the dziggetai or onager, a form intermediate between the true horse and the true ass, for drawing chariots. See Max Hilzheimer, "The Evolution of the Domestic Horse," *Antiquity*, 9: 133-139, 1935.

American Indian Pottery (p. 130). Quite recently it has been argued that two centers must be recognized for New World pottery—the southern one mentioned in the text; and an Asiatic place of origin for the pottery of the Woodland area of North America. See W. C. McKern, "An Hypothesis for the Asiatic Origin of the Woodland Culture Pattern," *American Antiquity,* 3: 138-143, 1937.

African Negro Metallurgy (p. 142). An authoritative recent study eliminates the theory that the Negroes originated the blacksmith's art, and also that of their having borrowed it from Egypt, whose influence is proved negligible. Cline discovers, rather, influences from the Berber region on the one hand, and from Arab or Indian traders on the other. See Walter Cline, "Mining and Metallurgy in Negro Africa," *General Series in Anthropology,* No. 5 (Menasha, Wis., 1937).

Potlatch (pp. 147, 151, 270). The statements in the text hold, but intense rivalry at potlatches with deliberate destruction of property to shame a competitor now appears rather as a local than a general phenomenon in the area. The most common form of the potlatch involves an assemblage of people ceremoniously bidden to participate as witnesses of some demonstration of family prerogative. See H. G. Barnett, "The Nature of the Potlatch," AA 40: 349-358, 1938.

Coins (pp. 151f.). In India, Assyria, and Crete, the custom of marking ingots of metal preceded the Lydian coinage; and punch-marked copper bars are described from Mohenjo-Daro in the third millennium B.C. E. M. Loeb, "The Distribution and Function of Money in Early Societies," *Essays in Anthropology presented to A. L. Kroeber* (Berkeley, 1936), 160f.

Negro Music (pp. 207f.). André Schaeffner, *Origine des instruments de musique* (Paris, 1936), 355, convincingly points out that the distinctive musical achievement of the Negroes lies in their handling of rhythm and timbre rather than in their use of stringed instruments.

Polyandry (p. 245). Some additional instances have come to light, especially from Shoshonean tribes of Nevada and their neighbors. See Julian H. Steward, *Basin-Plateau Aboriginal Sociopolitical Groups,* BAE-B 120 (Washington, 1938), 242. However, among these groups polyandry is not the dominant form of marriage.

Hereditary Classes (p. 269). Drucker ("Rank, Wealth, and Kinship in Northwest Coast Society," AA 41: 55-65, 1939) has shown that while there was a sharp cleavage between slaves and freemen, no corresponding demarcation existed among freemen, there being rather an unbroken series of gradings. However, he emphasizes the importance of individual prerogatives and shows that in aboriginal times a man of low rank could not have accumulated enough wealth to enhance his status even though more recently this has become possible. Thus, heredity remained vital under the old régime.

Restrictions on Willing Property (p. 283). Primitive notions are forcibly illustrated by the following case from the Boloki, a Bantu people of the Belgian Congo. A sick man went to a friendly medicine-man for treatment and, when dying, struck the doctor across the ankle with a long pod. For this the doctor demanded and received damages from the heirs, viz. a slave, three pots of wine, two spears, and some brass rods. The point was that the patient had *wanted* to leave this property to his friend, but that was impossible since he was not a kinsman. Accordingly, he deliberately went through the forms of assault and battery so that the doctor could claim the intended bequest as an indemnity. This is an excellent instance of a legal fiction. John H. Weeks, *Among Congo Cannibals* (Philadelphia, 1913), 193.

GLOSSARY

Aerophone: A musical instrument, such as our wind instruments, played so as to cause primarily the vibration of the air.

Alpine Race: The brachycephalic racial type of Western Europe, exemplified by the people of central France, northern Italy, and southwestern Germany.

Amitate: The special authority exercised over persons by their father's sister.

Avunculate: The special authority exercised by a person's maternal uncle.

Bull-roarer: A flat slab, usually of wood, swung by a string attached near one end so as to produce a humming noise. Sometimes a mere toy, it is frequently of ceremonial significance, especially in signaling uninitiated persons to remain at a distance.

Cat's Cradle: The pastime of making string figures with the hands, but sometimes also with the toes and teeth.

Chordophone: A musical instrument with stretched strings, the simplest example being the musical bow.

Clan: A social unit based on kinship through one parent only, and including either all actual blood-kin on that side or, in addition, persons regarded as kin by legal fiction.

Cross-Cousin: A person's mother's brother's child or father's sister's child, there being a *crossing* from the female to the male sex in the pair of connecting relatives.

Diffusion: The spreading of cultural elements from one people to another.

Dinaric Race: The brachycephalic racial type of Western Europe, exemplified by the Northern Albanians and Montenegrins.

Endogamy: The rule that persons shall marry within their group, as in the caste system. The practice of marrying within one's group from mere convenience is *not* endogamy.

Exogamy: The rule that persons shall marry outside their group; operative most commonly for clans and moieties, but also sometimes for local groups, whence the term "local exogamy".

Fetich: A material object revered because of an indwelling spirit or investment with impersonal supernatural power.

Idiophone: A musical instrument set to vibrate itself by the player. Tomtoms and rattles are examples.

Incorporeal Property: Immaterial property, such as the privilege of using names, songs, sacred objects; illustrated by our copyrights and patents.

Junior Right: The rule that the youngest child inherits the bulk of the estate.

Kumyss: Fermented mare's milk.

Levirate: The inheritance of a widow by her deceased husband's brother.

Lineage: A clan composed exclusively of actual, not at all of fictitious blood-kin.

Mana: Impersonal supernatural power; a term derived from Melanesian and Polynesian languages.

Matrilocal Residence: A husband's residence in the house or settlement of his wife's kin.

Membranophone: A musical instrument played on a membrane stretched over an opening; illustrated by the skin-headed drums.

Moiety: One of two intermarrying exogamous tribal halves, either undivided or comprising lesser clans. Sometimes the term is applied to the clearly defined half of a tribe irrespective of marriage regulations.

Neolithic Age: The New Stone Age; originally defined by the knowledge of the stone-grinding process, now by a complex of features of which the use of domestic beasts, cultivated plants, and pottery are most prominent.

Nordic Race: The fair, tall (as compared with Alpines), long-headed race of Northern Europe, best exemplified by the Swedes.

Paleolithic Age: The Old Stone Age; originally defined by the lack of the stone-grinding process, now rather by the lack of the Neolithic complex; or, positively, by exclusive reliance on a hunting-gathering economy and exclusive use of fracturing stone techniques.

Parallel Cousin: A person's father's brother's child or mother's sister's child; parallel cousins are commonly regarded as brothers and sisters, hence are not allowed to intermarry.

Patrilocal Residence: A wife' residence in the house or settlement of her husband's kin.

Phratry: A union, loose or close, of two or more clans. A phratry may or may not coincide with the subdivided type of moiety.

Pictograph: A picture having for its primary purpose communication rather than aesthetic effects.

Polyandry: The marriage of one woman to two or more husbands.

Polygyny: The marriage of one husband to two or more wives. It is not the same as polygamy, which technically includes both polygyny and polyandry since it simply suggests a plurality of mates irrespective of sex.

Potlatch: A festival at which gifts are presented to the witnesses of the host's (or his kin's) social advancement; usually with emphasis on the prestige acquired by lavish donations.

Section: One of the four marriage-regulating divisions of many Australian societies; formerly called "class".

Shaman: A person who has direct communication with supernatural beings through dreams, visions, or spirit possession. Since the word is of Siberian origin, some authors limit it to the

Siberian type of votary characterized by mediumistic possession.

Sibling: A brother *or* sister; e.g., "siblings must not intermarry".

Sororate: The marriage of a man with his deceased wife's sister.

Subsection: One half of an Australian section, i.e., one of the eight divisions of some Australian societies.

Survival: A trait preserved apart from its setting, hence not in harmony with its present context.

Teknonymy: The custom of calling a person according to his relationship to a child, e.g., "Father of Mary", "Mother of Philip".

Tort: A wrong against an individual, as distinguished from a crime, which is an offence against the community or state.

Totem: Usually an animal, more rarely a plant species, still more rarely some natural phenomenon or artifact connected with a clan or similar unit. The term has also been applied to the animals specially associated with males and females, respectively, in certain Australian tribes. "Individual totem", however, is a misnomer for a person's guardian spirit.

Tumbaga: The alloy, invented by Indians in Colombia, of copper, gold, and some silver. It is as hard as bronze and has the advantage of a melting-point 200° C. lower than either gold (1063° C.) or copper (1083° C.). The word comes from Malay tamboga, copper. A synonym for it in American literature is "guanin".

Ultimogeniture: *See* Junior Right.

Zebu: The humped ox domesticated in India.

ANNOTATED READING LIST

(This list, prepared by special request, is not meant to be in any sense complete. It offers merely a few readily accessible readings in English that will be useful to both teachers and students. The Bibliographical Notes that follow it contain the more important sources used by the author.)

C. Daryll Forde, Habitat, Economy and Society; a geographical introduction to ethnology. New York: Harcourt, Brace & Co., 1937.

Part IV furnishes probably the best English account of the history of cultivation and stock-breeding. Apart from the correlated discussion of economic life, the book gives suggestive descriptions of selected tribal cultures, with the emphasis on their material aspects.

Franz Boas (editor), General Anthropology. Boston: D. C. Heath & Company, 1938.

This text covers prehistory and physical as well as cultural anthropology. Attention is directed to the theoretical final chapter by the editor, as well as the chapters on Prehistoric Archaeology (N. C. Nelson) and Mythology and Folklore (F. Boas).

Paul Radin, Primitive Man as Philosopher. New York and London: D. Appleton-Century Co., 1927.

Besides vindicating the contemplative phase of primitive mentality, this book offers interesting samples of oral literature and discusses certain aspects of religious life.

Franz Boas, The Mind of Primitive Man. Revised edition. New York: The Macmillan Company, 1938.

This is the classical up-to-date critique of racial theories. There is also a clear consideration of theoretical problems, such as diffusion vs. parallelism.

Ralph Linton, The Study of Man. New York and London: D. Appleton-Century Co., 1936.

While avoiding a detailed topical summary of fact, this book concentrates on theoretical problems of special concern to the sociologist and psychologist, such as Discovery and Invention, Culture and Personality, and so on.

Robert H. Lowie, The History of Ethnological Theory. New York: Farrar & Rinehart, Inc., 1937.

This book indicates the classics of cultural anthropology as well as the more important monographs on special topics and regions.

Richard Thurnwald, Black and White in East Africa. London: G. Routledge & Sons, 1935.

Contains excellent material on the blending of cultures.

V. Gordon Childe, Man Makes Himself. London: C. A. Watts & Co., 1936.

A distinguished prehistorian's popular account of the rise of higher civilizations. Unusually successful in throwing into relief the significant correlations.

Elsie Clews Parsons, Pueblo Indian Religion. Chicago: The University of Chicago Press, 1939. 2 vols.

An unusually well-documented account of the supernaturalism of a particular area, the long Introduction providing an adequate sketch of the whole culture. The two final chapters are invaluable for their exemplification of cultural processes.

Leslie Spier, Yuman Tribes of the Gila River. Chicago: The University of Chicago Press, 1933.

The exceptionally competent monograph on the Maricopa and their neighbors.

Bronislaw Malinowski, Argonauts of the Western Pacific. London: George Routledge & Sons, Ltd., 1922.

The justly famous monograph on the economic system of a Melanesian people as correlated with their total culture.

Beatrice Blackwood, Both Sides of Buka Passage. London: Oxford University Press, 1935.

An exemplary monograph on a Melanesian group, paying due attention to all phases of native life.

John Roscoe, The Northern Bantu. Cambridge, 1915.

While not so full as many other recent monographs, this work gives an unusually clear picture of a native African state with distinct castes.

Edward E. Evans-Pritchard, Witchcraft, Oracles and Magic among the Azande. Oxford, 1937.

An admirable exposition of the relevant beliefs of a non-Bantu African people living in the Congo-Nile watershed area.

BIBLIOGRAPHICAL NOTES

The following abbreviations have been used for serial publications:

AA	American Anthropologist
AAA-M	American Anthropological Association, Memoirs
AMNH-AP	American Museum of Natural History, Anthropological Papers
AMNH-B	American Museum of Natural History, Bulletins
BAE-B	Bureau of American Ethnology, Bulletins
BAE-R	Bureau of American Ethnology, Reports
FMNH	Field Museum of Natural History, Publications, Anthropological Series
FMNH-G	Field Museum of Natural History, Guide
JRAI	Journal of the Royal Anthropological Institute
UC	University of California, Publications in American Archaeology and Ethnology

Numerals before colons indicate the volume of a series, those following a colon the pages.

Certain works have been used so constantly throughout this book that it seems best to segregate them at the beginning of these Bibliographical Notes rather than to repeat their citation for chapter after chapter. This list is followed by additional references for every chapter.

NORTH AMERICA

Kaj Birket-Smith, The Caribou Eskimos, Material and Social Life and their Cultural Position. I. Copenhagen 1929. (Report of the Fifth Thule Expedition 1921-1924, vol. V.)

Therkel Mathiassen, Material Culture of the Iglulik Eskimos. Copenhagen, 1928. (Ib., vol. VI, no. 1.)

A. L. Kroeber, Handbook of the Indians of California. Washington, 1925. (BAE-B 78.)

Leslie Spier, Havasupai Ethnography. (AMNH-AP 29:81-392, 1928.)

Leslie Spier, Yuman Tribes of the Gila River.[1] Chicago, 1933.

[1] All statements about the Maricopa are based upon this book.

SOUTH AMERICA

Erland Nordenskiöld, An Ethno-geographical Analysis of the Material Culture of two Indian Tribes in the Gran Chaco. (Comparative Ethnographical Studies, vol. 1.) Göteborg, 1919.

Erland Nordenskiöld, The Ethnography of South America seen from Mojos in Bolivia. (Ibid., vol. 3.) Göteborg, 1924.

Erland Nordenskiöld, Indianer und Weisse in Nordostbolivien. Stuttgart, 1922.

Erland Nordenskiöld, Indianerleben; el Gran Chaco (Südamerika). Leipzig, 1912.

Martin Gusinde, Die Selk'nam; vom Leben und Denken eines Jägervolkes auf der Grossen Feuerlandinsel. Mödling bei Wien, 1921.[2]

AFRICA

Wilhelm Hofmayr, Die Schilluk. Mödling bei Wien, 1925.

AUSTRALIA AND OCEANIA

N. W. Thomas, Natives of Australia. London, 1906.

K. Langloh Parker, The Euahlayi Tribe; a Study of Aboriginal Life in Australia. London, 1905.

Walter E. Roth, North Queensland Ethnography, Bulletins 3, 4, 5, 7, 8. Brisbane, 1901-1906.

Elsdon Best, The Maori as He Was. Wellington, N. Z., 1924.

Te Rangi Hiroa (P. H. Buck), Samoan Material Culture. (Bernice P. Bishop Museum, Bulletin 75.) Honolulu, 1930.

PREHISTORY OF THE NEAR ORIENT AND EUROPE

Max Ebert (editor), *Reallexikon der Vorgeschichte,* 15 vols., Berlin, 1924-1932.

CHAPTER I

A. C. Haddon, The Races of Man and their Distribution. New York, 1925.

Hugo Obermaier, Fossil Man in Spain. New Haven, 1924.

George Grant MacCurdy, Human Origins. 2 vols. New York, 1924.

V. Gordon Childe, The Most Ancient East. New York, 1929.

[2] This is the source for virtually all statements about the Ona (= Selk'nam).

CHAPTER II

A. R. Radcliffe-Brown, Former Numbers and Distribution of the Australian Aborigines. Official Year Book of the Commonwealth of Australia, No. 23 of 1930, pp. 687-696.

A. L. Kroeber, Native American Population, AA 36:1-25, 1934.

Gerhard Lindblom, Jakt-och Fangstmetoder bland Afrikanska Folk. I. (Etnografiska Riksmuseet, Stockholm, 1925. 138 pp.)

Julian H. Steward, "Ethnography of the Owens Valley Paiute," UC 33:233-350, 1933.

I. T. Kelly, "Ethnography of the Surprise Valley Paiute," UC 31:67-210, 1932.

CHAPTER III

A. L. P. P. de Candolle, Origine des plantes cultivées. Paris, 1883.

B. Laufer, Sino-Iranica, FMNH 15:185-630, Chicago, 1919.

E. Werth, Zur Natur- und Kulturgeschichte der Banana, in Eduard Hahn Festschrift, 22-58. Stuttgart, 1917.

H. F. Lutz, Viticulture and Brewing in the Ancient Orient. Leipzig, 1922.

Gilbert L. Wilson, Agriculture of the Hidatsa Indians; an Indian Interpretation. (The University of Minnesota, Studies in the Social Sciences, No. 9.) Minneapolis, 1917.

Ralph Linton, The Tanala; A Hill Tribe of Madagascar. FMNH, vol. 22, 1933.

J. H. Steward. See Notes for Chapter II.

CHAPTER IV

Eduard Hahn, Die Haustiere und ihre Beziehungen zur Wirtschaft des Menschen. Leipzig, 1896.

Glover M. Allen, in Bulletin, Museum of Comparative Zoology, Harvard, vol. 63:431-517, 1920.

O. Antonius, Grundzüge einer Stammesgeschichte der Haustiere, 1922.

W. Schmidt and W. Koppers, Völker und Kulturen. Regensburg, 1924.

B. Laufer, Some Fundamental Ideas of Chinese Culture. The Journal of Race Development, 5:160-174, 1914.

B. Laufer, The Reindeer and its Domestication. (AAA-M, 4:91-147, 1917.)

W. Radloff, Aus Sibirien. 2 vols. Leipzig, 1893.

Alois Musil, Arabia Petraea, 3:140 sq., 262-270. Wien, 1908.

C. W. and B. Z. Seligman, The Kababish, a Sudan Arab Tribe. (Harvard African Studies, 2:105-184, 1918), esp. 116-120.

Gilbert L. Wilson, The Horse and the Dog in Hidatsa Culture. (AMNH-AP 15:125-311, 1924.)

CHAPTER V

Albert B. Lewis, Ethnology of Melanesia. (FMNH-G, 5. Chicago, 1932.)

Paul Schebesta, Bambuti, die Zwerge vom Kongo. Leipzig, 1932.

CHAPTER VI

Fay-Cooper Cole, The Wild Tribes of Davao District, Mindanao. (FMNH 12:203, 1913.)

W. S. and K. Routledge, With a Prehistoric People; the Akikuyu of British East Africa. London, 1910.

Paul Schebesta, Bei den Urwaldzwergen von Malaya. Leipzig, 1927.

CHAPTER VII

W. Jochelson, Peoples of Asiatic Russia. New York, 1928.

Tr. Fr. Troels-Lund, Das tägliche Leben in Skandinavien während des sechzehnten Jahrhunderts. Copenhagen, 1882.

Arthur Young, Travels in France and Italy during the Years 1787, 1788 and 1789. London, 1915.

F. Staschewski and B. Ankermann, Die Banjangi. (Baessler-Archiv, Beiheft 8:1-66, 1917.)

CHAPTER VIII

Clark Wissler, Material Culture of the Blackfoot Indians, AMNH, 5: 1-175, 1910.

Baldwin Spencer and F. J. Gillen, The Arunta, 2:536-550. London, 1927.

B. Laufer, The Early History of Felt, AA, 32:1-18, 1930.

R. Karutz, Unter Kirgisen und Turkmenen. Leipzig, 1911.

Otis T. Mason, Aboriginal American Basketry. Washington, 1902.

Isabel T. Kelly, See Notes for Chapter II.

Hugo Ephraim, Über die Entwicklung der Webetechnik und ihre Verbreitung ausserhalb Europas. Jena, 1904.

S. Linné, The Technique of South American Ceramics. Göteborg, 1925.

B. Laufer, The Beginnings of Porcelain in China, FMNH 15:79-177, 1917.

Marshall H. Saville, The Wood-Carver's Art in Ancient Mexico. (Contributions from the Museum of the American Indian, Heye Foundation, vol. 9, 1925.)

Erland Nordenskiöld, The Copper and Bronze Ages in South America. (Comparative Ethnographic Studies, 4, Göteborg, 1921.)

Erland Nordenskiöld (editor), Comparative Ethnographical Studies, 9:101-114, 1931.

Paul Rivet et H. Arsandeaux, Contribution à l'étude de la métallurgie mexicaine. (Journal de la Société des Américanistes de Paris, XIII, 1921.)

Paul Rivet et H. Arsandeaux, Nouvelle note sur la métallurgie mexicaine. (Ibid., XXXIII, 1923.)

Samuel R. Lothrop, The Indians of Tierra del Fuego. (Contributions from the Museum of the American Indian, Heye Foundation, vol. X.) New York, 1928.

CHAPTER IX

Richard Thurnwald, Werden, Wandel und Gestaltung der Wirtschaft im Lichte der Völkerforschung. Berlin-Leipzig, 1932.

M. Mauss, Essai sur le don, forme archaïque de l'échange. (L'année sociologique, NF 1, 1923-24.)

B. Malinowski, Argonauts of the Western Pacific. London, 1922.

A. B. Lewis, Melanesian Shell Money, FMNH 19:1-36, 1929.

Hortense Powdermaker, Life in Lesu; the Study of a Melanesian Society in New Ireland. 1933. pp. 155-225.

Henri Labouret, Les tribus du Rameau Lobi. (Travaux et Mémoires de l'Institut d'Ethnologie, XV.) 1931. pp. 352-363.

CHAPTER X

Stewart Culin, Games of the North American Indians. (BAE-R 24, 1907.)

B. Laufer, in AA 21:88 f., 1919.

Henri A. Junod, The Life of a South African Tribe. 2 vols. Neuchâtel, 1912.

John R. Swanton, Source Material for the Social and Ceremonial Life of the Choctaw Indians. (BAE-B 103:140-160, 1931.)

K. G. Lindblom, The Use of Stilts, especially in Africa and America. id., Further Notes on the Use of Stilts. (Riksmuseets Etnografiska Avdelning, Smärre Meddelanden, nos. 3 and 6, Stockholm, 1927, 1928.)

N. B. Emerson, Unwritten Language of Hawaii. (BAE-B 38, 1909.)

CHAPTER XI

F. Boas, Primitive Art. Oslo, 1927.

A. C. Haddon, Evolution in Art. London, 1895.

I. Schapera, Some Stylistic Affinities of Bushman Art. (South African Journal of Science, 22:504-515, 1925.)

Paul Radin, Literary Aspects of North American Mythology. (Canada Geological Survey, Museum Bulletin No. 16, Ottawa, 1915.)

Edna Lou Walton and T. T. Waterman, American Indian Poetry, AA 27:25-52, 1925.

M. W. Beckwith, The Hawaiian Romance of Laieikawai. (BAE-R 33:285-666, 1919.)

R. B. Dixon, The Mythology of All Races: Oceanic. Boston, 1916.

W. Thalbitzer, The Ammassalik Eskimo, Language and Folklore. Copenhagen, 1923. (Meddelelser om Grönland, 193-564.)

Ella Deloria, Dakota Texts. (Publications American Ethnological Society, vol. XIV.) New York, 1932.

H. Junod, Les chants et les contes des Ba-Ronga. Lausanne, 1897.

A. Dirr, Kaukasische Märchen. Jena: Eugen Diederichs, 1922. p. 279.

E. M. von Hornbostel, The Ethnology of African Sound-Instruments, in *Africa,* 6:129-157, 277-311, 1933.

CHAPTER XII

K. G. Lindblom, Die Schleuder in Afrika und anderwärts (Riksmuseet, 2.) Stockholm, 1927.

B. Laufer, in AA 19:74, 1917.

H. Diels, Antike Technik. Leipzig, 1920.

Georg Friederici, Skalpieren und ähnliche Kriegsgebräuche in Amerika. Braunschweig, 1906.

Georg Friederici, Nachtangriffe bei Südsee-Völkern und Indianern. (Mitteilungsblatt der Gesellschaft für Völkerkunde, No. 2, 4-15, 1933.)

Fay-Cooper Cole, See Notes for Chapter VI.

Wm. Lloyd Warner, Murngin Warfare. (Oceania, 1:456-494, 1931.)

CHAPTER XIII

E. B. Tylor, On a Method of Investigating the Development of Institutions; applied to Laws of Marriage and Descent. (JRAI 18:245-272, 1889.)

A. R. Radcliffe-Brown, The Social Organization of Australian Tribes. (The "Oceania" Monographs, No. 1.) Melbourne, 1931.

B. Malinowski, The Sexual Life of Savages. 2 vols. New York, 1929.

Wm. Lloyd Warner, Morphology and Functions of the Australian Murngin Type of Kinship, AA 32:207-256, 1930.

W. H. R. Rivers, The Todas. London, 1906.

E. S. G. Handy, The Native Culture in the Marquesas. (Bernice P. Bishop Museum, Bull. 9:81 sq., 98 sq., Honolulu 1923.)

J. H. Driberg, The Status of Women among the Nilotics and Nilo-Hamitics, *Africa,* 5:404-421, 1932.

P. Amaury Talbot, The Peoples of Southern Nigeria. London, 1926.

Ella Deloria, Dakota Texts. New York, 1932. p. 159.

Paul Kirchhoff, Die Verwandtschaftsorganisation der Urwaldstämme Südamerikas. (Zeitschrift für Ethnologie, 63:85-193, 1931.)

Paul Kirchhoff, Verwandtschaftsbezeichnungen und Verwandtenheirat. (Ibid., 64:41-71, 1932.)

E. W. Gifford, California Kinship Terminologies, UC 18:1-285, 1922.

CHAPTER XIV

E. B. Tylor, see Notes for Chapter XIII.

L. H. Morgan, Ancient Society. New York, 1877.

John R. Swanton, The Social Organization of American Tribes, AA 7:663-673, 1905.

W. H. R. Rivers, Kinship and Social Organization. London, 1914.

B. Malinowski, Crime and Custom in Savage Society. London, 1926.

E. W. Gifford, Miwok Moieties, UC 12:139-194, 1916.

E. W. Gifford, Miwok Lineages and the Political Unit in Aboriginal California, AA 28:389-401, 1926.

Wm. D. Strong, Aboriginal Society in Southern California, UC 26, 1929.

T. T. Waterman and A. L. Kroeber, Yurok Marriages, UC 35:1-14, 1934.

A. A. Goldenweiser, On Iroquois Work. (Summary Report of the Geological Survey, Canada, Ottawa, 1912 and 1913, pp. 464-475, 365-373, respectively.)

F. G. Speck, Family Hunting Territories. (Memoirs, Canada Geological Survey 70, Ottawa, 1915.)

F. G. Speck, The Family Hunting Band as the Basis of Algonkian Social Organization, AA 17:289-305, 1915.

P. Kirchhoff, see Notes for Chapter XIII.

A. R. Radcliffe-Brown, see Notes for Chapter XIII.

CHAPTER XV

R. H. Lowie, Primitive Society. New York, 1920. (pp. 205-296, 338-357.)

R. H. Lowie, Incorporeal Property in Primitive Society. (Yale Law Journal, 37:551-563, 1928.)

F. Boas, The Social Organization and Secret Societies of the Kwakiutl Indians. (Report of the U. S. National Museum for 1895, pp. 315-733, Washington, 1897.)

E. Sapir, The Social Organization of the West Coast Tribes. (Transactions, Royal Society of Canada, 3d. series, pp. 355-374, 1915.)

W. Jochelson, The Yukaghir and the Yukaghirized Tungus. (AMNH, Memoirs 13. Leiden, 1910.)

Clark Wissler, The Social Life of the Blackfoot Indians. (AMNH 7:1-64, 1911.)

P. A. Talbot, See Notes for Chapter XIII.

CHAPTER XVI

H. Maine, Ancient Law. London, 1861.

H. Schurtz, Altersklassen und Männerbünde. Berlin, 1902.

H. Webster, Primitive Secret Societies. New York, 1908.

R. H. Lowie, The Origin of the State. New York, 1927.

B. Malinowski, see Notes for Chapter XIV.

R. F. Barton, Ifugao Law, UC 15:1-127, 1919.

D. Westermann, Die Kpelle, ein Negerstamm in Liberia. 1921.

P. A. Talbot, see Notes for Chapter XIII.

M. A. Poupon, Étude ethnographique de la tribe Kouyou, L'Anthropologie, 29:53-88, 397-435, 1918-1919.

C. G. Seligman, The Religion of the Pagan Tribes of the White Nile, *Africa* 4:1-21, 1931.

A. H. Gayton, Yokuts-Mono Chiefs and Shamans, UC 24: 361-420, 1930.

CHAPTER XVII

E. B. Tylor, Primitive Culture, 2 vols. London, 1913.

R. R. Marett, The Threshold of Religion. 2nd edition. London, 1914.

W. Schmidt, Der Ursprung der Gottesidee. I. Münster, 1926.

P. Radin, Primitive Man as Philosopher. New York, 1927.

H. A. Junod, See Notes for Chapter X.

B. Laufer, The Development of Ancestral Images in China, Journal of Religious Psychology, 6:111-123, 1913.

J. Spieth, Die Religion der Eweer in Süd-Togo. Göttingen, 1911.

J. Roscoe, The Baganda. London, 1911.

E. S. C. Handy, Polynesian Religion, Bernice P. Bishop Museum, Bulletin 34, 1927.

M. Vanoverbergh, Philippine Negrito Culture: Independent or Borrowed? *Primitive Man,* 6:25-35, 1933.

R. B. Dixon, The Northern Maidu, AMNH-B 17:119-346, 1905.

R. H. Lowie, The Religion of the Crow Indians, AMNH-AP 25:309-444, 1922.

CHAPTER XVIII

J. Eric Thompson, The Civilization of the Mayas. Chicago, 1927.

Sylvanus Griswold Morley, An Introduction to the Study of the Maya Hieroglyphs, BAE-B 57, 1915.

Wm. T. Sedgwick and H. W. Tyler, A Short History of Science. New York, 1917.

R. C. Archibald, Mathematics before the Greeks, *Science* 71: 109-121, 1930.

George P. Murdock, Our Primitive Contemporaries, p. 223. New York, 1934.

CHAPTER XIX

A. Meillet, Introduction à l'étude comparative des langues indoeuropéennes. Paris, 1937.

Leonard Bloomfield, Language. New York, 1933.

Edward Sapir, Language. New York, 1921.

Franz Boas, Handbook of American Indian Languages; Part I, Introduction. Washington, 1911.

CHAPTER XX

Robert H. Lowie, The History of Ethnological Theory. New York, 1937.

CHAPTER XXI

John M. Cooper, Analytical and Critical Bibliography of the Tribes of Tierra del Fuego and Adjacent Territory, BAE-B 63:218-228, 1917.

Samuel K. Lothrop, The Indians of Tierra del Fuego. New York, 1928.

Martin Gusinde, Die Selk'nam; vom Leben und Denken eines Jägervolkes auf der Grossen Feuerlandinsel. Mödling bei Wien, 1931. Id., Die Yamana; vom Leben und Denken der Wassernomaden am Kap Hoorn. Mödling bei Wien, 1937.

Junius Bird, Before Magellan, *in* Natural History: 4:16sq., 1938.

CHAPTER XXII

Wm. Lloyd Warner, A Black Civilization. New York and London, 1937.

CHAPTER XXIII

Curt Nimuendajú and R. H. Lowie, The Dual Organizations of the Ramkókamekra (Canella) of Northern Brazil, AA 39:565-582, 1937.

Curt Nimuendajú, The Social Structure of the Ramkókamekra (Canella), AA 40:51-74, 1938.

Curt Nimuendajú and R. H. Lowie, The Associations of the Šerénte, AA 41:408-415, 1939.

Curt Nimuendajú, The Apinayé (The Catholic University of America, Anthropological Series, No. 8), Washington, D. C., 1939.

CHAPTER XXIV

Hilde Thurnwald, Menschen der Südsee; Charaktere und Schicksale. Stuttgart, 1937.

Hilde Thurnwald, Woman's Status in Buin Society. (Oceania, 5:142-170, 1934.)

Richard Thurnwald, Ein vorkapitalistisches Wirtschaftssystem in Buin. (Archiv für Rechts- und Sozialphilosophie, vol. 31, Heft 1.)

Richard Thurnwald, Profane Literature of Buin. (Yale University Publications in Anthropology, No. 8, 1936.)

Richard Thurnwald, Pigs and Currency in Buin. (Oceania, 5:119-141, 1934.)

CHAPTER XXV

Alexander M. Stephen (Elsie Clews Parsons, ed.), Hopi Journal. New York, 1936. 2 vols.

Elsie Clews Parsons, Pueblo Indian Religion. Chicago, 1939. 2 vols.

C. Daryll Forde, Hopi Agriculture and Land Ownership, JRAI 61:357-405, 1931.

Ernest Beaglehole, Hopi Hunting and Hunting Ritual; id., Notes on Hopi Economic Life. (Yale University Publications in Anthropology, Nos. 4 and 15. New Haven, 1936, 1937.)

CHAPTER XXVI

Fay-Cooper Cole, The Wild Tribes of Davao District, Mindanao. FMNH 12:51-128, 1913.

Laura Watson Benedict, A Study of Bagobo Ceremonial, Magic and Myth. Annals N. Y. Acad. Sci., 25:1-308, 1916.

CHAPTER XXVII

Wilhelm Hofmayr, Die Schilluk. Mödling bei Wien, 1925.

C. G. and B. Z. Seligman, Pagan Tribes of the Nilotic Sudan. London, 1932.

CHAPTER XXVIII

B. Ya. Vladimirtsov, The Life of Chingis-Khan. (Tr. by Prince D. S. Mirsky.) London, 1930.

Alfred E. Hudson, Kazak Social Structure. (Yale University Publications in Anthropology, No. 20. New Haven, 1938.)

Wilhelm von Rubruk, Der Bericht des Franziskaners Wilhelm von Rubruk über seine Reise in das Innere Asiens in den Jahren 1253-1255. Leipzig, 1925. (First complete translation by Hermann Herbst from Latin original.)

Marco Polo, The Travels of Marco Polo. (Manuel Komroff edition) New York, 1926.

James Gilmour, Among the Mongols. London, no date (ca. 1875?).

Berthold Laufer, Skizze der mongolischen Literatur. (Extrait de la Revue Orientale, 165-261, 1907.)

Ferdinand Lessing, Mongolen; Hirten, Priester und Dämonen. Berlin, 1935.

CHAPTER XXIX

M. Edith Durham, High Albania. London, 1909.

M. Edith Durham, Some Tribal Origins, Laws and Customs of the Balkans. London, 1928.

Louis Adamic, The Native's Return. New York, 1934.

Nexhmie Zaimi, Daughter of the Eagle; the autobiography of an Albanian girl. New York, 1937.

J. G. von Hahn, Albanesische Studien. Jena, 1854.

Franz Baron Nopcsa, Albanien; Bauten, Trachten und Geräte Nordalbaniens. Berlin and Leipzig, 1925.

Norbert Jokl, Linguistisch-kulturhistorische Untersuchungen aus dem Bereiche des Albanischen. Berlin and Leipzig, 1923.

Maximilian Lambertz, Albanische Märchen. (Akademie der Wissenschaften in Wien: Schriften der Balkankommission, Linguistische Abteilung, XII.) Wien, 1922.

Franz Seiner, Ergebnisse der Volkszählung in Albanien in dem von den Österr.—Ungar. Truppen 1916-1918 besetzten Gebiete. (ibid., XIII). Wien, 1922.

Carleton Stevens Coon, The Races of Europe.[1] New York, 1939.

[1] Contains some of the author's original observations in Albania.

CHAPTER XXX

Conrad Arensberg, The Irish Countryman. New York, 1937.

Wm. I. Thomas and Florian Znaniecki, The Polish Peasant in Europe and America. New York, 1927. 2 vols.

Encyclopaedia of the Social Sciences, articles on Match Industry (Wm. Grotkopp), 10:203sq., 1933; Machines and Tools, ancient, medieval and early modern (F. M. Feldhaus), 10:14sq.; Sanitation (Thomas H. Reed), 13:538sq., 1934; Technology (Emil Lederer), 14:553sq., 1934.

Sources of Illustrations

1. Baumann, H., "Die materielle Kultur der Azande und Mangbettu," *Baessler-Archiv* Band XI, 1927, pp. 137.
2. Best, E., "The Maori as He Was," *New Zealand Board of Science and Art Manual,* No. 14, Wellington, N. Z., 1924, pp. 280.
3. Birket-Smith, K., "The Caribou Eskimos," *Report of the Fifth Thule Expedition,* Vol. V, Copenhagen, 1929, pp. 306.
4. Cartailhac, E. and Breuil, H., *La Caverne d'Altamira à Santillane près Santander,* 1906, pp. 287.
5. Cole, F.-C., "The Wild Tribes of the Davao District," *Field Museum of Natural History Anthropological Series,* Vol. XII, No. 2, Chicago, 1913, pp. 203 + 76 plates.
6. Ephraim, H., *"Über die Entwicklung der Webetechnik und ihre Verbreitung ausserhalb Europas,"* Leipzig, 1904, pp. 72.
7. Finsch, O., *Ethnologischer Atlas: Typen aus der Steinzeit Neu Guineas,* Leipzig, 1888, pp. 56, 24 Tafeln.
8. Gayton, A. H., "Yokuts and Western Mono Pottery Making," *University of California Publications in American Archaeology and Ethnology,* Vol. XXIV, No. 3, pp. 239-255, Berkeley, 1929.
9. Gusinde, M., *Die Feuerland-Indianer:* I, *Die Selk'nam,* Wien, "Anthropos"-Verlag, 1931, pp. 1173.
10. Gusinde, M., *Die Feuerland-Indianer:* I, *Die Selk'nam, Atlas,* Wien, *"Anthropos"-Verlag,* 1931, 45 Tafeln.
11. Handy, E. S. C., "The Native Culture of the Marquesas," *Bulletin of the Bishop Museum,* No. 9, Honolulu, Hawaii, 1923, pp. 358.

12. Harrington, M. R., "Cherokee and Earlier Remains on the Upper Tennessee River," *Indian Notes and Monographs,* Museum of the American Indian, New York, 1922, pp. 321.
13. Hofmayr, W., "Die Schilluk," *"Anthropos" Bibliothek Internationale Sammlung Ethnologischer Monographien* Band II, Heft 5, 1925, pp. 521. 32 Tafeln.
14. Horwitz, I. H. Th., "Die Drehbewegung in ihrer Bedeutung für die Entwicklung der materiellen Kultur," *Anthropos,* XXVIII: 721-758, September-December 1933.
15. Jochelson, W., "The Koryak," *American Museum of Natural History Memoirs,* Vol. X, Leiden, 1905-08, pp. 383-811.
16. Jochelson, W., *Peoples of Asiatic Russia,* American Museum of Natural History, New York, 1928, pp. 258.
17. Jochelson, W., "The Yukaghir and the Yukaghirized Turks," *Memoir of the American Museum of Natural History,* Vol. IX, Part 3, New York, 1926, pp. 343-469.
18. Kroeber, A. L. and Waterman, T. T., *Source Book in Anthropology,* University of California Press, Berkeley, 1920, pp. 565.
19. Kroeber, A. L., "Handbook of the Indians of California," *Bureau of American Ethnology Bulletin,* No. 78, Washington, 1925, pp. 995.
20. Kroeber, A. L., "The Arapaho," *Bulletin of the American Museum of Natural History,* Vol. XVIII, New York, 1902-07, pp. 1-229 and 279-455.
21. Labouret, H., "Les Tribus du Rameau Lobi," *Travaux et Mémoires de l'Institut d'Ethnographie,* Vol. XV, Université de Paris, 1931, pp. 510 + 31 plates.
22. Lewis, A. B., *Ethnology of Melanesia,* Field Museum of Natural History, Chicago, 1932, pp. 209 + 44 plates.
23. Lindblom, G., *Jakt-Och Fångstmetoder* Etnografiska Riksmuseet, Stockholm, 1925, pp. 138.
24. Linton, R., "The Tanala, A Hill Tribe of Madagascar," *Anthropological Series,* Field Museum of Natural History, Chicago, Vol. XXII, 1926, pp. 334.
25. Lothrop, S. K., "The Indians of Tierra del Fuego," *Contributions from the Museum of the American Indian,* Vol. X, 1928, pp. 244.
26. Lowie, R. H., "The Assiniboine," *Anthropological Papers of the Museum of Natural History,* New York, Vol. IV, Part 1, 1909, pp. 270.

27. Lowie, R. H., "The Material Culture of the Crow Indians," *Anthropological Papers of the American Museum of Natural History,* Vol. XXI, Part 3, 1922, pp. 203-270.
28. Mathiassen, T., "Material Culture of the Iglulik Eskimos," *Report of the Fifth Thule Expedition,* Vol. VI, No. 1, Copenhagen, 1928, pp. 242.
29. Nopcsa, Baron Fr., *Albanien; Bauten, Trachten, Geräte Nordalbaniens,* Berlin-Leipzig, 1925, pp. 257.
30. Nordenskiöld, E., *Indianer und Weisse in Nordostbolivien,* Stuttgart, 1922, pp. 220.[1]
31. Obermaier, H., in Ebert, *Reallexikon der Vorgeschichte,* Vol. VII, 1926.
32. Rogin, L., "The Introduction of Farm Machinery," *University of California Publications in Economics,* Berkeley, Vol. IX, 1921, pp. 260.
33. Roth, W. E., "Domestic Implements, Arts and Manufactures," *North Queensland Ethnography Bulletin* No. 7, 1901, Brisbane, pp. 34 + 26 plates.
34. Roth, W. E., "An Introductory Study of the Crafts and Customs of the Guiana Indians," BAE-R 38, Washington, 1924, pp. 745.
35. Saville, M. H., *The Woodcarver's Art in Ancient Mexico,* Museum of the American Indian, New York, 1925, pp. 120.
36. Schebesta, P., *Bei den Urwaldzwergen von Malaya,* Leipzig, 1927, pp. 278.
37. Schebesta, P., *Bambuti: die Zwerge vom Kongo,* Leipzig, 1932, pp. 270.
38. Schweinfurth, G., *Artes Africanae,* Leipzig, 1875, XXI plates with explanatory notes.
39. Smith, H. I., "An Album of Prehistoric Canadian Art," *Victoria Memorial Museum Bulletin,* No. 37, Ottawa, 1923, pp. 195.
40. Spinden, H. J., "Ancient Civilizations of Mexico and Central America," *Handbook Series of the American Museum of Natural History,* No. 3, New York, 1917, pp. 227.
41. Staschewski, F., "Die Banjangi," *Baessler-Archiv,* Beiheft VIII, 1917, pp. 59.
42. Stow, G. W., *The Native Races of South Africa,* London, 1905, pp. 618.

[1] Used by permission by Albert Bonnier, publisher of the Swedish original.

43. Thomas, N. W., *Natives of Australia,* London, 1906, pp. 256.
44. Umfreville, E., *The Present State of Hudson's Bay,* 1790.
45. Von Luschan, F., *Beiträge zur Völkerkunde der Deutschen Schutzgebiete,* Berlin, 1897, pp. 87 + 48 Tafeln.
46. Waterlot, E. G., "Les Bas-reliefs des Bâtiments royaux d'Abomey," *Travaux et Mémoires de l'Institut d'Ethnologie,* Université de Paris, 1926, 10 pp. + 23 plates.
47. Wilson, G. L., "Agriculture of the Hidatsa Indians," *The University of Minnesota Studies in the Social Sciences,* No. 9, Minneapolis, 1917, pp. 129.
48. Wissler, C., "Decorative Art of the Sioux Indians," AMNH-B 18, 1902-1907, pp. 230-278.
49. Yule, H., *The Book of Sir Marco Polo, the Venetian,* London, 1921 ed., 1:254.

INDEX

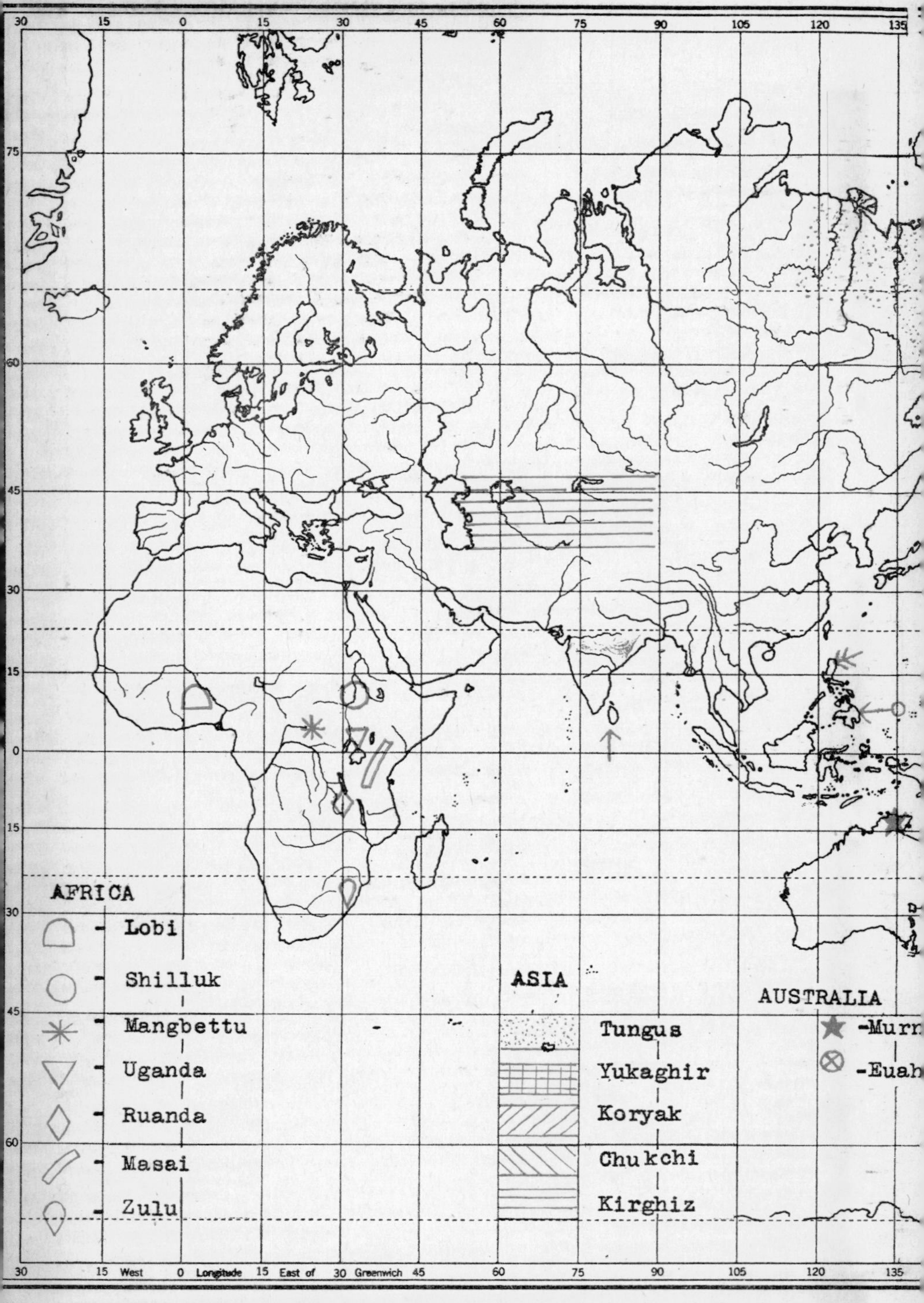

AFRICA
- Lobi
- Shilluk
- Mangbettu
- Uganda
- Ruanda
- Masai
- Zulu
ASIA
Tungus
Yukaghir
Koryak
Chukchi
Kirghiz
AUSTRALIA
-Murn
-Euah
West
Longitude
East of
Greenwich